MW01200525

INTERNATIONAL COURTS AND
TRIBUNALS SERIES

General Editors: Philippe Sands, Ruth Mackenzie,
and Cesare Romano

COMPLIANCE WITH DECISIONS OF THE INTERNATIONAL COURT OF JUSTICE

INTERNATIONAL COURTS AND
TRIBUNALS SERIES

A distinctive feature of modern international society is the increase in the number of international judicial bodies and dispute settlement and implementation control bodies; in their case-loads; and in the range and importance of the issues that they are called upon to address. These factors reflect a new stage in the delivery of international justice. The International Courts and Tribunals series has been established to encourage the publication of independent and scholarly works which address, in critical and analytical fashion, the legal and policy aspects of the functioning of international courts and tribunals, including their institutional, substantive and procedural aspects.

COMPLIANCE WITH DECISIONS OF THE INTERNATIONAL COURT OF JUSTICE

CONSTANZE SCHULTE

THE PROJECT ON INTERNATIONAL COURTS AND TRIBUNALS

This series has been developed in cooperation with the
Project on International Courts and Tribunals

OXFORD
UNIVERSITY PRESS

*This book has been printed digitally and produced in a standard specification
in order to ensure its continuing availability*

OXFORD
UNIVERSITY PRESS

Great Clarendon Street, Oxford OX2 6DP
Oxford University Press is a department of the University of Oxford.
It furthers the University's objective of excellence in research, scholarship,
and education by publishing worldwide in
Oxford New York
Auckland Cape Town Dar es Salaam Hong Kong Karachi
Kuala Lumpur Madrid Melbourne Mexico City Nairobi
New Delhi Shanghai Taipei Toronto
With offices in
Argentina Austria Brazil Chile Czech Republic France Greece
Guatemala Hungary Italy Japan South Korea Poland Portugal
Singapore Switzerland Thailand Turkey Ukraine Vietnam

Oxford is a registered trade mark of Oxford University Press
in the UK and in certain other countries

Published in the United States
by Oxford University Press Inc., New York

© C. Schulte 2004

The moral rights of the author have been asserted

Database right Oxford University Press (maker)

Reprinted 2011

ISBN 978-0-19-927672-1

To my parents

General Editors' Preface

The most striking feature of the pattern of use of the International Court of Justice since 1946 is its irregularity. The history of the ICJ, indeed, is rich with accounts of states that have given the institution a cold shoulder or left the courtroom slamming the door spectacularly. In turns, all regions of the world or political groupings of states seem to have found in a decision of the Court a reason to refuse to implement the ruling, or violently attack it. The communist countries had the *Corfu Channel* case, and the advisory opinions on the *Interpretation of Peace Treaties and the Reservations to the Genocide Convention*; the Latin Americans the *Asylum and Haya de la Torre* cases; the Asians *the Temple of Preah Vihear and Right of Passage* cases; the Africans the *South West Africa* cases; the United States the *Nicaragua* case; and France the *Nuclear Tests* cases. Other decisions that were not persuasive and which were read as a reason to utilize the Court sparingly were the *Icelandic Fisheries Jurisdiction* cases and, more recently, the advisory opinions on *Nuclear Weapons*.

By and large this is the relatively short list of the defeats suffered by the World Court. Yet, it is also a fact that the ICJ has been around for almost sixty years, holding its ground through radical changes in the fabric of the international community (for example, decolonization, the Cold War, the demise of communism, and the dawn of a yet-to-be-labeled tormented era). Over this period it has been submitted slightly more than a hundred disputes and has been requested advisory opinions a little more than two dozen times. Despite those widely publicized slaps, it has enjoyed many more hushed victories, playing a crucial role in settling for good some delicate disputes, to the point that nowadays it is as busy as it has ever been in its history. The Court's reputation is held high around the world, as witnessed by its widely diversified "clientele," including states of all regions and of all kinds, from the tiny (Liechtenstein) to superpowers (the U.S.).

This book is a careful, pragmatic, and dispassionate account not only of the cases handled by the ICJ to date but also, crucially, of their aftermath. Dr. Constanze Schulte, indeed, has followed the parties out of the courtroom and looked at whether they eventually complied with the ruling. This is something that typically, but wrongly, lawyers and legal scholars disdain to do. Once the case has been gaveled, follow-up of the judgment is left to political bodies, and the study of its consequences is usually the business of historians and political scientists. The judgment, those dozens of printed pages, seems to be the only thing that matters to way too many legal scholars, always anxious to find the law but little concerned with the impact that those words have on the real world.

However, since the ICJ is the judicial authority of an international society made of equals, and since it lacks its own enforcement powers, the only way it has to ensure actual compliance with its decisions is persuading the parties of the worth of its decisions. Rulings that are not legally sound will likely not go a great length. Knowing when and why decisions of the ICJ have been complied with is essential to understand properly not only international relations but also, ultimately, what international law is.

This book is a welcome addition to a regrettably small literature on the topic of compliance with decisions of international judicial bodies, and a very authoritative and determinative one, for that matter. It is to be hoped that this series will one day host also a book on compliance, so to speak, with advisory opinions of the ICJ, for that is a field where the Court's suasion powers face an even greater test, as the recent issue of the *Legal Consequences of the Construction of a Wall in the Occupied Palestinian Territory* clearly shows.

Cesare P. R. Romano
New York University
4 July 2004

Preface

The idea of this project was born in the aftermath of the provisional measures orders of the International Court of Justice (ICJ) in the Breard and LaGrand cases. The failure of the Court's orders to prevent the execution of Angel Francisco Breard and Walter LaGrand triggered a huge controversy as to the binding force of ICJ provisional measures and their alleged general inefficacy to provide actual interim protection. The Court was seized of cases with potential impacts for the domestic criminal system, raising the question whether states are ready to defer to the Court in such matters and obey its decisions. At the same time, the Court had a record number of cases on its docket, some of which were of a highly political character, which gave rise to fears as to possible non-compliance. All these issues made the question of the actual track record of the ICJ decisions appear a natural one—one frequently addressed, but never made the subject of a contextual study systematically exploring the state practice in relation to compliance with ICJ decisions.

This study was submitted as a Ph.D. thesis to the Faculty of Law of the University of Munich in the summer term 2003 under the supervision of Professor Bruno Simma, who was elected Judge to the International Court of Justice whilst the manuscript was being finalized. The present publication contains updated references to cover literature and jurisprudence up to the end of 2003; the decisions covered are all cases giving rise to an obligation of compliance and concerning matters sufficiently in advance so as to provide a reasonable factual basis for assessing compliance.

Many persons deserve credit for helping me to turn this project into a success. First of all, I wish to express my gratitude to His Excellency, Judge Bruno Simma, for tutoring my Ph.D. thesis as well as for his continuous support and inspiration during the seven years in which I worked at the Institute of Public International Law at the University of Munich. Already during my law studies and for several years thereafter, he gave me the opportunity to participate in challenging projects. Much more than only a working place, the Institute of Public International Law became the ideal place for me to live and explore my passion for public international law. It gave me a warm and collegiate as well as inspiring atmosphere to work in, and my particular thanks go to Daniel-Erasmus Khan and Andreas L. Paulus as well as all present and former members of the institute. My thanks also go to Professor Dietrich Rauschning at the University of Göttingen, Judge at the Human Rights Chamber for Bosnia and Herzegovina, who supported me in the early days of my studies and offered me interesting opportunities to take my first steps in public international law during my time as a research assistant at the University of Göttingen. He also enabled me to broaden my horizons and get acquainted with alternative, non-European perspectives to public international law through a stay as a special student at the University of Singapore in 1994.

The research for this study was mainly carried out at Harvard University and New York University, where I had the honor and privilege to work and study from January 2000 to June 2001 (Harvard Law School) and in fall 2001 (New York University School of Law) as an Emile Noël fellow and research associate of Professor Joseph H. H. Weiler. I am greatly indebted to Professor Weiler, not only for giving me wonderful research opportunities, but also for the multiple intellectual and human experiences which I encountered during those fellowships and for the many things I learned from working with him, in particular, an integral approach to law in context. My times at Harvard Law School and New York University School of Law were a gift for life and I am grateful to all who made this possible.

During a visit to the ICJ in March 2002, I had the honor to discuss my research results with several judges and clerks of the Court, which deepened my understanding of the matter. My warm thanks go to all who were ready to meet with me and discuss my research results. With more enthusiasm, thought, and diligence than I could have reasonably expected, Steven Bartels assisted me in editing and revising the manuscript and developed as much passion for this project as myself. Lasia Bloss contributed inspiring discussions and readily helped out in reply to many last-minute requests for material. Peter Schramm deserves credit for helping me in the final preparation of the thesis for submission; Imogen Fowler kindly advised on linguistic questions. Finally, my thanks go to Verena von Bomhard and Andreas Renck of Lovells Alicante for making it possible to find time and space for completing this project.

This thesis is dedicated to my parents, whose loving support and confidence in myself were of tremendous help throughout this project as well as in my life and career in general. The assistance of my family and friends helped me to get through all difficulties and rough phases, and in the name of all, I wish to thank my sister and brother-in-law, and my partner, Luis.

Last but not least, this study was made possible with the generous support of the Volkswagen Foundation, and I am greatly indebted to the Foundation for their belief in the promise of this research project.

C.S.

Contents

Table of Cases

Abbreviations

UN documents are cited according to their official UN document symbols. For further information, see the United Nations Documentation: Research Guide, Document Symbols, http://www.un.org/Depts/dhl/resguide/symbol. htm

General abbreviations

AIOC	Anglo-Iranian Oil Company
APRA	Alianza Popular Revolucionaria Americana— American People's Revolutionary Alliance
ANAD	Accord de non-aggression et d'assistance en matière de défense
BBC	British Broadcasting Corporation
CIA	Central Intelligence Agency
Decl.	Declaration
Diss. Op.	Dissenting Opinion
DRC	Democratic Republic of the Congo
ECOSOC	United Nations Economic and Social Council
EEC	European Economic Community
EEZ	Exclusive Economic Zone
EFZ	Exclusive Fishery Zone
FCN Treaty	Treaty of Friendship, Commerce, and Navigation
FRG	Federal Republic of Germany
GA	United Nations General Assembly
ICAO	International Civil Aviation Organization
ICJ	International Court of Justice
ICRC	International Committee of the Red Cross
ICJ Rep.	ICJ Reports
ICTY	International Criminal Tribunal for the Former Yugoslavia
ILC	UN International Law Commission
ILO	International Labor Organization

MONUC	United Nations Organization Mission in the Democratic Republic of the Congo
NATO	North Atlantic Treaty Organization
NGO	Non governmental organization
OAU	Organization of African Unity
OAS	Organization of American States
PCIJ	Permanent Court of International Justice
PRC	People's Republic of China
SEATO	South East Asian Treaty Organization
Sep. Op.	Separate Opinion
SG	UN Secretary-General
UK	United Kingdom of Great Britain and Northern Ireland
UN	United Nations
UNASOG	United Nations Aouzou Strip Observer Group
UNESCO	United Nations Educational, Scientific, and Cultural Organization
UNPROFOR	United Nations Protection Force
US/USA	United States of America
USSR	Union of Soviet Socialist Republics
VCCR	Vienna Convention on Consular Relations
WL	Westlaw
ZPO	Zivilprozessordnung (German Code of Civil Procedure)

Journals/serial publications

AdG	Archiv der Gegenwart
AdV	Archiv des Völkerrechts
AFDI	Annuaire française de droit international
Afr. JICL	African Journal of International and Comparative Law/Revue africaine de droit international et comparé
AJIL	American Journal of International Law
Am. Pol. Sci. R	American Political Science Review
ASIL Insights	(American Society of International Law) Insights

BDGVR	Berichte der Deutschen Gesellschaft für Völkerrecht
Bos. C. TWJ	Boston College Third World Law Journal
Br. LR	Brooklyn Law Review
BU ILJ	Boston University International Law Journal
BYIL	British Yearbook of International Law
Cal. W. ILJ	California Western International Law Journal
Can.–US LJ	Canada–United States Law Journal
Case W. Res. JIL	Case Western Reserve Journal of International Law
Cath. ULR	Catholic University Law Review
CILJSA	Comparative and International Law Journal of South Africa
Col. JTL	Columbia Journal of Transnational Law
Col. LR	Columbia Law Review
Crim. LF	Criminal Law Forum
CTK Daily News	(Ceska Tiskova Kancelar) Daily News
CYIL	Canadian Yearbook of International Law
Denv. JILP	Denver Journal of International Law and Policy
Dig. IL	Digest of International Law
DoS Bull.	(US) Department of State Bulletin
EELR	European Environmental Law Review
EJIL	European Journal of International Law
EPIL	Encyclopedia of Public International Law
Etudes Norm.	Etudes Normandes
EuGRZ	Europäische Grundrechte-Zeitschrift
Ford. ELJ	Fordham Environmental Law Journal
F-W	Die Friedens-Warte
Ga. JICL	Georgia Journal of International and Comparative Law
GYIL	German Yearbook of International Law
Harv. ILJ	Harvard International Law Journal
HYIL	Hague Yearbook of International Law
IBRU Int'l Bound & Sec. Bull	IBRU International Boundary and Security Bulletin
ICJ YB	ICJ Yearbook
ICLQ	International and Comparative Law Quarterly
IJ Glob.Env. Issues	International Journal of Global Environmental Issues

ILM	International Legal Materials
ILR	International Law Reports
ILSA JICL	(International Law Students' Association) Journal of International & Comparative Law
Indian JIL	Indian Journal of International Law
IO	International Organization
JDI	Journal de Droit International
Jers. LR	Jersey Law Review
JIL & Pract.	Journal of International Law and Practice
JiR	Jahrbuch für internationales Recht
JKaBA	Journal of the Kansas Bar Association
JuS	Juristische Schulung
JZ	Juristen-Zeitung
Leid. JIL	Leiden Journal of International Law
Lloyd's List Int'l	Lloyd's List International
LOS Bulletin	UN Law of the Sea Bulletin
MEED	Middle East Economic Digest
Mich. JIL	Michigan Journal of International Law
MLR	Modern Law Review
Nig. AIL	Nigerian Annual of International Law
NILR	Nederlands Tijdschrift voor Internationaal Recht/ Netherlands International Law Review
NQHR	Netherlands Quarterly of Human Rights
Nord. TIR	Nordisk Tidsskrift for International Ret
NYIL	Netherlands Yearbook of International Law
NYU JILP	New York University Journal of International Law and Politics
ODIL	Ocean Development and International Law
Ohio S. JDR	Ohio State Journal on Dispute Resolution
ÖZöR	Österreichische Zeitschrift für öffentliches Recht
Proc. ASIL	Proceedings of the American Society of International Law
RAGDI	Revista de la Asociación Guatemalteca de Derecho Internacional
RBDI	Revue belge de droit international
RDI	Rivista di diritto internazionale

RDICD	Revista de Derecho Internacional y Ciencias Diplomáticas
RdC	Receuil des Cours
Rec. NYCBA	Record of the Association of the Bar of the City of New York
REgyDI	Revue égyptienne de droit international
REspDI	Revista española de derecho internacional
RGDIP	Revue générale de droit international public
RIAA	Reports of International Arbitral Awards
RPDI	Revista peruana de derecho internacional
S.Ill.U. LJ	Southern Illinois University Law Journal
Stan. JIL	Stanford Journal of International Law
StV	Strafverteidiger
Syd. LR	Sydney Law Review
Temple ICLJ	Temple International and Comparative Law Journal
Tex. ILJ	Texas International Law Journal
U. Pitt. LR	University of Pittsburgh Law Review
UNYB	United Nations Yearbook
US–Qatar J Online	US–Qatar Journal Online Edition
Va. JIL	Virginia Journal of International Law
Vand. JTL	Vanderbilt Journal of Transnational Law
Wis. ILJ	Wisconsin International Law Journal
Yb WA	Yearbook of World Affairs
YIEnvL	Yearbook of International Environmental Law
ZaöRV	Zeitschrift für ausländisches öffentliches Recht und Völkerrecht

Treaty series

CTS	Consolidated Treaty Series
LNTS	League of Nations Treaty Series
TIAS	United States Treaties and other International Acts Series
UNTS	United Nations Treaty Series

Introduction

Business is booming for the International Court of Justice (ICJ). Its prestige and activity have reached unprecedented heights. At the time of writing, the Court's docket comprises twenty-one contentious cases involving litigants from four continents[1] and a noticeable contingent of African countries.[2] Although Asian states resort to the ICJ less frequently—cultural issues may be at play here—there are still a steady number appearing as parties.[3] The cases presently before the Court address a diverse range of topics, including use of force, genocide, maritime delimitation, title to territory, location of borders, law of treaties, state responsibility, international criminal law, immunity, treatment of aliens, and human rights. The impartiality and expertise

[1] Application of the Convention on the Prevention and Punishment of the Crime of Genocide (Bosnia v. Federal Republic of Yugoslavia), Gabčíkovo–Nagymaros (Hungary/Slovakia), Ahmadou Sadio Diallo (Republic of Guinea v. Democratic Republic of the Congo), Legality of use of force (Yugoslavia v. United Kingdom), Legality of use of force (Yugoslavia v. Portugal), Legality of use of force (Yugoslavia v. Netherlands), Legality of use of force (Yugoslavia v. Italy), Legality of use of force (Yugoslavia v. Germany), Legality of use of force (Yugoslavia v. France), Legality of use of force (Yugoslavia v. Canada), Legality of use of force (Yugoslavia v. Belgium), Armed activities on the territory of the Congo (Democratic Republic of the Congo v. Uganda), Application of the Convention on the Prevention and Punishment of the Crime of Genocide (Croatia v. Federal Republic of Yugoslavia), Maritime delimitation between Nicaragua and Honduras in the Caribbean sea (Nicaragua v. Honduras), Certain property (Liechtenstein v. Germany), Territorial and maritime dispute (Nicaragua v. Colombia), Frontier Dispute (Benin/Niger), Armed activities on the territory of the Congo (New application: 2002), (Democratic Republic of the Congo v. Rwanda), Avena and other Mexican Nationals (Mexico v. United States of America), Certain criminal proceedings in France (Republic of the Congo v. France), Sovereignty over Pedra Branca/Pulau Batu Puteh, Middle Rocks, and South Ledge (Malaysia/Singapore).

[2] They account for five of the cases reported in the preceding note. The proceedings instituted by Libya in 1992 against the United States and the United Kingdom concerning the Lockerbie incident (Interpretation and Application of the 1971 Montreal Convention (Libya v. USA) and (Interpretation and Application of the 1971 Montreal Convention (Libya v. UK)) were discontinued due to an agreement between the parties. The Court took note of the discontinuance and removed the cases from its list by orders of 10 September 2003. In two other cases launched by African states, final judgments were delivered in 2002 (Arrest warrant (Democratic Republic of the Congo v. Belgium) Judgment of 14 February 2002 (see in detail below Chapter 3 B XXVII) and Land and Maritime Boundary between Cameroon and Nigeria (Cameroon v. Nigeria), Judgment of 10 October 2002).

[3] Currently pending is a case submitted by Malaysia and Singapore in which the Court is asked to rule on the sovereignty over certain territories (Sovereignty over Pedra Branca/Pulau Batu Puteh, Middle Rocks, and South Ledge; the parties jointly notified the ICJ of their respective special agreement on 24 July 2003, see joint notification to the Registrar of the International Court of Justice, http://212.153.43.18/icjwww/idocket/imasi/imasiorder/imasi_iapplication_20030724.PDF). Recently, the Court delivered its judgments in two other cases involving Asian litigants, one in a case jointly submitted by Malaysia and Indonesia (Sovereignty over Pulau Litigan and Pulau Sipadan, Judgment of 17 December 2002); and another in a case instituted by Iran against the United States based on alleged violations of the Treaty of Amity, Economic Relations and Consular Rights through actions against Iranian oil platforms in 1987 and 1988 (Oil Platforms, Judgment of 6 November 2003).

of the Court are beyond question, as is the high quality of its jurisprudence. Certainly, the day when the Court handles all disputes between states remains a long way off; this reality should not detract from the impact of its jurisprudence on the development of international law, particularly since the Court has shed its former image as a Western-dominated body. The diversity of litigants, judges, and subject-matters seems to justify the institution's unofficial title of "World Court," even in the absence of universal compulsory jurisdiction. The Court's full docket has necessitated steps to increase the efficiency of its working mechanisms—not to mention its budget.[4]

The situation was quite different in the not-too-distant past when the Court faced numerous challenges to its authority. The Court's 1966 judgment in the South West Africa cases precipitated an outcry particularly from developing countries and was followed by a wave of instances of non-appearance and defiance in the 1970s. A climax was reached in the context of the Nicaragua case, where the open refusal of the United States to respect the judgment, its veto of Security Council action under Article 94(2) of the Charter, and the subsequent General Assembly resolutions urging compliance[5] bear witness that the success of the Court should not be taken for granted. The ICJ's ongoing challenge lies in winning over its state clientele through the quality and legitimacy of its work.[6]

The Nicaragua judgment in particular has drawn attention to the relative weakness of the enforcement procedures available to the ICJ in comparison to those available in municipal judicial proceedings.[7] Therefore, discussions of the role and significance of the Court will naturally bring up the question relating to its actual performance. The rate of compliance will provide a measurement for success. Moreover, it will have a decisive impact on the

---

[4] See Speech by President Guillaume to the General Assembly, 29 October 2002, http://212.153.43.18/icjwww/ipresscom/SPEECHES/iSpeechPresident_Guillaume_GA57_20021029.htm.

[5] See in detail *infra* Chapter 3 B XVIII g. Some commentators have pointed to the end of the Cold War as an explanation for the current success and, through a comparison with the Court's early phase, conclude that there is reason to fear the success is less a trend than part of a cycle, see *Scott/Bothwell/Pennell*, 3 ILSA JICL (1996), at 1–29. Yet the early ICJ years and the present situation are not quite comparable: the early years already saw various cases of refusals to comply—notably, the Corfu Channel case and the Anglo-Iranian Oil Company case—and the origin of litigants before the Court was far less representative then, with litigants almost exclusively coming from Western European and American states.

[6] Indeed, just recently, the Court delivered two decisions which could further test its current authority: the judgment in the Cameroon–Nigeria boundary dispute and an order for provisional measures in the dispute between Mexico and the US in the Avena case on the Vienna Convention on Consular Relations, see *infra* n. 12. In the latter case, it also remains to be seen whether any obligation of compliance that may arise from the judgment will be heeded.

[7] See on the development of the Court's image *Tomuschat*, 281 RdC (1999), at 411–12. In the aftermath of the Nicaragua judgment, commentators focused on the Court's limitations and saw its potential in a rather pessimistic light, questioning in particular the desirability of compulsory jurisdiction from an institution-building perspective. See *Scott/Carr*, 81 AJIL (1987), at 57–76.

Court's future role and self-understanding. Cases of open defiance constitute an institutional challenge, whereas instances of successful implementation strengthen the Court's position and prestige. In the 1970s, a series of snubs at the Court's authority encouraged similar behavior by other litigants, which was exacerbated by a general crisis of confidence in the ICJ. Conversely, a sustained streak of successfully implemented decisions will considerably heighten the stakes for non-compliance and tend to isolate the defiant state. While the need for a thorough analysis of the compliance record thus appears obvious, a comprehensive treatise on the issue is still wanting at present.[8] Indeed, this is a need which has been frequently identified in recent years—most notably from judges of the Court themselves.[9] The present study is a contribution to close this gap. As will be illustrated in detail, the record for judgments has generally been quite positive. The true test of the authority of provisional measures is yet to come, since the persistent controversy over their binding force was unequivocally settled by the Court only in 2001. All in all, the analysis of the practice will show that while much is left to be desired, the record for provisional measures deserves more praise than its reputation would suggest.

The increased workload and the numerous cases with security implications in particular certainly present risks from the perspective of compliance. The Court's revived role, increased prominence, and the effectively higher value of provisional measures after the LaGrand judgment might give new impetus for states to submit cases disingenuously in an attempt to exploit the Court for purely political purposes. The Court will have to refine its mechanisms to

---

[8] There is a Ph.D. thesis by Tuncel, *L'exécution des décisions de la Cour internationale de Justice selon la Charte des Nations Unies*, published in 1960, but his focus is on comparing Article 94 of the Charter to the League of Nations framework and there is only little practice analyzed, apart from the fact that there has been a large number of decisions delivered in the meantime. Only in the course of updating the present study for publication, the author became aware of a parallel research project with a similar title, *L'exécution des décisions de la Cour Internationale de Justice*, by Aida Azar, published in late 2003. The research agenda of that book, however, was rather different than the present author's. Ms Azar focused on an analysis of Article 94, developed a typology of execution techniques, and examined the legal consequences of non-compliance, explaining the enforcement mechanisms under Article 94(2) of the UN Charter and the rules of state responsibility. Her book does not aim, however, at giving a comprehensive picture of the Court's actual track record, covering all relevant decisions, which is the main subject of the present book (see *infra* Chapter 1 A).

[9] See, for example, Judge *Oda*'s statement, 59 ICLQ (2000), at 251: "In my view, one subject missing from contemporary studies on the function and work of the International Court of Justice is a pragmatic examination of the manner in which certain contentious cases presented to the International Court of Justice have disappeared from view and of whether a judgment, once handed down, has actually been complied with by the parties to the dispute." See also the statement by ICJ President Bedjaoui in an address to the Asian–African Legal Consultative Committee in 1994, ICJ YB 1994–1995, 230: "[Compliance with decisions of the ICJ] is a subject of capital importance—but one that is, paradoxically, disregarded or to some extent ignored or played down by legal writers."

tackle such problems.[10] Another potential ground for concern could lie in the large amount of cases which reached the Court on the basis of compulsory jurisdiction rather than by a joint submission of the parties.[11] The preliminary signs are somewhat mixed on the basis of two recent cases that will not be examined in detail because of lack of sufficient facts for evaluating compliance, but hopefully the states concerned can be persuaded to take the route of legality.[12]

It is interesting to step back and see how the Charter mechanism for compliance with and enforcement of ICJ decisions was perceived at the time of the Charter's adoption. Shortly after it entered into force, an early Charter commentary by two distinguished experts in this field, Leland Goodrich and Edvard Hambro,[13] offered the following appraisal of Article 94(2)—the provision on enforcement of ICJ judgments:

[10] The pending request for an advisory opinion concerning the legal consequences of the wall in the occupied Palestinian territory (http://212.153.43.18/icjwww/idocket/imwp/imwporder/imwp_iapplication_20031208.PDF) is an example of a highly political conflict brought before the Court. Regardless of the features of the eventual opinion of the Court, doubtlessly it will meet critique by parts of the international public opinion and voices will be heard stating that the Court's decision showed its inadequacy adequately to address the world's most serious crises and questioning whether the Court is worth while the effort at all.

[11] See in particular the concerns to this extent by *Oda*, 49 ICLQ (2000), at 265.

[12] In the Land and Maritime Boundary between Cameroon and Nigeria case, the Court decided in its Judgment of 10 October 2002 *inter alia* that sovereignty over the Bakassi peninsula belonged to Cameroon. Nigeria's initial reactions shed some doubts on whether it will heed its repeated commitment to obey the Court's decision and withdraw from the peninsula; in particular, there appears to be resistance on the local level, http://www.irinnews.org/report.asp?ReportID=30415&SelectRegion=West_Africa&SelectCountry=CAMEROON-NIGERIA http://www.irinnews.org/report.asp?ReportID=30673&SelectRegion=West_Africa&SelectCountry=WEST%20AFRICA. The promising sign is that, despite expressing its problems with accepting the decision, the parties are currently negotiating, with the involvement of Secretary-General Annan; the UN has sent an assessment mission to the peninsula, see http://www.irinnews.org/report.asp?ReportID=31251&SelectRegion=West_Africa&SelectCountry=CAMEROON-NIGERIA. At both parties' request, the Secretary-General established a Mixed Commission shortly after the judgment was delivered in order to facilitate its peaceful implementation; for details, see the Commission's website at http://www.un.org/Depts/dpa/prev_dip/africa/office_for_srsg/fst_office_for_srsg.htm. In the Avena case (Avena and other Mexican Nationals (Mexico v. United States of America), Order of 5 February 2003, at para. 59), the Court has ordered the United States to take all necessary measures to ensure that three Mexican nationals on death row in Texas and Oklahoma are not executed pending the final proceedings. While the response of Oklahoma authorities was ambiguous, the first reactions from the Texas governor were not quite promising, www.internationaljusticeproject.org/briefsWorldNews.cfm. When the Court issued its order, no execution dates had yet been set, and at the time of writing, all concerned individuals are still alive. As the judgment in that case is likely to have considerable domestic impacts, it remains to be seen how far it will be implemented.

[13] Goodrich was director of the World Peace Foundation from 1942 to 1946 and involved in the debate on the creation of the UN; he was member of the secretariat of the San Francisco Founding Conference, see http://www.bartleby.com/65/go/Goodrich.html. Hambro was Registrar of the ICJ from 1946 to 1953 and President of the 25th Session of the General Assembly, see http://www.un.org/ga/55/president/bio25.htm.

Judging from past experience, this paragraph is not likely to have great importance in practice. It has happened very rarely that states have refused to carry out the decisions of international tribunals. The difficulty has always been in getting states to submit their disputes to a tribunal. Once they have done so, they have usually been willing to accept even an adverse judgment.[14]

While the authors were right in predicting that Article 94(2) was not to exert a great degree of influence on future practice, compliance with ICJ decisions proved far more problematic than with PCIJ decisions. The scarcity of practice relating to Article 94(2) is due to the fact that in most cases where compliance was problematic, creditor states did not bring the matter before the Security Council, or the Security Council was unwilling or incapable of taking a decision. The year in which the first edition of Goodrich and Hambro's commentary appeared was also the year in which the ICJ issued the judgment on the merits in the Corfu Channel case—which was to become a case of non-compliance lasting over 40 years. Accordingly, in the next edition, published in 1969, the first sentence of the quotation is conspicuously omitted.[15]

---

[14] Goodrich/Hambro, *Charter of the United Nations*, at 485. Another author praises the article as innovation, see Dolivet, *The United Nations*, at 76: "This is an important provision, for it creates for the first time an enforcement procedure for the application of the decisions of the International Court of Justice [...] A new legal concept for juridical procedure in the international field has been established." This assessment is hardly understandable if one considers the fact that the League Covenant actually established a more far-reaching system, see critical *Vulcan*, 18 RGDIP (1947), at 196.

[15] See Goodrich/Hambro/Simons, *Charter of the United Nations*, at 557.

1

Methodology

A. PERSPECTIVE OF THIS STUDY

It would be impossible to cover all aspects related to the wide-ranging topic of compliance with decisions of the ICJ in one study. The topic could be approached from many different directions. For example, one might analyze the issue through the lens of compliance theory, considering why states obey international law in general, what motivates them to obey international courts, and how mechanisms inducing compliance could be enhanced from this perspective. Another approach would be to focus on the potential for enforcement in the post-adjudicative phase, suggesting ways to improve the efficiency of various enforcement mechanisms. Both these approaches would apply general theories to the particular case of the ICJ. Another perspective would be through a comparative lens. This approach would examine the ICJ in connection with its predecessor, the Permanent Court of International Justice, or other international and domestic tribunals, with the focus on functions, structures, compliance, and enforcement mechanisms. The topic could also be approached from a very broad understanding of "compliance." Such an analysis would go beyond the question of a state's obedience with regard to ICJ decisions binding upon it to include an examination of the impact of ICJ pronouncements on state behavior in general and the appropriateness of classifying ICJ decisions as a source of international law in their own right.

The present study has another focus: state practice. It assesses the extent to which states participating in ICJ proceedings have respected their obligation to comply with the decisions of the Court and the lessons that can be drawn for the future. While cases of non-compliance have been the main focus of earlier publications that tackled the issue of compliance with ICJ decisions, this study strives for an overall picture, although certainly due regard will be given to the problem cases. General assumptions will be questioned, such as those relating to the difficulty of proceedings based on compulsory jurisdiction versus those introduced by special agreement. Attention will also be paid to the different track records of judgments versus provisional measures. The study begins with an overview of the legal framework for compliance in terms of the scope of the obligation to comply with ICJ decisions and the Charter system for enforcing those decisions; in this context, reference to the Court's practice will be made to supplement the interpretation of the respective provisions. Moreover, other enforcement mechanisms such as self-help will be briefly explained.

The second part of the study analyzes state practice in all ICJ cases that are relevant for the question of compliance. A discussion of the post-adjudicative phase of these cases will certainly be an important aspect. Yet the discussion avoids a shortsighted approach that would merely examine whether the subsequent action of the parties squares with the formula contained in the operative part of the respective decision. A contextual examination is preferable in that it is often not possible to determine the scope of the obligation to comply and the action necessary for the decision's implementation without considering the concrete circumstances of the case. It would be naive to assume that the only aspect relevant for the state's decision to comply was the existence of Article 94(1) the Charter.[1] Indeed, only a contextual analysis, which takes into account a variety of factors—such as the origins of the dispute, the relationship between the parties, the competing interests involved, and the route by which the case reached the Court—will enable general conclusions to be drawn as to the reasons for a decision's (non-) implementation. Finally, compliance and efficient dispute settlement are related, but not identical, questions. While a priori the Court's inability to settle a dispute would appear less harmful for its authority than outright defiance by a party, the perceived inadequacy of the ICJ as a settlement mechanism despite compliance would still be prejudicial for the Court's image as an institution and might discourage states from submitting further cases. The efficiency of dispute settlement will therefore be among the questions addressed, although the emphasis will rest on the compliance practice of states.

The study concludes with a section synthesizing the various "lessons learned" from the actual practice of states with regard to the issue of compliance and evaluating prospects for the future. My modest aim is to stimulate debate on the revived role of the Court with particular focus on the post-adjudicative phase and to draw attention to the compliance issue from the specific perspective of state practice.

B. THE RELEVANT DECISIONS

In the context of the present study and in accordance with the terminology contained in the Charter, the Statute and the Rules of Court, the term "decision" refers to a formal judicial measure aimed at creating immediate legal effects; advisory opinions are therefore excluded.[2] More concretely, this study concentrates on compliance with judgments and provisional measures

---

[1] See *Magid* in Peck/Lee, Increasing the effectiveness, at 332–3, on factors relevant for the likelihood of success.
[2] See Article 94(1) of the Charter on decisions: "Each Member of the United Nations undertakes to comply with the decision of the International Court of Justice in any case to

of the Court, but not with interlocutory decisions other than provisional measures.

I. Final judgments

The usefulness of monitoring compliance with the Court's final decisions is apparent. Non-compliance with the final decision puts the very purpose of adjudication before the Court into question and could potentially diminish the Court's authority and prestige.

II. Interim measures of protection

Provisional measures serve to protect rights at stake in pending cases. Non-compliance can frustrate the object of the proceedings and render the adjudication process useless; therefore defiance of the Court's interim measures of protection similarly puts its authority and efficiency into question.

Until recently, the question whether provisional measures issued by the Court are binding on parties was a matter of substantial controversy.[3] The Court clarified this issue in the LaGrand judgment in clear and un-equivocal terms: "Orders on provisional measures under Article 41 [of the

---

which it is a party" and Article 96 on advisory opinions: "(1) The General Assembly or the Security Council may request the International Court of Justice to give an advisory opinion on any legal question. (2) Other organs of the United Nations and specialized agencies, which may at any time be so authorized by the General Assembly, may also request advisory opinions of the Court on legal questions arising within the scope of their activities." The Statute uses the term "decision" only with regard to the Court's internal practice and procedure on the one hand and to contentious proceedings on the other hand (see Articles 16(2), 17(2), 24(3), 31(5), (6), 36(6), 39(2), 41(2), 59, 62(2), 64. The term is not used in the context of advisory opinions, see Articles 65–8, in particular, Article 65 which stipulates:

"(1) The Court may give an advisory opinion on any legal question at the request of whatever body may be authorized by or in accordance with the Charter of the United Nations to make such a request.

(2) Questions upon which the advisory opinion of the Court is asked shall be laid before the Court by means of a written request containing an exact statement of the question upon which an opinion is required, and accompanied by all documents likely to throw light upon the question."

[3] Lengthy discussion of this settled question of law is unnecessary. There is abundant literature discussing the various arguments in favor and against binding force. For details on the prior debate, see Elkind, *Interim Protection*, at 153–66; *Mennecke/Tams*, 42 GYIL (1999), at 203–9; Oellers-Frahm, *Die einstweilige Anordnung*, at 107–15; Sztucki, *Interim Measures*, at 260–94; all with further references. See also the written pleadings in LaGrand: German memorial, Part 4, III 2, and the US Counter-memorial, Part VI, Chapter IV: http://212.153.43.18/icjwww/idocket/igus/iguspleadings/iGUS_ipleading_Memorial_Germany_19990916_Complete.htm; http://212.1 53.43.18/icjwww/idocket/igus/iguspleadings/iGUS_ipleading_CounterMemorial_US_20000327. htm; and Paraguay's Memorial of 9 October 1998, ICJ Pleadings, Vienna Convention on Consular Relations (Paraguay v. United States of America), 89–187, at 152–76 (Chapter 5 II).

Statute] have binding effect."[4] This finding garnered the support of an overwhelming majority within the Court;[5] although it did not form part of the judgment's operative section, the issue needed to be resolved before proceeding to the applicant's claim that the respondent had "violated its international legal obligation to comply with the Order on Provisional Measures issued by the Court."[6]

Although one might try to write off the significance of the decision by pointing to the *inter partes* effect of ICJ judgments under Article 59 of the Court's Statute, there are few doubts that the findings on provisional measures represent a landmark decision. It is unlikely that the Court, having affirmed the binding force of its orders of interim protection, would step back and decide differently in any future case. A state can no longer claim in good faith that it was not bound by an ICJ order of interim protection because of an alleged lack of binding force of such measures after the Court has clarified this issue in these general terms. The ICJ president stressed the general significance of the judgment in his speech to the General Assembly when presenting the ICJ report for 2000/2001:

[F]or the first time in its history, the Court took the opportunity to give a clear ruling on the effect of provisional measures [...] pursuant to Article 41 of its Statute. [...] Thus there is no longer any room for doubt: the provisional measures indicated as a matter of urgency by the Court for the purpose of safeguarding the rights of the parties are binding on them. The Court anticipates that in future these measures will as a result be better executed than when the matter was subject to doubt."[7]

The immediate reaction from Member States praising the decision[8] demonstrated the opinion of the international community that controversies

---

[4] LaGrand, Judgment of 27 June 2001 (hereinafter LaGrand judgment), at para. 109. In the concrete case, the Court found that the relevant order had been adopted pursuant to Article 41 and was therefore binding in character, creating legal obligations for the respondent, ibid., para. 110. See on this aspect of the judgment *Aceves*, 96 AJIL (2002), at 217–18; *Hillgruber*, 57 JZ (2002), at 98; *Mennecke*, 44 GYIL (2001), at 439–40, 445–9; *Oellers-Frahm*, 28 EuGRZ (2001), at 268–9; *Tams*, JuS 2002, at 328.

[5] The decision on the breach of the obligations under the order was reached by thirteen votes to two, LaGrand judgment, para. 128(5). Finding that the Court lacked jurisdiction for the decision on the breach of the order, Judge Parra-Aranguren did not express an opinion about the bindingness of the order, Sep. Op. Judge Parra-Aranguren, paras. 12–15. Judge Oda criticized the granting of the order as well as the Court's methodology concerning the findings on the binding force of provisional measures; yet, he took no clear stand on whether he considers the measures binding or not. His view was that the respondent complied with the measures, Diss. Op. Oda, paras. 28–35. *Mennecke*, 44 GYIL (2002), at 447–8, expresses some sympathy for Judge Oda's critique of the methodology.

[6] This was Germany's third submission in the case, see LaGrand judgment, para. 92.

[7] Speech by President Gilbert Guillaume, 30 October 2001, http://212.153.43.18/icjwww/ipresscom/SPEECHES/iSpeechPresident_Guillaume_GA56_20011030.htm, also printed at A/56/PV.32, 6–9.

[8] See the verbatim records of the General Assembly's meeting of 30 October 2001, A/56/PV.32, in particular, the representatives of Peru (at 10: "[The LaGrand decision] also produced valuable legal precedents on the juridical effects of the provisional measures provided for in

regarding the legal status of interim measures had been authoritatively settled by the Court.[9]

The discussion had mainly centered on the wording of the English text of Article 41(1) of the Statute, pursuant to which "[t]he Court shall have the power to indicate, if it considers that circumstances so require, any provisional measures which ought to be taken to preserve the respective rights of either party."

Some legal commentators, as well as the US in the LaGrand case, had argued that the language was merely exhortatory.[10] While the English text on its face permitted such a reading, the interpretation represented only one of several possible interpretations—including the contrary understanding that the language of the article was mandatory. This ambiguity is not evident in the equally authentic[11] French text, which suggests a compelling force: *"La Cour a le pouvoir d'indiquer, si elle estime que les circonstances l'exigent, quelles mesures conservatoires du droit de chacun doivent être prises à titre provisoire."*

---

article 41 of the Court's Statute"), Costa Rica (at 11: "We also note with satisfaction its decision that provisional measures dictated by the Court impose an obligation of compliance"), Mexico (at 15: "In [the LaGrand case and the dispute between Qatar and Bahrain], the Court has made significant contributions to international law and towards the objective of facilitating the future implementation of international legal norms. We are grateful to the Court for those two decisions. [. . .] The Court resolved a long-standing debate by determining that the provisional measures set forth in its decisions, in conformity with article 41 of its Statute, are binding and create a legal obligation for the States to which they are addressed."), Republic of Korea (at 21: "As pointed out by previous speakers, another landmark judgment of the Court was that of the LaGrand case. In its ruling, the Court recognized for the first time the binding nature of its orders for the indication of provisional measures under article 41 of the Statute. Given the ambiguity of the legal effect of provisional measures prior to this case, my delegation feels that the LaGrand judgment will serve to strengthen the role and authority of the Court and also encourage States to make use of it more frequently.") and Cameroon (at 22: [W]hat is particularly important is that the Court's ruling in the LaGrand case decides a question that has long been at the fore in debate on doctrine: the legal force of orders for the indication of provisional measures [. . .] The delegation of Cameroon welcomes this dictum of the judgment of 27 June 2001, which fully justifies the procedure of provisional measures before the International Court of Justice.")

[9] See *Oellers-Frahm*, 28 EuGRZ (2002), at 268, stating that the Court has terminated the debate on the binding force.

[10] See the US Counter-memorial in LaGrand, Part VI, Chapter IV, Section 2, http://212.153.43.18/icjwww/idocket/igus/iguspleadings/iGUS_ipleading_CounterMemorial_US_2000 0327.htm, with further references. The wording of the earlier Orders was also used as an argument: the Court's standard formulation was "should" instead of the less ambiguous "shall;" this was just changed after LaGrand, in Armed activities in the territory of the Congo (whose authoritative text was French, though, and the French versions of earlier orders had always employed the formulation "doivent," which denotes a legal obligation, see *infra* Chapter 3 C, in particular, the Armed activities case, *ibid.* at XI. The Avena case, the most recent example of provisional measures, now applied the formulation "shall" for the first time in an order with English as authoritative text, so that there is no further room for confusion, see Avena and other Mexican Nationals (Mexico v. United States of America), Order of 5 February 2003 at para. 59.

[11] Articles 111, 92 cl. 2 of the Charter.

This text was the original version of the corresponding provision of the PCIJ Statute, with the English text merely being the translation.[12] In the LaGrand judgment, the Court resorted to the rule in Article 33(4) of the Vienna Convention of the Law of Treaties, which in its view reflected customary law, that stipulates that in cases of a difference of meaning between the equally authentic texts, the one that best reconciles the divergent texts, "having regard to the object and purpose of the treaty," shall prevail.[13] The Court applied the object and purpose test to the Statute and pointed out that its intent was to enable the Court to settle international disputes by binding decisions, with Article 41 serving in this context "to prevent the Court from being hampered in the exercise of its functions because the respective rights of the parties to a dispute are not preserved"—an objective only achievable through an interpretation of provisional measures as binding. It apparently saw this point very clear, devoting only one paragraph to it.[14] Another factor in which the Court saw its conclusion of binding force confirmed was the existence of a general principle in international judicial proceedings pursuant to which parties to a case must abstain from acts that might have a prejudicial effect on the execution of the final decision or aggravate or extend the dispute.[15] Finally, the Court deemed it appropriate to explain that neither the drafting history nor the wording of Article 94(1) of the Charter were arguments against the affirmative finding on the binding force of provisional measures.[16]

The Court reached the correct result: in fact, only the power to make binding provisional measures enables the ICJ to provide effective protection, and it is to be presumed that its powers conferred are meant to be effective. The role of the Court as a judicial institution advocates against the assumption that such powers are meant to be purely recommendatory; exhortatory mechanisms belong to the diplomatic realm. In general, while the concept of an international court empowered merely to recommend interim measures is not an impossible construct, this will rather be the exception to the rule and

---

[12] See LaGrand judgment, para. 100. See also the German memorial in LaGrand, http://212.153.43.18/icjwww/idocket/igus/iguspleadings/iGUS_ipleading_Memorial_Germany_19990916_Complete.htm, at 4.137–4.140, 4.149–4.150 with references to the other authentic languages.

[13] See LaGrand judgment, para. 101. More precisely, Article 33(4) of the Vienna Convention on the Law of Treaties reads (and was restated to this extent by the Court) that "when a comparison of the authentic text discloses a difference of meaning which the application of articles 31 and 32 does not remove, the meaning which best reconciles the texts, having regard to the object and purpose of the treaty, shall be adopted." Articles 31 and 32 embody the general rule and supplementary means of interpretation.

[14] LaGrand judgment, para. 102. Critical on the brevity of the reasoning on this point *Mennecke*, 44 GYIL (2001) at 447, expressing worries "whether the brief reasoning offered will silence the critics and convince reluctant governments of its correctness."

[15] LaGrand judgment, para. 103. For details on the Court's reasoning, see *Oellers-Frahm*, 28 EuGRZ (2002), at 268–9.

[16] LaGrand judgment, paras. 104–7.

there will most likely be a clear provision to this extent: in general, courts *order* in contentious cases—they do not merely *recommend*.[17] In the case of the ICJ, the procedural requirements for granting of provisional measures, which require the balancing of multiple factors, including the presence of prima-facie jurisdiction, the urgency of the situation, and the necessity of protective measures, are unlikely to have been designed to produce a mere recommendation.[18]

The LaGrand judgment is of tremendous significance for the present study, as it has shifted the focus in research relating to compliance with provisional measures. The question of their binding force is no longer situated in a legal "grey area." Analyzing compliance in this field is the examination of observance of a legal obligation, not of mere respect for recommendations. There is no longer room for doubts on the bindingness that might influence the positions of the parties, UN organs, or third states in respect of giving effect to provisional measures or assisting in this field.[19] At the same time, the revalorization of provisional measures through the LaGrand judgment adds to the desirability of research on compliance in this field, as interim protection will receive more attention; the significance of cases of defiance and inefficiency can no longer be downplayed by pointing to an uncertainty about the legal force. More than ever, non-compliance will question the authority and efficiency of the Court and might function as a disincentive for the submission of further cases, as well as a green light for non-compliance in subsequent

---

[17] See, for example, the comparison of the structure of various international courts and tribunals in the research matrix of the Project on International Courts and Tribunals, www.pict-pcti.org/matrix/Matrix-main.html, which shows that the power to grant interim measures normally implies the bindingness of those measures. The European Court of Human Rights is an exception, as the European Convention on Human Rights has not explicitly conferred powers on it in this field. The ECHR's rules create a right to grant interim measures of a recommendatory character: see Sands, *Manual on International Courts*, 207.

[18] In the words of Sir Hersch Lauterpacht, *The Development of International Law by the International Court*, at 254: "It cannot be lightly assumed [...] that the Court weighs minutely the circumstances which permit it to issue what is no more than an appeal to the moral sense of the parties." While prior to LaGrand, the Court had not made an explicit pronouncement on the binding force of provisional measures as it had never been required to do so, indications for binding force could be found in its prior jurisprudence and individual judges had openly spoken out in favor of binding force: see German memorial, *supra* n. 12 Part 4, III 2 with further references. As will be shown in the analysis of the cases, *infra* Chapter 3 C, the reactions of the parties in prior cases also point in this direction. LaGrand was the only case where the respondent's main and central argument was that the Court's provisional measures are non-binding; in the Breard case, the argument appeared to have been tailored more to the language of the particular order. Another case in which non-bindingness was reached was Anglo-Iranian Oil Company, but more in passing: in the first place, Iran claimed an excess of powers.

[19] Besides clarifying the binding force of provisional measures, the judgment followed the applicant's request and declared that the respondent had breached its obligation to comply with the measures. This introduced a sanctioning mechanism with a potential to influence compliance in further cases; see on this aspect *infra* Chapter 4 B IV and on the details in LaGrand *infra* Chapter 3 C X.

cases.[20] Moreover, as provisional measures will now be given increased attention and are perceived to give rise to a separate set of obligations in and of themselves, states might more frequently seek interim protection to exert pressure on their opponents. The potential for states to exploit such proceedings for political purposes and claim protection of rights the existence of which is far from clear in proceedings where the existence of a jurisdictional link is dubious might increase.[21] The Court should be mindful of this danger of politicization of interim proceedings and make sure that there are clear and precise criteria which make the decisions on interim protection predictable—in particular, that the criterion of prima-facie jurisdiction is thoroughly considered, as the Court's function is based on the principle of consent to its proceedings.[22]

III. Interlocutory decisions other than provisional measures: no object of this study

Other interlocutory decisions raise questions of a rather different nature and will not be analyzed in the present study. Decisions regulating the conduct of the parties during the proceedings are designed as binding under the ICJ Statute and the Rules[23] as part of the power of international courts to regulate their procedure.[24] Arguably such a decision might be considered a "decision" under Article 94(1).[25] Yet, the impact of non-compliance with these measures is distinct from that of non-compliance with provisional measures and judgments in that such conduct presents no direct interference with the rights forming the subject-matter of the dispute, and the Court itself disposes of appropriate means to tackle non-compliance and counterbalance potential negative effects. Certain interlocutory decisions, such as the decision to admit a certain piece of evidence, are self-executing and require no

---

[20] See *Aceves*, 96 AJIL (2002), at 218: "A pattern of non-compliance—at least if it continues—may undermine the Court's credibility and the value of provisional measures orders."

[21] See for a recent example Armed activities on the territory of the Congo (New application: 2002) (Democratic Republic of the Congo v. Rwanda), Order of 10 July 2002 (rejecting the request for interim protection of 28 May 2002, http://212.153.43.18/cijwww/cdocket/ccrw_capplication_20020528_demand.PDF).

[22] Recent practice appears to confirm that the Court has refined the standard for prima-facie jurisdiction and now applies a stricter test: see *infra* Chapter 4 B II 1.

[23] See, for example, Article 48: "The Court shall make orders for the conduct of the case, shall decide the form and time in which each party must conclude its arguments, and make all arrangements connected with the taking of evidence." Article 49: "The Court may, even before the hearing begins, call upon the agents to produce any document or to supply any explanations. Formal note shall be taken of any refusal."

[24] See Schachter, *International Law*, at 230 using general rules to support obligation of providing all relevant evidence and power of the Court to draw adverse inferences for failure to do so.

[25] See *Ajibola* in Bulterman/Kuijer, Compliance with judgments, at 13; Rosenne, *Law and Practice I*, 215–16; Tuncel, *L'exécution des décisions*, at 51–2; *Weckel*, 42 AFDI (1996), at 430.

implementation; others, such as the decision on the participation of a particular judge under Article 24(3) of the Statute, are implemented by the Court itself. In other cases the where the Court requests action by the parties, the Court might not see non-compliance as an impediment to a decision on the merits. For instance, if the Court orders a party to deliver certain pieces of evidence and this evidence is not produced, the Court may ascertain the facts through other means and possibly draw negative inferences from the failure to deliver information; the respective party thus might not only lose the opportunity to present favorable evidence, but even suffer a procedural disadvantage. If the parties fail to observe a deadline, the Court will not be paralyzed, but can and will find some solution. In such cases, the impact on the Court's authority and functioning is entirely different from failure to comply with provisional measures and judgments, whose very purpose can only be achieved through compliance. Non-compliance with interlocutory decisions does not directly affect the subject-matter of the proceedings, as it will result in automatic sanctions.[26] Accordingly, the parties will normally comply with the respective decisions already out of their own interest. Therefore, compliance in this field is not perceived as a problem.[27]

It would be a matter for a different study to analyze the degree to which the parties cooperate with the Court and the impact this has on the efficiency of the Court's procedure and ability to settle disputes. In this context, compliance with interlocutory decisions would be one aspect to consider among many, as cooperation has more facets than merely obeying the terms of an order.[28]

IV. Advisory opinions: no object of this study

Although there is no doubt that the advisory function is an important function of the Court with the potential to influence the further development of the law, advisory opinions by their very nature are not binding, and therefore, the compliance issue does not arise. Neither Article 94 of the

---

[26] It should also be noted that the impact of a failure of a party to cooperate (e.g. in the production of evidence), for example, to produce evidence cannot be determined *in abstracto* (in this example, because it is possible that the requested information was not indispensable).

[27] See *Ajibola* in Bulterman/Kuijer, Compliance with judgments, at 14: "[E]ven though such interlocutory matters as have been discussed here may not be covered by Article 94(2) of the Charter, there is adequate procedural protection to promote intrinsic compliance [. . .]" See further Rosenne, *Law and Practice I*, at 214–15; Tuncel, *L'exécution des décisions*, at 52–4 (reporting the proceedings in the Corfu Channel case). Most studies on the topic of compliance with ICJ decisions do not mention these ICJ decisions or address them only very briefly. For details on the obligations of the parties relating to evidence and the possible responses by international courts, see Sandifer, *Evidence before international tribunals*, at 112–75.

[28] On the particular problem of non-appearance (i.e. a particularly high degree of non-cooperation), see the monographs by Elkind and Thirlway, both titled, *Non-appearance before the International Court of Justice* and published in 1984 and 1985, respectively.

Charter nor Articles 59–61 of the Statute cover advisory opinions.[29] The relevant provision for these opinions—Article 96 of the Charter—[30]does not provide for binding force and an enforcement mechanism. Neither the organizations requesting an opinion nor States are under the obligation to give effect to an advisory opinion by virtue of Charter law.[31] It would not be correct to equate advisory opinions with declaratory judgments that do not require implementing action and are nevertheless binding: the scope of the obligation to comply (which in concrete cases might not encompass obligations of implementation) and the binding force are two separate questions. The efficiency of the Court's advisory jurisdiction is certainly a matter deserving analysis; yet, it is beyond the scope of the present study.[32]

Confusion may arise in the special case of so-called "binding advisory opinions"—opinions under Article 96 of the Charter on which certain

---

[29] For the text of Article 94 of the Charter, see *supra* Chapter II A; for Articles 59–61 see *infra* Chapter 2, n. 1.

[30] For the text of Article 96 of the Charter, see *supra* n. 2.

[31] See *Ajibola* in Bulterman/Kuijer, Compliance with judgments, at 16; *Guillaume* in Jasentuliyana, Perspectives on international law, at 275; *Kapoor* in Dhokalia, International Court in transition, at 312; *Mosler/Oellers-Frahm* in Simma, Charter, Article 96 at nn. 1 and 35–40; *Bacot*, 84 RGDIP (1980), at 1030; *Hudson*, 42 AJIL (1948), at 630–32; Rosenne, *Law and Practice II*, at 989, and *Law and Practice III*, at 1754–9; *Tanzi*, 6 EJIL (1995), at 570; *Tuncel*, *L'exécution des décisions*, at 58–9. The Court has explicitly confirmed the non-binding nature of its advisory opinions on numerous occasions. See, for example, Interpretation of Peace Treaties with Bulgaria, Hungary, and Romania, Advisory Opinion of 30 March 1950, at 71: "The Court's reply is only of an advisory character: as such, it has no binding force." See also Judgments of the Administrative Tribunal of the ILO upon complaints made against UNESCO, Advisory Opinion of 23 October 1956, at 84, Certain Expenses of the United Nations, Advisory Opinion of 20 July 1962, at 168.

[32] See *Guillaume* in Jasentuliyana, Perspectives on international law, at 275–6: "In practice [...], most—if not virtually all—of the advisory opinions have been endorsed by resolutions of the bodies or agencies concerned. Problems of compliance that have been encountered in this area have therefore involved not the Court's opinions themselves, but compliance with the resolutions adopted in pursuance of those opinions, and such problems do not fall within the scope of this study [on enforcement of decisions of the ICJ]." An overall positive balance is also drawn by *Weckel*, 42 AFDI (1996), at 430–2. For cases where states have refused to behave in accordance with an advisory opinion, see *Charney* in Damrosch, The ICJ at a Crossroads, at 297–9. See further on the reception of ICJ advisory opinions *Daillier* in Cot/Pellet, Charte des Nations Unies, Article 96, at 1300–2; *Pomerance*, Advisory Function, at 341–71; Rosenne, *Law and Practice I*, at 309–10. The pronouncements of the Court will certainly enjoy great persuasive authority (see *Kapoor* in Dhokalia, International Court in transition, 312). While the Security Council could not take enforcement action under Article 94(2), it will have the right to take the Court's interpretation into account in the exercise of its competences under other provisions; thus, it could take action to give effect to an advisory opinion under Chapters VI or VII of the Charter, provided that the conditions of those provisions are fulfilled, see *Tanzi*, 6 EJIL (1995), at 570. In contentious proceedings, a state might refer to an advisory opinion as evidence of the existence or scope of a particular right that it seeks to enforce. The Court will likely endorse the position taken in the advisory proceedings, as it generally strives for consistency in its jurisprudence and relies on its case law, including advisory opinions: see Shahabuddeen, *Precedent in the World Court*, at 26–31, 165–71. Yet, this means of "enforcing" advisory opinions (in a non-technical sense) has its limitations. It would presuppose the existence of a jurisdictional link, and contentious proceedings are only open to states, see Article 35 of the Statute.

international instruments confer binding effect.[33] Such clauses are to be found especially in treaties involving the UN or specialized agencies, where they offer a mechanism for the authoritative settlement of disputes through advisory proceedings, a certain substitute for contentious proceedings where the Statute precludes international organizations from being a party.[34] Likely candidates for the inclusion of such clauses would be conventions on privileges and immunities, headquarters agreements, or statutes of specialized agencies; even some general international treaties contain clauses to that extent.[35] These "binding advisory opinions" are no exception to the rule that advisory opinions *per se* are non-binding: the binding force is not derived from the Charter or the Court's Statute, but from the respective instrument. In such cases, a conventional obligation to comply with the opinion will arise, but this fact cannot turn it into a Court decision acquiring the force of *res judicata*. Article 94 of the Charter will not apply; for the purposes of the Charter and the Statute, those opinions remain regular

[33] For details on these types of advisory opinions, see *Ago* in Montaldo (ed.), El derecho internacional, at 1081–98; *idem*, 85 AJIL (1991), at 439–51; *Benadava* in: Infante Caffi, Solución judicial de controversias, 85–94. The compatibility of such clauses with the Court's advisory function might be a matter for debate (see *Bacot*, 84 RGDIP (1980), at 1043–55), but the Court has not seen any obstacle for the exercise of its advisory jurisdiction and has rendered advisory opinions in cases where they existed, see, for example, Judgments of the Administrative Tribunal of the ILO upon Complaints Made against UNESCO, Advisory Opinion of 23 October 1956, at 84. For the most recent case of a "binding" advisory opinion, see Difference relating to immunity from legal process of a special rapporteur of the Commission on Human Rights, Advisory Opinion of 29 April 1999, ICJ Reports 1999, 62; for details, see *infra* Chapter 2, nn. 239, 246.

[34] Article 34(1) of the ICJ Statute: "Only States may be parties before the Court." Therefore, disputes with and within international organizations cannot become the subject-matter of contentious proceedings before the Court, although the legal validity of acts by international organizations might incidentally become relevant in contentious cases.

[35] See *Bacot*, 84 RGDIP (1980), at 1031–33: Such clauses can be found in treaties between States and international organizations or between international organizations and in constitutional instruments of international organizations. The wording of the conventional instruments can be ambiguous; it might be a matter for interpretation whether a particular provision merely obliges the competent organ to submit certain questions to the Court or whether it confers binding force on the Court's opinion. See, for example (with a clear wording), Convention on the Privileges and Immunities of the United Nations of 13 February 1946, 1 UNTS 15 (Article VIII Section 30); Convention on the Privileges and Immunities of the Specialized Agencies of 21 November 1947, 33 UNTS 261 (Article IX Section 32); Agreement on the Privileges and Immunities of the International Atomic Energy Agency of 1 July 1959, 374 UNTS 147 (Article X Section 34); Instrument for the amendment of the Constitution of the International Labor Organization, 9 October 1946, 15 UNTS 35 (Article 37). For general treaties, see Article 66(2)(e) of the Vienna Convention on the Law of Treaties between States and international organizations or between international organizations of 21 March 1986, UN Doc. A/CONF.129/15 (1986), reprinted in 25 ILM (1986), 543–92; United Nations Convention against Illicit Traffic in Narcotic Drugs and Psychotropic Substances of 19 December 1988, UN Doc. E/CONF.82/15 (1988), reprinted in: 28 ILM 493 (1989) (Article 32(3)). For headquarters agreements, see, for example (with a more ambiguous wording), Agreement regarding the headquarters of the United Nations between the UN and the US of 26 June 1947, 11 UNTS 11 (Article VIII Section 21(b)), and Agreement regarding the headquarters of UNESCO and the privileges and immunities of the organization on French territory, 357 UNTS 3 (Article 29(2)). For further references see *Ago*, 85 AJIL (1991), at 439 fn. 2.

advisory opinions.[36] Monitoring compliance with them is a matter of verifying the observance of the respective treaty rather than of the opinion proper.

---

[36] See *Bacot*, 84 RGDIP (1980), at 1038, 1063–7; *Hudson*, 42 AJIL (1948), at 631–2; *Tanzi*, 6 EJIL (1995), at 570–1. The Court itself has stressed that the binding effect in such cases does not derive from the Charter nor its Statute: see, for example, Application for Review of Judgment No.158 of the United Nations Administrative Tribunal, Advisory Opinion of 12 July 1973, at 182, para. 39, on the binding effect of its opinion under the Statute of the UN Administrative Tribunal: "Such an effect, it is true, goes beyond the scope attributed by the Charter and by the Statute of the Court to an advisory opinion. It results, however, not from the advisory opinion itself but from a provision of an autonomous instrument having the force of law for the staff members and the Secretary-General."

2

The Legal Framework

A. INTRODUCTION

The Charter and the ICJ Statute each contain provisions relevant to the duty of states to comply with the Court's decisions. Most notably, Article 94(1) of the Charter provides: "Each Member of the United Nations undertakes to comply with the decision of the International Court in any case to which it is a party." Articles 59 through 61 and Article 63(2) of the Statute[1] concern the legal effects of judgments, while Article 41(1) covers that of provisional measures.[2] These articles are supplemented by additional provisions in the Rules of Court.[3]

---

[1] Article 59: "The decision of the Court has no binding force except between the parties and in respect of that particular case."
Article 60: "The judgment is final and without appeal. In the event of dispute as to the meaning or scope of the judgment, the Court shall construe it upon the request of any party."
Article 61: "(1) An application for revision of the judgment may be made only when it is based upon the discovery of some fact of such nature as to be a decisive factor, which fact was, when the judgment was given, unknown to the Court and also to the party claiming revision, always provided that such ignorance was not due to negligence.
(2) The proceedings for revision shall be opened by a judgment of the Court expressly recording the existence of the new fact, recognizing that it has such character as to lay the case open to revision, and declaring the application admissible on this ground.
(3) The Court may require previous compliance with the terms of the judgment before it admits proceedings in revision.
(4) The application for revision must be made at latest within six months of the discovery of the new fact.
(5) No application for revision may be made after the lapse of ten years from the date of the judgment."
For Article 63(2), see *infra* C III.
[2] Article 41(1): "The Court shall have the power to indicate, if it considers that circumstances so require, any provisional measures that ought to be taken to preserve the respective rights of either party."
[3] Article 94(2) of the 1978 Rules of Court specifies the moment at which the judgment acquires binding force: "The judgment shall be read at a public sitting of the Court and shall become binding on the day of the reading." Article 74(4) provides for a basis for measures promoting compliance prior to the issuance of the order of provisional measures: "Pending the meeting of the Court, the President may call upon the parties to act in such a way as will enable any order the Court may make on the request for provisional measures to have its appropriate effects." Article 75(1) and (2) resonate the contents of Article 41 of the Statute: "(1) The Court may at any time decide to examine proprio motu whether the circumstances of the case require the indication of provisional measures which ought to be taken or complied with by any or all of the parties. (2) When a request for provisional measures has been made, the Court may indicate measures that are in whole or in part others than those requested, or that ought to be taken or complied with by the party which has itself made the request." Article 78 further amplifies the authority of the Court in proceedings relating to provisional measures: "The Court may request information from the parties on any matter connected with the implementation of any provisional measures it has indicated."

The provision for enforcement appears in the Charter, rather than in the ICJ Statute. This approach reflects the separation between the adjudicative and post-adjudicative phase in international relations. Non-compliance might give rise to new political tensions, and the efficacy of the post-adjudicative phase will not be determined by another judicial examination, but by immediate political action.[4] As a result, the Security Council—and not the Court—has primary competence among the main UN organs for ensuring compliance with an ICJ decision. Accordingly, Article 94(2) of the Charter provides:

If any party to a case fails to perform the obligations incumbent upon it under a judgment rendered by the Court, the other party may have recourse to the Security Council, which may, if it deems necessary, make recommendations or decide upon measures to be taken to give effect to the judgment.

B. HISTORY OF THE PROVISIONS ON COMPLIANCE AND ENFORCEMENT

The cited provisions of the Statute are based on the Statute of the Permanent Court of International Justice. The original text of those particular provisions was largely maintained as drafted in 1920, with occasional stylistic and consequential changes.[5] However, with regard to an enforcement mechanism, the drafters of the Charter took an approach somewhat different than the League of Nations Covenant when adopting Article 94(2).

I. The predecessor of Article 94 of the Charter: Article 13(4) of the League of Nations Covenant

The Covenant of the League of Nations contained in Article 13(4) a corresponding provision for compliance and enforcement for arbitral awards and judicial decisions, applicable *inter alia* for judgments of the PCIJ:

The Members of the League agree that they will carry out in full good faith any [arbitral] award or [judicial] decision that may be rendered, and that they will not resort to war against a Member of the League which complies therewith. In the event of failure to carry out such an [arbitral] award or [judicial] decision, the Council shall propose what steps should be taken to give effect thereto.[6]

---

[4] Rosenne, *Law and Practice I*, 249.

[5] *Hudson*, 40 AJIL (1946), at 37, 41–2: Articles 59 and 60 repeat the previous language; Articles 61 and 63(2) contain a few stylistic changes; in Article 41, a typographical error of the 1920 English text is corrected. There are also other stylistic and consequential changes ("Security Council" instead of "Council").

[6] League of Nations Covenant, as amended in 1924. The original version of Article 13(4) just referred to awards; this was changed to cover judicial decisions as well after the creation of the PCIJ: *Pillepich* in Cot/Pellet, Charte, Article 94, at 1276.

The differences between this provision and Article 94 of the Charter are significant. While the League provision covers compliance and enforcement with respect to all international judicial and arbitral decisions, Article 94 exclusively relates to decisions of the ICJ and provides an enforcement mechanism only for judgments. Article 13(4) seems to suggest that the proceedings were to be automatically launched irrespective of any formal complaint on the part of the judgment creditor; there was a duty of the League of Nations Council to examine the conduct of the litigants and act *proprio motu* in the moment there was non-compliance.[7] Article 94(2), on the other hand, establishes a right of recourse to the Security Council for the judgment creditor, not any other state[8] or organ. Noteworthy is the discretion retained by the Security Council relating both to the decision whether to act at all and to the choice of concrete means. Article 13(4) obliges the League of Nations Council, Article 94(2) empowers the UN Security Council.[9] Another important difference lies in the means available for given to these two organs under the respective instruments: while the League Council could propose steps that should be taken, the UN Security Council can adopt both recommendations and binding decisions.[10]

From a comparison of these provisions, one might think that there was more potential for enforcement action by the League of Nations Council than by the UN Security Council, as Article 13(4) provided for a role as an automatic enforcement agency.[11] However, as Article 5(1) of the Covenant required unanimity for Council decisions, it is unlikely that it would have been a truly efficient mechanism in critical situations, all the more since a state not member of the Council that was directly affected by a potential Council decision had a right to participate and vote pursuant to Article 4(5)

---

[7] As Reisman, *Nullity and revision*, explains at 702–03, this difference between Article 94(2) and 13(4) might actually not have had any practical relevance. The League of Nations Council never took action on its own initiative under the basis of Article 13(4), whereas the Security Council can take action *proprio motu* if there is a threat to the peace, see *infra* E II 1 a (2).

[8] Other states might bring such matters to the attention of the Security Council under Chapter VI, see *infra* E III 1 a (2) and *Mosler/Oellers-Frahm*, in Simma, Charter, Article 94, at n. 8; Reisman, *Nullity and revision* at 703.

[9] But see *supra* n. 7.

[10] Tuncel, *L'exécution des décisions*, at 59–64; *Ajibola*, in: Bulterman/Kuijer, Compliance with judgments, at 26–34; *Guillaume* in Jasentuliyana, Perspectives on international law, at 282; Reisman, *Nullity and revision*, at 701–4. Another difference is the fact that Article 13(4) obliges members to fulfill their obligation in good faith, whereas Article 94(1) does not explicitly take up that duty. This should, however, not be taken as a substantive shift, since Article 2(2) of the Charter contains a general obligation of UN members to fulfill their Charter obligations in good faith, see *Vulcan*, 18 RGDIP (1947), at 192; but see Tuncel, *L'exécution des décisions*, at 63. Finally, another difference is that Article 94 does not contain a provision relating to an obligation not to resort to war against a state in compliance with a PCIJ decision, which is obviated by the Charter's general prohibition of the unilateral use of force (with self-defense as the only exception).

[11] "Shall propose" for the League of Nations Council against "may" for the Security Council.

of the Covenant.[12] There is very little practice on the enforcement provision of Article 13(4). As there was no case of a refusal by a state to comply with a PCIJ judgment, there was no reason for Council action concerning any such decision under Article 13(4).[13] Council discussions based on Article 13(4) took place only once in a case of an arbitral award, but the matter was settled during the course of those very discussions. Accordingly, no need for enforcement action arose.[14]

II. The way from Article 13(4) League of Nations Covenant to Article 94 of the UN Charter

Article 94 found its way into the draft proposals for the UN Charter at a relatively late stage of the drafting process. The Dumberton Oaks proposals contained provisions on the establishment of the International Court of Justice, but none relating to the legal effect and the enforcement of its decisions.[15] The issue came up at the San Francisco Founding Conference after the Washington Committee of Jurists had drawn attention to the need of including

---

[12] If Article 5(1) of the Covenant had been applied as broadly as its text suggests, the debtor of a judgment would have possessed a right of veto and could have blocked the decision-making process, see Reisman, *Nullity and revision*, at 678.

[13] It is worth mentioning that in the majority of cases, no specific act was required to implement the judgment, see *Guillaume* in Jasentuliyana, Perspectives on international law, at 278, quoting Hudson, *Permanent Court of International Justice 1920–1942*, at §§ 449, 505. Factual circumstances, rather than bad faith or defiance, explain the two occasions in which judgments were not complied with, see *Pillepich* in Cot/Pellet, Charte, Article 94, at 1277 n. 14: in the S.S. Wimbledon case, Germany did not pay damages to France because this was not approved by the Committee of Guarantees of the Reparations Commission installed by the Treaty of Versailles (in which France participated); in the Société commerciale de Belgique case, the judgment was delivered in the year when the Second World War began.

[14] The case (the Central Rhodope forests case) concerned an award of 29 March 1933 delivered in a dispute between Greece and Bulgaria. When Bulgaria did not comply, Greece put the matter on the Agenda of the League of Nations by a letter of 6 September 1934, Annex 1517, C.394, 15 League of Nations Official Journal 1417 (1934). In the meeting of the Council of the League of Nations of 19 September 1934, the Bulgarian representative expressed his country's willingness to comply with the award, but asked Greece to accept substituted performance in lieu of a cash payment. The Council took note of the parties' agreement to continue negotiations. 15 League of Nations Official Journal 1432–3, 1477 (1934), Reisman, *Nullity and revision*, at 686; *Guillaume* in Jasentuliyana, Perspectives on international law, at 282; *O'Connell*, 30 Va. JIL (1990) 906; Rosenne, *Law and Practice I*, at 238. In the case of another claim of noncompliance with an arbitral award (in the Optants Case concerning an arbitral award between Hungary and Romania), the matter was considered under Article 11(2) of the League of Nations Covenant instead of 13(4). Article 11(2) reads: "It is also declared to be the friendly right of each Member of the League to bring to the attention of the Assembly or of the Council any circumstance whatever affecting international relations which threatens to disturb international peace or the good understanding of the nations upon which peace depends." The Council installed a committee that nullified the award, *O'Connell*, 30 Va. JIL (1990), at 906 fn. 66; Reisman, *Nullity and revision*, at 686–96.

[15] UNCIO Doc. G/1 The United Nations. Dumbarton Oaks Proposals for a General International Organization. 3 UNCIO 1–23, at 11–12 Chapter VII An International Court of Justice.

provisions on the execution of ICJ decisions in the Charter.[16] Three drafting committees[17] dealt with the issue of compliance with ICJ decisions.[18] Several states submitted proposals to fill the gap relating to legal effect and enforcement of ICJ decisions. Interestingly, there was no suggestion to transfer the provision of Article 13(4) League of Nations Covenant into the Charter. A proposal from Belgium came the closest to Article 13(4),[19] but was not taken up.

Australia suggested a provision that closely resembled what was later to become Article 94(1): "All members of the United Nations undertake to comply with any decision of the Court of International Justice to which they are parties."[20] It pointed out that such a provision could serve to mobilize public opinion against perpetrators.[21]

On enforcement, there were several further initiatives. Pursuant to a proposal by Norway that failed to convince the competent drafting committee, the Security Council was to have the necessary powers to ensure that all international judicial decisions were complied with regardless of whether the non-execution presented a threat to international peace.[22] Other States made suggestions aimed at limiting the Council's discretion and increasing the

---

[16] See *Hudson*, 40 AJIL (1946), at 12.

[17] In the San Francisco Founding Conference, the drafting was delegated to four commissions subdivided into twelve committees. The committees forwarded their work to the Commissions, which then submitted the texts to the Coordination Committee and the Advisory Committee, which referred the draft proposals back to the committees in case of substantial changes. The final text was submitted to the Plenary Assembly for vote and adoption. See *Grewe/Khan*, in Simma, Charter, History, at nn. 43–5.

[18] These were Committees III/1 (Security Council—structure and procedures), III/3 (Security Council—coercive measures), and IV/1 (Judicial organization—International Court of Justice).

[19] Dumbarton Oaks Proposals: amendments submitted by the Belgian delegation, 3 May 1945, Doc. 2 (English), G/7 (k) (1), 3 UNCIO 335–41, at 336: "The Security Council shall see to it that the engagements undertaken by the States with a view to a pacific settlement of their disputes are respected. In the case of non-observance of these engagements or of omission in the execution of court decisions or awards rendered in accordance with the procedures provided for, the Security Council shall advise as to the measures to be taken to insure their fulfilment."

[20] Amendments to the Dumberton Oaks Proposals submitted on behalf of Australia, Doc. 2 (English), G/14 (1), 5 May 1945, 3 UNCIO 543–53, at 553.

[21] Summary report of fourteenth meeting of Committee III/1, 11 UNCIO 393–8, at 396.

[22] Amendments and observations on the Dumberton Oaks Proposals, submitted by the Norwegian Delegation, 3 UNCIO 365–75, at 368–9: "The Security Council is empowered to enforce by appropriate means the execution of any final decision in a dispute between States delivered either by the Permanent Court of International Justice or by any other tribunal whose jurisdiction in the matter has been recognized by the States parties to the dispute." Norway explained that the number of international judgments was likely to increase and that there was a need to make sure that they were duly carried out, since an accumulation of instances of non-compliance could endanger peace. It also noted the importance of holding powerful states accountable to comply with unfavorable judgments and emphasized that its proposal merely empowered, but did not oblige the Security Council: Summary report of the fourteenth meeting of Committee III/1, 11 UNCIO 393, at 396. The proposal was rejected by the competent drafting committee III/1. Ibid., at 397.

probability for enforcement action for ICJ decisions,[23] but all initiatives to impose an obligation on the Council in this field or to enumerate acts of aggression and include non-compliance with ICJ decisions in such a catalogue were rejected by the drafting committee charged with designing the coercive measures available to the Council.[24]

Ultimately, a Cuban proposal in combination with the Australian proposal formed the basis for Article 94.[25] The drafting committee responsible for the set-up of the ICJ decided that the relevant provisions should not appear in the Statute, but in the Charter, thus following Australia's approach,[26] and adopted provisions very similar to the later Article 94.[27] Some changes were made[28] so as to give effect to recommendations of the Advisory Committee of Jurists and the Coordination Committee.[29] The words "if it deems it necessary" were added to the enforcement provision so as to emphasize the discretionary character of the power of the Security Council under the provision;[30]

[23] Turkey proposed that the Security Council should be under an obligation to render assistance to any party to a dispute that had agreed to "submit to judicial settlement and to the decision of the Court as required," and that assistance could range from "moral assistance" or "sympathy" to diplomatic, economic, or military measures: summary report of Third Meeting of Committee III/3, 9 May 1945, 12 UNCIO 288–90, at 290; Corrigendum to the Summary Report of the Fifth Meeting of Committee III/3, 12 UNCIO 312. Venezuela suggested an obligation for the Council, lower procedural requirements for the voting procedure in this context, and the suspension of UN membership rights for a state failing to respect ICJ jurisdiction or an ICJ decision: 4 UNCIO 283–334, at 322. Bolivia advocated that non-compliance with an ICJ judgment was to turn a state into an aggressor, 4 UNCIO 831–40, at 833, 835, 837.

[24] Report of Mr Paul-Boncour, Rapporteur, on Chapter VIII, Section B, 12 UNCIO 502–14, at 505.

[25] Cuba made several proposals. The first one envisaged a provision in the ICJ Statute, the first paragraph of which resembled the Australian proposal and the later Article 94(1) UN Charter; the second paragraph contained a right of recourse to the Security Council for cases of non-compliance, which would then be *obliged* to take the necessary measures for enforcement: 4 UNCIO 700–16, at 712. Cuba's second proposal foresaw enforcement action by the Court itself. In a case of non-compliance, the Court could, at the request of a party, ask other states with capacity to act before the ICJ to adopt the necessary commercial or economic measures. Should those measures remain unsuccessful, the Court could call for military action, 4 UNCIO 734–41 at 740–1. At the 20th meeting of Committee IV/1, it suggested that the Security Council should be empowered to make recommendations or take decisions, 13 UNCIO 296–9, at 298.

[26] Australia's proposals related to the Charter, Cuba's to the Statute, *supra* nn. 20 and 25.

[27] 13 UNCIO 296–9, at 297–8: "All members of the United Nations undertake to comply with the decision of the International Court of Justice in any case to which they are parties. [...] In the event of a state's failure to perform the obligations incumbent upon it under a judgment rendered by the Court, the other party may have recourse to the Security Council, which may make recommendations or decide measures to be taken to give effect to the judgment."

[28] 13 UNCIO 459–60, at 459.

[29] Texts as tentatively approved by the Advisory Committee of Jurists at its Fifth Meeting, 11 June 1945, 18 UNCIO 315–16, at 315 (Article 66); all articles approved by the Advisory Committee of Jurists at its Sixth Meeting, 12 June 1945, and by the Coordination Committee at its sixteenth meeting, 12 June 1945, 18 UNCIO 464–6, at 465 (Article 66).

[30] On this point, the Committee report pointed out: "It was observed that the use of this phrase might tend to weaken the position of the Court. In answer to this argument it was pointed out that the action to be taken by the Security Council was permissive rather than obligatory and that the addition of the aforementioned phrase merely made more clear the discretionary power of the Security Council"—*supra* n. 28.

the other changes were of a linguistic nature. The eventual text of Article 94 was complete at that point, save for one last rather insignificant stylistic matter.[31] The draft charter was approved by the Advisory Committee and the Coordination Committee on 22 June 1945,[32] and in the Plenary Session of 25 June 1945, the Charter was unanimously approved.[33]

C. THE ADDRESSEES OF THE OBLIGATION OF COMPLIANCE AND OF POTENTIAL ENFORCEMENT ACTION

I. *"The parties:" states in their entirety*

As international obligations generally apply to the states in their entirety, the obligation under Article 94(1) is in principle an obligation incumbent on the state as a whole, not on any of its organs in particular,[34] although in proceedings before the Court, the state will be represented by its government. This has consequences in two directions. First, it leaves the choice of the precise domestic means and mechanisms to bring about compliance to the state. It is a matter of its municipal law, and its system of attribution of competences will decide which branch will have to respond; the subject-matter of the decision might concern matters within the sphere of competences of organs other than the government. Hence, in order to monitor compliance, it might not be sufficient to limit the focus on the government's response to a decision. Second, the state cannot refer to its domestic legal system as an excuse for a failure to comply with ICJ decisions: all action by public officials will be attributed to the state, and it cannot evade responsibility for a failure to meet its obligations due to, for example, action by the judiciary.[35] Similarly, an organization as a federal system will be no excuse for a failure to fulfill the obligation under Article 94(1). Problems can arise

---

[31] Instead of "if it deems it necessary," as in Article 94(2), the draft provision as adopted by Committee IV/1 and subsequently by Commission IV (Revised Verbatim Minutes of Second Meeting of Commission IV, 15 June 1945, Commission IV, 13 UNCIO 90–106 at 95) reads "as it deems *it* necessary." The "it" was eliminated by the Coordination Committee in its Fortieth Meeting of 22 June 1945, 17 UNCIO 360–83, at 372.

[32] Draft Charter of the United Nations as finally approved in English by both the Coordination Committee and the Advisory Committee of Jurists on 22 June 1945. The French text was approved in part by the Advisory Committee of Jurists the same day. 18 UNCIO 602–44, at 637.

[33] Verbatim Minutes of the 9th Plenary Session, 1 UNCIO 612–32, at 631.

[34] In exceptional circumstances, an ICJ decision will be directed at the government in particular, see the measure (b) in the order indicating provisional measures in LaGrand: "The Government of the United States of America should transmit this Order to the Governor of the State of Arizona" (see *infra* Chapter 3 C X 1).

[35] See Jenks, *Prospects of international adjudication*, at 715–17 (suggesting means by which support from the legislature and the judiciary can be secured in advance); *Mosler/Oellers-Frahm* in Simma, Charter, Article 94, at n. 6; Rosenne, *Law and Practice I*, at 221–6; Schachter, *International Law*, at 237.

where the implementation of a decision requires action not on the federal but on the state or provincial level in a country with a constitutional order that accords only limited control to federal authorities. State or provincial organs might show less readiness to respect the countries' obligation to comply with the decision, as they might in general be less sensitive to foreign policy concerns since they have no general responsibility in this field, and they might not have been involved in the decision to submit the respective matter to adjudication. Yet, neither the reference of state or provincial authorities to the discretionary nature of their powers in relation to the federal authorities, nor the reliance of federal authorities on their limited capabilities to compel compliance by the state authorities can relieve either one from the international obligations, including Article 94(1), which remain incumbent on the state as a whole.[36]

II. A special case: parties to ICJ proceedings that are non-members to the United Nations

Despite its role as the principal judicial organ of the United Nations,[37] the ICJ is under certain conditions open to states that are not UN members. While this matter might appear nowadays more of historical interest than of practical relevance in view of the quasi-universal membership of states in the United Nations,[38] it can become significant in cases of the emergence of new states and uncertainty about a continuation of UN membership in the context of state succession.[39] In the first decades of ICJ activity, there were a significant number of cases involving non-UN members, including the first case taken up by the Court.[40]

Under Article 93(2) of the Charter, a state non-member of the UN may become a party to the ICJ Statute subject to conditions to be determined in each case by the General Assembly on recommendation of the Security

---

[36] See Jenks, *Prospects of international adjudication*, at 718.
[37] Article 92 UN Charter.   [38] See Rosenne, *World Court*, at 84.
[39] The Court sidestepped the issue of Yugoslavia's membership status in its Judgment on preliminary objections in the Genocide case. Yugoslavia itself had not challenged its membership in the Statute at that point, Application of the Convention on the Prevention and Punishment of the Crime of Genocide, Preliminary Objections, Judgment, Judgment of 11 July 1996. In April 2001, however, it applied for revision of that judgment, arguing that its admission to the United Nations on 1 November 2000 represented a decisive new fact, since it showed that at the time of the earlier judgment, it had not been a UN member and no party to the Statute and the Genocide Convention: application for revision of the Judgment of 11 July 1996 in the Case Concerning Application of the Convention on the Prevention and Punishment of the Crime of Genocide (Bosnia and Herzegovina v. Yugoslavia), Preliminary Objections (Yugoslavia v. Bosnia and Herzegovina), http://212.153.43.18/icjwww/idocket/iybh/iybhapplication/iybh_iapplication_200 10424.pdf. The Court found Yugoslavia's request inadmissible in its judgment of 3 February 2003.
[40] See Corfu Channel, *infra* Chapter 3 B I. Albania, the respondent, became a UN member of the United Nations in 1955.

Council. The General Assembly requested identical conditions in all cases—namely, the acceptance of the obligations under Article 94 of the Charter.[41] At present, all parties to the Statute are UN members as well, so that this provision currently has no relevance.[42]

In accordance with Article 35(2) of the Statute, the Court is also open to states that are not party to its statute upon conditions to be laid down by the Security Council.[43] The Council determined those conditions in 1946: states are required to deposit a declaration with the Court's registrar, in which, amongst other things, they have to undertake to "comply in good faith with the decision or decisions of the Court" and to accept "all the obligations of a Member of the United Nations under Article 94 of the Charter."[44]

Both Article 93(2) of the Charter and the Security Council resolution relating to Article 35(2) of the Court's Statute make reference to Article 94 in its entirety; therefore, not only the duty of compliance under Article 94(1) but also the enforcement mechanism of Article 94(2) UN Charter are applicable for non-UN members that are parties to proceedings before the Court, which implies that the Security Council could take enforcement measures against a non-UN member.[45] The right to take recourse to the Council under Article 94(2) is equally not limited to UN members, but is available for "parties."[46]

---

[41] For the first time, the Assembly laid down these conditions for Switzerland (GA Resolution 91(I) of 11 December 1946). The further conditions are acceptance of the provisions of the Statute and an undertaking to contribute to the expenses of the Court. See http://212.153.43.18/icjwww/ibasicdocuments/ibasictext/ibasicnonmembers.html and *Mosler/Oellers-Frahm* in Simma, Charter, Article 93, at n. 4.

[42] Until its accession to the UN in September 2002, Switzerland was the only member to the Statute which was not a UN member, www.un.org/Overview/unmember.html and www.uno.admin.ch/sub_uno/e/uno.html. Japan, Liechtenstein, San Marino, and Nauru were parties to the Statute of the Court pursuant to Article 93(2) of the Charter before becoming UN members. See http://212.153.43.18/icjwww/ibasicdocuments/ibasictext/ibasicnonmembers.html.

[43] See Article 35(2) of the Statute: "The conditions under which the Court shall be open to [States] not parties to the Statute) shall, subject to the special provisions contained in treaties in force, be laid down by the Security Council, but in no case shall such conditions place the parties in a position of inequality before the Court." UN members are *ipso facto* parties to the Statute (Article 93(1) UN Charter); the provision is therefore irrelevant for them.

[44] Security Council resolution 9(1946) of 15 October 1946, para. 1. The respective declaration can be either general or restricted to a particular dispute, ibid., para. 2. Article 35(2) of the Statute has been made use of by more states than Article 93(2) of the Charter. Particular declarations were filed by Albania (1947) and by Italy (1953), general declarations by Cambodia (1952), Ceylon (1952), the Federal Republic of Germany (1955, 1956, 1961, 1965, and 1971), Finland (1953 and 1954), Italy (1955), Japan (1951), Laos (1952), and the Republic of Viet Nam (1952); all are meanwhile UN members, see http://212.153.43.18/icjwww/ibasicdocuments/ibasictext/ibasicotherstates.htm.

[45] Nantwi, *Enforcement of international judicial decisions*, at 149. If non-UN members are parties to ICJ proceedings, it must be under the same conditions as UN members: see Article 35(2) of the Statute.

[46] See Satow, *A guide to diplomatic practice*, at 451.

III. Intervening states

Article 94 applies to "parties," raising the question of a decision's effects on intervening states; is such a state equally obliged to comply with a judgment and could enforcement under Article 94(2) be taken against it? The Statute provides for two forms of intervention. First is the "discretionary intervention" foreseen in Article 62, where a state asserts a legal interest that might be affected by the decision and where the Court has discretion on whether to grant permission to intervene. Second is the so-called "intervention of right" contained in Article 63, which gives contracting parties to a multilateral convention that are not litigants before the Court the right to participate in proceedings in which the interpretation of the convention is at stake.[47] Article 63(2) establishes that if a state avails itself of an intervention of right, "the construction given by the judgment will be equally binding upon it." There is no question of its legal interests being affected by the substantive decision proper, but by the Court's general legal findings independently of the specific case.[48] However, Article 94 of the Charter remains inapplicable as the provision does not elevate the intervening state to the status of a "party." It means, not more, not less, that the intervening state will be bound by the Court's interpretation, should it itself be involved in a future case concerning the application of this instrument. There is no provision on the legal effects of a permitted intervention under Article 62. However, the Court's recent jurisprudence has provided significant clarification. The Court distinguishes between states trying to intervene as a party (for which a jurisdictional link with the other parties must be demonstrated) and non-party interveners (for which Article 62 is actually designed.)[49] In the only two cases where the

---

[47] For details on intervention before the Court, Rosenne, *Law and Practice III*, at 1480–1555, *Torres Bernárdez*, 256 RdC (1995), at 193–457.

[48] In Haya de la Torre (Columbia v. Peru), Cuba's intervention under Article 63 was admitted, see Judgment of 13 June 1951, at 77. El Salvador's intervention under Article 63 in the Nicaragua case was declared inadmissible at the jurisdictional phase, Military and Paramilitary Activities in and against Nicaragua, Order of 4 October 1984, at 215. See on the interpretation of Article 63(2) *Torres Bernárdez*, 256 RdC (1995), 426–7.

[49] Land, Island and Maritime Frontier Dispute (El Salvador/Honduras), Application by Nicaragua for permission to intervene, Judgment of 13 September 1990, at 133–4, para. 97: "Intervention under Article 62 of the Statute is for the purpose of protecting a State's 'interest of a legal nature' that might be affected by a decision in an existing case already established between other States, namely the parties to the case. It is not intended to enable a third State to tack on a new case, to become a new party, and so have its own claims adjudicated by the Court. A case with a new party, and new issues to be decided, would be a new case. The difference between intervention under Article 62, and the joining of a new party to a case, is not only a difference in degree; it is a difference in kind." See further ibid. at 134–5, para. 99: "It is therefore clear that a State which is allowed to intervene in a case, does not by reason only of being an intervener, become also a party to the case. It is true, conversely, that, provided that there be the necessary consent by the parties to the case, the intervener is not prevented by reason of that status from itself becoming a party to the case. That the competence given to the Court in Article 62 of the Statute is not extendable to making an intervener a party to the case unless the parties to the case have consented to the change appears also to be the view of Nicaragua [. . .]."

Court thus far has granted permission to intervene under Article 62 (Land, Island and Maritime Frontier Dispute and Land and Maritime Boundary between Cameroon and Nigeria), the respective states were classified as non-party interveners.[50] In the first case, the Court described the legal effects of the intervention in the judgment on the merits: "[A] State permitted to intervene under Article 62 of the Statute, but which does not acquire the status of a party to the case, is not bound by the Judgment given in the proceedings in which it has intervened."[51] It went to discuss the intervener's statement in its application (revoked in its written observations after having been admitted as a non-party intervener)[52] that it intended "to submit itself to the binding effect of the decision" and pointed out that the force of *res judicata* operated in both directions, both obliging and entitling the state to which it applies; that a non-party once admitted as intervener (in this case, Nicaragua) could not claim an entitlement to rely on the judgment against the original parties; and that accordingly "in the circumstances of the present case, the Judgment is not *res judicata* for Nicaragua."[53] Thus, the Chamber appeared to reject the concept of the judgment as source of rights and obligations for the non-party intervener as a whole, giving intervention under Article 62 a more limited effect than under Article 63. While Article 94 of the Charter would only apply in the heretofore purely theoretical case in which a state intervenes as a new party, the Court's view seems to be that there is no legal basis for making its findings binding on the non-party intervener under Article 62. The decision was not uncontroversial, and doubts might be raised whether such an argumentation can stand in this generality.[54] Yet, for the purposes of the present study, there is no need to assess compliance of an intervener under Article 62: for the cases up to date

---

[50] Land, Island and Maritime Frontier Dispute, Judgment of 13 September 1990, at 99–100, 102; and Land and Maritime Boundary between Cameroon and Nigeria, Order of 21 October 1999, at paras. 11, 18. In the most recent case, Sovereignty over Pulau Litigan and Pulau Sipadan (Indonesia/Malaysia), the Court denied permission to intervene in its Judgment of 23 October 2001, but explained that as the Philippines did not seek to become a party, the absence of a jurisdictional link was no impediment to granting the intervention, paras. 31–6. The character of the judgment in Land, Island and Maritime Frontier Dispute as decision of a chamber did not appear to detract from its persuasive force. In subsequent decisions, the full Court has quoted relevant passages from that judgment with approval: Land and Maritime Boundary between Cameroon and Nigeria, Order of 21 October 1999, paras. 14–15; Sovereignty over Pulau Litigan and Pulau Sipadan, Judgment of 23 October 2001, para. 33.

[51] Land, Island and Maritime Frontier Dispute, Judgment of 11 September 1992, at 609, para. 423.

[52] Ibid., at 609, para. 421.   [53] Ibid., at 610, para. 424.

[54] See, for an opposing view Declaration of Vice-President Oda, ibid., at 619–20: "I do not share the views of the Chamber concerning the effect of Nicaragua's intervention [...] In my view, Nicaragua, as a non-party intervener, will certainly be bound by this judgment in so far as it relates to the legal situation of the maritime spaces of the Gulf." He reiterated those concerns in the judgment on the Philippine intervention in Sovereignty over Pulau Litigan and Pulau Sipadan, Judgment of 23 October 2001, Diss. Op. Oda, paras. 119–20. See also *Oda*, 244 RdC (1993), at 84–5,

of a granted intervention under Article 62, the Court explicitly stated that the respective judgment was not binding on the intervener.[55]

D. THE OBLIGATION OF COMPLIANCE

Since the subject of an international obligation must generally determine itself how it will give effect to that obligation, it will be up to each addressee of the Court decision to determine the action necessary to ensure compliance. This determination will not be binding on the other side, which might challenge it; thus, a new dispute might arise which the states concerned might refer to a dispute settlement mechanism again.[56] States will typically enter into negotiations on the implementation of the decision. Therefore, in many cases, it will be only after a certain time period that it can be ascertained whether a state is violating its obligation to comply with the decision; international law does not establish any general time limit for this purpose.[57]

The concrete circumstances of the case will be an important factor. Particularly in cases where implementation requires close cooperation between the parties, it will be difficult to attribute clear responsibility for the failure of negotiations. The judgment might lay down modalities for implementation, including timeframes, although the Court generally will be reluctant in this regard and cautious not to overstep its judicial function.[58] Similarly, special agreements for the submission of the case to the ICJ might already provide for implementation schedules in advance.

I. Compliance with final judgments

Article 94(1) of the Charter reflects the general principle of international law of the binding nature of a judgment of an international court, confirmed by

observing that the Chamber's approach would give the intervener an advantage over the original parties and an intervener under Article 63, and *Torres Bernárdez*, 256 RdC (1995), at 426–37. Critical on the Court's approach also Rosenne, *Law and Practice III*, at 1550–1. For a broad understanding of bindingness of a judgment on the intervener prior to the recent jurisprudence, see Fritzemeyer, *Die Intervention vor dem Internationalen Gerichtshof*, 146–9, with further references.

[55] See Land, Island and Maritime Frontier Dispute, Judgment of 11 September 1992 at 609, para. 421: "The terms on which intervention was granted [...] were that Nicaragua would not, as an intervening state, become party to the proceedings. The binding force of the Judgment for the Parties, as contemplated by Article 59 of the Statute of the Court, does not therefore extend also to Nicaragua as intervener." See also the Court's statement in the Land and Maritime Boundary between Cameroon and Nigeria, Judgment of 10 October 2002, at para. 238.

[56] See Rosenne, *Law and Practice I*, at 219.

[57] See *O'Connell*, 30 Va. JIL (1990), at 937–8.

[58] On the Court's reluctance to deal with questions of execution and enforcement, see its refusal to make a choice among the possible ways the asylum could be terminated in Haya de la Torre, *infra* Chapter 3 B II 3. See Rosenne, *Law and Practice I*, at 206–7, on the Court's reluctance to deal with questions of execution and enforcement.

Articles 59 and 60 of the Statute.[59] Article 59 limits the scope of the binding force to the parties to the dispute, thus excluding the common law rule of *stare decisis*.[60] In individual cases, there might be more than one final judgment on the merits, such as when the Court disposes of several claims in the first judgment and leaves single issues for continued proceedings, such as the Corfu Channel case, in which the judgment confirming Albania's obligation to compensate was followed by a judgment assessing the amount of obligation.[61]

The operative part of the judgment spells out the duties of the parties, which may entail performing a certain act or refraining from doing so. The degree of precision will vary as determined in each case by the applicable legal rules. While in some cases, the parties' obligation will be stated in unambiguous terms in the judgment's operative part,[62] in other cases, the parties will have a margin of appreciation for the implementation, such as when the Court affirms a duty to negotiate.[63] The Court's reasoning provides explanations on the correct interpretation of the specific obligations.[64]

The obligation is not construed as reciprocal, as is clear from the wording of Article 94(1), which states that "each member" individually undertakes certain responsibilities in the implementation of the judgment. The state concerned bears the primary duty to determine how to give effect to the decision. If the other party challenges this determination, the Court might be called upon to interpret the judgment pursuant to Article 60 cl. 2 of the Statute. It will defer to the parties to make political choices between various modes of compliance.[65] Joint modification of the Court's decision by the parties presents no reason for concern. A state remains free to renounce its rights under a judgment and thus the judgment debtor might eventually be relieved of its obligations under Article 94(1).[66]

---

[59] See *Ajibola*, in Bulterman/Kuijer, Compliance with judgments, at 17; Goodrich/Hambro, *Charter of the United Nations*, at 485, Goodrich/Hambro/Simons, *Charter of the United Nations*, at 555; Jenks, *Prospects of international adjudication*, at 663; Rosenne, *Law and Practice I*, at 218–19.

[60] See *Mosler/Oellers-Frahm*, in Simma, Charter, Article 94, at n. 2. On the question whether certain decisions (such as those referring to the status of territory) are valid *erga omnes*, see Rosenne, *Law and Practice I*, at 217, and *Law and Practice III*, at 1661–4.

[61] See Tuncel, *L'exécution des décisions*, at 44; for details on the Corfu Channel case, see *infra* Chapter 3 B I.

[62] See, for example, the operative part of the judgment on the merits in the Ambatielos Case: "The Court finds that the United Kingdom is under an obligation to submit to arbitration, in accordance with the Declaration of 1926, the difference as to the validity, under the Treaty of 1886, of the Ambatielos claim." Ambatielos (merits: obligation to arbitrate), Judgment of 19 May 1953, at 23.

[63] See *Weckel*, 42 AFDI (1996), at 439.

[64] See *Mosler/Oellers-Frahm* in Simma, Charter, Article 94, at n. 1.

[65] See the Haya de la Torre judgment, *infra* Chapter 3 B II 3.

[66] See on these general features Rosenne, *Law and Practice I*, at 216–21; *Weckel*, 42 AFDI (1996), at 435.

General guidelines cannot be made to gauge compliance in every kind of judgment. For some decisions, it will not be possible to determine *in abstracto* whether there is a need for implementing action or whether mere acquiescence is sufficient. The factual context, the route by which the dispute reached the Court, and the formal submissions of the parties all have an impact on the interpretation of the obligation stemming from the judgment.[67]

Certain types of decisions, such as judgments rejecting the claims for lack of jurisdiction or admissibility, are inherently self-executory and therefore do not raise the question of compliance;[68] the same will be true for judgments rejecting the applicant's claims on the merits,[69] unless they include some positive statement implying a need for action. However, the Court will decline to exercise its jurisdiction where the applicant or both parties do not request a judgment capable of legal effects and susceptible to any compliance or execution. If a declaratory judgment is sought, there must be some continuing applicability and legal relevance.[70] Nothing requires the parties to submit their dispute in its entirety for definitive settlement by the Court; they may indeed decide to request explanations from the Court on merely one aspect of the dispute in order to facilitate subsequent negotiations. For example, they might seek clarification on the content of a legal rule, but still prefer to retain control over the question of the actual applicability of that rule in their legal relations for their bilateral diplomatic settlement process.

The qualification of a decision as declaratory does not rule out a possible need for implementation. For example, a judgment on sovereignty over a certain territory will imply that if one party occupies territory awarded to the other side, it will be under the obligation to withdraw from that territory even absent an explicit statement by the Court to this extent. On the other hand, of course, if the territory is already in possession of the entitled state, there is no need for action by the other side, but it will be sufficient that it abstains from challenging this result. Therefore, the decision has to be analyzed in its context. The factual circumstances will determine the required action: there is no strict distinction (as might exist in municipal judicial proceedings)

---

[67] See Rosenne, *Law and Practice I*, at 216–17.

[68] See *Ajibola* in Bulterman/Kuijer, Compliance with judgments, at 17; *Weckel*, 42 AFDI (1996), at 434; *Jennings*, 47 ZaöRV (1987), at 4.

[69] See *Guillaume* in Jasentuliyana, Perspectives on international law, at 277, stating that judgments rejecting the claims of the applicant will normally be self-enforcing. See also Jenks, *Prospects of international adjudication*, at 688–90 for examples of self-executory decisions, highlighting decisions dismissing claims as the most obvious example.

[70] See Rosenne, *Law and Practice III*, at 1637, and *Law and Practice II*, at 548–51; see also the Court in Northern Cameroons, Judgment of 2 December 1963, at 33–4, 37–8, see in particular at 34 on the Court's function: "The Court's judgment must have some practical consequence in the sense that it can affect existing legal rights or obligations of the parties, thus removing uncertainty from their legal relations."

between judgments explicitly requiring a specific act and declaratory judgments.[71]

In special agreements submitting disputes to the Court (or in a separate agreement on the implementation of the judgment), the parties might include provisions for the post-adjudicative phase which amplify the obligation under Article 94(1) or give it a more concrete content, for example, by setting time limits for implementation or by providing for the establishment of auxiliary bodies or recourse to existing organizations. Moreover, they might provide for further steps ensuring the lasting settlement of their disputes beyond those requested by the judgment. In such cases, a dispute relating to the observance of the obligations established in the respective special agreement would not implicate Article 94(1) of the Charter but would rather relate to compliance with that agreement.

II. Compliance with provisional measures

1. Provisional measures as "decision" under Article 94(1)

The LaGrand judgment cleared any doubts as to the binding force of interim measures of protection.[72] Yet, the Court left open the question as to the actual source of the obligation to comply with such measures—whether it derives exclusively from Article 41 of the Statute or also from Article 94(1) of the Charter. This would not appear to have any practical consequences, as Article 41 forms an integral part of the Charter[73] and thereby participates in the particular status of Charter obligations under Article 103.

The Court's findings were based on an interpretation of Article 41 of the Statute, and it found it sufficient to point out that "Article 94 of the Charter does not prevent orders made under Article 41 from having binding character."[74] Article 94(1) lays down the duty of states to comply with "the decision of the International Court of Justice in any case" to which they are parties, whereas Article 94(2) provides for an enforcement mechanism for non-compliance with "a judgment." It was suggested that the terms are synonymous because Article 59 of the Statute speaks of "the decision" while being applicable to judgments only.[75] For Article 59, however, the context of

---

[71] See for categories of final decisions with examples of the respective scope of the obligation to comply with them Jenks, *Prospects of international adjudication*, at 667–88; for the case of title to territory ibid., 674–6. For other examples see *Mosler/Oellers-Frahm* in Simma, Charter, Article 94, at n. 5. See further on the concept of ICJ declaratory judgments Rosenne, *Law and Practice III*, at 1363–4; he states in *Law and Practice I* at 216 that not all declaratory judgments are executory (thereby implying that some are).

[72] *Supra* Chapter 1 B II.   [73] Article 92 cl. 2 of the Charter.

[74] LaGrand, Judgment of 27 June 2001, at paras. 108–9 (emphasis added).

[75] See *Pillepich* in Cot/Pellet, Charte, Article 94, at 1281–4; *Mosler* in Simma, UN Charter, 1st edn., Article 94, at n. 1. An additional factor may be that "decision" is used in the singular, which could suggest that it refers to one decision, namely the final.

Articles 56–60 of the Statute clarifies that it is indeed a provision for one particular type of decisions, namely judgments. It would be counterintuitive to suggest that the use of the term in Article 59 and Article 94(1) must be identical, all the more since the general usage of the term "decision" in the Statute is not limited to judgments.[76] The decisive point remains that Article 94 of the Charter uses two different terms for two different concepts—compliance on the one hand, enforcement on the other; as a general rule of interpretation, there is a presumption that such a difference in terminology aims at producing different legal effects. The UN Charter is admittedly the result of a political conference, and its drafting might as a consequence be at times more political than stringent in terms of legal logics. Still, the burden of proof for those terms being synonymous would be on the party claiming this, and the mere reference to Article 59 would not appear to be a sufficiently strong argument.[77]

2. Scope of the obligation

The very concept of provisional measures as measures that ought "to be taken" implies that they are measures requiring some kind of state response, be it through acts or omissions. The precise scope of the obligation will have to be assessed according to the particular measure; the measures will not always be framed so precisely as to facilitate the determination of the appropriate behavior. Sometimes an assessment of facts might be required to determine the required action. For example, the Court might order a withdrawal to positions occupied before a certain date without specifying the location, provoking controversy between the parties; in other cases, a legal rule might have to be interpreted where the Court urges adherence to that rule. The Court's decision may reaffirm obligations already incumbent on the parties as a matter of general international law.[78] A standard clause used with minor variations in many orders indicating provisional measures counters the risk of an aggravation or extension of the dispute and of measures prejudicing the rights under the future final decision, resonating a general principle of international law that parties to a case must abstain from

---

[76] It is used for procedural decisions as well; see *supra* n. 16 and Articles 16(2), 17(3), 24(3), 48 of the Statute.

[77] See *Mosler/Oellers-Frahm* in Simma, Charter, Article 94, at n. 1; Rosenne, *Law and Practice I*, at 216 (drawing also an a contrario argument to Article 13 of the League of Nations Covenant).

[78] Some measures are construed as general statements; one of the measures indicated in the Nicaragua case (see *infra* Chapter 3 C VI 1) was the affirmation that "the right to sovereignty and to political independence possessed by the Republic of Nicaragua, like any other State of the region or of the world, should be fully respected and should not in any way be jeopardized by any military or paramilitary activities which are prohibited by the principles of international law." The measure accordingly to be "taken" was an omission of acts interfering with that principle.

measures with a potential prejudicial effect for the execution of the decision on the merits or capable of extending or aggravating the dispute, as was highlighted by the Court in LaGrand.[79] In many cases, the reasoning will provide further information on the scope of the obligations, as the circumstances which according to the Court required the indication of interim measures[80] will shed light on the motives for the indication of the measures and will thus aid in their interpretation.

Regularly, the measures will remain valid until the delivery of the judgment unless the Court determines otherwise, for example, provides for their review at a certain date. Moreover, the parties might decide to substitute interim protection granted by the Court by another interim regime developed jointly.[81]

III. Non-compliance and possible defenses

We can conceive of a broad spectrum of possible reactions by the debtor of the decision. First of all, it might acknowledge its obligations under the decision and conform to what was mandated by the Court. While this would be the ideal outcome, a smooth implementation might still not be guaranteed and a new dispute might arise if the required behavior is not easily discernible at first sight because the decision requires further interpretation and/or an assessment of facts. It might happen that the decision's creditor will then make a complaint of non-compliance. Yet, usually in such conflicts, one will have to speak of difficulties in implementation rather than of non-compliance, unless there is conclusive evidence that the debtor acts in bad faith and it does not engage in attempts to settle the dispute with the other side. If, however, the creditor itself is responsible for the lack of knowledge about the mandated behavior, this will have to be qualified as non-compliance. Second, the debtor might acknowledge the decision and claim to conform to it, but it is doubtful whether its words are matched by the required action. The dispute then would center on facts—the actual behavior of the debtor—and not concern either the bindingness of the decision or its content and the scope of the resulting obligation. If the debtor, in fact, despite its announcements to the contrary, fails to conform to what is mandated, this is certainly non-compliance; moreover, if the debtor deceitfully claims to comply with the decision while being aware of its contravening

[79] LaGrand, Judgment of 27 June 2001, at para.103, quoting the principle as stated by the PCIJ in Electricity Company of Sofia and Bulgaria in its Order of 5 December 1939 and recalling the various orders in which the ICJ itself had made orders to this extent.
[80] See Article 41(1) of the Statute: "The Court shall have the power to indicate, if it considers that the circumstances so *require* (...)" (emphasis added).
[81] Both happened in the Fisheries Jurisdiction cases, see *infra* Chapter 3 C II 2.

action, we can even speak of (concealed) defiance. Third, the debtor might express respect for the decision, but fail to comply with it, either temporarily or permanently, while bringing justifications. It will then bear the burden of proof that its non-compliance is justified in accordance with the general rules of state responsibility. In all these scenarios, the authority of the Court is not directly attacked, as the parties in principle acknowledge the bindingness of the decision and their obligation of compliance under Article 94(1) of the Charter. This is different in cases of open defiance where the debtor rejects the decision as invalid and refuses to comply. Yet, an initial verbal rejection or statements of disapproval will be irrelevant if followed by action in conformity with the Court's decision: as long as the decision is properly executed, there will be no need to investigate the state's motives in order to assess the lawfulness of its behavior with Article 94(1).[82]

Non-compliance with the obligation under Article 94(1) of the Charter will normally constitute an international wrong entailing state responsibility, as in other cases of violations of international obligations; moreover, it takes on increased significance in its challenge to the authority of the ICJ, the principal UN judicial organ. This factor has induced some discussion on whether such non-compliance should have the character of an aggravated international wrong—in particular, whether it should be regarded as an act of aggression. Yet its seems inappropriate to make such a wholesale classification based on the mere fact that the right at stake is confirmed in an ICJ judgment, regardless of the subject-matter of the dispute and the terms of the judgment. The classification is only justified if the concrete action apart from violating Article 94(1) *per se* represents an act of aggression.[83]

As mentioned, non-compliance will not always be attributable to a willful decision to defy the authority of the ICJ judgment. The judgment debtor might contest the factual allegations used to found the claim of non-compliance or attempt to justify its action. Under the rules of state responsibility, there might be circumstances precluding the wrongfulness of action that fails to meet the prescribed requirements, as for example a state of necessity or the use of a lawful countermeasure.[84] The question is whether the obliged state might invoke nullity of the decision beyond the recognized grounds for precluding wrongfulness under the general law of state responsibility. There has been some practice with regard to arbitral decisions where parties have invoked nullity as a ground for invalidity—most notably an excess of power (*excès de pouvoir*).[85] However, the Charter and the Statute do not contain any provision on the basis of which invalidity could be claimed on such

---

[82] See *Weckel*, 42 AFDI (1996), at 437.   [83] See Rosenne, *Law and Practice I*, at 227–30.
[84] Ibid., at 230–1.
[85] *Anand*, 26 U. Pitt. LR (1965), at 673; *Schachter*, 54 AJIL (1960), at 3–5, with further references; at 3, Schachter reports three conditions usually cited as grounds for nullity: (1) excess of power, (2) corruption of a member of the tribunal, or (3) a serious departure from a

grounds. To assume a right for a party to proceedings before the Court to determine unilaterally whether the decision is valid would be incompatible with Article 94(1) of the Charter. It would run counter to the binding character of decisions (Article 59 of the Statute for judgments, Article 41 for provisional measures), to the judgment's final character and the absence of a possibility of an appeal (Article 60 cl. 1 of the Statute), and would circumvent the provisions on interpretation and revision of the judgment (Articles 60 cl. 2, 61 of the Statute).[86] The reference to a lack of jurisdiction on part of the Court would not accord with Article 36(6) of the Statute, pursuant to which a dispute as to jurisdiction shall be settled by the decision of the Court.[87]

Non-compliance and cases of difficulties in the implementation of a judgment are of a rather different nature. Whereas non-compliance, characterized by the disregard of a judgment by a state, is a serious blow to the authority of the Court—be it indirectly through a failure to stick to its words and honor Article 94(1) or even more directly through an open refusal to accept the decision as valid and binding—difficulties in the implementation are less worrisome as they are no direct attack on the Court's authority. Nevertheless, depending on the concrete circumstances, such cases might also be prejudicial for the Court, since they might raise doubts on the efficiency of the Court as a mechanism for the settlement of disputes.

E. ENFORCEMENT OF ICJ DECISIONS

I. *Preliminary remarks*

The enforcement mechanisms for ICJ decisions are significant in examining compliance with ICJ decisions: first, the availability of effective enforcement mechanisms will generally be a factor inducing compliance; and, second, on the other side of the coin, international law in general as well as international adjudication in particular are frequently described as weak given their scarce

---

fundamental rule of procedure. See also in detail on claims of nullity Reisman, *Nullity and revision*, at 265–634; Nantwi, *Enforcement of international judicial decisions*, at 114–18. On the concept of nullity in international law in general, see *Jennings*, in Cambridge Essays in International Law, at 64–87.

[86] See *Goodrich/Hambro*, Charter of the United Nations, at 485; see also (specifically on the Nicaragua case) *Rowles*, 80 AJIL (1986), at 581–3.

[87] For details on this provision see Shihata, *The power of the International Court to determine its own jurisdiction*. For a claim that a particular judge should not have participated, see Article 16(2), 17(3) of the Statute. *Vulcan*, 18 RGDIP (1947), at 196, argues that the process by which the Court is constituted and the presence of numerous procedural guarantees make it practically impossible to argue that a decision is null and void, even though he sees a risk that a state might raise a claim of nullity if recourse to the Court was to be taken more frequently in the future.

enforcement mechanisms.[88] In any case, however, one should bear in mind that an exclusive focus on enforcement does not adequately grasp the mechanisms influencing execution of ICJ decisions, for in many cases, the (non-) availability of enforcement will play no role. Potential enforcement will not be the only driving force for state behavior, as it neither will be for domestic actors.[89] In many cases, states will comply voluntarily with an ICJ decision regardless of whether they might contemplate enforcement action. Furthermore, as was explained before, not all decisions will require execution.

A basic distinction can be drawn between direct and indirect enforcement mechanisms: while the first concerns the physical transfer of what was decreed (be it through substitutive means), the second concerns the imposition of sanctions in order to persuade the defaulting state to comply.[90] Obviously, direct enforcement means will generally be the more efficient measures as they bring about the execution of the judgment by themselves and thereby, they provide immediate satisfaction to the creditor. Yet it will not be available in all cases (for instance, where the performance of a specific act is required, or where the creditor has no means of accessing assets owned by the creditor in cases of monetary judgments). Therefore, traditionally there has been more focus on indirect enforcement on the international level, although the potential for direct enforcement is certainly an issue worth while exploring.

Many questions on the applicable enforcement mechanisms are general issues of enforcement of international obligations and of decisions of international organizations: the conditions for permissibility of countermeasures; the possibility of involving domestic courts, etc. It would go beyond the scope of the present study to address all these questions in detail. Instead, the aim of the following explanations is to present the specific approach to enforcement of ICJ decisions in the Charter and, in particular, to explain the Security Council's special competence for enforcement of judgments under Article 94(2), indicate the potential for action by other UN main organs, and to give an overview of further enforcement mechanisms. While the procedure under Article 94(2) of the Charter has its limitations, the end of the Cold War has opened the way for more constructive Security Council action, as a result of which there is more likelihood for effective enforcement action. Hence, it is now worth while taking a look afresh at those provisions.

---

[88] See Schachter, *International Law*, at 227–9, who at 228 comments that, on the other hand, there is a contrary argument that states may be more ready to accept compulsory jurisdiction because of the absence of stronger enforcement mechanisms.

[89] See *Reisman*, 63 AJIL (1969), at 2–5 on different approaches to compliance and enforcement.

[90] See Reisman, *Nullity and revision*, at 651, and *idem*, 63 AJIL (1969), at 6–7.

II. Enforcement of ICJ decisions under the United Nations Charter

The Security Council has the special competence for the enforcement of ICJ decisions under Article 94(2) of the Charter, although it has never explicitly made use of this provision. UN organs have become involved in the implementation of only a few ICJ decisions.

This section will analyze the legal bases for enforcement action by the various UN organs other than the Court; it will make references to the Court's practice as far as it is useful for the interpretation of those provisions.

As was already described, the Charter conceives enforcement of ICJ decisions not as part of the judicial but of the political branch of government; the key provision of Article 94(2) thus empowers the Security Council and not the Court.[91] Yet the Court has some role in enforcement of ICJ decisions under the Charter and the Statute. Under Article 61(3) of the Statute, it can make compliance with the terms of a judgment a condition for admitting proceedings in revision, a provision never applied thus far.[92] The PCIJ's 1922 Rules of Court provided a mild sanction for non-compliance with provisional measures: the Court could place on record a refusal of a party to implement provisional measures (Article 57). The provision was revoked at the revision of the Rules of 1931 and not reintroduced ever since.[93] The Court has sanctioned violations of provisional measures *ex post* through pronouncements in the judgment, most notably, in the LaGrand judgment.[94] As concerns the violation of the obligation to comply with a judgment, the creditor might take this issue to the Court again by way of new proceedings, provided that there is a valid jurisdictional link. Unlike for interpretation and revision proceedings, this is not automatically given by the jurisdiction in the original proceedings.[95]

---

[91] Of course, the way the Court reaches and frames its decisions will affect the prospects of compliance (see further *infra* Chapter 4 B II); yet this is not a decision of enforcement proper. See further Article 74(4) of the Rules of Court for positive measures prior to the issuing of provisional measures: the president of the Court may call upon the parties to ensure that the order will have its appropriate effects, see *supra* n. 3.

[92] This provision serves to discourage proceedings for revision launched with the sole aim of delaying implementation of the original judgment. It cannot be applied in relation to different cases, however; therefore the ICJ President rightly refused Nicaragua's attempt to sanction US non-compliance with a provisional measures order by rendering its services unavailable in a different case, see *infra* Chapter 3 C VI 3.

[93] Rosenne, *Law and Practice I*, 215.

[94] The very existence of such a sanctioning mechanism might serve as a deterrent in further cases, particularly if the Court might even consider state responsibility claims under this heading. For further details, see *infra* Chapter 4 B IV.

[95] Unlike in case of interpretation and revision proceedings, the Court does not acquire jurisdiction for proceedings relating to non-compliance based on jurisdiction in the main proceedings, although proposals to this extent have been made in legal literature: *Reisman*, 63 AJIL (1969), at 27 suggests the addition of an Article 60a to the Statute with the following text: "In the event of any dispute as to the fact or manner of compliance, either party may apply to the

1. Enforcement of ICJ decisions through the Security Council

Although the Security Council has never actually founded measures to enforce ICJ decisions on Article 94(2),[96] there have been some instances where states have brought non-compliance with ICJ decisions before the Council invoking that provision and where related issues were discussed.[97] The only clear-cut instance of Council discussions based on a complaint of non-compliance by a judgment creditor was the Nicaragua case, in which ultimately no action was taken.[98] There are other cases where parties had filed complaints with the Security Council, but did not follow through with requests for a Council meeting. This behavior seems to demonstrate a lack of genuine desire to have the Council immediately confront the matter. Rather, the parties appear to have used such complaints as part of their strategy to urge compliance.[99] With regard to provisional measures, for which the applicability of Article 94(2) is doubtful, the Council did hold discussions in some cases in response to complaints of non-compliance—for example, in the Anglo-Iranian Oil Company case, the Tehran hostages case, and the Genocide case.[100]

Nature of the Council's jurisdiction under Article 94(2)   In order to examine the nature of the Council's powers under Article 94(2), the first question to consider is whether this provision represents an autonomous source of the Council's jurisdiction or, conversely, whether the Council can only take

Court." Special agreements might provide for a right of either party to seize the Court again in the post-adjudicative phase; on this basis, Slovakia has seized the Court with a complaint of non-compliance with the Gabčíkovo–Nagymaros judgment, see *infra* Chapter 3 B XXIV 4.

[96] In the South West Africa cases, it appeared that Security Council enforcement action might take place and that South Africa would not comply with a judgment against it. In 1964, the US Department of State announced that it would not tolerate a repudiation of the judgment. Ultimately, the applicants' request was held inadmissible for lack of standing (South West Africa, Second Phase, Judgment of 18 July 1966). See Reisman, *Nullity and revision*, at 728.

[97] See *Tanzi*, 6 EJIL (1995), at 540, 543–5, 564–8.

[98] Military and paramilitary activities in and against Nicaragua, see *infra* Chapter 3 B XVIII 6 b (1).

[99] See Portugal's complaint in Right of Passage over Indian Territory (without an explicit reference to Article 94(2)), *infra* Chapter 3 B VI 4 and the further reaching complaint by Honduras in Land, Island and Maritime Frontier Dispute invoking Article 94(2) and requesting Council intervention, yet not the scheduling of a meeting, *infra* Chapter 3 B IXX 4.

[100] See *infra* Chapter III C I 4, IV 2, and VII 3. As in the case of judgments, there have been complaints of non-compliance not accompanied by requests for Council meetings on the matters, see Cameroon's complaints in Land and Maritime Boundary between Cameroon and Nigeria, *infra* Chapter 3 C VIII 4. In Military and Paramilitary Activities in and against Nicaragua, Nicaragua's complaint related to the violation of provisional measures, although the Council meeting was requested for alleged aggression, *infra* Chapter 3 C VI 3. There were other cases where Council action was parallel to that of the Court and both organs pursued similar objectives, but the Council acted in fulfillment of functions other than Article 94(2), see Armed Activities in the Territory of the Congo, Chapter 3 C XI. See further *infra* Chapter 4 A VIII.

action in the execution of an ICJ decision if the conditions of Chapters VI or VII of the Charter are fulfilled.[101] The former interpretation seems more compelling.[102] Article 94(2) has not been designed as conditional on the prerequisites of Chapter VI or VII.[103] It appears in a separate chapter (Chapter XIV, dedicated to the ICJ) that is not subordinate to the former chapters. The drafting history of the provision indicates the intention of the framers to strengthen the enforcement mechanism for ICJ judgments and to give the aggrieved party a right of recourse, not merely to reiterate the other powers of the Security Council.[104] The provision's ordinary meaning, its context, drafting history, and purpose—all these factors point to the conclusion that the right contained in the article is not dependent on the existence of a potential threat to international peace and security.[105] If one were to

---

[101] This question has practical consequences for the applicable procedural rules. Moreover, if Article 94(2) provided no autonomous competence, Council action would not be possible in the absence of a potential threat to international peace and security. Admittedly, in its recent practice the Security Council has adopted a rather broad interpretation of the term "threat to the peace" (for details see *Frowein/Krisch* in Simma, Charter, Article 39, at nn. 16–25), and it is not very likely that it will be seized with cases of non-compliance where the determination of a potential threat to the peace would not be feasible. It will usually be in serious cases only that the judgment creditor will push for Council action and that the Council will be willing to act.

[102] The large majority of commentators therefore agrees that Article 94(2) is an independent source of competence for the Security Council: Goodrich/Hambro, *Charter of the United Nations*, at 486–7; Goodrich/Hambro/Simons, *Charter of the United Nations*, at 556–7; *Schachter*, 54 AJIL (1960), at 18–20; *Mosler/Oellers-Frahm* in Simma, Charter, Article 94, at n. 11; *Tanzi*, 6 EJIL (1995), at 571; *Kapoor* in Dhokalia, International Court in transition, at 305; *Magid* in Peck/Lee, Increasing the effectiveness, at 327–8; Reisman, *Nullity and revision*, at 709–13; but see Jiménez de Aréchaga, *Derecho constitucional de las Naciones Unidas*, at 560; *Kerley* in Gross, The future of the International Court of Justice, at 277–8.

[103] *Mosler/Oellers-Frahm* in Simma, Charter, Article 94, at n. 11.

[104] The intention of the members of Committee IV/1 who drafted the provision was to give the aggrieved party an effective right of recourse to the Security Council, see the respective discussion in the 20th meeting of the committee, 13 UNCIO, 266–9. In the session of the Coordination Committee of 12 June 1945, the Soviet delegate Golunsky pointed out that the article "made a considerable change in the functions of the Security Council. Formerly, the Security Council had jurisdiction only in matters concerned with the maintenance of international peace and security. This article would give the Council authority to deal with matters which might have nothing to do with security." Other committee members stressed that there had been no intention to confer an additional obligation on the Security Council, which leaves room for the inclusion of an additional *right*. The Chinese delegate argued that non-compliance would automatically affect peace and security and that therefore Article 94 was not unrelated to questions of international peace and security. Only the US delegate Dr Pasvolsky argued that there might be an actual *duplication* of provisions. The Committee deferred further discussion of this article. No further discussion of the provision is documented in the conference materials. Summary report of 16th meeting of Coordination Committee, 17 UNCIO 96–101, at 97–8. As a whole, the documents of the San Francisco conference rather support the view that Article 94(2) is a separate competence: *Schachter*, 54 AJIL (1960), at 19, 21.

[105] Article 24 with its catalogue of Security Council competences in paragraph (2) is no evidence to the contrary since that catalogue is non-exhaustive (see *Delbrück* in Simma, Charter, Article 24, at n. 11). Article 24 reads: "(1) In order to ensure prompt and effective action by the United Nations, its Members confer on the Security Council primary responsibility for the

assume that Article 94(2) had no independent significance, the provision would be superfluous; a result incompatible with the presumption that a treaty does not contain redundant provisions.[106]

Several arguments have been raised to challenge the autonomous character of Article 94(2). A position against an autonomous character was defended by two US delegates to the San Francisco Conference in their testimony before the Committee of Foreign Affairs of the US Senate.[107] However, this testimony was no more than a subjective assessment of two US State Department officials and might have been motivated by an attempt to lower the risk of resistance against the UN Charter in the not enthusiastically internationalist US Senate,[108] making ratification more palatable by

maintenance of international peace and security, and agree that in carrying out its duties under this responsibility the Security Council acts on their behalf. (2) In discharging these duties the Security Council shall act in accordance with the Purposes and Principles of the United Nations. The specific powers granted to the Security Council for the discharge of these duties are laid down in Chapters VI, VII, VIII, and XII. (3) [...]." Paragraph (2) concerns *specific* competences for the fulfillment of the responsibilities for the maintenance of international peace and security and leaves room for specific competences in other fields as well as general competences. It is therefore not surprising that Chapter XIV and Article 94(2) are not mentioned, as well as other chapters that clearly confer competences on the Security Council, such as Chapter IV (Article 12(1)) and V (Article 26).

[106] See *Kapoor* in Dhokalia, International Court in transition, 305; *Magid* in Peck/Lee, Increasing the effectiveness, at 328; *O'Connell*, 30 Va. JIL (1990), at 908; Reisman, *Nullity and revision*, at 709–10; *Schachter*, 54 AJIL (1960), at 19–20; *Tanzi*, 6 EJIL (1995), at 561. Shortcomings in the drafting (i.e. the inclusion of redundant provisions) may owe to the political character of the conference, which essentially took place in committees and commissions, and it is not impossible that there might be some shortcomings in the drafting; there is therefore some possibility that some redundant provisions might have been included (the counter-argument used by *Kerley* in Gross, The future of the International Court of Justice, 277); still, it would be an anomaly for the occurrence of which conclusive evidence would have to be presented.

[107] The testimony of Dr Leo Pasvolsky, US delegate to the San Francisco conference and chairman of the Coordination Committee, before the US Senate Committee on Foreign Relations was quoted as the main authority for the view that Article 94(2) is not an autonomous competence. Pasvolsky held that enforcement of an ICJ judgment could take place only under Chapter VI and VII, and that Article 94(2) did not confer additional powers on the Council: "The Council may proceed, I suppose, to call upon the country concerned to carry out the judgment, but only if the peace of the world is threatened, and if the Council has made a determination to that effect. [...] The Council is not a sheriff in the sense that the Council enforces the Court's decision when the Court asks it to enforce it. The Council simply handles a political situation which arises out of the fact that the judgment of the Court is not being carried out by one of the parties." Hearings before the Senate Committee on Foreign Relations on the Charter of the United Nations, 9–13 July 1945, 79th Cong., 1st Sess. (rev.) (1945), at 287. Similarly, Mr Hackworth, legal advisor to the State Department, pointed out during the same session: "There was no intention to increase the duties of the Council under Article 94 [...] all that was intended by these provisions was to show that the States expected that the decision of the Court would be complied with, the complaining party would have a right to bring the matter to the attention of the Council for whatever it might be worth, but the Council would be entirely free to do what it might seem fit." He confirmed that there was no desire or intention to increase the Council's jurisdiction. Ibid., at 331–2.

[108] See Reisman, *Nullity and revision*, 712–13.

downplaying worries about any automatism for Council enforcement action.[109] Another argument was the omission of any reference to Article 94 in the Provisional Rules of Procedure of the Security Council.[110] Yet these rules should not be understood as forming a practice of the Council not to treat Article 94 as an autonomous provision.[111] There is no indication that the Council had intended to interpret Article 94 or to make any final and comprehensive assessment of its powers in its adoption of these Rules; it cannot be lightly assumed that the Council wanted to subject itself to stricter requirements in the application of Article 94 than those of the Charter. The likely reason for the lack of an explicit reference to Article 94 was that the Council felt no need for it given the low probability of a call for action in the enforcement of a judgment in a situation where the threshold of at least Chapter VI is not passed.[112]

The Council's limited practice sheds only little light on this issue. The *Nicaragua* case was the only case of enforcement of a judgment being discussed, and this precedent rather lends support to an understanding of this provision as autonomous competence. The sole basis of Nicaragua's request was Article 94(2),[113] and the matter was put on the agenda without the specification of a legal basis. There were no debates on the Council's jurisdiction and on any further requirements beyond those of Article 94(2).[114]

---

[109] As stated above, *supra* n. 104, the drafting history rather points to the contrary result, with Dr Pasvolsky himself as the only delegate who had pointed to an alleged "duplication of provisions" during the discussion on the provision. *Kerley* in Gross, The future of the International Court of Justice, acknowledges, at 277: "The legislative history of Article 94(2) does not conclusively confirm or contradict the position taken by the State Department representative."

[110] S/96/Rev.7 (as revised on 21 December 1982), also retrievable at http://www.un.org/Docs/sc/scrules.htm. Rule 3 reads: "The President shall call a meeting of the Security Council if a dispute or situation is brought to the attention of the Security Council under Article 35 or under Article 11(3) of the Charter, or if the General Assembly makes recommendations or refers any question to the Security Council under Article 11(2), or if the Secretary-General brings to the attention of the Security Council any matter under Article 99." There is no explicit reference to Article 94 in the Rules of Procedure.

[111] But see *Kerley* in Gross, The future of the International Court of Justice, at 277.

[112] If the Council was seized under Article 94(2) in situations beyond Chapters VI and VII, the President would most likely see no obstacles against proceeding in the same manner as described in Rule 3 of the Provisional Rules of Procedure and call a meeting; if the request under Article 94(2) came from a Council member, Rule 2 would be directly applicable ("The President shall call a meeting of the Security Council at the request of any member of the Security Council.").

[113] S/18415.

[114] For further details see *infra* Chapter 3 B XVIII 6 b (1). The draft resolution (S/18428) that failed due to the US veto did not indicate its legal basis. *Magid* in Peck/Lee, Increasing the effectiveness, at 328 fn. 5, suggests that the US practice in the Nicaragua case is indicative of a perception of Article 94(2) as an autonomous competence, since the application of the procedural rules of Chapter VI would have prevented the US from casting a veto. On the other hand, the applicability of Chapter VI and the fulfillment of its procedural conditions (and the legal consequences of a breach) are two separate matters. Moreover, it may be debatable whether the rule of obligatory abstention remains applicable to permanent members, see *O'Connell*, 30 Va. JIL (1990), at 908–9. In general, the Council does not always give a clear indication of the legal

The practice with regard to provisional measures is somewhat inconclusive;[115] yet, this might rather reflect doubts on the applicability of Article 94(2) to provisional measures than on its independent character as a Council competence. In the two cases of provisional measures where the Council took action, the Court was actively seized with the overall situation and had already adopted resolutions, so it was unsurprising that non-compliance with the orders of interim protection did not occupy a central place and that there was no cause to engage in a general discussion on the nature of the Council jurisdiction under Article 94(2). Moreover, there was little reason for a debate on the "nature" of the competences under this article as in all cases[116] there were no doubts that at least the threshold of Chapter VI had been passed.

A related issue would be whether Article 94(2) leaves room for action under other chapters or whether as a special rule it trumps all other competences in accordance with the rule of *lex specialis derogat legi generali*, representing an exclusive competence as far as the enforcement of ICJ judgments is concerned.[117] The former reasoning appears more persuasive for a number of reasons.[118]

First, Article 94(2) empowers the Security Council, but in no way affects the potential for other actors to become involved. Second, as far as action by

basis for its action, so it might not see a need to engage in general discussions about the delimitation of competences between Article 94(2) and Chapters VI and VII in any future cases: see *Kerley* in Gross, The future of the International Court of Justice at 277–8: "[I]t seems probable [...] that the Security Council would follow its usual practice of avoiding as far as possible a clear articulation of the legal basis of its action in cases such as this where the law is open to dispute."

[115] In Anglo-Iranian Oil Company, the UK request for the meeting was based on Article 94(2) as well as to Article 35 of Chapter VI (S/2357), and the UK took the position in the discussions that there was a basis for Council action under both provisions (S/PV.559, at 20, para. 93). The discussions did not address the nature of Article 94(2), in particular, its applicability beyond or in connection with Chapter VI. The British representative held that Article 94(2) applied to provisional measures while the Iranian representative argued that such measures were not binding. The Council adjourned the discussions because of doubts concerning jurisdiction in the main proceedings, which were subsequently confirmed in the Court's judgment. Those doubts may have been an additional reason for the UK to refer to Chapter VI as well. See further *infra* Chapter 3 C I 4. In the Tehran Hostages case, the US complaint did not explicitly mention Article 94(2) (S/13705), and no related issues were discussed at the Security Council meetings, see further *infra* Chapter 3 C IV 2. In the Genocide case, two letters from Bosnia preceded the Council meeting, in one of which Article 94(2) was invoked and "measures under Chapter VII" were requested, see *infra* Chapter 3 C VII 3; it would be inappropriate to interpret this as acknowledgment of a lack of independent nature of Article 94(2), as the situation in Bosnia and Herzegovina was already under Council consideration under Chapter VII.

[116] Including the Anglo-Iranian Oil Co. case where no action was taken.

[117] See Tuncel, *L'exécution des décisions*, at 72.

[118] See *Pillepich* in Cot/Pellet, Charte, Article 94, at n. 21, 1284–5; Goodrich/Hambro/Simons, *Charter of the United Nations*, at 556; Rosenne, *Law and Practice I*, at 258. One might think that the practice in the three cases of provisional measures (see *supra* n. 115) confirms this result; yet, the applicability of Article 94(2) to such measures is questionable, see *infra* pp. 60–2.

the Council itself is concerned, Article 94(2) neither explicitly excludes action under other provisions nor can any exclusive effect be understood as being implied. Article 94(2) and Chapters VI and VII have different prerequisites;[119] they cannot be perceived as forming a relationship of the special *vis-à-vis* the general norm. Rather, these provisions reasonably complement each other if taken as separate and autonomous competences.[120] Moreover, the maintenance of international peace and security is one of the principal purposes of the United Nations, elaborated in Article 1(1) of the Charter, and primary responsibility is conferred on the Security Council for the achievement of this objective pursuant to Article 24(1). To construct Article 94(2) as a limitation for Security Council action under Chapters VI and VII would run counter to that primary goal. The right of recourse under Article 94(2) cannot be construed in a manner that would result in a threat to international peace and security.

Range of measures   A discussion of the array of measures for Security Council action available under Article 94(2) remains necessarily on a theoretical level, as the Council has never explicitly based action on this provision. A basic distinction is to be made as to whether scenarios of non-compliance represent threats to international peace and security. If so, the full range of measures under Chapter VII will be available with broad discretion and powers for the Council up to military action. Otherwise, the question of the available means under Article 94(2) will become relevant.[121]

---

[119] This would be different if the Bolivian proposal at the San Francisco Conference had prevailed and non-compliance with an ICJ judgment was regarded as an act of aggression (see *supra*, n. 23). This would have automatically opened the field for Chapter VII. However, it would not seem appropriate to equate a state not complying with an ICJ judgment without further particulars to a state launching a military attack on another state, unless such an evaluation would seem justified by the particular norm involved: see *Vulcan*, 18 RGDIP (1947), at 200. The respective proposal was therefore appropriately rejected at the San Francisco Conference. Moreover, the General Assembly Resolution on the Definition of Aggression (Res. 3314 (XXIX) of 14 December 1974) does not mention non-compliance with ICJ decisions.

[120] In cases where there is no threat to international peace and security, only the state creditor of the judgment can seize the Security Council. There is no reason why the Council should deal with the situation absent that state's wish. In cases where there might arise a threat to peace and security, Chapter VI allows action without that state's initiative. Chapters VI and VII on the one hand and Article 94(2) on the other thus have overlapping, but not identical, fields of application.

[121] Of course, the question of the available means under Article 94(2) only comes up under the assumption that Article 94(2) is an autonomous source of competence for the Security Council; otherwise, it would merely be a reiteration of other powers. The practical significance of the question of the available means under Article 94(2) absent a Chapter VII situation might be limited since the Council has adopted a broad interpretation of Article 39 (see *supra* n. 101) and will most likely be ready to consider non-compliance as a threat to international peace and security if it is committed to act: see *Tanzi*, 6 EJIL (1995), at 561, n. 87. On the other hand, in scenarios where there is clearly no such threat and where there is only a disagreement between two states that maintain good relations, it is unlikely that Article 94(2) would ever come into

Under Article 94(2), the Council is free to decide not to take action; the provision empowers the Council without obligating it to act.[122] If the Security Council decides to become active, the means available under Article 94(2) are "recommendations" and "measures," without a further specification. For example, the Security Council could make recommendations on the modalities for implementation, the desirability of third-party assistance, possible self-help measures open to the judgment creditor, and the role of third states.[123] Beyond recommendations, the Security Council might reiterate the Court's decision and order compliance—be it through an explicit call for compliance[124] or implicitly through a parallel call for the action ordered by the Court without labeling it as call for compliance with the respective decision. Apart from adding authority to the judgment and exerting political pressure on the recalcitrant state, such a resolution could make the operative part of the decision extend beyond its *inter partes* effect under Article 59 of the ICJ Statute and thereby binding for all states under Article 25 of the Charter—a step that might be particularly appropriate in cases of obligations *erga omnes*.[125] For further measures, reference can be made to the catalogue in Article 41, which provides a non-exhaustive list of coercive measures: complete or partial interruption of economic relations and of rail, sea, air, postal, telegraphic, radio, and other means of communication; and the severance of diplomatic relations.[126] One has to bear in mind, though, that this catalogue provides for collective responses to a threat to the peace, a breach of the peace, or acts of aggression, and might be too drastic in many cases of non-compliance with an ICJ judgment unless the conditions of Chapter VII are fulfilled.[127] Yet some of those measures might be appropriate beyond the context of Chapter VII. For example, an economic embargo, limited to a certain category of goods if appropriate, might serve as effective tool: it could involve third states and publicly expose the non-compliance,

play, or that particular drastic measures such as military enforcement would ever be discussed as an option.

[122] *Vulcan*, 18 RGDIP (1947), at 197–8; Tuncel, *L'exécution des décisions*, 88–9. But see *Kapoor* in Dhokalia, International Court in transition, at 304, who argues that the Security Council is *obliged* to act and that it has discretion only regarding the nature of measures. Yet, this cannot be reconciled with the clear wording, the drafting history, and object and purpose of Article 94(2).

[123] On the question on how far the Council is bound by the Court's findings and whether it could recommend a solution entirely different from the one reached by the Court, see *infra* section C.

[124] This was the case of the failed draft resolution aimed at urging compliance with the Nicaragua judgment; see *infra* Chapter 3 B XVIII 6 b (1).

[125] See *Tanzi*, 6 EJIL (1995), at 562.

[126] See *Schachter*, 54 AJIL (1960), at 22. But see *Vulcan*, 18 RGDIP (1947), at 199, who argues that the sanctions enumerated in Articles 41 and 42 can only be taken in accordance with Article 39.

[127] *Tanzi*, 6 EJIL (1995), at 561–2.

apart from pressuring the recalcitrant state through economic disadvantages.[128]

In general, one may ask whether the array of measures under Article 94(2) must be construed narrower than that under Articles 41 and 42. Neither the San Francisco records nor the practice of the Council give any indications on whether there are any restrictions.[129] Could the Security Council order a third state to transfer assets of the recalcitrant state to the judgment creditor or use military means to enforce an ICJ judgment, even though it does not see a threat to international peace and security? From the wording of Article 94(2), there are no explicit limits to the Court's powers to adopt "recommendations" or "measures". Some commentators conclude that the Charter contains no obstacles to prevent the Council from taking any measures identical to what is specified in Articles 41 and 42, as long as they are appropriate to secure compliance, and that these measures would be binding pursuant to Article 25 of the Charter.[130] Accordingly, the Council would have broad powers, including, for example, the power to make orders to third states to seize and transfer funds of the recalcitrant state located within their territory. Other commentators have expressed doubt, though, whether Council powers are broad enough to include an order to effect such a transfer in the absence of a threat to international peace and security.[131] Economic embargoes would then similarly pose problems, as the harmful effect of collective economic sanctions for a third state might be more serious than in case of a transfer of certain funds.[132] Consequently, every measure asking for third-state action with a potential prejudicial effect on that state would have to be excluded. This would severely limit the enforcement means available to the Council and might make effective action in certain cases impossible—an interpretation incompatible with the object and purpose of Article 94(2). There is no indication for such a far-reaching restriction. Article 25 makes clear that the Security Council's power to issue binding decisions to Member States is not restricted to Chapter

---

[128] In this context, however, it has to be considered whether such sanctions might be counterproductive because they might cause the defaulting state to stick to its position for reasons of national pride: see ibid., 562.

[129] See *infra* B II and *Schachter*, 54 AJIL (1960), at 21.

[130] Jenks, *Prospects of international adjudication*, at 694. Under this view, the Council would have broad powers to adopt measures, and military action would be possible as well as orders to third states to transfer funds.

[131] *O'Connell*, 30 Va. JIL (1990), at 910, seems to suggest that the powers under Article 94(2) cannot be as broad as those under Chapter VII.

[132] *O'Connell*, 30 Va. JIL (1990), does not draw this consequence, though: at 909 she argues that the Council could call on Member States to apply sanctions. However, if the reason for denying the permissibility of a transfer order was to be seen in the fact that rights and interests of third states would be unduly affected, this may be the case for sanctions just as easily as for transfer orders.

VII decisions.[133] Hence, the powers under Article 94(2) a priori could comprise an order to Member States to attach or seize and transfer assets in their territory.[134] As a milder measure, the Security Council could also make a recommendation to the same effect rather than order third states, which might still increase the readiness of third states to provide assistance to the judgment creditor.

Yet, the powers under Article 94(2) are not unfettered. There are good reasons to believe that the only measures available under Article 94(2) are peaceful ones, and that Chapter VII is the sole basis for military action or an express authorization for use of force by the judgment creditor or third states.[135] The Charter lays down a comprehensive system for regulating the use of force, and Chapter VII contains detailed provisions on the permissibility of collective military measures as well as of self-defense. The Council must make a determination under Article 39 and verify whether peaceful measures under Article 41 are not sufficient before ordering coercive action.[136] Article 94 contains no such requirements. If Article 94(2) were perceived as enabling military action, its conditions would effectively be less strict than those of Chapter VII, where the interests of the international community are affected to a much larger interest and where an essential purpose of the United Nations is touched upon—hardly a reasonable result. Chapter VII is the basis for the use of force under the UN Charter, and Article 94(2) cannot form an independent basis for military action.[137]

The Security Council could direct the UN specialized agencies to assist in the enforcement of judgments. For example, it could order the World Bank to turn over funds of the debtor to the creditor or order the ICAO to ask

---

[133] Proposals to limit the binding force of Security Council decisions to certain chapters of the Charter did not find support at the San Francisco conference. The ICJ has explicitly confirmed that binding decisions can be taken outside of Chapter VII, as explicitly confirmed by the ICJ, Legal Consequences for States of the Continued Presence of South Africa in Namibia (South West Africa) notwithstanding Security Council Resolution 276 (1970), Advisory Opinion of 21 June 1971, at 52–4, paras. 113–16. See further *Delbrück* in Simma, Charter, Article 25, at nn. 8–15, and *Higgins*, 21 ICLQ (1972), at 270–86.

[134] See *Magid* in Peck/Lee, Increasing the effectiveness, at 328; *Schachter*, 54 AJIL (1960), at 22.

[135] See *Mosler/Oellers-Frahm* in Simma, Charter, Article 94, at n. 11; *Magid* in Peck/Lee, Increasing the effectiveness, at 329; but see Jenks, *Prospects of international adjudication*, at 694; Tuncel, *L'exécution des décisions*, 95–7; and *Vulcan*, 18 RGDIP (1947) (who, at 199–201, makes a distinction between the availability of sanctions under Chapter VII—which he denies—and the possibility of a Council authorization of use of force by the creditor—which he affirms).

[136] See Article 42: "Should the Security Council consider that measures provided for in Article 41 would be inadequate or have proved to be inadequate, it make take such action by air, sea or land forces [...]."

[137] Adjudication is a mechanism for the *peaceful* settlement of disputes, and Article 94(2) is part of the Chapter on the International Court of Justice a certain institution created for that purpose. This context favors the interpretation according to which military measures can be taken only under Chapter VII. See *Mosler/Oellers-Frahm* in Simma, Charter, Article 94, at n. 11; *Magid* in Peck/Lee, Increasing the effectiveness, at 329.

its members to deny air space and landing rights. Many of the specialized agency agreements concluded pursuant to Article 57(1) of the Charter lay down obligations for those agencies to assist the Council under certain conditions.[138]

Finally, for further sanctions in extreme cases of non-compliance with ICJ decisions, one could think of suspension from membership rights under Article 5 or exclusion from the organization under Article 6.[139] However, these sanctions are so drastic that they have never been applied in UN practice[140] and it is unlikely that non-compliance with ICJ decisions will be regarded as a reason substantial enough to merit their application, particularly given the fact that the persuasive effect of such sanctions will usually be doubtful.[141]

The Security Council and the Court decision   As for the limits of the Council's powers under Article 94(2), it is necessary to analyze how far the Council is bound to give effect to the Court's decisions. An important issue is whether the Council could, for example, ignore an ICJ order on interim protection and adopt measures of a different nature, even aimed at opposite results, or issue a moratorium on the legal effects of the judgment by suspending the operation of Article 94(2) of the Rules of Court when it determines that there are reasons not to give immediate effect to a judgment.[142]

Article 94(2) empowers the Council to "make recommendations or decide upon measures to be taken to give effect to the judgment." Thereby, it establishes that Council measures under this article must aim at the

---

[138] See *O'Connell*, 30 Va. JIL (1990), at 910–11, Reisman, *Nullity and revision*, at 741–53.

[139] Article 5: "A member of the United Nations against which preventive or enforcement action has been taken by the Security Council may be suspended from the exercise of the rights and privileges of membership by the General Assembly upon the recommendation of the Security Council. The exercise of these rights and privileges may be restored by the Security Council."
Article 6: "A member of the United Nations which has persistently violated the Principles contained in the present Charter may be expelled from the Organization by the General Assembly upon the recommendation of the Security Council." See *Kerley* in Gross, The future of the International Court of Justice, at 284; *Tanzi*, 6 EJIL (1995), at 563; Tuncel, *L'exécution des décisions*, at 90–1; *Vulcan*, 18 RGDIP (1947), at 199.

[140] See *Schütz* in Simma, Charter, Article 5, at n. 6; *Tams* in Simma, Charter, Article 6, at n. 22.

[141] But see *Kerley* in Gross, The future of the International Court of Justice, at 284, who sees a potential for Article 5 to serve as an "effective, if somewhat drastic" sanction. On the arguments for and against an exclusion, see *Tams* in Simma, Charter, Article 6, at nn. 4–6.

[142] Article 94(2) of the 1978 Rules of Court reads: "The judgment shall be read at a public sitting of the Court and shall become binding on the parties on the day of the reading." In favor of the availability of such a measure, *Schachter*, 54 AJIL (1960), at 22; *Rosenne*, 57 RGDIP (1953), at 573 (commenting on the equivalent Article 76 of the 1946 Version of the Rules of Court: "The judgment becomes binding on the parties on the day on which it is read in open Court.")

implementation of the verdict; this would exclude measures interfering with the judgment. The view has been put forward, though, that the phrase "to give effect to the judgment" only relates to measures but not to recommendations under Article 94(2), where the Council would be free to proceed as if the Court had never decided, up to the point of recommending a solution entirely different from that of the Court, and qualifying a non-compliance with its own recommendation as a threat to the peace. Thus, Article 94(2) would be understood as a right of appeal: the Council could effectively replace the judgment through its recommendation or measure, and the states' obligations under Article 94(1) would accordingly be modified.[143] A more convincing interpretation of the phrase "to give effect to the judgment" relates it to both recommendations and decisions.[144] The purpose of Article 94(2) is to give the judgment creditor a right of recourse to the Council so that compliance with Article 94(1) is achieved; it would turn this purpose on its head if the Council could take away rights adjudicated by the Court through this very procedure. An understanding of Article 94(2) as a mechanism of "appeal to a higher authority" would be at odds with numerous other provisions, including: Article 60 of the ICJ Statute (an integral part of the Charter),[145] according to which the judgment is final and without appeal and the Court has jurisdiction to give an interpretation of its scope in case of controversies; Article 61 of the ICJ Statute, which provides for a Court revision procedure; and Article 7(1) of the Charter, which establishes both the Court and the Council as principal UN organs without creating a hierarchy between them. To advocate a right for the Council to destroy the *res judicata* would run counter to the binding force of the judgment (Article 94(1) of the Charter, Article 59 of the Statute); under such a reading, the judgment would effectively be reduced to an advisory opinion in relation to the Council.

These considerations would be equally valid for the general question of whether the Security Council has a right of review of ICJ decisions, be it in the exercise of its powers under Article 94 or Chapters VI and VII. A general right of review of judgments must be rejected.[146] It is not the role of the Council to interfere with the findings of the Court as the principal judicial

---

[143] Kelsen, *The Law of the United Nations*, at 539–41. He concedes, however, that this is only a possible, but not a compelling reading of the Article. See also Satow, *A guide to diplomatic practice*, at 452; Vulcan, 18 RGDIP (1947), at 197, arguing that, while there is a risk that the Court takes up the role of a court of cassation, this was a risk intended by the drafters of the Charter.

[144] *Rosenne*, 57 RGDIP (1953), at 571 and *Law and Practice I*, at 253–4; the same result is reached by *Mosler/Oellers-Frahm*, in Simma, Charter, Article 94, at n. 10.

[145] See Article 92 of the Charter.

[146] For an affirmative answer, see Kelsen, *The Law of the United Nations*, 539–41, and Statement of Leo Pasvolsky, Hearings before the Committee on Foreign Affairs of the US Senate on the Charter of the United Nations, 79th Cong. 1st Session, 1945, 288: "If the matter is referred to the Council, the Council is not limited in its method of enforcement or adjustment

organ of the United Nations (Article 92 of the Charter); the Council cannot destroy rights adjudicated by the Court.[147] The Council should not reopen the *res judicata* by examining a State's claim that a judgment is null and void *ab initio*:[148] this can be no valid defense because it would be a violation of Article 94(1). Valid claims of nullity of an ICJ judgment are hardly imaginable.[149] Neither would it seem open to the Council to decide that a judgment is no longer valid because of events subsequent to its delivery, as the Statute provides for a revision procedure addressing precisely situations of subsequent events with a potential impact on the judgment's findings.[150]As for concerns that in single cases, the Court's findings might be "bad law" deserving no respect by the Council, it is worth remembering that the Court, a judicial organ, is more likely to reach a sound legal result than the Security Council, a political organ. The judgment is the outcome of a thorough judicial procedure and the Court is composed of a carefully screened panel of judges.[151]

The preceding questions dealt with the issue of whether the Council can make a pronouncement on the legal validity of the judgment and directly interfere with the *res judicata* through the adoption of measures or recommendations contrary to the judgment's findings. This question will rarely come up so directly; states will regularly raise other arguments besides a challenge to the legality validity of the judgment, arguing that the judgment did not cover all relevant political issues and that the broader context must be taken into account. The Council might be more likely to act pragmatically

---

to anything that happened in the Court, but it would have the same power, within the scope of its authority, that it would have had if the case had originally been brought before the Council."

[147] *O'Connell*, 30 Va. JIL (1990), at 907–8; Rosenne, *Law and Practice I*, at 254; *Kapoor* in Dhokalia, International Court in transition, at 306; *Magid* in Peck/Lee, Increasing the effectiveness, 329; *Kerley* in Gross, The future of the International Court of Justice, at 78–9, who, however, makes an exception for manifestly unjust judgments and judgments raising difficult political problems. Even in such cases (which, as Kerley concedes, are unlikely to happen), though, a direct review of the *res judicata* should be avoided, and the Council should solve the problem on the political level rather than putting the Court's authority at risk.

[148] In the Council's discussions on the Nicaragua case, the United States was the only state to claim that the judgment was not valid because the Court had exceeded its jurisdiction, and the only state that voted against the draft resolution. The abstaining states framed their arguments purely in political terms and did not put the authority of the Court in question. In the debate, no attacks on the authority of the Court were made except for those by the US delegate, see Chapter 3 B XVIII 6 b (1). Neither was a formal review undertaken in the Council discussions on the Court's provisional measures in Anglo-Iranian Oil Company; the validity of the measures was not questioned (except on part of the Iranian representative), see *infra* Chapter 3 C I 4 and *Tanzi*, 6 EJIL (1995), at 545.

[149] Tuncel, *L'exécution des décisions*, at 70, and *supra* D III.   [150] Tuncel, ibid.

[151] See *O'Connell*, 30 Va. JIL (1990), at 907–8, fn. 70. The Court consists of fifteen independent judges "elected from among persons of high moral character, who possess the qualifications required in their respective countries for appointment to the highest judicial offices, or are jurisconsults of recognized competence in international law" (Articles 2 and 3 of the Statute).

and base its action on such considerations rather than to pass upon the judgment's validity.[152] This leads to the question whether the Council has to enforce the decision "blindly," even if there are important reasons to refrain from any action or to take action that affects single aspects of the *res judicata*. *Fiat iustitia, pereat mundus* can hardly be the function of Article 94(2) and even less of Chapter VII. The Council is precisely not an automatic enforcement agency under Article 94(2), but its discretion allows for a consideration of other factors, in particular, its primary responsibility for the maintenance of international peace and security.[153] The Council cannot neglect the potential impacts of a decision to enforce an ICJ judgment, but on the contrary has to examine them before taking action; the dispute submitted to the Court as resolved by the judgment and the dispute arising out of the implementation of the judgment are two separate matters.[154] For example, the Council can take into consideration difficulties in the implementation from the debtor's sphere[155] by establishing a schedule for implementation, taking into account practical difficulties. Where the Council for exceptional circumstances finds it inappropriate to support the Court's verdict, it might refrain from taking action.[156] In this sense, one can speak of a permissible "political revision" of the judgment by the Council.[157] Yet, the decision not to take enforcement action might cast a certain doubt on the legitimacy of the judgment creditor's claims; therefore, the Council should carefully examine whether security interests outweigh the interest in enforcement of ICJ decisions, and it should base its decisions on reasons other than doubts as to the judgment's validity.[158]

[152] See *Schachter*, 54 AJIL (1960), at 20. Even in the Nicaragua case, the US brought political arguments against Security Council action alongside its claim that the ICJ had acted *ultra vires*, see *infra* Chapter 3B XVIII 6 b (1). If the Council is uncertain as to the legal effects of a judgment, it might consider requesting an advisory opinion. It has also been suggested that the Council might want to search advice on legal questions from a committee of jurists (see *Schachter*, 54 AJIL (1960), at 21; *Vulcan*, 18 RGDIP (1947), at 197; on the corresponding provision of the League of Nations Covenant, *Scelle*, 55 RdC (1936), at 160).

[153] The Court's function, on the other hand, is "to decide disputes in accordance with international law," Article 38(1) of the Statute.

[154] See Rosenne, *Law and Practice I*, at 204–5; and *Tanzi*, 6 EJIL (1995), at 549, 572.

[155] See *Mosler/Oellers-Frahm* in Simma, Charter, Article 94, at n. 12. In municipal enforcement procedures, there are mechanisms to protect basic interests of the debtor such as social factors with the aim of preventing certain forms of execution while leaving the *res judicata* intact. The ICJ Statute does not contain such provisions (it is not a matter for revision as it does not aim at changes to the *res judicata*), so the Council should fill this gap.

[156] See *Magid* in Peck/Lee, Increasing the effectiveness, at 329.

[157] See *Tanzi*, 6 EJIL (1995), at 543. This is no conflict with Articles 59–61 of the Statute as there would be no interference with the *res judicata*: it is a situation entirely different from the one where the Council would take a decision aimed at invalidating a judgment, because in the latter case, a conflict between Article 94(1) and Article 25 of the Charter would arise. Thus, the Security Council's rejection of the draft resolution calling for compliance with the judgment in Military and Paramilitary Activities in and against Nicaragua was a lawful decision.

[158] *Tanzi*, 6 EJIL (1995), at 547–50. At 549–50 and 572, suggests a GA resolution "codifying" a rule of self-restraint for the UN political organs *vis-à-vis* decisions of the Court, which would

Could the Council impose a moratorium on the legal effects of the judgment by suspending the operation of Article 94(2) of the Rules of Court?[159] Under Article 94(2) of the Charter, this would not seem possible, as a moratorium would run contrary to the requirement "to give effect to the judgment" since it would, in fact, deprive the judgment of its legal effects, even if just for a limited time.[160] Such a measure seems possible under Chapter VII, however;[161] it would leave the *res judicata* intact and would not violate Article 60 of the ICJ Statute because the validity of the ICJ verdict as such would not be questioned, but only some of its legal effects would be suspended for a limited time.[162]

The procedure before the Security Council Council proceedings under Article 94(2) take place at the initiative of the judgment creditor only. Irrespective of such an initiative, action under Chapter VI and VII remains possible.[163] Regardless of the legal basis for Council discussions and the way they were initiated, where the recalcitrant state is not a member of the Security Council, it shall be invited to participate in the pertinent discussions without a right to vote.[164] It might happen that a state lodges a complaint of non-compliance as a political maneuver without a genuine desire for Council action and therefore does not request a meeting on the matter. In such situations, the Council will likely be reluctant to get involved.[165]

The requirement of the initiative of the judgment creditor should not be seen as a flaw of Article 94(2).[166] To the contrary, this seems quite sensible

primarily have symbolic significance and remind Member States of a rule of conduct that they have spontaneously applied to preserve "the delicate balance between law and politics which is essential for the functioning of the United Nations system."

[159] For its text see *supra* n. 142.   [160] But see Tuncel, *L'exécution des décisions*, at 91.

[161] Or Chapter VI (only for recommendations).

[162] See Rosenne, *Law and Practice I*, at 254; *Schachter*, 54 AJIL (1960), at 22; *Magid* in Peck/Lee, Increasing the effectiveness, at 329. Such action would affect the rights of the judgment creditor, but the powers of the Security Council under Chapter VII are broad enough as to allow for an interference with states' individual rights in the overwhelming general interest of international peace and security.

[163] Under Chapters VI and VII, the Security Council can act *proprio motu*, and the dispute or situation can be brought to its attention by states or the General Assembly: Articles 11(3), 34, 35. Non-UN members can address the Council under the conditions of Article 35(2).

[164] See Article 32 of the Charter (including a provision on the conditions for the participation of non-members), for details, see Dolzer in Simma, Charter, Article 32, at nn. 1–10). This article presupposes that the disagreement over the non-compliance has reached the threshold of a "dispute." Otherwise, Article 31 would provide another basis for participation of UN members, see Tuncel, *L'exécution des décisions*, at 69. The Council's Rules of Procedure contain provisions on the participation of non-members, see *Dolzer* in Simma, Charter, Article 31, at nn. 6–10.

[165] See, for example, Portugal's complaint in Right of Passage over Indian territory and Honduras's complaint in Land, Island and Maritime Frontier Dispute (El Salvador/Honduras), *infra* Chapter 3 B VI 4 and IXX 4.

[166] Article 13(4) of the League of Nations Covenant did not require such an initiative, see further *supra* B I.

since, in general, it is the free decision of the holder of a right—in this case, the right confirmed by an international court—whether or not to require the debtor to comply with its obligation. A state might have a variety of reasons not to make use of the right.[167] A legal victory might be sufficient satisfaction in itself. The state might want to use the outcome of the judgment as a bargaining chip in negotiations about other problems and wish to give up its entitlement confirmed by the judgment in exchange for concessions from the other side. The subject matter of the dispute could just be one aspect of a broader conflict and the Court's solution might require adaptations in order to fit into the overarching settlement. Article 94(2) is in conformity with litigation theory, according to which it is up to the judgment creditor to determine how much compliance is required.[168] By expanding the circle of actors that could take action under Article 94(2), one would put the creditor state at a disadvantage by taking away its options regarding enforcement of its rights.

There might be some exceptional cases where non-compliance affects not only the creditor, but the entire international community, and where it is not open to the judgment creditor to renounce the right adjudicated. For situations involving a threat to international peace and security, those interests will be met by Chapter VI or Chapter VII of the Charter, where Council action remains possible regardless of an initiative from the creditor.[169]

The voting procedure applicable to Article 94(2) is governed by the rules in Article 27(2) and (3) of the Charter, where procedural matters (paragraph 2) are distinguished from other matters (paragraph 3) for which under certain conditions the obligatory abstention rule applies and the veto of a permanent member can prevent a decision.[170] The rationale of Article 27(3) is to require unanimity between the permanent members for Council action in politically

---

[167] *Vulcan*, 18 RGDIP (1947), at 192–3.

[168] Rosenne, *Law and Practice I*, at 252; Tuncel, *L'exécution des décisions*, at 85. Usually, municipal enforcement proceedings will not be launched without the initiative of the creditor.

[169] Under Article 34, the Security Council may investigate any dispute, or any situation that might lead to international friction or give rise to a dispute, in order to determine whether the continuance of the dispute or situation is likely to endanger the maintenance of international peace and security; under Articles 35(1) and (2), any UN Member State can bring to the attention of the Security Council or the General Assembly any such dispute or situation. As stated above, *supra* n. 101, with the rather extensive interpretation of the term international peace and security in the recent practice of the Council, the Council will not be likely to consider the absence of a request from the creditor as the decisive obstacle if it is truly committed to act.

[170] Article 27(2) and (3) read: "(2) Decisions of the Security Council on procedural matters shall be made by an affirmative vote of nine members. (3) Decisions of the Security Council on all other matters shall be made by an affirmative vote of nine members including the concurring votes of the permanent members; provided that, in decisions under Chapter VI, and under paragraph 3 of Article 52, a party to a dispute shall abstain from voting." When talking about voting procedures, it is important to note that a significant number of Security Council decisions are taken by consensus, i.e. without a formal vote: see the table by *Tavernier* in Cot/Pellet, Charte, Article 27, at 510; and Bailey/Daws, *The Procedure of the UN Security Council*, at 259–63. On the permissibility of this practice, see *Simma/Brunner/Kaul* in Simma, Charter, Article 27, at nn. 111, 116.

sensitive issues, in particular, to prevent coercive action against such a member by excluding the operation of the principle of *nemo iudex in re sua*, enabling parties to a dispute to vote unless it falls within the field of decisions under Chapter VI and Article 52(3).[171] The Charter does not define procedural and substantive questions; nevertheless, it is generally understood that recommendations or measures under Chapter VI or VII of the Charter are substantive matters since, rather than having implications for the internal practice of the Council or its relationship to other organs, they involve numerous political considerations and could culminate in enforcement measures.[172]

For similar considerations, a decision on action under Article 94(2) should be classified as a substantive rather than a procedural matter. In its nature and content, action under Article 94(2) is comparable to measures under Chapter VI or VII. The Security Council examines the situation, exercises its discretion, and possibly adopts enforcement action against a state; this can hardly be considered a matter concerning the internal organization of the UN organs only.[173] Consequently, voting is governed by Article 27(3) and the veto threat remains. In the decision on a draft resolution on the judgment

---

[171] See *Simma/Brunner/Kaul* in Simma, Charter, Article 27, at nn. 1–10. Article 27 has its origin in the Yalta Formula, a compromise on the decision on whether to require unanimity or majority voting for Council action. On the history of the Article, see Goodrich/Hambro/Simons, *Charter of the United Nations*, 216–21.

[172] See *Simma/Brunner/Kaul* in Simma, Charter, Article 27, at nn. 13–14, and at nn. 16–20 for details on the distinction between procedural and other matters, including the explanation of the "chain of events theory," according to which decisions requiring unanimity of permanent members—substantive matters—are those that relate to decisions or actions that may have major political consequences and initiate a chain of events that might require the Security Council to take enforcement action. This theory has its roots in the San Francisco Declaration of 8 June 1945, a joint declaration on voting procedure in the Security Council of the sponsoring governments of the San Francisco UN founding conference, for the text, see ibid., at n. 154.

[173] This is the predominant view of legal commentators; see *Simma/Brunner/Kaul* in Simma, Charter, Article 27, at n. 16; Kelsen, *The Law of the United Nations*, at 541, at 543–4; *Magid* in Peck/Lee, Increasing the effectiveness, at 330–1; *Schachter*, 54 AJIL (1960), at 23; Tuncel, *L'exécution des décisions*, at 70; *Vulcan*, 18 RGDIP (1947), at 201; but see *Mosler/Oellers-Frahm* in Simma, Charter, Article 94, at n. 13. Even in the unlikely event that in any future proceedings a member of the Security Council would claim that Article 27(2) is applicable instead of Article 27(3), no decision could be taken against the will of a permanent member. If the procedural character of an action is in controversy, a decision would be taken on this preliminary question pursuant to Article 27(3), since Article 27(3) is the regular procedure ("all other matters") and Article 27(2) the exception the applicability of which would have to be determined. See UN Office of Legal Affairs, Memorandum to the Secretary-General, 18 July 1986, United Nations Juridical Yearbook 1986, ST/LEG/SER.C/24, 283–5, at 284. Although attempts have been made to restrict this so-called double veto, recourse to this procedure in the context of the enforcement of an ICJ judgment could not be considered an abuse, for severe doubts would exist as to the applicability of Article 27(2). According to an interpretation of the Charter supported by the broad majority of scholars and confirmed by UN practice, the matter is not procedural; if a permanent member has the same view, this is no sign of bad faith. Thanks to informal agreement, the double veto procedure has not been used since 1959, see *Simma/Brunner/Kaul* in Simma, Charter, Article 27, at n. 44.

in the Nicaragua case, the US veto was considered to have prevented the resolution from being taken, a conclusion that presupposes its character as a decision under Article 27(3).[174]

The obligatory abstention rule under Article 27(3) will prevent the creditor of an ICJ decision from participating in the vote only if the Council were to proceed under Chapter VI or Article 52(3). The Charter lacks a provision incorporating the principle *nemo iudex in causa sua* in general terms; Article 27(3) is a compromise formula covering just two particular instances, although it might also be appropriate for an affected state to abstain in other cases. Obligatory abstention is neither required for decisions under Chapter VII[175] nor under Article 94(2).[176] Hence, a judgment debtor member of the Security Council is not barred from participating in a vote on a decision under Article 94(2);[177] if it is a permanent member, it might even prevent any kind of

---

[174] See *infra* Chapter 3 B XVIII 6 b (1). The Interim Committee of the General Assembly was unable to make a recommendation on whether matters under Article 94(2) were procedural or not, see 3 GAOR Supp.10 (A/578) 3, 14 (1948); the General Assembly did not take a definite stand on this issue either in Resolution 267 (III) of 14 April 1949 in which it defined instances where the veto should not apply, see Rosenne, *Law and Practice I*, at 257; Schachter, 54 AJIL (1960), at 23. The representative of Nicaragua argued in the General Assembly on 6 November 1986 that its draft resolution that had been vetoed by the US in the Security Council had been a procedural matter according to the terms of GA Resolution 267 (III) since it was a decision "to remind members of their obligations under the Charter." Statement by the Minister for Foreign Affairs of Nicaragua, Mr D'Escoto Brochmann, in the General Assembly on 6 November 1986 (A/41/PV.53, at 62 ff.) This argument is unconvincing for several reasons. First, General Assembly Resolution 267(III) was a recommendation (see Article 10 of the Charter) incapable of amending Article 27 of the Charter. Second, what Nicaragua wanted was not a decision abstractly reminding members of their obligations under the Charter, but instead one urging compliance with a specific judgment. See *Tanzi*, 6 EJIL (1995), at 551–2.

[175] The rationale of Article 27(3) is precisely a requirement of unanimity among the permanent members, or at least acquiescence or abstention, for cases of enforcement under Chapter VII, see *supra* n. 171.

[176] Jenks, *Prospects of international adjudication*, at 693. The language of Article 94(2) ("enforcement") is reminiscent of Chapter VII rather than Chapter VI: *Simma/Brunner/Kaul* in Simma, Charter, Article 27, at n. 78. Authors who deny the character of Article 94(2) as autonomous competence would have to make the decision on the rule of obligatory abstention dependent on the existence of a "dispute" under Chapter VI: see *Kerley* in Gross, The future of the International Court of Justice, at 281–2; Jiménez de Aréchaga, *Derecho constitucional de las Naciones Unidas*, at 557–8. However, even under this hypothesis, unless the Council determines there is a "dispute" and proceeds accordingly, the rule of obligatory abstention is irrelevant. The UN Office of Legal Affairs expressed doubts on whether the situation envisaged in Article 94(2) could qualify as a "dispute", Memorandum of 18 July 1986, *supra* at 284–5. Authors who consider the decision under Article 94(2) a procedural one under Article 27(2) would have to conclude that there is no requirement of obligatory abstention. *Tanzi*, 6 EJIL (1995), suggests at 554–7 that the applicability of the obligatory abstention rule was to be made dependent on whether the concrete dispute falls in the scope of Chapter VII or VI; in the latter case, he postulates an application of Article 27(3) *in fine* by way of analogy. However, such an analogy would be incompatible with the character of Article 27(3) as an exception.

[177] This is the predominant view among legal commentators and in many cases is not even discussed as a problem, *Kapoor* in Dhokalia, International Court in transition, at 307; Kelsen, *The Law of the United Nations*, at 541; *Pillepich* in Cot/Pellet, Charte, Article 94, at 1282 n. 17; Ross, *Constitution of the United Nations*, at 102; Schachter, 54 AJIL (1960), at 23; Tuncel,

Council action through the exercise of its veto right.[178] One may deplore that this makes some litigants "more equal" than others in the post-adjudicative phase[179]—but it is hardly any news that the permanent members of the Security Council have a privileged position within the United Nations. Efficient Security Council action against one of its permanent members or a recalcitrant state with strong political ties to a permanent member is usually unlikely if not impossible. Yet, the conclusion that the Charter provisions concerning the enforcement of Court decisions "are unlikely to be effective in more than a limited number of relatively unimportant cases"[180] might now be too pessimistic in view of the new climate since the end of the Cold War. While proceedings in the Security Council still are not always free of tensions, there is nowadays no general paralysis as in former decades, and it does not seem impossible that Council members might approach enforcement of ICJ judgments from a less politicized perspective and reach common ground at least in cases where the permanent members are not directly involved.[181] Even in cases against a permanent member like the Nicaragua case, it cannot be entirely ruled out that a permanent member might abstain for reasons of propriety and that some form of "mild" resolution expressing regret about the lack of compliance might be adopted; however, it is hard to ever imagine military enforcement, economic sanctions, or similar actions against a permanent member.[182]

L'exécution des décisions, 71; *Vulcan*, 18 RGDIP (1947), at 201. Where parties that are not members of the Council are invited to participate in the discussions, they have no voting rights: see Article 32 of the Charter and Kelsen, *The Law of the United Nations*, at 541.

[178] This happened in the Nicaragua case, where the US veto met with no protests, see *infra* n. 174. However, the subject-matter involved the use of force, and it could be argued that the controversy fell under Chapter VII and not Chapter VI: *Tanzi*, 6 EJIL (1995), at 560. It is not impossible that in cases not involving the use of force, the Council might proceed differently: *idem*, at 561. But see *Magid* in Peck/Lee, Increasing the effectiveness, at 330–1 who claims that the Council practice in the Nicaragua case now has answered the questions relating to Article 27. The memorandum of the UN Office of Legal Affairs (see *supra* n. 173), providing information on the applicability of Article 27(3) in preparation of the Council proceedings on the first initiative of a draft resolution urging compliance with the Nicaragua judgment, delivered a variety of arguments effectively supporting the right of the US to participate in the vote.

[179] See *Vulcan*, 18 RGDIP (1947), at 201.

[180] Jenks, *Prospects of international adjudication*, at 693, similarly, *Kapoor* in Dhokalia, International Court in transition, at 306.

[181] See for an optimistic assessment *O'Connell*, 30 Va. JIL (1990), at 912: "Long dismissed as irrelevant, recent events have shown that the Security Council may yet prove to be an effective enforcer of judgments." See also *Magid* in Peck/Lee, Increasing the effectiveness, at 331.

[182] But see Ross, *Constitution of the United Nations*, at 102: "[N]o enforcement of a judgment in the case of a great power will ever come into question." Yet permanent members have not always prevented decisions affecting them, even if the existence of an obligation to abstain was unclear or entirely absent. For example, when the Council adopted Resolution 437 (1978) of 10 October 1978 on the situation in Southern Rhodesia, the US delegate voluntarily abstained from the decision "in the spirit of Article 27(3)"; in the resolution, the Council criticized that the US had permitted the entry of some members of the illegal Southern Rhodesian regime to its territory and stated that thereby the US had acted contrary to relevant Security Council resolutions and Article 25 of the Charter. As the issue concerned a "situation" rather than a "dispute," the US had not been required to abstain, see Blum, *Eroding the United Nations Charter*, at 207.

Obligatory abstention in the field of enforcement of ICJ decisions might become relevant only if the Council proceeds under Chapter VI alone—and even there, the obligatory abstention rule will in most cases be an insufficient tool to prevent an affected member from participating in the vote. First, it is often unclear whether the Council acts under Chapter VI or Chapter VI; if this was raised as a preliminary question, the Council will take a decision for which the obligation to abstain will not apply.[183] Second, Article 27(3) requires abstention only for parties to a "dispute," not for those affected by a "situation."[184] It is the Council's discretion whether to deal with a matter as "dispute" or "situation"; its general tendency seems to show a preference for a qualification as "situation,"[185] and absent a clear determination to approach the matter as a "dispute," there would be no obligation to abstain.[186] Third, even the current validity of the obligatory abstention rule under Article 27(3) is debatable; there are some indications that it might have been modified by subsequent practice and is thus no longer applicable, at least for permanent members.[187] Irrespective of whether one regards the

---

[183] *Simma/Brunner/Kaul* in Simma, Charter, Article 27, n. 89; Kelsen, *The Law of the United Nations*, at 261; Memorandum of the UN Office of Legal Affairs to the Secretary General of 18 July 1986, ST/LEG/SER.C/24, UN Juridical Yearbook 1986, 283–5, at 284. It would be a non-procedural vote, as the applicability of Chapter VII would open the way for enforcement measures, and it would involve the determination under Article 39 whether world peace is endangered, hence there is no obligation to abstain, and a permanent member could cast its veto.

[184] Only in disputes, the Security Council has a quasi-judicial settlement function under Article 37, where the rationale of the principle of *nemo iudex in causa sua* applies. "Dispute" and "situation" are terms that are not mutually exclusive: situation is the broader term that encompasses "dispute". A "situation" relates to facts that might lead to international friction; a "dispute" to the communication between the actors (claims and counter-claims are raised). They are functional terms which open the way for crisis management or quasi-judicial dispute settlement. It is therefore the Security Council that determines whether there the conditions to deal with a "dispute" are actually fulfilled; it is not bound by the parties' opinion on the existence of a dispute: Kelsen, *The Law of the United Nations*, at 263; *Simma/Brunner/Kaul* in Simma, Charter, Article 27, at nn. 86–7.

[185] See *Tavernier*, 22 AFDI (1976), at 287, who criticizes that in some of the cases, there was "clearly a dispute".

[186] *Simma/Brunner/Kaul* in Simma, Charter, Article 27, at n. 90, arguing that the duty to abstain arises only if the Council "expressly decides" to deal with the matter as a dispute. But see Conforti, *Le nazioni unite*, at 79–80, who suggests that the immediate addressees of a draft resolution are the states obliged to abstain; however, this would be too broad a criterion because there may be addressees in case of situations as well.

[187] See *O'Connell*, 30 Va. JIL (1990), at 908–9: "[T]oday it appears that no permanent member of the Council may be expected to recuse itself." See also *Tavernier*, 22 AFDI (1976), at 283–9. Evidence of a treaty modification is dubious. In the instances where directly affected members have taken part in the vote, it will generally be difficult to prove that all requirements for an abstention had been present, in particular, whether it had been a "dispute" under Chapter VI dealt with as such by the Council. Moreover, in critical cases, the silence on the participation of an affected member might have stemmed from the fact that that participation was harmless as the respective decision had a solid majority anyway and it would have been adopted also without that state's participation, which makes the probative value of silence appear very limited. The UN continues to keep track of the cases of obligatory abstention under Article 27(3) in the publication Repertoire of the Practice of the Security Council.

evidence to this extent as sufficient, it may ultimately be unlikely that the Council would treat the vote of a permanent member as void, even though theoretically the respective member had been obliged to abstain.[188]

As to the legal consequences of the participation in a vote of a state obliged to abstain pursuant to Article 27(3), in principle, its vote must not be counted;[189] its participation will only be harmful for the decision if it had otherwise not been taken.[190] If a resolution has failed due to the vote of a permanent member actually obliged to abstain under Article 27(3), one could hardly ignore this fact and take the resolution as if it had been adopted. If a resolution is vetoed, for example, the President will state that the resolution was not adopted. One might argue that the decision not to adopt the resolution was taken illegally, but it would yet be another step to deduce the existence of a valid affirmative decision. Finally, mention should be made of the case of voluntary abstention, in which a state abstains without a respective obligation. Voluntary abstention has been broadly accepted in UN practice and does not prevent a decision from being taken, even if the abstaining state is a permanent member, in spite of the text of Article 27(3) that requires the concurring votes of all permanent members.[191]

Desirability of an automatic procedure?   Some observers have pointed at possibilities of enhancing the efficiency of the Security Council in the enforcement of ICJ judgments through creating more automatism in the enforcement procedure. These ideas are to be seen in the broader context of Security Council reform (in particular, relating to the role of the veto) and are likely to meet resistance from the current roster of permanent members, whose affirmative vote would be required for the corresponding amendments to the Charter.[192]

---

[188] In future cases, permanent members may cast a veto in violation of Article 27(3) and the Security Council will nevertheless not adopt a decision as a result, see *Tanzi*, 6 EJIL (1995), at 558.

[189] *Simma/Brunner/Kaul* in Simma, Charter, Article 27, at n. 90; Kelsen, *The Law of the United Nations*, at 263–4.

[190] *Simma/Brunner/Kaul* in Simma, Charter, Article 27, at n. 91. In such cases, there is only a formal defect which can easily be cured and cannot be a reason to challenge the validity of the decision in its entirety. In the practice of the Security Council, the issue has only led to discussions when another state has explicitly invoked Article 27(3). Most likely, the legality of a vote under Article 27(3) will only be examined if there is a claim against the participation of a certain member prior to the taking of the vote; otherwise, the controversial vote will be counted. On the other hand, in most cases where states abstained pursuant to Article 27(3), this happened without a formal request. See Blum, *Eroding the United Nations Charter*, at 204–5.

[191] UN practice to this extent has been uniform since the abstention of the Soviet Union over the Spanish question of 29 April 1946; the ICJ has confirmed the acceptance of the practice of voluntary abstention in the Namibia Advisory Opinion, Legal Consequences for States of the Continued Presence of South Africa in Namibia (South West Africa) notwithstanding Security Council Resolution 276 (1970), Advisory Opinion of 21 June 1971, at 22, para. 22. See *Simma/Brunner/Kaul* in Simma, Charter, Article 27, at nn. 46–74 on the requirement of the "concurring votes."

[192] Article 108 of the Charter.

One suggestion aims at the abolition of the veto and the application of the obligatory abstention rule to decisions under Article 94(2); another one at the creation of a subsidiary body (the "United Nations Judgment Enforcement Council") with a different composition and without operation of the veto. It seems very unlikely that the permanent members might give their consent to either suggestion; there would seem to be no reason for the Council—and even less so, of course, for its permanent members—to cede its powers under Article 94(2) to such a subsidiary body.[193] Whether such utopian proposals are desirable depends on one's general attitude towards the veto for the permanent members—whether it is seen as an arbitrary barrier to efficient action, as an inevitable recognition of existing power distributions, or as a sensible system of checks and balances. In any case, the veto could not be abolished for Article 94(2) alone and in that context trump the provisions of Chapter VII, as Article 94(2) certainly has to be interpreted in harmony with the primary responsibility of the Council for international peace and security. Only a comprehensive reform of the Security Council could restrain the veto's influence.

The Council's chief function in maintaining peace and security advocates against the concept of reducing its discretion under Article 94(2), as do the very features of the organic structure of the decentralized international community. Unlike general international law, domestic law relating to execution of judicial decisions provides for fast and efficient means to verify whether there are legitimate reasons for non-compliance, or whether enforcement is to be suspended for the moment for superior reasons such as social concerns. The Security Council's discretion enables it to pay due regard to such concerns. The international community also lacks a central legislative authority; on the domestic level, this body can take steps to mitigate undesirable consequences of a judgment and change the law rapidly and effectively if it is found to contradict the requirements of justice.[194]

A more modest proposal aims at the establishment of an automatic monitoring procedure by the Council. This might have a certain positive effect in so far as it would make the implementation process more transparent, and it would enable the Security Council to act rapidly and well informed if later seized by the judgment creditor.[195] Still, those advocating for such a procedure should not forget that the procedure under Article 94(2) is created as a

---

[193] Both suggestions were made by *Ajibola*, in Bulterman/Kuijer, Compliance with judgments, at 29. See also *Kapoor* in Dhokalia, International Court in transition, at 306 in favor of a change of the voting procedure.

[194] See Rosenne, *Law and Practice I*, at 277. See also *supra* n. 155.

[195] *Kerley* in Gross, The future of the International Court of Justice, at 283, suggests that the President of the Council should ask the parties how they intend to implement the judgment. In cases of non-response or an open refusal to comply, the President would appoint a committee consisting of Security Council members to consult with the parties how compliance can be brought about, and the committee would report its results to the Security Council, so that it is fully informed in case the aggrieved party brings the issue before the Council under Article 94(2).

right of the aggrieved state demanding compliance. It does not provide for Council action *proprio motu*, but at the initiative of the aggrieved party. Therefore any automatism—be it only for a monitoring process—is to be rejected if it ignores the attitudes of the parties towards third-party involvement.[196] If neither party wishes such involvement in the post-adjudicative phase, there is not only no reason for the Security Council (or any auxiliary body possibly to be created) to intervene, but such intervention might even be counterproductive. Especially in cases where the Court's judgment has merely clarified some aspect of a bigger controversy and where its implementation has to be embedded in a larger context, outward pressure for immediate compliance with the judgment will not be constructive if undesired by both sides. A further issue is that automatism in enforcement might discourage states from submitting cases to the ICJ, as they might wish to retain control over the post-adjudicative process.

Finally, one must bear in mind that enforcement action by the Security Council might not always produce the effective implementation of the judgment either; indirect enforcement measures, even the use of force, will not be efficient under all circumstances, and means of direct enforcement will often be unavailable.

Enforcement of provisional measures   In the Council's practice, Article 94(2) was invoked for the purpose of enforcing ICJ provisional measures in the context of Chapters VI and VII proceedings, but the Council has never explicitly based action on this provision. In its complaint of non-compliance with provisional measures in the Anglo-Iranian Oil Company Case, the UK requested the respective Council meeting under Articles 34 and 35, and it was only in the meeting itself that it invoked Article 94(2). The Council did not express an opinion on the applicability of Article 94(2)[197] and adjourned the discussions so as to await a clarification on the Court's jurisdiction in the main proceedings.[198] In the Genocide case, Bosnia and Herzegovina requested a Council meeting under Article 94(2),[199] but in the same letter

---

[196] *Kerley* ibid., at 283 concedes that his proposal is not fully compatible with Article 94(2).

[197] While the Iranian representatives pointed to invalidity of the measures rather than to a lack of enforcement mechanisms, the Ecuadorian delegation stated that Article 94(2) did not apply. The interpretation of Article 94(2) in general did not appear to have played a significant role. For details, see *infra* Chapter 3 C I 4.

[198] The doubts on jurisdiction were apparently a main reason, *infra* Chapter 3 C I; and *Schachter*, 54 AJIL (1960), at 23–4.

[199] But see *Guillaume* in Jasentuliyana, Perspectives on international law, at 283, who reports that it has never been claimed before the Security Council that the examination of an alleged failure to comply with provisional measures was within the scope of Article 94(2). From the letter of the Bosnian representative, it can be inferred that they considered Article 94(2) as applicable; nevertheless the Genocide case is a special case because it dealt with issues of international peace and security that were already pending before the Council independently of the existence of the interim measures anyway. See also *Tanzi*, 6 EJIL (1995), at 566.

asked for "action under Chapter VII." There were no doubts as to the applicability of Chapter VII situation and the provisional measures were not, in fact, the central matter—another Bosnian communication of the same day did not mention the provisional measures. Article 94(2) was not discussed in the Security Council meeting, and the resolution subsequently adopted addressed the general situation rather than affording a central place to the provisional measures. The resolution did not explicitly indicate its legal basis; its terms would most likely have been largely identical if there had not been any ICJ order.[200] The precedential value of those two instances for the interpretation of Article 94(2) is therefore limited. Where states have lodged complaints on the breach of provisional measures to the Security Council in other cases, they did so under headings other than Article 94(2).[201]

The argument has been made that the term "judgment" in Article 94(2) could be interpreted in a material sense rather than a formal one so as to apply to provisional measures as well, with reference to the binding force of provisional measures and the obligation of the Court under Article 41(2) of its Statute to give the Council notice of an order indicating interim measures.[202] However, the bindingness of a decision does not necessarily imply the applicability of a certain enforcement mechanism—the questions of the obligation of compliance and of enforceability have to be kept separate.[203] Article 41(2) of the ICJ Statute is a provision of cooperation; the information on the provisional measures can be helpful for the Council properly to carry out its function under Chapters VI and VII.[204] While one might reasonably

---

[200] See *infra* Chapter 3 C VII 3 for details.

[201] See the United Kingdom in the Fisheries Jurisdiction Case, *infra* Chapter 3 C II 2 (where no debate followed as a meeting on this issue had not been requested), the United States in United States Diplomatic and Consular Staff in Tehran, *infra* Chapter 3 C IV 2 (where the respective discussions did not accord a central place to the order), Nicaragua in Military and Paramilitary Activities in and against Nicaragua, *infra* Chapter 3 C VI 3 (with the debate centering on the issues of aggression and intervention rather than on the ICJ Order), Cameroon in Land and Maritime Boundary between Cameroon and Nigeria, *infra* Chapter 3 C VIII 4 (with no Council debate and action being requested). While the applicants' complaints in those cases do not lend authority for an applicability of Article 94(2) of the Charter, they confirm the understanding that provisional measures are binding.

[202] See *Mosler/Oellers-Frahm* in Simma, Charter, Article 94, at nn. 15–16; *Schachter*, 54 AJIL (1960), at 23–4, argues that the Council might decide to take action under Article 94(2), particularly if the preservation of the *res* was considered essential for the judicial proceedings. See also Jenks, *Prospects of international adjudication*, at 693: "There would appear to be nothing in the Charter to debar the Security Council from deciding on measures to enforce an interlocutory order, particularly if the preservation of the *res* is essential to permit of justice being done in the subsequent proceedings." The question then remains *on which basis* Council action would be permissible.

[203] Sep. Op. Weeramantry to Application of the Genocide Convention, Order of 13 November 1993 at 374–5.

[204] See the argument of the Iranian representative in the discussions in the AIOC case, 6 SCOR S/PV.560, 12 quoted by Rosenne, *Law and Practice I*, at 263–4 as "plausible."

argue that it would be desirable for Article 94(2) to apply for provisional measures, one cannot overcome its clear wording referring only to "judgments."[205] Although the different wording in paragraphs 1 and 2 can be taken as an indication that "decision" is broad enough to comprise provisional measures,[206] it would stretch rules of interpretation too far to classify such measures as "judgments" although they are issued as orders. It would contradict the term's ordinary meaning to qualify them as "judgments in a material sense" and this interpretation would find no basis in the Charter and the Statute either, where "judgment" is not used as a term comprising interlocutory orders. Consequently, Article 94(2) only relates to judgments proper.[207] Yet, this does not rule out action by the Council for the enforcement of provisional measures in the exercise of other competences:[208] the Council can take action under Chapters VI and VII if the conditions of the respective provisions are fulfilled.[209]

2. Enforcement by other UN organs

Even though Council action to enforce an ICJ decision does not seem quite as unlikely at present as in former times, there is no denying the fact that it is a political organ and that national sensibilities—in particular, those of the permanent members—will play a role in the decision of whether enforcement action will be taken. The existence of the veto right restrains the Council's ability to take efficient action, and the rule of obligatory abstention is no sufficient counterweight since it has only a limited field of application and there are ways to circumvent it. Moreover, adherence to the rule has not been meticulous and there are no efficient sanctions in case of a breach. Consequently, hopes for Council action might not materialize in particular cases, and thus it is useful to investigate how other principal organs of the UN—the

---

[205] *Magid* in Peck/Lee, Increasing the effectiveness, at 330; Tuncel, *L'exécution des décisions*, at 108, Sep. Op. Ajibola, Application of the Genocide Convention, Order of 13 November 1993, at 401–3.

[206] See Tuncel, *L'exécution des décisions*, 51. But see *Pillepich* in Cot/Pellet, Charte, Article 94, n. 15. The different language in paras. 1 and 2 hints at a different meaning: see *Mani*, 10 Indian JIL (1970), at 368.

[207] *Ajibola*, in Bulterman/Kuijer, Compliance with judgments, at 14; *Magid* in Peck/Lee, Increasing the effectiveness, at 330; *Pillepich* in Cot/Pellet, Charte, Article 94, at n. 16; Rosenne, *Law and Practice I*, at 216; Tuncel, *L'exécution des décisions*, at 108.

[208] No *a contrario* argument can be made from Article 94(2) that provisional measures were meant to be entirely excluded from any kind of enforcement action, because such a limitation of the Council's general competences, in particular, of its primary responsibility for the maintenance of international peace and security, cannot be presumed. See Rosenne, *Law and Practice I*, at 264.

[209] *Tanzi*, 6 EJIL (1995), at 570; Tuncel, *L'exécution des décisions*, at 109. But see *Mani*, 10 Indian JIL (1970), at 368–72.

General Assembly, the Economic and Social Council, and the Secretariat—
may play helpful roles in enhancing compliance.[210]

The General Assembly   The General Assembly is perhaps the international
community's most prominent forum for political discussion and is occasionally referred to as the "open conscience of humanity"[211]—a term reflecting the
hopes and aspirations vested in that forum, which have not always been
realized to their full extent. Debates in the Assembly are usually anything
but immune from politics, even in comparison with the Council, particularly
after the rapid increase in membership in the 1960s and 1970s, when the
Assembly's increasing diversity gave rise to new rivalries besides those in the
Council.[212] Yet the non-existence of a veto right substantially reduces the
influence of single countries in comparison to the Security Council, which
gives some basis to assume that there will be cases in which the Assembly will
show more awareness than the Council of the need to protect the ICJ's
authority against special interests of individual countries. The only case to
date where the Assembly took a role in the post-adjudicative phase was the
Nicaragua case,[213] where its call for compliance might have been more conducive to the prestige of the Court and more reflective of the opinion of the
international community than the omission of action by the Security Council
due to the veto of one country—the state directly involved in the litigation.

The Assembly's efforts to give effect to the Court's advisory opinions[214]
have led to hopes that it may take up a more constructive role in contentious
proceedings[215] than the Council.[216] However, this assumption can only be

---

[210] The Trusteeship Council is a principal UN organ pursuant to Article 7(1) of the Charter,
but it actually has the function of assisting the General Assembly and the Security Council and
operates under their authority; the Charter does not contain any explicit power for the Trusteeship Council to make recommendations. It suspended operation in 1994 with the independence
of the last UN trust territory in 1994: *Rauschning* in Simma, Charter, Article 86, at nn. 1, 5.
Unless new functions and powers are assigned to it, there is nowadays no basis for any role of this
organ in compliance with ICJ decisions.
[211] Yearbook of the United Nations 1946–7, at 51, see also Kelsen, *The Law of the United
Nations*, at 199–200; and *Heilbronner/Klein* in Simma, Charter, Article 10, at n. 2.
[212] For a description of the different alliances in the General Assembly over time, see
Tomuschat in Wolfrum, United Nations Law, at 556–7.
[213] See *infra* Chapter 3 B XVIII 6 b (2).
[214] Although strictly speaking, there is no enforcement for advisory opinions, the General
Assembly has made efforts to ensure that the obligations restated by the Court therein were
complied with. For example, after the Advisory Opinion on the International Status of South
West Africa, the General Assembly accepted the Court's findings, urged the Government of
South Africa to take the necessary measures to give effect to the advisory opinion, and established a committee of five in order to confer with the Union of South Africa on the procedural
measures for the implementation of the advisory opinion and to report to the General Assembly.
See Nantwi, *Enforcement of international judicial decisions*, at 159–60.
[215] Rosenne, *Law and Practice I*, at 260.
[216] Nanwti, *Enforcement of international judicial decisions*, at 160, highlights: "[T]he [...]
resolution of the General Assembly on the advisory opinion of the International Court of Justice

made with caution, bearing in mind the differences of contentious and advisory proceedings. In the cases where it did become involved, advisory proceedings had been instituted by the Assembly itself. The Assembly had therefore been interested in the matter from the outset, which makes its action after the opinions less surprising.[217] Its proactive behavior under these circumstances is comparable to that of the Council in the one instance where it had requested an advisory opinion.[218]

In contentious proceedings, on the other hand, the Assembly or Council normally will have no influence on the decision whether and under which circumstances a matter is brought before the Court, which might lead to more controversy concerning a role in the follow-up.

Yet, one might refer to the Assembly's practice relating to advisory opinions in order to appeal the Assembly to take a similarly positive role for

regarding the International Status of South-West Africa is an outstanding effort, and stands in marked contrast to the weak and inconclusive handling by the Security Council, under the provisions of Article 94(2), of the United Kingdom's complaint regarding Iran's refusal to comply with the interim measures indicated by the International Court of Justice in the Anglo-Iranian Oil Company Case." Similarly, Rosenne, *The International Court of Justice*, at 113. For several reasons, this comparison is not quite fair. There was huge consensus in the international community regarding South West Africa, whereas in the Anglo-Iranian Oil Company case, there were substantial doubts as to the Court's jurisdiction, and the question of bindingness of interim measures was still controversial. Moreover, in the former case the General Assembly had requested the advisory opinion and was therefore interested in the follow-up. The Security Council on the other hand had been seized in the Anglo-Iranian Oil Company case by the UK and had not acted *proprio motu*. For further details on the Anglo-Iranian Oil Company case, see *infra* Chapter 3 C I 4.

[217] The Assembly did not take up the role of a "guardian" of the implementation of advisory opinions requested by ECOSOC or specialized agencies. This is appropriate: if the GA authorizes other organs or specialized agencies to request advisory opinions under Article 96(2) of the Charter (for ECOSOC, by GA Resolution 89 (I) of 11 December 1946, for other bodies and agencies, see ICJ YB 1998–9, pp. 83–8), it should be those bodies' primary responsibility to monitor the follow-up. Generally, these cases have not caused problems, with the exception of the opinion on the difference relating to immunity from legal process of a Special Rapporteur of the Commission of Human Rights, which had been requested by ECOSOC in the case of the Malaysian national Dato' Param Cumaraswamy. Here, ECOSOC and the Secretary-General continue to deal with the matter, see Press Releases SG/SM/6974 ICJ/570 of 29 April 1999, ECOSOC/5880 of 16 December 1999, and ECOSOC/5883 of 4 February 2000, not the General Assembly (for details, see *infra* n. 239).

[218] In the only case where the Security Council requested an advisory opinion, concerning Legal Consequences for States of the Continued Presence of South Africa in Namibia (South West Africa) notwithstanding Security Council Resolution 276 (1970), it gave support to the Court's opinion, namely the Opinion of 21 June 1971 (ICJ Reports 1971, 16). On 20 October 1971, it adopted Resolution 301(1971), in which it noted the advisory opinion with appreciation, agreed with its conclusions in the operative clause, and called upon all states to conform to the statements set out in the advisory opinion. Here again, the decision of the Security Council requesting the advisory opinion—Res. 284 (1970) of 29 July 1970 (taken by 12 votes to 0, with Poland, the USSR, and the UK abstaining)—had been indicative of its willingness to deal with the matter and its interest in the Court's opinion: see the Preamble of Res. 284 (1970): "Considering that an advisory opinion from the International Court of Justice would be useful for the Security Council in its further consideration of the question of Namibia and in furtherance of the objectives of the Council in seeking."

decisions, i.e. to show the same respect for the Court and, in particular, not to question the authority of its findings.[219]

Articles 10 and 11(2) of the Charter, which allow the Assembly to discuss Charter issues and give recommendations, are the principal sources of the Assembly's authority to take a role in the enforcement of ICJ decisions.[220] Non-compliance with an ICJ decision is a matter within the scope of the Charter, as the duty to comply is a Charter obligation,[221] and in most cases where the Assembly will consider itself fit to deal with such questions, there will be a scenario at least potentially leading to international friction, where Chapters VI and VII would apply. The Assembly may discuss any matter even while it is being dealt with by the Council, but its power to make recommendations is qualified by the Council's primary (albeit not exclusive)[222] responsibility in matters of international peace and security.[223] In order to protect that primary responsibility, Article 12 imposes a temporary ban on the adoption of Assembly recommendations while the Security Council exercises its Charter functions "in respect of any dispute or

---

[219] For advisory opinions, the General Assembly has shown awareness of the need to uphold the authority of the International Court; it carefully avoided to question the Court's authority and did not undertake formal "reviews" of the findings: the general view was that advisory opinions should either be accepted or rejected in total without a discussion of the Court's findings: *Kerley* in Gross, The future of the International Court of Justice, at 278–9; and *Tanzi*, 6 EJIL (1995), at 548–9 with further references. For a suggestion of a General Assembly resolution codifying such self-restraint, see *Tanzi*, 6 EJIL (1995), at 549–50 and 572.

[220] Article 10: "The General Assembly may discuss any questions or any matters within the scope of the present Charter [. . .] and, except as provided in Article 12, may make recommendations to the Members of the United Nations or to the Security Council or both on any such questions or matters." Article 11(2): "The General Assembly may discuss any questions relating to the maintenance of international peace and security brought before it by any Member of the United Nations, or by the Security Council, or by a State which is not a Member of the United Nations in accordance with Article 35, paragraph 2, and, except as provided in Article 12, may make recommendations with regard to any such questions to the State or States concerned or to the Security Council or to both. [. . .]."

[221] See Nantwi, *Enforcement of international judicial decisions*, at 158–9.

[222] It is clear from Articles 10, 11(2), 14, and 35(1) that the maintenance of international peace and security is also a legitimate concern for the General Assembly. The ICJ confirmed the General Assembly's powers in this field in the Certain Expenses Advisory Opinion, see Certain Expenses of the United Nations (Article 17, para. 2 of the Charter), Advisory Opinion of 20 July 1962, at 163. In the Uniting for Peace Resolution of 3 November 1950 (GA Res. 377 (V), printed in UNYB (1950), 193–5), the Assembly asserted its own responsibility in this field in an attempt to overcome the Council's inability to act (due to the Cold War power patterns) and to create a stronger parallelism between the Council's and the Assembly's powers. While the resolution was highly controversial and its legality was challenged by the Soviet Union and its allies, the critical points were the question of the circumstances under which the Security Council was supposed to be discharging its functions—and whether the General Assembly could recommend coercive measures, not the general question of whether the mere existence of a Chapter VII scenario excludes a competence of the General Assembly.

[223] Goodrich/Hambro/Simons, *Charter of the United Nations*, at 130; Nantwi, *Enforcement of international judicial decisions*, at 155.

situation."[224] While the precise understanding of an "exercise of its functions" is controversial, it will not necessarily require enforcement action, but at least some form of active Council involvement.[225] As the provision is a temporary and not a substantive limitation on the Assembly's powers, the Assembly is free to make recommendations if Council deliberations are closed such as when a veto thwarts Council action.[226] Accordingly, the adoption of resolutions in the Assembly calling for compliance with the Nicaragua judgment met with no protest from the Council. On the other hand, Article 12(1) could arguably be held to apply where the Council is dealing with a matter without reaching consensus on concrete steps or in an inefficient manner.[227] In practice, the Assembly has interpreted Article 12(1) very narrowly and has felt free to make recommendations even on matters pending before the Council,[228] an interpretation not quite reconcilable with the wording of the article, but sustained by state practice.[229] Hence, if the

---

[224] See *Hailbronner/Klein* in Simma, Charter, Article 12, at n. 1; Goodrich/Hambro/Simons, *Charter of the United Nations*, at 129. Article 12(1) reads: "While the Security Council is exercising in respect of any dispute or situation the functions assigned to it in the present Charter, the General Assembly shall not make any recommendation with regard to that dispute or situation unless the Security Council so requests." The provision is taken up by Articles 10 and 11(2). According to *Hailbronner/Klein* in Simma, Charter, Article 12, at n. 8, Article 12(1) only refers to the functions of the Council under Chapters VI and VII; however, the wording is broad enough to apply to Article 94(2) as well. This question is rather theoretical, as it is unlikely that a case of non-compliance will, on the one hand, be taken as seriously as to lead to a conflict of jurisdiction between the Council and Assembly, while on the other hand being considered to lack any potential impact on the maintenance of international peace and security, particularly given the broad interpretation of these terms by the Council, see *supra* n. 101.

[225] If the Council does not include the matter in its agenda, there are no concerns against Assembly action. According to Article 11(3) of the Charter, the Assembly has the *right* to call the attention of the Council to situations likely to endanger international peace and security; an *obligation* only arises if the Assembly considers that Council action is necessary, see Article 11(2) *in fine*.

[226] The Assembly's reasoning in the Uniting for Peace Resolution had a somewhat different emphasis, stating that the Council actually failed to exercise its functions in cases where it was unable to act because of a lack of consensus among the permanent members. An adjournment of a matter by the Council would also allow the General Assembly to proceed with recommendations, since it would show that the Council has decided not to deal with the matter for the moment. See *Hailbronner/Klein* in Simma, Charter, Article 12, nn. 30 and 15 on the impact of a veto.

[227] One has to bear in mind that the permanent members might have legitimate reasons for casting the veto, that this is a right provided for by the Charter, and that it is not the Assembly's task to supervise the Council. Therefore, it would be problematic to give the Assembly the right to assess whether or not the Council "fulfills its functions." See *Hailbronner/Klein* in Simma, Charter, Article 12, at nn. 13–16.

[228] See White, *The United Nations*, at 103–5, 113–39.

[229] See *Hailbronner/Klein* in Simma, Article 12, nn. 19–22; see also Goodrich/Hambro/Simons, *Charter of the United Nations*, at 131: "[The] initial effort to impose a broad restriction upon the Assembly's powers has not been sustained" and 133: "Article 12(1) has become somewhat of a dead letter in so far as strict adherence to its language is concerned. Nonetheless, the Assembly has for the most part respected the intent of the article by not interfering, when the Council was making active efforts to bring about a satisfactory solution." Tomuschat in Wolfrum, United Nations, at 548–57 goes even further and refers to Article 12 as a rule that

Assembly is firmly committed to take action to bring about compliance with an ICJ decision, it will not likely consider Article 12 an obstacle. The obligation under Article 11(2) *in fine* to refer questions relating to international peace and security on which "action" is necessary to the Council is no substantive limitation of the Assembly's competences either. It is instead a procedural rule of cooperation between the two organs reflective of the Council's monopoly for coercive measures.[230]

There are substantive limitations, though, in Articles 59 to 61 of the ICJ Statute. The same considerations as described above for the Security Council apply for the Assembly. It must abstain from damaging the Court's authority and from action contrary to the judgment's *res judicata*. Similarly, it may not undertake a formal review of the Court's verdict.[231]

"Recommendations" are the sole means available to the Assembly under Articles 10 and 11(2). Although this restriction to non-binding instruments has been perceived as a great impairment of effective Assembly action under Article 10, it would be shortsighted to assume that binding decisions alone can produce beneficial effects and that recommendations are doomed to failure.[232] The pressure of world opinion should not be underestimated. Moreover, the discussion in this world forum *per se* may be useful for the state demanding compliance, as it might enable it to gain publicity and support for its cause and isolate the recalcitrant state.

Assembly recommendations for compliance with ICJ decisions might take many different forms. The Assembly might decide to address the Security Council,[233] the parties to the dispute, third states,[234] or other international

---

has lost its practical relevance: "[T]he General Assembly seems to feel less than bound by this rule. The terms [...] are read in practice as preventing the General Assembly from making a statement only in those cases where the Security Council has already acceded to its wishes." Similarly, White, *The United Nations*, at 138–9 and 103: "Article 12 is probably the most difficult provision, in constitutional terms, to reconcile with the practice of the General Assembly."

[230] See *Hailbronner/Klein* in Simma, Charter, Article 10, at nn. 23–32, Article 11, at n. 31. It does not set limits to the Assembly's powers additional to Article 12: White, *The United Nations*, at 102. This is confirmed by the practice of the Organization. See *Tomuschat* in Wolfrum, United Nations Law, at 555, stating that the Assembly "is not prepared to acknowledge Article 11(2) as restricting its power to make recommendations in any way."

[231] Rosenne, *Law and Practice I*, at 259–60.

[232] See Nantwi, *Enforcement of international judicial decisions*, at 155 and 161, according great significance to Article 10 in this context.

[233] The impact of reverting with the matter to the Security Council will usually be doubtful if the case came to the General Assembly precisely because of a deadlock in the Security Council. Yet occasionally even in such a scenario, the Assembly might give new impulses to a blocked situation and exert a certain political pressure on Council members to justify their lack of action.

[234] Recommendations could be directed at particular states which have a special role or at the community of states as a whole. Such recommendations could increase the pressure on the debtor, make it easier for the judgment creditor to get the assistance of others, and serve as a basis for legitimization for a third state to provide assistance, for example, in the form of a transfer of assets of the recalcitrant state.

organizations, including specialized agencies. As for their substance, recommendations might call for compliance in general terms and reaffirm the duty under Article 94(1) of the Charter or condemn the non-compliance outright.[235] The recommendations may take the form of suggestions on concrete steps to be taken to bring about compliance, such as recourse to peaceful settlement mechanisms. In cases that concern compliance with *erga omnes* obligations, a confirmation of this *erga omnes* character might cause third states to see themselves not only entitled but obliged to assist in the enforcement of the decision.[236] Even though the Assembly cannot order collective enforcement action, it can recommend the use of lawful enforcement measures against the recalcitrant state (thus effectively legitimizing unilateral steps). For example, it could recommend that particular or all Member States make use of their right to collective self-defense under Article 51 of the Charter,[237] apply countermeasures such as economic sanctions,[238] or proceed to direct enforcement such as the seizing of assets to satisfy pecuniary claims.

The legality of such a resolution will depend on the lawfulness of the recommended countermeasure. A breach of the obligation under Article 94(1), for instance, will generally not entitle the creditor to enforcement through military means, unless there is an "armed attack" pursuant to Article 51; only in such a scenario could the Assembly recommend military enforcement. Below this threshold, it should instead address the Security Council and request action under Chapter VII on its part.

As impressive as this array of measures appears, the Nicaragua case marks the furthest the General Assembly has gone to date in terms of bringing about compliance with an ICJ decision. Even in this case, it urged full and immediate compliance with the judgment rather than condemning the behavior of the US—still a rather soft call.

ECOSOC   According to Article 62(1) and (2) of the Charter, the Economic and Social Council may make recommendations with respect to "international economic, social, cultural, educational, health, and related matters" to the General Assembly, the UN members and to the specialized agencies, as well as "recommendations for the purpose of promoting respect for, and

---

[235] See the action taken by the General Assembly with regard to South Africa's disregard of advisory opinions, *supra* n. 214 and Schachter, *International law*, at 235.

[236] Schachter, *International law*, at 235 and 246 fn. 25: counsel for the UK had pursued such an argumentation in the Monetary Gold case.

[237] Verdross/Simma, *Universelles Völkerrecht*, at 151. This would remain a recommendation, not an authorization. States would therefore have to justify their behavior through a legal rule such as Article 51 and could not directly base their action on the GA recommendation, ibid., 152. The Assembly resolution will yet have significance as persuasive authority.

[238] For example, a call to interrupt trade relations or to block assets, see Schachter, *International law*, at 235.

observance of, human rights and fundamental freedoms for all." Individual states might be addressees of such recommendations, and recommendations can relate to specific situations, so one could imagine a potential for ECO-SOC action to promote compliance with ICJ decisions relating to matters within ECOSOC jurisdiction. As for the effectiveness of recommendations in this field, similar considerations as for General Assembly resolutions would hold true. ECOSOC has not yet taken up such a role for ICJ judgments and provisional measures, but it has been actively involved in urging implementation of advisory opinions where its interests were affected.[239]

The Secretary-General Another organ with a potential role in bringing about compliance with ICJ decisions is the Secretariat.[240] The Secretary-General is not only the chief administrative officer of the organization[241] but is also entrusted with political powers. By virtue of Article 99, he has the right to direct the Council's attention to all matters that in his opinion may threaten the maintenance of international peace and security—a provision broadly interpreted as a right of political initiative and investigation. On many occasions, the Secretary-General takes a discrete, but influential, role in conflict prevention and settlement, conducting investigations, offering good offices, and mediating by way of "quiet diplomacy."[242] In some situations, an initiative by the Secretary-General will be more promising than action by the UN political organs: the Secretary-General is a person well

[239] Just recently, ECOSOC became involved in the case of Malaysian jurist Dato' Param Cumaraswamy, Special Rapporteur on the Independence of Judges and Lawyers to the United Nations Commission on Human Rights, a subsidiary organ of ECOSOC. A dispute had arisen between the UN and Malaysia concerning the immunity of Mr Cumaraswamy from litigation for certain comments he had made in an interview with a magazine in 1995 about the Malaysian judicial system. Civil defamation suits were launched against him before Malaysian Courts, and a dispute arose on whether he was entitled to immunity under Section 22 of the Convention on the Privileges and Immunities of the United Nations (1 UNTS 15); ECOSOC made a request for an ICJ advisory opinion, ECOSOC Decision 1998/297. In its advisory opinion of 29 April 1999, binding on the United Nations and Malaysia under Section 30 of the same convention, the ICJ affirmed Cumaraswamy's immunity and stated that he was to be held financially harmless for any costs imposed upon him by Malaysian Courts, Difference relating to immunity from legal process of a special rapporteur of the Commission on Human Rights, Advisory Opinion of 29 April 1999, at 89–90, para. 67. Despite this opinion, the litigation before Malaysian Court continued; in response, ECOSOC adopted a resolution that stressed Malaysia's obligation to ensure Cumaraswamy's immunity, ECOSOC Resolution 1999/64, E/1999/INF/2/Add.2, 152–3. ECOSOC continued to be seized of the matter, Press Release ECOSOC/5883 of 4 February 2000. The Secretary-General has several times reported that all lawsuits were dismissed, but that Malaysia has not yet reimbursed the UN for the legal expenses paid on behalf of Cumaraswamy despite various requests to do so: Letters dated 26 April 2002 and 27 May 2003 from the Secretary-General to the President of the Economic and Social Council, E/2002/5, E/2003/78. See for further information on the case Human Rights Watch, Significant cases: Param Cumaraswamy, http://www.hrw.org/campaigns/malaysia/2000/cases-param.htm.
[240] On the fact that the Secretariat and not the Secretary-General is termed principal organ, see *Fiedler* in Simma, Article 97, at n. 3.
[241] Article 97 cl. 3 Charter.   [242] See *Fiedler* in Simma, Charter, Article 99, nn. 8–56.

known by the parties with whom they can hold confidential discussions removed from the political organs and controversies. He will generally have a rather cooperational than confrontational role.[243] An interesting example of a role of the Secretary-General in promoting compliance is provided in the Land and Maritime Boundary case between Cameroon and Nigeria. In the wake of the delivery of the Court's final judgment, Secretary-General Kofi Annan met with the parties to discuss related issues, and a variety of positive measures promoting compliance were agreed upon.[244] He is continuing his efforts in favor of compliance now that the judgment has been delivered and implementation raises some problems.[245]

The Secretary-General has taken up an active role in urging the implementation of ICJ advisory opinions concerning the relationship between the UN and single states.[246] Yet this should not be taken as a basis for considering him a watchdog for compliance with ICJ rulings, as with regard to such advisory opinions, the Secretary-General rather acts out of his function as the chief administrative officer of the UN than because of a general interest in the observance of ICJ decisions and opinions.

In addition, the political organs might confer tasks upon the Secretary-General relating to supervision of the implementation of their resolutions. In the Nicaragua case, for example, the Assembly asked the Secretary-General to report on the implementation of its resolutions on compliance with the respective judgment. In the Territorial Dispute (Libya/Chad) case, the Secretary-General became involved in the post-adjudicative phase in the preparation and deployment of a UN observer mission.[247]

---

[243] *Morr* in Wolfrum, United Nations Law, at 1143. The imposition or recommendation of sanctions is neither covered by his competencies, nor would it be desirable because this might be perceived as setting aside his neutrality.

[244] Press Release SG/SM/8368 ADR/576 of 5 September 2002. Both parties undertook to respect and implement the forthcoming ICJ ruling on the Bakassi Peninsula, to establish an implementing mechanism with the support of the United Nations, and to resume ministerial-level meetings of a joint commission. They agreed on the need for confidence-building measures, including the eventual demilitarization of Bakassi with the possibility of international observers to monitor the withdrawal of troops.

[245] See *supra* Introduction n. 12, in particular, on the Mixed Commission.

[246] In the case of Cumaraswamy, see *supra* n. 239, the Secretary-General had an active role. In the advisory opinion, the Court had upheld the Secretary-General's assessment that Cumaraswamy had acted in an official capacity and was entitled to immunity; the Court stressed the "pivotal role" of the Secretary-General in making the determination on the entitlement to immunity and his "authority and [. . .] responsibility to exercise the necessary protection where required" as well as his "primary responsibility and authority to protect the interests of the Organization and its agents"—*supra* at paras. 50–1. The Secretary-General monitored the follow-up of the opinion and kept ECOSOC updated, see Letters from the Secretary-General to the President of the Economic and Social Council dated 21 July 1999 (E/1999/49/Add.1), 19 October 1999 (E/1999/121), and 15 December 1999 (E/1999/124). In the letter of 19 October 1999, he suggested concrete steps under Malaysian law for giving effect to Cumaraswamy's immunity in accordance with the Convention on Privileges and Immunities, the ICJ advisory opinion and ECOSOC Resolution 1999/64.

[247] See *infra* Chapter 3 B XVIII 6 b (2) and XXII.

III. Unilateral Enforcement and Assistance by Other Actors

1. Availability of regular unilateral enforcement measures

Although this is not explicitly restated in the Charter or Statute, the victorious state may take certain unilateral measures to bring about compliance with an ICJ decision which international law generally provides, such as self-help—albeit the general rules might require certain adaptations.

A distinction must first be made between the enforcement of final judgments and provisional measures. While the final judgment concludes the adjudicatory process, interim measures come at a stage where it is incumbent on both parties to refrain from any measure capable of aggravating or extending the dispute or prejudicing the rights of the other party under any future decision—a general duty of parties to proceedings before the Court that will in many cases be restated in its orders on interim protection.[248] This obligation will be in tension with the right of a party to enforce an order. Unilateral enforcement action during ICJ proceedings—even to give effect to rights confirmed in an order—might undermine the Court's authority. It is particularly appropriate that the party instituting proceedings or requesting provisional measures demonstrates its faith in the adjudicative process (which it had launched itself) by—at least initially—refraining from self-help. On the other hand, it would be inapposite to deprive that state of all means of enforcement in situations where the other party has repeatedly defied the Court's order and shows no willingness to comply, and where other enforcement mechanisms—for example, through the Council or an additional Court order—are unavailable or futile. The entitled state cannot be expected to suffer irreparable harm only because it has chosen the route of adjudication; such a construction would effectively reward a state that not only fails to observe its obligations but even challenges the Court's authority, and turn the purpose of interim protection on its head. As Oscar Schachter has observed on the duty not to take action to aggravate the dispute: "This duty cannot be categorical, it must allow, as the Charter does, for legitimate self-defense even during the period of judicial deliberation. [. . .] To deny this right in the hope that judicial protection would be adequate is less than realistic. It would make the best the enemy of the good."[249] Accordingly, a balance must be struck between the duty not to aggravate the dispute and the interests of the creditor in the enforcement of the order, taking into account factors such as, *inter alia*, the concrete behavior of the opposite side— whether it ignores the order, takes steps which the creditor regards as

---

[248] See the ICJ's clear statement to that extent in LaGrand, Judgment of 27 June 2001, at para. 103.

[249] *Schachter* in Kreisberg, American Hostages in Iran, at 345.

insufficient, or is prepared to negotiate; the time passed since the order—whether the entitled state can be legitimately expected to postpone self-help to determine whether the adversary's subsequent conduct will provide satisfaction; the imminence of the harm and the danger of an aggravation of the situation; the potential impact of the envisaged enforcement action on the further development of the dispute; and the prospects for help from the Security Council.[250]

As for judgments, one might wonder whether recourse to the Security Council must be made prior to applying any unilateral measures. However, Article 94(2) of the Charter has established a right for the aggrieved state, thus widening the mechanisms available to it. There is no indication that this recourse is meant as mandatory or sets restrictions to other mechanisms normally available.[251]

2. The concrete measures available

The available means are generally limited to peaceful measures. Non-compliance with an ICJ decision *per se* does not entitle the creditor to take recourse to force, let alone to engage in a full-fledged *guerre d'exécution* (war of execution). As explained above, proposals in the Charter's drafting process that non-compliance with a judgment should automatically qualify as an act of aggression were rejected;[252] the Charter contains no special rules exempting the creditor of a judgment or provisional measure from the prohibition of the use of force for the purposes of enforcing ICJ decisions. The permissibility of armed action will thus be determined by the general rules, and only if the concrete situation was such as to amount to an armed attack under Article 51 would recourse to force be legal, up to the extent that the Charter allows for self-defense. Accordingly, the substantive consequences of non-compliance—be it the post-adjudicative dispute in case of judgments or the dispute following the indication of provisional measures—will decide on the legality of recourse to force. The mere fact that the state's objective is the enforcement of an ICJ decision will not be a sufficient justification.[253]

---

[250] The Court carried out a differentiated examination in the Tehran Hostages case, evaluating economic sanctions differently than military action, see further *infra* Chapter 3 C IV 3.

[251] But see *O'Connell*, 30 Va. JIL (1990), 928, regarding the existence of an obligation of prior recourse to the Council as unclear. In any event, in the concrete circumstances of the case, it was clear that Security Council action would not take place; therefore, no such obligation could be sustained, as a state should not be held to make use of a mechanism on the futility of which there are no doubts, see ibid., at 939.

[252] See the proposal by Bolivia during the San Francisco conference, *supra* n. 23.

[253] See (referring to judgments) *Magid* in Peck/Lee, Increasing the effectiveness, 333–4; Schachter, 54 AJIL (1960), at 14–17; *O'Connell*, 30 Va. JIL (1990), 928; Rosenne, *Law and Practice I*, 233–6. For the view that unilateral military enforcement of ICJ judgments is legal, see

A full account on the conditions for self-help and lawful countermeasures under the general law of state responsibility is obviously beyond the scope of the present study; a few remarks must suffice here.[254] To qualify as lawful self-help the measures taken must be necessary to terminate or remedy the violation and not out of proportion to the violation and the injury.[255] As self-help carries an inherent risk of escalating the dispute, the respect for the principle of proportionality deserves particular attention, and the potential efficiency should be considered carefully in advance.

One might think of self-help either through direct enforcement or coercive measures to pressure the recalcitrant state to compliance. For example, if assets of the defaulting state are located on the judgment creditor's territory, the judgment creditor might seize those assets, be it as a means of direct (i.e. measures effecting the execution of a monetary judgment) or as indirect enforcement (i.e. countermeasures in order to compel the state to execute). International law will not require the state first to launch proceedings before its domestic courts.[256] As to the question which property can be taken, the principle of proportionality has to be respected: the seizing of military or diplomatic property would generally appear to be excluded, as international law grants a particular status to this type of property and such action might intensify the dispute. If the creditor wants to seize property of nationals of the recalcitrant state rather than of the state itself, human rights standards would have to be observed besides proportionality.[257] Turning to means of indirect enforcement, there is a wide array of measures available, all of which are subject to the proportionality principle, including the suspension of treaties, the freezing and confiscation of assets, economic sanctions, and the termination of assistance or overflight rights.[258]

The efficiency of unilateral sanctions is a subject of general discussion and will depend on the concrete circumstances of each case. In general, direct enforcement measures would appear more promising than measures aimed at

Wright in Stanger, Essays on Espionage and International Law, at 6–7. For an intermediate position see Reisman, *Nullity and Revision*, at 844–51, who agrees that the mere objective of non-compliance cannot in itself justify use of armed force. However, his general interpretation of Article 2(4) of the Charter does not limit the permissible cases to situations involving an armed attack, instead determining the lawfulness by the potential impact on world order and considering forcible self-help excluded only in so far as the UN itself is an effective enforcer. At 668 he suggests criteria for a valid *guerre d'exécution*. Against the understanding that Article 2(4) only prohibits use of force not inconsistent with the purposes of the United Nations see *Schachter*, 54 AJIL (1960), at 15–16.

[254] For details, see the Draft Articles on the Responsibility of States for Internationally Wrongful Acts adopted by the International Law Commission in 2001, Report of the International Law Commission of its Fifty-Third Session, UN Doc. A/56/10, Chapter IV, E 1.

[255] See *O'Connell*, 30 Va. JIL (1990), at 930.

[256] Municipal law might provide for such a requirement, however; for the mechanisms of enforcement before national courts, see *infra* section 5.

[257] See *O'Connell*, 30 Va. JIL (1990), at 929–30.   [258] Ibid., at 929.

compelling compliance, as the former lead to immediate satisfaction of the creditor's claims and sanctions often turn out inefficient and fail to target the debtor precisely enough. Where direct enforcement is possible, it will therefore generally be the preferable mechanism. Before resorting to indirect enforcement, it would be wise for the state to consider whether direct enforcement is possible, if not through its own action, then through assistance from third states.

3. Assistance by third states

While countermeasures are as a general rule only available to the state directly injured,[259] most commentators recognize that states may provide assistance in the enforcement of ICJ decisions, even though there is no explicit provision in the Charter or the Statute to this extent.[260] An attempt to obtain satisfaction through third-party assistance was made by the UK with regard to the Corfu Channel judgment, resulting in another case before the ICJ, the Monetary Gold case, which was dismissed because of the absence of Albania, the necessary third party.[261] Proceedings before the domestic courts of a third state will be a likely route for the entitled state in such a situation.[262]

---

[259] See ILC draft articles on state responsibility, *supra* n. 254, at Articles 49, 54. An exception is made for obligations owed to the international community as a whole or to a group of states, including the state wishing to apply countermeasures, and established for the collective interest of that group (ibid., Article 48(1)).

[260] See Jenks, *Prospects of international adjudication*, at 705; *Schachter*, 54 AJIL (1960), at 11–12; Nantwi, *Enforcement of international judicial decisions*, at 175; *O'Connell*, 30 Va. JIL (1990), at 931–7. The right of assistance is further confirmed by the provisions on enforcement in treaties concerning regional organizations and specialized agencies, see *infra* III 4. *Reisman*, 63 AJIL (1969), at 18 even refers to an obligation of assistance.

[261] For details, see *infra* Chapter 3 B I 3. The ICJ did not take any substantive decision regarding the third-party assistance in that case. *Schachter*, 54 AJIL (1960), at 11–12, draws the following lessons: states have the right to assist in the execution of ICJ decisions that are not complied with if requested by the successful party; this assistance might take the form of transfer of assets without the necessity of an authorization by the Security Council or another ICJ decision, subject to the obligation to take necessary measures to safeguard competing claims (e.g. by providing judicial control).

[262] There were suggestions for the creation of a uniform system of domestic enforcement mechanisms for ICJ monetary judgments by the Security Council; no such initiative has been taken thus far. *Kerley* in Gross, The future of the International Court of Justice, at 284, suggests that in a first resolution, the Council should require all Member States to inform the Secretary-General whether they have provisions in their domestic laws enabling a state creditor of a money judgment to obtain recovery our of assets of the debtor in their territories; the Secretary-General would then compile and distribute a report of the replies. In a second resolution, the Security Council would urge Member States to establish such a remedy and inform the Security Council accordingly. Kerley argues that the fact that a significant number of states offer such a remedy would be a deterrent to non-compliance. Yet, although such system might admittedly have a certain deterring effect and enable the creditor to take more efficient action, it might be difficult to convince the Council to take such kind of action, and there would not appear to be any legal basis to oblige states to participate in such a system; it would stretch the wording of Chapter VII or Article 94(2) too far to imagine a binding decision to this extent.

Whether assistance in the enforcement of ICJ decisions rises to the status of an obligation for third states is a matter of debate; it is doubtful whether there is sufficient evidence to support the existence of such an obligation.[263]

4. Enforcement action by specialized agencies and regional organizations

The constitutions of various specialized agencies contain enforcement mechanisms for certain ICJ decisions: final decisions reached in the framework of the respective constitution's dispute settlement system. Examples can be found in the Constitution of the International Labor Association and in the International Civil Aviation Convention.[264] Those provisions have not been applied as there was no case of non-compliance with a judgment delivered in context of such an enforcement mechanism.[265] If such scenarios were to arise, enforcement action by these organizations may be quite efficient, as some of those organizations have control over state assets which would open the way for direct enforcement, and suspension of membership rights might significantly hurt the respective state's interests.[266] To avoid a politicization of their activities, specialized agencies will yet most likely display reluctance to take a role in enforcing ICJ decisions beyond the

---

[263] In favor of the existence of such an obligation Reisman, *Nullity and revision*, at 781; skeptical *O'Connell*, 30 Va. JIL (1990), at 936–7.

[264] *Guillaume* in Jasentuliyana, Perspectives on international law, at 284; Nantwi, *Enforcement of international judicial decisions*, at 162–8. See the Constitution of the International Labor Organization as amended on 9 October 1946, 15 UNTS 35. Articles 26–34 set up a mechanism for the settlement of disputes relating to the observance of the ILO conventions, which might include decisions of the ICJ under the terms of Articles 31 and 32. In the event that a state fails to respect an ICJ decision thus taken, the ILO Governing Body "may recommend to the Conference such action as it may deem wise and expedient to secure compliance therewith" pursuant to Article 33. See also Convention on International Civil Aviation of 7 December 1944, 15 UNTS 295, at Articles 84–8: disputes relating to the interpretation or application of the Convention are decided by the Council, subject to appeal to the PCIJ or arbitration; all states parties undertake to prohibit overflights for airlines of a state party not in conformity with a final decision; as penalty for non-conformity by a state, the Assembly shall suspend the voting power of that state in the Assembly and the Council. See further Article 17 of the Statute of the International Atomic Energy Agency (26 October 1956, 276 UNTS 3), which confers jurisdiction on the ICJ for disputes concerning its interpretation or application; for non-compliance with Statute obligations (which might include obligations adjudicated upon by the Court), Article 19B opens the possibility to effect a suspension from membership or a suspension from the exercises of the privileges and rights; Article 12C enables the Board under certain conditions to order curtailment or suspension of assistance and call for return of materials and equipment.

[265] In the Appeal relating to the jurisdiction of the ICAO Council, the ICJ's judgment was complied with by the parties, so there was no need for enforcement action; in any case, it is doubtful whether the enforcement mechanism could have been applied as the decision only concerned the competence of the ICAO Council, not the substantive issues relating to overflight rights. See further Chapter 3 B XI.

[266] See Nantwi, *Enforcement of international judicial decisions*, at 168.

context of dispute settlement under the respective treaty, as will other international organizations with sanctioning mechanisms.[267]

Regional organizations might also provide for mechanisms to promote compliance with ICJ decisions through diplomatic means, with the potential benefit of greater responsiveness on the part of the recalcitrant state to opinion and pressure from its own region, a sense of regional responsibility and solidarity conducive to involvement of further states, and more effective voting arrangements than for the UN organs.[268] A few examples illustrate, such as Article 50 of the American Treaty on Pacific Settlement (the "Pact of Bogotá"), which supplements the enforcement mechanism under Article 94(2) of the UN Charter by requiring the proposition of a meeting of consultation of the OAS ministers of foreign affairs[269] prior to recourse to the UN Security Council.[270] This provision was applied with regard to the ICJ judgment in the Arbitral Award case between Honduras and Nicaragua.[271] Another mechanism has been established under the 1957 European Convention for the Peaceful Settlement of Disputes: in a case of noncompliance, the Committee of Ministers of the Council of Europe may, at the initiative of the judgment creditor, make recommendations in order to

[267] See Reisman, *Nullity and revision*, at 745–53, on international financial institutions. The constitutive instruments of international organizations might provide for sanctions in the general case of non-compliance with obligations under the respective treaty. See, for example, Articles of Agreement of the International Bank for Reconstruction and Development, 2 UNTS 39, Article VI Section 2, Articles of Agreement of the International Monetary Fund, ibid.; Article XV, Section 2, Articles of Agreement on the International Finance Corporation, 264 UNTS 117 Article V Section 2.

[268] See Jenks, *Prospects of international adjudication*, at 699–702; and *Anand*, 26 U. Pitt. LR (1965), at 702.

[269] The OAS Charter (119 UNTS 3) establishes the Conference, which only meets every five years, as the Organization's supreme organ; foreign ministers meet for consultations in the interval "in order to consider problems of an urgent nature and of common interest to the American States": Articles 33, 35.

[270] American Treaty on Pacific Settlement (Pact of Bogotá) of 30 April 1948, 30 UNTS 449, Article 50: "If one of the High Contracting Parties should fail to carry out the obligation imposed upon it by a decision of the International Court of Justice or by an arbitral award, the other party or parties concerned shall, before resorting to the Security Council of the United Nations, propose a Meeting of Consultation of Ministers of Foreign Affairs to agree upon appropriate measures to ensure the fulfillment of the judicial decision or arbitral award." For details on dispute settlement in the Inter-American System see Reisman, *Nullity and revision*, at 758–68.

[271] *Guillaume* in Jasentuliyana, Perspectives on international law, at 285; Nantwi, *Enforcement of international judicial decisions*, at 171–2. More precisely, a bilateral agreement concluded for submitting their dispute to the Court had almost literally taken up the provisions of the Pact of Bogotá, so the recourse to the regional dispute settlement machinery in the post-adjudicative phase was an application of that agreement as well as of the Pact: Agreement between Honduras and Nicaragua for submitting to the International Court of Justice their differences with respect to the award of his majesty the King of Spain of 23 December 1906, 22 June 1957, 277 UNTS 159, Section 5. For details on the case, see *infra* Chapter 3 B VIII.

ensure compliance.[272] This mechanism has not yet been applied for ICJ decisions.[273]

5. Enforcement through proceedings before domestic courts

Litigation before domestic courts might represent an efficient mechanism for enforcement of ICJ decisions, as there is a huge potential for a role of domestic courts in the enforcement of international law in general.[274] The form and degree to which domestic courts might defer to ICJ decisions and perceive them as part of its own legal system or of a foreign one upon the general status of international law in their domestic legal order;[275] a comprehensive discussion of this issue would be a matter for a study of its own. The following explanations merely aim at providing an overview of this potential enforcement mechanism.[276] Practice is still limited. While there were two cases of provisional measures in which the creditors made an attempt of enforcement through domestic judicial proceedings, there has not been any such case for the creditor of an ICJ judgment, but in some cases, private parties have made the attempt to invoke ICJ decisions in their favor, as will be shown below.[277]

These examples already indicate that domestic litigation aimed at enforcement of ICJ decisions[278] might come up in many different situations that can

---

[272] European Convention for the Peaceful Settlement of Disputes of 29 April 1957, 320 UNTS 243, Article 39: (1) Each of the High Contracting Parties shall comply with the decision of the International Court of Justice or the award of the Arbitral Tribunal in any dispute to which it is a party.
(2) If one of the parties to a dispute fails to carry out its obligations under a decision of the International Court of Justice or an award of the Arbitral Tribunal, the other party to the dispute may appeal to the Committee of Ministers of the Council of Europe. Should it deem necessary, the latter, acting by a two-thirds majority of the representatives entitled to sit on the Committee, may make recommendations with a view to ensuring compliance with the said decision or award.

[273] *Guillaume* in Jasentuliyana, Perspectives on international law, at 285.

[274] *O'Connell*, 30 Va. JIL (1990), at 913; Reisman, *Nullity and revision*, at 802–4.

[275] See *O'Connell*, 30 Va. JIL (1990), at 916; *Ordonez/Reilly* in Franck/Fox, International law decisions in national courts, at 346 and 368–70 (for patterns of deference).

[276] Another issue is voluntary compliance with ICJ decisions through action of municipal courts: see Rights of United States Citizens in Morocco, *infra* Chapter 3 B III, where domestic courts followed the Court's interpretation on the extent of consular jurisdiction.

[277] There is one example of an attempt to enforce a PCIJ judgment before national courts (Société Commerciale de Belgique (Belgium v. Greece)), Judgment of 15 June 1939. The private party for whom the Belgian government had exercised diplomatic protection brought a claim before Belgian courts to attach Greek assets, which the Belgian court refused absent an *exequatur* that would have given the ICJ judgment the status of a Belgian judgment, effectively treating the ICJ verdict like a judgment of a foreign country, see *Ordonez/Reilly* in Franck/Fox, International law decisions in national courts, at 354; and *O'Connell*, 30 Va. JIL (1990), at 915.

[278] On the treatment of ICJ advisory opinions before domestic courts, see *Bedjaoui*, in Franck/Fox, International law decisions in national courts, at 32–4; *Ordonez/Reilly* in Franck/Fox, International law decisions in national courts, at 357–9.

only be sketched in the framework of the present study. The likelihood of successful implementation might vary according to these different situations.

First, one might differentiate according to the subject instituting proceedings: not only the parties to the decision (i.e. the winning party, be it the applicant that gained a decision in its favor or the respondent that defended itself successfully) might want to launch domestic proceedings, but also other actors: third states with an interest in the decision, even private actors, such as a person on whose behalf the decision creditor had taken action (say, in the exercise of diplomatic protection),[279] or further private parties with an interest in the implementation of the decision. In fact, it was private persons and groups who made the attempt to bring about compliance with the Nicaragua judgment before US domestic courts. In Breard and LaGrand, parallel action was taken by the states creditors of the provisional measures and the individuals for whose protection they had taken action. In the Anglo-Iranian Oil Company case, the company invoked the Court's provisional measures as evidence for a prima-facie title in domestic proceedings against private companies various countries in order to obtain injunctions.[280] Second, we can distinguish according to the jurisdiction in which the proceedings are launched: i.e. action before the courts of the judgment debtor, of the judgment creditor, and of third states. Third, the objectives of the litigation will differ; in some cases, the creditor might seek immediate satisfaction, in others, securities or pressure through sanctions. Fourth, we can distinguish between measures for the enforcement of provisional measures, on the one hand, and of judgments, on the other. Fifth, one might think of action the objective of which is the actual enforcement of the obligation under Article 94(1) of the Charter against the judgment creditor *vis-à-vis* the scenario where the Court's jurisprudence is invoked as persuasive authority beyond the immediate context of the prior ICJ litigation.[281] The latter scenario is currently arising where non-German nationals sentenced to death in the United States under violation of the Vienna Convention on Consular Relations invoke the LaGrand judgment as authority to achieve a review and reconsideration of their sentence.[282] Finally, the identity of the

---

[279] As in the Socobelge case relating to a PCIJ judgment, see *supra* n. 277.

[280] *Ordonez/Reilly* in Franck/Fox, International law decisions in national courts, at 351–2; *O'Connell*, 30 Va. JIL (1990), at 933–4; Rosenne, *Law and Practice I*, at 225 fn. 47.

[281] As explained by *Bedjaoui* in Franck/Fox, International law decisions in national courts, at 22, a distinction is to be made between enforcement proper (i.e. judicial proceedings launched by the successful state or a third party directly concerned aimed at securing that decision's benefit), and other forms of reference to the Court's decisions, which might be called "reception." On the practice of ICJ decisions being cited as evidence of law or fact see ibid., at 30–2; *Ordonez/Reilly* in Franck/Fox, International law decisions in national courts, at 359–67. For example, French courts followed the indications of the ICJ in Rights of United States Nationals on the extent of French jurisdiction, see ibid., at 365, and *infra* Chapter 3 B III.

[282] See *infra* Chapter 3 B XXVI B.

respondent is another factor for differentiation: one could conceive of proceedings against the judgment debtor as well as against third states or further actors.

A fundamental issue is whether national courts will recognize ICJ decisions as binding or at least as persuasive authority.[283] Another issue is whether they will recognize them as enforceable without further particulars (i.e. whether merely on the basis of authenticity of the decision they will proceed to enforcement or whether on the contrary they will demand an *exequatur*, i.e. an additional procedure in order to confer on decisions emanating from a non-domestic jurisdiction the effect of a domestic decision, a requirement which a Belgian court regarded as applicable for a PCIJ judgment, thus equating that judgment to one of a foreign state).[284] Furthermore, the interpretation of Article 94(1) will be an important issue: for instance, the understanding of the subjects obliged under that provision[285] or the question of who might derive therefrom a right of action.[286] Another issue could be the scope of the respondent state's immunity from jurisdiction.[287]

Support by domestic courts would doubtlessly represent a powerful tool for improved compliance with ICJ decisions. Governments will generally be more responsive towards decisions of their domestic courts, as non-observance would then represent a defiance of their own constitutional order. Thus, in a liberal democracy with an effective observance of the rule of law, it is not imaginable that governments will openly defy judgments of their national highest courts urging compliance with an ICJ decision, whereas they might

---

[283] One might deduce bindingness from Article 41 or 60 of the Statute or the doctrine of issue preclusion. See *Ordonez/Reilly* in Franck/Fox, International law decisions in national courts, at 350: issue preclusion means that questions adjudicated upon in the original decision need not be reopened even between different parties. For example, US courts relied on the ICJ jurisprudence in United States Diplomatic and Consular Staff in Tehran for the assessment of the Iran–US legal relations in private litigation, ibid., 353; *Bedjaoui* in Franck/Fox, International law decisions in national courts, at 31. On the Tehran Hostages case, see *infra* Chapter 3 B XIV.

[284] *Supra*, n. 277. There are good reasons against the requirement of a domestic procedure expressly endorsing an ICJ decision, as national courts should not be empowered to invalidate an international decision. One could refer to analogous provisions for the direct enforcement of arbitral awards, such as the New York Convention on the Recognition and Enforcement of Foreign Arbitral Awards, 330 UNTS 38, or to a corresponding rule of customary international law. See *Bedjaoui* in Franck/Fox, International law decisions in national courts, at 23; *O'Connell*, 30 Va. JIL (1990), at 915–24; Rosenne, *Law and Practice I*, at 221–6; Schachter, 54 AJIL (1960), at 13–14.

[285] See *supra* C I; national courts might perceive the obligation as one incumbent on the government only and regard the matter to be within the government's discretion.

[286] In particular, it might be questionable whether there is a right for private persons to enforce an ICJ decision: a US court ruled that Article 94(1) of the Charter does not aim at enabling individuals to bring respective claims against their own government). See *infra* Chapter 3 B XVIII 6 a and *Ordonez/Reilly* in Franck/Fox, International law decisions in national courts, at 356–7.

[287] See Schachter, 54 AJIL (1960), at 13–14.

act differently where the implementation of an international decision is outside domestic judicial control. In fact, cooperation between the European Court of Justice and domestic courts (in particular, the procedure of preliminary references under Article 234 EC Treaty) has been identified as one of the key factors for the success of the European Community legal order.[288] There is no guarantee, however, that national courts will come to assistance of decisions of international courts in this respect, as the example of the provisional measures in the Breard and LaGrand cases shows: in both cases, the United States Supreme Court did not help to give effect to the ICJ provisional measures.[289]

---

[288] See *Jones* in Franck/Fox, International law decisions in international courts, at 221–45; *Weiler*, The Constitution of Europe, at 27–9, 192–7.

[289] On reasons for reluctance of domestic judges see *Ordonez/Reilly* in Franck/Fox, International law decisions in national courts, at 370.

3

The ICJ Practice Analyzed

A. ANALYSIS OF THE PRACTICE: WHICH PRACTICE AND HOW?

The present chapter will analyze the practice of the Court with regard to judgments and provisional measures from the perspective of compliance.

I. Form of the presentation

This analysis cannot limit itself to an examination of whether subsequent action matched the dictates of the operative part of a decision. First of all, the determination of the scope of the obligation under Article 94(1) will not be apparent in each case and thus an interpretation of the respective decision is required. Moreover, knowledge gained by a narrow examination of the follow-up would not be very significant, as only an analysis of the decisions in their context will enable the identification of factors favorable or unfavorable to compliance. This chapter will therefore also discuss the disputes and proceedings before the Court; their historical and political contexts (where appropriate); the decisions of the Court; and the post-adjudicative phase. Of course, the complexity of the respective case will determine the extent and nature of the analysis. The analysis will center on those aspects relevant for compliance.[1]

The study considers those cases in which the Court issued orders on provisional measures and/or a judgment requiring implementation. Provisional measures will be analyzed separately from final judgments. This approach naturally entails some duplications and the need for cross-references; however, a separate analysis has the advantage of highlighting the structural differences between the two types of decisions, the standards applied by the Court, the development of the pertinent jurisprudence, and the reactions of the parties. The stark difference between compliance rates for provisional measures and for judgments could cause the impression that the Court is simply not an adequate organ to provide interim protection and that its

---

[1] It would exceed the scope of this study to provide a full account of the Court's jurisprudence, explain the complex legal issues for each decision, discuss whether the Court took the right decision, or even describe how the decisions influenced the further development of the law. See also *supra* Chapter 1 A on the possible approaches and the selected methodology.

provisional measures are therefore doomed to failure. Yet the analysis of the practice will show a more nuanced picture.

II. Selection of decisions for the analysis

Not all of the contentious cases on the Court's docket are or have been relevant for the question of compliance.[2] The entire list of contentious cases from 1946 to 2003 is shown in Table 3.1 and follows information available on the Court's website and in the ICJ Yearbooks.[3] The cases appear in chronological order based on the date of institution of proceedings; cases that pursuant to these sources[4] were instituted by means of a special agreement are separated by an oblique stroke.[5]

As can be seen from Table 3.1, cases with several judgments in the course of continuing proceedings—as occurs when the Court confirmed its jurisdiction in a first judgment before delivering a decision on the merits or issues a judgment on compensation that is followed by proceedings on the precise form and amount of that compensation—are presented as one case. However, where separate proceedings raising new legal questions are launched in the aftermath of completed proceedings—such as proceedings aimed at revision or interpretation, the Court treats these proceedings as separate cases, even though the underlying dispute might still be the same. Where the proceedings are joined in related cases, they appear as one case, although remaining technically separate.

The relevant cases for this study are those in which the decision produced a need for compliance. Yet if a case is thus excluded although intrinsically linked with another case that *does* give rise to a duty of implementation, the former will be mentioned in context with the latter case. The study will consider closely related cases together, as subsequent decisions on requests

---

[2] See discussion of the obligation under Article 94(1), Chapter 2 D.

[3] http://212.153.43.18/icjwww/idecisions.htm, ICJ YB 1999–2000, 3–7. There are some differences between these sources as regards the order of some cases in which applications instituting proceedings were filed the same day. Where this occurred, the table has followed the presentation of the ICJ Yearbook (YB).

[4] See *infra* Chapter 4 A IV 1 on the determination of whether a case was launched based on a special agreement and why the Court's practice does not appear fully consistent.

[5] The numbers indicated are given only for the purposes of the present study and are not meant to correspond to the respective case's number in the Court's general list. Differences from the registry's numbering will arise as all cases, whether in contentious or advisory proceedings, will be consecutively numbered by date of application, and cases concerning various litigants that were later joined by an order of the Court—South West Africa (Ethiopia v. South Africa; Liberia v. South Africa) and North Sea Continental Shelf (Federal Republic of Germany v. Denmark; Federal Republic of Germany v. Netherlands). See the list of cases of the ICJ 1946–96 in Eyffinger, The International Court of Justice 1949–96, at 374–84. As in the Court's Yearbooks and website, the cases are taken up here as one case. As for the names of cases involving the Federal Republic of Yugoslavia/Serbia and Montenegro, the nomenclature of the Court's website was adopted in this table; see further on this issue *infra* n. 1545.

Table 3.1. The Court's docket for contentious cases, 1946–2003

1. Corfu Channel (United Kingdom v. Albania)
2. Fisheries (United Kingdom v. Norway)
3. Protection of Egyptian Nationals and Protected Persons in Egypt (France v. Egypt)
4. Asylum (Colombia/Peru)
5. Rights of Nationals of the USA in Morocco (France v. United States of America)
6. Request for the Interpretation of the Judgment of 20 November 1950 in the Asylum case (Colombia v. Peru)
7. Haya de la Torre (Colombia v. Peru)
8. Ambatielos (Greece v. United Kingdom)
9. Anglo-Iranian Oil Co. (United Kingdom v. Iran)
10. Minquiers and Ecrehos (France/United Kingdom)
11. Nottebohm (Liechtenstein v. Guatemala)
12. Monetary Gold removed from Rome in 1943 (Italy v. France, United Kingdom, and United States of America)
13. Electricité de Beyrouth Company (France v. Lebanon)
14. Treatment in Hungary of Aircraft and Crew of the United States of America (United States of America v. USSR)
15. Treatment in Hungary of Aircraft and Crew of the United States of America (United States of America v. Hungary)
16. Aerial Incident of 10 March 1953 (United States of America v. Czechoslovakia)
17. Antarctica (United Kingdom v. Argentina)
18. Antarctica (United Kingdom v. Chile)
19. Aerial Incident of 7 October 1952 (United States of America v. USSR)

20. Certain Norwegian Loans (France v. Norway)
21. Right of Passage over Indian Territory (Portugal v. India)
22. Application of the Convention of 1902 Governing the Guardianship of Infants (Netherlands v. Sweden)
23. Interhandel (Switzerland v. United States of America)
24. Aerial Incident of 27 July 1955 (Israel v. Bulgaria)
25. Aerial Incident of 27 July 1955 (United States of America v. Bulgaria)
26. Aerial Incident of 27 July 1955 (United Kingdom v. Bulgaria)
27. Sovereignty over Certain Frontier Land (Belgium/Netherlands)
28. Arbitral Award made by the King of Spain on 23 December 1906 (Honduras v. Nicaragua)
29. Aerial Incident of 4 September 1954 (United States of America v. USSR)
30. Barcelona Traction, Light and Power Company, Limited (Belgium v. Spain)
31. Compagnie du Port, des Quais et des Entrepôts de Beyrouth and Société Radio-Orient (France v. Lebanon)
32. Aerial Incident of 7 November 1954 (United States of America v. USSR)
33. Temple of Preah Vihear (Cambodia v. Thailand)
34. South West Africa (Ethiopia v. South Africa; Liberia v. South Africa)
35. Northern Cameroons (Cameroon v. United Kingdom)

(Continued)

Table 3.1. *(Continued)*

36. Barcelona Traction, Light and Power Company, Limited-new application (Belgium v. Spain)
37. North Sea Continental Shelf (Federal Republic of Germany/Denmark; Federal Republic of Germany/Netherlands)
38. Appeal relating to the jurisdiction of the ICAO Council (India v. Pakistan)
39. Fisheries Jurisdiction (United Kingdom v. Iceland)
40. Fisheries Jurisdiction (Federal Republic of Germany v. Iceland)
41. Nuclear Tests (Australia v. France)
42. Nuclear Tests (New Zealand v. France)
43. Trial of Pakistani Prisoners of War (Pakistan v. India)
44. Aegean Sea Continental Shelf (Greece v. Turkey)
45. Continental Shelf (Tunisia/Libyan Arab Jamahiriya)
46. United States Diplomatic and Consular Staff in Tehran (USA v. Iran)
47. Delimitation of the Maritime Boundary in the Gulf of Maine Area (Canada /United States of America)
48. Continental Shelf (Libyan Arab Jamahiriya/Malta)
49. Frontier Dispute (Burkina Faso/Republic of Mali)
50. Military and Paramilitary Activities in and against Nicaragua (Nicaragua v. United States of America)
51. Application for Revision and Interpretation of the Judgment of 24 February 1982 in the Case concerning the *Continental Shelf (Tunisia/Libyan Arab Jamahiriya)* (Tunisia v. Libyan Arab Jamahiriya)

52. Border and Transborder Armed Actions (Nicaragua v. Costa Rica)
53. Border and Transborder Armed Actions (Nicaragua v. Honduras)
54. Land, Island and Maritime Frontier Dispute (El Salvador/Honduras)
55. Elettronica Sicula S.p.A. (ELSI) (United States of America v. Italy)
56. Maritime Delimitation in the Area between Greenland and Jan Mayen (Denmark v. Norway)
57. Aerial Incident of 3 July 1988 (Islamic Republic of Iran v. United States of America)
58. Certain Phosphate Lands in Nauru (Nauru v. Australia)
59. Arbitral Award of 31 July 1989 (Guinea-Bissau v. Senegal)
60. Territorial Dispute (Libyan Arab Jamahiriya/Chad)
61. East Timor (Portugal v. Australia)
62. Maritime Delimitation between Guinea-Bissau and Senegal (Guinea-Bissau v. Senegal)
63. Passage through the Great Belt (Finland v. Denmark)
64. Maritime Delimitation and Territorial Questions between Qatar and Bahrain (Qatar v. Bahrain)
65. Interpretation and Application of the 1971 Montreal Convention arising from the Aerial Incident at Lockerbie (Libyan Arab Jamahiriya v. United Kingdom)
66. Interpretation and Application of the 1971 Montreal Convention arising from the Aerial Incident at Lockerbie (Libyan Arab Jamahiriya v. United States of America)

(Continued)

Table 3.1. (*Continued*)

96. Application for Revision of the Judgment of 11 July 1996 in the Case Concerning Application of the Convention on the Prevention and Punishment of the Crime of Genocide (Yugoslavia v. Bosnia and Herzegovina)
97. Certain Property (Liechtenstein v. Germany)
98. Territorial and Maritime Dispute (Nicaragua v. Colombia)
99. Frontier Dispute (Benin/Niger)
100. Armed Activities on the territory of the Congo (New application: 2000) (Democratic Republic of the Congo v. Rwanda)
101. Application for Revision of the Judgment of 11 September 1992 in the case Concerning the Land, Island and Maritime Frontier Dispute (El Salvador/Honduras: Nicaragua intervening) (El Salvador v. Honduras)
102. Avena and other Mexican Nationals (Mexico v. United States of America)
103. Certain Criminal Proceedings in France (Republic of the Congo v. France)
104. Sovereignty over Pedra Branca/Pulau Batu Puteh, Middle Rocks and South Ledge (Malaysia/Singapore)

for interpretation, for example, might give indication on the scope of the obligation of compliance.[6]

III. Compliance with judgments

Many of the cases listed in Table 3.1 can be excluded for the purposes of the analysis of compliance with judgments.[7] These include the 20 cases pending before the Court which have not yet yielded a judgment on the merits.[8] Cases that were completed without a judgment on the merits were also left unconsidered. Falling in this category are 8 cases removed from the Court's list after having been launched without any jurisdictional basis,[9] 20 cases in

---

[6] For example, the chapter "Asylum/Haya de la Torre" will report all three judgments made in context with the respective dispute between Peru and Colombia, although in Table 3.1 they appear as three cases under 4, 6, and 7.

[7] See on the scope of the obligation under Article 94(1) for various types of judgments *supra* Chapter 2 D I.

[8] Application of the Convention on the Prevention and Punishment of the Crime of Genocide (Bosnia v. Federal Republic of Yugoslavia), Ahmadou Sadio Diallo (Republic of Guinea v. Democratic Republic of the Congo), Legality of use of force (eight parallel cases by Serbia and Montenegro against the UK, Portugal, the Netherlands, Italy, Germany, France, Canada and Belgium, respectively), Armed activities on the territory of the Congo (Democratic Republic of the Congo v. Uganda), Application of the Convention on the Prevention and Punishment of the Crime of Genocide (Croatia v. Federal Republic of Yugoslavia), Maritime Delimitation between Nicaragua and Honduras in the Caribbean Sea (Nicaragua v. Honduras), Certain property (Liechtenstein v. Germany), Territorial and maritime dispute (Nicaragua v. Colombia), Frontier Dispute (Benin/Niger), Armed activities on the territory of the Congo (New application: 2002), (Democratic Republic of the Congo v. Rwanda), Avena and other Mexican Nationals (Mexico v. United States of America), Certain criminal proceedings in France (Republic of the Congo v. France), Sovereignty over Pedra Branca/Pulau Batu Puteh, Middle Rocks and South Ledge (Malaysia/Singapore). On the other hand, there was already a judgment on the merits in the Gabčíkovo–Nagymaros case, so that this case will be considered regardless of its remaining on the docket.

[9] Treatment in Hungary of Aircraft and Crew of the United States of America (USA v. USSR), Treatment in Hungary of Aircraft and Crew of the United States of America (USA v. Hungary), Aerial Incident of 10 March 1953 (USA v. Czechoslovakia), Antarctica (United Kingdom v. Chile), Aerial Incident of 7 October 1952 (USA v. USSR), Aerial Incident of 4 September 1954 (USA v. USSR), Aerial Incident of 7 November 1954 (USA v. USSR). The applications in those cases had been made as a political signal only, without any likelihood for actual proceedings taking place. Applications of this type were treated as regular applications until the adoption of the 1978 Rules of Court; now they are no longer entered in the Court's General List until the state concerned explicitly gives its consent to the Court's jurisdiction for the purposes of the case: Article 38(5) of the Rules of Court. The pending case launched by the Republic of the Congo against France (Certain criminal proceedings in France) is the first case ever for the respondent to consent to proceedings instituted this way. On 9 December 2002, the Republic of the Congo filed an application instituting proceedings and a request for provisional measures, indicating that the jurisdiction was based on "the consent of the French Republic, which certainly will be given" in accordance with Article 38(5) Rules of Court (http://212.153.43.18/icjwww/idocket/icof/icoforder /icof_iapplication_20020209.pdf). France informed the Court on 11 April 2003 that it consented to the Court's jurisdiction to entertain the Congolese application, which enabled the Court to open the proceedings and to include the case in its docket (http://212.153.43.18/icjwww/ipresscom/ ipress2003/ipresscom2003-14_xx_20030411.htm).

which the Court rejected the applicants' claims on the basis of lack of jurisdiction or admissibility,[10] and 18 cases that were discontinued without any prior judgment on the merits.[11] Two cases were excluded because the judgment on the merits was delivered so shortly before the completion of this manuscript that no reliable assessment of compliance can yet be made.[12] Included in the study, however, are cases where remaining proceedings were discontinued only after a judgment on the merits[13] as well as a pending case in which such a judgment has already been issued by the Court.[14]

---

[10] Anglo-Iranian Oil Company (United Kingdom v. Iran), Request for the Interpretation of the Judgment of 20 November 1950 in the Asylum Case (Columbia v. Peru), Nottebohm (Liechtenstein v. Guatemala), Monetary Gold Removed from Rome in 1943 (Italy v. France, United Kingdom and USA), Certain Norwegian Loans (France v. Norway), Interhandel (Switzerland v. United States of America), Aerial Incident of 27 July 1955 (Israel v. Bulgaria), Northern Cameroons (Cameroon v. United Kingdom), Nuclear Tests (Australia v. France), Nuclear Tests (New Zealand v. France), Aegean Sea Continental Shelf (Greece v. Turkey), East Timor (Portugal v. Australia), Fisheries Jurisdiction (Spain v. Canada), Request for an Examination of the Situation in Accordance with Paragraph 63 of the Court's Judgment of 20 December 1974 in the Nuclear Tests Case (New Zealand v. France), Request for an Interpretation of the Judgment of 11 June 1998 (Nicaragua v. Cameroon), Legality of use of force (Yugoslavia v. United States of America), Legality of use of force (Yugoslavia v. Spain), Aerial Incident of 10 August 1999 (Pakistan v. India), Application for Revision of 11 July 1996 in the Genocide case (Yugoslavia v. Bosnia and Herzegovina), Application for Revision of the Judgment of 11 September 1992 in the Case concerning the Land, Island and Maritime Frontier Dispute (El Salvador v. Honduras: Nicaragua intervening) (El Salvador v. Honduras).

[11] Protection of Egyptian Nationals and Protected Persons in Egypt (France v. Egypt), Electricité de Beyrouth Company (France v. Lebanon), Aerial Incident of 27 July 1955 (United States of America v. Bulgaria), Aerial Incident of 27 July 1955 (United Kingdom v. Bulgaria), Barcelona Traction, Light and Power Company (first application, instituted 1958) (Belgium v. Spain), Compagnie du Port, des Quais et des Entrepôts de Beyrouth and Société Radio-Orient (France v. Lebanon), Trial of Pakistani Prisoners of War (Pakistan v. India), Border and Transborder Armed Actions (Nicaragua v. Costa Rica), Border and Transborder Armed Actions (Nicaragua v. Honduras), Certain Phosphate Lands in Nauru (Nauru v. Australia), Aerial Incident of 3 July 1988 (Iran v. USA), Maritime Delimitation between Guinea-Bissau and Senegal (Guinea-Bissau v. Senegal), Passage through the Great Belt (Finland v. Denmark), Vienna Convention on Consular Relations (Paraguay v. United States of America), Armed Activities on the Territory of the Congo (Democratic Republic of the Congo v. Rwanda), Armed Activities on the Territory of the Congo (Democratic Republic of the Congo v. Burundi), Interpretation and Application of the 1971 Montreal Convention (Libya v. USA), Interpretation and Application of the 1971 Montreal Convention (Libya v. UK).

[12] Land and Maritime Boundary between Cameroon and Nigeria (Cameroon v. Nigeria), Judgment of 10 October 2002; Sovereignty over Pulau Litigan and Pulau Sipadan (Indonesia/Malaysia), Judgment of 17 December 2002. In view of the parties' first positive reactions to the latter, it appears unlikely that any problems will arise in this regard, see the statements by the respective ministers of foreign affairs, http://www.indonesianembassy.org.uk/nnv_2002_12_17b.html; http://www.snni.org/cgi-bin/snni2/list_item.cgi?archives/2002_12_20/malaysia/ma2012_6.txt; see further "Malaysia gets disputed islands," BBC News, http://news.bbc.co.uk/1/hi/world/asia-pacific/2583457.stm; for details of the judgment, see *Colson*, 97 AJIL (2003), at 398–406.

[13] As will be explained, pending proceedings on the assessment of compensation were discontinued in the cases of US Diplomatic and Consular Staff in Tehran and Military and Paramilitary Activities in and against Nicaragua, see infra B XIV 5 and XVIII 7.

[14] Gabčíkovo–Nagymaros (Hungary/Slovakia).

From the remaining 36 cases with a judgment on the merits, 6 cases are nevertheless irrelevant from the perspective of compliance. In these decisions, the applicant's claim was rejected with no positive statement beyond that rejection that could possibly imply a duty of acceptance and implementation.[15] The remaining 30 cases suitable for analysis can be reduced to 27 by treating parallel cases relating to the same dispute as one case. Table 3.2 lists the cases to be analyzed, indicating the time frame from the introduction of the proceedings to their termination.[16] The order of the cases is based upon the date of application.

The cases in this study include judgments that explicitly required implementing action; judgments of a declaratory nature that indirectly restate obligations; and judgments in which the apparent duty of the parties is no more than to acquiesce to the ruling, as the precise scope of obligations can often not be determined without further analysis.[17]

IV. Compliance with provisional measures

By their very nature, provisional measures, as measures that "ought to be taken," are measures requiring some response by the parties.[18] Therefore, all cases in which the Court *indicated* provisional measures are relevant for the purposes of this study, except for 1 case where the order was delivered so shortly before the completion of this study that compliance cannot yet be

---

[15] In South West Africa and the Barcelona Traction, the claims were rejected because of a lack of *locus standi* on part of the applicants; in the Fisheries case (United Kingdom v. Norway), the Application of the Convention of 1902 Governing the Guardianship of Infants (Netherlands v. Sweden), and the Elettronica Sicula S. p. A. (ELSI) case (United States of America v. Italy), the applicant lost on the basis of the substantive law. On the other hand, the case concerning the appeal relating to the jurisdiction of the ICAO Council will be examined because the Court did not only make a negative statement rejecting the applicant's claim but also a positive statement in confirming the validity of the decision of the ICAO Council. In the Oil Platforms (Iran v. United States of America) case, the Court did not uphold the parties' claims and counterclaims relating to alleged violations of Article X(1) of the Treaty of Amity, Economic Relations and Consular Rights and reparation. Its statement, equally included in the operative part of the decision, that the US actions could not be justified under Article XX(1)(d) of that Treaty did not trigger an obligation of compliance because the Court ultimately did not found a breach of the obligation which the basis of jurisdiction allowed it to examine, see Judgment of Judgment of 6 December 2003 (Merits).

[16] This does not rule out, of course, that some of the excluded cases might be referred to in the discussion. The table of cases was exclusively made for the purposes of showing which cases will be analyzed from the perspective of compliance with judgments.

[17] For a slightly different approach to the question which decisions are relevant from the perspective of compliance, see *Guillaume* in Jasentuliyana, Perspectives on international law, at 277–8, who makes the distinction on the basis whether judgments have to be carried out, or whether the parties are required "only to comply with them". In the latter case, he regards them as self-enforcing and unproblematic. This is a narrower understanding than the one adopted for the present study.

[18] See on the obligation under Article 94(1) for provisional measures *supra* Chapter 2 D II.

Table 3.2. Compliance with judgments: list of cases relevant for this study

- Corfu Channel (United Kingdom v. Albania) (1947–9)
- Asylum (Colombia/Peru) (1949–1950) and Haya de la Torre (Colombia v. Peru) (1950–1)
- Rights of Nationals of the USA in Morocco (France v. USA) (1950–2)
- Ambatielos (Greece v. United Kingdom) (1951–3)
- Minquiers and Ecrehos (France/United Kingdom) (1951–3)
- Right of Passage over Indian Territory (Portugal v. India) (1955–60)
- Sovereignty over Certain Frontier Land (Belgium/Netherlands) (1957–9)
- Arbitral Award made by the King of Spain in 1906 (Honduras v. Nicaragua) (1958–60)
- Temple of Preah Vihear (Cambodia v. Thailand) (1959–62)
- North Sea Continental Shelf (FRG/Denmark; FRG/Netherlands) (1967–9)
- Appeal relating to the jurisdiction of the ICAO Council (India v. Pakistan) (1971–2)
- Fisheries Jurisdiction (United Kingdom v. Iceland) and Fisheries Jurisdiction (FRG v. Iceland) (1972–4)
- Continental Shelf (Tunisia/Libya) (1978–82) and Application for Revision and Interpretation of the Judgment of 24 February 1982 Tunisia–Libya (1984–5)
- United States Diplomatic and Consular Staff in Tehran (USA v. Iran) (1979–81)
- Delimitation of the Maritime Boundary in the Gulf of Maine Area (Canada/USA) (1981–4)
- Continental Shelf (Libya/Malta) (1982–5)
- Frontier Dispute (Burkina Faso/Mali) (1983–6)
- Military and Paramilitary Activities in and against Nicaragua (Nicaragua v. USA) (1984–91)
- Land, Island and Maritime Frontier Dispute (El Salvador/Honduras) (1986–92)
- Maritime Delimitation in the Area between Greenland and Jan Mayen (Denmark v. Norway) (1988–93)
- Arbitral Award of 31 July 1989 (Guinea-Bissau v. Senegal) (1989–91)
- Territorial Dispute (Libya/Chad) (1990–4)
- Maritime Delimitation and Territorial Questions between Qatar and Bahrain (Qatar v. Bahrain) (1991–2001)
- Gabčíkovo–Nagymaros (Hungary/Slovakia) (1994–present)
- Kasikili/Sedudu Island (Botswana/Namibia) (1996–9)
- LaGrand (Germany v. USA) (1999–2001)
- Arrest Warrant of 11 April 2000 (2000–2)

assessed.[19] There are a total of 37 decisions on interim protection in 34 cases. In 14 cases, the Court indicated provisional measures, with 3 cases giving rise to 2 orders each. In 20 cases, requests for provisional measures were rejected. Taking into consideration the fact that basically identical decisions were taken in parallel cases—as, for example, in connection with 2 applicants challenging the same behavior by the respondent[20]—and counting such cases as 1 case only, there are 9 cases in which interim protection was rejected by the Court. This study will consider compliance in the remaining 11 cases in which the Court granted measures. Table 3.3 presents the decisions in chronological order based on the date of the request for provisional measures.[21]

B. COMPLIANCE WITH JUDGMENTS

I. The Corfu Channel case

For a long time, legal scholars could cite the Corfu Channel case[22] as the only instance of non-compliance with an ICJ judgment. The case was eventually settled through a memorandum of understanding reached in 1992 and implemented in 1996, forty-seven years after the original judgment.

1. Background and proceedings before the Court

On 22 October 1946, two British destroyers struck mines in the Corfu Channel, resulting in serious loss of life and damage to the vessels, for which the UK government held Albania responsible. Over the protests of Albanian authorities, the British conducted mine-sweeping operations in the channel on 12 and 13 November 1946 and discovered twenty-two that had been laid only shortly before the incident of 22 October.[23] The UK

---

[19] Avena and other Mexican nationals, Order of 5 February 2003, in which the Court asked the United States to take all necessary measures to ensure that three Mexican nationals on death row in the US were not executed pending the proceedings.

[20] Of course, the role as "applicant" or "respondent" of provisional measures is not necessarily identical to the role the respective party has in the main proceedings, although regularly the requests for provisional measures came from the party that had instituted the proceedings.

[21] All the listed decisions on interim protection were made in the form of separate orders, with the exception of the 1995 Request for an examination of the situation, where the request for interim protection was part of the order dismissing New Zealand's application and closing the proceedings. In the LaGrand case, the Court indicated provisional measures *proprio motu*, although in response to a request from Germany. Cases where requests were made, but where no Court decision followed (due to a withdrawal or discontinuance), are not listed.

[22] For details of the three judgments in the case and the background, see *Bernhardt* in EPIL I, at 831–3; *Jully*, 48 F-W (1948); *Jully*, 49 F-W (1949); Verzijl, *Jurisprudence of the World Court II*, at 3–6, 22–36.

[23] For the facts, see Judgment of 9 April 1949, at 12–15.

Table 3.3. Decisions on requests for interim protection (in chronological order by date of decision)

Request for interim protection granted	Request for interim protection rejected
Anglo-Iranian Oil Company (1951) Fisheries Jurisdiction (United Kingdom v. Iceland), Fisheries Jurisdiction (Federal Republic of Germany v. Iceland)—(two cases, two orders in each (1972, 1973))	Interhandel (1957)
Nuclear tests (Australia v. France), Nuclear Tests (New Zealand v. France)—(two cases, one order in each (1973)) US Diplomatic and Consular Staff in Tehran (1979) Military and Paramilitary Activities in and against Nicaragua (1984) Frontier Dispute (1986)	Aegean Sea Continental Shelf (1976)
	Arbitral Award of 31 July 1989 (1990) Passage through the Great Belt (1991)
Application of the Convention on the Prevention and Punishment of the Crime of Genocide—two orders (1993) (partially acceding to Bosnia's requests while rejecting Yugoslavia's parallel ones)	Questions of Interpretation and Application of the 1971 Montreal Convention arising from the Aerial Incident at Lockerbie (two cases—one order in each) (1992)
Land and Maritime Boundary between Cameroon and Nigeria (1996)	Request for an examination of the situation (1995)
Case concerning the Vienna Convention on Consular Relations (1998)	Use of force (ten cases—ten orders) (1999)
LaGrand (1999) Armed activities on the territory of the Congo (Democratic Republic of the Congo v. Uganda) (2000)	Arrest warrant of 11 April 2000 (2000) Armed activities on the territory of the Congo (New application 2002; Democratic Republic of the Congo v. Rwanda) (2002)
Avena and other Mexican nationals (2003)	Certain criminal proceedings in France (2003)

subsequently demanded compensation for the damage and loss of life, while Albania questioned the lawfulness of the mine-sweeping operations. The dispute was discussed in the UN Security Council with the participation of Albania (in accordance with Article 32 of the UN Charter), but could not be settled.[24] In its resolution of 9 April 1947,[25] the Security Council advised the parties to submit their dispute to the ICJ.

The UK seized the Court by its unilateral application of 22 May 1947, in which it maintained that Albania had violated international law by failing to notify the presence of mines in the straits and that it was therefore responsible for the loss and injury caused by the incident.[26] The UK based the Court's jurisdiction on the Security Council resolution, arguing that this resolution was binding upon Albania pursuant to Article 25 of the Charter, a provision to which Albania had consented in accepting the Council's invitation under Article 32 of the Charter.[27] Albania protested against the unilateral action of the UK in a diplomatic note on 2 July 1947, but affirmed its willingness to appear before the Court. At the same time, it emphasized that its acceptance of the Court's jurisdiction for that case should not be construed as constituting a precedent for the future.[28]

In an abrupt about-face, Albania filed a preliminary objection challenging the Court's jurisdiction on 9 December 1947.[29] Relying on the acceptance of its jurisdiction as expressed in Albania's diplomatic note, the Court dismissed the objection in its judgment of 25 March 1948[30] and saw no need to consider additional British arguments relating to compulsory jurisdiction.[31] Shortly before the delivery of this judgment, the two parties had concluded a special agreement which defined the questions to be decided by the Court and provided a clear consensual basis for the Court's jurisdiction. Accordingly, the proceedings would have continued even if Albania's preliminary objection had been upheld.[32]

---

[24] Documents and records of the Security Council relating to the dispute are collected in Annex 23 of the Memorial of the United Kingdom, ICJ Pleadings, Corfu Channel, Vol. I, at 174–397.

[25] Resolution 22 (1947) of 9 April 1947, S/324. The resolution is also reprinted in Judgment of 25 March 1948, at 17. The relevant text reads: "The Security Council having considered statements of representatives of the United Kingdom and Albania concerning a dispute between the United Kingdom and Albania arising out of an incident on 22nd October, 1946 [...] recommends that the United Kingdom and Albanian Governments should immediately refer the dispute to the International Court of Justice in accordance with the provisions of the Statute of the Court."

[26] Letter from the UK Agent to the Registrar, ICJ Pleadings, Corfu Channel, Vol. I, 8–17.

[27] UK Application, ICJ Pleadings, Corfu Channel, Vol. I, at 8–9.

[28] Le ministre adjoint aux affaires étrangères d'Albanie au greffier, ICJ Pleadings, Corfu Channel, Vol. V, 136–8; also reprinted in the Judgment of 25 March 1948, at 18–19.

[29] Exception préliminaire du gouvernement albanais, ICJ Pleadings, Corfu Channel, Vol. II, 9–13.

[30] Judgment of 25 March 1948, at 29. The decision was taken by 15 votes to 1, with the only negative vote coming the judge *ad hoc* who was appointed by Albania.

[31] Ibid., at 26. It is highly doubtful that the UK arguments on compulsory jurisdiction would have been accepted.

[32] Special agreement concluded on 25 March 1948, ICJ Pleadings, Corfu Channel, Vol. II, 29. The agreement's text makes it clear that it precedes the delivery of the judgment and was designed to provide a basis for jurisdiction irrespective of the outcome of the case: "The parties agree that the present Special Agreement shall be notified to the International Court of Justice immediately after the delivery on the 25th March of its judgment on the question of jurisdiction."

Apart from the questions already raised by the UK application of 22 May 1947, the Court was asked to decide whether the UK had violated international law by traversing Albanian waters and by conducting the minesweeping operations and whether it was under a duty to give satisfaction. The special agreement thereby extended the scope of the Court's inquiry, taking into account Albania's grievances and allowing the Court to carry out a comprehensive assessment of their differences. Uncertainty about the Court's decision on the preliminary objection might have motivated both sides to conclude the special agreement. For the UK, the agreement guaranteed a continuation of the proceedings; for Albania, the agreement enabled it to shape the terms of references and to make sure its own grievances would be addressed. The agreement contained no reference to the post-adjudicative phase, however.

Since the Security Council had recommended the submission of the dispute to the ICJ and Albania had given its consent, Albania could be a party in proceedings before the Court pursuant to Article 35(2) of the Statute, although it was not a party to the Statute and had not deposited a declaration under Security Council Resolution 9 (1946).[33] By consenting to the proceedings, Albania had also accepted the obligation under Article 94(1) of the Charter to comply with the judgment of the Court.[34]

2. The judgments of 1949

In its judgment of 9 April 1949, the ICJ ruled that Albania had incurred international responsibility for the incident of 22 October 1946 and was obliged to pay compensation, and that the Court had jurisdiction to assess the amount of compensation due.[35] Since the amount of compensation could not be assessed without additional inquiry, it reserved this issue for further proceedings.[36] With regard to the passage of UK warships, the Court held that the acts of the British navy on 22 October 1946 in Albanian waters did not infringe upon Albania's sovereignty, since the warships in question had been entitled to pass through those waters based on the right to innocent passage through straits used for international navigation.[37] On the other hand, the Court decided that the mine sweep had violated Albania's sovereignty and that this declaration alone constituted appropriate satisfaction.[38] Hence, the judgment required no implementation on the part of Britain.

[33] For details on Article 35 of the Statute, see Rosenne, *Law and Practice II*, at 605–55.

[34] Rosenne, *Law and Practice II*, at 636–7; and Order of 31 July 1947, at 5.

[35] Judgment of 9 April 1949, at 32–6. That decision was taken by 11 votes to 5. The responsibility of Albania was determined by 11 votes to 5, the postponement of the assessment of damages by 10 votes to 6.

[36] Ibid., at 23–6, 36. The decision was taken by 10 votes to 6.

[37] Ibid., at 28–32, 36. That decision was taken by 14 votes to 2.

[38] Ibid., at 32–6. That decision was taken unanimously.

Albania refused to participate in the proceedings on compensation, arguing that the special agreement did not confer jurisdiction upon the Court to assess the precise amount due[39]—an argument that the Court had preemptively rejected in its judgment of 9 April 1949.[40] Albania's self-judging behavior ran afoul of Article 36(6) of the ICJ Statute, pursuant to which jurisdictional disputes are settled by the decision of the Court. The proceedings could continue despite the non-appearance, as Article 53 of the ICJ Statute allows the Court to rule in such cases after verifying that it has jurisdiction and that the claim is well founded in fact and in law. Albania suggested an out-of-court settlement, but refused to discuss any British claims apart from pensions and loss of life, an offer the UK rejected.[41]

On 15 December 1949, the ICJ delivered its assessment and ordered Albania to pay £843,947 to the United Kingdom,[42] precisely the sum claimed by the UK.[43] Although the amount may not seem high, it represented a substantial burden for Albania, where political turmoil and lack of access to sterling currency combined to create weak economic conditions.[44]

3. Albania's response: non-compliance

In response to Albania's failure to pay the compensation due, the UK considered recourse to the Security Council, but dismissed that option because of the high probability of a Soviet veto.[45] There were no Albanian assets in British territory from which satisfaction could have been sought.[46] Discussions started between the two countries on how the compensation was

[39] Judgment of 15 December 1949, at 246–8.

[40] Judgment of 9 April 1949, at 23–26. The Court found that the first question in the special agreement (on the evaluation of Albania's behavior) comprised two parts: one concerning the responsibility of Albania; the other, the existence of a duty to pay compensation. In the Court's view, this second part would be superfluous if understood as a request for a mere declaration that compensation was due. The Court's finding was based on the text of the special agreement and on its connection with the unilateral British application that had included a claim for the assessment of compensation. The special agreement did not show an intention to limit the British claims; moreover, the Court assumed that the parties strived for a comprehensive settlement, which required a finding on compensation.

[41] Gray, *Much fine gold*, at 21; see also ICJ Pleadings, Corfu Channel, Vol. IV, 706 (without details on the settlement proposals by the Albanian side).

[42] Judgment of 15 December 1949, at 250. It was a decision made by 12 votes to 2. The Court refused to deal with the issue of jurisdiction again, holding at 248 that it had decided this question with force of *res judicata* in its judgment of 9 April 1949.

[43] See ibid., at 247. Prior to the first judgment on the merits, it had claimed £875,000: Judgment of 9 April 1949, at 23.

[44] Gardiner, *The Eagle spreads his claws*, at 235–46 (1966).

[45] Gray, *Much fine gold*, at 21. The Soviet Union had previously expressed little sympathy for the UK complaint relating to the incident of 22 October 1946 and had abstained from the resolution recommending the submission of the dispute to the ICJ. See Statement of the USSR representative Gromyko in the Security Council, 127th meeting of 9 April 1947, S/PV.127, at 723–6, 727.

[46] *Anand*, 26 U. Pitt. LR (1965), at 676; *Schachter*, 54 AJIL (1960), at 8.

to be paid. UK officials balked at a final settlement offer of £20,000 (later increased to £40,000), and negotiations broke down in January 1951.[47] The non-compliance continued to complicate Albanian–British relations for decades.[48] Furthermore, Albania appeared to have violated the spirit of the judgment in its refusal until 1958 to acknowledge its duty to grant innocent passage through the Corfu Channel.[49] All in all, however, it seems that the right of passage through the straits was respected, despite the Albanian rhetoric.

The UK, denied compensation, engaged in an attempt at self-help,[50] which was to give rise to yet another case before the Court.[51] It tried to satisfy its claims out of gold reserves that originally had belonged to the National Bank of Albania and that the Nazis had brought from Rome to Berlin in 1943. The French, British, and US governments had pooled these reserves with the monetary gold found in Germany at the end of the war and brought it under the administration of the Tripartite Commission for the Restitution of Monetary Gold.[52] According to an arbitrator's decision, the gold was Albanian property and its value was sufficient to cover Albania's financial obligations under the judgment.[53]

Italy also had claims against Albania for which it demanded the gold and filed an application against the Western allies before the Court, in which it argued that its claim to the Albanian gold was superior to the British claim

[47] Gray, *Much fine gold*, at 27–8.

[48] Rosenne, *Law and Practice I*, at 241–2. He notes at 242 fn. 72 that as late as 1981, the British government resisted establishing diplomatic ties with Albania due in part to the issue of non-payment. Another commentator observed: "[I]f the trouble and discussion, the bitterness and spite and gradual descent into farce of the Corfu Channel case could have been foreseen when the International Court of Justice pronounced Albania guilty of the mining [. . .], then it is possible that a Foreign Secretary would have declared publicly that his Government was satisfied, and would not press for payment of a sum which meant little to it, but much to its adversary." (Gardiner, *The Eagle spreads his claws*, at 249.)

[49] Gardiner, *The Eagle spreads his claws*, at 243–4, 272–3. There was no actual non-compliance under Article 94(1) of the Charter because the right of passage was not included in the operative part of the judgment, although the operative part did allude to that right. Moreover, the judgment is just binding inter partes; third parties could not petition the Court to compel compliance.

[50] For details, see *Schachter*, 54 AJIL (1960), at 8–12.

[51] Monetary gold removed from Rome in 1943 (Italy v. France, United Kingdom of Great Britain and Northern Ireland and United States of America), Preliminary Question, Judgment of 15 June 1954.

[52] This Commission was established between France, the United States, and the United Kingdom in September 1946 on the basis of the Paris Agreement on Reparation, 14 January 1946, reprinted in 40 AJIL Supplement 117 (1946). The agreement provided that the monetary gold looted by Nazi Germany from banks in occupied Europe was to be pooled for distribution among the entitled countries (ibid., part III). The task of the Commission was to adjudicate and execute claims against this gold pool. See Judgment of 15 June 1954, *supra* n. 51, at 25–6; US Department of State, Tripartite Gold Commission, 24 February 1997, www.state.gov/www/regions/eur/tripartite_gold_commission.html. For further details, see also *Wühler*, EPIL III, at 445–6.

[53] Gardiner, *The Eagle spreads his claws*, at 247.

and that Italy should be entitled to retrieve it. The ICJ held in its judgment of 15 June 1954[54] that it could not address the merits of the case in the absence of Albania's consent to the proceedings, since Albania's legal interests would form the very subject-matter of the decision. After that judgment, the gold therefore continued to be held by the Bank of England in the name of the Tripartite Commission, given the lack of an agreement on whether and how the gold should be divided.[55]

The UK was unwilling to write off Albania's debts despite the low probability that Albania would eventually pay.[56] This position was taken as a matter of principle, so as not to set an undesirable precedent undermining the Court's authority.[57] New efforts were launched in 1980 to settle the dispute and to tie a payment of the awarded sum to a restitution of the gold reserves, whose value had in the meantime increased to thirteen times the amount of the Corfu award. On the other hand, interest on the original damages would also have justified a substantially higher claim, but the UK regarded the issue of interest as negotiable, as the settlement might otherwise become more difficult since the US insisted on the settlement of its claims as well. Albania continued a hard-line approach in public fora, although unofficially Albanian diplomats expressed the hope for improved relations with the UK.[58]

Discussions between the Albanian and British governments started in April 1985—the first direct contact between the two governments since 1951. Still, Albania found the linkage between a return of the gold and payment of British and in particular American damages hard to digest. The negotiations reached a stalemate in October 1988 after Albania had refused to accept simultaneity of payment and gold restoration as a precondition with regard to the US claims.[59]

4. The settlement

The revolutions in Central and Eastern Europe paved the way for a final settlement. Reacting to the events in other communist countries, Albania adopted a more conciliatory tone in an effort to improve relations with the West even before the collapse of its own communist regime. A new round of talks started in November 1990 and diplomatic relations between the UK and Albania were restored in May 1991.[60]

---

[54] Judgment of 15 June 1954, *supra* n. 51. For details on the judgment, see *Johnson*, 4 ICLQ (1955), at 93–115; *Oliver*, 49 AJIL (1955) at 216–21; and *Wühler* in EPIL III, at 446–7.
[55] Between 1953 and 1979, British officials had greater difficulty handling the Italian claims. Several options were discussed, including turning all the gold over to the UK or splitting it, either between the UK and Italy; between these two countries and Albania; or between all three and the US, see Gray, *Much fine gold*, at 33–42. See also *Wühler* in EPIL III, at 445–7; Rosenne, *Law and Practice I*, 242–8; *Goy*, 41 AFDI (1995), at 385–9.
[56] Gardiner, *The Eagle spreads his claws*, at 277.   [57] Gray, *Much fine gold*, at 46.
[58] Ibid., at 46–53 (for the period between 1980 and 1984).   [59] Ibid., at 45–63.
[60] Ibid., at 64–74.

A solution was finally brokered after Albania's communists fell from power. In a joint statement of 8 May 1992, both sides expressed their regret at the Corfu Channel incident. A memorandum of understanding provided that Albania would pay $2,000,000 in exchange for the UK's approval for the transfer of the 1574 kilograms of gold kept by the Tripartite Commission to Albania; the UK affirmed that its financial claims were to be settled once Albania had paid the full amount.[61] The sum had been set taking into account the original ICJ award, the length of time elapsed, and Albania's weak economic position.[62] Since the decision to return the gold reserves required the consent of the Tripartite Commission, the settlement could not be completed without the approval of the two other Member States of the Commission.[63] The US and France concluded agreements with Albania with regard to their outstanding claims on 10 March 1995 and 22 February 1996, respectively.[64] Finally, on 29 October 1996, a meeting of the Tripartite Commission and Albania took place, and the gold allocated to Albania was transferred after Albania had given irrevocable instructions to the US Federal Reserve to pay $4,000,000 to the American and British governments as agreed.[65] A spokesman of the British Foreign Office stated simply: "The matters remaining in dispute between the UK and Albania have now been settled."[66] A long period of non-compliance with the judgment of the Court had thus come to an end.

5. Conclusion

In this case, there was a long period of non-compliance despite several encouraging factors for successful implementation: the presence of a special agreement (the problem being the extent of commitment assumed therein), the clarity of the applicable law (Albania's opposition in the aftermath had not related to the finding of responsibility, but rather to the jurisdiction for the assessment), and the precise determination of damages. Admittedly, Albania found itself in a precarious financial situation, yet it could not earnestly maintain that it was unable to fulfill its duty to pay given the monetary gold, all the more since it could have made a serious attempt at

---

[61] The joint statement and the memorandum of understanding are reprinted at Marston, 63 BYIL (1992), at 781–2 (1994).

[62] Gray, *Much fine gold*, at 74.

[63] Ibid., at 74–6; Rosenne, *World Court*, 248.

[64] Agreement between the US and Albania on the settlement of certain outstanding claims, 34 ILM (1995) 597; Accord relatif au règlement de la question de l'Or monétaire (France–Albania), 100 RGDIP (1996) 898. See also *Goy*, 41 AFDI (1995), at 390–1.

[65] Gray, *Much fine gold*, at 76; and US Department of State, Tripartite Gold Commission, 24 February 1997, *supra* n. 52.

[66] See e.g. Albania and the Tripartite Gold Commission Meeting, 29 October 1996; M2 Presswire, 31 October 1996; and Documents to return gold to Albania signed, Albanian Telegraphic Agency, 30 October 1996, http://www.hri.org/news/balkans/ata/1996/96-10-31.ata.html.

least at *discussing* the implementation of the judgment at an earlier time. However, after the judgment of 9 April 1949, Albania charted a course of fundamental opposition to the Court to whose involvement it had consented, and its non-appearance surely did not bode well for the prospects of compliance. Since it ignored the Court's ruling relating to the jurisdiction to assess damages, there was reason to assume that the decision on the merits of assessment would also be disregarded.

The case revealed the limitations of the enforcement system of ICJ judgments. The likelihood of a Soviet veto stymied enforcement by the Security Council. Self-help was not possible given the lack of Albanian assets in British territory. The UK was also hindered by the fact that it could not unilaterally dispose of the monetary gold, but only in cooperation with other states whose claims equally had to be satisfied.

The judgment was complied with in the end. Important political developments made a settlement possible. Albania's break with China at the end of the 1970s made the UK and the US more susceptible to compromise, as it allayed Western fears of a growing Soviet influence. Moreover, political change in Central and Eastern Europe from 1989 onwards, followed by the collapse of Albania's own communist regime and the country's increasing desire to relieve its domestic economic crisis and improve the relations with the West, caused the British Treasury to adopt a more accommodating position as to the sum to be paid.[67]

II. Asylum/Haya de la Torre

The case concerning the diplomatic asylum granted to the Peruvian national Víctor Raúl Haya de la Torre in the Colombian embassy in Lima gave rise to no less than three judgments by the International Court of Justice.[68] Due to difficulties in the implementation of the Court's rulings, nearly two years and

[67] Gray, *Much fine gold*, at 77–9.
[68] Asylum case (Colombia v. Peru), Judgment of 20 November 1950; Request for interpretation of the judgment of November 20th, in the Asylum case (Colombia v. Peru), Judgment of 27 November 1950; Haya de la Torre case (Colombia v. Peru), Judgment of 13 June 1951 (in this section hereinafter cited without reference to the titles).
For a discussion of these decisions, see *Evans*, 45 AJIL (1951), at 755–62; *idem*, 46 Am. Pol. Sci. R (1952), at 142–57; *Gonidec*, 55 RGDIP (1951), at 547–92; *Hudson*, 46 AJIL (1952), at 8–12; *Jully*, 51 F-W (1951), at 20–58; *Van Essen*, 1 ICLQ (1952), at 533–9; and Verzijl, *Jurisprudence of the World Court II*, at 81–99. On the first judgment, see *Barcía Trelles*, 3 REspDI (1950), at 753–801; Conte, *El derecho de asilo y el caso Haya de la Torre*, at 39–57; Planas-Suárez, *El asilo diplomático*, at 43–93; Ursúa, *El asilo diplomático*. For some representative Latin American perspectives, see Fernandes, *El asilo diplomático*, at 127–57; Luque Angel, *El derecho de asilo*, 203–62, 273–96; Moreno Quintana, *Derecho de asilo*, at 67–78; Urrutia-Aparicio, *Diplomatic asylum in Latin America*, at 71–100; Zárate, *El asilo en el derecho internacional americano*, at 155–312.

ten months elapsed between the delivery of the last judgment and the termination of the asylum.

1. Background of the proceedings

Haya de la Torre was the leader of the Peruvian party *Alianza Popular Revolucionaria Americana* (American People's Revolutionary Alliance, hereinafter APRA). Peruvian authorities had banned the party on 4 October 1948 on charges that it had organized an unsuccessful military rebellion that had taken place the previous day. Criminal proceedings were opened against party members, including Haya de la Torre, who emerged from hiding on 3 January 1949, at which time he obtained asylum at the Colombian embassy in Lima. Colombia informed Peru that it had granted this asylum in accordance with the 1928 Havana Convention on Asylum.[69] Having qualified Haya de la Torre as a political refugee pursuant to the 1933 Montevideo Convention,[70] it demanded safe conduct for him to leave the country.[71] Although Peru had granted such permission with regard to other APRA members who had sought asylum in other embassies,[72] it refused to do so for Haya de la Torre and contested the legality of his asylum.

The two countries agreed to submit the case to the International Court of Justice in the Act of Lima, a joint declaration signed on 31 August 1949.[73] Thereby, they demonstrated their common understanding that the ICJ was an appropriate forum to settle their dispute. The precise question to be presented to the Court remained undefined, however, since the parties could not agree on the terms of reference. The specific subject-matter of the proceedings was thus not determined by the Act of Lima, but was left for the parties' submissions to the Court. Accordingly, the proceedings were not to be introduced by the notification of the Act, but by unilateral application.[74]

---

[69] Convention fixing the rules to be observed for the granting of asylum, 20 February 1928, 132 LNTS 323.

[70] Convention on Political Asylum, 26 December 1933, reprinted in 28 AJIL 70 (Supplement, 1934). Article 2 reads: "The judgment of political delinquency concerns the state which offers asylum," which Colombia took as basis for a right for the state granting asylum unilaterally to qualify the nature of the crime. Peru had not ratified the Montevideo Convention, however. Judgment of 20 November 1950, at 276–8.

[71] Judgment of 20 November 1950, at 272–3.

[72] *Anand*, 26 U. Pitt. LR (1965), at 679, fn. 36; Memorial of Colombia, ICJ Pleadings, Asylum, Vol. 1, 13, at 40–1.

[73] The Act of Lima is reprinted in Judgment of 20 November 1950, at 267–8.

[74] In the Act, the parties declared first, that each approved referring the matter for a decision to the ICJ, in accordance with the agreement concluded by the two governments; and second, that, as they had been unable to reach consensus on the terms for a joint referral, proceedings could be instituted by unilateral application by either of them. Each party agreed that a unilateral application by the other party would not be regarded as without this being regarded as an unfriendly act toward the other, or as an act likely to affect the good relations between the two countries. See Judgment of 20 November 1950, at 268.

Technically, the Act constituted a framework agreement[75] rather than a special agreement,[76] although it might have served as a basis for the Court's jurisdiction. The Act made no mention of the post-adjudicative phase.[77]

On 15 October 1949, Colombia filed an application instituting proceedings against Peru, asserting Article 7 of the 1934 Protocol of Friendship and Co-operation[78] as a jurisdictional basis while at the same time making reference to the Act of Lima.[79] The application asked the Court to declare that Colombia, as the country granting asylum, was competent to determine the nature of the offense for the purposes of that asylum and that Peru was to give the necessary guarantees for the refugee's safe departure. Peru countered by requesting a finding that the grant of asylum violated Articles 1(1) and 2(2) item 1, first indent[80] of the Havana Convention, and that in any case the maintenance of the asylum itself constituted a further breach of the treaty. Article 1(2) of the Havana Convention provides a right for the local government to request the surrender of a common criminal;[81] yet the Peruvian submission did not explicitly ask the Court to decide whether Colombia was under the obligation to turn over the fugitive.[82]

---

[75] Rosenne, *World Court*, at 164.

[76] See Rosenne, *Law and Practice II*, 663–4: a special agreement in the sense of the Statute and the Rules of Court is an agreement conferring jurisdiction in a concrete case and which is formally notified to the Court and thereby produces the effect of the introduction of the proceedings. Some commentators nevertheless call the Act of Lima a *compromis*, although technically it was none. See e.g. Urrutia-Aparicio, *Diplomatic asylum in Latin America*, at 76–7. See *infra* Chapter 4 A IV.

[77] Ibid. The only provision with any practical effect was the stipulation that the case be conducted in French. As for the rest, the agreement declares the ordinary procedure applicable and stresses the parties' right to appoint a judge *ad hoc*, not adding anything to the normal course of proceedings.

[78] Protocol of Friendship and Co-operation between Colombia and Peru of 24 May 1934, 164 LNTS 21.

[79] Application instituting proceedings of 15 October 1949, ICJ Pleadings, Asylum, Vol. 1, 8–11. The reference to the Act of Lima was made in the following manner: Colombia stated that the two governments had in vain tried to set up a special agreement and had agreed in the Act of Lima that each party could bring the case unilaterally (at 10). It added "For some aspects of the procedure, the attention of the Court is called to the provisions of the Act (*Acta*) of August 31st, 1949, which has been duly notified to the Court." (at 11).

[80] Article 1(1) reads: "It is not permissible for States to grant asylum in legations, warships, military camps or military aircraft, to persons accused or condemned for common crimes, or to deserters from the army or navy." Article 2(2) item 1, first incise reads: "Asylum may not be granted except in urgent cases and for the period of time strictly indispensable for the person who has sought asylum to ensure in some other way his safety." Judgment of 20 November 1950, at 327 and 329.

[81] Article 1(2) reads: "Persons accused of or condemned for common crimes taking refuge in any of the places mentioned in the preceding paragraph, shall be surrendered upon request of the local government." Judgment of 20 November 1950, at 329.

[82] For a summary of the parties' submissions, see Judgment of 20 November 1950, at 270–1.

2. The judgments of 20 and 27 November 1950

In its judgment of 20 November 1950, the Court decided that Peru was not obliged to guarantee safe conduct and that the asylum granted to Haya de la Torre was not in conformity with the Havana Convention.[83] On this latter point, the Court noted that, given that three months had elapsed from the time of the failed coup and the granting of the asylum, no "urgency" existed as required under Article 2(2) of the Convention.[84] Furthermore, while ruling that Colombia did not have a unilateral right to determine in a manner binding on Peru whether Haya de la Torre was a political offender, the Court observed that Peru had failed to present any proof of common crimes. As a result, Haya de la Torre could not be considered a common criminal, and the claimed violation of Article 1(1) of the Havana Convention was rejected.[85] The Court provided no explicit ruling on an obligation to surrender Haya de la Torre, but its finding that he did not qualify as a common criminal implied that Article 1(2) of the Havana Convention could *not* provide a basis for such an obligation in this case.

On the day the Court delivered its ruling, Colombia filed a request for the interpretation of the judgment, asking for clarification on whether compliance with the judgment necessitated the release of Haya de la Torre and whether the Colombian ambassador's determination of Haya de la Torre's eligibility for asylum had been valid.[86] Colombia appeared committed to abide by the judgment, but remained uncertain as to the required response. In its judgment of 27 November 1950, the Court rejected this request as inadmissible on grounds that it concerned issues which had not been addressed in the judgment of 20 November and thus could not be deemed a request for "interpretation,"[87] and that a "dispute" on the scope of the

[83] Judgment of 20 November 1950, at 288. Both parties appointed judges *ad hoc*: Colombia selected José Joaquín Caicedo Castilla; Peru, Luis Alayza y Paz Soldán. Ibid., at 269. The decision on safe conduct was taken by 15 votes to 1; the decision on Article 2(2), by 10 votes to 6. Colombia's Judge *ad hoc* Caicedo Castilla dissented on both points. See ibid., Diss. Op. Caicedo Castilla, at 359, 372–4 and 374–81. It is interesting to note that the Court did not follow the Peruvian request to order that Colombia had *violated* the Havana Convention, instead of using the more cautious formula that the grant of asylum "was not made in conformity with Article 2, paragraph 2" of the Havana Convention.

[84] Judgment of 20 November 1950, at 282–3. The Court emphasized the criterion of urgency: "It is certainly the most important of [the conditions of Article 2 paragraph 2 of the Havana Convention], the essential justification for asylum being in the imminence or persistance of a danger for the person of the refugee." Ibid., at 282.

[85] Judgment of 20 November 1950, at 273–8, 281–2, and 288. The decision on the unilateral qualification was reached by 14 votes to 2. See ibid., at 360–72 (with Judge Caicedo Castilla dissenting). The decision on Article 1(1) was made by 15 votes to 1. See ibid., at 288 (dissenting judge not specified). For further details of the judgment, see Jully, 51 F-W (1951/53), at 20–43.

[86] Request for the interpretation of the judgment of November 20th, 1950, ICJ Pleadings, *Asylum*, Vol. 1, 466–9.

[87] The Court explained that the questions of an obligation to surrender, the correctness of the qualification of the offense and the consequences arising therefrom had not been answered in

judgment (as required by Article 60 of the Statute)[88] did not exist. The Court was unambiguous in its reasoning: "In reality, the object of the questions submitted by the Colombian government is to obtain, by the indirect means of interpretation, a decision on questions which the Court was not called upon by the parties to answer."[89] The Court thus implicitly acknowledged that Article 94(1) of the Charter did not require Colombia to surrender Haya de la Torre, regardless of whether such an obligation might derive from other legal principles: since the question of surrender had not been dealt with at all, Peru could not then claim that surrender was required in order to comply with the judgment.

This decision made clear that the Court's ruling of 20 November 1950 was a declaratory judgment on the evaluation of the asylum under the Havana Convention, not one ordering the surrender.[90] Whether Colombia was at this point required by the applicable rules of international law to turn over the fugitive to Peru constituted a separate matter that the Court would take up in due course.

3. The judgment of 13 June 1951

Not surprisingly, as the legal consequences of the judgments remained unclear, they had contributed little to the settlement of the dispute. Peru maintained that compliance with the judgment of 20 November 1950 was contingent upon the release of Haya de la Torre by the Colombian embassy.[91] Colombia responded by arguing that not only had the judgment provided no basis for requiring the surrender, but that in fact it would be in defiance of the judgment, were it to release the accused despite the Court's

the judgment because they had not been submitted by the parties. Judgment of 27 November 1950, at 402–4. The decision was taken by 12 votes to 1, against the vote of Colombia's judge *ad hoc* Caicedo Castilla. Ibid., at 404.

[88] Article 60 of the Statute reads: "The judgment is final and without appeal. In the event of a dispute as to the meaning or scope of the judgment, the Court shall construe it upon the request of any party."

[89] Judgment of 27 November 1950, at 403. For a critical comment, see Verzijl, *Jurisprudence of the World Court II*, 93–5 (arguing that gaps in judgment of 20 November justified Colombia's request because they rendered fulfillment impossible under Article 94(1) of the Charter and because of the judgment's extreme formalism).

[90] See *Van Essen*, 1 ICLQ (1952), at 533.

[91] Note from the Peruvian Minister of Foreign Affairs to the Colombian ambassador in Lima of 28 November 1950, printed in: ICJ Pleadings, Haya de la Torre case, at 12–13, 34–5, 103–4, Note from the Peruvian Minister of Foreign Affairs to the Colombian Minister of Foreign Affairs of 14 December 1950, ibid., 39–45, 109–15. An excerpt from the note of 28 November 1950 is quoted in Judgment of 13 June 1951, at 77–8. For the Spanish originals, see 10 RPDI (1950), at 223–5 and 230–41. See also *Información oficial del gobierno de Perú*, 10 RPDI (1950), at 241–70. The Peruvian perspective found support by Planas-Suárez, *El asilo diplomático*, 91–3.

rejection of Peru's claim that he was a common criminal.[92] This argument, however, was as unconvincing as Peru's argument on the surrender, since the Court had affirmed in the judgment of 27 November 1950 that it had not ruled on the legal consequences on the rejection of Peru's claim of a violation of Article 1(1) of the Havana Convention.[93]

Actually, the controversial questions concerned general international law rather than compliance with the judgment, although in a broader sense the issue was one of the practical consequences of the Court's findings. The parties perceived the dispute as relating to the execution of the judgment: in the new proceedings launched by a unilateral application of Colombia on 13 December 1950,[94] both parties requested in their first submission that the Court state in what manner the judgment of 20 November 1950 was to be executed.[95] Colombia also asked the Court to declare that it was not obliged to surrender Haya de la Torre in execution of the judgment nor under general international law, should the Court not deliver judgment on the first submission.[96] Peru asked the Court to dismiss Colombia's submissions relating to the surrender of Haya de la Torre, and to adjudge, in case it was not to decide on the first decision relating to the execution of the judgment, that the asylum ought to have ceased immediately after the delivery of the judgment of 20 November 1950 and in any event had to cease forthwith.[97]

As basis of jurisdiction, Colombia's application indicated Article 7 of the Protocol of Friendship and Co-operation, just as in its application of 15 October 1949.[98] Peru did not contest the Court's jurisdiction and filed arguments on the merits. Accordingly, the Court concluded that the "conduct of the parties is sufficient to confer jurisdiction on the Court."[99]

On 13 June 1951, the Court delivered its judgment. First, it rejected the request for guidance on how the judgment of 20 November 1950 was to be executed. It understood this request as relating to the termination of the asylum and pointed out that the judgment "confined itself, in this connection, to defining the legal relations which the Havana Convention had established between the parties. It did not give any directions to the Parties, and entails for them only the obligation of compliance therewith."[100] This confirmed the ruling of 27 November 1950, according to which the judgment

---

[92] Note from the Minister of Foreign Affairs of Colombia to the Minister of Foreign Affairs of Peru of 6 December 1950, ICJ Pleadings, Haya de la Torre, 13–16, 35–8, 105–8. For the Spanish original, see 10 RPDI (1950), at 225–30.

[93] With regard to Peru's counterclaim concerning a violation of Article 1(1) of the Havana Convention, the Court determined that the Peruvian government had not proved that Haya de la Torre was accused of common crimes prior to the granting of asylum. Judgment of 27 November 1950, at 402–3.

[94] Application instituting proceedings, ICJ Pleadings, Haya de la Torre, 7–16.

[95] Judgment of 13 June 1951, at 75, 78.   [96] Ibid., at 79.   [97] Ibid., at 75, 80, 82.

[98] See *supra* nn. 78 and 79.   [99] Judgment of 13 June 1951, at 78.

[100] Judgment of 13 June 1951, at 79, 83. This decision was taken unanimously.

of 20 November had merely answered the questions relating to the evaluation of the asylum itself, but had not decided on the legal consequences; therefore, the legal consequences were not a question of execution *per se*. Since the Court was aware of the parties' desire to receive guidance on how the asylum could be terminated, it explained further:

The interrogative form in which [the parties] have formulated their submissions shows that they desire that the Court should make a choice amongst the various courses by which the asylum should be terminated. But these courses are conditioned by facts and by possibilities which, to a large extent, the Parties alone are in a position to appreciate. A choice among them could not be based on legal considerations, but only on considerations of practicability or of political expediency; it is not part of the Court's judicial function to make such a choice.[101]

Hence, the Court regarded the determination of the way in which the asylum would be terminated as one of policy instead of law and beyond its judicial function. Later, it repeated:

[The Court] is unable to give any practical advice as to the various courses which might be followed with a view to terminating the asylum, since, by doing so, it would depart from its judicial function.[102]

Beyond the issue of execution of the judgment, it remained for the Court to decide on an obligation to surrender Haya de la Torre under general international law. In a seemingly contradictory decision, the Court held that while Peru had the right to demand an end to the asylum,[103] Colombia was not obliged to surrender Haya de la Torre to Peru.[104] The Court held that it had not ruled on Peru's right to claim a termination of the asylum in the first judgment,[105] hence it was the third judgment that gave rise to a duty to terminate the asylum as a duty under Article 94(1) of the Charter. The Court

---

[101] Ibid., at 79.   [102] Ibid., at 83.

[103] Ibid., at 82: The Court argued that its decision that the asylum had not been granted in conformity with Article 2, para. 2 of the Havana Convention entailed "a legal consequence, namely that of putting an end to an illegal situation: the Government of Colombia which had granted the asylum irregularly is bound to terminate it." The decision on this point was taken unanimously. Ibid., at 83.

[104] The Court held that whereas the Havana Convention contained an obligation to surrender common criminals (Article 1(2), see *supra* n. 81), no such obligation had been established for persons accused of political offences. This silence could not be interpreted as imposing a similar obligation for cases of asylum granted contrary to Article 2 of the Convention. Instead, in accordance with Latin American tradition, such situations were to be adjusted by decisions inspired by considerations of convenience or political expediency. For the question of surrender, Haya de la Torre was to be treated as a person accused of a political offence, for Peru had not brought evidence for common crimes committed by him, as stated in the judgment of 20 November 1950. Judgment of 13 June 1951, at 80–2. The decision on the obligation to surrender was taken by 13 votes to 1, against the vote of Peru's judge *ad hoc* Alayza y Paz Soldán. Ibid., at 83–4.

[105] Judgment of 13 June 1951, at 79–80. For an opposing view, see Planas-Suárez, *El asilo diplomático*, 91–2 (arguing that the execution of the original judgment clearly required the surrender of the accused).

maintained that these facially incompatible findings could be reconciled with one another: "There is no contradiction between these two findings, since surrender is not the only way of terminating asylum."[106] Was this assessment correct? One might tend to think that there *was* a contradiction if the Court on the one hand stated that even in the case of irregular asylum, one cannot assume a duty actively to assist in the prosecution, and on the other hand highlighted the responsibility of Colombia to terminate the asylum as a consequence of the findings of the judgment of 20 November 1950.[107] Accordingly, Colombia had to take action to terminate the asylum, but was not bound to surrender Haya de la Torre because there was no obligation to render positive assistance in the prosecution.[108] Were there any other ways of terminating the asylum? All other unilateral acts Colombia could reasonably take would either have to be equated to surrender and positive assistance in the prosecution—things it was not obliged to do—or would have resulted in violations of international law.[109]

A closer look at the Court's reasoning reveals what the Court intended: it stated that that the Havana Convention did not impose an obligation to surrender in cases of irregular asylum and that the silence of the Convention on this issue implied "that it was intended to leave the adjustment of the consequences of this situation to decisions inspired by considerations of convenience or of simple political expediency."[110] It concluded that

it can be assumed that the parties, now that their mutual legal relations have been made clear, will be able to find a practical and satisfactory solution by seeking guidance from those considerations of courtesy and good-neighborliness which, in matters of asylum, have always held a prominent place in the relations between the Latin-American republics.[111]

This reference to diplomatic means of dispute settlement makes clear that the Court saw the answer in negotiations. Peru was entitled to have the asylum

---

[106] Judgment of 13 June 1951, at 82.
[107] Ibid., at 82: "This decision [the judgment of 20 November 1950] entails a legal consequence, namely that of putting an end to an illegal situation: the Government of Colombia which has granted the asylum irregularly is bound to terminate it."
[108] Ibid., at 81 (stating that obligation to render assistance to prosecution would exceed Court's findings and would not be recognized without an express provision to that effect in the Havana Convention).
[109] *Jully* suggests and rejects several possibilities of a termination of the asylum, 51 F-W (1951), at 56: it would have amounted to surrender to expel Haya de la Torre or to have him escape secretly because the embassy was surrounded by Peruvian police and military forces. Verzijl, *Jurisprudence of the World Court II*, at 98–9 ironically suggests to disguise Haya de la Torre as nun and send him abroad in a nun's choir, or to snatch him away from the embassy's roof with a helicopter. Luque Angel, *El derecho de asilo*, argues, at 214–15, 223, that it was impossible to comply with the Court's judgment because there was no possibility to terminate the asylum, he does not mention negotiations. Moreno Quintana, *Derecho de asilo*, at 77, sustains that Colombia was obliged to restore the *status quo ante*, but does not provide details.
[110] Judgment of 13 June 1951, at 81.   [111] Judgment of 13 June 1951, at 83.

terminated, and this had to be brought about by negotiations between the parties—not by a unilateral act of Colombia, bearing in mind that the latter was not bound to surrender the accused.[112] Hence, if Peru was to make use of its right to require the termination of the asylum, the parties were obliged under international law to engage in negotiations, thus resolving the judgment's apparent internal inconsistency.[113] The Court's judgments were welcomed by some observers while meeting harsh criticism from others.[114]

4. The post-adjudicative phase: a difficult implementation

Relations between the two countries continued to deteriorate. After the judgment, the parties still disagreed on in its interpretation and had difficulties arriving at a practical solution.[115] Colombia understood the decision as requiring the two states to develop a common solution and thus suggested several compromises.[116] Peru rebuffed the Colombian initiatives,. arguing that it was under no obligation to take action, refrain from action, or even to collaborate with Colombia, but that it was in any event incumbent on Colombia to terminate the asylum.[117] Although the Court had not definitively settled the dispute, its findings had left the parties with a clearer understanding of their respective rights and obligations under the Havana Convention, thereby facilitating negotiations; on the other hand, the judgments included

[112] *Evans*, 45 AJIL (1951), at 760–1. But see *Gonidec*, 55 RGDIP (1951), at 580–1, 591 (arguing that Court's judgment indicates *lacuna* in international law, instead of explaining legal rule).

[113] *Hudson*, 46 AJIL (1952), at 12, calls the judgment to be one "of the best reasoned and most persuasive rendered by the Court in thirty years." For the opposite view, see *Zárate*, *El asilo en el derecho internacional*, at 176–8, who vehemently criticizes the Court for being contradictory and having put itself in an impasse; he refuses to consider a duty to negotiate as applicable legal rule and argues that the outcome of this case is a lesson for countries not to submit their dispute to the ICJ. However, admitting that the outcome was not a really fortunate one, one has to bring legal arguments for the fact that a duty to negotiate was not the applicable rule, apart from the sheer fact that it did not conclusively solve the conflict.

[114] For positive assessments, see Fernandes, *El asilo diplomático*, at 147–57; *Hudson*, 46 AJIL (1952), at 12; *Jully*, 51 F–W (1951), at 57–8; Moreno Quintana, *Derecho de asilo*, at 76–8. On the first judgment only, see *Barcía Trelles*, 3 REspDI (1950), at 771–801; Planas-Suárez, *El asilo diplomático*, at 43–93. For criticism, see Luque Angel, *El derecho de asilo*, at 213–23; *Van Essen*, 1 ICLQ (1952), at 538–9; Verzijl, *Jurisprudence of the World Court II*, at 90, 93–5, 99; Zárate, *El asilo en el derecho internacional*, at 176–8, 209–55; on the first judgment only, Conte, *El derecho de asilo y el caso Haya de la Torre*, 49–57.

[115] For a summary of the events, see Urrutia-Aparicio, *Diplomatic asylum in Latin America*, at 96–100.

[116] Nota del gobierno de Colombia al gobierno de Perú, número 255, Bogotá, 7 July 1953, reprinted in: República de Colombia, Ministerio de Relaciones Exteriores, Nota del gobierno de Colombia ante la Comisión Interamericana de Paz sobre el asilo de Víctor Raúl Haya de la Torre presentada en Washington el día 18 de noviembre de 1953 (Bogotá 1953) [hereinafter Colombian Materials], at 15.

[117] Respuesta del gobierno de Perú al gobierno de Colombia, No. (D)-6/8-Lima, 18 July 1953, reprinted in: Colombian Materials, *supra* n. 116, at 23.

favorable and unfavorable arguments for both sides, which were made use of accordingly. Peru insisted that it had no duty to grant safe passage, resulting in a "literal state of siege" at the Colombian embassy, effectively making Haya de la Torre a prisoner, and presenting a practical nuisance for the embassy staff.[118]

On 18 November 1953, Colombia brought the case to the attention of the Inter-American Peace Commission. It complained about the various disruptions to its diplomatic and consular services in Lima—including a constant police watch over the embassy compound—while emphasizing its own respect for the Court's judgments and its desire to find a solution to terminate the asylum.[119] Peru objected to these proceedings because all relevant questions had in its view been authoritatively settled by the International Court of Justice; revisiting them in another forum thus would be inappropriate.[120] It chastized Colombia for its "obstinate refusal to honor decisions of the Court" in violation of its obligations under Article 94(1) of the Charter[121] and maintained that the Court had required Colombia to terminate the asylum of Haya de la Torre without laying down any reciprocal obligation for Peru itself. Given the scope of obligations deriving from the judgment as explained above, this hint of non-compliance was hardly more than a political maneuver: if the matter was to be resolved by diplomatic talks, Peru itself was under the obligation to negotiate in good faith, and yet it had refused to discuss all Colombian proposals. Colombia's defense of diplomatic asylum received the general support of public opinion in Latin America and the rest of the world.[122]

Peru and Colombia finally reached a compromise in an agreement concluded in Bogotá on 22 March 1954: Colombia was to hand over Haya de la Torre for him to be expelled from Peru.[123] The agreement was properly carried out. After Haya de la Torre had been interrogated in the Colombian embassy on the night of 5 April 1954, the Colombian embassy terminated the asylum at 5.30 p.m. the next day and turned him over to the Peruvian Minister of Justice. The Peruvian government issued a decree of expulsion[124]

---

[118] *Anand*, 26 U. Pitt. LR (1965), at 680–1.   [119] Colombian Materials, *supra* n. 116, at 3.

[120] Note addressed by the Minister of Foreign Affairs of Peru to the Chairman of the Inter-American Peace Commission, reprinted in: Peru, Ministry of Foreign Affairs, The case of the inrighteous asylum granted in the embassy of Colombia in Lima (Lima 1953) [hereinafter Peruvian Materials], at 1.

[121] Note addressed by the Minister of Foreign Affairs of Peru to the various Ministers of Foreign Affairs of the American republics, reprinted in: Peruvian Materials supra n. 120, 5, at 9.

[122] *Anand*, 26 U. Pitt. LR (1965), at 681.

[123] Acuerdo de Bogotá, reprinted in: 2 RAGDI (1955), at 206. See Luque Angel, *El derecho de asilo*, 282–6 (strongly criticizing agreement as being unfavorable to Colombia); *Anand*, 26 U. Pitt. LR (1965), at 681 (suggesting as motivations for Peru to settle the pressure of public opinion and the concern that matter would become focus of the Inter-American Conference of March 1954).

[124] Decreto Supremo No. 2679, reprinted in: 2 RAGDI (1955) 208.

and on 7.45 p.m. the same day, Haya de la Torre embarked on a plane to Mexico,[125] having spent more than five years in the Colombian embassy. Almost three years had passed from the last decision of the Court—the judgment of 13 June 1951—to the termination of the asylum.

5. Reasons for the difficulties in the implementation

Why did it take so long to settle the dispute and implement the Court's judgments, and who was responsible for this delay? One critical point has to be seen in the narrow formulation of the claims and the failure of the parties to define the dispute jointly, which made it impossible for the Court to decide on more than isolated aspects of the overall problem.[126]

The means by which the seeming contradictions in the judgment of 13 June 1951 could be resolved have already been discussed. It might have been desirable for the Court to state more explicitly that the solution lay in an obligation to negotiate; it is unlikely, however, that this would have made a difference for the parties, since negotiations were in any event the only reasonable consequence.

The problem was rather one of the law itself and the solution it provided: as many commentators criticized,[127] the Court sent the parties back to negotiations, although it had been seized by the parties precisely for the reason that they had been unable to settle the dispute by negotiations. While it is certainly regrettable that the contribution of the ICJ to a settlement of the dispute was limited,[128] and that there was an inherent risk that the asylum could have continued for a long time,[129] it is unfair to put the full blame on the Court.[130]

One can deplore that the law did not provide for an easier solution, yet under the given circumstances, what the Court did when it returned the matter to the parties' negotiation was not "acting like Pilate,"[131] but instead applying the law and thus fulfilling its judicial task. Ultimately, the case would probably have been better dealt with by a conciliation commission or an arbiter with ample powers than by a judicial tribunal.[132]

---

[125] Government of Peru, Comunicado oficial, 6 April 1954, reprinted in: 2 RAGDI (1955) 210.
[126] See Fernandes, *El asilo diplomático*, at 154–5; Jully, 51 F-W (1951), at 57; Luque Angel, *El derecho de asilo*, at 215–16; Van Essen, 1 ICLQ (1952), at 533–4; Verzijl, *Jurisprudence of the World Court II*, at 99; Rosenne, *World Court*, at 165–6.
[127] Zárate, *El asilo en el derecho internacional*, at 176–8.
[128] Urrutia-Aparicio, *Diplomatic asylum in Latin America*, at 95.
[129] Godinec, 55 RGDIP (1951), at 581.
[130] Jully, 51 F-W (1951), at 58; Van Essen, 1 ICLQ (1952), at 533.
[131] See Zárate, *El asilo en el derecho internacional*, at 177; Moreno Quintana, *Derecho de asilo*, at 74.
[132] Jully, 51 F-W (1951), at 57.

III. Rights of nationals of the United States of America in Morocco

This case related to a dispute between France and the United States about the treatment of US nationals in the French zone of Morocco.[133] While an ongoing disagreement on US capitulatory rights in the French zone had existed since the establishment of the French protectorate, the dispute's immediate origins lay in a decree of the French resident general of 30 December 1948 imposing a licensing requirement on all imports, except those from France and other parts of the French Union, in order to prevent excessive loss of capital.[134] The decree prejudiced American economic interests in the area, which had increased markedly after the end of the Second World War, and the US protested that it affronted Morocco's official regime of economic non-discrimination ("economic liberty without inequality").[135] Key issues included the differential treatment with regard to imports, the extent of the US consular jurisdiction,[136] the applicability of laws and regulations to US citizens, fiscal immunity, and valuation of merchandise for customs purposes under Article 95 of the General Act of Algeciras of 7 April 1906.[137]

Discussions between the parties proved futile. Although France had proposed submitting the matter for adjudication—an idea to which the US expressed no fundamental objections—the parties could not reach a joint agreement on the matters to be litigated.[138] France initiated proceedings before the ICJ in its unilateral application of 28 October 1950, based on both parties' declarations accepting the compulsory jurisdiction of the Court.[139] Thus, even though the primary dispute centered on American objections to France's behavior, it was France, and not the US, that acted as applicant in the case. France had a significant interest in having its rights clarified after the passage of the Hickenlooper Amendment to the American Foreign Aid Act in 1950, which threatened to withdraw credits from any

---

[133] For details, see *Silagi* in EPIL IV, at 1229–30; *Cheng*, 2 ICLQ (1953), at 345–67; *Johnson*, 29 BYIL (1952), at 401–23.

[134] See *Johnson*, 29 BYIL (1952), at 407–8. See also the Application instituting proceeings on behalf of the government of the French Republic, ICJ Pleadings, US Nationals in Morocco, Vol. 1, 9–13.

[135] *Cheng*, 2 ICLQ (1953), at 356.

[136] Consular jurisdiction, i.e. the exercise of judicial functions by a consul, played an important role in the relations of Europe with the Ottoman Empire and the Far East, although it would be considered an infringement on sovereignty in the present era. See *Münch* in EPIL I, at 763–5.

[137] The Act of Algeciras appears in Annex 32 of the US Counter-memorial, ICJ Pleadings, US Nationals in Morocco, Vol. 1, at 577.

[138] For background on efforts to seize Court, see French Memorial, ICJ Pleadings, US Nationals in Morocco, 15–234, at 25–6, 28–9, which were not disputed by the US.

[139] Application instituting proceedings on behalf of the Government of the French Republic, ICJ Pleadings, US Nationals in Morocco, Vol. 1, 9–13. The two declarations were the US declaration of 14 August 1946 (effective on 26 August 1946), 1 UNTS 9, and the French declaration of 18 February 1947, 26 UNTS 91.

country having a dependent territory in which the US president considered treaty rights as being violated.[140]

The United States filed a preliminary objection claiming that the French memorial did not specify the parties to the case;[141] in response, France clarified that it acted on its own behalf as well as in its capacity as protecting power of Morocco, so that both France and Morocco were to be bound by the Court's decision.[142] The United States then withdrew its objection[143] and filed various counterclaims.[144]

The parties' declarations under Article 36(2) of the ICJ Statute had contained far-reaching reservations: both countries had exempted from their acceptance of the compulsory jurisdiction of the Court disputes essentially within their domestic jurisdiction as determined by their respective governments.[145] The danger that the Court's jurisdiction would be challenged under this reservation did not materialize as the US made no determination as to whether the matter lay within its domestic jurisdiction. In its counter-memorial, the US did not contest the Court's jurisdiction, instead going so far as to manifest a positive attitude towards the Court's involvement;[146] it nevertheless retained the right to rely on its reservations in later cases.[147]

The Court delivered its judgment on 27 August 1952,[148] whereby both parties saw gains and losses. The Court ruled that the decree of 30 December 1948 unlawfully discriminated in favor of France and other parts of the French Union.[149] It also recognized the jurisdiction of the US consular courts, albeit to a more limited extent than the US had claimed.[150] It stated

[140] De Laubadère, *Le statut international du Maroc*, at 5; *Cheng*, 2 ICLQ (1953), at 357; *Soto*, 80 JDI (1953), at 516–83; *Silagi* in EPIL IV, at 1229.
[141] Preliminary objections filed by the Government of the United States of America, ICJ Pleadings, US Nationals in Morocco, 235–47.
[142] Observations du gouvernement français, ICJ Pleadings, US Nationals in Morocco, 248–56. See *Sweeney*, 4 ICLQ (1955) at 145–6; *Cheng*, 2 ICLQ (1953), at 358.
[143] Judgment of 27 August 1952, at 179; *Cheng*, 2 ICLQ (1953), at 357.
[144] See US submissions as reported in Judgment of 27 August 1952, at 180–1.
[145] *Supra* n. 139. The popular name for this US reservation is the "Connally amendment," having been added to the draft US declaration under Article 36(2) of the Statute at the initiative of Senator Tom Connally. See *Franck/Lehrman* in Damrosch, The ICJ at a crossroads, at 16–17.
[146] US Counter-memorial, ICJ Pleadings, US Nationals in Morocco, 257, at 257–8. The US pointed out that the case was appropriate for judicial settlement and that the controversial questions were "submitted to the Court in the belief that resort to judicial settlement will not only promote a just decision satisfactory for both parties, but will also contribute to the development of the tradition of law and order which both the United States and France desire to promote."
[147] Ibid., at 262.
[148] For details on the judgment, see *Johnson*, 29 BYIL (1952), at 410–22; de Laubadère, *Le statut international du Maroc*, at 8–47; Verzijl, *Jurisprudence of the World Court II*, at 134–48.
[149] Judgment of 27 August 1952, at 181–6, 212 (unanimous decision).
[150] Ibid., at 186–201. Unanimously, it decided that pursuant to the US–Moroccan Treaty of 16 September 1836, the US was entitled to to exercise consular jurisdiction in all cases between its citizens or protégés; by 10 votes to 1, it decided that the US was also entitled to exercise consular jurisdiction in all cases brought against its citizens or protégés under the Act of Algeciras to the extent required by that Act's provisions relating to consular jurisdiction. By 6 votes to 5, it rejected further US claims on consular jurisdiction, ibid., at 212. See also *Cheng*, 2 ICLQ (1953), at 360–7.

that the applicability of Moroccan laws and regulations to US citizens did not depend on prior assent of the US government, but that the US consular courts were free to disregard legal rules that had not received such an assent.[151] Moreover, the Court held that American citizens were not exempt from taxes in general and from consumption taxes in particular. In assessing the value of merchandise for customs purposes pursuant to Article 95 of the Act of Algeciras, its value in the country of origin as well as in the Moroccan market were relevant factors. That provision laid down no strict rule.[152]

The decision was quickly implemented. The US authorities withdrew all matters erroneously brought before its consular courts and informed the protectorate authorities accordingly.[153] Beyond US consular jurisdiction, the French courts in Morocco, for their part, asserted their jurisdiction in cases involving US nationals based on the ICJ judgment.[154] The French resident general informed the US chargé in Tangier that the disputed residential decrees of 11 March and 30 December 1948 providing for differential treatment were rescinded, concluding: "Thus, the principles established by the Act of Algeciras and referred to by the Hague Court are being rigorously observed."[155]

The litigation lost significance for the Franco-American relations[156] in view of the efforts to restore Moroccan sovereignty, which culminated in the recognition of Morocco's independence and the termination of the protectorate on 2 March 1956.[157] US President Eisenhower relinquished US consular jurisdiction in Morocco on 15 September 1956 and all cases pending before the consular courts were disposed of by 1960.[158] Moroccan independence did not mean that the judgment became *de jure* obsolete: since France had explicitly argued to act not only in its own behalf but also on behalf of Morocco, the latter was bound by the judgment as well. However, very little of the decision remained of relevance; all the aspects of the decision involving extraterritoriality became purely academic.[159] Basically, there remained only the issue of the assessment of the value of imported merchandise for customs purposes as a matter of potential relevance, to which the

---

[151] Judgment of 27 August 1952, at 201–3, 213 (unanimous decision).

[152] Ibid., at 207–13 (unanimous decision).

[153] 27 DoS Bull. (20 Oct. 1952), 620, 623; de Soto, 80 JDI (1953), at 559.

[154] See Famchon, *Le Maroc d'Algésiras à la souveraineté économique*, at 275–9; *de Soto*, 80 JDI (1953), at 559–61 (with references from the jurisprudence); Cour d'Appel de Rabat, 8 July 1952 and Tribunal Criminel de Casablanca, 6 November 1952, 80 JDI 667–71 (1953).

[155] 27 DoS Bull. 623 (20 Oct. 1952), 623; *Anand*, 26 U. Pitt. LR (1965), at 682; see also *Hudson*, 47 AJIL (1953), at 15 .

[156] Jessup, *The birth of nations*, at 133–4.

[157] For details, see de Laubadère, 2 AFDI 122 (1956), at 122–49.

[158] See 35 DoS Bull. 844 (26 Nov. 1956). 22 USC Sec. 183 was thereby repealed. See Sec. 183. Repealed. Aug. 1, 1956, ch. 807, 70 Stat. 774. The announcement to relinquish jurisdiction was already made on 26 January 1956. See 34 DoS Bull. 204 (6 Feb. 1956).

[159] *Anand*, 26 U. Pitt. LR (1965), at 682.

Court had given wide latitude as to its application.[160] The judgment presented no obstacles to US–Moroccan relations and no claims of non-compliance were raised against independent Morocco.[161]

IV. Ambatielos

In the Ambatielos case, the judgment was complied with without problems.

The Greek government exercised diplomatic protection on behalf of its national Nicolas Eustache Ambatielos, whose claims under a sales contract with the British government on ships had been the subject of dispute since the 1920s, first in the form of judicial proceedings by Ambatielos himself before English Courts and later between the Greek and British governments.[162] On 9 April 1951, Greece instituted proceedings before the ICJ by unilateral application, asking it to act as an arbitral tribunal or at least to confirm that Britain was obliged to submit the dispute to arbitration.[163] Jurisdiction was based on Article 29 of the 1926 Treaty of Commerce and Navigation between Greece and the UK in connection with Article 37 of the ICJ Statute.[164] The UK objected to the Court's jurisdiction.[165] In its judgment on jurisdiction of 1 July 1952, the Court stated that it was not competent to deal with the merits of the Ambatielos claims, but that it had jurisdiction for the question of the existence of an obligation to arbitrate.[166]

On 19 May 1953, Court delivered the judgment on the merits (i.e. the obligation to arbitrate) and found that the UK was under an obligation to submit the dispute to arbitration.[167] The UK relented, thereby putting an end to a controversy that had been dragging on for decades.

---

[160] See *de Soto*, 80 JDI (1953), at 579 (criticizing Court's "refusal to decide on the determination of the customs value"). As for the continued validity of Morocco's international economic régime in accordance with the terms of the Act of Algeciras, see *de Laubadère*, 2 AFDI 122 (1956), at 143–4; Famchon, *Le Maroc d'Algésiras à la souveraineté économique*, 427–56 (discussing ways Morocco could abrogate the Act).

[161] See Rosenne, *World Court*, at 175 (stating that "case had no long-term significance" after Moroccan independence). See also *Anand*, 26 U. Pitt. LR (1965), at 682–3 (citing unpublished US State Department memorandum).

[162] For details on the background of the case, see *Wühler*, "Ambatielos", in EPIL I, at 123–5; Clericetti, *L'affaire Ambatielos*, at 23; *Hambro*, 6 AdV (1957), at 154–6, Puig, *Caso Ambatielos/caso de las pesquerías*, at 15–22.

[163] Application instituting proceedings, ICJ Pleadings, Ambatielos, 8–12.

[164] Treaty of Commerce and Navigation, 16 July 1926, 61 LNTS 125 (1927). Article 29 of the Treaty provided for the settlement of disputes by the Permanent Court of International Justice, a clause which confers jurisdiction on the International Court of Justice by virtue of Article 37 of the ICJ Statute.

[165] Counter-memorial submitted by the Government of the United Kingdom of Great Britain and Northern Ireland (Preliminary Objection), ICJ Pleadings, Ambatielos, 129–220.

[166] Judgment of 1 July 1952 at 44 and 46. Because of a Greek–British Declaration to the Treaty of 16 July 1926 from the same day (61 LNTS 40) according to which no prejudice to the arbitration provisions of an earlier commercial treaty was intended, the Court found itself excluded from adjudging the claim's merits.

[167] Judgment of 19 May 1953, at 23.

After this judgment, the parties started negotiations on the establishment of an arbitral tribunal and reached an agreement on 24 February 1955.[168] Following a written phase, the arbitration commission held the oral proceedings from 25 January to 16 February 1956, ultimately rejecting the Greek claim in its decision of 6 March 1956.[169]

V. Minquiers and Ecrehos

In this case, the Court had to rule on the sovereignty over two small groups of islands and rocks in the English Channel between Jersey and the French coast. Some of them were uninhabitable; others contained a few buildings, but were not used for permanent habitation.[170] The main interests at stake were fishing rights and hydroelectric energy—strategic interests supposedly played no role.[171] France and the United Kingdom agreed to submit the dispute to the ICJ in a special agreement signed on 29 December 1950.[172] The UK notified the Court of the agreement on 5 December 1951 in accordance with Article 40(1) of the Court's Statute.[173] The application included a request for a declaratory judgment on the question of which state had sovereignty over the islands.

The special agreement did not provide for the post-adjudicative phase, a matter unlikely to present significant problems since the islands were uninhabited and a separate agreement had already been reached on the main point of controversy—fishing rights, "without prejudice to the determination of the question of sovereignty [...]."[174] The terms of this agreement were partly made dependent on the Court's judgment: special zones in the Minquiers and Ecrehos were established where the country that would be granted sovereignty would be able to allocate special fishing

---

[168] Agreement regarding the submission to arbitration of the Ambatielos claim, Greece–UK, 24 February 1955, 209 UNTS 187.

[169] Award of 6 March 1956, 12 RIAA (1963), 83–153. For details, see *Hambro*, 6 AdV (1957), at 159–73; *Lipstein*, 6 ICLQ (1957), at 643–56; Puig, *Caso Ambatielos/caso de las pesquerías*, at 83–93; *Wühler*, "Ambatielos" in EPIL I, at 125.

[170] See the Description in the UK Memorial, ICJ Pleadings, Minquiers and Ecrehos, Vol. 1, 11, at 21–6, and in the French Counter-memorial, 353, at 355.

[171] On the background of the dispute, see Roche, *The Minquiers and Ecrehos case*, at 11–18; *Hudson*, 48 AJIL (1954), at 6–12; *Johnson*, 3 ICLQ (1954), at 192–207; *Orcasitas Llorente*, 7 REspDI (1954), at 531–3; *Hambro*, 4 AdV (1953), at 493 (suggesting significance of French plans to develop hydroelectricity given that fishing rights were already regulated at time special agreement concluded).

[172] Special Agreement for submission to the International Court of Justice of differences between the United Kingdom of Great Britain and Northern Ireland and the French Republic concerning sovereignty over the Minquiers and Ecrehos Islets, 29 December 1950, 118 UNTS 150 (1952).

[173] The instruments of ratification of the special agreement had been exchanged on 24 September 1951, Judgment of 17 September 1953, at 49.

[174] Agreement Regarding Rights of Fishery in Areas of the Ecrehos and Minquiers, 30 January 1951, 121 UNTS 97.

concessions.[175] However, these zones comprised only a minor part of the waters in question and the respective concessions therefore had little significance.[176] The general regime provided for common fishing by French and UK fishermen, in addition to areas of exclusive fishery by one or the other side.[177]

In its judgment of 17 November 1953, the Court ruled that Britain held title to the territories in question.[178] Implementing action was not required since the judgment was declaratory, and the economic importance was limited since the question of fishery rights had already been resolved, although the outcome resulted in a slightly better position for the UK under the 1951 fisheries agreement.[179] France did not oppose the ruling.[180]

When Western European countries concluded a Fisheries Convention on 9 March 1964,[181] a clause was included to preserve the special regime between France and the UK with respect to the Minquiers and Ecrehos,[182] a point confirmed in an exchange of notes between the French and UK governments on 10 April 1964.[183]

The judgment definitively settled the dispute between the two countries, although the area did not remain entirely free of conflict. There were some incidents between privately operated French and British vessels,[184] although none posed a serious challenge to UK sovereignty over the territories and the French government never put that sovereignty in question.[185] Long after the judgment, there were symbolic "French invasions" of the contested island groups by private persons. On 24 June 1993, for instance, a group of some 50 French fishermen sailed to La Marmotière, an island part of the Ecrehos,

---

[175] Articles II and III mention "the contracting party which is held to have sovereignty" over certain parts; Article IV sets up certain hypotheses for a finding confirming UK or French sovereignty, respectively.

[176] Rodwell, *Les Ecréhous*, at 332 (reporting no concessions were granted following the ICJ judgment).

[177] Article I of the Agreement, *supra* n. 174.

[178] Judgment of 17 November 1953, at 47–72. For a detailed description, see Roche, *The Minquiers and Ecrehos case*, at 52–144. On the parties' submissions and on the judgment, see Bishop, 48 AJIL (1954), at 316–26; Johnson, 3 ICLQ (1954), at 207–16; Orcasitas Llorente, 7 REspDI (1954), at 536–47; Rodwell, *Les Ecréhous*, at 333–44. For a critical comment, see *de la Morandière*, 21 Etudes Norm. (1956), at 17–36.

[179] See *Honig*, 15 ZaöRV (1953–4), at 726 (1953–54); *Anand*, 26 U. Pitt. LR (1965), at 684 (stating that decision's only practical consequence was "exclusion of French fishermen from two small fishing reserves").

[180] Roche, *The Minquiers and Ecrehos Case*, at 188 fn. 2 (calling 1951 agreement and ICJ decision "entirely successful," with only one reported incident by French fishermen). See also *Anand*, 26 U. Pitt. LR (1965), at 684 (praising France's "sportsmanlike spirit" in accepting judgment).

[181] 581 UNTS 57. The participating States were Belgium, Denmark, the Federal Republic of Germany, France, Ireland, Italy, Luxembourg, the Netherlands, Portugal, Spain, Sweden, and the UK.

[182] Ibid., Article 10(d). [183] 648 UNTS 73. [184] Rodwell, *Les Ecréhous*, at 346.

[185] See Rodwell, *Les Ecréhous*, at 352 (stating that "[i]t is unlikely that the sovereignty of Les Ecréhous will ever again be challenged at the international level").

replaced the British flag with French and Norman flags, and absconded with the Union Flag.[186] About a year later, a much larger group of around 150, composed of fishermen and other individuals with diverse political motivations, landed at various places in the Ecrehos, tried to remove the British flag, planted a Norman flag, and held a mass in which the priest prayed for a return of the Channel Islands to the Catholic fold—an incident that might have been triggered by Jersey's intention to extend the territorial sea to 12 sea miles and resulting fears of the potential impact of such action on French fishing rights, although local authorities had attempted to appease such fears by affirming that fishing rights would not be negatively affected.[187] On 1 September 1998, the French novelist Jean Raspail landed on the Minquiers accompanied by three persons and claimed the reef for the imaginary kingdom of Patagonia.[188] The French government was not involved and regarded it as a domestic matter of Britain.[189]

In July 2000, France and the UK concluded agreements on the delimitation of the territorial waters between Jersey and France and on a new fishing regime in the hopes of ending conflicts in the area.[190] Although there is no guarantee preventing future recurrence of such events, these incidents are in any event anecdotal and present no genuine test of the Court's authority. There is no reason to assume that the question of sovereignty over the Minquiers and Ecrehos will ever be reopened between the two governments or that the validity of the judgment would be put in question.[191]

---

[186] Rodwell, *Les Ecréhous*, at 47.

[187] See Binney/Hornsby, "Jersey Polic outwits Norman invasion," The Times, 11 July 1994, 1994 WL 9157112; Brown, "Three Policemen halt new Norman conquest," The Sunday Telegraph, 10 July 1994, 1994 WL 11326956; Rodwell, Les Ecréhous, at 347–52.

[188] Woodward, "Invaded! But British again within a few hours," Daily Mail, 2 September 1998, 1998 WL 18503106. The novelist later returned the British flag to the British Embassy in Paris. See "A matter of honour as flag returned," Birmingham Post, 4 September 1998, 1998 WL 18498739.

[189] Tanner, "Husband and Wife interrupt day trip to reconquer Channel isle for Britain," The Independent, 2 September 1998, 1998 WL 16749666 (quoting spokeswoman from the French foreign ministry).

[190] Agreement concerning fishing in the Bay of Granville, http://www.fco.gov.uk/Files/KFile/CM6139.pdf; Agreement concerning the establishment of a maritime boundary between Jersey and France, http://www.fco.gov.uk/Files/KFile/CM6138.pdf. Both entered into force on 1 January 2004 (see ibid.). See also "Accord de pêche avec Jersey," French Ministry for Agriculture and Fisheries, Pêche-info no. 10, 10 October 2000, http://www.agriculture.gouv.fr/spip/IMG/pdf/peche-info10.pdf, at 3; Birt, 4 Jers. LR (2000), at 290–9.

[191] Rodwell, Les Ecréhous, at 352: "[I]t would be unrealistic to believe that the French will not, at some time in the future, be tempted once more to tweak the tail of the British lion. When that happens, there will be adequate support on a summer's day to hoist the Normandy banner, to renew the ancient presence of the church and to sing songs of anarchy. The Jersey taxpayer may begrudge the cost of restraining excessive nationalism on such occasions, but would appear to have little to fear in the overall context of a breach of States' sovereignty."

VI. Right of passage over Indian territory

1. The institution of the proceedings

This case concerned overland routes between Portuguese-occupied enclaves on the Indian subcontinent.[192] The Portuguese colonial possessions on the Indian subcontinent consisted of the districts of Goa, Diu, and Daman. Since its independence in 1947, India had demanded that Portugal relinquish control over those territories, a claim which Portugal rejected, leading to deterioration in their diplomatic relations. The district of Daman comprised a littoral territory on the west coast of the peninsula and Dadra and Nagar-Aveli, two enclaves entirely surrounded by Indian territory. Portugal held that it had a right of passage between those two enclaves as well as between them and the main territory of Daman based on custom as well as on instruments from the eighteenth century.[193] Insurrectionist movements in July and August 1954 had resulted in the overthrow of Portuguese authority in Dadra and Nagar-Aveli, and attempts by the Portuguese to restore their rule had failed since India denied passage to Portuguese troops through its territory.[194]

Portugal made a unilateral application to the ICJ on 22 December 1955, requesting a declaration that it was beneficiary of a right of passage over Indian territory and that this right was being violated by India.[195] The application was founded on both countries' declarations recognizing the compulsory jurisdiction of the Court:[196] India's declaration of 28 February 1940[197] and Portugal's declaration of 19 December 1955[198] deposited only

---

[192] For details on the background of the case, see Bains, *India's international disputes*, 165–8.

[193] See Judgment of 12 April 1960, at 27, 33, 37. In particular, Portugal claimed that it had gained full sovereignty over the enclaves by virtue of a treaty of 1779 and decrees of 1783 and 1785 by the Maratha rulers and that it consequently possessed a right of passage, ibid., at 37. For a description of the enclaves, see Krenz, *International enclaves and rights of passage*, at 61–5.

[194] This fact was uncontroversial, see Preliminary objection by India, ICJ Pleadings, Right of Passage, Vol. 1, 97, at 158–9.

[195] Application insituting proceedings, ICJ Pleadings, Right of Passage, Vol. 1, 1960, 2–7.

[196] Ibid., at 6.

[197] Further acceptance of the Optional Clause under New Conditions, 200 LNTS 489–90; the declaration contained some reservations, of which India were to invoke the one relating to "disputes with regard to questions which by international law fall exclusively within the jurisdiction of India." The declaration conferred jurisdiction on the ICJ by virtue of Article 36(5) of the ICJ Statute. Shortly after the introduction of proceedings by Portugal, on 9 January 1956, India terminated this declaration (Termination of the declaration of 28 February 1940, 226 UNTS 388) and submitted a new declaration under Article 36(2), Declaration of India recognizing as compulsory the jurisdiction of the International Court of Justice of 7 January 1956, 226 UNTS 235–9, applicable for disputes submitted after 26 January 1950, in which the exemption of matters of domestic jurisdiction was framed more broadly to encompass "disputes in regard to matters which are essentially within the domestic jurisdiction of India as determined by the Government of India" (similar to the US Connally amendment, see *supra* n. 145.)

[198] Declaration of Portugal recognizing as compulsory the jurisdiction of the International Court of Justice, 224 UNTS 275.

three days prior to the institution of the proceedings and five days after its admission to the UN.[199] Taken by surprise,[200] India opposed the proceedings and filed six preliminary objections against the Court's jurisdiction, challenging the validity of Portugal's declaration, the existence of a legal dispute, and the applicability of India's declaration to the dispute.[201] Still during the proceedings, it terminated its 1940 declaration and replaced it by another one with more restricted conditions under which a lawsuit such as Portugal's could no longer possibly be launched;[202] this action left the Court's jurisdiction in the present case untouched.

2. The judgments of 1957 and 1960

By its judgment of 26 November 1957, the Court rejected four of India's preliminary objections and joined two others to the merits.[203] A judgment on the merits was delivered on 12 April 1960.[204] After dismissing India's fifth and sixth preliminary objections,[205] the Court held that in 1954 Portugal had indeed had a general right of passage over intervening Indian territory with respect to private persons, civil officials, and goods,[206] but not with respect to armed forces, police, and munitions.[207] The Court based the right of passage solely on local custom and dismissed Portugal's claims that it had gained sovereignty over the enclaves (and thereby a right of passage) by a 1779 treaty and decrees of 1783 and 1785.[208] Finally, the Court ruled that India had not contravened its obligations relating to the right of passage, since in the aftermath of the events of July 1954, India's refusal of passage was

---

[199] Portugal was admitted to the United Nations on 14 December 1955, GA Res. 995 (X) following the recommendation of the Security Council of the same day. It had not been a member of the ICJ Statute before.

[200] Rosenne, *World Court*, at 188.

[201] Preliminary objection by India, *supra* n. 194, at 97–188.

[202] Declaration of 14 September 1959, ICJ YB 1960–61, at 203, 204; the earlier declaration was terminated by a notice of 8 February 1957, ibid. 203 n. 2.

[203] The voting pattern varied for the different objections, within a range of 16 to 1 to 13 to 4. See Judgment of 26 November 1957, at 152–3. The objections joined to the merits were the fifth and sixth objections: the submissions that the matter was within India's exclusive domestic jurisdiction and that the dispute related to a situation antecedent to 5 February 1930 and was therefore *ratione temporis* excluded from India's acceptance of jurisdiction by the declaration of 28 February 1940, see ibid., at 149–52. For details, see Bains, *India's international disputes*, at 169–77.

[204] For details, see Bains, *India's international disputes*, at 177–91; *Chacko*, 1 Indian JIL (1960), at 293–9; Krenz, *International enclaves and rights of passage*, at 132–7; de Visscher, 64 RGDIP (1960), at 697–710.

[205] Judgment of 12 April 1960, at 32–6. By 13 votes to 2 and 11 votes to 4, respectively, ibid., at 45.

[206] Ibid., 39–40. The decision on this point was reached by eleven votes to four, ibid., at 45.

[207] Ibid., at 40–3. This was the most controversial point within the Court, decided by 8 votes to 7, 46.

[208] Ibid., at 37–9 and Krenz, *International enclaves and rights of passage*, at 107–10.

covered by powers of regulation and control of the passage, taking into consideration the prevailing tensions. As for the period between October 1953 and July 1954, it found that Portugal had not claimed that there had been a *violation* of the right of passage, although it had complained on continuous restrictions on that right.[209]

Both India and Portugal considered the judgment a victory, although Portugal had hardly any reason to be satisfied; it is doubtful whether it had gained any benefit.[210]

3. Scope of the Court's findings

The Court had explicitly rejected Portugal's claims that it had gained sovereignty over the enclaves by the historical treaty and decrees, a decision hardly conducive to Portugal's desire to reassert control over the territories it had occupied on the Indian peninsula. The operative part of the judgment had a very limited scope. Contrary to what Portugal claimed after its delivery, the verdict did *not* recognize the existence of a right of passage on the time it was delivered, but *just with regard to 1954*.[211] In its application, Portugal had asked the Court "to recognize and declare that Portugal is the holder or beneficiary of a right of passage"; in its memorial and final submissions, it furthermore had requested a ruling that "India is under the obligation to respect that right."[212] Yet, the Court answered with a more nuanced formulation: "The Court finds [. . .] that Portugal *had in 1954* a right of passage over intervening Indian territory [. . .]."[213] In the view of the Court, the Portuguese application had referred to 1954 as the decisive date, not to the date of the application or that of the judgment; hence it held that Portugal merely wished to have a finding for the past, but not for the present. The judgment explicitly left open whether the right in question might have lapsed as a result of the events of July and August 1954,[214] which, according to the Court, "brought about a new situation."[215] It maintained that Portugal had

---

[209] Ibid., at 44–6; this finding was made by 9 votes to 6.

[210] See *Anand*, 26 U. Pitt. LR (1965), at 685; *Chacko*, 1 Indian JIL (1960), at 294–9; Bains, *India's international disputes*, at 192–3 and 179 (stating that "[o]n the merits, the decision of the Court is favourable to India"). See also Rosenne, *World Court*, at 189 (describing Portugal's victory as "pyrrhic").

[211] *Mathy*, 10 RBDI (1974), at 173.

[212] Portuguese Memorial, ICJ pleadings, Right of Passage, Vol. 1, 1960, at 33: "May it please the Court (. . .) to adjudge and declare (a) that the Government of India must respect that right; (b) that it must therefore abstain from any act capable of hampering or impeding its exercise, (c) that neither may it allow such acts to be carried out on its territory;" (English translation from the Judgment of 12 April 1960, at 10; final submissions, ibid., at 12: "May it please the Court to adjudge and declare that the right of passage [. . .] is a right possessed by Portugal and which must be respected by India."

[213] Judgment of 12 April 1960, at 45–6 (emphasis added).   [214] Ibid., at 29.

[215] Ibid., at 28.

not indicated an exact date in relation to which the existence of the right of passage was to be ascertained, but since the dispute was a consequence of obstacles to passage created by India in 1954, Portugal's application had to be understood as relating to times before the creation of these obstacles.[216]

The reasoning of the Court might raise doubts: Portugal's claims had always been unambiguously formulated in the present tense. Its claims were not only retrospective in character, but also directed to the present and the future. Portugal sought a resolution of the current conflict, not a judgment on the past. The Court failed to rule on the subject-matter of the application, and its interpretation contravened the explicit intentions of the applicant.[217] In view of the unequivocal wording, there was little need for interpretation, and if the Court had doubts, these should have been clarified during the oral proceedings. One can hardly assume that Portugal referred to a time prior to the date of the application, but surely not July 1954.[218] A likely reason for the Court's restrictive approach was its reluctance to decide on the delicate issues concerning the current status of the enclaves,[219] which directly related to the question of colonialism. The Court did not want to be seen as acting as a proxy to reimpose colonial rule by the Portuguese.[220] Judge Moreno Quintana voiced a clear opinion in this respect: "To support the Portuguese claim in this case, which implies survival of the colonial system, without categorical and conclusive proof is to fly in the face of the United Nations Charter."[221]

In sum, the judgment affirmed Portugal's qualified right of "civil" passage for the past—subject to Indian regulation and control[222]—while denying a similar right for military passage and remaining silent as to the continuing existence of the right or an obligation on part of India to assist Portugal in restoring its authority over the enclaves.[223] For the Court, the only claim relating not to the past, but to the present and the future, was the question of the remedy for the failure of India to respect the right of passage in 1954.[224] Hence, any pronouncement of the Court requiring implementing action on the part of India would have required a prior finding of a breach of India's obligations in 1954, but the Court found that India had not committed such a breach.[225]

---

[216] Ibid., at 28–9.

[217] Critical, see *de Visscher*, 64 RGDIP (1960), at 698; *Verzijl*, 7 NILR (1960), at 217, 219.

[218] Judgment of 12 April 1960, at 47 (Decl. Klaestad) and 125 (Diss. Op. Fernandes).

[219] See *de Visscher*, 64 RGDIP (1960), at 698–9.

[220] Bains, *India's international disputes*, at 190–1.

[221] Judgment of 12 April 1960, Diss. Op. Moreno Quintana, at 88, 95.

[222] See Bains, *India's international disputes*, at 193 (submitting that addition of clause giving control to India "whittled [right sanctioned by Court] down to a nullity").

[223] *Verzijl*, 7 NILR (1960), at 242.

[224] Judgment of 12 April 1960, at 31–6.

[225] See also Bains, *India's international disputes*, at 184 (stating that Court neither accepted Portuguese claim nor called for action or omission on the part of India).

4. Portugal's complaint of non-compliance

Despite the fact that the judgment provided hardly any grounds to demand implementing action, Portugal alleged that India did not comply with the Court's judgment and took recourse to the UN Security Council. On 16 August 1961, Portugal sent a complaint to the president of the Security Council for circulation among the Council members. The complaint was triggered by India's Dadra and Nagar Haveli Act, which regulated administration of the former Portuguese enclaves and conferred on the Indian central government all rights, liabilities, and obligations of administration and representation of the territories in the Union parliament.[226] Portugal argued that this legislation constituted "[...] a clear violation of the judgment of the International Court of Justice, the highest judicial body, which on 12 April 1960 recognized both the Portuguese sovereignty over the two territories and the right of access to them, which Portugal can rightfully exercise in all matters concerning private persons, civil officials and goods in general."[227] It requested India to clarify whether it intended to abide by the Court's decision and announced that it would exercise the right of passage recognized by the Court.[228] Portugal's complaint to the Council neither invoked Article 94 of the Charter[229] nor included a request for a Council meeting; the matter was therefore not officially discussed in the Council.

At a later stage, on 18 December 1961, the Council discussed the Indian takeover of all Portuguese colonial possessions (Goa, Daman, and Diu) that had taken place in the meantime.[230] Apart from very brief references by

[226] Act 35 of 1961, Gazette of India, 4 Sept. 1961, pt. II-S.1, Ext., 295. It was approved by the Indian president on 2 September 1961. *Whiteman*, 2 Dig. IL 1213 (1963).

[227] Official Communiqué issued by the Portuguese government, dated 16 August 1961, on the Portuguese enclaves of Dadra and Nagar-Aveli, Annex 1 to Letter dated 16 August 1961 from the representative of Portugal to the President of the Security Council concerning the enclaves of Dadra and Nagar-Aveli, UN Doc. S/4929, reprinted in: *Whiteman*, 2 Dig. IL 1213 (1963).

[228] Note transmitted by the Portuguese government to the Indian government and released on 16 August 1961, Annex II to UN Doc. S/4929: "The judgment passed by the International Court of Justice [...] recognized that there exists a in favour of Portugal a right of passage over intervening Indian territory [...] Since the Government of the Indian Union has always stated that it respects international judicial order and defends the principles of compliance with the decisions of the highest judicial body in the community of nations, the Portuguese Government has been waiting for the Indian Government to define, within this spirit, its attitude toward the judgment given on 12 April 1960, and in particular, its intentions regarding the arrangements for Portugal to exercise its right of passage in compliance with and within the terms of said judgment. [...] Because the Indian Government has not yet made known how it intends to fulfil the decision of the International Court, the Portuguese Government feels that it cannot delay any longer the steps required to exercise its right, as recognized by the International Court of Justice." *Whiteman*, 2 Dig. IL 1214 (1963).

[229] The complaint that the judgment had been violated appeared in the annexes to the letter to the Security Council president; the letter itself used more moderate language. There was no explicit reference to Article 94, nor was the Council asked to take action to enforce the judgment.

[230] UN Doc. S/PV.987 and S/PV.988. Portugal's complaint to the Council (Letter dated 18 December 1961 from the representative of Portugal to the President of the Security Council, S/5030) did not mention the judgment.

Portugal and India to the ICJ judgment, the judgment was not a topic of the discussion:[231] since Portugal had lost its possessions on the Indian subcontinent in their entirety, the issue of a right of passage had lost any importance. The Council could not agree on a resolution to the general situation.[232]

The Portuguese complaint about non-compliance with the judgment of 12 April 1960 was unfounded. The judgment had not confirmed Portuguese sovereignty over the enclaves; it had merely affirmed a right of Portuguese civil passage for the past and had explicitly not made a statement on the continued existence of that right following the overthrow of Portuguese authority. There was no basis for deducing from those findings that India had no right to exercise sovereignty in territories formerly occupied by Portugal. It is therefore unsurprising that the Portuguese cries of non-compliance fell on deaf ears.

The judgment was already a defeat for the Portuguese. They did not reach their political goal in the end—i.e. regaining control over the territories in question, and it cannot be argued that this was a consequence of India's failure to respect a judgment of the Court,[233] since the Portuguese title to the enclaves was precisely what the judgment did not address.

VII. *Sovereignty over certain frontier land*

The case concerning sovereignty over certain frontier land concerned two tiny plots of land which between 1836 and 1843 had been known as Nos. 91 and 92, Section A, Zondereygen. These plots of land—a total of about 14 hectares, or 35 acres—were situated in the Belgian enclave Baarle-Hertog,[234] which was itself surrounded by the Dutch commune of Baarle-Nassau. Belgium contested Dutch claims that the land was actually part of Baarle-Nassau. The

---

[231] The Portuguese representative Garin referred to Dadra and Nagar-Aveli and the judgment, but just in passing: S/PV.988, 10, para. 47: "Those enclaves were recently unilaterally annexed by the Indian Union in total disregard of a decision of the International Court of Justice." The only one who commented on that statement was the Indian representative Jha (at 17, para. 80), arguing that the International Court of Justice had not accepted Portuguese sovereignty over the said enclaves, citing p. 38 of the Court's judgment ("Article 17 of the Treaty is relied upon by Portugal as constituting a transfer of sovereignty. From an examination of the various texts of that article placed before it, the Court is unable to to conclude that the language employed therein was intended to transfer sovereignty over the villages to the Portuguese.")

[232] A draft by the United Arab Republic, Liberia, and Ceylon rejecting the Portuguese complaints and calling upon Portugal to terminate hostile action against India did not receive the majority, a draft by the US, the UK, France, and Turkey calling for a cease-fire and an Indian withdrawal was vetoed by the Soviet Union, S/PV.988, 26–7.

[233] Krenz, *International enclaves and rights of passage*, 65: "Ever since the rising, however, the Portuguese have lost all control over the territories in question, a situation in which the Court seems to have acquiesced tacitly."

[234] Baarle-Hertog is the Flemish name; the French denomination is Baerle-Duc. See Old and new toponyms in Belgium, Luxembourg, Netherlands, and France, www.users.skynet.be/luc.ockers/plaatsnamen.htm. For details of the history of Baarle and the current situation, see *Whyte*, 53 The Globe (2002), at 45–9.

enclave of Baarle-Hertog is not a continuous territory, but made up of many small plots of land, two of which for their part contain Dutch enclaves. As a result, small sections of the Dutch Baarle-Nassau lay within the borders of the Belgian Baarle-Hertog enclaves.[235]

In 1836, the communes of Baarle-Nassau and Baarle-Hertog tried to define their respective boundaries. In the Dutch copy of the communal minutes dated 29 November 1936, which were completed by mid-1839 and signed on 22 March 1841, plots 91 and 92 belonged to the Netherlands; the Belgian copy could not be found. The Boundary Treaty between the Netherlands and Belgium of 5 November 1842 did not define the Dutch–Belgian border in the area between markers 214 and 215 (which included the plots); Article 14 called for maintenance of the status quo concerning the villages of Baarle-Hertog and Baarle-Nassau. Following the work of a Mixed Boundary Commission, a Boundary Convention was concluded on 8 August 1843. Integral to the convention was an annex containing the descriptive minute prepared by the Mixed Boundary Commission.[236] Article 14(5) of the Convention repeated the call of the Boundary Treaty for the maintenance of the status quo with regard to Baarle-Hertog and Baarle-Nassau, a provision that was also recalled in the descriptive minute itself. However, unlike the communal minute (according to the Dutch copy), the descriptive minute accorded plots 91 and 92 to Belgium, not to the Netherlands.[237] Both countries had asserted their sovereignty over the plots in some form and included them in their respective land registers, and since 1922 there was an official controversy regarding the sovereignty over the plots.[238]

Given that only tiny plots of land without any particular significance were involved, the controversy garnered little notice until the actions of a Belgian citizen brought the matter to national attention. In 1953, Franciscus Gerard (Sooi) van den Eijnde, a Belgian pig-breeder and landlord, acquired the plots of land. He had purchased ten former railway houses and properties located in a place called Moleriet along the road from Turnhout to Baarle. Van den Eijnde wanted to charge his tenants rents permissible under Belgian law which exceeded by three times the sum permissible under Dutch law. The tenants protested; local authorities and, eventually, the national governments and parliaments got involved when van den Eijnde took obstructive action against the Dutch authorities, convinced that his land was Belgian. Local emotions ran high, despite the good relations between the two states,

---

[235] *Franckx*, 31 RBDI (1998), at 340; *Whyte*, 53 The Globe (2002), at 46–7.

[236] Article 3.

[237] See the summary of facts in the Judgment of 20 June 1959, at 212–22. See also *Cocâtre-Zilgien*, 5 AFDI (1959) at 284–6; Verzijl, *Jurisprudence of the World Court II*, 353–5; Whyte, *En Territoire Belge* (unpublished manuscript).

[238] Judgment of 20 June 1959, at 227–30.

and negotiations proved unsuccessful since each side insisted that the plots were located on its respective territory.[239]

It might seem ridiculous[240] that the World Court had to settle a dispute over such miniscule plots of land between two countries that had formed a customs union and were on the eve of entering into an economic union.[241] But there were some arguments for submitting the matter to adjudication: it was a situation which received little national, but great local, attention, and it had to be solved quickly because of the problems with van den Eijnde. In June 1954, the parties had agreed on an interim regime for the exercise of authority in the plots concerned, but this was understood as a temporary solution.[242] It did not seem an unreasonable step to take the matter to an impartial, international body removed from the heated emotions of local politics.[243] Still, the time and resources necessary for the proceedings before the World Court seem somewhat out of proportion to the significance of the matter for both countries' relations. The relative insignificance might explain why the parties did not make use of their right to appoint a judge *ad hoc* under Article 31(3) of the ICJ Statute.[244]

On 7 March 1957, Belgium and the Netherlands concluded a special agreement to submit the dispute to the ICJ, which entered into force on 19 November 1957.[245] The special agreement did not include any reference to the post-adjudicative phase; this was probably not considered necessary since the parties requested a declaratory judgment and there was no apparent need

---

[239] *Franckx*, 31 RBDI (1998), at 340 fn. 5; Whyte, *En territoire Belge* (unpublished manuscript).

[240] Verzijl, *Jurisprudence of the World Court II*, refers to the case at 358 and 353 as a "ridiculous case," an "absurd dispute." But see Rosenne, *World Court*, 193 (stating that an important conflict of economic interests underlay the "seemingly insignificant" dispute). Yet one might doubt whether the case would have been considered as important were it not for the actions of Mr van den Eijnde.

[241] The treaty on economic union between Belgium, the Netherlands and Luxemburg was concluded on 3 February 1958 and entered into force on 1 November 1960. For details on the cooperation between the Benelux countries, see *Fayat*, 25 ÖZöR (1974), at 247.

[242] Exchange of notes constituting an agreement between the Netherlands and Belgium concerning the exercise of authority over the registered lands known as the "Commune of Zondereygen," Section A, Nos. 91 and 92, 26 and 28 June 1954, 272 UNTS 235; Exchanges of notes constituting an agreement extending the above-mentioned agreement, 5 and 7 December 1956, 272 UNTS 240. The latter agreement explicitly stated that it might not be invoked in support of either party's claim before the ICJ and that the extension was to be valid for a year from the date of the reply of the Dutch Ministry of Foreign Affairs, which took place on 7 December 1956. Hence, the agreement expired shortly after the dispute was submitted to the ICJ.

[243] Whyte, *En Territoire Belge* (unpublished manuscript).

[244] See the composition of the Court, Judgment of 20 June 1959, at 209.

[245] Arrangement to submit to the International Court of Justice the difference between the Kingdom of Belgium and the Kingdom of the Netherlands concerning sovereignty over certain lots situated along the Belgian–Netherlands frontier, 7 March 1957, 282 UNTS 241. It was received by the Court's Registry on 27 November 1957, Judgment of 20 June 1959, at 210. The question submitted to the Court was whether the sovereignty over the defined plots belonged to Belgium or the Netherlands (Article I).

for any action of implementation. A week later, the Netherlands notified the Court's Registrar of the agreement.[246]

In its judgment of 20 June 1959, the Court found by 10 votes to 4 that Belgium had sovereignty over the plots,[247] thus giving priority to the wording of the descriptive minute annexed to the 1843 Convention. The judgment was declaratory: an agreement for implementation was not required because the territory was Belgian by virtue of the Convention of 1843, had always been considered as such by Belgium, and was part of its administrative structure. The Netherlands was bound to refrain from steps asserting sovereignty such as retaining the plots in the land register and producing maps showing them as Dutch territory, but this posed no real problems. The dispute over the two plots of land was settled and the person that had created all the attention, van den Eijnde, was confirmed in his opinion that his property was indeed Belgian; problems with the judgment were thus not to be expected.

The case gave an impulse to new efforts to carry out a proper delimitation of the area between boundary pillars 214 and 215. Another Mixed Boundary Commission was established.[248] A solution was eventually reached for the remaining gaps in the border and *procès-verbaux* for the delimitation were signed on 26 April 1974[249] and 31 October 1995, respectively.[250] The second *procès-verbal* defined all the Belgian enclaves of Baarle-Hertog, among them

---

[246] Le ministre des affaires étrangères a. i. du Royaume des Pays-Bas au greffier, ICJ Pleadings, Sovereignty over Certain Frontier Land, 596. The relevant article of the agreement reads: "Upon the entry into force of the present Agreement, it shall be notified to the Court under Article 40 of the Statute of the Court by the Kingdom of the Netherlands." (Article III).

[247] Judgment of 20 June 1959 at 230. For details of the judgment, see *Whiteman*, Dig. IL, at 626–33; *Bishop*, 53 AJIL (1959), at 937–43; *Orcasitas Llorente*, 13 REspDI (1960) at 519–29; Verzijl, *Jurisprudence of the World Court II*, at 353–8.

[248] Whyte, *En Territoire Belge* (unpublished manuscript).

[249] Convention fixant les limites entre le Royaume de Belgique et le Royaume des Pays-Bas, signée a Maastricht le 8 août 1843. Procès-verbal de délimitation de la frontière entre les Royaumes des Pays-Bas et les communes belges de Poppel, Weelde, Baerle-Duc, Turnhout, Baer le-Duc, Merksplas, Baer le-Duc, Wortel, Minderhout, Baer le-Duc, Minderhout et Meerle, à l'exception de toutes les enclaves de la commune de Baerle-Duc, situées à l'intérieur de la circonsription de la circonscription communale de Baarle-Nassau, signé à Turnhout le 26 avril 1974, Moniteur Belge, 5 March 1975, 2575–81. This protocol was not a late execution of the judgment as apparently suggested by *Rousseau*, 79 RGDIP (1975), at 166. As indicated by its title and content show, the Belgian enclaves of Baarle-Hertog within Baarle-Nassau (including the plots in question) were not defined therein, but the main section of the borderline between the border posts 214 and 215. See also Whyte, *En Territoire Belge* (unpublished manuscript); *Franckx*, 31 RBDI (1998), at 343–4. Moreover, the judgment did not require an execution by an agreement between the parties. But see *Guillaume* in Jasentuliyana, Perspectives on international law, at 279 (holding that judgment was implemented slowly).

[250] Convention fixant les limites entre le Royaume de Belgique et le Royaume des Pays-Bas, 8 August 1843. Procès-verbal de délimitation de la frontière des enclaves de la commune de Baarle-Duc, situées sur le territoire de la commune de Baarle-Nassau et des enclaves de Baarle-Nassau, situées sur le territoire de la commune de Baarle-Duc, 31 October 1995. Moniteur Belge, 26 June 1996, 17565–94.

the plots that had been in dispute before the ICJ; they are now designated as enclave H17.[251]

VIII. *Arbitral award made by the King of Spain on 23 December 1906*

This case[252] deserves closer attention because of a special feature of its post-adjudicative phase: the implementation took place within the framework of the Inter-American system of dispute settlement. The dispute centered on the validity of an arbitral award concerning the land frontier between Nicaragua and Honduras[253] and the question whether Nicaragua was bound to give effect to it and withdraw from an area of land that it had attributed to Honduras.

On 7 October 1894, Nicaragua and Honduras had concluded the Gámez–Bonilla Treaty,[254] which contained rules for the delimitation of their boundary and for the establishment of a Mixed Boundary Commission to carry out the demarcation and settle remaining differences; the issue of points of the boundary line still unsettled after the Commission's final session was to be submitted to arbitration. While the Commission managed to fix the boundary from the Pacific Coast to the Portillo de Teotecacinte, no agreement could be reached on the remaining part of the frontier leading to the Atlantic Coast.[255] Spanish King Alfonso XII delivered an arbitral award[256] with terms favorable to Honduras.[257] Nicaragua contested the validity of the arbitral award from 12 March 1912[258] onwards and proceeded to occupy the disputed territory. This led to an ongoing controversy between the two

---

[251] Ibid., 17570.   [252] Judgment of 18 November 1960, at 192–239.

[253] The arbitral award did not concern the maritime boundary; that issue was unilaterally submitted to the Court by Nicaragua on 8 December 1999 based on XXXI of the American Treaty on Pacific Settlement, 30 April 1948, 30 UNTS 55 (also known as the "Pact of Bogotá") as well as the two countries' declarations under Article 36(2) of the Statute. The case is still pending before the Court at the time of writing. In that application, Nicaragua asks the Court to to determine the course of the single maritime boundary between areas of the territorial sea, continental shelf, and exclusive economic zone appertaining respectively to Nicaragua and Honduras: http://212.153.43.18/icjwww/idocket/iNH/iNH_orders/Inh_iapplication_19991208.pdf. These proceedings do not put in question the Court's judgment in the Arbitral Award case in any way, but concern the area beyond the coordinates fixed by the award, i.e. the maritime zones.

[254] Printed as annex I to Honduras's application instituting proceedings of 1 July 1958, ICJ Pleadings, Arbitral Award Made by the King of Spain, Vol. I, 2, at 12–16, and in the Judgment of 18 November 1960, at 199–202.

[255] Judgment of 18 November 1960, at 202.

[256] Printed as annex II to Honduras's application, *supra* n. 254, at 18–26, and in the judgment of 18 November 1960, at 202–3. The king did not make declaration on the position of an existing border, but defined the border himself: "the dividing line between the Republics of Honduras and Nicaragua from the Atlantic to the Portillo de Teotecacinte [...] is now fixed in the following manner [...]": Application at 25 and Judgment of 18 November 1960, at 202.

[257] *Johnson*, 10 ICLQ (1961), at 329.

[258] The date of Nicaragua's first protest against the award was the subject of controversy during the proceedings. Nicaragua claimed that it had immediately criticized the award after it was delivered: Counter-memorial of Nicaragua, ICJ Pleadings, Arbitral Award Made by the

States which attempts at negotiation and mediation had been unable to resolve.[259]

Faced with the prospects of an armed conflict—there were fights between the two states in the disputed area—the Council of the Organization of American States, at Honduras's request, became active as an organ of consultation on 1 May 1957,[260] based on Article 12 of the Inter-American Treaty of Reciprocal Assistance (Rio Treaty).[261] It appointed an investigating committee that succeeded in brokering a cease-fire[262] and issued a report suggesting the International Court of Justice as an appropriate forum for the solution of the conflict, in addition to the Inter-American Peace Committee and other means of dispute settlement mentioned in the Pact of Bogotá.[263] An *ad hoc* committee appointed by the OAS Council drafted a proposal for an agreement to bring the case before the World Court[264] which formed the framework of the eventual agreement concluded between the two parties in June 1957.[265]

The agreement included clauses on the post-adjudicative phase: Section 3 determined that the Court's decision was to be final and executed without delay. For cases of non-compliance, Section 4 provided that the aggrieved party had to request a meeting of consultation of ministers of foreign affairs of the American states so that appropriate implementation measures could be decided upon before taking recourse to the UN Security Council. Pursuant to Section 5, the arbitral procedure of the Pact of Bogotá[266] was to be applied in the event that the ICJ proceedings did not definitively settle all phases of disagreement.

In a resolution of 5 July 1957, the OAS Council praised the cooperation of the parties with the *ad hoc* committee and the Council itself.[267] Shortly

King of Spain, Vol. I, at 142–53. The Court found that the first time that Nicaragua had raised the question of the validity of the award on the grounds that the King of Spain had not been validly designated arbitrator, that the conditions of the Gámez–Bonilla Treaty had not been fulfilled and that it was not a "clear, really valid, effective and compulsory Award" was on 19 March 1912, see Judgment of 18 November 1960, at 213; the argument that the Gámez–Bonilla Treaty had lapsed had not even been made before 1920, ibid., at 209.

[259] For additional details on the factual background, see *Guyomar*, 6 AFDI (1960), at 362–3; *Johnson*, 10 ICLQ (1961), at 328–30; *Ortiz García*, 14 REspDI (1961), at 197–9; *Wühler*, "Arbitral Award," in EPIL I, at 210–11.

[260] The steps taken in this framework are documented in: OAS/OEA, Secretaría General, Tratado Interamericano de Asistencia Recíproca, Vol. 1, 1948–59, 5th edn., Washington, D.C: 1973, at 233–306. Nicaragua, on 2 May 1957, equally called for an assembly of consultation of the foreign ministers: ibid., at 242–4.

[261] Signed at Rio de Janeiro on 2 September 1947, entered into force on 3 December 1948, 21 UNTS 93.

[262] OAS/OEA, *supra* n. 260, at 245.   [263] Ibid., at 273.   [264] Ibid., at 290–1.

[265] Agreement (with related documents) for submitting to the International Court of Justice their differences with respect to the Award of His Majesty the King of Spain of 23 December 1906. Signed at Tegucigalpa and at Managua on 21 and 22 June 1957, respectively. 277 UNTS 159.

[266] *Supra* n. 253.

[267] Printed as related document to the agreement under 288 UNTS 159, at 180–1.

thereafter, the two countries concluded another agreement in Washington on the submission of the matter to the ICJ.[268] Section 1 reiterated the parties' undertaking to submit the dispute to the ICJ; Section 2 stated that the proceedings were to be launched by an application of Honduras within a determined period of time.[269] Thus, although the parties had specifically agreed to submit the dispute to the ICJ for the institution of proceedings, they opted for the unilateral application route over that of notification of the special agreement—perhaps because of a lack of agreement on the terms of reference: the questions to be submitted were hardly defined.[270] No new arrangements were made for the post-adjudicative phase, but the respective provisions of the June agreement were taken up.[271]

Honduras submitted an application instituting proceedings on 1 July 1958[272] basing the Court's jurisdiction on the Washington agreement and the parties' declarations under Article 36(2) of the ICJ Statute.[273] Honduras claimed that the arbitral award was valid and binding on Nicaragua. Nicaragua countered that the king's decision did not constitute an arbitral award in conformity with the Gámez–Bonilla Treaty as he had improperly been designated as arbitrator and as the treaty had in any event lapsed before he agreed to assume that role. Moreover, it claimed that the award was void on the basis of excess of jurisdiction, essential errors, and inadequate reasoning. Nicaragua pleaded that the award was incapable of execution and asked the Court to declare that the two countries were in the same legal situation with respect to their borders as before 23 December 1906.[274]

---

[268] Agreement on the procedure for submitting to the International Court of Justice their differences with respect to the award of his Majesty the King of Spain of 23 December 1906, 21 July 1957, 277 UNTS 159.

[269] Ibid., Section 2: "[. . .] Honduras shall, within a period of not more than ten months from 15 September 1957, and in accordance with Article 40 of the Statute of the International Court of Justice, submit to the Court a written application bringing the case before it and stating the claim [. . .]."

[270] See Section 1 of the June agreement: "The Parties [. . .] shall submit thereto the disagreement existing between them with respect to the Arbitral Award handed down by [. . .] the King of Spain on 23 December 1906, with the understanding that each, within the framework of its sovereignty, shall present such facets of the matter in disagreement as it deems pertinent." Section 1 of the Washington agreement is worded almost identically.

[271] See Section 5 (reinforcing Sections 4 and 5 of the June agreement): "Should any of the situations arise which are envisaged in the Agreement between the two Governments embodied in the resolution adopted on 5 July 1957 by the Council [. . .], the two governments shall have recourse to the measures specified in that agreement." Section 4 corresponded to Section 3 of the June agreement.

[272] *Supra* n. 254.

[273] Ibid., at 7–9. Since there were two clear bases for the Court's jurisdiction undisputed within the proceedings, the Court did not need to discuss this issue beyond repeating what Honduras had indicated.

[274] See the summary of the submissions in the judgment, 195–7 (Honduras), 197–9 (Nicaragua). See also *Ortiz García*, 14 REspDI (1961), at 199–200; and *Johnson*, 10 ICLQ (1961), at 330–2.

The Court delivered its judgment on 18 December 1960, deciding by 14 votes to 1 that "the arbitral award [...] is valid and binding and [...] Nicaragua is under an obligation to give effect to it."[275] It held that, given the considerable delay between the time of the award and the legal challenge to it, Nicaragua could not challenge[276] the king's designation as arbitrator, the proper application of the Gámez–Bonilla Treaty or the validity of the award itself. Moreover, the Court rejected Nicaragua's arguments in favor of a nullity of the award. Finally, it found that the award was capable of execution and concluded that Nicaragua was under the obligation to give effect to it.[277] In explicitly requiring action for its implementation, the judgment goes beyond confirming the validity of the award; regardless of how one constructs the scope of the *res judicata* of a judgment upholding an arbitral award in general, the terms of the judgment in question cover the legal consequences of the validity of the award.

On the day of the delivery of the judgment, the government of Nicaragua declared that it would comply with the Court's judgment and carry it out "in common agreement with her sister republic Honduras."[278] The implementation of the judgment was no easy matter, given that Nicaragua had to withdraw from an inhabited area that it had been occupying for several decades. A variety of steps was required. Inhabitants not wishing to be subject to Honduran jurisdiction had to be resettled. A solution had to be found for acquired rights concerning private property in the region, and the boundary was to be demarcated.[279] Faced with these practical difficulties, it is not surprising that Nicaragua asked the Inter-American Peace Committee on 16 February 1961[280] for assistance in resolving questions arising from the execution of the ICJ judgment. On 24 February 1961, the government of

---

[275] Judgment of 18 November 1960, at 217. Nicaragua's judge *ad hoc*, the Colombian Urrutia Holguín, dissented.

[276] The Court did not use the term estoppel, but applied a principle related to acquiescence or estoppel. See *Johnson*, 10 ICLQ (1961), at 333–4.

[277] See ibid., 205–17; *Guyomar*, 6 AFDI (1960), at 364–69; *Johnson*, 10 ICLQ (1961), at 332–4; *Ortiz García*, 14 REspDI (1961), at 200–2; *Wühler*, "Arbitral Award," in EPIL I, at 210–11.

[278] Comisión Interamericana de Paz, Informe de la Comisión Interamericana de Paz a la Octava Reunión de Consulta de Ministros de Exteriores, OEA/Ser.L/III/CIP/1/62, 14 January 1962, 3, Press release, The American Embassy, Managua, to Secretary of State Herter, telegram, 18 Nov. 1960, MS. Department of State, file 615.173/11–1860, as quoted in: *Whiteman*, 3 Dig. IL (1964), at 646.

[279] *Anand*, 26 U. Pitt. LR (1965), at 688.

[280] The basis for the Inter-American Peace Committee goes back to a resolution on the second meeting of consultation of the Foreign Ministers of the American Republics in Havana 1940, but it did not become operative and did not receive its name until 1948. It was not mentioned in the OAS Charter (30 April 1948, 119 UNTS 3). According to its statutes (first adopted in 1950 and modified in 1956), the committee's function was "to keep constant vigilance, within the scope of its authority, to ensure that states between which any dispute or controversy exists will solve it as quickly as possible, to which end it shall suggest measures and steps conducive to a settlement [...]." Whereas before 1956, it could act on the initiative of any OAS member, under the 1956 statutes it could only act at the request of a party to the dispute and with the assent of the other

Honduras gave its consent to the Committee's intervention, but made it conditional on an immediate and unconditional Nicaraguan withdrawal from the territory in question, a demand that was dropped on 1 March after further negotiations.[281]

There were no complaints of non-compliance, and neither Sections 4 nor 5 of the special agreement[282] were invoked. Yet the fact that Nicaragua had unilaterally resorted to the Committee and that Honduras at first had demanded the immediate withdrawal as a condition for the Committee's involvement revealed existing tensions and obstacles to implementation. On 12 March 1961,[283] the two governments accepted the Committee's proposal for *bases de arreglo* (bases of arrangement) designed to bring about the withdrawal of the Nicaraguan authorities from the zone of Teotecacinte after the demarcation of that zone, an immediate withdrawal from other parts of the disputed territory,[284] and the establishment of a binational commission headed by the chairman of the Inter-American Peace Committee. This mixed commission was installed on 21 March 1961[285] and had numerous functions: to ensure that persons living in the territory were given a choice as to their nationality; to assist in the relocation of those opting for Nicaraguan citizenship; to fix the boundary line on the ground and verify the starting-point for the natural boundary at the mouth of the Coco River; and to supervise the setting of landmarks, as well as any other power conferred to it by the two governments at the suggestion of the Inter-American Peace Committee. In case of disagreement between the Honduran and Nicaraguan representatives of the Mixed Commission, the chairman had a non-delegable power to make the final decision. Finally, Section 8 of the *bases de arreglo* provided that the Inter-American Peace Committee would suggest measures conducive to a settlement of all questions that might arise between the two governments in carrying out the arbitral award that were not submitted to the Mixed Commission and that acquired rights to private property in the

---

party or parties. It was *de facto* integrated into the OAS and in the Protocol of Buenos Aires (27 February 1967, 721 UNTS 266) was replaced by the Inter-American Committee on Peaceful Settlement (see Article XV, ibid., 346, 352–4), which was founded as a subsidiary of the Permanent Council (see Articles 83–90 of the revised OAS Charter, reprinted in: Sohn, *International organisation and integration*, at 977–96). See Ball, *The OAS in transition*, at 365–73; Kutzner, *Die Organisation Amerikanischer Staaten*, at 338–47; Honegger, *Friedliche Streitbeilegung durch Regionalorganisationen*, at 19–21; Brandt, *Das interamerikanische Friedenssystem*, at 317–25. See also Inter-American Institute, *The Inter-American System*, at 82–104.

[281] Comisión Interamericana de Paz, *supra* n. 278, at 3–4.

[282] The provisions on the post-adjudicative phase.

[283] Whiteman, *supra* n. 278, at 646.

[284] The reason for this different treatment was that there was a natural boundary for the territory, with the exception of the zone of Teotecacinte, where there was a need for demarcation. Comisión Interamericana de Paz, *supra* n. 278, at 12.

[285] Ibid., at 11; Inter-American Institute, *The Inter-American System*, at 102.

territory would be respected in conformity with the constitution and laws of Honduras.[286]

Nicaragua had pulled out of all areas except for Teotecacinte by 12 April 1961; in May, the commission reported that the approximately 4,000 persons desiring relocation to Nicaragua had left. In its report to the Assembly of Foreign Ministers of the OAS, the Inter-American Peace Committee observed that the cooperation of the two governments and the presence of civil servants of the Pan-American Union had significantly contributed to this successful outcome.[287] A disagreement within the Commission concerning the delimitation in the Teotecacinte area was resolved by a decision of the chairman on 2 August 1961 that was accepted by the two governments.[288] In December 1962, the Commission verified the starting-point of the natural border and undertook a final inspection of the boundary markers.[289]

In its report to the OAS Council of 16 July 1963,[290] the Inter-American Peace Committee stated that the verification had been carried out, that all boundary markers in the area of Teotecacinte had been placed and inspected and that the Mixed Commission had thus successfully completed its mandate. The controversy over the arbitral award was definitively settled.[291] With regard to the contribution by the Inter-American system, the Committee expressed its "conviction that the success of the work carried out by it and by the other organs of the Inter-American System that have taken part in this case was due essentially to the genuine spirit of understanding of the parties and their sincere desire to resolve the controversy that existed between them."[292] The UN Secretary-General was informed of the successful implementation of the Court's judgment.[293]

---

[286] The bases of agreement are printed in Whiteman, *supra* n. 278, at 646–8; and Inter-American Institute, *The Inter-American System*, at 100–1.

[287] See *Anand*, 26 U. Pitt. LR (1965), at 689; Inter-American Institute, *The Inter-American System*, 102; and Comisión Interamericana de Paz, *supra* n. 278, at 14: the civil servants had supervised the withdrawal of the Nicaraguan authorities and their presence was intended to avoid the occurrence of incidents.

[288] Informe, *supra* n. 278, at 16–17; Secretaría de Relaciones Exteriores, República de Honduras, Decisión del embajador Vicente Sánchez Gavito sobre el desacuerdo surgido en la Comisión Mixta, Tegucigalpa 1961; *Anand*, 26 U. Pitt. LR (1965), at 689.

[289] *Anand*, 26 U. Pitt. LR (1965), at 689; Inter-American Institute, *The Inter-American System*, at 102.

[290] Report of the Inter-American Peace Committee to the Council of the Organization of American States on the Termination of the Activities of the Honduras-Nicaragua Mixed Commission, OEA/Ser.L/III/II.9.

[291] Ibid., at 8–9. See also *Anand*, 26 U. Pitt. LR (1965), at 689; Inter-American Institute, *The Inter-American System*, at 102.

[292] Report, *supra* n. 290, at 9.

[293] Letter dated 20 October 1963 from the Chairman of the Inter-American Peace Committee addressed to the Secretary-General transmitting the report of the Committee to the Council of the Organization of American States on the termination of the activities of the Honduras–Nicaragua Mixed Commission, UN Doc. S/5452, 7 November 1963.

This result can be attributed to a variety of factors. For starters, the two countries share cultural similarities and values, as well as a common language. Both conceived the dispute as a legal one and seemed genuinely committed to settling it by submitting it to the ICJ and making use of the Inter-American system in the pre- and post-adjudicative phases. The availability of assistance from the OAS and the Inter-American Peace Committee was a plus, but could not have realistically achieved a satisfactory outcome without cooperation from both parties. Nevertheless, a number of factors existed that were adverse to a peaceful solution, including the gravity of the dispute, which had led to the outbreak of hostilities, and its prolonged duration over several decades. Logistical arrangements had to be made for the assignment of nationality and property rights to the thousands of residents of the territory, not to mention for their relocation. Moreover, the loss of face in a matter of national sovereignty could not be taken lightly by the Nicaraguan government. Considering these circumstances, the implementation of the judgment was surprisingly efficient, representing a successful case of the ICJ as a dispute settlement mechanism.

IX. Temple of Preah Vihear

This case concerned the question of sovereignty over the precincts of a temple situated in the Dangrek mountain range in the border zone between Cambodia and Thailand. France[294] and Thailand (then Siam) had reached a boundary settlement for the disputed area between 1904 and 1908. A 1904 treaty established the watershed line as the frontier and left the determination of the exact course of the boundary to a Mixed Boundary Commission. In 1907, French topographical officers mapped the frontier region at the request of the Siamese government; the map for the area in question showed the temple on the Cambodian side, which Phnom Penh pointed to as proof that the temple was Cambodian territory.[295] Thailand relied on the boundary treaty's stipulations, arguing that the application of the true watershed line placed the temple on Thailand's territory, that the map was therefore incorrect, and that it had not been intended to be a binding instrument.[296]

Beginning in 1949, Thailand had stationed keepers at the temple and did not react to protests from France and later from independent Cambodia.[297] From 1954 onwards, Thailand posted troops in the temple. The area as such was not of fundamental importance, but the dispute was symptomatic of the tense relations between the two countries. For Cambodia, the temple represented its independence and resistance to Thai claims to sovereignty over

---

[294] Until its independence in 1953, Cambodia was part of French Indo-China, and its foreign relations were conducted by France as protecting power, see Judgment of 15 June 1962, at 16.
[295] See ibid., at 16–21. For a description of the temple, see ibid., at 15.
[296] Ibid., at 21.   [297] Ibid., at 31; *Johnson*, 11 ICLQ (1962), at 1188–9.

Cambodian territory; for Thailand, it served as a symbol of its desire for control in the region. Different political affiliations[298] and personal resentments between the countries' leaders[299] tainted negotiations in August 1958; diplomatic relations were suspended in late November 1958. Tempers calmed and the two governments announced on 6 February 1959 that their ambassadors would return to their posts, although a true reconciliation was still beyond reach.[300]

Cambodia suggested two alternative solutions to the dispute: a joint administration of the temple site by both countries; or the submission of the case to the ICJ. Since the Thai side did not respond to these proposals,[301] Cambodia seized the ICJ by unilateral application on 6 October 1959,[302] indicating the declarations of Cambodia and Thailand under Article 36(2) of the Court's Statute[303] and several treaty clauses[304] as jurisdictional bases.

---

[298] Thailand was an ally of the United States and, unlike Cambodia, a member of the Southeast Asia Treaty Organization (SEATO), that had been created by the Southeast Asia Collective Defence Treaty, 8 September 1954, 209 UNTS 28. During the Geneva Conference on Indochina of 1954, the PRC urged that Vietnam, Laos, and Cambodia remain neutral; as a consequence, these three states were not offered SEATO membership when the pact was concluded, but were accorded protection by SEATO under a special protocol, 8 September 1954, 209 UNTS 36. Cambodia had committed to neutrality, albeit in a rather lax form: it had assumed the obligation not to join military alliances not conforming with the principles of the UN Charter and not to allow foreign military bases in its territory unless its security was threatened. See Article 7, Agreement on the cessation of hostilities in Cambodia, 20 July 1954, 935 UNTS 184, 189–91; and Declaration of Cambodia, 935 UNTS 99. Cambodia affirmed after the conclusion of the Manila Treaty that it was not barred from joining. Modelski, *SEATO*, at 88, 140–4. Cambodia's initial positive attitude towards SEATO soured as relations with its neighbors South Vietnam and Thailand deteriorated. Non-alignment then became a core element of the foreign policy of Cambodia's ruler, Sihanouk, who refused to join SEATO and even rejected protection under the Protocol, ibid., at 150–3. Cambodia received US military aid based on the Military Aid Agreement of 16 May 1955 (ibid., at 151), nevertheless there were suspicions that Cambodia might orient itself towards the communist bloc, see US National Security Council report of 25 July 1960, printed in US Department of State, Foreign Relations of the United States 1958–1960, Vol. XVI East-Asia Pacific Region, Cambodia, Laos, Washington 1992, 209–23 at 218–19.

[299] The resentment was of such a dimension that Cambodia announced official celebrations upon the death of the Thai prime minister in December 1963, see AdG (1963) 10958 B.

[300] Leifer, *Cambodia*, at 85–8. See also *Rousseau*, 63 RGDIP (1959), at 99–100.

[301] Smith, *Cambodia's Foreign Policy*, at 145. See also Judgment of 15 June 1962, at 32.

[302] Application introducing proceedings, ICJ Pleadings, Temple of Preah Vihear, Vol. I, 4–15. The application was dated 30 September 1959, but handed over to the Court's Registrar by the minister-counsellor of the Cambodian embassy in Paris on 6 October 1959, see Judgment of 26 May 1961, at 19.

[303] See application, at 4 and Declaration recognizing as compulsory the jurisdiction of the International Court of Justice, in conformity with Article 36, para. 2, of the Statute of the International Court of Justice. Phnom-Penh, 9 September 1957, 277 UNTS 77, Declaration recognizing as compulsory the jurisdiction of the Court, in conformity with Article 36, para. 2, of the Statute of the International Court of Justice, Bangkok, 20 May 1950, 65 UNTS 157.

[304] The treaties referred to were the General Act for the Pacific Settlement of International Disputes of 26 September 1928 (see application, 4), the Franco-Siamese Treaty of Friendship, Commerce and Navigation of 7 December 1937, and the settlement agreement of 12 November 1946 (see written observations on the preliminary objections, ICJ Pleadings, Temple of Preah Vihear, Vol. I, 153–67, at 163–7).

Thailand expressed its displeasure about the proceedings before the World Court,[305] claimed that Cambodia was acting under the influence of the communist bloc,[306] and filed preliminary objections contesting the Court's jurisdiction.[307] It conceded that, with its declaration of 20 May 1950, it had had the intention to accept the jurisdiction of the International Court of Justice. However, it argued that this declaration had been intended to extend a declaration recognizing the jurisdiction of the Permanent Court of International Justice of 20 September 1929, a declaration which had lapsed on 19 April 1946; accordingly, the 1950 declaration had been aimed at extending a void declaration, could not produce legal effects, and was equally void. In support of its argumentation, Thailand relied on the Court's decision in the case concerning the Aerial Incident of 27 July 1955 (Israel v. Bulgaria).[308] In its judgment on preliminary objections of 26 May 1961, the Court unanimously found that it had jurisdiction to adjudicate the dispute.[309] It held that there were no doubts it had been Thailand's clear intention to accept the compulsory jurisdiction of the ICJ in its declaration and that this intention was not nullified by some defect in the consent given.[310]

After this judgment, relations between the parties continued to worsen. Cambodia broke off diplomatic relations with Thailand on 23 October 1961 in response to a speech by Thai prime minister, Sarit Thanarat, perceived as an insult to Cambodia's ruler, Sihanouk. Thailand countered by sealing its border with Cambodia, and both countries put their armies into a state of alert.[311] The oral proceedings before the ICJ took place in March 1962.[312] Remarks by the Thai counsel during the proceedings added fuel to the fire and increased Cambodia's concerns that Thailand would pursue a policy

---

[305] Leifer, *Cambodia*, at 88; Smith, *Cambodia's Foreign Policy*, at 145.

[306] Smith, *Cambodia's Foreign Policy*, at 145.

[307] Preliminary objections of the Government of Thailand, ICJ Pleadings, Temple of Preah Vihear, Vol. 1, 133–52.

[308] See Judgment of 26 May 1961, at 20–5. On the aerial incident case, see Aerial incident of 27 July 1955 (Israel v. Bulgaria), Preliminary Objections, Judgment of 26 May 1959; *Hailbronner* in EPIL I, at 51–4. The Court decided that Bulgaria's declaration recognizing the jurisdiction of the PCIJ did not confer jurisdiction on the ICJ under Article 36(5) of the ICJ Statute because Bulgaria had not been represented at the San Francisco Conference and was no signatory of the Charter and the Statute, and it had not become a UN member until after the dissolution of the PCIJ. Bulgaria's declaration lapsed with that dissolution and was not "revived" by its admission the United Nations. (Judgment, ibid., at 135–46).

[309] Judgment of 26 May 1961, at 35. Judges *ad hoc* had not been appointed. For details of the judgment, see *Carrillo Salcedo*, 15 REspDI (1962), at 1190–7; Verzijl, *Jurisprudence of the World Court II*, at 426–33.

[310] Judgment of 26 May 1961, at 27–35. Since the Court regarded this declaration as a sufficient basis for its jurisdiction, it did not regard it necessary to examine Thailand's opposition to the treaties allegedly providing for jurisdiction, ibid., at 35.

[311] Leifer, *Cambodia*, at 89; Smith, *Cambodia's Foreign Policy*, at 147–8. See also 31 AdG (1961) 9411 A.

[312] Judgment of 15 June 1962, at 8.

based on power rather than on law.[313] In the judgment on the merits of 15 June 1962, the Court found in a 9 to 3 decision that the sovereignty over the temple area was vested in Cambodia and that Thailand was under an obligation to withdraw from the temple premises and Cambodian territory in their vicinity. It argued that for a long time, Thailand had not objected to the map according to which the temple belonged to Cambodia, that both parties had by their conduct recognized the boundary line as depicted in the map, and that Thailand was now precluded from asserting non-acceptance of that map.[314] Furthermore, the Court decided by 7 votes to 5 that Thailand had to return any objects removed from the temple since 1954.[315] This last point, however, merely represented a finding for Cambodia in principle, since there was no evidence that objects had in fact been removed.[316]

The first reactions to the judgment were not promising for compliance. Whereas Cambodia celebrated the victory, with Prince Sihanouk treating the matter as a personal and national triumph, Thailand assailed the judgment as being "contrary to usage and international law" and a "miscarriage of justice." Adding insult to injury was from Thailand's perspective the participation of former US secretary of state Dean Acheson as counsel for Cambodia; although he had acted in his private capacity, the Thai government felt betrayed by the US.[317] It threatened to withdraw its ambassador from Paris because two French professors had represented Cambodia before the Court and announced its intention to boycott the sessions of SEATO and the Geneva Conference for Laos. The judges themselves were not immune to criticism. Thailand cut off trade with Poland as a personal snub to Polish ICJ President Winiarski,[318] whom Thai officials suspected of being a communist; other judges were seen as front men for colonial powers.[319] Thai border guards were ordered to shoot on sight every Cambodian trying to enter the temple.[320] The flagrant defiance towards the Court's authority had no precedent at the time. True, Albania had refused to pay damages in the Corfu Channel case; however, this refusal was not coupled with a virtual declaration of war against the Court and any country whose nationals had engaged in an attempt to settle the dispute peacefully before the ICJ.[321]

[313] Smith, *Cambodia's Foreign Policy*, at 148–9.
[314] Judgment of 15 June 1962, at 32–7. Accordingly, the Court did not regard it as necessary to examine whether the line corresponded to the true watershed line: ibid., at 35.
[315] Judgment of 15 June 1962, at 36–7. There were no judges ad hoc. For details, see *Johnson*, 11 ICLQ (1962), at 1199–204; *Kelly*, 39 BYIL (1963), at 462–72; *Thornberry*, 26 MLR (1963), at 448–51; Verzijl, *Jurisprudence of the World Court II*, at 433–61.
[316] Judgment of 15 June 1962 at 36.
[317] See Smith, *Cambodia's Foreign Policy*, at 149–50; 32 AdG (1962) 9923 G; *Anand*, 26 U. Pitt. LR (1965), at 691.
[318] *Cot*, 8 AFDI (1962), at 246; *Anand*, 26 U. Pitt. LR (1965), at 691.
[319] Smith, *Cambodia's Foreign Policy*, at 149.
[320] *Cot*, 8 AFDI (1962), at 246; *Rousseau*, 70 RGDIP (1966), 1009; Smith, *Cambodia's Foreign Policy*, 150.
[321] *Cot*, 8 AFDI (1962), at 247; see also *supra* I 3 and 4 on the Corfu Channel case.

Fortunately, the ruling was implemented in spite of these first reactions, and the temper of the Thai government quickly subsided following visits of the American ambassador and the Australian foreign minister. On 21 June 1962, Marshal Sarit Thanarat announced that Thailand would honor its commitments under the UN Charter;[322] on 6 July 1962, Thailand sent a note to the UN Secretary-General in which it confirmed its intention to comply with the decision, albeit with the addition that this had no impact on any future rights on part of Thailand to recover the area by "having recourse to any existing or subsequently applicable legal process."[323] This last reservation caused concerns on part of Cambodia, particularly since Thailand had erected barbed-wire barriers around the temple before it withdrew its troops.[324] Cambodia, on its part, tried to ease tensions: as a gesture of reconciliation, it offered objects removed from the temple during the occupation as a gift to the Thailand, and declared that every non-armed Thai citizen could visit the temple for prayers without formalities.[325] In early January 1963, Cambodia took possession of the temple.[326]

In April 1966, two attacks on Cambodian temple guards from the Thai territory were reported. Thailand attributed the behavior to Cambodian rebels, but Cambodia countered that the attacks could not have occurred without Thailand's consent, since they had been launched from Thai territory and there were witnesses who testified that the first incident had been carried out by Thai elements using machinery that the rebels never possessed.[327] Even assuming there were indications for Thailand's responsibility for these incidents,[328] they were isolated events that did not serve as open challenges to the Court.

Compliance took place, but only after great difficulty, which is understandable given the hostile relations and mutual suspicions between the parties,[329] Thailand's initial opposition to judicial settlement and unwillingness to reconcile during the proceedings, and the symbolic importance of the issue at stake.

---

[322] *Anand*, 26 U. Pitt. LR (1965), at 691.

[323] Smith, *Cambodia's Foreign Policy*, at 150–1.

[324] *Rousseau*, 70 RGDIP (1966), at 1009; Smith, *Cambodia's Foreign Policy*, 151.

[325] *Cot*, 8 AFDI (1962), at 247.

[326] Ibid., at 247; *Rousseau*, 70 RGDIP (1966), at 1009 (both reporting that this took place on 5 January); compare Smith, *Cambodia's Foreign Policy*, 151 (stating it occured on 4 January).

[327] *Rousseau*, 70 RGDIP (1966), at 1009–10; compare also Leifer, *Cambodia*, 90.

[328] See *Rousseau*, 70 RGDIP (1966), at 1010.

[329] The climate of mutual resentments and lack of trust becomes visible, for example, in US Department of Commerce, Cambodia's relations with its neighbors—an analysis by Norodom Sihanouk, Washington D.C. 1963, at 5–28, reprinting articles by the Cambodian head of state, Sihanouk, in the newspaper Réalités Cambodgiennes, 22 June 1962, 1–3, 6 July 1962 1–5, 13 July 1962 1–4, and Thailand, Ministry of Foreign Affairs, Facts about the relations between Thailand and Cambodia, Bangkok 1961.

X. North Sea continental shelf

These cases concerned the delimitation of the continental shelf between the Federal Republic of Germany, on the one hand, and Denmark and the Netherlands, on the other. The continental shelf had been partly delimited between the three countries by a German–Dutch Treaty of 1964 and a German–Danish Treaty of 1965, but only for the area in the vicinity of the coast.[330] The negotiations for points beyond ground to a halt after Denmark and the Netherlands insisted on the applicability of the equidistance principle, a method rejected as inequitable by the Germans, who would have had a disproportionately small share of the shelf if it had been employed.[331]

The parties decided to bring the matter before the ICJ in special agreements dated 2 February 1967.[332] The Court was not asked to determine the boundary, but rather to indicate the applicable rules of international law.[333] The definitive settlement thus was to remain a matter for subsequent negotiations; for that purpose, the parties undertook in the special agreement to effect the delimitation of the continental shelf in pursuance of the judgment.[334] The trilateral character of the dispute was reflected in the way the Court was approached: the special agreements were the result of tripartite

[330] Treaty concerning the lateral delimitation of the continental shelf in the vicinity of the coast, 1 December 1964, Netherlands–Federal Republic of Germany, 550 UNTS 123; Agreement concerning the delimitation, in the coastal regions, of the continental shelf of the North Sea, 9 June 1965, Denmark–Federal Republic of Germany, 570 UNTS 91.

[331] *Jaenicke* in EPIL III, at 657. On the background of the case, see also *Monconduit*, 15 AFDI (1969), at 213–17; Reynaud, *Les différends du plateau continental de la Mer du Nord devant la Cour international de Justice*, 15–47.

[332] ICJ Pleadings, North Sea Continental Shelf, Vol. 1: Danish–German special agreement, 2 February 1967, 6–7, German–Dutch special agreement, 2 February 1967, 8–9. The Federal Republic of Germany was not yet a party to the Court's Statute, but on 29 April 1961, it had made a general declaration of acceptance of the jurisdiction of the ICJ in conformity with Article 3 of the European Convention for the Peaceful Settlement of Disputes of 29 April 1957 (320 UNTS 243), Article 35(2) of the ICJ Statute and Security Council Resolution 9 of 15 October 1946, see the preamble of the special agreements. See for further details on the availability of the Court for states not parties to the Statute *supra* Chapter 2 C II.

[333] See Judgment of 20 February 1969, at 13 para. 2: "The Court is not asked actually to delimit the further boundaries which will be involved, this task being reserved by the special agreement to the parties, which undertake to effect such a limitation 'by agreement in pursuance of the decision requested from the [. . .] Court'—that is to say on the basis of, and in accordance with, the principles and rules of international law found by the Court to be applicable." See Article 1(1) of both special agreements, defining the question submitted to the Court: "What principles and rules of international law are applicable to the delimitation as between the Parties of the areas of the continental shelf in the North Sea which appertain to each of them beyond the partial boundary determined by the above-mentioned Convention [. . .]." The term "convention" referred to the bilateral delimitation treaties of 1964 and 1965, respectively.

[334] Article 1(2) ibid. "The Governments of [the contracting parties] shall delimit the continental shelf in the North Sea as between their countries by agreement in pursuance of the decision requested from the International Court of Justice."

negotiations, and at their signature, the three states agreed in a protocol that the Netherlands would make a notification to the Court under Article 40(1) of the Statute and that they would ask the Court to join the two cases.[335] The Dutch notification was received by the Court's Registry on 20 February 1967.[336] While the Court joined the proceedings in the two cases by an order of 26 April 1968, the cases remained formally separate.[337]

The Netherlands and Denmark submitted that the relevant legal principle was the equidistance/special circumstances principle as expressed in Article 6(2) of the Geneva Convention on the Continental Shelf, despite the fact that the Federal Republic of Germany had never ratified that convention; they argued that this principle was inherent in the concept of the continental shelf or at least part of customary international law. Germany, on the other hand, maintained that delimitation had to be carried out in such a way as to leave each side "a just and equitable share" and that the equidistance principle was just one method that under certain conditions might bring about an equitable solution, but not as between the parties in the present case, and it contested the principle's binding character beyond the Geneva Convention.[338]

On 20 February 1969, the Court delivered its judgment:[339] by 11 votes to 6, it found that the use of the equidistance method was not obligatory as between the parties, that there was no other single method of delimitation applicable in all circumstances, and that the applicable rules and principles were that the delimitation had to "be effected by agreement in accordance with equitable principles, and taking account of all the relevant circumstances, in such a way as to leave as much as possible to each Party all those parts of the continental shelf that constitute a natural prolongation of its land territory [...]." If overlap resulted, the areas were to be divided in agreed proportions or, failing agreement, equally, unless the parties were to establish some form of a joint régime. The Court gave a non-exhaustive list of relevant circumstances to be taken into account in the course of the negotiations, including the general configuration of the coast, the geological

---

[335] Protocol between Denmark, the Netherlands, and the Federal Republic of Germany of 2 February 1967, ICJ Pleadings, North Sea Continental Shelf, Vol. I, 10. Furthermore, they agreed that Denmark and the Netherlands would be regarded as parties in the same interest under Article 31(5) of the ICJ Statute for the purposes of appointing a judge *ad hoc*. Denmark and the Netherlands chose Max Sørensen; the Federal Republic of Germany Hermann Mosler; see Judgment of 20 February 1969, at 8.

[336] Judgment of 20 February 1969, at 5.

[337] Order of 26 April 1968, at 9–11. This order followed the request of the parties, despite some differences between the two cases; the aim of the joinder was to produce a single set of pleadings and a single judgment. See Rosenne, *World Court*, 203–4.

[338] For a summary of the parties' submissions, see *Jaenicke* in EPIL III, at 658; and Judgment of 20 February 1969, at 8–12. For details on the equidistance rule, the respective sumissions, and the decision on the Court on this point, see *Griesel*, 64 AJIL (1970), at 562–93.

[339] As the Court's conclusions in the two cases were identical, it was a single judgment. See *Jaenicke* in EPIL III, at 658.

structure of the seabed, and the location of natural resources, and a reasonable degree of proportionality between the extent of the continental shelf and the length of the coast of each state measured in the general direction of the coastline.[340] It rejected the German claim to a "just and equitable share" on grounds that the task was delimitation and not apportionment, i.e. the establishment of boundaries in an area already in principle appertaining to the coastal state.[341] Furthermore, the Court recalled the parties' obligation to enter into "meaningful negotiations" without any party insisting on one specific method, emphasizing that the negotiations conducted in 1965 and 1966 had not fulfilled this condition because of the reliance on the equidistance method on part of the Netherlands and Denmark.[342] From the broad guidelines indicated by the Court, it was impossible to suggest one particular line as the sole correct outcome; there was a broad margin of appreciation for future negotiations, particularly since the list of the relevant circumstances was non-exhaustive.

The judgment was respected by the parties and served as a guideline in their negotiations;[343] the Netherlands and Denmark could not insist any longer on the applicability of the equidistance principle. On 28 January 1971, Germany concluded separate treaties on the continental shelf's delimitation with Denmark and the Netherlands; a tripartite protocol was made on the same day.[344] These instruments explicitly invoked the Court's judgments as a basis for the establishment of the boundaries;[345] hence, the parties saw the delimitation as an implementation of the principles indicated by the Court. For the question of compliance with the judgment, it is not necessary to assess for whom the settlement was more favorable and who had made the best use of the margin provided by the Court's findings—what is relevant is

---

[340] Judgment of 20 February 1969, at 53–4, para. 101. The dissenting judges were Judges Bengzon (Philippines), Koretsky (USSR), Tanaka (Japan), Morelli (Italy), Lachs (Poland), and Judge *ad hoc* Sørensen (appointed by the Netherlands and Denmark); the German Judge *ad hoc* Mosler voted with the majority (ibid., at 56). For details, see *Monconduit*, 15 AFDI (1969), at 219–44; *Rothpfeffer*, 42 Nord. TIR (1972), at 94–137 (particularly on Court's concept of equity).

[341] Judgment of 20 February 1969, at 21–3, paras. 18–20. One might doubt whether this was more a difference in approach than in the actual result. See *Jaenicke* in EPIL III, at 659; *Friedmann*, 64 AJIL (1970), at 235–6; *Chaturvedi*, 13 Indian JIL (1973), at 484.

[342] Judgment of 20 February 1969, at 47–8, paras. 85–6.

[343] See *von Schenck*, 15 JiR (1971), at 391 (observing that intense negotiations required for implementation).

[344] Treaty concerning the delimitation of the continental shelf under the North Sea, Denmark–Federal Republic of Germany, 28 January 1971, 857 UNTS 109; Treaty concerning the delimitation of the continental shelf under the North Sea, Netherlands–Federal Republic of Germany, 28 January 1971, 857 UNTS 131; Protocols to the Treaties of 28 January 1971 between the Federal Republic of Germany and Denmark and the Netherlands, respectively, concerning the delimitation of the continental shelf under the North Sea, 28 January 1971, 857 UNTS 155. The treaties were simultaneously ratified on 7 November 1972.

[345] Treaties, preamble, Protocol, I (1).

that the principles explained by the Court were not put into question and that the parties had reached a result that they considered equitable.[346]

Factors that might have been unfavorable to an effective settlement of the dispute[347] were the lack of precision of the applicable law and the fact that the Court merely had to rule on the applicable legal principles and was not asked to carry out the delimitation itself. However, since the legal principles were the controversial issue and the willingness of the parties to engage in negotiations had not been in question, this did not turn out to be a problem.[348] In the end, the positives outweighed the negatives, most notably the common desire of the parties to settle the dispute and to have the disputed principles clarified by the Court. The matter was of important, though not vital, interest. Both special agreements included a precisely framed question for the Court as well as a provision on the post-adjudicative phase. Overall, the Court's intervention brought an end to the deadlock in the negotiations between the traditional allies and enabled the amicable settlement of a multilateral problem within a multilateral framework.[349]

XI. Appeal relating to the jurisdiction of the ICAO Council

In this case, India challenged a decision which the Council of the International Civil Aviation Organization had delivered on 29 July 1971.[350] In that decision, the ICAO Council had dismissed India's preliminary objections to its jurisdiction over a complaint brought by Pakistan on 3 March 1971; there was not yet a decision on the merits.[351] Pakistan had introduced proceedings before the ICAO Council after India barred Pakistani civilian planes from Indian airspace in response to a hijacking incident in which an

---

[346] For details on the settlement, see *Auburn*, 16 AdV (1974/75), at 28–36; Reynaud, *Les différends du plateau continental*, at 169–91 (arguing at 176–8 that settlement somewhat contradicts aspects of Court's reasoning); *von Schenck*, 15 JiR (1971), at 379–82. See also *Jaenicke* in EPIL III, at 659 (reporting that the Federal Republic of Germany nearly received the sector claimed before the Court). On the negotiations and the nature of the result, see *Rothpfeffer*, 42 Nord. TIR (1972), at 128–30.

[347] Not necessarily to compliance with the judgment, though: the question of compliance, on the one hand, and effective dispute settlement, on the other, must remain distinct. They can coincide if the judgment as such definitively resolves *all* disputed issues; if, however, a judgment is supposed to solve only one aspect of a dispute, a final settlement might be far off.

[348] See *von Schenck*, 15 JiR (1971), at 378.

[349] See *Auburn*, 16 AdV (1974/75), at 33 (calling Court's intervention "external pressure" enabling the Netherlands and Denmark to make concessions embodied in final settlement). See also *Rothpfeffer*, 42 Nord. TIR (1972), at 129 (reporting that the Netherlands and Denmark were particularly interested in rapid settlement after judgment delivered). On the impact of the judgment on the development of the law of the sea, see *Jaenicke* in EPIL III, at 659–60 with further references.

[350] See India's application instituting proceedings, ICJ Pleadings, Appeal relating to the jurisdiction of the ICAO Council, 4–21; the decision of the ICAO Council is printed in the annex, at 16–17.

[351] See the ICAO Council's decision, *supra* n. 350.

Indian aircraft had been diverted to Pakistan and blown up.[352] The suspension of overflights seriously disrupted movement between what was then West and East Pakistan[353] at a moment in which Pakistani unity had become fragile and East Pakistan was shortly to become an independent state, Bangladesh. The dispute came at a moment when relations between the two countries were extremely volatile.[354]

India considered the ICAO Council decision as either illegal, null and void, or erroneous because of a lack of jurisdiction of the Council. It argued that the two treaties upon which Pakistan's application and complaint were based—the International Civil Aviation Convention and the International Air Services Transit Agreement[355]—were no longer applicable between the parties and as a result the Council had no jurisdiction to decide the dispute. India and Pakistan had become members of the International Air Services Agreement in 1945 and 1947, respectively, and of the International Civil Aviation Convention in 1947.[356] On the basis of these treaties, Pakistan asserted the right for its civil aircraft to fly across Indian territory. Hostilities between the parties had interrupted flights across their respective territories from August 1965 onwards; however, in February 1966, they agreed in an exchange of letters on an immediate resumption of overflights "on the same basis as that prior to 1 August 1965 [...]." India argued that this exchange of letters had created a new legal regime for the overflights, and that the International Civil Aviation Convention and the International Air Services Transit Agreement were no longer valid between them. Consequently, it regarded the clauses of those treaties establishing the jurisdiction of the ICAO Council as inapplicable.[357] When the ICAO Council rejected the preliminary objections, India immediately appealed the decision

---

[352] See the summary of the facts in the Judgment of 18 August 1972, at 50–1, paras. 9–10; *Fitzgerald*, 12 CYIL (1974), at 159–72; *Manin*, 19 AFDI (1973), at 294–8.

[353] Rosenne, *World Court*, 204.

[354] The state of Bangladesh was proclaimed after a civil uprising broke out in East Pakistan in March 1971. India supported the secessionist forces and engaged in border clashes with Pakistan from April 1971 onwards, culminating in a war between the two countries in December 1971 both on the eastern and the western fronts. On 6 December, diplomatic relations were interrupted when India recognized Bangladesh; Bangladesh achieved recognition by a large number of states in the subsequent months. A cease-fire became effective on 17 December following Pakistan's capitulation the preceding day. See Brown, *The United States and India, Pakistan, Bangladesh*, 206–26; Heß, *Bangladesh*; Rousseau, 76 RGDIP (1972), at 538–64. The tensions resonated in the language used before the Court. See e.g. India's memorial, ICJ Pleadings, Appeal relating to the jurisdiction of the ICAO Council, at 32–7 (32: "Pakistan's posture of confrontation bordering on hostility against India").

[355] Both treaties were signed at Chicago on 7 December 1944. The Convention on International Civil Aviation is published at 15 UNTS 295, the International Air Services Transit Agreement at 84 UNTS 389.

[356] The Convention on International Civil Aviation entered into force for India on 4 April 1947, for Pakistan on 6 December 1947, 15 UNTS 374, the International Air Services Transit Agreement for India on 2 May 1945, for Pakistan on 15 August 1947, 84 UNTS 390.

[357] See Judgment of 18 August 1972, at 49–50, para. 8 and 51, para. 10.

to the International Court of Justice,[358] filing an application on 30 August 1971.[359] It based the Court's jurisdiction on Article 84 of the International Civil Aviation Convention and on Article II Section 2 of the International Air Services Transit Agreement.[360] Those articles provide for the possibility of an appeal against decisions of the ICAO Council to the PCIJ;[361] by virtue of Article 37 of the ICJ Statute, such clauses confer jurisdiction on the ICJ.[362]

Pakistan objected to the ICJ's jurisdiction. It argued that the respective appeal provisions of the International Civil Aviation Convention and the International Air Services Transit Agreement were applicable only to final decisions of the Council disposing of the case, not to interlocutory ones. It submitted that India was precluded from invoking the appeal provisions as a basis for the Court's jurisdiction because of its reasoning that those treaties were inapplicable in its relationship with Pakistan. Nevertheless, in the event that the Court found that it had jurisdiction in the case, Pakistan urged the Court to uphold the Council's own jurisdictional ruling.[363]

In its judgment of 18 August 1972, the Court found by 13 votes to 3 that it had jurisdiction to entertain India's appeal[364] and, by 14 votes to 2, that the ICAO Council was competent to entertain the Application and Complaint

---

[358] See Statement of the Indian representative Gidwani, minutes of the 6th meeting of the 74th Session of the Council, ICAO Doc. 8956/1001, C-Min. LXXIV/6 (Closed), printed in the Memorial submitted by the Republic of India, ICJ Pleadings, Appeal relating to the jurisdiction of the ICAO Council, 25 at 266 (annex E (e)), at 289, para. 152.

[359] See letter of the Indian agent to the registrar, 30 August 1971, ICJ Pleadings, Appeal relating to the jurisdiction of the ICAO Council, at 3, and the application, *supra* n. 350.

[360] See Judgment of 18 August 1972 at 48, para. 1 and application, *supra* n. 350, 4 para. 2.

[361] Article 84 of the Convention reads: "If any disagreement between two or more of the contracting States relating to the interpretation or application of this Convention and its Annexes cannot be settled by negotiation, it shall, on the application of any State concerned in the disagreement, be decided by the Council. No member of the Council shall vote in the consideration by the Council of any dispute to which it is a party. Any contracting State may, subject to Article 85, appeal from the decision of the Council to an *ad hoc* arbitral tribunal agreed upon with the other parties to the dispute or to the Permanent Court of International Justice. Any such appeal shall be notified to the Council within sixty days of receipt of notification of the decision of the Council." Article II Section 2 of the Transit Agreement reads: "If any disagreement between two or more contracting States relating to the interpretation or application of this Agreement cannot be settled by negotiation, the provisions of Chapter XVIII of the above-mentioned Convention shall be applicable in the same manner as provided therein with reference to any disagreement relating to the interpretation or application of the above-mentioned Convention." This is a reference to the International Civil Aviation Convention (see Article I Section 2 Transit Agreement); its Article 84 is the first provision in chapter XVIII.

[362] For further details on the Court's ability to act as an instance of appeal against decisions of other bodies when such authority is expressly conferred upon it, see Rosenne, *World Court*, at 38 and 105–6.

[363] Judgment of 18 August 1972, at 50, para. 8, and Pakistan's Counter-memorial, ICJ Pleadings, Appeal relating to the jurisdiction of the ICAO Council, 369–404, at 379–94.

[364] Judgment of 18 August 1972, at 52–61, paras. 13–26 and 70, para. 46. President Zafrulla Khan (Pakistan) and judges Petrén (Sweden) and Onyeama (Nigeria) voted against this section of the operative part, but concurred in the finding that the ICAO Council had jurisdiction (ibid., at 71, 76, 86). For a critical comment on the Court's finding of jurisdiction, see *Böckstiegel* in Festschrift für Hermann Jahrreiß, at 15–18.

by Pakistan of 3 March 1971, thus rejecting India's appeal against the Council's decision.[365] It explained that the Council had jurisdiction since the dispute related to the interpretation or application of the International Civil Aviation Convention and the International Air Services Transit Agreement: both the charges of breaches of the Convention and the Agreement and the issue of the possibility to replace the treaties by another regime or terminate them involved such questions of interpretation or application.[366] Finally, the Court clarified that its task was not to investigate the proceedings in which the Council had arrived at the decision, but to establish, as an objective question of law, whether the Council had jurisdiction in the case.[367]

Prior to the delivery of judgment, the parties had concluded an agreement on their bilateral relationships at Simla on 2 July 1972,[368] in which they affirmed their intentions to put an end to conflict and confrontation and to withdraw forces to their side of the international border and respect the line of control in Jammu and Kashmir resulting from the cease-fire of 17 December 1971.[369] In an effort to normalize relations, they undertook to take steps to resume airlinks, including overflights.[370] While this agreement did not conclusively settle all disputes between the two countries,[371] the climate between the parties had improved by the time the judgment was delivered, making resistance to it less likely.

The ICJ had confirmed Pakistan's position on the merits and thus objections from its side were not to be expected. India, on the other hand, was not yet faced with a ruling directly affecting its policy of suspending overflight for Pakistani aircraft; the result of the judgment was that the ICAO Council proceedings could go ahead to the merits stage, but there was not yet a final decision on whether India had been bound by the treaties to permit overflights.[372] Thus, it was not the ICJ's judgment, but, if anything, a future

---

[365] Judgment of 18 August 1972, at 61–71, paras. 27–46. The dissenting judges were the Soviet Morozov and India's judge *ad hoc* Nagendra Singh. For details, see *Huntzinger*, 78 RGDIP (1974), at 975–1016; *Fitzgerald*, 12 CYIL (1974), at 173–85; *Magiera*, 17 JiR (1974), at 327–31; *Manin*, 19 AFDI (1973), at 299–318.

[366] See Judgment of 18 August 1972, at 66–9, paras. 35–43.

[367] See ibid., at 69–70, paras. 44–5.

[368] Agreement on bilateral relationships, India–Pakistan, 858 UNTS 71 (entered into force 4 August 1972).

[369] Ibid., Sections 1 and 4.   [370] Ibid., Section 3(i).

[371] Most notably, the dispute over Jammu/Kashmir problem remains unsettled up to the present day; from the large news coverage, see, for example, the section "Kashmir Flashpoint" on the BBC website, http://news.bbc.co.uk/2/hi/in_depth/south_asia/2002/kashmir_flashpoint. Section 6 of the Simla agreement stated that both sides were to meet to discuss further on arrangements to achieve durable peace, including among other things a final settlement of Jammu and Kashmir.

[372] This had not yet been decided by the ICAO Council's decision of 29 July 1971, see the minutes of the 6th meeting of the 74th Session of the Council, ICAO Doc. 8956/1001, C-Min. LXXIV/6 (Closed), printed in the Memorial submitted by the Republic of India, ICJ Pleadings, Appeal relating to the jurisdiction of the ICAO Council, 25 at 266 (annex E (e)).

decision of the ICAO Council that could restrict India's freedom of action, and that decision again could be appealed to the ICJ. India therefore had no compelling reasons to protest the judgment, especially in view of warming relations with Pakistan. It accepted the judgment by taking part in the proceedings before the ICAO Council and submitting a counter-memorial on 28 August 1972.[373] Ultimately, the proceedings did not advance to a further stage, since the parties engaged in complementary efforts to re-establish the overflights.[374] The proceedings were officially discontinued in 1976[375] after a period of continuous improvement in the relations between the two countries.[376]

XII. Fisheries Jurisdiction

The Fisheries Jurisdiction cases concerned the validity of an exclusive fishery zone (EFZ) established by Iceland and its impact on traditional fishing rights of the United Kingdom and the Federal Republic of Germany within that zone.

1. Background of the dispute

Since 1948, Iceland had pursued a policy of claiming exclusive jurisdiction over the fishery resources in the waters adjacent to its coast. The establishment of a 12-mile EFZ in 1958 led to a conflict with the UK and the FRG. Settlements were reached by bilateral exchanges of notes between those two countries and Iceland in 1961.[377] Acknowledging the importance of coastal fisheries for Iceland's economy, the UK and the FRG agreed no longer to object to the 12-mile-zone, subject to the proviso that Iceland not object to fishing by UK and German vessels in certain parts of the fishery zone for three subsequent years. Iceland declared that it would continue its policy of extending its fishery zone, but undertook to give notice six months before such an extension. It was agreed that "in case of a dispute in relation to such extension, the matter shall, at the request of either party, be referred to the International Court of Justice."[378] The exchanges of notes did not contain a termination clause or a time limit.

---

[373] ICAO, Action of the Council, 88th Session, 7–30 June 1976, Doc. 9171-C/1033, 22; *Manin*, 19 AFDI (1973), at 318.

[374] Manin, 19 AFDI (1973), at 318–19.

[375] ICAO, Action of the Council, 88th Session, 7–30 June 1976, Doc. 9171-C/1033, 22.

[376] On 14 May 1976, they agreed to re-establish diplomatic relations. Ambassadors were exchanged on 21 July 1976. See *Klein/Klein*, "Chronologie des faits internationaux d'ordre juridique, année 1976," 22 AFDI (1976), 1029, 1934.

[377] Exchange of notes with the UK, 11 March 1961, 397 UNTS 275; Exchange of notes with the Federal Republic of Germany, 19 July 1961, 409 UNTS 47.

[378] Ibid., penultimate paragraph, respectively.

On 14 July 1971, Iceland's newly elected[379] government issued a policy statement in which it announced its intention to terminate the agreements with the UK and the FRG and to extend the EFZ to 50 miles as from 1 September 1972. Despite protests from the British and the Germans, who challenged the legality of the extension of the fishery zone and insisted on the validity of the 1961 exchanges of notes,[380] the Icelandic parliament adopted a resolution on 15 February 1972 that the fishery zone be extended and that the UK and the FRG be informed that "because of the vital interests of the nation and owing to changed circumstances the Notes concerning fishery limits exchanged in 1961 are no longer applicable and that their provisions do not constitute an obligation for Iceland."[381] It therefore contested the continued validity of the agreements in their entirety, supposedly on a *clausula rebus sic stantibus* argument. In *aides-mémoires* of 31 August 1971 and 24 February 1972, the government of Iceland elaborated its position, stressing the vital interests of the Icelandic people and maintaining that the object and purpose of the provisions in the 1961 notes for recourse to judicial settlement in certain eventualities had been fully achieved and were therefore to be regarded as terminated.[382] Accordingly, Iceland did not contest at that point that the dispute settlement clause had originally provided for jurisdiction by the Court, nor did it advance a right to terminate this agreement, instead claiming that the respective clauses had lapsed because their object and purpose of the clause had been achieved. Such a position appears highly dubious since the clause referred to disputes arising out of further extensions—precisely the scenario presented by the proposed 50-mile fishery zone.

The conflict on the limits of Iceland's EFZ flared up again.[383] The extension of the fishery limits threatened to inflict substantial losses on British and German fishermen, who had traditionally fished in the region and had few if

---

[379] Following elections, a new center-left government was formed in July 1971, with a communist in the important post of fisheries minister. See Jónsson, *Friends in conflict*, at 122–4 and *Favoreu*, 18 AFDI (1972), at 293.

[380] Judgments of 25 July 1974, 13–14 paras. 27–8 (UK), and 185–6 paras. 27–8 (FRG).

[381] Resolution of the Althing on Fisheries Jurisdiction, printed in the Judgments of 2 February 1973, at 18 para. 37 (UK), and 63 para. 37 (FRG v. Iceland); Annex G to the British Application, ICJ Pleadings, Fisheries Jurisdiction, Vol. I, 25.

[382] Government of Iceland's Aide-mémoire of 31 August 1971, printed as Annex C to the UK Application, ICJ Pleadings, Fisheries Jurisdiction, Vol. 1, 14, Government of Iceland's Aide-mémoire of 24 February 1972 printed as Annex H to the UK Application, ICJ Pleadings, Fisheries Jurisdiction, Vol. 1, 26. The *aides-mémoires* communicated to Germany were shorter, but equally stressed the changed circumstances and the achievement of the objectives of the dispute settlement clause: Government of Iceland's Aide-mémoire of 31 August 1971, Annex D to the German Application, ICJ Pleadings, Fisheries Jurisdiction, Vol. 2, 15, and Government of Iceland's Aide-mémoire of 24 February 1972, Annex H to the German Application, ICJ Pleadings, Fisheries Jurisdiction, Vol. 2, 17–18.

[383] For history of the dispute, see *Briney*, 5 Ga. JILC (1975), at 248–51; *Jaenicke* in EPIL II, at 386; Jónsson, *Friends in conflict*; *Langavant/Pirotte*, 80 RGDIP (1976), at 60–6; *Weil*, 16 Harv. ILJ (1975), at 474–7.

any alternative fishing opportunities. As negotiations proved fruitless, the UK and the FRG decided to take the matter before the International Court of Justice.[384]

2. The proceedings before the Court

By unilateral applications of 5 April and 5 June 1972, the UK and the FRG brought the matter before the ICJ[385] and based the Court's jurisdiction on Article 36(1) of the Statute in connection with the notes of 1961.[386] Both countries challenged Iceland's claim to a 50-mile EFZ and argued that the conservation of fish stocks was to be effected by mutual agreement, not by a unilateral extension of fisheries jurisdiction.[387]

Talks between the parties continued after that point,[388] although Iceland made no effort formally to participate in the ICJ proceedings. It did transmit its legal opinions through communications to the Registrar, essentially adopting the line that the Court lacked jurisdiction. It observed that the exchanges of notes had taken place under extremely difficult circumstances; that the clause in question gave the applicants the opportunity of recourse to the Court should Iceland further extend the limits of the fishery zone *without warning*; and finally that the agreement had not been of a permanent nature.[389] It did not specify the legal rules on which it based its objections, although the reasoning evokes issues such as temporal application, *clausula rebus sic stantibus*, use of coercion (for the exchange of notes with the UK), and the content of the dispute settlement clause (i.e. the statement that it related to disputes arising out of an extension *without warning*, which seems to imply that it was irrelevant for disputes in which a warning was issued).

---

[384] See *Anderson*, in Götz, Liber amicorum Günter Jaenicke, at 446–7.

[385] Application submitted by the UK, Fisheries Jurisdiction Cases, ICJ Pleadings, Vol. 1, 3–68, Application submitted by the Federal Republic of Germany, ibid., Vol. 2, 3–20.

[386] UK application, German application, 3. The Federal Republic of Germany was not a party to the ICJ Statute at the time, but accepted the Court's jurisdiction in relation to the dispute and the respective obligations in accordance with Article 35(2) of the Statute and the Security Council resolution of 15 October 1946, German application at 3, 12 (see *supra* Chapter 2 C II).

[387] UK application, 10, German Application, 11. While the UK requested a declaration that the extension of the fisheries jurisdiction was invalid, the Federal Republic of Germany's claim was that it was not opposable to Germany: ibid. The UK Memorial included non-opposability as a second claim besides its first claim regarding the invalidity; in the hearings, the UK stated that a ruling on the first submission was not necessary if the Court decided on the second submission, Argument of Mr Slynn on behalf of the United Kingdom, Public Sitting of 29 March 1974, ICJ Pleadings, Fisheries Jurisdiction, Vol. I, 479–508, at 487–8. The Court decided the case on the basis of non-opposability, see Judgment of 25 July 1974 at 29–31 paras. 67–72 (UK).

[388] *Rousseau*, 76 RGDIP (1972), at 894–5; *Rüster* in Blumenwitz/Randelzhofer, Festschrift für Berber, at 456–7.

[389] Letters from the Minister for Foreign Affairs of Iceland to the Registrar of 29 May 1972 and of 27 June 1972, ICJ Pleadings, Fisheries Jurisdiction, Vol. 2, 374–6 and 380–2, and for further communication from Iceland, see ibid., at 388–90, 397–9, 404–5, 447–8, 462–3.

Given their relative vagueness, these arguments could hardly rebut the seemingly straightforward texts of the notes.[390] In view of the non-appearance and non-participation of Iceland, the UK and the FRG requested the Court to proceed under Article 53 of its Statute.[391]

Even though Iceland never made formal pleadings to the Court, the Court took its legal arguments seriously. For certain, the Court was obliged by Article 53(2) of its Statute to examine whether there was jurisdiction and whether the claims were well founded in fact and law; the Court is not authorized to make a judgment by default.[392] Yet it is noteworthy that the Court thoughtfully took up the Icelandic argumentation even though it had not been formally submitted. This was emphasized by the Court in its judgment on the merits: "In ascertaining the law applicable in the present case the Court has had cognizance not only of the legal arguments submitted to it by the Applicant but also of those contained in various communications addressed to it by the Government of Iceland, and in documents presented to the Court. The Court has thus taken account of the legal position of each party."[393] On the other hand, the Court did not order a further examination of the facts because it held that they were either not in dispute or attested by documentary evidence which partly emanated from the government of Iceland and had not been specifically contested, and the Court saw no reason to doubt its accuracy. In the Court's view, Iceland's general declaration that it "did not accept or acquiesce in any of the statements of fact" was not sufficient to put into question the establishment of the facts by documentary evidence.[394]

In view of the Icelandic objections to jurisdiction and its refusal to participate in the proceedings, the Court regarded it as appropriate to address the question of jurisdiction at the outset and determined in orders of 18 August 1972 that the first pleadings were to be dedicated to that question.[395] The Court proceeded in this manner although Iceland had not formally raised

---

[390] See Elkind, *Interim Protection*, 115 (calling 1961 agreements "clearest sort of jurisdictional clause possible").

[391] Judgments of 25 July 1974, 8–9, para. 14 (UK), and 180 para. 15 (FRG).

[392] For details on Article 53 of the Statute, see Rosenne, *Law and Practice III*, at 1401–18.

[393] Judgments of 25 July 1974, at 9 para. 17 (UK) and 181 para. 18 (FRG). See Anderson, at 453–4: "The Court can be said to have acted most fairly in its handling of the cases, especially at the stage of the merits. [. . .] [T]he Court proceeded to consider Iceland's case fully, even in the absence of an appearance on the merits. At the same time, the absence of the respondent did nothing to make the position of the two applicants more difficult, but it would be idle at this time to speculate over the likely result had Iceland been present in Court in 1974." (at 454).

[394] Judgments of 25 July 1974, at 9, para. 16 (UK), and 181, para. 17 (FRG).

[395] Orders of 18 August 1972 at 182 (UK) and 189 (FRG). Judges Bengzon and Jiménez de Aréchaga appended a joint dissenting opinion, arguing that the Court should have followed the normal procedure first, and that it was not possible to treat the Icelandic letter as a preliminary objection because such an objection could not be validly raised before the filing of the memorial. Ibid., at 184–6 (UK), 191–3 (FRG).

preliminary objections in accordance with the Rules of Court[396]—further proof of the substantial attention paid to Iceland's perspective in spite of its non-participation in the proceedings. A day earlier, the Court had indicated provisional measures of protection, which Iceland ignored.[397]

In its judgments of 2 February 1973, the Court confirmed its jurisdiction by 14 votes to 1, ruling that there was no ground for a termination of the compromissory clause and that the clause had been precisely intended for disputes such as the present one.[398] It reached this decision after addressing and rejecting the arguments raised by Iceland in favor of a termination.[399] Although the basic facts of the cases brought by the United Kingdom and the Federal Republic of Germany were the same, the Court decided on 17 January 1974 not to join the two cases since the legal argumentation was not entirely the same and a joinder was not desired by the applicants.[400]

3. The judgments on the merits

On 25 July 1974, the Court delivered the judgments on the merits. It held that Iceland's regulations extending its exclusive fishing rights to 50 nautical miles were not opposable to the UK and Germany. Moreover, Iceland was not entitled unilaterally to exclude vessels of these countries from fishing between the area agreed to in the exchanges of notes in 1961 and the limits specified in the regulations of 1972 nor to impose restrictions on those vessels' activities in that area. The Court ruled that the parties were under the obligation to undertake negotiations in good faith for the equitable resolution of their differences, taking into account various factors such as the special needs of Iceland and its right to a preferential share in the waters adjacent to its coast beyond the 12-mile zone, the traditional rights of the UK and Germany, the

---

[396] See Article 67(1) and (2) of the Rules of Court adopted on 6 May 1946, as amended on 10 May 1972.

[397] See *infra* C II.

[398] Judgments of 2 February 1973, at 22–3 (UK) and 66–7 (FRG). Judge Padilla Nervo (Mexico) dissented. For details, see *Ferrer Sanchis*, 29 REspDI (1976), at 431; *Magiera*, 17 JiR (1974), at 332–5; *Martin*, 78 RGDIP (1974), at 435–58.

[399] The Court engaged in a comprehensive assessment of the aspects of the case, addressing even issues brought forward in general terms such as that the 1961 agreements took place "under extremely difficult circumstances": on this point, the Court stated that it could not consider "an accusation of this serious nature on the basis of a vague general charge unfortified by evidence in its support," and that the history of the negotiations that led to the 1961 Agreement showed that they were conducted on the basis of "perfect equality and freedom of decision." Judgments of 2 February 1973 at 14 para. 24 (UK) and 59 para. 24 (FRG).

[400] Ibid., at 5 para. 8 (UK) and 177, para. 8 (FRG). *Favoreu*, 20 AFDI (1974), at 260–1 (speculating that this decision, apart from coinciding with the parties' wishes, might also have been based on desire to prevent an "objective" character for the proceedings). On the implications for the pleadings, see *Anderson*, in Götz, Liber amicorum Günter Jaenicke, at 448–9 and 454–5 (commenting on absence of German judge *ad hoc*).

interests of other states, and the need for conservation and development of the fishery resources.[401]

The Court refrained from ruling on the issue of whether Iceland's claim to extend its EFZ to 50 nautical miles could be founded in international law.[402] It noted, however, that a 12-mile EFZ was generally accepted, as were preferential rights in adjacent waters for the coastal state dependent on fisheries, and that the exceptional dependence of Iceland on fishery resources was undisputed.[403] The decision on the opposability of the EFZ *vis-à-vis* the applicants rather than on its validity was in line with the FRG's submissions and did not contradict the British submissions either.[404]

The Court found itself in an uncomfortable situation. It was well aware of the fact that the international law of the sea was in flux: "[...] [T]he Court must add that its Judgment obviously cannot preclude the parties from benefiting from any subsequent developments in the pertinent rules of international law."[405] The fact that the issue was being discussed at an international conference better equipped to take all aspects of the law of the sea into consideration raises doubts on whether the decision to submit the case before the Court was well advised in the first place.[406] One might question whether the Court is equipped to take over a role filling in lacunae

[401] Judgments of 25 July 1974, at 34–35 (UK) and 205–206 (FRG). The decisions were reached by 10 votes to 4, with Judges Gros, Petrén, Onyeama, and Ignacio-Pinto dissenting: ibid., at 35–8 and 126–73 (UK); at 208–11 and 234–51 (FRG). The Court dismissed the German claim for compensation; the decision was equally made by 10 votes to 4, ibid., at 206 (FRG). For details of the judgments on the merits, see *Castillo Daudí*, 29 REspDI (1976), at 437–45; *Fahmi*, 30 REgyDI (1974), at 141–56; *Foucheaux*, 10 Tex. ILJ (1975), at 150–71; *Obozuwa*, Nig. AIL (1976), at 101–23.

[402] Critical, see *Briney*, 5 Ga. JILC (1975), at 248 and 256 (arguing that thereby the Court refused to answer the most important issue raised); *Churchill*, 24 ICLQ (1975), at 90 (arguing that Court failed to meet the duty to examine arguments that might have supported Iceland's claim, namely evidence for existence of a rule permitting a 50-mile fisheries zone). See also *Langavant/ Pirotte*, 80 RGDIP (1976), at 99.

[403] Judgments of 25 July 1974, at 23 para. 52 and 26–7, paras. 58–9 (UK) and 192, para. 44, 195, paras. 50–1 (FRG).

[404] The UK had primarily focused on invalidity, but had conceded that the Court could decide the case on the basis of opposability without the need to tackle invalidity, see *supra* n. 387. It has been suggested by *Churchill*, 24 ICLQ (1975), at 88–90, that the Court's reasoning implies that a 50-mile EFZ was generally unlawful because the notion of "preferential" and "exclusive" rights were incompatible with each other. However, this might be too far-fetched an argument: in their joint separate opinion, Judges Forster, Bengzon, Jiménez de Aréchaga, Nagendra Singh, and Ruda emphasized that they concurred in the decision precisely because it did *not* rule on the invalidity of the fishery zone *erga omnes* (Judgments of 25 July 1974, at 45, para. 1 (UK), and at 217, para. 1 (FRG)). Moreover, the concept of exclusive economic zone as it evolved after the delivery of the judgment leaves room for some (albeit limited) rights by other states and is therefore not quite as exclusive as might be inferred from its denomination; for details, see Kwiatkowska, *The 200 Mile Exclusive Economic Zone in the New Law of the Sea*, 60–74.

[405] Judgments of 25 July 1974 at 33 para. 77 (UK) and 203 para. 70 (FRG). The word "obviously" was only included in the UK judgment, apart from that, the wording of that sentence in the two judgments was identical.

[406] *Churchill*, 24 ICLQ (1975), at 104.

in the law and the tasks of redistribution.[407] The Court was faced with a dilemma—either to adopt a conservative approach ignoring current developments, potentially exerting a restrictive influence on the ongoing conference, or to anticipate the law before it was laid down. It chose the middle path, finding a solution based on bilateral relations rather than setting a general standard for the extension of EFZs. This approach was probably the most prudent one under the circumstances—the Court gave an answer to the central question of the dispute and thereby fulfilled its judicial task.[408]

4. The scope of the obligations arising from the judgment

The judgments went beyond a declaration of the law to prohibit Iceland from unilaterally imposing restrictions on the fishing of British and West German vessels beyond the fishery limits agreed to in 1961. Moreover, it obliged both sides to undertake negotiations in good faith to arrive at an equitable solution of their differences and to take into account a variety of specified factors in this regard. The judgment had immediate relevance for the legal relations between Iceland and the FRG. As between Iceland and the UK, however, the obligation to implement the judgment was modified by an interim agreement on 13 November 1973 regulating the British fishing in the 50-mile zone for the subsequent two years, which had created a temporary regime that was to remain valid irrespective of whether a judgment would be delivered in the meantime.[409] The agreement might point to a lack of faith in the Court's ability to settle the dispute; nevertheless, the UK could have pursued the proceedings with the expectation that a favorable judgment might improve its position in the next round of negotiations.[410] Seeing the controversy as an ongoing one, the Court did not consider itself constrained in delivering its judgment by the interim agreement[411]—even though this implied taking a decision on a legal standard that might be superseded by the UN Conference on the Law of the Sea, a possibility that might have justified withholding any judgment until the lapse of the agreement in November

[407] *Weil*, 16 Harv. ILJ (1975), at 488–90.

[408] Foucheaux, 10 Tex. ILJ (1975), at 171. For the opposing view, see *Obozuwa*, Nig. AIL (1976), at 119 (arguing that main issue was illegality *erga omnes*, with preferential rights constituting a peripheral issue). Similarly, see *Langavant/Pirotte*, 80 RGDIP (1976), at 78–94 (arguing that refusal to answer essential question of general international law and focus on finding practical solution to dispute made judgment resemble more closely an arbitral award than a judicial decision, and that verdict represents visible compromise between judges). However, it must be borne in mind that the Court's findings conformed to the applicants' submissions, which had not insisted on a ruling on the general questions.

[409] Exchange of notes constituting an interim agreement in the fisheries dispute between the government of the United Kingdom of Great Britain and Northern Ireland and the government of the Republic of Ireland, ICJ Pleadings, Fisheries Jurisdiction, Vol. II, 459–61.

[410] *Foucheaux*, 10 Tex. ILJ (1975), at 170.

[411] Judgment of 25 July 1974 (UK), 17–20, paras. 35–41.

1975.[412] On the other hand, there was no question that the limits of Iceland's fishery zone remained highly controversial. Generally, it is to be welcomed if the parties agree on a *modus vivendi* pending the proceedings. Particularly in a situation serious enough as to lead to military action and brought to the attention of the Security Council (as in the present case),[413] every understanding between the parties decreasing tensions is positive and should not have a negative impact on the proceedings, unless the parties desire their discontinuance. As the Court itself pointed out, a contrary finding would have had the inevitable result of discouraging "the making of interim agreements in future disputes with the object of reducing friction and avoiding risk to peace and security. This would run contrary to the purpose enshrined in the provisions of the United Nations Charter relating to the pacific settlement of disputes."[414] Moreover, the Court itself had drawn the parties' attention to the possibility of an interim agreement in the second orders indicating provisional measures: in this light, its decision not to regard the interim agreement as an impediment to delivering the judgment appears justified.[415]

5. Follow-up to the judgment

Iceland did not comply with the judgment.[416] It never pretended that its action conformed to the ICJ judgment nor that the judgment had become moot because of subsequent developments. Instead, in so far as it mentioned the judgment at all,[417] Iceland continued to toe the line that the Court had

---

[412] Critical, see *Weil*, 16 Harv. ILJ (1975), at 478 fn. 21 (arguing that because of infrequency of Court cases, ICJ "is not inclined to let pass an opportunity to clarify and define the law as it views it").

[413] When Iceland refused to comply with the Court's interim measures and proceeded to enforce its regulations against British vessels, the Royal Navy was deployed, resulting in the "second cod war," see *infra* C II 2.

[414] Judgment of 25 July 1974 (United Kingdom v. Iceland), at 20, para. 41.

[415] For a positive assessmnet, see *Anderson*, in Götz, Liber amicorum Günter Jaenicke, at 459. At the time of the judgment, it was not obvious that the applicable customary law would undergo a fundamental change within an extremely short time.

[416] *Ajibola* in: Bulterman/Kuijer, Compliance with judgments, at 35; *Schwebel*, ibid., at 40; *Elkind*, Interim protection, 117; Anderson, in Götz, Liber amicorum Günter Jaenicke, at 351 (author, the UK's agent, reporting that "[a]lthough not represented, the Icelandic Government in Reykjavik somehow still managed to issue a statement rejecting the verdicts even before the UK Agent had left the Peace Palace, following a courtesy call upon President Lachs"); *Jaenicke* in EPIL II, at 388. But see Kapoor, *Enforcement of Judgments and Compliance with advisory opinions of the International Court of Justice*, at 309: "Iceland [...] later reached agreements with the United Kingdom and West Germany which by and large conformed to the guidelines laid down by the International Court." This assessment is hardly compatible with the evidence to the contrary.

[417] In Iceland's complaints to the UN Security Council during the third "cod war" (see *infra* C II 2), there was no reference to the International Court of Justice: see the various letters from the Icelandic representative to the Security Council S/11905, S/11907, S/11944, S/11954 (11 and 12 December 1975, 23 and 29 January 1976). Similarly, in the sitting of the Security Council where the matter was being discussed, Iceland's representative Ingvarsson did not mention the International Court of Justice, UN Doc. S/PV.1866, 2–3.

not been competent to render a decision on the merits[418]—flouting Article 36(6) of the ICJ Statute.[419] Although some further negotiations were held, they did not conform to the indications given by the Court.[420]

Stakes were raised after an incident on 24 November 1974 in which the Icelandic coastguard seized a West German vessel fishing within the 50-mile zone, but outside the 12-mile zone. A local court imposed a fine on the basis that the ICJ judgment was not binding on Iceland, followed by the FRG's imposition of a landing ban for Icelandic fish.[421] Rather than retreat from its claims to a 50-mile fishery zone, Iceland took a step in the opposite direction on 15 July 1975, extending its EFZ to 200 miles.[422] Enforcement action was taken against West German and UK fishermen who did not respect the new limits.[423] Neither Germany nor the UK took recourse to the UN Security Council under Article 94(2) of the UN Charter; there was good reason to doubt that they could have gathered substantial support there, and most likely, there would have been little desire to impose sanctions on Iceland.[424] Germany reached a settlement without insisting on its position under the judgment. On 28 November 1975, it concluded a fisheries agreement with Iceland which regulated fishing by German vessels on a limited scale in the 200-mile zone for a period of two years.[425] The conflict with the UK, however, became increasingly critical. In another incident, the British navy escorted UK ships to enable them to fish in areas 12 miles from the Icelandic shores in what could later be billed as the third "cod war."[426] When in December 1975 Iceland complained to the Security Council about use of force by the UK, the UK referred to the ICJ judgment in its favor. In a message to the President of the Security Council, the UK government pointed out:

---

[418] Jónsson, *Friends in conflict*, 167 (suggesting that "Iceland was jumping somewhat ahead of the evolutionary process of the law, but the law was evolving in line with Iceland's action"). See also *Anand*, 16 Indian JIL (1976), at 53 (concluding Iceland was "swimming with the current").

[419] Article 36(6) provides: "In the event of a dispute as to whether the Court has jurisdiction, the matter shall be settled by the decision of the Court." See *supra* Chapter 2 D III.

[420] *Anderson*, in Götz, Liber amicorum Günter Jaenicke, at 452.

[421] 44 AdG (1974) 19073 A and 19083 F. The landing ban was revoked on 16 October 1975 in order to improve the climate for negotiations. 45 AdG (1975) 19774 A.

[422] Iceland had already paved the way for this extension by amending the Fundamental Conservation Law of 5 April 1948 by law no. 45 of 13 May 1974. The 1973 agreement exempted Britain from these regulations until 14 November 1975. See Jónsson, *Friends in conflict*, 153–5, 158, 161.

[423] 44 AdG (1974) 19073 A; 45 AdG (1975) 19774 A, 19854 D.

[424] *Schwebel* in Bulterman/Kuijer, Compliance with judgments, at 41.

[425] "Fisheries Agreement between Iceland and the Federal Republic of Germany relating to the extension of the Icelandic fishery limits to 200 nautical miles," 15 ILM 43 (1976). See 45 AdG (1975) 19868 A.

[426] 46 AdG (1976) 20057 C. On the first and second "cod wars," see *infra* C II 2.

On 25 July 1974, the International Court of Justice found that the Government of Iceland was not entitled unilaterally to exclude British fishing vessels from the waters around Iceland 'or unilaterally to impose restrictions on the activities of those vessels in such areas.' Between 15 and 25 November 1975, the Icelandic Coastguard vessels, supported by their aircraft, attacked a number of British trawlers in the area, damaging the equipment of at least seven of them. This marked a serious failure to comply with the decision of the Court. [...] Whilst the general question of fishing rights between Iceland and the United Kingdom will be taken up again in March 1976 at the Third United Nations Conference on the Law of the Sea, at present the question of fishing rights between Iceland and the United Kingdom is governed by the decision of the Court.[427]

The Security Council dealt with Iceland's complaints on 16 December 1975. Only representatives of Iceland and the UK made statements on the matter.[428] The UK's representative, while complaining about the harassment of British fishermen, referred to the Court's judgments and stated bluntly in this context: "May I take this opportunity to remind the Council that decisions of the International Court of Justice are binding under the United Nations Charter on the States concerned."[429] The Council took no action,[430] and there were no further sessions on the matter.[431] On 19 February 1976, Iceland broke off diplomatic relations with the UK[432] and even put its NATO membership into question.[433] Finally, on 1 June 1976, the two countries reached an agreement allowing British fishers limited rights within the 200-mile zone;[434] the agreement had a duration of six months only, following which British vessels were allowed to fish in the zone "only to the extent provided for in arrangements agreed with the Government of Iceland."[435]

---

[427] Note by the President of the Security Council circulating a message of the UK government of 11 December 1975, S/11914. See also Jónsson, *Friends in conflict*, at 166–7; and the letters of Iceland's representative to the President of the Security Council quoted *supra* n. 417.

[428] UN Doc. S/PV.1866, at 2–5.

[429] Ibid., at 4, para. 29.

[430] S/PV.1866, at 5: The President concluded: "As no other representative has asked to be allowed to speak on the question before the Council, I shall adjourn the debate on the item. The Security Council will remain seized of the question so that it may resume consideration of it at an appropriate date."

[431] See Repertoire of the Practice of the Security Council, Supplement 1975–1980, ST/PSCA/1/Add.8, 253–5 (recording no other Council discussions on the matter beyond those of the 1866th meeting).

[432] 46 AdG (1976) 20058 (reporting that was a first in relations between two NATO partners), Jónsson, *Friends in conflict*, at 169.

[433] 46 AdG (1976) 20058; Jónsson, *Friends in conflict*, at 173–5.

[434] Agreement concerning British Fishing in the Icelandic Waters, 1 June 1976, 15 ILM 878 (1976). Diplomatic relations were restored the following day. See Jónsson, *Friends in conflict*, 180; 46 AdG (1976) 20261 C.

[435] Agreement, *supra* 880 no.10.

The FRG[436] and the UK[437] themselves established 200-mile fishery zones in the waters adjacent to their territorial waters at the end of the same year, following a resolution adopted by the EEC Council on 6 November 1976.[438] The new policies resonated with the rapidly emerging consensus at the Third UN Conference on the Law of the Sea and the prevailing practice of many coastal states in the late 1970s and the 1980s to establish 200-mile exclusive economic zones (EEZs) or EFZs.[439] One might doubt whether the Court's statements remained valid at the moment the Federal Republic and the UK themselves established 200-mile EFZs.[440] The concept of a 200-mile EEZ was incorporated in the 1982 UN Convention on the Law of the Sea[441] and held to form part of customary international law by the ICJ in the Tunisia/Libya case of 1982 and the Libya/Malta case of 1985.[442] In view of these developments, the concepts of a 12-mile EFZ and of preferential rights were no longer sustainable.[443] As Judge Waldock, then ICJ President,[444] commented on the Fisheries Jurisdiction cases as early as 1979, it was "to be expected that the Court's findings as to the law would be short-lived, and so it appears to be proving." Subsequent events quickly overtook the findings.[445]

[436] Proclamation of the Federal Republic of Germany of 21 December 1976 on the establishment of a fishery zone of the Federal Republic of Germany in the North Sea, printed in: United Nations, The Law of the Sea. National Legislation on the Exclusive Economic Zone and the Exclusive Fishery Zone, New York 1986, 116 and in Bundesgesetzblatt 1976, Part II, Vol. 2, 1999–2000. One and a half years later, a fishery zone was established in the Baltic Sea as well, Proclamation concerning the establishment of a Fishery Zone in the Baltic Sea of 18 May 1978, Bundesgesetzblatt 1978 Part II, Vol. 1, 867.

[437] Act to extend British Fishery Limits and make further provision in connection with the regulation of Sea Fishing, 22 December 1976, United Nations, Law of the Sea, *supra* n. 436, 322–9.

[438] "European Communities: Council Resolution on External Aspects of the Creation of a 200-Mile Fishing Zone," 15 ILM (1976), 1425: see in particular the second paragraph: "[The Council] agrees that, as from 1 January 1977, member states shall, by means of concerted action, extend the limits of their fishing zones to 200 miles off their North Sea and North Atlantic coasts [...]." For further details, see Churchill, *EEC Fisheries Law*, 69–72.

[439] See *Anderson*, in Götz, Liber amicorum Günter Jaenicke, at 451–2; Smith, *Exclusive Economic Zone Claims*, at 17–23 (table on territorial sea and fishing zone claims); Attard, *The Exclusive Economic Zone in international law*, 285–7 ("a 200-n.m. FZ is now part of international law"). Similarly, see Barbara Kwiatkowska, *The 200 Mile Exclusive Economic Zone in the New Law of the Sea*, at 27–37. An EFZ is one element of the establishment of an EEZ. See Article 56(1)(a) of the United Nations Convention on the Law of the Sea, the recognition of the latter concept therefore necessarily implies the recognition of the former.

[440] Attard, *The Exclusive Economic Zone*, 148 ("By 1976 there was considerable evidence to suggest a general acceptance of a maximum fishery limit of 200 n.m."). See also *Anderson*, in Götz, Liber amicorum Günter Jaenicke, at 451–2.

[441] Part V United Nations Convention on the Law of the Sea, 1833 UNTS 397, 418–28.

[442] Continental Shelf (Tunisia/Libyian Arab Jamahiriya), Judgment of 24 February 1982 at 74, para. 100; Continental Shelf (Libyan Arab Jamahiriya/Malta), Judgment of 3 June 1985, at 32–3, paras. 31–4.

[443] Attard, *The Exclusive Economic Zone*, at 287.

[444] Sir Humphrey Waldock, who took part in the proceedings of the Icelandic Fisheries cases, was President of the Court from 1979 until his death on 15 August 1981. ICJ YB 1982–3, 9.

[445] Waldock, *The International Court and the Law of the Sea*, 15–16. Similarly, see *Anderson*, in Götz, Liber amicorum Günter Jaenicke, at 446. See also Guillaume, in Jasentuliga, *Perspectives on International Law*, at 280.

The judgment did not have much of an impact on the Law of the Sea conference: few references to the Court's findings were made,[446] the Conference produced a very different outcome, and customary law rapidly developed in another direction.[447] In any event, even assuming that a transformation of the law had not yet taken place when the UK and West Germany made their claims to a 200-mile EEZ, they were precluded from subsequent challenges to the validity of Iceland's EFZ. And in fact, when their respective agreements with Iceland expired,[448] the countries did not continue to object to the Icelandic fishery zone.[449]

6. Conclusion

All in all, these cases marked an unfortunate chapter in the history of the ICJ. Iceland showed disrespect for the Court by not participating in the proceedings (in spite of having conferred jurisdiction on the Court in 1961 in rather clear terms) and by rejecting the judgments both on jurisdiction and on the merits. Its boycott of the proceedings was indicative of a lack of any readiness to compromise and a bad sign for the prospects for compliance. As a matter of domestic policy, the Icelandic government felt unable to capitulate to any reduction in its EFZ, given the domestic economy's extraordinary dependence on fishing (dependence not put into question by the applicants). The extension of the fishery zone enjoyed support across party lines;[450] no opposition existed to push for compliance with the Court's judgment. Even though some temporary arrangement was reached, there can be no doubt that those agreements were not designed to implement the judgments; they were not perceived as such implementation, and the rights of the UK and the Federal Republic of Germany under the agreements compared very poorly

---

[446] *Hafner*, 15 BDGVR (1975), at 198. *Langavant/Pirotte*, 80 RGDIP (1976), state at 102 that the judgment said so little about the law that it was invoked as an arguments by both coastal states and states engaged in offshore fisheries in the course of the UN Conference on the Law of the Sea.

[447] See Attard, *The Exclusive Economic Zone*, 284–309; Kwiatkowska, *The 200 Mile Exclusive Economic Zone in the New Law of the Sea*, at 27–37; *Anderson* in Götz, Liber amicorum Günter Jaenicke, at 451–2.

[448] The Icelandic–German agreement was valid for two years and expired on 28 November 1977, *supra* n. 425 at point 9, the Icelandic–British agreement was valid for half a year and expired on 1 December 1976, *supra* n. 434 at point 10. Neither one was renewed: Jónsson, *Friends in conflict*, 178, 181.

[449] Jónsson, *Friends in conflict*, 186. The agreements included clauses that after their expiry, fishing in the waters defined in the Icelandic Regulations of 15 July 1975 could take place only as provided for in arrangements with the Icelandic government, *supra* n. 434 point 10, Note of the Icelandic Government, 880. This could be interpreted as implicit recognition of the Fishery Zone: Jónsson, *Friends in conflict*, 184–6. The last British trawlers left the zone on 1 December 1976, see 46 AdG (1976) 20633 E.

[450] As the extension of the EFZ to 50 miles, the new extension to 200 miles took place after elections on 30 June 1974 that brought about a change in government. Jónsson, *Friends in conflict*, 122–4, 158.

to those adjudicated by the Court. The case presents the unusual circumstance of non-compliance by a state that was without doubt in general committed to the rule of law and democracy[451] relating to a judgment concerning fellow-members of NATO and the Council of Europe.[452]

The most striking aspect of this case was the unexpectedly rapid transformation of the applicable customary law at the time the judgment was delivered, which created an impetus for its rejection. Yet the change in the law may also have softened the perceived blow to the Court's authority. What had been unlawful at the time of the decision was quickly legitimated at the Third UN Conference on the Law of the Sea: Iceland had anticipated a trend in the law and thus was to be regarded as a pioneer. Apart from diplomatic squabbles with the two affected parties, no protest arose from the rest of the international community as more and more coastal states adopted similar policies and hence regarded Iceland's position as equitable.[453]

There are some other features of the case with potential relevance for the prospects for compliance, although they probably did not significantly influence Iceland's behavior under the circumstances. One is the fact that the Court's solution referred only to bilateral structures, although the problem was a multilateral one—the freedom of the high seas.[454] Apart from considerations of *inter partes* effect of the judgment, the Court was no doubt cognizant of the ongoing UN conference, which might give some explanation for its rather cautious approach. It has been suggested that the Court's silence on the *erga omnes* validity of the fishery zone encouraged Iceland to go ahead with broader claims extending its EFZ to 200 miles.[455] Yet it might go too far drawing a causal link between the reasoning of the judgment and the extension of the EFZ. The judgment found that the extension to 50 miles was not opposable to the UK and Germany; this implied that an extension to 200 miles would not be either. Still, Iceland proceeded with the extension, enforcing the new limits without trying to justify them *vis-à-vis* the judgment.

[451] See *Schwebel* in Bulterman/Kuijer, Compliance with judgments, at 40 ("In the Icelandic Fisheries case a most democratic State, perhaps the state with the oldest existing democratic system in the world and a history of compliance with international law, declined to argue whether the Court had jurisdiction—although it was obvious that it did—and paid no attention to the judgment of the Court when it came down.").

[452] The UK and Iceland were among the signatories of the North Atlantic Treaty, 34 UNTS 243; the Federal Republic of Germany acceded on 6 May 1955, 243 UNTS 313. The UK was also a signatory of the Statute of the Council of Europe, 5 May 1949, 87 UNTS 103; Iceland and the Federal Republic of Germany acceded on 9 March 1950 and 13 July 1950, respectively, 100 UNTS 302.

[453] *Anand*, 16 Indian JIL (1976), at 49–51.

[454] *Hafner*, 15 BDGVR (1975), at 206–8, 229–32.

[455] See Attard, *The Exclusive Economic Zone*, at 30 and fn. 184 (seeming to advocate this point).

The nature of the Court's findings presented difficulties for implementation, even if all parties had taken efforts to comply. No single solution was prescribed. Pursuant to the judgment, Iceland was barred from enforcing its regulations; at the same time, the UK and Germany had to respect Iceland's preferential rights and arrive at a negotiated solution.[456] Certain questions remained open: if Iceland had preferential rights, but no unilateral right to exclude the UK and Germany from fishing, how were the preferential rights in practice to be exercised until a settlement could be reached? How could Iceland's management and conservation interests over the fish stocks be protected if it was not entitled to impose any restrictions on the activities of British and German vessels in the meantime? Moreover, the judgment could have benefited from a clearer and more extensive presentation of the Court's legal reasoning. The examination of the legal status of the doctrine of preferential rights is somewhat cursory, for example, with primary emphasis given to a joint amendment adopted by majority vote at the end of the 1960 Geneva Conference on the Law of the Sea.[457] Similarly, the basis of the obligation to negotiate called for a more detailed explanation.[458]

On the other hand, the Court did address Iceland's objections in a comprehensive fashion—despite the fact that they were communicated informally. For instance, the Court determined the need for an initial jurisdiction phase even though Iceland had not filed preliminary objections. Nevertheless, this was of little help as Iceland appeared determined to follow its course.

The case is a clear instance of non-compliance, albeit an atypical one in that the judgment would shortly be superseded by developments in the law. Regardless of this transformation, the recalcitrance of a democratic state committed to the rule of law such as Iceland in resisting the Court's authority is perhaps surprising. As the policy on the extension of the exclusive fisheries zone was generally supported on the domestic level, there was no significant domestic protest against this defiance of the UN's principal judicial organ.

---

[456] Some commentators argue that the Court thus assumed the functions of other dispute settlement organs since it acted primarily in order to *settle* the dispute. See, e.g. *Foucheaux*, 10 Tex. ILJ (1975), at 162–4; *Langavant/Pirotte*, 80 RGDIP (1976), at 101. Yet, the Court found that the applicable legal rules included an obligations to negotiate; it based its reasoning on its findings on customary international law and not on political expediency.

[457] Judgments of 25 July 1974, at 25–6, para. 57 (UK), and 194, para. 49 (FRG). Opposing views should have been discussed as well. See *Weil*, 16 Harv. ILJ (1975), at 482.

[458] Judgments of 25 July 1974, at 23, paras. 74–5 (UK) and 201, paras. 66–7 (FRG): the Court held that the obligation to negotiate was inherent in the concept of preferential rights, then it mentioned the 1958 Geneva Reolution on Special Situations relating to Coastal Fisheries, and it concluded by stating that the obligation flew from the "very nature of the respective rights of the Parties." Bearing in mind the strict standard the Court has set up for the emergence of customary law in the North Sea continental shelf cases, one would have wished a more detailed reasoning on this point. Critical, see *Langavant/Pirotte*, 80 RGDIP (1976), at 98.

Despite the findings in their favor, the UK and West Germany gained no concrete advantages from the litigation.[459] The international community seemed to show little sympathy for their cause. It is doubtful whether the applicants would have instituted the proceedings had they anticipated the further legal developments.

XIII. Continental shelf (Tunisia/Libya)

1. The special agreement and the proceedings before the Court

The Court's next case again took up the matter of maritime delimitation, this time concerning the continental shelf between Tunisia and Libya in the Mediterranean Sea. Delimitation became contentious after the two countries unilaterally started granting concessions for offshore petroleum drilling in the 1960s, which led to overlapping claims.[460] From 1968 onwards, the issue was the subject of negotiations, and in 1976, both countries formally protested against one another's claims.[461] On 10 June 1977, they concluded an agreement to the submit the dispute to the ICJ, notified to the Court by each of them individually.[462] The Court was asked to indicate the rules and principles applicable for the delimitation of the area of the continental shelf appertaining to the two countries and to give indications for a practical implementation (Article 1)—although to what extent remained in question. The linguistic ambiguity arose from the differing Libyan[463] and Tunisian[464] translations of

---

[459] *Anand*, 16 Indian JIL (1976), at 49.

[460] Judgment of 24 February 1982, at 36–7, para. 21; *Christie*, 13 Ga. JICL (1983), at 3–4; *Hodgson*, 16 Case W. Res. JIL (1984), at 4; *Sonenshine*, 24 Harv. ILJ (1983), at 225. Libya had enacted legislation to grant unilateral concessions in 1955. See Judgment of 24 February 1982, at 36, para. 21.

[461] *Christie*, 13 Ga. JICL (1983), at 4; Judgment of 24 February 1982, at 37, para. 21.

[462] 1120 UNTS 103. Notification of this special agreement was received by the Court's registry on 1 December 1978 (by Tunisia) and 19 February 1979 (Libya). Le greffier au ministre des affaires étrangères de Tunisie, 1 December 1978, ICJ Pleadings, Continental Shelf (Tunisia/Libyan Arab Jamahiriya), Vol. 5, 445, The Registrar to the Secretary for Foreign Affairs of the Libyan Arab Jamahiriya, 20 February 1979, ibid., 448. During the proceedings, Malta asked for permission to intervene, which was opposed by both parties. Application for permission to intervene by the Government of the Republic of Malta dated 28 January 1981, ICJ Pleadings, Continental Shelf (Tunisia/Libyan Arab Jamahiriya), Vol. III, 257–62. The Court unanimously rejected this request: Judgment of 14 April 1981, at 20.

[463] The Libyan version of the text (submitted in English) reads in relevant part: "[T]he Court is further requested to clarify the practical method for the application of these principles and rules in this specific situation, so as to enable the experts of the two countries to delimit these areas without any difficulties." Judgment of 24 February 1982, at 23, para. 4.

[464] The Tunisian version (submitted in French) provides: "[T]he Court is further requested to specify precisely the practical way in which the aforesaid principles and rules apply in this particular situation so as to enable the experts of the two countries to delimit those areas without any difficulties." Translation into English by the Registry; the French text furnished by Tunisia was: "[I]l est demandé également à la Cour de clarifier avec précision la manière pratique par laquelle lesdits principes et règles s'appliquent dans cette situation précise, de manière à mettre

the authentic Arabic text. The lack of precision in the texts as to the division of tasks between Court and the parties in the post-adjudicative phase was to become controversial during the proceedings.

Articles 2 and 3 of the special agreement concerned the post-adjudicative phase. Article 2 required the parties to meet in order to determine the line of delimitation and conclude a treaty on the matter. If the conclusion of such a treaty could not be achieved within a period of three months from the date of delivery of the judgment (a period of time renewable by agreement), they assumed the obligation to return to the Court for binding clarifications under Article 3.[465]

2. The judgment on the merits of 1982

On 24 February 1982, the Court delivered its judgment on the merits of the case with a 10 to 4 decision.[466] It ruled that delimitation was to be effected in accordance with equitable principles taking into account all relevant circumstances,[467] so as to achieve an equitable result.[468] Disagreements persisted as to the practical application of these principles. The parties had agreed that the correct route lay somewhere between the approach of the North Sea Continental Shelf case, in which the Court had merely been asked to decide on rules and principles,[469] and that of the Franco-British Arbitration[470] of 1977, in which the court of arbitration had had to define the course of a boundary between the portions of the continental shelf.[471] While Tunisia had essentially argued that the Court made the final determination up to the

---

les experts des deux pays en mesure de délimiter lesdites zones sans difficultés aucunes." Judgment of 24 February 1982, at 21, para. 2.

[465] *Supra* n. 462.

[466] Judgment of 24 February 1982, at 18–94. Judge *ad hoc* Jiménez de Aréchaga appointed by Libya voted with the majority, Judge *ad hoc* Evensen appointed by Tunisia voted against. For details, see *Christie*, 13 Ga. JICL (1983), at 219–38; *Herman*, 33 ICLQ (1984), at 825–68; *Oellers-Frahm*, 42 ZaöRV (1982), 804–14.

[467] Judgment of 24 February 1982, at 92–3, para. 133. Although the Court stated that it did not take a decision *ex aequo et bono*, but applied legal principles, at 60 para. 71, commentators have criticized the judgment for blurring the distinction between a decision based on the law and a decision *ex aequo et bono*, arguing that the relevant criteria were not clear: see *Johnston*, The theory and history of ocean boundary-making, 177; *Hodgson*, 16 Case W. Res. JIL (1984), at 36. This critique is also made in the dissenting opinions of Judge Oda, *ibid.*, at 157 para. 1 and Judge *ad hoc* Evensen, at 291. See also the related workshop of the American Society of International Law, "ICJ Decision in the Libya–Tunisia Continental Shelf Case," [1982] Proc. ASIL 150–65. Article 38(2) of the ICJ Statute authorizes the Court to decide cases *ex aequo et bono* if requested by the parties, but there was never a request to that extent. For more comments on the treatment of equity in this judgment, see *Bermejo*, 1 HYIL (1988), at 59–76.

[468] Judgment of 24 February 1982, at 59–60, paras. 70–1.

[469] *Supra* Section X.

[470] Continental Shelf (UK–France), Decision of 30 June 1977, 18 RIAA 3, reprinted in: 18 ILM 397 (1979).

[471] Judgment of 24 February 1982, at 38, para. 25.

ultimate point before the purely technical work, Libya had taken a decidedly contrary position, arguing that the Court was not invited to set out the specific method of delimitation itself[472]—again, partly attributable to the different translations of the Arabic original.[473]

The Court saw "no fundamental difference in opinion" between the parties, however, considering the divergent emphases as to the respective roles of the Court and the parties' experts a controversy of "minor importance." It rejected Libya's request for "guidance"—a call for an advisory opinion rather than a judgment; it viewed its proper role as providing a definitive assessment of the factors to be taken into account for the calculations of the coordinates, leaving only technical details to the experts.[474] Following Tunisia's broader interpretation, the Court's decision had a precise and enforceable content:[475] it contained a practical method for the delimitation and decided that it was to be effected in two sectors, the first one to be formed by a straight line between two precisely specified coordinates. For the second sector, it was necessary to ascertain the coordinates of "the most westerly point on the shoreline" (low-water mark) of the Gulf of Gabes, a task remaining for the experts; the Court offered a likely candidate at "approximately 34° 10′ 30″ North".[476] The judgment included a map with the boundary lines described by the Court,[477] but with the comment that this map was "for illustrative purposes only."[478] A lesson learned from the controversy is the need for clarity in drafting agreements for the Court; the parties should have agreed on an authentic translation when submitting documents in multiple languages.

3. Tunisia's request for revision, correction, and interpretation
   and the judgment of 1985

After the judgment was delivered, several meetings took place concerning its implementation. These talks failed when the two states disagreed on the

---

[472] Judgment of 24 February 1982, at 39, paras. 27–8.

[473] Ibid., at 39, para. 28, and supra nn. 463 and 464. *Christie*, 13 Ga. JICL (1983), at 7.

[474] Judgment of 24 February 1982, at 38–40, paras. 25–30. In this context, the Court pointed to Article 3 of the special agreement, which envisioned that an implementing agreement should be reached within three months from the delivery of the judgment, and explained that the only remaining task would be the technical one: ibid., at 40, para. 30.

[475] See *Bermejo*, 1 HYIL (1988), at 67; *Herman*, 33 ICLQ (1984), at 828; *Sonenshine*, 24 Harv. ILJ (1983), at 226. For a critical comment on the Court's approach see *Sonenshine*, 24 Harv. ILJ (1983), at 234, arguing that the Court's reasoning was poor, that it could have rendered an advisory opinion and instead "usurped the parties' consensual responsibility." However, this leaves out of account that the Court's advisory jurisdiction cannot be used by states, see Article 96 United Nations Charter. See also *Feldman*, 77 AJIL (1983), at 222: "The Court was clearly concerned with the efficacy of its judgments." The Court emphasized that its task was to deliver a judgment with "the effect and the force attributed to it under Article 94 of the Charter of the United Nations and the said provisions of the Statute and the Rules of Court." Judgment of 24 February 1982, at 40, para. 29.

[476] Ibid., at 87.   [477] Ibid., at 90.   [478] Ibid., at 89–90.

proper interpretation of the judgment.[479] On 17 July 1984, Tunisia filed an application based on Articles 60 and 61 of the Statute of the Court and Articles 98, 99, and 100 of the Rules of Court.[480] The application called for a revision of the original judgment, alleging that it had been unable to submit a piece of evidence: the text of a resolution of the Libyan Council of Ministers of 28 March 1986 that determined the "real course" of the north-western boundary of a petroleum concession granted by Libya, known as Concession No. 137 and mentioned in the 1982 judgment.[481] The application also re-quested a correction of the coordinates of the first sector of the boundary and an interpretation for both the first and the second sector. In particular, Tunisia asked the Court to confirm the westernmost extreme of the Gulf of Gabes at 34° 05′ 20 and, as a subsidiary claim, to order an expert survey to ascertain the precise location of the delimitation line from those coordinates.[482]

A unanimous judgment came on 10 December 1985.[483] Tunisia's request for revision was rejected because the Court found that the conditions of Article 61 of the ICJ Statute were not fulfilled: the failure to introduce the document earlier was due to negligence, and the substantive decision would not have been changed if the document had been considered.[484] The Court dismissed the request for correction, as there was no reason to alter the judgment.[485] As for the interpretation, the Court held Tunisia's request admissible as far as it related to the "most westerly point of the Gulf of Gabes." On this point, the Court clarified that the coordinates it had indicated (34° 10′ 30″ North) were not conclusively established and that it was incumbent on the parties to determine the most westerly point of the shoreline.[486] The Court refused to confirm the specific coordinates sug-

---

[479] Application instituting proceedings submitted by the Government of Tunisia, 17 July 1984, ICJ Pleadings, Application for Revision and Interpretation of the Judgment of 24 February 1982, 3, Observations of the Socialist People's Libyan Arab Jamahiriya on the application submitted by Tunisia for revision and interpretation, ibid., at 51–112.

[480] Application instituting proceedings submitted by the Government of Tunisia, 17 July 1984, ICJ Pleadings, Application for Revision and Interpretation of the Judgment of 24 February 1982, at 3–47; it was received by the Registrar on 27 July 1984, Le greffier au ministre des affaires étrangères de Tunisie, 30 July 1984, ibid., at 274.

[481] Judgment of 10 December 1985, at 198, para. 11.

[482] For a summary of the parties' submissions, see Judgment of 10 December 1985, at 195–6, para. 6.

[483] Judgment of 10 December 1985, at 192–231. For details, see *Decaux*, 32 AFDI (1985), at 324–49; *Oellers-Frahm*, "Continental Shelf Case (Tunisia/Libyan Arab Jamahiriya)," in EPIL I, at 802–3.

[484] Judgment of 10 December 1985, at 198–214, paras. 11–40.

[485] Ibid., at 230, para. 69C.

[486] This was the point on the shoreline furthest to the west on the low-water mark and might be a point within a channel or the mouth of a wadi: ibid., at 229–30, para. 69D.

gested by Tunisia, deferring to the experts to make a precise determination.[487] It explained the tasks for the experts of the parties[488] and declined ordering an expert survey of its own since it had left this task to the parties' experts in its original judgment.[489] The Court recalled in this regard that the parties still were under the obligation to carry out the special agreement to the very end and fully implement the 1982 judgment.[490] It would perhaps have been helpful had the Court included a similar paragraph summarizing the experts' tasks in its original judgment; on the other hand, it is uncertain whether that would have resulted in its quicker implementation, since Tunisia's application seemed to have been directed against the verdict as such.[491]

It is worth noting that the Court made an effort to deal with all the parties' submissions, even where that was not strictly necessary, as in the part on the admissibility of the request for revision.[492] The clarifications provided a better understanding and paved the way for the eventual settlement.

4. The final settlement

After the judgment, the parties met again to establish the delimitation line and concluded an agreement implementing the Court's decision on 8 August 1988.[493] The area, which is rich in oil and gas, was set to be exploited by the Libyan–Tunisian Joint Oil Company (JOC).[494] The desire of the parties to settle the dispute—as evidenced by the special agreement—was a positive factor ensuring compliance; a more precise drafting of that agreement leaving less room for interpretation would perhaps have contributed to a speedier implementation.

---

[487] Ibid., at 226–7, para. 62.

[488] Ibid., at 227, para. 63.

[489] Ibid., at 227–8, paras. 64–6. The Court pointed out that Article 50 enabled it to request expert opinions in order to arrive at a judgment on the dispute submitted to it; in the present case of a request for interpretation, however, the desired expert survey would not actually aim at interpretation of the original judgment. It clarified that it could have carried out an expert survey in the original proceedings in order to ascertain the coordinates, but as it had left this matter to the parties' experts, this decision had the force of *res judicata*. Article 50 reads: "The Court may, at any time, entrust any individual, body, bureau, commission, or other organization that it may select, with the task of carrying out an enquiry or giving an expert opinion."

[490] Judgment of 10 December 1985 at 229, paras. 67–8.

[491] *Decaux*, 32 AFDI (1985), at 349.   [492] Ibid., at 348.

[493] Leanza in: Starace/Villan, *Studi in ricordo di Antonio Filippo Panzera I*, at 465–6; Lucchini/Vœlckel, *Droit de la mer II*, at 120. The text is reprinted at Charney/Alexander, *International Maritime Boundaries II*, at 1663.

[494] Country Analysis Brief—Libya, http://www.eia.doe.gov/emeu/cabs/libya.html; Libyan Oil and Gas, http://www.emerging-markets.com/reports/R139/summary.asp.

XIV. United States diplomatic and consular staff in Tehran

1. Background: the events of 1979

The facts of the Tehran hostage case received worldwide media attention.[495] The 1978–9 revolution in Iran brought about the overthrow of the Shah's US-friendly regime. Many supporters of the revolution considered the US the "Great Satan" and channeled their hatred against the Shah into hatred against the US, making the American embassy a focal point for protests. An armed group first seized the mission on 14 February 1979, taking 70 people as prisoners; two persons connected with the embassy staff were killed. The Iranian authorities intervened promptly and restored control to the American officials. Fears of another attack rose in October 1979 when the Shah flew to the US for medical treatment. Despite demands for the extradition of the exiled leader to Iran, the new regime gave assurances that the mission compound would be protected. On 4 November 1979, a large demonstration took place in front of the embassy. A mob of several hundred militants attacked the building and took the diplomatic and consular staff—as well as two unfortunate visitors—hostage. The Iranian security forces stood aside as revolutionaries took control of the buildings as well as of the US consulates in Tabriz and Shiraz the following day. The archives and other documents were ransacked. The Islamic radicals released thirteen hostages on 18 and 20 November 1979 pursuant to a decree of Ayatollah Khomeini to "hand over the blacks and the women, if it is proven that they did not spy"; on 22 November 1979, an additional five non-Americans were freed. The other 53 hostages[496] remained in captivity. The hostage-takers announced that their captives were guilty of espionage and would be put to trial if the Shah was not returned. While Iran officially claimed that the hostages were well treated, it did not refute specific allegations of ill treatment, as, for example, the parading and blindfolding of some hostages before chanting crowds. The resignation of moderate Iranian prime minister Bazargan one day after the taking of the hostages did not augur well for US negotiators. The Revolutionary Council took over the government,[497] with the primary power being vested *de facto* in religious leader Khomeini, who had stirred anti-American sentiments and endorsed the hostage-taking

---

[495] As the Court observed, Judgment of 24 May 1980, at 9, para. 12, "The essential facts of the present case are, for the most part, matters of public knowledge which have received extensive coverage in the world press and in radio and television broadcasts from Iran and other countries."

[496] The exact number of hostages had still been unclear at the time of the judgment: it speaks of at least 50 persons. Judgment of 24 May 1980, at 13, para. 22; 52 hostages were retained until the final settlement, see 51 AdG (1981) 24215–26; the seriously ill vice-consul had been released on 10 July 1980: 51 AdG (1981) 24216.

[497] 50 AdG (1980) 23172.

from an early point.[498] US attempts to end the crisis proved futile: Khomeini prohibited Iranian officials from contact with American representatives.[499]

2. The reaction by the international community

States and international organizations around the world demanded the swift release of the hostages.[500] On 9 November, the US permanent representative to the UN addressed the President of the Security Council with a call for urgent consideration.[501] The latter made a public statement on behalf of the members of the Council on the same day, urging "in the strongest terms that the diplomatic personnel being held in Iran should be released without delay and provided protection."[502] The President of the General Assembly sent a similar message to Khomeini.[503] Iranian foreign minister Abolhassan Bani-Sadr sent a letter to the UN Secretary-General requesting a meeting of the Security Council on the basis that the US was creating a "war psychosis" threatening international peace and security. The letter made no mention of the hostages while vehemently criticizing the US for "false propaganda" and its protection for "an international criminal," the former Shah. The letter stated that "if the United States government were not so reluctant to hand over to us those who have betrayed our people and if it recognized its wrongful actions during the bloody, illegitimate and destructive régime of the former Shah, the best possible relations would exist between the Iranian people and the United States." Bani-Sadr demanded that the US recognize the guilt of the exiled leader and turn over the Shah's substantial wealth to the Iranian government.[504]

UN Secretary-General, Kurt Waldheim, on his part, requested an urgent meeting of the Security Council based on Article 99 of the Charter and stated: "in my opinion [...] the present crisis poses a serious threat to international peace and security".[505] Iran had been invited to participate in the Council's deliberations and had initially indicated that it would accept

---

[498] Judgment of 24 May 1980, at 29–30, para. 59 and 33–5, paras. 71–5.

[499] See the summary of facts, ibid., at 10–15, paras. 14–27, the report in 50 AdG 23195–210 (1980), and Elkind, *Interim protection*, 131–2.

[500] See, for example, the various references in 50 (1980) AdG 23199.

[501] Letter dated 9 November 1979 from the representative of the United States of America to the President of the Security Council, S/13615.

[502] Statement by the President of the Security Council, 9 November 1979, S/13616. It was reiterated by the President in the Council's meeting of 27 November, S/PV.2172, at 2.

[503] GA/6076 of 9 November; he reiterated his call on 20 November 1979, GA/6096. Both documents are reprinted as Annex 44 to the US Memorial, ICJ Pleadings, US Diplomatic and Consular Staff in Tehran, 221–2.

[504] Letter dated 13 November 1979, S/13626.

[505] Letter dated 25 November 1979 from the Secretary-General to the President of the Security Council, S/13646.

this invitation and be represented by the foreign minister himself,[506] but when the matter was debated in the Council on 1 December, the Iranian representatives failed to show.[507] While there is no obligation for a state to follow an invitation of the Security Council based on Article 31, this non-participation was a bad sign that showed Iran's unwillingness to engage in any discourse on the matter, even in the framework of the Security Council, where the discussion would not be limited to questions of law and where there might have been a certain sympathy for Iran's grievances on the part of some members. On the same day, the new foreign minister Sadegh Ghotbzadeh[508] directed a letter to the Secretary-General emblematic of an escalating anti-American rhetoric of Khomeini's consolidating regime: "The United States imperialism and international zionism have now embarked on a new plot. While you are endeavoring to defuse the crisis created by the United States on a world-wide scale, the agents of United States imperialism and zionism are spreading malicious rumours [...]."[509] Again, the letter contained no allusion to the hostage crisis nor to the potential for its resolution. On 4 December, the Security Council unanimously adopted Resolution 457, which called for the immediate release of the hostages.[510] This demand was repeated in Resolution 461 of 31 December;[511] however, a draft resolution imposing economic sanctions failed on 13 January 1980 due to the negative vote of the USSR.[512]

---

[506] S/PV.2172 of 27 November 1979, at 2; the date of the deliberations had been postponed out of respect for Islamic religious holidays, following a request by Iran, so as to permit the participation of foreign minister Bani-Sadr.

[507] Iran's permanent representative had informed the Security Council's president about his country's changed decision not to attend the meeting, S/PV.2175 (1 December). See also the subsequent meetings S/PV.2176 (2 December), 2177 (3 December), and 2178 (4 December), in which Iran was not represented either.

[508] He took over for Bani-Sadr on 28 November. Bani-Sadr, who was considered rather moderate (although he had cooperated with Khomeini already during his exile) and who took a more distanced stance in relation to the occupants of the embassy (see 50 AdG (1980) 23469) would be elected president in January 1980; he had popular support, yet not enough political power, and eventually lost the power struggle against the clerics; he was forced out of his office on 1 June 1981 and subsequently escaped to France. See Mohammad Mehdi Khorrami, The Islamic Revolution, http://www.internews.org/visavis/BTVPagesTXT/Theislamicrevolution.html. Foreign minister Ghotbsadeh apparently also would have preferred to talk with US officials, but could not act contrary to Khomeini's Order, see Greenberg, 20 Stan. JIL (1984), at 263.

[509] Letter dated 1 December from the minister for foreign affairs of Iran addressed to the Secretary-General, S/13671. The letter of 13 November had presented Iran's grievances in a more moderate form and was less loaded with hatred.

[510] See Resolution 457 (1979): "The Security Council [...] urgently calls upon the Government of Iran to release immediately the personnel of the Embassy of the United States of America being held at Tehran, to provide them with protection and to allow them to leave the country." The resolution does not explicitly mention its legal basis, which apparently was Chapter VI: see preamble: "Deeply concerned at the dangerous level of tension between Iran and the United States of America, which could have grave consequences for international peace and security."

[511] Resolution 461 (1979) was adopted by 11 votes to 0 with 4 abstentions (Bangladesh, Czechoslovakia, Kuwait, USSR).

[512] The efforts of the United Nations to bring about a release of the hostages will be explained in detail below in the report on the provisional measures in the case: see *infra* C IV.

The United States also adopted a series of unilateral economic and diplomatic sanctions; notably, on 14 November 1979, President Carter issued an executive order freezing all Iranian governmental assets after it seemed likely that Iran might withdraw its assets from US banks and repudiate its obligations to US firms.[513] Despite the diplomatic and economic pressure, the hostages were not released.

3. The proceedings before the Court

On 29 November 1979, the United States seized the International Court of Justice by unilateral application[514] and filed a request for the indication of interim measures of protection.[515] It based the Court's jurisdiction on the optional protocols[516] on compulsory dispute settlement to the Vienna Conventions on diplomatic and consular relations, as well as other international agreements, including a 1955 bilateral friendship treaty.[517] Iran refused to participate in the proceedings before the ICJ as it had before the Security Council, airing its objections to an involvement of the Court in two communications to the Court's President in December and March. Iran contended that the issues concerned only a marginal aspect of a larger problem involving a quarter century of violations of international law on the part of the United States and that the repercussions of its revolution were essentially within the national jurisdiction of Iran.[518] These statements included legal arguments

[513] See Judgment of 24 May 1980, at 16–17, paras. 30–1; and *Malloy*, Wisc. ILJ (1984), at 19–22.

[514] Application instituting proceedings submitted by the Government of the United States of America, ICJ Pleadings, United States Diplomatic and Consular Staff in Tehran, 1–8.

[515] Ibid., 11–12.

[516] Optional Protocol to the Vienna Convention on Diplomatic Relations concerning the compulsory settlement of disputes of 18 April 1961, 500 UNTS 241, ratified by Iran on 3 February 1965 and by the US on 13 November 1972, ST/LEG/SER.E/19, 111, Optional Protocol to the Vienna Convention on Consular Relations concerning the compulsory settlement of disputes of 24 April 1963, 596 UNTS 487, ratified by the US on 24 November 1969, acceded to by Iran on 5 June 1975, ST/LEG/SER.E/19, 123. The text of Article I of the two protocols is identical: "Disputes arising out of the interpretation or application of the Convention shall lie within the compulsory jurisdiction of the International Court of Justice and may accordingly be brought before the Court by an application made by any party to the dispute being a Party to the present Protocol."

[517] Treaty of Amity, Economic Relations, and Consular Rights, USA–Iran, 15 August 1955, 284 UNTS 93. Article XXI para. 2 provides: "Any dispute between the High Contracting Parties as to the interpretation or application of the present Treaty, not satisfactorily adjusted by diplomacy, shall be submitted to the International Court of Justice, unless the High Contracting Parties agree to settlement by some other pacific means." Moreover, the US referred to Article 13(1) of the Convention on the Prevention and Punishment of Crimes against Internationally Protected Persons, included Diplomatic Agents, of 14 December 1973. See application, *supra* n. 514, at 5.

[518] ICJ Pleadings, US Diplomatic and Consular Staff in Tehran, at 18, 500 (letter of 9 December 1979, also printed in the Order of 5 December 1979, at 10–11), 511, 253–4 (letter of 16 March, also printed in the Judgment of 24 May 1980, at 8–9, para. 10).

only with a view to challenging the proceedings before the ICJ rather than substantive justifications for the acts—indicative of Iran's unwillingness to perceive the dispute as a legal one. In fact, Khomeini issued several statements rejecting the concept of international law as such.[519] Underlying the dispute were such legal questions as whether Iran's actions violated its treaty obligations or whether a trial of the hostages would be permissible on any grounds; nevertheless, it was political issues—not legal ones—that predominated. Both parties, in fact, shared skepticism about the ability of the international legal system to redress the wrongs adequately. Iran felt that international law served the interest of powerful states; the US, on the other hand, regarded recourse to the UN and ICJ as useful steps in the political process while doubting prospects for actual compliance.[520] These doubts proved correct. In its order indicating provisional measures of 15 December 1979, the Court asked Iran among other things to release the hostages, in line with the request of Security Council Resolution 457. Neither the order nor the Security Council resolution was obeyed, and at the time of the delivery of the judgment, the hostages remained in detention.[521]

4. The judgment of 24 May 1980

The Court delivered its judgment on 24 May 1980.[522] By 13 votes to 2, it determined that Iran had acted and continued to act in violation of its obligations towards the United States under international law and that this entailed Iran's international responsibility.[523] Unanimously, it ordered Iran to free the hostages and ensure they could leave Iranian territory. Iran could not retain them for any form of judicial proceedings and was required to restore the premises, property, archives, and documents of the missions.[524] Furthermore, the Court held by 12 votes to 3 that Iran had to make reparation,[525] and by 14 votes to 1, it decided that the form and amount was to be determined at a later stage, should negotiations between the parties fail. It reserved for this purpose the subsequent procedure in the case.[526]

The non-participation of Iran in the proceedings raised the issue of Article 53 of the Statute. The Court confirmed its jurisprudence that this article

---

[519] *Greenberg*, 20 Stan. JIL (1984), at 267–8.

[520] *Schachter* in Kreisberg, American Hostages in Iran, at 325.

[521] For futher details on the provisional measures, see *infra* C IV.

[522] Judgment of 24 May 1980, at 65. For details, see *Papachristou*, 21 Harv. ILJ (1980), at 748–56; *Zoller*, 84 RGDIP (1980), at 973–1026.

[523] Judgment of 24 May 1980, at 44 para. 95(1), (2). Judges Morozov (USSR) and Tarazi (Syria) dissented.

[524] Ibid., at 44–5, para. 95(3), (4).

[525] Ibid., at 45, para. 95(5). Judges Lachs (Poland), Morozov and Tarazi dissented.

[526] Ibid., at 45, para. 95(6). Judge Morozov dissented. In line with its decision to boycott the proceedings, Iran had not appointed a judge *ad hoc*.

allows it "to convince itself by such methods as it considers suitable that the submissions are well founded."[527] It did not draw negative inferences from Iran's non-appearance and comprehensively addressed the arguments informally advanced by Iran.[528]

With regard to its jurisdiction, the Court found a clear basis in the protocols to the Vienna Conventions of 1961 and 1963[529] as well as the 1955 Treaty of Amity.[530] As for the merits of the case, the Court addressed the impact of the proceedings simultaneously before the Security Council. It held that the fact that the Security Council was seized of the matter did not preclude the Court from exercising its function to solve legal questions.[531] The political dimension of the dispute and its broader context likewise presented no major obstacles for the Court; it stated that:

[L]egal disputes between sovereign States by their very nature are likely to occur in political contexts, and often form only one element in a wider and long-standing political dispute between the States concerned. Yet never has the view been put forward before that, because a legal dispute submitted to the Court is only one aspect of a political dispute, the Court should decline to resolve for the parties the legal questions at issue between them. Nor can any basis for such a view of the Court's function or jurisdiction be found in the Charter or the Statute of the Court; if the Court were, contrary to its settled jurisprudence, to adopt such a view, it would impose a far-reaching and unwarranted restriction upon the role of the Court in the peaceful solution of international disputes.[532]

As to the substantive law, the Court quoted the clear and unequivocal provisions concerning the inviolability of the diplomatic and consular premises and staff, and the obligations of the receiving state to give effect to it.[533] Moreover, it pointed out that submitting the hostages to any trial or investigation would result in a breach of Article 31 of the 1961 Vienna Convention on Diplomatic Relations.[534] It went on to say that Iran had failed to sub-

---

[527] Ibid., at 9, para. 11.

[528] A different approach was suggested by *Schachter* in Kreisberg, American Hostages in Iran, at 343–4, according to whom the Court "could have declared Iran's objections irreceivable and thus made it clear that a state's failure to plead on the jurisdictional issue would have adverse consequences." (footnote omitted).

[529] Judgment of 24 May 1980, at 24–6, paras. 45–9. The text of Article 1, identical in both protocols, is as follows: "Disputes arising out of the interpretation or application of the Convention shall lie within the compulsory jurisdiction of the International Court of Justice and may accordingly be brought before the Court by an application made by any party to the dispute being a Party to the present Protocol."

[530] Ibid., at 26–8, paras. 50–4. The Court did not find it necessary to examine the applicability of the third basis of jurisdiction invoked (Article 13 of the 1973 Convention on the Prevention and Punishment of Crimes Against Internationally Protected Persons), ibid., at 28, para. 55.

[531] Ibid., at 21–4, paras. 40–4.   [532] Ibid., at 20, para. 37.

[533] These included Articles 22, 24–27 of the 1961 Convention and the equivalent provisions of the 1963 Convention as well as Article II paragraph 4 of the 1955 Treaty of Amity; ibid., at 28–37, paras. 56–78.

[534] Ibid., at 37, para. 79.

stantiate its claim of criminal activities of the US diplomatic and consular missions, and stated *arguendo* that even if this claim were correct, the Iranian action could not be justified, because Article 9 of the Convention on diplomatic relations and Article 23 of the Convention on consular relations already provided for a remedy for such situations: the receiving state can declare a person abusing diplomatic functions *persona non grata* or, as a more radical measure, break off relations with the sending state.[535]

5. The follow-up to the judgment

Despite the unambiguous terms of the judgment, almost eight months passed before the release of the hostages. Numerous obstacles to a settlement can be identified, including the intense animosity against the US; a lack of common standards (in particular, the unwillingness on the part of Iran to perceive the dispute as legal); linguistic and cultural barriers; and domestic political requirements. Ultimatums from both sides, coupled with the impossibility of face-to-face negotiations, also worked against an amicable resolution.[536]

After a failed mediation effort by West Germany in fall 1980,[537] Iran's hardline policies softened to a degree. Having sustained its defiance toward a powerful foe, Iran realized that a prolonged crisis ran counter to its interests, given the outbreak of the Iran–Iraq war in September and the potential for a tougher US administration after the upcoming presidential elections. Moreover, the Khomeini regime had less of a need for the hostages as political capital after having consolidated its power in Tehran.[538] The Shah died in Egypt on 27 July 1980,[539] which removed a significant obstacle for a settlement as Iran had requested his extradition. Algeria finally brokered a settlement between the two countries on 19 January 1981 (the Algiers Accords).[540]

Algeria was an adequate intermediary[541] since it was one of the few countries that enjoyed the trust of both Iran and the US. It had strong trade links with the US, but at the same time, was an Islamic nation with a history of anti-colonial struggle; it had assisted Iran in a previous dispute.[542] It had condemned the taking of the hostages while acknowledging that the

---

[535] Ibid., at 37–41, paras. 80–9. In this context, the Court, at 40, para. 86 referred to the rules of diplomatic law as a self-contained regime in a phrase that was to become famous and give rise to extensive discussions. For details, see *Simma*, 16 NYIL (1985), at 111–36.

[536] *Greenberg*, 20 Stan. JIL (1984), at 262–73.   [537] Ibid., at 276.

[538] See *Chinkin/Sadurska*, 7 Ohio S. JDR (1991), at 67; *Greenberg*, 20 Stan. JIL (1984), at 272–3.

[539] See 50 AdG (1980) 23727.

[540] "Iran–United States: Settlement of the Hostages Crisis," 20 ILM (1981), 223–40. On the validity of the settlement agreements, see *Schachter* in Kreisberg, American Hostages in Iran, at 369–73.

[541] The Algerians called themselves intermediaries instead of negotiators, see *Greenberg*, 20 Stan. JIL (1984), at 284.

[542] *Chinkin/Sadurska*, 7 Ohio S. JDR (1991), at 65; for greater detail, see *Greenberg*, 20 Stan. JIL (1984), at 277–83.

dispute was embedded into a broader situation.[543] The Algerian government served as an effective go-between—Iran rebuffed direct contact with the Americans[544]—by acting as a "cultural interpreter," engaging in confidence-building and refusing to transmit ultimatums.[545] The ultimate form of the settlement speaks to the difficulties of the resolution of this dispute: a declaration by Algeria to which both parties subsequently adhered to avoid the necessity of entering into a direct treaty relationship.[546]

The Algiers Accords were aimed at settlement of the dispute in its broader context. The main elements of the agreement included the return of Iranian assets blocked in the US and the establishment of an arbitral tribunal for claims of US nationals against Iran (the Iran–US Claims Tribunal). This tribunal would have exclusive jurisdiction over claims against Iran. The US was to withdraw the case for reparation pending before the ICJ and bar any judicial actions relating to the events in its courts, including litigation brought by former hostages.[547]

US President Carter immediately informed the UN Secretary-General about the agreement and that a prompt return of the hostages to the United States was to be expected; he stated: "With the release of our hostages, the United States considers that Iran has fully complied with Security Council resolutions 457 of December 4, 1979 and 461 of December 31, 1979, and with the Judgment of the International Court of Justice of May 24, 1980."[548] The release took place the following day, after 444 days of captivity. On 6 April, the US requested the discontinuance of the pending case for reparations at the ICJ.[549] The case was discontinued by an order of the ICJ President of 12 May 1981.[550]

---

[543] *Chinkin/Sadurska*, 7 Ohio S. JDR (1991), at fn. 115.

[544] There was one attempt of a direct dialogue. See *Greenberg*, 20 Stan. JIL (1984), at 288–9.

[545] Ibid., at 283–9.

[546] This created a face-saving process for both sides. See *Chinkin/Sadurska*, 7 Ohio S. JDR (1991), at 66; *Greenberg*, 20 Stan. JIL (1984), at 284. Algeria issued two documents: the General Declaration and the Claims Settlement Declaration, to which the US and Iran adhered, see ILM, *supra* n. 540, at 224–8, 230–3, and Wallace-Bruce, *The settlement of international disputes*, 41.

[547] General Declaration, *supra* n. 540, para. 11.

[548] Printed in ICJ Pleadings, US Diplomatic and Consular Staff, at 522.

[549] The deputy agent of the United States of America to the President of the Court, 6 April 1981, ibid., at 524. On 1 May 1981, the US clarified its request for discontinuance of 6 April, expressing its understanding that the effects of discontinuance were exclusively procedural and that it did not renounce any right of action should Iran fail to fulfill its obligations: the deputy agent of the United States of America to the president of the Court, ibid., at 526.

[550] Order of 12 May 1981, at 45–47. On the details, see *Wegen*, 76 AJIL (1982), at 731–6. Discontinuance is regulated by Articles 88 and 89 of the Rules of Court. It has procedural character—i.e. the case is removed from the Court's list, but there is no *res judicata*. This had been disputed until the adoption of the 1978 Rules of Court. See *Wegen*, 76 AJIL (1982), at 724–5, 730–1; Guyomar, *Commentaire du règlement de la CIJ*, at 562–78. Depending on the particular circumstances of a case, a party might be estopped from invoking the same claim again; see *Wegen*, 76 AJIL (1982), at 730–1.

Some observers have contended that the release of the hostages could not be regarded as compliance with the judgment since it did not actually take place in response to the judgment.[551] However, a party's actual motivations become less material when the Court's demands—in this case, the release of the hostages—are fulfilled. The US itself regarded the release of the hostages as compliance with the judgment, as official statements show.[552]

Actual compliance proved only partial.[553] The US secretary of state clarified that the release represented compliance with the judgment only as far as the part requiring the freeing of the hostages was concerned, whereas other obligations remained intact.[554] Despite the Court's decision, Iran has not yet handed over the premises of the US embassy;[555] they were taken over by the Revolutionary Guards, a hardline military force, and used as a high school and training camp. The former embassy now houses exhibitions on "crimes of America against Iran."[556]

6. Conclusion: the Court's role in the Tehran Hostages dispute

In sum, the Court did play a role in the settlement of the dispute, albeit a rather limited one.[557] The settlement was reached after negotiations at the government level, and only when Iran was willing to moderate its position to serve its interests. Interestingly enough, the Algiers Accords hardly mention the ICJ; there is only a reference to the withdrawal of pending claims before the Court.[558]

The case was filled with signs warning of eventual non-compliance. A common theme in all of Iran's official statements is the refusal to perceive the dispute as a legal one. The highly political climate did not bode well for a quick solution. Iran had charted a course of total opposition to the Court,

---

[551] *Ajibola* in Bulterman/Kuijer, Compliance with judgments, at 21 (conceding that "it cannot be said that the counter measures by the United States in this regard failed altogether to achieve the desired effect of enforcing the judgment of the Court"); and *Schwebel* in Bulterman/Kuijer, Compliance with judgments, at 41.

[552] See the President, *supra* n. 548 and the secretary of state, *infra* n. 554.

[553] But see *Guillaume* in Jasentuliyana, Perspectives on international law, at 279, who refers to the judgment as one that "could only be carried out at the price of a wider agreement settling additional issues that divided the states involved."—apparently implying that the Algiers Accords settled all underlying issues and that the judgment was eventually complied with completely.

[554] Telex from the legal counsel of the UN to the Registrar transmitting a message from the US secretary of state to the Secretary-General, 10 March 1981, ICJ Pleadings, US Diplomatic and Consular Staff, at 523.

[555] *Ajibola* in Bulterman/Kuijer, Compliance with judgments, at 20; Schwebel, ibid., at 41.

[556] Nazila Fathi, "Step Right up! On show in Iran, Sins of Uncle Sam," New York Times, 2 November 2001, at A3; Jim Muir, "Iran marks US embassy seizure," 4 November 2003, http://news.bbc.co.uk/1/hi/world/middle_east/3241217.stm.

[557] But see *Malloy*, Wisc. ILJ (1984), at 67: "Unfortunately, this exercise in international dispute resolution through judicial means was completely ineffective."

[558] *Supra* n. 540, Algiers Accords (see in particular the general declaration, Section 11).

the UN, and world opinion; its non-participation in the proceedings and non-appearance before the Court were part of that policy. Another issue was Iran's allegation that just a part of a broader dispute was submitted to the Court. On this point, it has been argued that the Court had, in fact, discouraged compliance by failing to address Iran's grievances and that the Court's narrow appraisal intensified Third-World views that the Court was a pawn of the West.[559] It is naturally problematic if just a piece of a broader dispute is subject to adjudication. It is not fair, though, to put the blame on the Court, as it was the Iranian government's own decision not to participate in the proceedings, where it would have had ample opportunities to present its perspective and to raise its complaints. However, the issues raised by Iran were too vague to enable the Court to examine them at depth.[560] If not all aspects of a dispute are brought before a certain dispute settlement mechanism, it seems important to address the other aspects elsewhere in order to ensure a lasting solution. Here, an attempt to provide for such a role was made by the establishment of a commission by the UN Secretary-General "to undertake a fact-finding mission to Iran to hear Iran's grievances and to allow for an early solution of the crisis."[561] While this mission supposedly was not very successful, the initiative as such was a good idea.[562]

Positive elements included the clear basis for jurisdiction and the precision of the applicable law[563] as well as of the decision, and the certainty about the facts that were directly relevant[564]—all this being of limited use, though, when the respondent generally opposes any legal evaluation. Yet the US achieved greater legitimacy in pursuing its claims (be it through the Court or by other means) and recourse to adjudication was considered worth while given a jurisdictional basis and clear evidence for the existence of a treaty violation.[565] The US had little to lose by involving the Court. The judgment was helpful in gathering international support and applying pressure to a diplomatically isolated opponent.[566]

---

[559] *Rafat*, 10 Denv. JIL (1981), at 458–9.

[560] Furthermore, they were not formally raised as counterclaims, and not as intrinsically linked to the American application as to be an obstacle for a decision of the Court.

[561] Judgment of 24 May 1980, at 21, para. 40.

[562] *Schachter* in Kreisberg, American Hostages in Iran, at 352–3.

[563] See *Schwebel* in Bulterman/Kuijer, Compliance with judgments, at 41: "There is no area of international law more securely established and acceptably codified than that of the law of diplomatic immunities."

[564] As the Court observed, Judgment of 24 May 1980, at 9, para. 12, the essential facts were "matters of public knowledge which have received extensive coverage in the world press and in radio and television broadcasts from Iran and other countries."

[565] *Chinkin/Sadurska*, 7 Ohio S. JDR (1991), at 56.

[566] Ibid., at 73. See also *Franck*, 79 AJIL (1985), at 384: "The Court deserves some credit for helping to generate the diplomatic climate in which Iran felt impelled to release the hostages and, incidentally, to submit the rival monetary claims of the United States and Iran to another system of international adjudication. The unilateral use of U.S. power had failed utterly to achieve that desired result."

XV. Delimitation of the maritime boundary in the Gulf of Maine area

In the Gulf of Maine case, a chamber of the Court defined a section of the maritime boundary between the United States and Canada. While issues of fish and fishing rights in the Gulf of Maine had been controversial since the Revolutionary War,[567] the more immediate origins of the case date to the 1960s and a dispute over the delimitation of the continental shelf, to which an additional dimension was added in 1977 when Canada and the US established 200-mile exclusive fishery zones (EFZs).[568] This led to overlapping claims, in particular in the Georges Bank, one of the richest fishing grounds in the world and an area with hydrocarbon resources.[569] The two countries realized that there was an imminent need to resolve the delimitation dispute.[570]

1. The efforts to submit the dispute to an ICJ chamber

On 29 March 1979, the US and Canada signed a series of interdependent agreements: an agreement on East Coast fisheries resources; a treaty on maritime delimitation dispute settlement that envisaged the submission of the dispute to the ICJ or alternatively to arbitration; a special agreement to submit the dispute to a chamber of the ICJ; and an agreement to submit the delimitation to a court of arbitration.[571] The special agreement was to take effect on the date of the entry into force of the maritime delimitation dispute settlement treaty;[572] the agreement to submit the delimitation to a court of

---

[567] *Rogoff*, 7 BU ILJ (1989), at 279–80; *Robinson/Colson/Rashkow*, 79 AJIL (1985), at 578.

[568] See Judgment of 12 October 1984, at 278–87, paras. 60–76. In early 1977, 200-mile exclusive fishery zones were established by both the US (the Fishery Conservation and Management Act of 13 April 1976 entered into force on 1 March 1977) and Canada (the Territorial Sea and Fishing Zones Act of 1 November 1976 became effective on 1 January 1977): ibid., at 283, para. 68. On the history of the dispute, see *Clain*, 25 Va. JIL (1985), at 532–5; and *Shelley*, 26 Harv. ILJ (1985), at 646. *Trendl*, 12 S. Ill. U. LJ (1988), at 606–10. See also *Brauer*, 23 Va. JIL (1983), at 465–7.

[569] On the history of fishing on Georges Bank, see *Clain*, 25 Va. JIL (1985), at 528–31. The fish stocks had become depleted in the 1960s due to increased fishing, including distant-water fishing by other nations: ibid., at 523.

[570] *Robinson /Colson/Rashkow*, 79 AJIL (1985), at 579; *Brauer*, 23 Va. JIL (1983), at 467; *Trendl*, 12 S.Ill.U. LJ (1988), at 605–6; *Rogoff*, 7 BU ILJ (1989), at 280.

[571] The original text of the treaty between the US and Canada to submit to binding dispute settlement the delimitation of the maritime boundary in the Gulf of Maine Area is printed at 20 ILM 1377 (1981); the Special Agreement to submit to a Chamber of the International Court of Justice the delimitation of the Maritime Boundary in the Gulf of Maine Area at 1288 UNTS 33, 20 ILM 1378 (1981); the agreement between the Government of Canada and the Government of the United States of America to submit to a Court of Arbitration the delimitation of the maritime boundary in the Gulf of Maine area at 20 ILM 1380 (1981). The fisheries agreement allocated various percentages of catches of different species to the parties: Agreement between the Government of Canada and the Government of the United States of America on East Coast Fishery Resources, Annex 20 to the Memorial of Canada, ICJ Pleadings, Gulf of Maine Area, Vol. 1, at 223–59.

[572] Article VIII special agreement, *supra* n. 571.

arbitration, in the event of a termination of the special agreement.[573] Both sides had to ratify the fisheries agreement as well for the dispute settlement treaty to enter into force.[574] Opposition by New England fishermen and US senators doomed the fisheries agreement to failure. Ultimately, the treaties were de-linked so as to resolve the delimitation dispute[575] and allow the issue of the management of fishery resources to be dealt with separately.[576] The parties jointly notified the ICJ of the special agreement on 25 November 1981.[577]

The two governments had incentives to have the ICJ rule upon the matter. A negotiated compromise had turned out to be impossible:[578] the comprehensive solution that the 1979 Fisheries Treaty had tried to provide had been rejected by the US, and the New England fishing lobby seemed to prefer the risk of an unfavorable judgment rather than accept an agreement that would have provided for access for fishermen from both sides to the entire Georges Bank area.[579] For both countries, it was important to have the dispute finally settled rather than to continue for years with negotiations whose ultimate success was highly doubtful.[580] The matter had a low national profile,[581] yet was significant on the local level as the economic well-being of fishermen who had had access to the Georges Bank for generations depended on the outcome.[582] Submission to the Court was a way for domestic politicians to have the matter settled without having to bear the political responsibility for the result and to face the reproach of their constituents.[583] In the event of a loss or major concessions, the governments could claim to have made all efforts,

---

[573] *Supra* n. 571, Article XIV, and Maritime Delimitation Dispute Settlement Treaty, Articles II, III.

[574] Art. IV of the Maritime Delimitation Dispute Settlement Treaty (original version, *supra* n. 571, at 1378).

[575] With slight amendments accepted by Canada, the Maritime Dispute Settlement Treaty entered into force on 20 November 1981 at the exchange of the instruments of ratification. For the final version, see Treaty to submit to binding dispute settlement the delimitation of the boundary in the Gulf of Maine area, 1288 UNTS 27, 28–9.

[576] Report of the Committee on Foreign Relations of the US Senate, U.S. Congress, Senate (97th Congress, 1st Session, Executive Report No. 97–5, 1 April 1981), printed in 20 ILM (1981), 1383–90. On the method how this delinkage was achieved, see ibid.; *Clain*, 25 Va. JIL (1985), at 534; and *Robinson/Colson/Rashkow*, 79 AJIL (1985), at 580.

[577] Letter from the Ambassadors of Canada and the US to the Netherlands to the Registrar, ICJ Pleadings, Gulf of Maine, Vol. I, 3–4.

[578] *Robinson*, 26 Can.–US LJ (2000), at 40 speaking about the "necessary level of desparation" that caused the parties to submit the matter to adjudication instead of solving it themselves through negotiations.

[579] Critical on the US refusal to ratify the 1979 Fisheries Agreement: *Clain*, 25 Va. JIL (1985), at 602–3.

[580] See *Brauer*, 23 Va. JIL (1983), at 474, mentioning the case as one where "the substantive need is to find *some* answer to the issue posed, and it matters little which."

[581] *Brauer*, 23 Va. JIL (1983), at 484 (calling dispute a "relatively unimportant" one).

[582] *Clain*, 25 Va. JIL (1985), at 535.

[583] *Brauer*, 23 Va. JIL (1983), at 474; and *Rogoff*, 7 BU ILJ (1989), at 280–1.

and convince their local constituencies that they were obliged to abide by the verdict of the Court.[584]

Several aspects of the manner in which the dispute was submitted to the Court deserve particular attention. The Court was asked to determine a maritime boundary, not merely to decide on pertinent rules and their practical application, and this maritime boundary was to be a single one, valid for the continental shelf and the EFZs.[585] The special agreement's degree of precision is also noteworthy. The Court was asked to determine the single maritime boundary in an area that was clearly defined by geographical coordinates. The agreement called for the appointment of an expert to assist the chamber on technical matters and, in particular, to prepare the description of the boundary.[586] These provisions are to be welcomed as a method to minimize problems in implementation.[587] The special agreement's foresightedness merits similar praise: another provision concerns the extension of the maritime boundary "as far seaward as the parties may consider desirable,"[588] ordering negotiations and potential adjudication by the chamber.[589]

The case marked the first time in the Court's history that parties availed themselves of the chamber procedure laid out in Articles 26(2) and 31 of the ICJ Statute. Moreover, the parties had a particular composition of the chamber in mind and took precautions for the possibility that the Court would not follow their ideas. Under the terms of the Dispute Settlement Treaty, the chamber would be officially constituted once the Registrar was informed of the names of the judges *ad hoc*.[590] Additional clauses allowed for the termination of the special agreement if the chamber was not formed within a six-month time frame, in which case the matter would be submitted to arbitration,[591] or if a vacancy in the chamber was not filled to a party's satisfaction.[592] The special agreement stipulated that the chamber would be composed of five judges (or judges *ad hoc*) and be constituted after consultation with the parties.[593] Those provisions resulted in a veto right over the chamber's composition: even though the Court was to select three of the judges, the parties could stall their appointments of judges *ad hoc* for six months, thereby gaining the right to terminate the special agreement.[594] Both the US and Canada made it clear that if the chamber was not composed as they wished, the case would be withdrawn.[595]

---

[584] Collier/Lowe, *The settlement of disputes in international law*, at 9.

[585] See *Schneider*, 79 AJIL (1985), at 541–2, 544–6; *Clain*, 25 Va. JIL (1985), at 522.

[586] *Supra* n. 571, Article II (3).   [587] Merrills, *International dispute settlement*, at 162.

[588] *Supra* n. 571, Article VII.

[589] Merrills, *International dispute settlement*, at 162.   [590] *Supra* note 571, Article I.

[591] Ibid., Article II.   [592] Ibid., Article III.

[593] Ibid., Article I (with a reference to Article 31 of the Statute concerning judges *ad hoc*).

[594] *Brauer*, 23 Va. JIL (1983), at 481.

[595] Merrills, *International dispute settlement*, 140. See also the dissenting opinion of Judge Morozov, who argued that the proposals of the US and Canada for the composition of the

In its order of 20 January 1982, the Court, by 11 votes to 2, acceded to the parties' wish to form a chamber of five judges.[596] The chamber consisted only of Western judges, and the composition had been effected entirely in accordance with the parties' wishes.[597] While this drew mixed comments,[598] the majority of the Court was certainly aware that if they had acted otherwise, the parties would have withdrawn the case and submitted it to arbitration.

Nevertheless, the chamber did not take a narrow, "Western" approach, instead proceeding in line with the Court's jurisprudence. The Gulf of Maine judgment was referred to extensively by the full Court in the subsequent Libya–Malta Continental Shelf judgment, which demonstrates that the full Court regarded this chamber judgment as part of its jurisprudence and not as the result of a non-representative fraction. In spite of the risk of parochialism inherent in giving the parties influence on the composition of the Court, this risk should not be exaggerated.[599] What had motivated the Court in 1978 to revise Articles 17 and 18 of its Rules had been precisely the intention to make recourse to it more attractive by allowing the parties to express preferences for chamber compositions.[600] It is then hard to imagine why the Court should ignore those preferences.[601]

The special agreement referred to the post-adjudicative phase only in passing, stating that the parties shall accept the chamber decision as final and binding.[602] Moreover, it made clear that the Court was asked to determine the boundary and not only to indicate how the parties were to establish it; the judgment to be rendered would thus not require any action by the US

chamber had been presented to the Court "in the form of some ultimatum." Order of 1 February 1982, Diss. Op. Morozov, at 11; similarly, Diss. Op. El-Khani, at 12.

[596] As a result of an election held on 15 January 1982, the chamber was composed of Judges Gros (France), Mosler (Federal Republic of Germany), Ago (Italy), Schwebel (USA), and Ruda (Argentina), who was asked to give place to the judge *ad hoc* to be chosen by Canada. The Canadian ambassador at the Hague informed the Court on 26 January 1982 that Maxwell Cohen was chosen as a judge *ad hoc*. Order of 1 February 1982, at 8–9. The dissenting judges were Morozov (USSR) and El-Khani (Syria).

[597] This was not openly acknowledged in the order, a matter that was criticized by Judge Oda in a declaration: "[I]t should in my view have been made known that the Court, for reasons best known to itself, has approved the composition of the Chamber entirely in accordance with the latest wishes of the Parties as ascertained pursuant to Article 26, paragraph 2, of the Statute and Article 17, paragraph 2, of the Rules of Court." Order of 20 January 1982, Decl. Oda, at 10.

[598] For a positive assessment, see *Brauer*, 23 Va. JIL (1983), at 483: "The Court's willingness to accommodate the interests of the parties in the composition of the chamber seems likely to elicit more confidence in the Court's impartiality and flexibility."

[599] Merrills, *International dispute settlement*, at 141–4. For an account of the current practice and arguments against its correctness, see *Moore*, 24 Case W. Res. JIL (1992), at 678–83, 693–97.

[600] The procedure had already been substantively amended for that purpose in 1972, see Judge *Jiménez de Aréchaga*, 67 AJIL (1973), at 2–3. It was revised and included as Article 17 of the 1978 Rules of Court: *Brauer*, 23 Va. JIL (1983), at 478–9; on the details, see Rosenne, *Law and Practice III*, at 1389–92.

[601] *Brauer*, 23 Va. JIL (1983), at 478–9.

[602] Article II(4), special agreement, *supra* n. 571. This reiterated their obligation under Article 94(1) of the Charter.

Congress or the Canadian parliament.[603] The judgment only obliged the states to refrain from acts in violation of this finding. In this light, the lack of further provisions on implementation seems less problematic, although one could have conceived arrangements for joint management of resources in the area as it was obvious that not all of the problems would be solved by the judgment and that further cooperation would be required. Still, while it might have been reasonable to include provisions to this extent, their inclusion was not indispensable for the special agreement.

2. The judgment of the Chamber

On 12 October 1984, the Chamber delivered its judgment and by 4 votes to 1 determined the precise coordinates of the maritime boundary between the two countries.[604] This boundary was a compromise, lying approximately halfway between the claims of the two parties.[605] Georges Bank was divided, with a small, but particularly resource-rich, part for Canada. This division entailed a need for further cooperation, since many of the fish species range over the entire Georges Bank.[606]

Both parties accepted the judgment.[607] While Canadian federal and provincial officials welcomed the decision, fishermen were more skeptical. All in all, though, the judgment was received more positively in Canada than in the US.[608] The New England fishing industry was disappointed and feared substantial economic losses.[609] To minimize hardships on the fishermen, the US secretary of state on 11 December 1984 suggested a one-year suspension of the Chamber's decision. Unsurprisingly, Canada rejected this proposal.[610] The Agreement on Fisheries Enforcement of 26 September 1990[611]

---

[603] *Schneider*, 79 AJIL (1985), at 544.

[604] Judgment of 12 October 1984, at 345. Judge Gros from France dissented. For details on the judgment, see *Oellers-Frahm* in EPIL II, at 648–50; *Legault/Hankey*, 79 AJIL (1985), at 961–91; *Schneider*, 79 AJIL (1985), at 566–75; *Shelley*, 26 Harv. ILJ (1985), at 647–54; *Trendl*, 12 S.Ill.U. LJ (1988), at 618–34; *De Vorsey/De Vorsey*, 18 Case W. Res. JIL (1986), at 415–42.

[605] Canada–United States (Gulf of Maine), in: Charney/Alexander, *International Maritime Boundaries I*, at 402. See *Robinson*, 26 Can.–US LJ (2000), at 44, who criticizes that the Court's approach might encourage excessive claims in the future.

[606] *Schneider*, 79 AJIL (1985), at 577; *Rogoff*, 7 BU ILJ (1989), at 281.

[607] *Clain*, 25 Va. JIL (1985), at 605–8 (1985). See also *Robinson*, 26 Can.–US LJ (2000), at 44, reporting that the matter was taken as settled by the two governments.

[608] *Schneider*, 79 AJIL (1985), at 540.

[609] *Clain*, 25 Va. JIL (1985), at 605–6: complaints came up although it appeared that the US was better off with the Chamber decision than with the quotas that would have been applicable under the 1979 agreement. Still, the decision brought about a change for the fishermen; earlier, they had access to the entire area, whereas now there is a delimitation line through Georges Bank that has to be respected: see *Trendl*, 12 S. Ill. U. LJ (1988), at 635 fn. 248.

[610] *Clain*, 25 Va. JIL (1985), at 607. *Trendl*, 12 S.Ill.U. LJ (1988), reports at 635 fn. 249 claims that Canada's rejection has injected a "spur of bitterness" into the countries' relations.

[611] TIAS 11753.

formed the basis for increased cooperation and made explicit reference to the ICJ judgment:

The parties reaffirm their commitment to ensure full respect for maritime boundaries between them delimited by mutual agreement or third-party dispute settlement, including by the International Court of Justice. Nothing in this Agreement, and no acts or activities taking place pursuant thereto, shall prejudice the position of either Party with respect to the location of any disputed maritime boundary or the legal status of waters and zones claimed by either Party.[612]

After its entry into force on 16 December 1991, the cooperation of the Canadian Department of Fisheries and the Oceans and the US Coast Guard succeeded in bringing about a substantial decrease in violations of the "Hague line", which is patrolled by both sides.[613] Neither government endorsed the occasional, inevitable, infractions by regional fishermen. This tortious conduct by private citizens did not represent an official challenge to the verdict.

There were several reasons for optimism about the prospects for compliance. First, the parties had clearly expressed their desire to have the dispute decided by the Chamber.[614] Second, their decision to do so had been motivated by a genuine will to have the dispute finally settled and thereby remove this irritant from their bilateral relations. This remained true even though both sides might have hoped for a result more favorable to their respective position. A definitive solution had been considered more important than the actual result.[615] Finally, the close relations and common values between the two trading partners,[616] as well as a shared interest in the conservation of the fish stocks concerned,[617] contributed to the ease of compliance.

XVI. Continental shelf (Libyan Arab Jamahiriya/Malta)

The delimitation of the continental shelf between Libya and Malta represented another controversial chapter in the history of maritime boundaries in the Mediterranean.[618] As in the case between Libya and Tunisia,[619] the

---

[612] Article V.

[613] Canadian Department of Fisheries and Oceans, Backgrounder: Enforcement of Canada/ US Boundary–Hague Line, Update July 1995, http://web.archive.org/web/20021017030018/ http://www.gfc.dfo.ca/communic/maritime/back95e/s95008.htm, with statistics about violations.

[614] See *Rogoff*, 7 BU ILJ (1989), at 282–3.

[615] *Brauer*, 23 Va. JIL (1983), at 474 (see the quotation *supra* n. 580).

[616] Ibid., at 464–5, 468, 473; *Robinson*, 26 Can.–US LJ (2000), at 38–40, at 39–40 speaks of an "unusual commonality in attitude" and an "almost family relationship."

[617] See on this point *Schneider*, 79 AJIL (1985), at 577.

[618] For a description of the overall situation relating to the Mediterranean continental shelf, see Leanza/Sico, *Mediterranean Continental Shelf*.

[619] See the Continental Shelf (Libyan Arab Jamahiriya/Tunisia) case *supra* XIII.

parties had already granted petroleum exploration concessions in the disputed area.[620]

On 23 May 1976, Libya and Malta concluded a special agreement to submit the issue to the ICJ.[621] At first, the ratification process in Libya was delayed; the dispute escalated in 1980 when Libyan warships forcefully halted drilling activities carried out on the basis of a Maltese permit. The matter came before the Security Council, and only after over a year of bilateral negotiations with the assistance of a special representative of the UN Secretary-General,[622] the parties finally agreed that the case should proceed to the ICJ, and the special agreement entered into force with the exchange of the documents of ratification on 20 March 1982.[623]

In terms similar to those of the special agreement in the case between Libya and Tunisia, the Court was asked to decide what principles and rules of international law were applicable to the delimitation of the areas of the continental shelf. As for the tasks in carrying out the delimitation, the language was different from that chosen between Libya and Tunisia: the Court was asked to decide "how in practice such rules and principles can be applied by the Parties in this particular case in order that they may without difficulty delimit such areas by an agreement as provided in Article III."[624] Following the Court's judgment, Article III of the special agreement called for negotiations and the conclusion of another agreement to determine the area of their continental shelves in accordance with the Court's decision.[625] While the agreement had been negotiated, the precise tasks to be delegated to the Court had generated controversy. Libya had wanted it to be asked only to decide on the rules and principles applicable for the delimitation. Malta's

---

[620] Judgment of 3 June 1985, at 22, para. 17. On the background, see *Mcdorman*, 24 CYIL (1986), at 336.

[621] Special agreement for the submission to the International Court of Justice of difference, Malta–Libya, 1275 UNTS 192.

[622] See *Mcdorman*, 24 CYIL (1986), at 337; Complaint by Malta against the Libyan Arab Jamahiriya, 34 UNYB 465 (1980); Questions concerning the Libyan Arab Jamahiriya, 35 UNYB 358 (1981) with further references.

[623] The Secretary of the People's Committee for the People's Foreign Liaison Bureau of the Socialist People's Libyan Arab Jamahiriya and the Minister for Foreign Affairs of the Republic of Malta to the Registrar of the International Court of Justice, 19 July 1982, ICJ Pleadings, Continental Shelf (Libya/Malta), Vol. I, at 3, Procès-verbal of the exchange of instruments of ratification of the special agreement between the Socialist People's Libyan Arab Jamahiriya and the Republic of Malta for the submission to the International Court of Justice of difference, http://diplowizard.diplomacy.edu/tara/getxDoc.asp?ParentLink=none&Idconv=355.
The Court's Registry received the joint notification of this special agreement on 26 July 1982, ICJ Pleadings, Continental Shelf (Libya/Malta), Vol. IV, 483.

[624] Article I of the special agreement.

[625] Article III reads: "Following the final decision of the International Court of Justice, the Government of the Republic of Malta and the Government of the Libyan Arab Republic shall enter into negotiations for determining the area of their respective continental shelves and for concluding an agreement for that purpose in accordance with the decision of the Court."

wish had been that the Court be requested to draw the delimitation line. The result was a compromise formula.[626]

Linguistic difficulties such as in the Tunisia–Libya case did not occur; both the English and the Arabic texts were authentic, and there was no claim of a difference of meaning between the two versions.[627] Yet, the parties disagreed on the interpretation of this article and the Court's tasks: Malta insisted that the only way to carry out the delimitation without difficulty was for the Court to indicate a possible line in the judgment, which was contested by Libya.[628] The Court was not called on to determine the actual boundary, however; it was clear that the final line had to be determined through negotiations between the parties.

In its judgment of 3 June 1985,[629] the Court ruled by 14 votes to 3[630] that the delimitation had to be carried out in accordance with equitable principles so as to achieve an equitable result and explained the relevant circumstances for achieving such an equitable result. With regard to the concrete application, the Court pointed out that since it was requested to ensure that the parties could carry out the delimitation "without difficulty", its task encompassed the indication of the appropriate method or methods, and that it was not debarred from indicating a line but that this indication was in fact necessary to discharge its task in the concrete circumstances of the case.[631] The decision included a map for illustrative purposes;[632] as the wording of the operative part of the judgment makes clear, the indicated line was only one possible solution.[633] This was in conformity with the special agreement, where the formulation had been used "how in practice such principles and

---

[626] Judgment of 3 June 1985, at 23, para. 18

[627] See the concluding sentence of the special agreement, *supra* n. 621. The proceedings were largely conducted in English, see ICJ Pleadings, Continental Shelf (Libya/Malta), Vols. I–IV.

[628] See the summary of the parties' arguments in the Judgment of 3 June 1985, at 23, para. 18.

[629] An application by Italy to intervene in the case was rejected in the Judgment of 21 March 1984, at 3–29. Nevertheless, the Court took Italy's interests into account and framed its decision so as to leave Italian claims unaffected: ibid., at 25–8, paras. 21–3, an approach that received mixed comments in literature. For details on the judgment, see *Brown*, in Cheng/Brown, Contemporary Problems of International Law, at 3–18; *Conforti*, 90 RGDIP (1986), at 313–43; *Leigh*, 80 AJIL (1986), at 645–8; *Oellers-Frahm* "Continental Shelf Case (Libyan Arab Jamahiriya/Malta)", in EPIL I, at 795–8; *Orihuela Calatayud*, 40 REspDI (1988), at 105–20; *Thomas*, 27 Harv. ILJ (1986), at 304–13.

[630] See 56–8, para. 79. The two judges *ad hoc* voted with the majority, but filed separate opinions. It should be observed that the split within the Court was higher than the 14 to 3 result suggests. Six judges appended a separate opinion, one a declaration. The divergence in some of the separate opinions from the judgment was substantial: five of the concurring judges argued that the delimitation line should be elsewhere: see *Orihuela Calatayud*, 40 REspDI (1988), at 120. It was argued that the result was closer to 9–8 than to 14–3: see Johnston, *The theory and history of ocean boundary-making*, 209.

[631] Judgment of 3 June 1985, at 23–4, para. 19.

[632] Ibid., at 46–56, paras. 60–78; the map is printed at p. 54.

[633] See Letter D of the operative part of the judgment, ibid., at 57, para. 79: "an equitable result *may* be arrived at by drawing [. . .]."

rules *can* be applied"[634] instead of "must be applied." As the decision stated, "an equitable result *may* be arrived at" by drawing[635] the line suggested by the Court. The actual final delimitation remained a matter for negotiations.

Although the decision sparked criticism and disappointment on Malta's part, the delimitation was rapidly carried out on the basis of the judgment:[636] on 10 November 1986, the parties concluded an agreement to implement the ICJ decision.[637] The agreement entered into force on 11 December 1987,[638] ending a dispute that had once been serious enough to attract the attention of the Security Council. At the time the judgment was delivered, relations between the parties had improved. In late 1984, an agreement on friendship and cooperation and a trade agreement had been concluded.[639] This improved climate might have contributed to a speedy implementation of the verdict.[640]

XVII. Frontier dispute (Burkina Faso/Mali)

The border between Mali and Upper Volta/Burkina Faso[641] had been the subject of dispute between these two former French colonies since their independence and had at several points led to armed conflict; joint efforts to agree on a demarcation were only partially successful. The concrete dispute submitted to the Court centered on the control over a stretch of land known as the Agacher strip, a remote and thinly populated area of some 1,200 square miles, rich in mineral resources.[642] Burkina Faso based its sovereignty claim on the frontier delimitation by the French colonial administration as shown in colonial maps. Mali, on the other hand, focused on the ethnicity of inhabitants and on legal documents attributing the region to the

---

[634] Special agreement, Art. I (emphasis added).

[635] Judgment of 3 June 1985, at 57, para. 79(C) (emphasis added).

[636] See Johnston, *The theory and history of ocean boundary-making*, 210.

[637] Agreement implementing Article III of the special agreement and the judgment of the International Court of Justice, Libya–Malta, printed in 81 ILR (1990), 726–7 and retrievable under http://diplowizard.diplomacy.edu/tara/getxDoc.asp?ParentLink=none&Idconv=357. See also Leanza in: Starace/Villan, *Studi in ricordo di Antonio Filippo Panzera I*, at 467–8.

[638] *Procès-verbal* of the Exchange of Instruments of Ratification of the Agreement between the Republic of Malta and the Great Socialist People's Libyan Arab Jamahiriya to implement Article III of the Special Agreement and the Judgment of the Court, http://diplowizard. diplomacy.edu/tara/getxDoc.asp?ParentLink=none&Idconv=358.

[639] Treaty of Friendship and Cooperation of 19 November 1984; Trade agreement of 19 December 1984, see http://docs.justice.gov.mt/lom/legislation/english/leg/vol_7/chapt311.pdf.

[640] Despite the assessment of *Mcdorman* in 1986 (24 CYIL (1986), at 366), who apparently did not consider it likely that implementation would take place soon: "Past practice indicates that despite the 1985 judgment between Libya and Malta, it may be some time before a formal bilateral agreement is entered into."

[641] Upper Volta changed its name to Burkina Faso as from 4 April 1984, during the proceedings before the Court: Judgment of 22 December 1986, at 558, para. 4.

[642] 55 AdG (1985) 29457 A.

French Sudan.[643] Following unsuccessful mediation efforts by the OAU, the two states submitted their dispute to a Chamber of the ICJ, marking the second occasion in which the chambers procedure was invoked. A special agreement[644] concluded on 16 September 1983 foresaw the creation of a five-judge Chamber, including two judges *ad hoc*.[645] The agreement spelled out the Chamber's role in defining the frontier within a determined area.[646] By explicitly referring to "the principle of the intangibility of frontiers inherited from colonization,"[647] the parties affirmed the relevance of the doctrine of *uti possidetis juris* in their legal relations.[648] In addition to miscellaneous procedural provisions, the agreement included the following article on the post-adjudicative phase:

Article IV. Judgment of the Chamber
(1) The Parties accept the Judgment of the Chamber given pursuant to the Special Agreement as final and binding upon them.
(2) Within one year after that Judgment the Parties shall effect the demarcation of the frontier.
(3) The Parties request the Chamber to nominate, in its Judgment, three experts to assist them in the demarcation process.

While the first paragraph reiterated the parties' obligation under Article 94(1) of the UN Charter,[649] the second paragraph gave that obligation a particular form by setting a time frame. The final paragraph anticipated the need for third-party assistance during the post-adjudicative phase and gave

---

[643] On the background, see Allcock, *Border and territorial disputes*, at 221–5; Tredano, *L'intangibilité*, at 182–6; *Naldi*, 36 ICLQ (1987), at 893–4; Rosenne, *World Court*, at 223–4.

[644] Special agreement between Upper Volta and Mali for the submission to a Chamber of the ICJ of the frontier dispute between the two states, 1333 UNTS 102–3. In accordance with Article 40(1) of the ICJ Statute, the parties jointly notified the ICJ Registrar of the special agreement in a letter of 14 October 1983. Judgment of 22 December 1986, at 556–7, para. 1.

[645] Agreement between Mali and Upper Volta concerning the submission to a Chamber of the International Court of Justice of the frontier dispute between the two States, 1333 UNTS 97. By order of 3 April 1985, the Court followed the parties' request and constituted a Chamber, which consisted of Judges Bedjaoui, Lachs, and Ruda and Judges *ad hoc* Luchaire (for Burkina Faso) and Abi-Saab (for Mali). Order of 3 April 1985, at 6–8.

[646] Special agreement, *supra* n. 645, Article I.

[647] Ibid., Preamble, second indent.

[648] The Court, nevertheless, felt compelled to pronounce on the general features of this principle under international law in the Judgment of 22 December 1986, at 565–7, paras. 20–6, and rightly so: the Court is asked to decide disputes "in accordance with international law" (Article 38(1) of the Statute) and can treat facts, but not the law, as givens. While the Court should give particular attention to the fact that the parties concur in a particular point of law, it should still bear in mind that its role in judging upon international law as such. At 565, para. 20, the Court stated first that the Court cannot "disregard" the principle of *uti possidetis juris* since both parties have agreed on its applicability. It proceeded to say that there was no need in the present case to show that it was an established principle in the decolonization context, but that it wished to emphasize its general scope "in view of its exceptional importance for the African continent and for the two parties."

[649] *Decaux*, 33 AFDI (1986), at 217–18 criticizes this provision, warning that it might dilute the obligatory force of the judgment *per se*.

the Court a role in this context: an unusual provision, as the Court normally fulfills its task with the delivery of the final judgment and is not involved in its implementation.[650]

The Chamber issued a series of decisions in the case. On 10 January 1986, after hostilities had broken out in the area, the Chamber indicated interim measures of protection at the request of both parties. The parties observed those measures and tensions calmed.[651] In its favorably received judgment of 22 December 1986, the Chamber unanimously fixed a borderline between the lines suggested by the two parties, dividing the disputed territory approximately in half.[652] The Chamber chose to defer the nomination of experts to carry out the demarcation until practical aspects had been clarified, and announced an order for that purpose at a later stage.[653]

Since the request to appoint the experts had come from both parties, the Chamber saw no obstacle against carrying out the nomination and constituted the three-person panel by an order of 9 April 1987.[654] The three-person panel was directed to assist in the judgment's implementation—not to deliver an expert opinion pursuant to Article 50 of the ICJ Statute.[655] Accordingly, the panel was not accountable to the Chamber, and its costs were not paid by the Court; the Swiss government provided financial support for the demarcation. The case was one of the factors that gave impetus for the establishment of the UN Secretary-General's Trust Fund.[656]

A variety of factors contributed to the successful outcome of the case. The parties shared a commitment to reach a settlement and had concluded a special agreement with clear provisions for the litigation itself as well as for the post-adjudicative phase. Regional organizations stood ready to render assistance in the event of difficulties in implementation.[657] The parties brought elements of objectivity and automatism to the post-adjudicative

---

[650] See *supra* Chapter 2 E.   [651] For details, see *infra* C V.

[652] Judgment of 22 December 1986, at 554–663. For details of the judgment, see Allcock, *Border and territorial disputes*, at 225–7; *Decaux*, 33 AFDI (1986), at 220–38; Leigh, 81 AJIL (1987), at 411–13; Naldi, 36 ICLQ (1987), at 893–903. Both parties accepted the verdict and expressed their satisfaction, see Tredano, *L'intangibilité*, 189; *Leigh*, 81 AJIL (1987), at 414, quoting messages from the President of Burkina Faso and the President of Mali to the President of the ICJ, dated 24 December 1986 and 10 January 1987, respectively, ICJ Communiqué No.87/ 1, 16 Jan. 1987, Stern, *20 ans de jurisprudence*, at 423. See also 56 AdG (1986) 30624 A, reporting statements from Mali's governing party and from Radio Ouagadougou.

[653] Judgment of 22 December 1986, at 648, para. 176. It did not voice any general concerns as to the appropriateness of including measures on the post-adjudicative phase in a *judgment*, but explained its way of proceeding by the circumstances of the case.

[654] Order of 9 April 1987, at 7–8. The panel included nationals of France, Algeria, and the Netherlands.

[655] Article 50 relates to an opinion that assists the Court on its way to a judgment; for details, see Rosenne, *Law and Practice III*, at 1364–71.

[656] See Rosenne, *Law and Practice I*, 274 fn. 121, and 514 fn. 86.

[657] The OAU had engaged in mediation efforts; the structures of the regional defence pact ANAD had helped to bring about a cease-fire after armed clashes took place, see *infra* C V.

phase by providing for the involvement of a non-political, Chamber-appointed expert panel in advance.[658] The eventual judgment was clearly framed; the Chamber's willingness to nominate the expert panel manifested deference to the wishes of the parties. The availability of external financing for the demarcation effort is a practical matter that cannot be ignored. In sum, the case marked an important triumph for the Court's institutional position—all the more so when bearing in mind that the underlying dispute had led at various times to armed clashes, even in the midst of proceedings.

XVIII. *Military and paramilitary activities in and against Nicaragua*

1. Background of the case

In July 1979, a revolutionary government came to power in Nicaragua, dominated by the Sandinista National Liberation Front. The initial support of the US for the new government waned after growing concerns over their assistance for insurgents in neighboring states, in particular El Salvador, and their ties to communist states such as Cuba and the Soviet Union; the US decried the regime as oppressive and undemocratic. Nicaragua, on its part, objected to US interference in its domestic affairs, and denied any involvement in the internal conflict in El Salvador. For both countries, important principles were at stake: the US saw its security interests, prestige, and influence in a neighboring region endangered; Nicaragua opposed US intrusion in Central America in general. The rhetoric of the American presidential campaign—in which incumbent Jimmy Carter was blamed for having "lost Nicaragua to the Marxists"—translated into a shift in policy with the election of the vocal anti-communist Ronald Reagan, who openly encouraged the overthrow of the Sandinista regime. The US cancelled its Nicaraguan aid program in 1981 and threw its support behind the Contras, a counterrevolutionary group in Nicaragua. This took the form of covert support in the beginning, by financial assistance, training, and the provision of military equipment; from late 1983, the US government began providing direct assistance. The US Central Intelligence Agency mined Nicaraguan harbors and launched armed raids on port facilities and oil depots.[659]

The US actions provoked intense national and international debate. The Reagan administration was committed to a tough line against Nicaragua, but

---

[658] See the statement of Mali's governing party as quoted in AdG, *supra* n. 652, attributing the success to the support of friendly nations, the desire of both countries to settle the dispute peacefully, and the wisdom of the two heads of state.

[659] See on the background Rosenne, *World Court*, 113–14; Gill, *Litigation Strategy at the World Court*, 128–40; Forsythe, *The politics of international law*, 31–8. See also *Moore*, 80 AJIL (1986), at 44–80 for a presentation on the background of the case from the perspective of a special counsel for the US.

its Contra aid package faced opposition in the Congress.[660] At Nicaragua's instigation, the UN Security Council discussed the matter on multiple occasions;[661] because of US objections, the Security Council could take no action beyond the adoption of a resolution addressing the situation in general terms and expressing support for the Contadora process, a diplomatic process designed to achieve a comprehensive peaceful settlement for the conflicts in the region.[662] The US vetoed wider ranging drafts, including one submitted by Nicaragua condemning the mining of Nicaraguan ports and calling on all states to refrain from any type of military action and support for any such action in Central America.[663]

Rumors circulated that Nicaragua might bring the matter before the ICJ.[664] The US responded by modifying its declaration under Article 36(2) of the ICJ Statute. On 6 April 1984, the US secretary of state, George Shultz, filed a document with the UN Secretary-General (the "Shultz letter"), pursuant to which the US excluded from the applicability of its 1946 declaration accepting the compulsory jurisdiction of the Court "disputes with any Central American State or arising out of or related to events in Central America," a proviso that was to "take effect immediately" and to "remain in force for two years, so as to foster the continuing regional dispute settlement process which seeks a negotiated solution to the interrelated political, economic and security problems of Central America."[665] It is dubious whether this step was tactically advisable, as the withdrawal from the Court's jurisdiction only with respect to Central America could be interpreted as an admission of guilt and an attempt to avoid litigation brought by Nicaragua.[666]

---

[660] Forsythe, *The politics of international law*, 40–9.

[661] See S/PV.2347, 2 April 1982, S/PV.2420–1, 23–4 March 1983, S/PV.2431–7, 9–19 May 1983.

[662] See SC Resolution 530 (1983) of 19 May 1983 adopted unanimously at the Security Council's 2437th meeting of 19 May 1983, S/PV.2437, 3; it was based on a draft resolution submitted by Guyana, Jordan, Malta, Nicaragua, Pakistan, Togo, Zaire, and Zimbabwe, S/15770.

[663] Draft resolution by Nicaragua, S/16463, put to vote at the 2529th meeting of the Security Council; 13 states voted in favor, the UK abstained, the US was the only country voting against, see S/PV.2529, at 26. A draft resolution submitted by Guyana and Panama on 1 April 1982 had not made any condemnation, but had emphasized the obligations relating to non-use of force and non-intervention and non-interference in domestic affairs and had appealed to all Member States to refrain from any use of force against any country in the Central American region, S/14941; it was put to vote on on 2 April 1982, 12 countries voted in favor, 2 abstained (the United Kingdom and Zaire), the US was the only country voting against, see S/PV.2347.

[664] See Gill, *Litigation Strategy at the World Court*, at 141; *Reichler* (one of the counsels for Nicaragua), 42 Harv. ILJ (2001), at 30–1; *Piñol i Rull*, 39 REspDI (1987), at 100.

[665] Letter from US Secretary of State Shultz to the UN Secretary-General, 6 April 1984, printed in 23 ILM (1984) 670.

[666] See *Reichler*, 42 Harv. ILJ (2001), at 31–2, reporting the reactions in the media.

2. The parties' submissions and the judgment on jurisdiction

On 9 April 1984, Nicaragua filed an application instituting proceedings before the ICJ[667] along with a request for interim measures of protection.[668] The lawsuit was part of a two-pronged strategy to prevent further aid to the Contras and to muster support for the Sandinistas. A corollary tactic was to influence US public opinion—particularly in the Congress, which held the purse strings for future aid and where the Reagan Nicaragua policy was already the subject of debate[669]—against continued involvement in the region.[670] The application asked for a declaration that the US actions constituted continuing violations of its obligations under international law, including the prohibitions on the use of force and intervention and the freedom of high seas, and that the US was obliged to pay reparation. The Reagan administration, on the other hand, was interested in thwarting the Nicaraguan strategy. It had little to gain in the World Court, but faced substantial risks because it was on the defensive. Its support for the Contras was a matter of public knowledge; it was in the difficult position of justifying its behavior as collective self-defense. The US government therefore had an interest that the matter did not reach the merits stage.[671] Consequently, it was not surprising that it strongly contested the Court's jurisdiction and demanded that the case be removed from the Court's docket.[672] Nicaragua's application had referred to both countries' declarations accepting the compulsory jurisdiction of the Court as a preliminary jurisdictional basis.[673] In the course of initial written proceedings, Nicaragua also referred to a 1956 Treaty of Friendship, Commerce and Navigation as grounds for jurisdiction.[674] In its order of 10 May 1984, the Court unanimously rejected the American request, calling for written proceedings on the questions of jurisdiction and admissibility and indicating various provisional measures to safeguard Nicaragua's rights.[675]

---

[667] Application instituting proceedings submitted by Nicaragua, ICJ Pleadings, Military and Paramilitary Activities, Vol. 1, 3–24.

[668] Request for the indication of provisional measures of protection submitted by Nicaragua, ICJ Pleadings, Military and Paramilitary Activities, Vol. 1, 27–9.

[669] *Reichler*, 42 Harv. ILJ (2001), at 22–3.

[670] See Gill, *Litigation Strategy at the World Court*, 134–5, *Rogoff*, 27 BU ILJ (1989), at 85.

[671] See Gill, *Litigation Strategy at the World Court*, 135–40.

[672] Letter of 13 April 1984 from the US ambassador to the Netherlands to the Registrar, ICJ Pleadings, Military and Paramilitary Activities, Vol. V, 359–60.

[673] US declaration of 14 August 1946 (effective on 26 August 1946), 1 UNTS 9 and Nicaragua's declaration accepting the jurisdiction of the Permanent Court of International Justice of 24 September 1929, printed in: ICJ YB 1984–5, 89.

[674] Treaty of Friendship, Commerce and Navigation, 21 January 1956, 367 UNTS 3. Article XXIV (2) provides for compulsory dispute settlement by the ICJ: "Any dispute between the parties as to the interpretation or application of the present Treaty, not satisfactorily adjusted by diplomacy, shall be submitted to the International Court of Justice, unless the Parties agree to settlement by other pacific means."

[675] Order of 10 May 1984, at 186–8. For details on the provisional measures, see *infra* C VI.

The Court's jurisdiction was controversial for various reasons. First, the validity of Nicaragua's declaration under the optional clause was doubtful. This issue was probably the strongest point for the US. Nicaragua had made a declaration accepting the compulsory jurisdiction of the Permanent Court of International Justice, but it had never deposited its ratification to the PCIJ Statute with the League of Nations Secretariat, as a result of which, as the parties agreed, it had never been bound by the compulsory jurisdiction of the PCIJ. Nicaragua claimed that the declaration of 24 September 1929 nevertheless had conferred jurisdiction on the ICJ under Article 36(5) of the ICJ Statute.[676]

Second, with regard to its own declaration under Article 36(2) of the ICJ Statute, the US referred to the Vandenberg reservation (a proviso of the 1946 declaration) and the Shultz letter. According to the Vandenberg reservation, the declaration under Article 36(2) was not to apply to disputes arising under a multilateral treaty unless all parties to the treaty affected by the decision were also parties to the case before the Court or the US agreed to the jurisdiction in the special case. The US identified Honduras, Costa Rica, and El Salvador as affected parties and argued that the Court lacked jurisdiction absent the consent of those states.[677] With regard to the Shultz letter, it was doubtful whether it could have had immediate effect since the 1946 declaration provided for a six-month notice for its termination. The US argued that the letter was a modification and not a termination of the declaration and that, in any event, in relation to Nicaragua it could be changed with immediate effect on the basis of reciprocity, since the Nicaraguan declaration had no temporal restrictions for changes.[678] With regard to the friendship treaty, the US objected to its consideration since this instrument had not been included as a basis for jurisdiction in the original application, and on the ground that Nicaragua had failed to establish a reasonable connection between its claims and the treaty.[679]

Interestingly, the US did not invoke the Connally amendment, a reservation to its 1946 declaration under Article 36(2) of the ICJ Statute according to which it had excluded from its acceptance of the Court's jurisdiction "disputes with regard to matters which are essentially within the domestic jurisdiction of the United States of America as determined by the United States of America."[680] The effects of such self-judging reservations to declarations under Article 36(2) are controversial; a similar reservation by France

---

[676] See Judgment of 26 November 1984 (Jurisdiction), at 399–401, paras. 15–18.
[677] See ibid., at 421–3, paras. 67–9.   [678] See ibid., at 415–17, paras. 52–5.
[679] See ibid., at 426, para. 78; 427–8, para. 81.
[680] See already *supra* n. 145. See *Reichler* (one of the counsels for Nicaragua), 42 Harv. ILJ (2001), at 29: "Our team assumed that the Reagan Administration would use the Connally Amendment to escape the Court's jurisdiction and kill Nicaragua's case. We considered this the biggest problem we would face, and we had no solution."

had been successfully invoked by Norway by way of reciprocity in the Norwegian Loans case.[681] The Connally amendment might have been a powerful defensive tool for the US government, and in view of its fundamental opposition to any ICJ involvement, it is surprising that it did not come into play. On the other hand, the claim that allegations of armed actions in another country were exclusively domestic matters would have been difficult to justify in substance, despite its efficiency as a tool to escape the Court's jurisdiction, and might have created the impression that the Reagan administration used unfair tools to avoid an involvement of the Court, putting the legitimacy of the US Nicaragua policy in question. In any event, since the US government declined to make the requisite determination of an exclusively domestic matter in the first place, the Court had no occasion to address the Connally amendment's validity.

Apart from these issues of jurisdiction, the US submitted that Nicaragua's claims were inadmissible in that Costa Rica, El Salvador, and Honduras were necessary third parties. On 15 August 1984, prior to the closure of the written proceedings on jurisdiction and admissibility, El Salvador filed a declaration of intervention under Article 63 of the ICJ Statute "for the sole and limited purpose of arguing that the Court has no jurisdiction over Nicaragua's application," reserving its other rights to make its views known.[682] In an order of 4 October 1984, the Court declared this intervention as inadmissible at that stage of the proceedings.[683] El Salvador did not try to intervene at a later point.

The US raised additional objections to the admissibility of Nicaragua's application. It maintained that the Court had no competence to deal with disputes involving armed conflict and the right to self-defense since the Charter entrusted such matters to the Security Council and that Nicaragua could not bring the matter to the ICJ because it had failed to exhaust the Contadora Process, the regional diplomatic process for the settlement of the Central American conflicts.[684]

---

[681] Certain Norwegian Loans (France v. Norway), Judgment of 6 July 1957, ICJ Reports 1957, 9. See also the analysis of the effect of such a clause in the Separate Opinion of Judge Lauterpacht in the Interhandel Case (where the US had invoked the Connally amendment during the interim proceedings): Interhandel (interim measures of protection), Order of 24 October 1957, at 117–20.

[682] Declaration of Intervention of the Republic of El Salvador, ICJ Pleadings, Military and Paramilitary Activities, Vol. II, 451–8.

[683] Order of 4 October 1984, at 215–16. The decision not to hold a hearing was reached by 9 votes to 6, the decision on the inadmissibility by 14 votes to 1, with the US Judge Schwebel dissenting. The order was very short and did not indicate its reasons, which was certainly not conducive to greater commitment of the US to the proceedings; for details on the intervention, see Gill, *Litigation Strategy at the World Court*, at 145–8; *Rogers et al.*, 7 BU ILJ (1989); *Beat/Wolf*, 78 AJIL (1984), at 929–36; and *Sztucki*, 79 AJIL (1985), at 1005–36.

[684] Judgment of 26 November 1984 (Jurisdiction), at 430–3, paras. 86–7, 89, 91, and at 436–8, paras. 99, 102.

The Court delivered its judgment on jurisdiction and admissibility on 26 November 1984.[685] It based its jurisdiction on Article 36(2) and (5) of the ICJ Statute[686] and Article XXIV of the bilateral friendship treaty[687] and unanimously declared Nicaragua's application admissible.[688]

As to the validity of Nicaragua's declaration under the optional clause, the Court held that the reference to "[d]eclarations [...] which are in force" appearing in Article 36(5) of the Statute included declarations with "potential effect"—i.e. those which would have been effective, had the respective state been party to the PCIJ Statute—and that this potential effect had been realized through Article 36(5). The Court also relied on its own practice of listing Nicaragua as a state having made a declaration under the optional clause in its yearbooks, maintaining that Nicaragua's constant attitude showed its intent to recognize the Court's compulsory jurisdiction.[689] As to the Shultz letter, the Court held that it intended to secure a partial and temporary termination of the 1946 declaration, that the US was bound by the six-month notice provision in its declaration, and that there was no reciprocity as to the continuance of the legal operation of declarations under Article 36(2). Moreover, even if reciprocity applied, a termination could only be made by "reasonable notice," which had not been satisfied since the US filed its notice only three days prior to the initiation of the proceedings.[690] The Court deferred on the issue of the Vandenberg reservation, finding that the reservation did not have an exclusively preliminary character and that the question of the states that might be affected was one for the merits.[691] The Court ruled that it was entitled to consider bases of jurisdiction brought to its attention subsequent to the submission of the application as long as they did not alter the nature of the dispute as originally described; it thus proceeded to find a basis for its jurisdiction under the friendship treaty as well.[692] On the issue of admissibility, these questions were less controversial than those relating to jurisdiction, since the Court could refer to its settled case law. The Court unanimously rejected the American indispensable third-party argument on the basis that the rights of the third states invoked did not constitute the very subject-matter of the dispute. "Political questions" were not immune from its review, it stated,

---

[685] For details, see *Briggs*, 79 AJIL (1985), at 373–8; *Chimni*, 35 ICLQ (1986), at 960–70; *Piñol i Rull*, 39 REspDI (1987), at 103–9; *Greig*, 62 BYIL (1991), at 118–281.

[686] Judgment of 26 November 1984, at 442, para. 113, No. 1(a). This decision was made 11 votes to 5. The dissenting judges were Mosler (Federal Republic of Germany), Oda (Japan), Ago (Italy), Schwebel (USA), and Sir Robert Jennings (UK).

[687] Ibid., No. 1(b). The dissenting judges were Schwebel (USA) and Ruda (Argentina). Finally, it drew the general conclusion that it had jurisdiction by 15 votes to 1, with Judge Schwebel dissenting, No. 1(c).

[688] Ibid., No. 2.   [689] Judgment of 26 November 1984, at 398–413, paras. 14–47.

[690] Ibid., at 415–21, paras. 52–65.   [691] Ibid., at 425–6, para. 76.

[692] Ibid., at 426–9, paras. 77–83.

affirming its earlier jurisprudence that the fact that the dispute involved the use of force and the involvement of the UN Security Council did not prevent it from exercising its jurisdiction and that there was no requirement of prior exhaustion of regional negotiation mechanisms before the Court could become involved.[693]

The Court took great pains in comprehensively dealing with the issues raised by the parties, an approach particularly suited to situations where one side vehemently opposes the proceedings. Yet the decision was controversial, in particular with regard to the validity of Nicaragua's declaration, where the dissenting judges expressed their opposition strongly.[694] There is no doubt that the Court adopted a broad interpretation of Article 36(5) of its Statute. Yet although other interpretations would have been tenable, the Court's was thoroughly explained.[695] Nicaragua could hardly have relied on a lack of validity of its 1929 declaration if the tables had been turned, with Nicaragua as the target of litigation, given that it had constantly been treated as a party of the optional clause and had behaved as such.[696] The Court's decision was founded on Article 36(6) of the Statute, according to which its decision shall settle disputes on its jurisdiction. There was thus no justification for the storm of criticism the judgment provoked from the Reagan administration.

3. The US reaction to the judgment on jurisdiction

Nicaragua had gained an important partial victory: it would have a forum to present its grievances to a world-wide public.[697] The US government refused to accept the ruling; its harsh critique had two dimensions relating to the

---

[693] Ibid., at 429–41, paras. 84–108. The less controversial character of this part of the decision is visible in the fact that the decision on admissibility was reached unanimously; the Court could address those issues on the basis of its settled jurisprudence.

[694] See the comments in the separate opinions of Judges Mosler (461–70 at 461–5), Oda (472–513 at 473–89), Ago (514–32 at 517–32), Jennings (533–57 at 533–45), and the dissenting opinion of Judge Schwebel (558–637 at 563–600).

[695] See *Franck*, 79 AJIL (1985), at 382–4, for an analysis of the decision from the perspective of whether "the findings of the Court [are] so patently unreasonable [. . .] as to permit no other conclusion than that they reflect the willful anti-American bias of the judges"—a question he answers in the negative, concluding at 384: "No part of that decision [. . .] appears to this American international lawyer to be insupportable in law and thus, evidently, a manifestation of 'politicization.' It is a decision as to which reasonable men and women versed in the law can and will differ." For positive comments on the judgment, see *Briggs*, 79 AJIL (1985), at 378: "[O]ne may take great satisfaction in a Judgment in which patient and careful legal analysis of the varied arguments presented resulted in upholding legal obligations voluntarily assumed." See further *d'Amato/O'Connell*, in Damrosch, The ICJ at a crossroads, at 418; but see *Reisman*, 80 AJIL (1986), at 130–4, for a vehement critique of the judgment, in particular, at 132 on the Court's reasoning on the Nicaraguan declaration: "The Court's creation of a valid Nicaraguan declaration is so ill-founded in the facts, in the law and in the Court's own jurisprudence as to constitute a ground of nullity."

[696] *d'Amato/O'Connell* in Damrosch, The ICJ at a crossroads, at 417.

[697] Rosenne, *World Court*, 136.

substance of the decision as well as to a lack of trust in the institution as such. On 18 January 1985, the US State Department issued an announcement that the US had, "with great reluctance, decided not to participate in the further proceedings in the case" along with a critical analysis of the Court's judgment.[698] It repeated its arguments against jurisdiction and admissibility, stating that

[f]ew if any other countries in the world would have appeared at all in a case such as this which they considered to be improperly brought. [...] [The decision of 26 November 1984] is erroneous as a matter of law and is based on a misreading and distortion of the evidence and precedent.[699]

It argued that the Court's findings contradicted its earlier jurisprudence. The decision's dissenting opinions provided welcome fuel for the US critique.[700]

Several US arguments revealed a lack of trust towards the Court. The US stated that the haste with which the Court had proceeded to give a judgment added "to the impression that the Court is determined to find in favor of Nicaragua in this case." It also maintained that much of the evidence establishing Nicaragua's aggression against its neighbors was of a highly sensitive intelligence character and that it would not "risk US national security by presenting such sensitive material in public or before a Court that includes two judges from Warsaw Pact nations."[701] It expressed its grave concern that a tendency of politicization of international organizations against the interests of Western democracies, as it had detected in the UN, might affect the Court as well.[702]

In addition, the US government took action with regard to both documents which, according to the judgment of the 26 November 1984, provided for the Court's jurisdiction. As the Treaty on Friendship, Commerce and Navigation of 1955 could be terminated with a one-year written notice,[703] the US terminated the treaty effective 1 May 1986.[704] On 7 October 1985, the US

---

[698] US Department of State, Statement on the US withdrawal from the proceedings initiated by Nicaragua in the International Court of Justice, 24 International Legal Materials (1985), 246–9; *idem*, Observations on the International Court of Justice's November 26, 1984 Judgment on Jurisdiction and Admissibility in the Case of Nicaragua v. United States of America, ibid., 249–63.

[699] Statement on withdrawal, *supra* n. 698, at 247.

[700] See ibid., at 247 on the question of the acceptance of the Court's compulsory jurisdiction on part of Nicaragua: "On this pivotal issue in the November 26 decision—decided by a vote of 11–5—dissenting judges called the Court's judgment 'untenable' and 'astonishing' and described the US position as 'beyond doubt.' We agree." See also Observations, *supra* n. 698, at 256, 258.

[701] Statement on withdrawal, *supra* n. 698, at 248.

[702] Ibid. On the Reagan administration's general attitude of skepticism toward the UN System, see Chimni, 35 ICLQ (1986), at 965, and against the US assertion of a bias of the Court ibid., at 966.

[703] Article XXV(3): Either party may, by giving one year's written notice to the other party, terminate the present treaty at the end of the initial ten-year period or at any time thereafter.

[704] US Diplomatic Note concerning the termination of the FCN Treaty, 24 ILM (1985), 815–16. See also Judgment of 27 June 1986, at 28, para. 36.

withdrew its declaration under Article 36(2) of 1946 as a further sign of its disapproval of the Court.[705] It explained that the expectations behind the 1946 declaration and the hopes that the Court would not be abused for political reasons had not been fulfilled. At the same time, it expressed its support for the Court "in performing its proper role" and its willingness to make use of the Court to solve disputes "whenever appropriate" and announced that an agreement had been reached with Italy to bring a dispute before a special Chamber of the Court.[706] The US has since appeared before the Court on several occasions without, however, renewing its declaration under Article 36(2).[707]

Neither the decision not to participate in the further proceedings nor the decision to withdraw from the compulsory jurisdiction *per se* affected the continuation of the proceedings.[708] Nicaragua asked the Court to proceed under Article 53 of the Statute, and the withdrawal of a declaration under Article 36(2) of the Statute cannot prevent the continuation of proceedings instituted under a valid basis of jurisdiction.[709] Yet these events did not bode well for prospects for compliance with the judgment and constituted a blow to the Court as an institution by a country that had traditionally been rather supportive of its role. The US decision to withdraw its declaration under Article 36(2) left the United Kingdom as the only remaining permanent member of the Security Council to have made a declaration under the optional clause; France had already terminated its declaration under Article 36(2) eleven years earlier.[710]

4. The proceedings on the merits

The proceedings on the merits took place without participation by the US, and there was no counter-memorial; yet the US Department of State transmitted a brochure entitled "'Revolution beyond our Borders': Sandinista

---

[705] Letter of US Secretary of State Shultz to the UN Secretary-General, 24 ILM (1985), 1742; it was to take effect six months from that date, in accordance with the terms of the 1946 declaration.

[706] US Department of State, Press Statement concerning termination of acceptance of ICJ compulsory jurisdiction, 24 ILM (1985), 1743–5. The new case was the ELSI case, see Elettronica Sicula S.p.A. (ELSI), Judgment of 20 July 1989.

[707] For a proposal for a new US declaration under Article 36(2) see *d'Amato*, 80 AJIL (1986), at 331–6. The US decisions to walk out of the Court and to withdraw from the compulsory jurisdiction under Article 36(2) triggered an intense debate, See *Franck/Lehrman* in Damrosch, The ICJ at a crossroads, at 3–18; *Franck*, 79 AJIL (1985), at 379–84; *Highet*, 79 AJIL (1985), at 992–1005. For a positive assessment of the rejection of the judgment on jurisdiction, see *Reisman*, 80 AJIL (1986), at 134: "[...] [I]t is an affirmation and not a repudiation of law to reject a decision by a tribunal that had no jurisdiction to make such a decision."

[708] Judgment of 27 June 1986, at 23–6, paras. 26–31 and at 28–9, para. 36.

[709] See on Article 53 *Highet*, 79 AJIL (1985), at 993–7.   [710] See *infra* C III 4.

Intervention in Central America" that explained the US position.[711] The brochure had also been circulated as a document of the General Assembly and the Security Council.[712]

The Court took efforts to carry out a thorough review of the facts; five witnesses had been called by Nicaragua, to whom questions were put by members of the Court, most notably by Judge Schwebel, an American.[713] The absence of the respondent impeded the ascertainment of the true facts; whether the Court's findings of the fact were correct or whether the Court had been misled remains a point of controversy.[714] The Court made efforts to arrive at an objective assessment of the situation and took into account the US brochure, although it had not been submitted to the Court in accordance with the Statute and the Rules of Court;[715] it also considered the arguments which the US had brought forward at the earlier stages of the proceedings. Yet the Court acknowledged in its judgment on the merits that it could not, by its own enquiries, entirely make up for the absence of one party and that this absence must necessarily limit the extent to which the Court was informed of the facts; it emphasized the inability of the absent party to counter the factual allegations of its opponent.[716] Since the main controversy aside from the legal questions of the applicability and scope of the Vandenberg reservation and the interpretation of the right to collective self-defense was the extent of Nicaragua's involvement (if any) in insurgent activities in neighboring countries, the Court's limited ability to ascertain the facts was highly problematic. Article 50 of the ICJ Statute would have allowed the Court to appoint an independent investigative body to carry out on-the-spot

---

[711] ICJ Pleadings, Military and Paramilitary Activities, Vol. IV, 459–532. It is not clear, though, whether collective self-defense was really the issue or whether the Reagan administration's principal goal was to remove the Sandinista régime: for the latter view, See *d'Amato*, 79 AJIL (1985), at 657–8.

[712] A/40/858, S/17612.

[713] See Oral arguments on the merits, ICJ Pleadings, Military and paramilitary activities, Vol. V, at 12–102. For details on the Court's approach to evidence, see *Highet*, 81 AJIL (1987), at 1–56.

[714] See for the view that the Court had been deceived by Nicaragua and that facts later discovered proved that Nicaragua had furnished considerable support for insurgents in El Salvador. Rosenne, *World Court*, 152–3; *Schwebel*, 27 NYU JILP (1995), at 739–41; Franck, in Lillich, *Fact-finding before International Tribunals*, at 28–32 (stating, at 31, that Court had taken "wrong guess as to the facts"). For a staunch critique of the Court's findings on the facts, see *Moore*, 81 AJIL (1987), at 151–9.

[715] Judgment of 27 June 1986, at 44, para. 73.

[716] Ibid., at 25, para. 30. See *Highet*, 81 AJIL (1987), at 2: "[T]he United States made the job of the Court virtually impossible from a factual point of view and, as some observed, perhaps effectively foreclosed almost all other options other than those adopted by the Court in its Judgment." See also ibid., at 3–5, 49–51. See *d'Amato*, 81 AJIL (1987), at 105, extending the argument of the impediment for the Court through the defendant's absence to the legal evaluation as well: "[T]he biggest missing element might not be judicial erudition as much as adversarial clash. More than we usually admit of what we admire about judges on any court may be due to the quality of the briefs and arguments handed to them [...]." He suggests that the Court should have encouraged the submission of *amicus curiae* briefs on behalf of the US.

investigations; it might have been useful to make use of that mechanism as the Court recognized its difficulties in parsing the truth in contradictory versions of facts.[717] Yet the Court discarded this possibility as impracticable since such a body, in order properly to fulfill its functions, would find it necessary to go not only to the applicant state but also to several other neighboring countries and even to the US itself.[718] Why this should be so serious an obstacle as to make an independent fact-finding mission undesirable is unclear and not explained further in the judgment. In any event, the Court drew mainly on indirect evidence[719] to find the facts as sufficiently established so as to decide in Nicaragua's favor. Judge Schwebel, who pointed out in his dissenting opinion that the facts were significantly different from how they had been presented by Nicaragua, failed in convincing the Court's majority.[720]

On 27 June 1986, the Court delivered its judgments on the merits.[721] It found that the Vandenberg reservation was applicable because El Salvador would be "affected" by the decision under the terms of that reservation, and that it thus was prevented from assessing the legality of the US action under the multilateral treaties invoked; however, the effect of the reservation was limited to barring the examination of those treaties and had no impact on the other sources of law which the Court had to apply under Article 38 of the Statute—customary law in particular.[722] The Court held that it had been established that US military personnel or persons in the pay of the US had engaged in the mining of Nicaraguan ports and waters, operations against oil installations and a naval base, and infringements of Nicaraguan airspace.[723] It was not persuaded by Nicaragua's claim that the Contras could be regarded as an organ of the American government whose actions were directly attributable to the US. The Court maintained that the Contras themselves bore responsibility for unlawful acts they committed, even though they had received support from the US.[724] While it found that Nicaragua had supported the armed opposition in El Salvador up to the early months of 1981, the Court held that the evidence did not indicate an arms flow on a significant scale afterwards, even though it imputed certain trans-border military incursions in Honduras and Costa Rica to the Sandinista govern-

---

[717] *Franck*, 81 AJIL (1987), at 116–21. Critical on the Court's failure to make use of its fact-finding powers *Moore*, 81 AJIL (1987), at 158.

[718] Judgment of 27 June 1986, at 40, para. 61.   [719] See *Highet*, 81 AJIL (1987), at 49–51.

[720] Judgment of 27 June 1986, Diss. Op. Schwebel, at 273–83, 395–527.

[721] For an overview, see *Bernstein*, 28 Harv. ILJ (1987), at 146–55; *Crawford* in EPIL III, at 375–6.

[722] Judgment of 27 June 1986, at 29–38, paras. 37–56 and at 92–7, paras. 172–82. This decision was reached by 11 votes to 4, with Judges Ruda, Elias, Sette-Camara, and Ni dissenting, 146, para. 292(1).

[723] Ibid., at 45–53, paras. 75–92.

[724] Ibid., at 53–69, paras. 93–122. On this particular aspect, see *Boyle*, 81 AJIL (1987), at 86–93.

ment.[725] The US justification of collective self-defense fell short on the basis that neither the arms supply nor the incursions had passed the threshold of an armed attack, that there was no evidence that the states in question saw themselves as victims of an armed attack, and that the requirements of necessity and proportionality were not fulfilled.[726]

The Court ruled that the US had committed a series of violations of the friendship treaty as well as customary international law. US support of the Contras had violated the prohibition of intervention, whereas that support as well as certain attacks by US personnel on Nicaraguan territory ran afoul of restrictions on the use of force. Together with the flights over Nicaraguan territory, these actions amounted to an infringement of Nicaragua's sovereignty. In addition, the mining activities in the internal and territorial waters of Nicaragua violated customary obligations not to interrupt peaceful maritime commerce[727] as well as a conventional obligation contained in Article XIX of the friendship treaty.[728] By failing to make known the existence and location of mines, the US had also violated customary international law. The CIA had encouraged the violation of humanitarian law[729] (although the single acts committed subsequently were attributable to the Contras, not the US).[730] The US trade embargo and attacks on Nicaraguan territory were acts calculated to deprive the friendship treaty of its object and purpose, and violated Article XIX of that accord.[731]

The Court held that the US was under a duty "immediately to cease and refrain from all such acts as may constitute breaches of the foregoing legal obligations" and to make reparation to Nicaragua for all breaches of obligations under customary international law and under the friendship treaty. A unanimous Court reminded the parties of "their obligation to seek a solution to their disputes by peaceful means in accordance with international

---

[725] On the method for the establishment of the facts and the facts imputable to the parties, see Judgment of 27 June 1986, at 38–92, paras. 57–171.

[726] This decision was reached by 12 votes to 3, with Judges Oda, Schwebel, and Sir Robert Jennings dissenting, ibid., at 146, para. 292(2). On the interpretation of the right to self-defense by the Court, see *Farer*, 81 AJIL (1987), at 112–16; *Hargrove*, 81 AJIL (1987), at 135–43.

[727] Those decisions were taken by 12 votes to 3, the dissenting judges were Oda, Schwebel, and Sir Robert Jennings: Judgment of 27 June 1986, at 146–47, para. 292(3)–(6). Critical on the Court's approach to customary law see *d'Amato*, 81 AJIL (1987), at 101–5; *Franck*, 81 AJIL (1987), at 118–19.

[728] This decision was made by 14 votes to 1, with Judge Schwebel dissenting. Judgment of 27 June 1986, at 147, para. 292(7).

[729] The intelligence agency had produced and distributed a manual to the Contras entitled "Operaciones sicológicas en guerra de guerrillas" containing advice contrary to humanitarian law, ibid., at 66–9, paras. 118–22.

[730] Both decisions were made by 14 votes to 1, with Judge Oda dissenting, ibid., at 147–8, para. 292(8)–(9).

[731] See ibid., at 112–13, paras. 215–16 and at 129, paras. 254–6. Those decisions were made by 12 votes to 3, with Judges Oda, Schwebel, and Sir Robert Jennings dissenting, at 148, para. 292 (10)–(11).

law."[732] It declined to follow Nicaragua's request for an immediate award of $370,200,000,[733] deferring the issue of the form and amount of reparation for subsequent proceedings in the event that negotiations between the parties on that issue failed.[734]

Since the Treaty on Friendship, Commerce and Navigation was already terminated at the time of the judgment, the pronouncements on that instrument were relevant only as a declaration of illegal behavior in the past and findings on a duty to make reparation; they did not call for future action in compliance with that treaty. The legality of a trade embargo in the future was therefore not discussed. The duties to refrain from further action, therefore, were relevant for the obligation under customary law rather than that accruing under the treaty.

Despite the rather comfortable majority for all points of the operative part (ranging from a unanimous decision to an 11 to 4 decision), the judgment splintered the Court, as manifested by the extensive separate and dissenting opinions, totaling 435 pages,[735] which reflected the diverse viewpoints held by the judges.[736] "To say that I dissent with the Court's Judgment," began Judge Schwebel's dissent, "is to understate the depth of my differences with it."[737] Although he sided with the majority on some points, he considered the judgment as misconceived, misconstruing essential facts relating to Nicaragua's behavior and the legal evaluation of Nicaragua's action. He reaffirmed his objections to the Court's jurisdiction and found the matter non-justiciable.[738] The main focus of his critique was ultimately the Court's evaluation of the facts.[739] He questioned the soundness of basing the judgment

---

[732] Judgment of 27 June 1986, at 149; the voting pattern was as follows: duty to cease and refrain from breaches of the obligations and duty to make reparation for injury caused by violations of customary law: 12 votes to 3 (Judges Oda, Schwebel, and Sir Robert Jennings dissenting), duty to make reparation for injury caused by violation of the Treaty of Friendship and deferral of the decision on form and amount of compensation: 14 votes to 1 (Judge Schwebel dissenting).

[733] Ibid., at 142–3, paras. 283–5.

[734] The decisions on the duty to refrain from further violations and on the obligation to make reparation for injury caused by violations of customary law was made by 12 votes to 3 (with Judges Oda, Schwebel, and Sir Robert Jennings dissenting), on the duty to make reparation under the Treaty of Friendship, the decision was taken by 14 votes to 1, with Judge Schwebel dissenting. Ibid., at 149, para. 292(12)–(15).

[735] See ICJ Reports 1986, 151–546: President Nagendra Singh, Judges Lachs, Ruda, Elias, Ago, Sette-Camara, and Ni appended separate opinions, Judges Oda, Schwebel, and Sir Robert Jennings appended dissenting opinions.

[736] See a personal controversy between Judges Elias and Schwebel: Sep. Op. Elias, 178–80 and Diss. Op. Schwebel, 259–527, Judgment of 27 June 1986, at 313–15, paras. 109, 115.

[737] *Ibid.*, Diss. Op. Schwebel, at 266, para. 1. *Piñol i Rull*, 39 REspDI (1987), at 117, calls Schwebel's opinion a "counter-judgment" ("*contra-sentencia*").

[738] Judgment of 27 June 1986, Diss. Op. Schwebel, at 266, para. 1. He agreed with the majority *inter alia* on the responsibility for the distribution of the manual urging violations of the laws of war, and the mining of Nicaraguan harbors without proper notification to international shipping.

[739] For his presentation of the facts, see ibid., at 273–83, paras. 17–41, and factual appendix, at 395–527, paras. 1–227.

on what he considered false testimony by the Sandinista representatives and stated: "The effect of the Court's treatment of that false testimony upon the validity of the Judgment is a question which only others can decide"[740]—a declaration that might be understood as an open challenge to the judgment's validity. He acknowledged that his were "uncommonly critical words"[741] requiring full justification, given that he was a national of a party to the case; he proceeded to criticize the Court's findings in a 268-page opinion. At the same time, though, Judge Schwebel's dissent is important in so far as it diverges from the US position:[742] despite his sharp critique, he agrees with several of the Court's legal conclusions and conceded that there was room for some others.[743] He expressed regret at the US boycott of the proceedings.[744]

5. The parties' reactions

The US rebuffed Nicaragua's requests for negotiations on compensation, an expected reaction taking into account the reactions to the earlier judgment on jurisdiction and admissibility.[745] The US flouted its obligations under Article 94(1) of the UN Charter and continued to support the Contras, thus engaging in precisely the activities that the Court had found to be unlawful. After Congress had rejected funding for the Contras in previous years, White House pressure eventually won over the US House of Representatives on 25 June 1986, two days before the delivery of the judgment.[746] The margin was rather close—221 votes to 209—leaving open speculations on the vote's outcome had it been taken after the judgment.[747] The bill had already won Senate approval in February, and was signed into law on 18 October 1986.[748] Nicaragua addressed a letter of protest to US secretary of state Shultz the following day, decrying this "open contempt for the Judgment of the International Court of Justice."[749] Over time, however, Reagan's Nicaragua

---

[740] Ibid., at 266, para. 1.   [741] Ibid., at 266, para. 2.

[742] See *Falk*, 81 AJIL (1987), at 110–11.

[743] Judgment of 27 June 1986, at 266, para. 1 and at 272, para. 15.

[744] Ibid., at 316–17, para. 119.

[745] See Keith Highet, 79 AJIL (1985), at 1003, prior to the judgment on the merits: "The January 1985 withdrawal of the United States [...] appears to be an anticipatory repudiation of this Charter obligation. It is difficult to read the departmental statement in any serious manner other than that of advance notice that the United States does not and will not consider itself bound by the final judgment of the Court, under either Article 59 of the Statute or Article 94 of the Charter."

[746] For fiscal year 1985, no Contra funding had been approved, for fiscal year 1986 only humanitarian assistance. For details on the US legislation, see United States, 26 ILM (1987), 433–78; the bill discussed here concerned fiscal year 1987, see ibid., at 467–78. See further *infra* Chapter VI 3.

[747] *Reichler* (one of the counsels for Nicaragua), 42 Harv. ILJ (2001), at 42.

[748] See 26 ILM (1987), 467.

[749] Letter dated 21 October 1986 from the representative of Nicaragua to the President of the Security Council transmitting a note from the Nicaraguan foreign minister to the US secretary of

policy became increasingly untenable, particularly after the Iran–Contra affair came to light, the biggest scandal to shake the Reagan administration over its eight years of office.[750] This course of events and the electoral defeat of the Sandinistas in Nicaragua would open the door for a settlement after several years of attempts to secure compliance with the judgment.

6. Action undertaken to bring about US compliance

An initiative of interested private persons: domestic litigation in the US The drive to end US government support of the Contras extended beyond Nicaragua. Certain US citizens living in Nicaragua and various organizations opposed to US policy in Central America filed a suit in the US federal courts. Their suit aimed at injunctive and declaratory relief against the funding of the Contras for the reason, *inter alia*, that this funding violated the UN Charter, the ICJ judgment on the merits, and customary international law. The district court dismissed the complaint on the ground that it involved nonjusticiable political questions. The Appeals Court rejected the plaintiff's request to reconsider the dismissal on 14 October 1988. It looked askance at the District Court's interpretation of the political question doctrine, but went on to affirm the ruling on reasons of American law and public international law.[751] The Court ruled that private parties had no cause of action to enforce an ICJ judgment in an American Court. Relying on the wording of Articles 92 and 94 of the UN Charter, it held that the ICJ was designed to settle disputes between governments and that the cited articles did not confer rights on individuals; it rejected the concept of a right of individuals to force their state to abide by a judgment of the ICJ as well as the plaintiffs' argument that the obligation to abide by the judgment was a rule of *jus cogens*.[752]

---

state of 19 October 1986, circulated under the double symbol A/41/741–S/18419. On 23 October 1986, Nicaragua also filed a document with the UN Secretary-General describing acts of aggression committed by the Contras after the judgment that was circulated as an official document of the Security Council and the General Assembly, Letter dated 23 October 1986 from the representative of Nicaragua to the Secretary-General, A/41/769–S/18429. Several other complaints were filed by Nicaragua against the US, A/41/871–S/18475, A/41/943–S/18497, A/41/944–S/18498 (Letters from representative of Nicaragua to the Secretary-General of 21 November and 3 December 1986).

[750] The affair centered on the administration's covert support for the Contras during a period when this had been prohibited by Congress; the funds for that purpose had been acquired through secret weapon sales to Iran. *Reichler*, 42 Harv. ILJ (2001), at 34–5, 43–4. See also *infra* Section B VI3.

[751] Committee of United States Citizens Living in Nicaragua v. Reagan, United States Court of Appeals, District of Columbia Circuit, 859 F. 2d 929 (1988), reprinted in: 85 International Legal Reports (1991), 252–73.

[752] Ibid., 937–41 (257–62). For further details, see *Wald*, 83 AJIL (1989), at 380–4; see also *O'Connell*, 30 Va. JIL (1990), at 926–7.

Initiatives by Nicaragua   Nicaragua itself tried unsuccessfully to enforce the judgment through various mechanisms. It took recourse to the Security Council, the General Assembly, and again the Court. These open discussions of Nicaragua's complaints kept the matter in the public's awareness. The departure of the Sandinistas would finally pave the way for a settlement.

Nicaragua took recourse to the Security Council various times in 1986. It turned to the Security Council for the first time immediately after the delivery of the judgment as part of a campaign to prevent $100 million of further aid to the Contras. On the day of the delivery of the judgment, it requested an emergency meeting of the Security Council relating to "the United States Government's policy of aggression against Nicaragua, which threatens international peace and security."[753] Nicaragua's foreign minister sent a letter to the US secretary of state complaining about the House of Representative's approval of a Contra aid package.[754] Nicaragua forwarded the text of the Court's judgment to the President of the Security Council;[755] the US, in turn, sent the separate and dissenting opinions to the UN Secretary-General.[756]

On 22 July 1986, Nicaragua again requested a meeting of the Security Council, indicating that the dispute threatened international peace and security—words to invoke Chapter VII enforcement mechanisms rather than Article 94(2) of the Charter.[757] The matter was discussed in the Security Council from 29 to 31 July 1986; the delegation of Nicaragua was invited to participate in the discussions. Nicaragua's President Ortega complained that the situation in Central America had worsened since the judgment. He lambasted the US "militarist policy against Nicaragua" and the congressional aid for the Contras, whom he derided as "mercenary forces organized, guided and trained by the US Government itself." In no uncertain terms, he made the stakes clear:

---

[753] Letter dated 27 June 1986 from the representative of Nicaragua to the President of the Security Council, S/18187.

[754] This letter was transmitted to the UN: Letter dated 27 June 1986 from the representative of Nicaragua to the Secretary-General, S/18189–A/40/1135.

[755] Letter dated 11 July 1986 from the representative of Nicaragua to the President of the Security Council transmitting the text of the Judgment of the International Court of Justice dated 27 June 1986 in the case "Military and Paramilitary Activities in and against Nicaragua (Nicaragua v. United States of America)", S/18221.

[756] Letter dated 18 July 1986 from the representative of the United States of America transmitting the text of the separate and dissenting opinions of the Judgment of the International Court of Justice in the case "Military and Paramilitary Activities in and against Nicaragua (Nicaragua v. United States of America)", S/18227–A 40/1147.

[757] Letter dated 22 July 1986 from the representative of Nicaragua to the President of the Security Council, S/18230: "I have the honor to write you to request the convening of a meeting of the Security Council on Tuesday, 29 July 1986, for the purposes of considering the dispute between the United States of America and Nicaragua, which was the subject of a Judgment of the International Court of Justice of 27 June 1986 (S/18221) and which threatens international peace and security." Thus, reference was made to the judgment, but the meeting was requested to consider the dispute and not the issue of compliance with the judgment.

The future of international law, the future of the international legal order and all it represents are now in the Council's hands. If the decision of the International Court of Justice, which was based on fundamental principles of international law, is not respected and supported, what will be the fate of the Court?[758]

The US representative launched a verbal counter-attack against Nicaragua. He stressed his country's commitment to the international legal system and declared that it was not ready to take lessons on international law from Nicaragua, a country which in its view consistently violated international law. He stated:

Nicaragua has now obtained a ruling from the International Court of Justice which it finds useful in its propaganda war against the United States. The United States regrets that Nicaragua has sought to misuse the Court in this manner. The United States has said from the beginning that this case is inappropriate for judicial resolution. The Court has been asked to address one small, carefully selected part of the crisis in Central America. To ask for the Court to solve this crisis does it a disservice, for the only way to solve the crisis is through negotiations involving all parties. This is neither the time nor the place for a detailed exposition concerning the Court's decision of 27 June and the compelling dissents that accompanied it. Suffice it to say now, we believe that the Court has fundamentally misperceived the situation in Central America. It is simply wrong on many of its facts, and the Court's conception of the relevant international law is seriously flawed in important respects.

He went on to criticize the Nicaraguan government's oppression of its own population, including serious human rights violations and religious persecution, as well as Managua's support for insurgent movements in the entire region. He condemned Nicaragua's hypocrisy and contended that Nicaragua planned to ally itself with Cuba and the Soviet bloc.[759] After several countries, led by the USSR, voiced criticism at the failure of the Americans to comply with the Court's judgment, the US representative responded:

It is interesting to note that of the many countries that have criticized the United States for its alleged failure to accept the judgment of the International Court of Justice, only one of them accepts the compulsory jurisdiction of the Court, and that country has carefully excluded from its acceptance any possibility of being brought before the Court on claims such as those at issue here today.[760]

In the further debate, several speakers referred to the need for compliance with the ICJ judgment, with only El Salvador and Honduras (who were not members of the Council, but who had been invited to participate without a right to vote pursuant to Article 31 of the UN Charter) fully supporting the US and blaming Nicaragua for aggression.[761] In its session of 31 July 1986,

---

[758] S/PV.2700 of 29 July 1986, reprinted in: 25 ILM (1986), 1338–42.

[759] S/PV.2701 of 29 July 1986, reprinted in: 25 ILM (1986), 1342–7, at 1343–6.

[760] S/PV.2702 of 30 July 1986, reprinted in: 25 ILM (1986), 1347–51, at 1349. Moreover, he again alluded to Nicaragua's own international law transgressions.

[761] S/PV.2702 of 30 July 1986, reprinted in: 25 ILM (1986), 1347–51, S/PV.2704 of 31 July 1986, reprinted in: 25 ILM (1986) at 1352–65.

the Council proceeded to vote on a draft resolution submitted by Congo, Ghana, Madagascar, Trinidad and Tobago, and the United Arab Emirates asking for full compliance with the ICJ judgment. This draft resolution did not indicate its legal basis and was couched in rather soft terms, not even condemning the non-compliance; the US was not mentioned explicitly, although it was clearly the intended addressee.[762] The resolution was torpedoed by an American veto. The US was the only country to cast a negative vote; 11 countries had voted in favor, with 3 abstaining.[763] The US representative, Vernon Walters, defended his negative vote, stating that the resolution would not have contributed to the achievement of peace in Central America. Moreover, he repeated attacks on the judgment, arguing that the Court had acted *ultra vires* and arrived at wrong findings on the facts and the law. He explained that a discussion of the weaknesses of the decision would have obscured the "real matter at issue before this Council,"[764] which he identified as the general crisis in Central America, not the ICJ decision. As a consequence, the first attempt of a resolution relating to compliance with the judgment had failed. The American arguments had been political rather than legal, but what is notable is that the US made no attempt to actually justify the non-compliance with the judgment beyond the affirmation of the lack of jurisdiction and deficiencies in the establishment of the facts and the legal reasoning, and it had made reference to the dissenting opinions.

In a letter of 17 October 1986, one day before President Reagan was to approve the bill providing for US aid to the Contras, Nicaragua requested another meeting of the Security Council, this time explicitly "in accordance with the provisions of the Charter, to consider the non-compliance with the Judgment of the International Court of Justice dated 27 June 1986 [...]."[765] This marked the first occasion on which Article 94(2) was invoked for the purposes of ensuring compliance with a judgment of the Court. Another draft resolution brought by the same group of states as the earlier one was placed on the Council's docket.[766] Even though it neither condemned the US

---

[762] S/18250.

[763] The affirmative votes came from Australia, Bulgaria, China, Congo, Denmark, Ghana, Madagascar, Trinidad and Tobago, USSR, the United Arab Emirates, and Venezuela; the abstentions came from France, Thailand, and the United Kingdom. S/PV.2704, 25 ILM (1986), at 1363.

[764] S/PV.2704, 25 ILM (1986), at 1364–5, see in particular, at 1365: "In the view of the United States, the Court has asserted jurisdiction and competence over Nicaragua's claims without any proper basis. Moreover, the Court failed to give any meaningful significance to the multilateral treaty reservation or the very substantial evidence of Nicaraguan misbehavior. Many of the principles asserted by the Court to constitute customary international law have no basis in authority or reason. We do not accede to these baseless assertions. For us to have discussed in detail here the factual and legal weaknesses of the Court's 27 June decision would only have obscured the real matter at issue before this Court, and for that reason we have chosen to reserve such a discussion for another place and time."

[765] Letter dated 17 October 1986 from the representative of Nicaragua to the President of the Security Council, S/18415.

[766] Congo, Ghana, Madagascar, Trinidad and Tobago, and the United Arab Emirates, S/18428.

action nor provided for any kind of enforcement action proper, the tone had become more pointed as compared to the July draft. It was shorter and more focused than the earlier resolution that had contained several paragraphs relating to the general obligations of peaceful dispute settlement. It did not indicate its legal basis, but since it was exclusively aimed at compliance with an ICJ judgment and the meeting had been requested under Article 94, that basis would have been Article 94(2) of the Charter. Although as in the case of the former draft resolution, the operative part still did not name an addressee, there is no doubt to whom it was destined:

The Security Council [...] considering that Article 36, paragraph 6, of the Statute of the Court provides that 'In the event of a dispute as to whether the Court has jurisdiction, the matter shall be settled by the decision of the Court', [...] having considered the events that have taken place in and against Nicaragua after the said judgment, in particular, the continued financing by the United States of military and paramilitary activities in and against Nicaragua [...]

1. urgently calls for full and immediate compliance with the Judgment of the International Court of Justice in the case of 'military and paramilitary activities in and against Nicaragua' in conformity with the relevant provisions of the Charter,
2. requests the Secretary-General to keep the Council informed on the implementation of this resolution.[767]

The reference to Article 36(6) can be understood as a response to the repeated affirmation on part of the US that the Court had had no jurisdiction in the case; the comment on the follow-up implied that the US was not complying with the judgment. The request to the Secretary-General to keep the Council informed on the implementation of the resolution added an interesting feature as it provided for a role for the Security Council in the post-adjudicative phase.

The Council dealt with the matter at the end of October 1986, with the final vote on the draft resolution identical to the July results, the same 11 countries voting in favor, the same 3 abstaining, and the US preventing the adoption of the resolution through its veto. The discussions rehashed the same arguments, with the US representative criticizing the Court's arrogation of jurisdiction and its findings in fact and law; US assistance to the Contras was defended as necessary so as to dissuade Nicaragua from its policy of exporting revolution. No other state tried to put the validity of the judgment into question—not even Honduras (again admitted to the debate under Article 31 of the Charter), which blamed Nicaragua for using the Court "for propagandistic purposes" without challenging the Court's rulings as such. The abstentions of France, Thailand, and the United Kingdom rested on political considerations and not on doubts on the validity of the judgment.

---

[767] Congo, Ghana, Madagascar, Trinidad and Tobago, and the United Arab Emirates, S/18428.

The US was, hence, alone in its vote against the draft resolution and its resistance to the judgment.[768]

The Council President stated that because of the US veto, the draft resolution was not adopted.[769] The representative of Nicaragua contested the ruling of the Security Council President one week later in the General Assembly and claimed that the US had been barred from exercising its right of veto as party to the dispute by virtue of Article 27(3).[770] However, after the vote had been taken in the Security Council, no objections had been made to the ruling, and no one had expressed doubts on the validity of the US vote. Even Nicaragua's representative framed the protest in vague terms as opposed to Nicaragua's protest in the General Assembly.[771] A representative of Ghana, one of the co-sponsors of the draft resolution in the Security Council, had commented after the vote: "The Council has just failed to make a decision on a landmark case. This failure has been made possible by the use of the veto by a permanent member of the Council. That course of action is within the competence of the Council and legitimate, and we respect the decision so made."[772]

The situation therefore remained unchanged: a US veto had prevented Nicaragua from obtaining a Security Council resolution in its favor. The draft resolution aimed at no more than reasserting the US's obligations under Article 94(1); no concrete action such as sanctions had been envisaged. Consequently, its objective would have been to maintain the matter in the public's awareness, to increase the pressure on the US to comply with the judgment, and to isolate the US in its position of defiance of the Court. In a certain sense, already the Security Council meetings themselves had the desired effect. At the meetings, Nicaragua received broad support from a majority of Council members backing a resolution that the US could only thwart by exercising its veto and thereby taking on the role of a judge in its own cause. Hence, despite the failure of the Council to adopt the resolution, the proceedings had been highly useful for Nicaragua.[773]

After the failed attempt to urge the US into compliance in the Security Council, the Nicaraguan representative turned to the General Assembly and submitted a draft resolution very similar to the one scuttled by the US veto in the Security Council. The General Assembly accepted the proposal and adopted Resolution 41/31 on 3 November 1986 by 94 affirmative votes,

---

[768] S/PV.2715–18; and "Security Council does not adopt text calling for compliance with International Court ruling regarding Nicaraguan case," XXIV UN Chronicle (1987), No. 1, 62–3.
[769] S/PV.2718, at 51.   [770] A/41/PV.53, at 61.   [771] S/PV.2718, at 57.
[772] S/PV.2718, at 53.
[773] See Gill, *Litigation Strategy at the World Court*, at 286: "[A]lthough Nicaragua's attempt had predictably failed, it had succeeded in gaining yet another diplomatic and propaganda success against its adversary."

3 negative votes, and 47 abstentions.[774] The resolution made an urgent call "for full and immediate compliance with the Judgment of the International Court of Justice" and requested the Secretary-General to keep the General Assembly informed on the implementation of the resolution.[775] In the preceding debate, the US had again claimed that the ICJ had had no jurisdiction; apart from that, no challenges to the legal authority of the judgment had been made.[776] Some states had even pointed out that although politically they disagreed with the Court's findings, they had not voted against the resolution out of respect for the ICJ judgment.[777] El Salvador, which had voted against the resolution, founded its rejection on the terms of the draft resolution and not on the Court's decision.[778] The US therefore found itself in a rather isolated position with its refusal to accept the judgments.

In its three subsequent sessions, the General Assembly adopted similar resolutions.[779] The Secretary-General filed reports on the implementation of the resolutions, but they were limited to the statement that no new developments had taken place.[780] At the 45th session, as the new Nicaraguan government re-evaluated its relations to the US and pursued a course of cooperation rather than confrontation, the General Assembly deferred consideration of the matter.[781]

Even though the hortatory character of General Assembly resolutions meant they were not "enforcement measures" in the proper sense of that phrase, diplomatic pressure was maintained on the US and the matter remained in the public's awareness; therefore, they served as part of Nicaragua's overall strategy to discredit US policy.[782] Statements by other international groups are to be seen in a similar light. On 28 July 1986, for example, the coordinating bureau of the countries of the Non-Aligned

---

[774] UN Doc. A/41/PV.53, at 92. The negative votes were cast by El Salvador, Israel, and the US. A difference between the General Assembly resolution and the draft resolution in the Council lay in the provision that the Secretary-General was asked to report on the implementation of the resolution to the General Assembly and not to the Security Council, as the draft voted upon in the Security Council did; of course, it makes sense that the reports on the implementation of a resolution are made to the organ emitting the respective resolution.

[775] GA Res. 41/31, Sections 1 and 2.   [776] A/41/PV.53, at 67.

[777] See the statements in A/41/PV.53 by the representatives of Ecuador (at 93), Luxembourg (at 93), and Mexico (at 77).

[778] Ibid., at 83–6.

[779] Resolutions 42/18 of 12 November 1987, 43/11 of 25 October 1988, 44/43 of 7 December 1989. The change to Resolution 41/31 was that the resolutions contained another paragraph pursuant to which the matter was to be included in the provisional agenda of the General Assembly's next session, thus, an element of automatism for the treatment of the topic was added.

[780] A/42/712, 4 November 1987, A/43/728, 19 October 1988, A/44/760, 22 November 1989.

[781] Decision 45/402, 21 September 1990, A/45/PV.3, 8, following a recommendation of the General Committee to that extent, Organization of the 45th regular session of the General Assembly, First Report of the General Committee, A/45/250, at 10, para. 28.

[782] Gill, *Litigation Strategy at the World Court*, at 286.

Movement issued a communiqué asking the US to comply strictly and immediately with the Court's judgment.[783]

7. The proceedings on compensation before the ICJ and the final settlement

With regard to the further proceedings before the ICJ, Nicaragua informed the Court on 7 September 1987 that no agreement on the form and amount of compensation had been reached and that it therefore wanted to take advantage of the opportunity afforded in the 1986 judgment to satisfy the Court that its claims were well founded as regarded the nature and the amount of compensation.[784] When the ICJ President scheduled a meeting of the parties to discuss the further procedure, the US deputy-agent answered that the US position remained unchanged, and the US did not participate in the proceedings.[785] The proceedings continued; on 28 March 1988, Nicaragua filed its memorial and specified its claims for damages, costs, and interest.[786]

Elections in Nicaragua in February 1990 fundamentally changed the situation. The Sandinistas lost power to the *Unión Nacional Opositora*, a coalition of 14 opposition parties, whose US-backed[787] presidential candidate, Violeta Chamorro, was elected new president.[788] The US terminated its economic sanctions against Nicaragua and announced plans to provide economic assistance; President Bush determined that the election had ended the threat to US national security.[789] A few weeks before Mrs Chamorro took office, outgoing President Ortega signed into law a bill of protection of the rights of Nicaragua in the framework of the International Court of Justice on 6 April 1990, according to which the proceedings in the Court were to be continued and the compensation claims fully recovered, a last act of protest by a

[783] It is quoted in the statement of the Indian representative, Krishnan, in the Security Council's 2701st meeting of 29 July 1986 (S/PV.2701 at 18–19); the US representative Walters called that communiqué a "scandalously one-sided document" (ibid., at 17).

[784] Letter from the agent of the Republic of Nicaragua to the Deputy-Registrar, 7 September 1987, ICJ Pleadings, Military and Paramilitary Activities, Vol. V, 465–6.

[785] Letter of the Deputy-agent of the United States of America to the Registrar, 13 November 1987, 469; and Order of 17 November 1987, at 189.

[786] Memorial of Nicaragua (Compensation), 29 March 1988, ICJ Pleadings, Military and Paramilitary Activities, Vol. V, 245–352.

[787] See, for example, the Letter of President George Bush to Republican and Democratic Leaders on Support for the Nicaraguan National Opposition Union of 24 January 1990, http://web.archive.org/web/20030327012359/http://bushlibrary.tamu.edu/papers/1990/90012405.html.

[788] 60 AdG (1990) 34260 A.

[789] 60 AdG (1990) 34315 A 2; White House Fact Sheet on Economic Assistance for Nicaragua, 13 March 1990, http://web.archive.org/web/20030611005923/http://bushlibrary.tamu.edu/papers/1990/90031303.html, Message of President Bush to the Congress reporting on the economic sanctions against Nicaragua, 1 May 1990, http://web.archive.org/web/20030610094732/http://bushlibrary.tamu.edu/papers/1990/90050102.html.

lame-duck government.[790] After Mrs Chamorro's inauguration,[791] the civil war was declared over on 10 June 1990.[792]

The ICJ President called a meeting to ascertain the parties' views as to the opening of the oral proceedings on 22 June 1990. In the course of this meeting, the Nicaraguan agent explained that his country's new government was studying the cases pending before the Court and was not yet in a position to take a decision. The Court consequently took no action for the time being.[793]

The prospects for enforcement of the ICJ judgment had been assessed negatively, unless seen in the context of a comprehensive diplomatic settlement.[794] The change in government had circumvented the impasse. President Chamorro made an official visit to the US from 15 to 17 April 1991. In speeches before Congress and at a White House reception, she thanked the US for its assistance in Nicaragua's reconstruction and expressed the commitment of the majority of her people to strengthen ties with the US. President Bush on his part announced a $500 million aid package, support for Nicaragua through international financial institutions, and opportunities for trade and investment.[795]

On 12 September 1991, Nicaragua informed the Court that it did not wish to continue the proceedings and renounced all further right of action in the matter. This decision was reached "taking into consideration that the Government of Nicaragua and the Government of the United States of America have reached agreements aimed at enhancing Nicaragua's economic, commercial and technical development to the maximum extent possible."[796] The US welcomed the discontinuance,[797] and the Court removed the case

---

[790] Ley de protección de los derechos de Nicaragua en el marco de la corte internacional de justicia, reprinted in: Letter of the President of the National Assembly of Nicaragua to the Registrar, 10 April 1990, ICJ Pleadings, Military and Paramilitary Activities, Vol. V, 474–7.

[791] 60 AdG (1990) 34463 B.   [792] 60 AdG (1990) 34771 A.

[793] Order of 26 September 1991, at 47–48.

[794] See Gill, *Litigation Strategy at the World Court*, 297. But, for a less pessimist statement, see *Falk*, 81 AJIL (1987), at 112 ("It might be that governmental defiance will not take the day. Support for President Reagan's Nicaragua Policy is shaky in Congress and among the citizenry. If the effect of the World Court decision is to shift even slightly the internal and international balance of opinion of further uses of force against the Sandinista government, it may yet contribute to a political process whereby legal claims are indirectly upheld.")

[795] 61 AdG (1991) 35536 A 7; White House, Remarks at the Welcoming Ceremony for President Violeta Chamorro of Nicaragua, http://web.archive.org/web/20030421023609/http:// bushlibrary.tamu.edu/papers/1991/91041700.html.

[796] Letter of the Agent of Nicaragua to the Registrar, 12 September 1991, ICJ Pleadings, Military and Paramilitary Activities, Vol. V, 484. Supposedly, the US had exerted considerable pressure on the Chamorro government to drop the case: "U.S. Urges Nicaragua to Forgive Legal Claim," New York Times, 30 Sept. 1990, at A18, col. 1.

[797] Letter from the legal advisor of the US Department of State to the Registrar, ICJ Pleadings, Military and Paramilitary Activities, Vol. V, 485.

from its general list on 25 September 1991.[798] The US and Nicaragua concluded another friendship treaty on 6 January 1992.[799]

8. Conclusion

There was a troubling period in which the Court's judgment was openly
defied by the respondent. Due to a variety of factors, it was to be expected
that compliance would raise problems. Among these factors were the Reagan
administration's fixation in its Nicaragua policy and its determination that
the ICJ was not the appropriate body to deal with the matter, a conviction
which it pursued to the point of boycotting the proceedings. It had blocked
Security Council action and increasingly isolated itself from the majority
world opinion. The administration's adamant refusal to seek compromise
was unlikely to endure domestic opposition in the long run.

It is unfortunate that the Reagan administration resorted to discrediting
the Court; its continued insistence on the lack of jurisdiction of the Court (in
contradiction to Article 36(6) of the ICJ Statute) could not justify its
action.[800] It is highly doubtful whether it would be compatible with Article
94(1) of the Charter for a state to invoke *excès de pouvoir* on the part of the
ICJ as a reason to treat a judgment as null and void and refuse to comply
with it.[801] Even if one assumes that such an action were permissible, it would
have to be limited to extreme cases and could not be justified by the assertion
that the arguments against the findings of the Court outweighed those in
favor. Although one may differ as to the persuasiveness of the Court's
reasoning, the Court did undertake a thorough legal analysis addressing all
the arguments raised by the US, be it in the judgment on jurisdiction or on
the merits.[802]

Some commentators have suggested that various factors could possibly
have bolstered the impression that the Court was biased against the United
States, among them the name given to the case itself and the treatment of El

---

[798] Order of 26 September 1991, at 47–8. The related case against Honduras was discontinued
in 1992: Border and Transborder Armed Action (Nicaragua v. Honduras), Order of 27 May 1992
at 222–3. The case against Costa Rica had already been discontinued in 1987: Border and
Transborder Armed Actions (Nicaragua v. Costa Rica), Order of 19 August 1987, at 182–3.

[799] TIAS 11844.   [800] See *Briggs*, 81 AJIL (1987), at 85–6.

[801] See *supra* Chapter 2 D III. But see *Reisman*, 80 AJIL (1986), at 128–34, arguing that the
judgment on the jurisdiction was an excess of jurisdiction and null and void.

[802] For a positive assessment of the judgment on the merits see *Briggs*, 81 AJIL (1987), at
78–86; *Falk*, 81 AJIL (1987), at 112. Generally positive also *Dhokalia*, in *idem et al.*, International
Court in Transition, at 124–5. But see *d'Amato*, 81 AJIL (1987), at 105, criticizing the Court's
methodology and observing that "only decisions that command respect by virtue of their
inherent soundness and scholarly thoroughness are likely to have a real impact." For the view
that the judgments were an *excès de pouvoir* resulting in their nullity, see *Reisman*, 80 AJIL
(1986), at 128–34; and *Moore*, 80 AJIL (1986), at 93–9 (on the judgment on jurisdiction), against
the excess of powers argument see *Rowles*, 80 AJIL (1986), at 580–4 (against the existence of any
legal justification for a non-compliance with an ICJ judgment).

Salvador's declaration of intervention. Doubts were also raised when ICJ President Elias had given an interview in 27 December 1984 in which he had criticized the US invasion of Grenada and commented that the Court was not used for propagandistic purposes in the Nicaragua case.[803] However, it is doubtful whether any of these factors can be taken as seriously as to cast doubt on the impartiality of the Court. The denomination of the case does not seem to presuppose any responsibility on part of the US, and it is therefore not quite clear why it should be an embrace of Nicaragua's side.[804] One might discuss the appropriateness of the treatment of the Salvadoran declaration of intervention; yet, the exclusion of Salvador had only related to the jurisdictional phase and it is not clear how the Court would have decided if El Salvador had tried to intervene at a later stage. Judge Elias perhaps might have been better advised to display greater discretion in commenting on US policy, yet his comments had related to the then closed jurisdiction and admissibility phase of the Nicaragua case and other events, and it would be too far-reaching to assume that this put the integrity of the Court as a whole in question. Although certainly the Court should take the utmost care to avoid any impression of bias, these factors alone offer unconvincing proof to substantiate claims of a politicized Court.[805] Neither could the order indicating provisional measures be taken as a sign of a bias, for as "measures to protect the rights of either party" it is impossible for such orders to be formulated in entirely neutral terms and to both sides' liking under all circumstances.[806]

The US non-appearance at the merits stage impeded the establishment of evidence. The Court was thus put in the awkward position of having to counterbalance the negative effects of this non-participation—a situation for which the Reagan administration bore responsibility. Still, one might ask whether the Court could have done more in its investigation of the facts, such as encouraging *amicus curiae* briefs or establishing an independent investigative body to conduct on-the-spot investigations.[807]

---

[803] See *d'Amato/O'Connell* in Damrosch, The ICJ at a crossroads, at 420–1, relying on the dissenting opinion of Judge Schwebel, Judgment of 27 June 1986, at 312–13, paras. 107–8; 314–15, para. 115, and 320–1, paras. 128–31.

[804] But see *Moore*, 81 AJIL (1987), at 159. An alternative title suggested by Nicaragua was "Case concerning an application of Nicaragua against the United States of America:" Letter of the Agent of the United States of America to the Registrar of 2 May 1984, ICJ Pleadings, Military and paramilitary activities, Vol. 5, 377, at 378. A name as indistinctive as this suggestion does not seem to be in conformity with the general practice of the Court. For details how names are given to cases see *Kamto*, 34 RBDI (2001), at 5–22.

[805] But see *d'Amato/O'Connell*, in Damrosch, The ICJ at a crossroads, at 421: "The United States is now in a position to argue that the tribunal was biased."

[806] For details on the alleged bias visible in the order indicating provisional measures, see *infra* C VI 2.

[807] See *Franck*, 81 AJIL (1987), at 116.

Another critical factor was that, in reality, the dispute was multilateral in character, while the proceedings before the Court were decidedly bilateral, concerning only the relations between the US and Nicaragua. Of course, the participation of all the states involved would have been advantageous for ensuring a comprehensive and lasting settlement, yet the Court had to rule on the legal relations between the *parties*. Probably in reaction to the US decision not to participate further in the proceedings, El Salvador did not declare its intervention at the merits stage—a request which, unlike at the jurisdictional phase, could have hardly been denied.

Finally, the subject-matter (involving security interests and the use of force) was particularly delicate and highly political,[808] and settlement was just possible after a change of the situation.

9. Evaluation

The judgment on the merits was disregarded by the US, and one might tend to regard this non-compliance as a severe problem for the Court's role in the settlement of the dispute and a loss for Nicaragua since it could not enforce an immediate compliance. Yet, assessing the usefulness of the litigation for the applicant requires an examination of Nicaragua's objectives in bringing the matter before the Court. Nicaragua's strategy had been to ensure maximum publicity for its cause and to prevent further Contra aid. While official aid was given after the judgment on the merits, it had been halted during the proceedings, at a stage critical for the Nicaraguan government. On 25 May 1984, after the Court had indicated interim measures at the request of Nicaragua and ordered the US to cease any support for military and paramilitary activities in and against Nicaragua, the House of Representatives rejected the White House's request for Contra aid for the first time, and subsequent requests were denied until 25 June 1986, two days before the delivery of the judgment on the merits. There was thus a period of over two years in which there was no official assistance for the Contras. As later revealed, however, the White House and the CIA had engaged in illegal covert support of the Contras.[809] Yet, despite this secret action, the Nicaraguan government gained increasing control over the Contras while Congress blocked aid to the group. The Contras never again posed a serious threat to the Nicaraguan government, although they continued to inflict damage.[810] The 1986 judgment and the

---

[808] On the inherent danger of non-compliance in a case of use of force such as the present one where the facts, the legal evaluation and the consent to the Court's jurisdiction are disputed, see *Rogoff*, 7 BU ILJ (1989), at 284–5.

[809] See *supra* n. 750; and *infra* C VI 3.

[810] *Reichler*, 42 Harv. ILJ (2001), at 34–5, 42; Gill, *Litigation Strategy at the World Court*, 320, who explain that while numerous factors contributed to the defeat for Contra aid in Congress, the ICJ litigation had a role and strengthened the opposition to Reagan's Nicaragua policy.

subsequent proceedings in the Security Council and the General Assembly subjected the anti-Sandinista Reagan administration to increased international isolation. Focusing solely on the question of how compliance should ideally have happened ignores the important question of the extent to which the rights of an applicant would have been violated without a judgment. Even in the face of official defiance, the existence of that judgment might act as a restraint and create domestic pressure for the enforcement of the rights.[811] Therefore, the fact that the judgment was first met with resistance should not detract from the fact that the proceedings fulfilled a useful purpose for the Nicaraguan government; Contra aid might have been far more significant and enduring without them and might have thrown Nicaragua into a full-scale civil war. The litigation before the Court, as well as its action before UN organs, was thus an integral part of Nicaragua's strategy to discredit the US policy *vis-à-vis* the Sandinistas.

Apart from this question of the usefulness for the litigant, one may ask what kind of an impact the litigation had for the role of the Court. Opinions are still divided.[812] Should the Court have taken into account that compliance might not take place and therefore have denied its jurisdiction or held the dispute non-justiciable?[813] The judgments and their follow-up triggered a major debate on the Court's proper role, particular among American writers.[814] In hindsight, those who expected or feared a further demise in the Court's prestige[815] after this judgment were proven wrong.[816] The Court became increasingly active in the late 1980s and 1990s and at present has

[811] See *Falk*, 81 AJIL (1987), at 112: "We must rethink the question of judicial effectiveness in the broader setting of public opinion and political democracy, and not confine our evaluation to conventional concerns about governmental non-responsiveness."

[812] *Highet*, 81 AJIL (1987), at 51–6, for an assessment of the possible impact of the judgment shortly after its delivery, expressing the expectation that a strengthening of the Court rather than a weakening would take place. Somewhat more cautious and arguing that both seems possible: *Piñol i Rull*, 39 REspDI (1987), at 118.

[813] For a proposal that the Court should have denied its jurisdiction (because of invalidity of the US declaration due to the Connally amendment) and at the same time reprimanded the US behavior in the form of *obiter dicta* see *Glennon*, 81 AJIL (1987), at 121–9, however, as the proceedings included a jurisdiction and admissibility and a merits stage, this was hardly feasible; Glennon's suggestion not to treat the invalidity of the US declaration as an exclusively preliminary matter (at 128) cannot quite convince.

[814] See the panel of the American Society of International Law on "The jurisprudence of the Court in the Nicaragua decision," Proc. ASIL, 81st annual meeting 1987, 258–77.

[815] See *Dhokalia* in *idem et al.*, International Court in transition, at 147, expressing the fear that the US attitude would "greatly undermine" the World Court as an institution. Some commentators argued that the case was a sign for a lack of efficiency of the Court in cases of compulsory jurisdiction, as it stood in line with other cases of defiance, which made the Court appear weak and put the very system of compulsory jurisdiction in question: see *Janis*, 81 AJIL (1987), at 144–6; *Scott/Carr*, 81 AJIL (1987), at 65–6.

[816] See the assessment already in 1991 of *Bilder*, 40 Cath. ULR (1991), at 255: "One of the most interesting developments in the last several years is that, despite dire United States predictions that the Nicaragua decision would broadly discredit the World Court and so discourage states from submitting cases as to virtually end its usefulness, the Court has never been busier."

record numbers of cases on its docket. Whether this trend emerged because of the Nicaragua judgments or despite them is another matter. Certainly, it would have created a crisis for the Court's authority if the impression had arisen that it had rejected the case on the basis of jurisdiction or justiciability out of fear that the US might not comply. Third-World countries in particular might have lost faith in the Court, temporarily putting it out of business for all but some Western states. Such an impression might have been similarly harmful for the Court as its decision in the South West Africa cases of 1966, which had led to a crisis of confidence.[817] The fact that the Court did not stand down against a superpower in a case involving the use of force might have enhanced its legitimacy with developing states, a factor that might have contributed to a "revival" of the Court.[818] On the other hand, this consideration could not have justified an automatic finding against the US, but the Court cannot be reprimanded for having been biased: its decision included a thorough review of the facts and the law. It would have been up to the US to provide the Court with the evidence that in its opinion correctly depicted the truth.

IXX. Land, Island and Maritime Frontier Dispute

1. Background of the case

Numerous diplomatic efforts had been unable to resolve the dispute between El Salvador and Honduras over their land frontier, the legal status of maritime spaces, and sovereignty over certain islands, a conflict which reached back to the nineteenth century. In 1969, a series of border incidents culminated in a brief war from 14 to 18 July (the "soccer war"); a cease-fire and troop withdrawal was rapidly brokered by the OAS, although a formal peace treaty was only signed on 30 October 1980.[819] The treaty delimited seven sections of the land boundary and created a Joint Frontier Commission charged, *inter alia*, with determining the frontier line in the remaining sectors in a way acceptable to the parties. Additional provisions specified how delimitation was to take place. The commission also had to determine the status of the islands and maritime spaces within a period of five years from the treaty's entry into force. In the event that the disputes concerning the land frontier were not completely settled within the five-year period, the parties agreed that they would negotiate a special agreement to submit jointly

---

[817] South West Africa Cases (Ethiopia v. South Africa; Liberia v. South Africa), Second Phase, Judgment of 18 July 1986. For details on the proceedings, the decisions, and the reactions, see Dugard, *The South West Africa/Namibia Dispute*, 239–375 (in particular on the political reactions, 374–5).

[818] *Keohane/Moravcsik/Slaughter*, 54 IO (2000), at 481.

[819] General Peace Treaty, El Salvador–Honduras, 30 October 1980, 1310 UNTS 213. On the history of the dispute before the conclusion of the General Peace Treaty, see Judgment of 11 September 1992 at 380–3, paras. 27–36.

any controversies to the ICJ.[820] The Joint Frontier Commission was to initiate the demarcation of the line defined in the ICJ decision within six months of the date of the judgment.[821]

2. The proceedings before a Chamber of the Court

A large part of the land boundary was successfully delimited, with six sectors remaining controversial at the end of the five-year period, as well as issues relating to the legal status of the islands and maritime spaces. The parties proceeded to negotiate a special agreement to submit the matters to a chamber of the International Court of Justice.[822] The special agreement was concluded on 24 May 1986;[823] the Court's registry was notified accordingly by the parties jointly on 11 December 1986.[824]

The special agreement requested the chamber to "delimit the boundary line in the zones or sections not described in ... the General Treaty of Peace of 30 October 1980" and "determine the legal situation of the islands and maritime spaces." The applicable law was agreed to include the rules of international law applicable between the parties, including the provisions of the peace treaty, where pertinent. With regard to the post-adjudicative phase, the agreement stipulated that the parties would "execute the Judgment of the Chamber in its entirety and in complete good faith," and that the Special Demarcation Commission established by an agreement of 11 February 1986[825] would begin the demarcation of the frontier line fixed by the decision not later than three months after the date of the judgment.[826] The General

[820] General Peace Treaty, *supra* n. 819, Article 31. Article 32 named points which that special agreement was to regulate:
(a) The submission of the Parties to the jurisdiction of the International Court of Justice so that it may settle the controversy or controversies referred to in the preceding article; (b) The time-limits for the presentation of documents and the number of such documents; (c) The determination of any other question of a procedural nature that may be pertinent.
[821] Ibid., Article 36.   [822] Judgment of 11 September 1992, at 385, para. 38.
[823] Agreement to submit the frontier dispute concerning land, island, and maritime areas between the two states to a decision of the International Court of Justice, El Salvador–Honduras, 24 May 1986, 1437 UNTS 157.
[824] Judgment of 11 September 1992, at 356, para. 1. Article 8 of the special agreement had regulated how the notification was to take place.
[825] Agreement setting up a special commission for the demarcation of the frontier line between El Salvador and Honduras pursuant to the General Peace Treaty of 30 October 1980, 11 February 1986, 1459 UNTS.
[826] See Article 6:
(1) The Parties will execute the Judgment of the Chamber in its entirety and in complete good faith. To this end, the Special Demarcation Commission established by the Agreement of 11 February 1986 will begin the demarcation of the frontier line fixed by the Judgment not later than three months after the date of the said Judgment and will diligently continue its work until after demarcation is completed.
(2) For this purpose, the procedures established in respect of this matter in the above-mentioned Agreement concerning the establishment of the Special Demarcation Commission will be applied.

Treaty of Peace was thus modified in so far as the special agreement involved a commission other than the Joint Frontier Commission.[827]

On 8 May 1987, the Court formed a Chamber in accordance with the special agreement and Articles 26 and 31 of the ICJ Statute.[828] On 13 September 1990, the Chamber unanimously acceded to Nicaragua's request for intervention in the proceedings under Article 62 on the ICJ Statute, but with a limited scope: only with regard to the decision on the legal regime of the waters of the Gulf of Fonseca (the coastline of which is divided between El Salvador, Honduras, and Nicaragua).[829] The Chamber stated that the intervention did not make Nicaragua a party to the proceedings.[830]

Although the parties had reached consensus on the subject of the litigation in the special agreement, they disagreed on the precise tasks conferred upon the Court by that agreement and on the applicable law. While the parties concurred that the reference to "islands" in the agreement was a reference to those located in the Gulf of Fonseca, it was controversial whether the Court was to rule upon all of those islands: El Salvador asked the Court to extend the ruling to all islands in the Gulf of Fonseca since there was no limitation to a certain group of islands in the special agreement. Honduras, on the other hand, argued that the Chamber was requested only to determine the status of the islands of Meanguera and Meanguerita.[831] Concerning the maritime zones, the parties agreed that both the areas inside and outside the Gulf of Fonseca were subject of the litigation; they disagreed, however, on the precise task of the Court. In Honduras's view, the Chamber was to carry out a full delimitation of the maritime zones since the object and purpose of the agreement had been to bring a definitive end to the dispute. El Salvador claimed that the Chamber had no authority to effect any kind of maritime delimitation.[832]

---

[827] Article 36 of the General Peace Treaty had conferred that task on the Joint Frontier Commission, see *supra* n. 819. On the role of the demarcation commission, see Judgment of 11 September 1992, at 385–6, para. 39.

[828] Order of 8 May 1987, at 10–13. The Chamber initially included Judges Sette-Camara, Jennings, and Oda, and Judges *ad hoc* Valticos and Virally. Virally was replaced after his death by Judge *ad hoc* Torres Bernárdez by Order of 13 December 1989, at 162–3.

[829] Judgment of 13 September 1990, at 136–7, paras. 104–5. It was the first case in the Court's history for a request under Article 62 of the Statute to be granted, see ibid., at 135, para. 102. Nicaragua had filed its request for intervention on 17 October 1989, ibid., at 98, para. 14; the full Court had decided in its order of 28 February 1990, that it was for the *Chamber* to decide whether the application for permission to intervene should be granted or not, Order of 28 February 1990, at 6. For further details on the Nicaraguan Intervention, see *Evans*, 41 ICLQ (1992), at 896–906. On intervention, see *supra* part 1.

[830] Judgment of 13 September 1990, at 135–6, para. 102.

[831] Judgment of 11 September 1992, at 553–54, paras. 323–4.

[832] Judgment of 11 September 1992, at 582–4, paras. 372, 374. See also the Memorial of Honduras, ICJ Pleadings, Land, Island and Maritime Frontier Dispute, Vol. II, at 217–18; and the Counter-memorial of Honduras, ibid., Vol. III, at 663–6.

With regard to the applicable law, the parties agreed on the relevance of the principle of *uti possidetis juris*, although the special agreement had not explicitly asked the Chamber to give its ruling on the basis of that principle.[833] Honduras claimed that *uti possidetis* was the sole legal principle to be used and based this assertion on the General Treaty of Peace, whereas El Salvador suggested the applicability of "arguments of a human nature" and *effectivités*.[834]

3. The judgment of 11 September 1992

The Chamber's judgment of 11 September 1992[835] delimited the six areas of the land frontier,[836] as a result of which about two-thirds of the disputed territory was held to belong to Honduras and one-third to El Salvador.[837] Although the Chamber agreed with El Salvador that it had jurisdiction to rule on the legal status of all the islands in the gulf, it found by 4 votes to 1 that it should only exercise that jurisdiction with regard to those islands that were actually under dispute,[838] a condition which it saw fulfilled for the islands of El Tigre, Meanguera, and Meanguerita, as they were the subject of specific expressed claims.[839] It decided that El Tigre belonged to Honduras, and Meanguera and Meanguerita to El Salvador.[840] With regard to the maritime zones, it held that in the absence of an agreement effecting a delimitation, the Gulf of Fonseca was a historic bay whose waters were in the joint sovereignty of El Salvador, Nicaragua, and Honduras, with the exception of zones of exclusive sovereignty 3 miles from the coastline of each state where the other states nevertheless retained a right of innocent passage.[841] The Chamber further decided that the agreement conferred no jurisdiction to effect a limitation of maritime spaces, whether within or

---

[833] Compare Frontier Dispute case between Burkina Faso and Mali (*supra* XVII), in which the principle was specifically invoked by the parties as a source of applicable law.

[834] Judgment of 13 September 1990, at 386, para. 40 (relating to the land frontier). For the islands, see 557–8, paras. 331–2. See also *Rottem*, 87 AJIL (1993), at 619.

[835] For details, see *Hartzenbusch*, 34 Harv. ILJ (1993), at 241–57; *Rottem*, 87 AJIL (1993), at 619–26; and *Shaw*, 42 ICLQ (1993), at 929–37.

[836] Judgment of 11 September 1992, at 610–15, paras. 425–30. The decision on the delimitation was taken unanimously, except for the one on the fourth sector, where Judge *ad hoc* Valticos dissented: ibid., at 613–14, para. 428. On the treatment of the prinicple of *uti possidetis* by the Chamber see *Hartzenbusch*, 34 Harv. ILJ (1993), at 244–50; and *Kohen*, 97 RGDIP 939 (1993), at 939–73.

[837] *Hartzenbusch*, 34 Harv. ILJ (1993), at 244, 257.

[838] Judgment of 11 September 1992, at 553–5, paras. 323–6 and at 615, para. 431. The dissenting judge was judge *ad hoc* Torres Bernárdez.

[839] Ibid., at 555–7, paras. 326–30, and at 615–16, para. 431: the decision on El Tigre was taken by 4 votes to 1, the dissenting vote was cast by judge *ad hoc* Torres Bernárdez.

[840] Ibid., at 616, para. 431. Judge *ad hoc* Torres Bernárdez dissented from the finding on Meanguerita; the other two decisions were taken unanimously.

[841] Ibid., at 586–606, paras. 381–414; and at 616–17, para. 432.

outside the gulf.[842] It then defined the status of the waters outside the gulf and concluded that since there was joint sovereignty over the area inside the gulf, each of the three joint sovereigns was entitled to territorial sea, continental shelf, and exclusive economic zone outside the bay closing line. The question of whether and how delimitation should be carried out was for the three states to decide.[843] The Chamber noted that Nicaragua, the intervening state, was not bound by the judgment as it had not become a party to the proceedings.[844]

The disagreement over the tasks conferred on the Chamber by the special agreement made the proceedings more complicated, but the careful way the Chamber interpreted the respective provisions of the agreement was not such as to make problems of acceptance likely to occur.[845] With regard to the islands, the Chamber had adopted a compromise approach narrower than that suggested by El Salvador, but broader than that suggested by Honduras. The sovereignty of El Salvador over the territories in which it had been the most interested, Meanguera and Meanguerita, was confirmed;[846] even though the status of El Tigre had been considered despite Honduran objections, the Chamber ultimately found in favor of Honduras. Concerning the maritime zones, the Chamber had followed closely the text of the agreement and thereby rejected the overly liberal interpretation of its tasks advanced by Honduras in this regard.

4. The aftermath of the decision

Both countries affirmed their acceptance of the verdict.[847] It was a declaratory judgment, and with the acceptance of the definition of the land boundary and the legal status of the islands and the waters, the parties complied with their obligation under Article 94(1) of the UN Charter. Practical

---

[842] Ibid., at 528–86, paras. 372–80, and at 617, para. 432(2): the Court relied on an interpretation of Article 2(2) of the special agreement.

[843] Ibid., at 606–9, paras. 415–20 and at 617, para. 432. The decision was taken by 4 votes to 1, against the vote of Judge Oda.

[844] Ibid., at 609–10, paras. 421–4. For the opposite view see Decl. of Judge Oda, at 619–20, and Sep. Op. Judge *ad hoc* Torres Bernárdez, at 730–1, para. 208.

[845] See *Rottem*, 87 AJIL (1993), at 626: "[T]he caution expressed by the Chamber—the determination of sovereignty over only those islands that were clearly in dispute and its reluctance to effect a maritime delimitation—is a clear signal to future litigants that the Court will seek to limit the remedy strictly to the jurisdiction in which is invited to operate." See also *Hartzenbusch*, 34 Harv. ILJ (1993), at 255: "This decision confirms [...] the Chamber's reluctance (and one may presume likewise the reluctance of the Court) to engage in a delimitation process unless it is absolutely clear that all relevant parties have given all relevant consent."

[846] El Salvador had given particular emphasis to its claim to Meanguera and Meanguerita in its final submissions: see Judgment of 11 September 1992, at 553, para. 323.

[847] 62 AdG (1992), 37147 A 5, Joint Communiqué of the Presidents of El Salvador and Honduras of 11 September 1992, www.sre.hn/despliega.asp?Documento=696&Banner=TIT6. gif&Text01=&Text02=, *Hartzenbusch*, 34 Harv. ILJ (1993), at 257.

difficulties remained, however, as to the demarcation of the land boundary, to which both countries had committed in the special agreement and in the General Treaty of Peace.[848] While the demarcation was a matter for implementation of the judgment in a broader sense, the source of the obligation to demarcate was to be seen in those two treaties and not in the judgment: a judgment defining a land boundary *per se* does not give rise to a duty to demarcate that boundary, as there is no general obligation to carry out a demarcation, as desirable as it may be from the point of view of an effective, lasting settlement (as a result of which the provisions to that extent were laudable).[849]

Another critical point was the treatment of the population in the respective areas, raising questions relating to the laws of nationality and the guarantee of property rights for the approximately 15,000 Honduran and Salvadoran nationals living in territory awarded to the other side.[850] The Chamber had anticipated these difficulties in its judgment:

> It cannot be excluded [. . .] that [. . .] the situation may arise in some areas whereby a number of nationals of one Party will, following the delimitation of the disputed sectors, find themselves living in the territory of the other, and property rights apparently established under the laws of the one Party will be found to have been granted over land which is part of the territory of the other. The Chamber has every confidence that such measures as may be necessary to take account of this situation will be framed and carried out by both parties, in full respect for acquired rights, and in a humane and orderly manner.[851]

For example, a long-standing practice of Salvadorans of harvesting wood in the area of Nahuaterique (attributed to Honduras) was not in conformity with Honduran conservation laws.[852] Another sticking point was that the

---

[848] Special agreement, *supra* n. 823, Article 6(1), General Peace Treaty, *supra* n. 819, at Articles 24–5, 29, and in particular 36 ("The parties agree to execute in its entirety and in complete good faith the decision of the International Court of Justice, empowering the Joint Frontier Commission to initiate, within six months from the date of the Court's decision, the demarcation of the frontier line laid down in that decision. For the demarcation in question the norms laid down in this respect in this Treaty shall apply.")

[849] Admittedly, Article 6(1) of the special agreement (see *supra* n. 823) set the demarcation in the context of the implementation of the judgment; yet, this is not to be understood as technical reference to Article 94(1) of the Charter—anyhow, the content of the obligation under Article 94(1) is determined by the *judgment* and not by special agreements.

[850] The indicated numbers vary: 14,000 (10,000 Salvadorans, 4,000 Hondurans) are cited in Procuradora salvadoreña denuncia "maltrato" en frontera con Honduras, Diario Tiempo, www.tiempo.hn/EDICANTE/2001/septiembre/11%20septiembre/sucesos/sucesos.htm and in Con Maduro resolverá conflicto limítrofe dice Presidente de El Salvador, Terra/La Prensa, www.terra.com.hn/noticias/articulo/html/act61436.htm; the following article refers to 15,000 persons: Ex-bolsones: el "espaldarazo" de los presidentes, Proceso, Año 20, núm.868, 1 September 1999, www.uca.edu.sv/publica/proceso/proc868.html.

[851] Judgment of 11 September 1992, at 400–1, para. 66.

[852] Center for International Policy, Central America Update, 19–25 April 1997, El Salvador/ Honduras border agreement, http://web.archive.org/web/20030622134737/http://www.us.net/ cip/970425.htm.

Constitution of Honduras contained a prohibition for persons who had not been Hondurans from their birth to own property within an area of less than 40 kilometers from the country's land and maritime boundaries.[853] Negotiations between the parties brought about the conclusion of an agreement on nationality and acquired rights on 19 January 1998.[854] This agreement provided for a right for the residents in the border areas to choose their nationality and guaranteed the acquired rights regardless of the choice taken.[855] It entered into force with the exchange of the instruments on ratification on 27 August 1999.[856] In November 1999, delegations of both countries, including their foreign ministers, met in Nahuaterique to get a first-hand impression of the situation and to ascertain the needs of the local population.[857] While there were still some complaints that those needs were not properly addressed in practice,[858] the two countries have launched a project to promote economic and social development in the border region.[859]

With regard to the demarcation, it did not begin within three months of the delivery of the judgment as laid out in the special agreement.[860] On 19 January 1998, the parties concluded an agreement creating a twelve-month time frame for the demarcation;[861] nevertheless, when the parties

---

[853] Article 107 of the Constitution of Honduras of 1982, www.honduras.net/honduras_constitution2.html.

[854] Convención sobre nacionalidad y derechos adquiridos en las zonas delimitadas por la sentencia de la Corte Internacional de Justicia de 11 de septiembre de 1992, www.rree.gob.sv/sitio/convenio.nsf/bf25ab0f47ba5dd785256499006b15a4/65ec9de0ef91569b062566320068f4d1?OpenDocument. The preamble of the Convention makes a reference to paragraph 66 of the judgment.

[855] On the solution of the problem of ownership under the Honduran Constitution see www.elsalvador.com/noticias/EDICIONESANTERIORES/agosto28/NACIONAL/nacio21.html.

[856] See Article 21 of the Convention and "Presidentes dan vida a convenio fronterizo", El Diario de Hoy, www.elsalvador.com/noticias/EDICIONESANTERIORES/agosto28/NACIONAL/nacio20.html, María Eugenia Brizuela de Avila (Foreign Minister of El Salvador), Las fronteras salvadoreñas: los nuevos polos de desarrollo nacional, www.rree.gob.sv/sitio/sitio.nsf/1d09b9c58a509f1106256665004e7755/d65d0394173e874a0625688e00562d90?OpenDocument.

[857] María Eugenia Brizuela de Avila, *supra* n. 856; Héctor González Urrutia, El amanecer de las fronteras salvadoreñas, www.rree.gob.sv/sitio/sitio.nsf/1d09b9c58a509f1106256665004e7755/d8cc827470e63f22062569ab00711dd7?OpenDocument.

[858] Procuradora salvadoreña denuncia "maltrato" en frontera con Honduras, Diario Tiempo, www.tiempo.hn/EDICANTE/2001/septiembre/11%20septiembre/sucesos/sucesos.htm; Ex-bolsones: el "espaldarazo" de los presidentes, Proceso, Año 20, núm.868, 1 September 1999, www.uca.edu.sv/publica/proceso/proc868.html.

[859] These efforts have received financial support from the EU. Héctor González Urrutia, *supra* n. 857.

[860] It was as late as on 11 February 1996 that the demarcation was announced to start, 11/02/1996, El Salvador–Honduras, Border Demarcation Begins, in: NOTIMEX NEWS AGENCY, MEXICO CITY, 11/2/96 (SWB AL/2538).

[861] Acuerdo para la ejecución del programa de demarcación de la frontera El Salvador–Honduras, www.rree.gob.sv/sitio/convenio.nsf/c317180a11767f0785256499006b15a3/83d77787a67f46cc0625663200696573?OpenDocument.

received outside assistance through the OAS in 2003,[862] only the part of the land boundary that had been delimited by the General Treaty of Peace has been demarcated—therefore not those sectors defined by the Chamber. Lack of financial resources seems to have played a role, as well as natural disasters in the area that shifted priorities.[863]

Honduras has claimed that El Salvador bears the sole blame for the delays,[864] although the finger-pointing does not relate to non-compliance with the judgment in a technical sense. The special agreement and the General Treaty of Peace had created the obligation to carry out a demarcation, not the judgment.[865] Honduras has nevertheless made a formal claim of non-compliance with the judgment on the part of El Salvador: on 22 January 2002, a letter from the Honduran foreign minister was submitted to be distributed as a document of the Security Council.[866] The letter stated that "[t]he failure of the Government of El Salvador to execute the [. . .] judgment of the International Court of Justice poses a challenge to the authority, validity and binding nature of the decisions of the main judicial organ of the United Nations" and explained that Honduras turned to the Security Council "pursuant to Article 94(2) of the UN Charter [. . .] to request it to intervene and assist in securing the execution of [. . .] the judgment [. . .]." In the first place, Honduras complained that none of the sectors of the land boundary defined by the Court had been demarcated "due to unjustified delays by the Government of El Salvador." Passing mention was given to El Salvador's unwillingness to accept joint sovereignty in the Gulf of Fonseca and its refusal to give effect to the Court's findings with regard to the maritime spaces in the Pacific Ocean, claims not explained further. Honduras asked the Council "to make the necessary recommendations to ensure the execution of the judgment," particularly with regard to the start of negotiations to delimit certain maritime spaces in the Gulf of Fonseca, the observance of the Gulf's legal régime, and the demarcation of the land boundary. It also requested that the Secretary-General monitor the follow-up to those recommendations. In case this

---

[862] The members of the Demarcation Commission met with Mr John Gates, an engineer appointed by the Panamerican Institute for Geography and History, from May 2003 onwards, http://www.sre.hn/Despliega.asp?Documento=14996&Banner=Tit4–1.gif; "La demarcación es vital," http://www.elsalvador.com/noticias/2003/06/09/nacional/nacio10.html.

[863] See No se ha demarcado ni una pulgada en frontera con El Salvador, www.tiempo.hn/EDICANTE/2002/enero/ene14/NACION~1/NACIONAL.HTM, Congreso pide explicaciones al gobierno porque El Salvador no cumple fallo de La Haya, Terra/La Prensa, www.terra.com.hn/noticias/articulo/html/act72904.htm.

[864] Congreso pide explicaciones al gobierno porque El Salvador no cumple fallo de La Haya, Terra/La Prensa, www.terra.com.hn/noticias/articulo/html/act72904.htm.

[865] It is therefore unnecessary for the purposes of the present study to investigate further whether the allegations of Honduras on El Salvador's responsibility are well founded.

[866] Letter dated 22 January 2002 from the chargé d'affaires a.i. of the Permanent Mission of Honduras to the United Nations addressed to the President of the Security Council, S/2002/108 (transmitting a letter from the minister of foreign affairs, Flores Bermúdez, with appendix).

procedure did not achieve the desired effect, it furthermore asked the Council to set a deadline of twelve months for the execution of the judgment and after the expiry of that deadline to dictate "the measures it deems appropriate in order to ensure that the judgment is executed." For the most part, Honduras demanded compliance with obligations that had not been part of the judgment under the heading of "execution of the judgment."[867] While its demand for "faithful observance of the legal regime established in the Gulf of Fonseca by the judgment of the Court" in fact related to compliance with the judgment, Honduras has hardly substantiated why El Salvador would fail to observe the ruling in this respect.

It is not clear how serious Honduras was in its recourse to the Security Council or whether it was merely a means to exert pressure on El Salvador; the fact that the letter did not include a request for a meeting of the Security Council on the matter (and neither made such a request subsequently) might speak for the latter view; no Council debates have taken place. El Salvador expressed its regret about the complaint to the Security Council and refuted the allegations of non-compliance. It maintained that the letter has been a domestic ploy timed to coincide with the inauguration of Honduran president-elect Maduro, and expressed the hope that the matter would be settled with the new government.[868] However, while the new government apparently made no new moves urging the Security Council to consider the issue, it endorsed the original letter's request in another note on 11 March 2002.[869] Yet recently some progress seems to have been reached, and there are hopes that the demarcation will be concluded in the near future.[870]

The judgment was accepted, but the delivery of a judgment cannot always be the final point for the solution of difficulties between the parties. More than a decade later, Honduras and El Salvador still conflict over their land

---

[867] This is the case for the demarcation of the land boundary and the start of negotiations to delimit the maritime spaces.

[868] Demandan a El Salvador ante la ONU, El Diario de Hoy, www.elsalvador.com/noticias/2002/1/24/nacional/nacio12.html; El Salvador lamenta denuncia de Honduras ante la ONU, www.elpanamaamerica.com.pa/archive/01242002/hispano06.html; Con Maduro resolverá conflicto limítrofe dice Presidente de El Salvador, Terra/La Prensa, www.terra.com.hn/noticias/articulo/html/act61436.htm.

[869] Letter dated 11 March 2002 from the chargé d'affaires a.i. of the Permanent Mission of Honduras to the United Nations addressed to the President of the Security Council, S/2002/251 (transmitting a communication from Foreign Minister Pérez-Cadalso Arias, the immediate occasion of which was a reservation to the Convention for Cooperation in the Protection and Sustainable Development of the Marine and Coastal Environment of the Northeast Pacific, signed on 19 February 2002; it is not explained further why precisely that reservation would "disregard both the letter and the spirit of the Judgment of the International Court of Justice.")

[870] La demarcación se terminará en diciembre, www.tiempo.hn.edicante/2004/febrero/27/NACION~1/nacio06.htm; Maduro exigirá a El Salvador cumplir plan de 18 meses, www.tiempo.hn.edicante/2003/sept/sept20/NACION~1/NACIONAL.htm; El Salvador confía en solucionar problema fronterizo con Honduras, http://www.elsalvador.com/noticias/2003/06/09/nacional/notacanciller.html.

and maritime boundaries; yet neither of the parties has taken a course of opposition to the judgment, and there seems to be little basis for the claim of non-compliance recently advanced by Honduras. After seemingly having settled the legal questions and problems of a practical nature, El Salvador in September 2002 turned to the Court to request a revision of the 1992 judgment concerning the sixth sector of the land boundary, claiming to have discovered evidence affecting the basis of the Chamber's findings,[871] but to no avail: the Chamber dismissed the request as inadmissible.[872] This request related only to a limited part of the judgment. Honduras's complaint of non-compliance relates to questions not directly decided upon by the Chamber. The judgment as such was straightforward, and the delay in demarcation does not seem to stem from any difficulty in its interpretation, but it appears to be rather a question of priorities and allocation of resources. It is perhaps to be expected that resolution will come slowly, especially where a transfer of territory concerns an area with a settled population, unless the practical problems likely to arise were already addressed earlier or perhaps even made subject of the litigation where appropriate.

XX. *Maritime delimitation in the area between Greenland and Jan Mayen*

This case concerned the delimitation of the continental shelf and the exclusive fishery zones (EFZs) between the Norwegian island of Jan Mayen and Greenland, a self-governing part of Denmark.[873]

Jan Mayen, located approximately 550 nautical miles off the Norwegian coast and 250 nautical miles off the coast of East Greenland, north-east of Iceland, is a volcanic island with no settled population.[874] The area's principal fishery resource is capelin, a migratory species.[875] Norwegian vessels had engaged in whaling, sealing and fishing for capelin and other species in the waters between Jan Mayen and Greenland.[876]

The dispute on maritime delimitation in the Jan Mayen area began in the late 1970s after large catches of capelin were made off Jan Mayen's shores and Norway planned the establishment of a 200-nautical mile EFZ around the island, which was to bring about overlapping claims with Iceland and

---

[871] Application for Revision, 10 September 2002, http://212.153.43.18/icjwww/idocket/iesh/iesh_iorders/ieshiapplicationtoc.htm.

[872] Application for Revision of the Judgment of 11 September 1992 in the Case concerning the Land, Island and Maritime Frontier Dispute (El Salvador/Honduras: Nicaragua intervening) (El Salvador v. Honduras), Judgment of 18 December 2003.

[873] Greenland is a former Danish colony and has been part of the Kingdom of Denmark since 1953; home rule was introduced in 1979. The population at the time of the proceedings totalled about 55,000. See Judgment, at 44, 46, paras. 13–14.

[874] The island is inhabited by the staff of a meteorological station and a radio station, however. Judgment, at 46, para. 15.

[875] Judgment of 14 June 1993, at 46, para. 14; and at 70, para. 73.

[876] Ibid., at 44, para. 11; and at 46, para. 15. See also *Politakis*, 41 NILR (1994), at 2.

Denmark (for zones around Greenland). The matter was settled between Iceland and Norway in 1980 and 1981.[877] As of 29 May 1980, Norway claimed a 200-mile EFZ around Jan Mayen not extending "beyond the median line in relation to Greenland."[878] By an executive order effective on 1 June 1980, Denmark extended its EFZ to 200 miles off the east coast of Greenland, indicating that fisheries jurisdiction would not be exercised beyond the median line *vis-à-vis* Jan Mayen "until further notice." An executive order of 31 August 1981 claimed Danish jurisdiction over the full 200 nautical miles.[879] Negotiations between the two countries from 1980 onwards failed to produce concrete results.[880] Denmark emphasized the dependency of Greenland's indigenous population on fishing;[881] Norway countered that catches in the Jan Mayen area accounted for 8 per cent of its total haul and contributed to the fragile economy of its coastal communities.[882]

On 16 August 1988, Denmark seized the Court by unilateral application, based on both countries' declarations accepting the compulsory jurisdiction of the ICJ[883]—the first instance in which a case of maritime delimitation was not introduced by notification of a special agreement.[884] Denmark asked the Court to declare that it was entitled to a full 200-mile EFZ and continental shelf and to draw a single delimitation line in the waters between Greenland and Jan Mayen at a distance of 200 nautical miles. Norway did not oppose the Court's jurisdiction, but objected to the Court drawing a delimitation line and stated that the Court should limit itself to a declaratory judgment on the bases for the delimitation, with the details to be negotiated by the parties subsequently. Norway maintained that a distinction had to be made between the boundary of the continental shelf and that of the fishery zones, both being conceptually different, but to be constituted by the median line.[885]

On 12 June 1989, while the case was still pending before the Court, Iceland, Denmark (on behalf of Greenland), and Norway concluded an agreement on

---

[877] Norway and Iceland concluded two agreements: the first agreement dealt with the delimitation of Iceland's exclusive economic zone and the future Norwegian fishery zone, providing for the establishment of a conciliation commission on the continental shelf boundary. The second agreement followed the conciliation commission's report and adopted as a boundary the same line as the one delimiting the exclusive economic zones. See *Richardson*, 82 AJIL (1988), at 443–58; *Stummel*, in EPIL III, at 1.

[878] Judgment of 14 June 1993, at 46, para. 17.   [879] Ibid., at 46, para. 16.

[880] *Dipla*, 98 RGDIP (1994), at 903–4.

[881] Judgment of 14 June 1993, at 44–6, paras. 13–14.

[882] Ibid., at 71, para. 74. Sea-bed resources played no substantial role. Ibid., at 70, para. 72. See *Charney*, 83 AJIL (1994), at 105.

[883] For the Danish declaration see ICJ YB 1998–9, at 97 (declaration of 10 December 1956); for Norway's declaration, see ICJ YB 1994–5, at 106–7 (declaration of 2 April 1976 replacing that of 17 December 1956).

[884] See *Charney*, 83 AJIL (1994), at 107; *Pozo Serrano*, 49 REspDI (1997), at 118–19.

[885] For a summary of the submissions, see *Politakis*, 41 NILR (1994), at 2–14; Judgment of 14 June 1993, at 42–4, paras. 9–10; and at 77–8, para. 88 on the task conferred on the Court.

the capelin stock in the waters between Greenland, Iceland, and Jan Mayen. This agreement obliged the parties to cooperate in the conservation and management of allotted quotas of the total allowable catch that was to be determined separately for each season.[886] Although the capelin stocks were a matter of essential interest, this agreement was in essence a short-term fix set to expire after three years[887] that did not eliminate the need for a final delimitation. On the other hand, the delimitation would not remove the need for cooperation in the area. Nevertheless, the fact that an agreement was reached on this matter was a good sign for the proceedings since it indicated the parties' willingness to negotiate and might itself have removed some tensions. During the oral proceedings, it was announced that the tripartite agreement was extended for another two years.[888]

In its judgment of 14 June 1993 the Court, by 14 votes to 1,[889] defined the (single) delimitation line for the continental shelf and the fishery zones.[890] The Court rejected Norway's submissions that it should limit itself to a judgment "declaratory as to the bases of delimitation, and which leaves the precise articulation (or demarcation) of the alignment to negotiation between the parties," since such a limitation would not completely discharge the Court's duty to decide the dispute. It regarded as its task "to define the delimitation line in such a way that any questions which might still remain would be matters strictly relating to hydrographic technicalities which the Parties, with the help of their experts, can certainly resolve."[891] In the absence of a an agreement between the parties that there should be a single maritime boundary, it examined the delimitation of the continental shelf and of the EFZs separately and found the Geneva Convention on the Continental Shelf of 1958 applicable to the former, customary law to the latter.[892] However, the result was that both lines coincided since the Court

---

[886] Agreement between Greenland/Denmark, Iceland, and Norway on the stock of capelin in the waters between Greenland, Iceland, and Jan Mayen, 12 June 1989, 1548 UNTS 170.

[887] Ibid., Article 13.

[888] Statement of Denmark's agent, Mr Tyge Lehmann, at the public sitting of 11 January 1993, Verbatim Record, http://212.153.43.18/icjwww/Icases/igjm/iGJM_cr/iGJM_iCR9301_19930111.PDF at 10; he stresses the desire of all the concerned countries toward conservation of the natural resources.

[889] Denmark's judge *ad hoc* Fischer appended a dissenting opinion. Judgment of 14 June 1993, at 304–14.

[890] Judgment of 14 June 1993, at 79–82, paras. 91–4. Unlike in other cases, the Court did not stop at suggesting a *possible* line. Commentators are divided as to how much the Court's judgment contributes to more predictability in maritime delimitation cases. For praise, see e.g. *Dipla*, 98 RGDIP (1994), at 921–5; *Kwiatkowska*, 28 ODIL (1997), at 101; *Pozo Serrano*, 49 REspDI (1997), at 131–2 (giving judgment credit for enhancing predictability in maritime delimitation cases, despite isolated criticisms). For mainly critical comments, see *Evans*, 43 ICLQ (1994), at 702–4; *Charney*, 88 AJIL (1994), at 253–4 (contending that Court failed to promote consistency by insufficiently analyzing relevant state practice).

[891] Judgment of 14 June 1993, at 77–8, paras. 88–9. See *Dipla*, 98 RGDIP (1994), at 917–21.

[892] Ibid., at 57–8, paras. 43–4.

in effect followed the same methodology for the fishery zones as for the continental shelf.[893] The line it drew was situated between the lines advanced by the parties,[894] somewhat less generous to Denmark than to Norway.[895]

Both parties declared that they were satisfied with the result, and their relevant official practice was temporarily based on the delimitation according to the coordinates indicated by the Court, until they had calculated final coordinates and formally agreed on them.[896]

On 18 December 1995, the delimitation was established by an agreement between the parties, which entered into force immediately upon signature.[897] In its preamble, the parties referred to the judgment: they expressed their agreement on drawing the borderlines between the fishery zones and the continent shelf according to its terms, and stated that they had completed a geodetic calculation of the delimitation criteria laid down by the ICJ. Article 1 described the course of the delimitation line of the continental shelf, and Article 3 stipulated that the boundary of the fishery zones coincided with this line. Moreover, another issue that was not touched upon by the Court's judgment was regulated: the exploitation of possible transboundary oil and gas fields. The fact that this clause had to be negotiated in order to reach a comprehensive solution was mentioned as the reason why it took some time until the agreement implementing the judgment was reached.[898]

The indicated coordinates for the delimitation in the judgment and the agreement are not identical;[899] there is a difference between the judgment and

---

[893] Ibid., at 61–4, paras. 52–8. Critical on this point, see *Politakis*, 41 NILR (1994), at 21; Separate Opinion Oda, at 117. On the specific line adopted, see *Pozo Serrano*, 49 REspDI (1997), at 122–31.

[894] See sketch map no. 2, Judgment of 14 June 1993, at 80.

[895] *Charney*, 83 AJIL (1994), at 108. See also *Scott et al.*, 3 ILSA JICL (1996), at 13, commenting that the Court found in favor of Norway. This view can hardly be sustained given that the Court disagreed with Norway's suggested delimitation line (Judgment of 14 June 1993, at 77, para. 87) and drew the actual line between the median line and the 200-mile zone claimed by Denmark (see sketch map no. 2, ibid., at 80).

[896] See *Magid* in Peck/Lee, Increasing the Effectiveness, at 333 fn. 23 (author was agent for Denmark in the case).

[897] Agreement between the Kingdom of Denmark and the Kingdom of Norway concerning the delimitation of the continental shelf in the area between Jan Mayen and Greenland and concerning the boundary between the fishery zones in the area, 18 December 1995, LOS Bull. no. 31 (1996), 59–61. The entry into force is governed by Article 4. The parties concluded an additional protocol on 11 November 1997: www.un.org/Depts/los/LEGISLATIONAND TREATIES/STATEFILES/DNK.htm.

[898] Mr Hans Wilhelm Longva, Legal Advisor of the Norwegian Foreign Ministry, Discussion Comment, in Peck/Lee, *Increasing the effectiveness of the ICJ*, at 362: "[T]he question that did come to the Court was only one element of what was needed for an agreement on maritime delimitation."

[899] Compare Article 1 of the agreement, *supra*, n. 897, with paras. 93 and 94 of the judgment of 14 June 1993, at 81–2.

the instrument used for its implementation.[900] However, even assuming that the delimitation has been carried out in a slightly different manner, this is no reason for the Court to worry, nor could it be considered as a case of non-compliance. The decisive factor is that the parties regarded their delimitation as an implementation of the Court's judgment and did not call its authority into question. Even after a judgment is delivered, the rights and obligations can be modified by agreement. This is a normal feature of adjudication, be it on the international or on the national plane. One should therefore not worry too much on whether such a slight modification has taken place or not. The fact is that both of the two parties expressed their respect for the Court's judgment and reached a comprehensive final solution of their dispute, with the Court playing a substantial role. The background was such as to expect such a positive result: the parties had good relations and close ties.[901] This spirit of good neighborliness was so strong as not to be possibly endangered by the proceedings:[902] Norway did not oppose the involvement of the ICJ although it had been seized by unilateral application of Denmark and fully participated in the proceedings.[903] The matter had significance, but was not of vital importance for either country and it had been predictable that the result would involve some degree of compromise.

XXI. *Arbitral award of 31 July 1989*[904]

In this case, the Court was asked to rule upon the existence, validity, and bindingness of an arbitral award on the maritime boundaries of Guinea-Bissau and Senegal.

---

[900] *Ranjeva*, in Peck/Lee, Increasing the effectiveness, at 324, 325 ("The accordance with these various points shows the boundaries, but they are not the same as those which were proposed by the Court in its judgment."). But see *Magid* in Peck/Lee, Increasing the effectiveness, at 364 ("[T]here was no dispute between the parties as to how to implement the judgment, or to try to negotiate around the judgment, which means, in fact, that the result is in accordance with the judgment. [...] [T]here may be a misunderstanding in reading the final result of the treaty compared with the judgment. My guess about the misunderstanding is that it might have something to do with base points.")

[901] The Nordic states (Denmark, Finland, Norway, Iceland, and Sweden) closely cooperate in many areas; cooperation is channeled through the Nordic Council and the Nordic Council of Ministers. Background of the Nordic cooperation are close ties between the Scandinavian states based on their proximity, common history, similarity in culture, language, the legal and social systems, and shared values. See *Berg*, EPIL III, at 634–8; Nordic Council/Nordic Council of Ministers, Facts on Nordic Co-operation—The Nordic Community, www.norden.org/faktab/uk/nr_generel.pdf.

[902] See *Magid* in Peck/Lee, Increasing the effectiveness, at 365 ("[B]asically, it was a very amicable case, because there was not too much strain on substance.").

[903] See *Scott et al.*, 3 ILSA JICL (1996), at 13 (suggesting that case could have ended up before the ICJ even without compulsory jurisdiction).

[904] See generally *Beveridge*, 41 ICLQ (1992), at 891–6; *Cotterau*, 96 RGDIP (1992), at 753–76.

1. The arbitral award of 31 July 1989

The dispute between the two countries dates back to colonial times. In an exchange of letters of 26 April 1960, France and Portugal had agreed on the maritime delimitation between Senegal—then an autonomous, but not yet independent, state within the Communauté Française—and the Portuguese province of Guinea, which gained independence as Guinea-Bissau in 1974. The agreement addressed the boundary between the territorial seas, the contiguous zones and the continental shelf, becoming the subject of controversy once both countries gained full independence. Guinea-Bissau contested Senegal's assertion that the exchange of letters had effected a valid delimitation of maritime boundaries. The establishment of an exclusive economic zone by Guinea-Bissau and an EFZ by Senegal—issues not considered by the former colonial powers—raised additional problems for delimitation.[905] The two countries began talks in 1977 and on 12 March 1985 concluded an agreement to submit the dispute to a three-member arbitral tribunal. The tribunal was asked to decide whether the 1960 agreement had the force of law in the relations between the parties and in case of a negative answer to that question, to define the delimitation line of the maritime territories.[906]

In its award of 31 July 1989, the tribunal decided that the agreement had the force of law for the delimitation of the areas explicitly mentioned therein—namely the territorial sea, the contiguous zone, and the continental shelf—but not for maritime spaces not yet existent in 1960, "whether they be termed exclusive economic zone, fishery zone or whatever...." Given its affirmative response to the first question, the tribunal ignored the second question relating to the delimitation itself and declined to effect the delimitation, as it considered not to be called upon to do so given its answer to the first question.

A declaration by the tribunal's President, who cast one of the positive votes in a split decision, prompted doubts as to whether there was a proper majority decision at all. He stated that he would have included a partially negative decision in the operative part on the first question as far as the exclusive economic zone and fishery zone are concerned, which would have

---

[905] Guinea-Bissau established an EEZ of 200 nautical miles on 19 May 1978 by Act 3/78, reprinted in: Smith, *Exclusive Economic Zone Claims*, at 191. See also Act No. 3/85 of 17 May 1985 on the Maritime Boundaries, available under www.un.org/Depts/los/LEGISLATION ANDTREATIES/PDFFILES/GNB_1985_Act3.pdf. Senegal established an EFZ of 50 nautical miles on 2 July 1976 by Act 76–89, reprinted in: Nordquist/Lay/Simmonds, *New directions VII*, at 171. The zone was extended to 200 nautical miles on 18 August 1987 by Act 97–27, available under www.un.org/Depts/los/LEGISLATIONANDTREATIES/PDFFILES/SEN_1987_Act.pdf.

[906] The panel was presided over by Julio Barberis, with Mohammed Bedjaoui (then member of the ICJ) and André Gros (former member of the ICJ) as the additional members. See judgment of 12 November 1991, at 59, para. 15. For a summary of the history of the dispute prior to the arbitral proceedings see ibid., at 57–9, paras. 12–15.

enabled the Court to deal with the second question and carry out the delimitation for the zones not covered by the 1960 agreement. The dissenting judge seized upon this declaration: "Since it emanates from the President of the Tribunal himself, that Declaration, by its very existence as well as by its contents, justifies more fundamental doubts as to the existence of a majority and the reality of the Award."[907]

2. The proceedings before the ICJ

The dissent seemed to question the authoritativeness of the tribunal's award and thus it was not surprising that on 23 August 1989 Guinea-Bissau launched proceedings before the ICJ by unilateral application challenging the existence and validity of the arbitral award.[908] It argued that Senegal could not demand compliance with an award that Guinea-Bissau considered non-existent, given the inconsistency between the decision and the President's declaration and, as a subsidiary claim, null and void in that it did not conform to the requests in the arbitration agreement.[909] Guinea-Bissau's application was based on both countries' declarations of the acceptance of the compulsory jurisdiction of the ICJ under Article 36(2) of the ICJ Statute. The Senegalese declaration contained a reservation for disputes in regard to which the parties had agreed on another settlement method. However, as it was advanced by Guinea-Bissau that the proceedings were no request for an appeal or a revision, but related to the inexistence or nullity, Senegal did not contest the Court's jurisdiction.[910]

In its order of 2 March 1990, the Court turned down a request for indication of provisional measures by Guinea-Bissau because the request related to the protection of rights that were not the subject-matter of the proceedings.[911] On 12 March 1991, shortly before the judgment was delivered, Guinea-Bissau filed a second application instituting further proceedings against Senegal.[912] This application related to the delimitation of all maritime spaces between the two states, since the judgment in the pending case would not settle that issue comprehensively given the arbitral award's silence

---

[907] See the summary of the tribunal's findings, President Barberis's declaration and Judge Bedjaoui's dissenting opinion in the judgment of 12 November 1991, at 59–61, paras. 16–21.

[908] Ibid., at 55, para. 1.   [909] Ibid., at 56–7, para. 10.

[910] Ibid., at 61–2, paras. 22–5.

[911] Order of 2 March 1990, at 64–71. The Court held that the request related to the rights of the parties in the maritime zones; issues that did not form part of the current proceedings concerned the question of the existence and validity of the award: ibid., at 70, paras. 25–7. Guinea-Bissau indicated "acts of sovereignty by Senegal which prejudge both the judgment on the merits to be given by the Court and the maritime delimitation to be effected subsequently between the states" as grounds for interim protection, ibid., at 67–8, paras. 15–18. See *Beveridge*, 41 ICLQ (1992), at 892–4; *Cotterau*, 36 AFDI (1990), at 368–89.

[912] Retrievable under http://212.153.43.18/icjwww/icases/idm/idm_iorders/idm_iapplication _19910312.pdf.

on the issue of the EEZ delimitation. The parties agreed with the ICJ President that no measure should be taken in this second case prior to a final decision in the arbitral award case.[913]

3. The judgment of 12 November 1991 and its aftermath

The Court released its judgment on 12 November 1991.[914] It rejected Guinea-Bissau's claims that the award was non-existent (unanimously) and that it was null and void (by 11 votes to 4). By 12 votes to 3, it found that the award was valid and binding for the parties and that they were under the obligation to apply it[915]—a finding requiring concrete action: the implementation of the arbitral award.

The Court had indicated in its judgment that it regarded a comprehensive settlement expedient: "[T]he Court considers it highly desirable that the elements of the dispute that were not settled by the Arbitral Award [...] be resolved as soon as possible, as both Parties desire."[916] Nevertheless, questions relating to important economic interests remained unanswered.[917] One of Guinea-Bissau's main criticisms of the arbitral award had been its failure to decide on the delimitation of all maritime areas.[918] Senegal had already stated during the proceedings that it had no objections against negotiations on the EEZ delimitation.[919] Guinea-Bissau transmitted a communiqué to the UN in which it affirmed its readiness to abide by the judgment despite its disappointment that Senegal's arguments had not been rejected.[920] Senegal, on its part, expressed its willingness to search for a comprehensive solution and to strengthen its cooperation with Guinea-Bissau.[921] Negotiations

---

[913] Maritime delimitation between Guinea-Bissau and Senegal (Guinea-Bissau v. Senegal), Order of 8 November 1995, at 424.

[914] Judgment of 12 November 1991, at 53–76.

[915] Ibid., at 75–6, para. 69. Senegal's judge *ad hoc* Mbaye (a former member of the Court whose term had ended during the proceedings, ibid., at 56 paras. 7) voted with the majority; Guinea-Bissau's judge *ad hoc* was among the dissenters on the second and the third parts of the decision. As Judge Bedjaoui had been one of the arbitrators, he recused himself pursuant to Article 17 of the ICJ Statute. See Rosenne, *World Court*, 235; *Cotterau*, 36 AFDI (1990), at 370–6. For details on the judgment see *Beveridge*, 41 ICLQ (1992), at 894–6; *Hartzenbusch*, 86 AJIL (1992), at 553–8; *Quéneudec*, 37 AFDI (1991), at 419–43.

[916] Judgment of 12 November 1991, at 75, para. 68.

[917] See *Kamto*, 101 RGDIP (1997), at 697.

[918] Judgment of 12 November 1991, at 56, para.10. In particular, Guinea-Bissau had submitted that the arbitral tribunal had been asked to draw a single line for delimitation.

[919] Ibid., at 75, para. 67.

[920] *Note verbale* from Guinea-Bissau: Communiqué on the ruling of the International Court of Justice in the case relating to the disputes between Guinea-Bissau and Senegal. LOS Bull., No. 20, 1992, 52.

[921] *Note verbale* from Senegal: Statement of the Senegalese Government following the decision of the International Court of Justice at The Hague confirming the award of 31 July 1989 finding for Senegal in its dispute with Guinea-Bissau over their maritime boundary. LOS Bull., No. 20, 1992, 53.

resumed and proved more fruitful than those during the pre-adjudicative phase. The countries presented progress reports in meetings with the ICJ President in February and October 1992 and March 1994.[922] The Court remained seized by Guinea-Bissau's second application of 12 March 1991, the issue of maritime delimitation was still pending: it was therefore the President's task to ascertain the parties' views as to the continuation of the proceedings in that second case. Strictly speaking, the meetings took place only in the context of the second case and thus represented no exercise of a function in the post-adjudicative phase. However, the implementation of the judgment was interrelated with the issues raised in second proceedings, so that a report of the progress of the negotiations was relevant for the post-adjudicative phase of the first case as well.

On 14 October 1993, the two states concluded a management and cooperation agreement that provided for joint exploitation of a specifically delimited maritime zone,[923] covering in that zone both areas that had been delimited by the 1960 exchange of letters (as affirmed by the 1989 award) and areas not yet delimited (Guinea-Bissau's EEZ and Senegal's EFZ). While the agreement does not effect any kind of delimitation,[924] it does provide that the parties shall have recourse to negotiation, and, failing this, to arbitration or the ICJ in respect of any unsettled delimitation in the event the agreement expires or is suspended; the same dispute settlement mechanisms apply for disputes concerning the agreement itself.[925] Hence, the parties adopted an equitable compromise that makes the delimitation unnecessary as long as the joint management works and creates precautionary measures for the event this cooperation breaks down.[926] The parties established an international agency for joint exploitation of the area's resources. The details on the

---

[922] Maritime delimitation, Order of 8 November 1995, at 424–5; Stern, *20 ans de jurisprudence*, at 628.

[923] Management and Cooperation Agreement, Senegal–Guinea-Bissau, 14 October 1993, www.un.org/Depts/los/LEGISLATIONANDTREATIES/PDFFILES/TREATIES/SEN-GNB 1993MC.PDF. The relevant zone was situated between the 268° and 220° azimuths drawn from Cape Roxo beyond the territorial seas.

[924] Article 6 contained a safeguard clause for the parties' claims in this respect: "By the present Agreement, the Parties shall pool the exercise of their respective rights, without prejudice to legal titles previously acquired by each of them and confirmed by judicial decisions, and without prejudice to claims previously formulated by them in respect of non-delimited areas."

[925] Article 9: "Disputes concerning the present Agreement or the international agency shall be resolved initially by direct negotiations and, should these fail, after a period of six months, arbitration or by the International Court of Justice. In the event of suspension of the present Agreement, or upon its expiry, the States Parties shall have recourse to direct negotiation, arbitration or the International Court of Justice in respect of any delimitations remaining unsettled." Article 8 provides that the agreement is concluded for twenty years and automatically renewable.

[926] On this aspect and the novel approach of the parties see *Kamto*, 101 RGDIP (1997), at 723–8, 733–5.

establishment and functioning of the agency were laid down in a protocol on 12 June 1995.[927]

By a letter of 2 November 1995, Guinea-Bissau notified the Court of its decision to discontinue the case; Senegal agreed, and the Court removed the case from its list by order of 8 November 1995.[928] On 21 December 1995, the instruments of ratification of both agreements were exchanged and the dispute was formally settled.[929] The ultimate settlement went beyond the mere implementation of the award,[930] and instead of the traditional solution of adopting a delimitation agreement, a new framework for cooperation was created.

After losing the case in 1991, Guinea-Bissau never put the validity of the Court's judgment in question. A positive factor was the parties' willingness to submit the issue to adjudication as evidenced in the arbitration treaty, which indicated their desire to have the issue settled and their capacity to perceive the dispute as a legal one. A faster settlement might have been achieved if the arbitration agreement had been framed in more precise terms and more comprehensively.[931]

XXII. Territorial dispute

This case centered on a dispute between Libya and Chad over an area of 330,000 square miles that included the Aouzou strip, a scarcely populated area rich in minerals occupied by Libya in 1973 and annexed in 1975.[932] The conflict erupted into a war from 1986 to 1987.[933] Chad claimed that its

---

[927] Protocol of agreement relating to the organization and operation of the agency for management and cooperation between the Republic of Guinea-Bissau and the Republic of Senegal instituted by the Agreement of 14 October 1993, LOS Bull. No. 31 (1996), 42–58. The parties undertook to establish this agency in Article 4 of the 1993 agreement.

[928] ICJ Reports 1995, 423. For details on the drafting of the two agreements see *Diaité*, 41 AFDI (1995), at 700–10; *Kamto*, 101 RGDIP (1997), at 698–735.

[929] *Diaité*, 41 AFDI (1995), at 709–10.

[930] See *Kamto*, 101 RGDIP (1997), at 717 and 725 (arguing that the parties have set aside the 1989 award on their way to an equitable solution). The 1993 and 1995 agreements do not explicitly refer either to the arbitral award or to the ICJ judgment. But see Article 6 of the 1993 agreement ("By the present Agreement, the Parties shall pool the exercise of their respective rights, without prejudice to legal titles previously acquired by each of them and confirmed by judicial decisions, and without prejudice to claims previously formulated by them in respect of non-delimited areas"). It is to be assumed that the line confirmed by the tribunal had an impact on the concrete features of the agreements. See *Kamto*, ibid., at 725–7; *Diaité*, 41 AFDI (1995), at 702. There is no reason for concern if the parties modify their rights and obligations by agreement, see *supra* Chapter 2 D I.

[931] See *Hartzenbusch*, 86 AJIL (1992), at 558 (arguing that case was lesson for drafters of arbitral agreements to take successive questions into account).

[932] *Munya*, 7 JIL & Pract. (1998), at 218–19; *Naldi*, 44 ICLQ (1995), at 683; *Pukrop*, "The Aouzou Strip," www.american.edu/ted/ice/aozou.htm (singling out strategic advantage of uranium deposits as reason for Libyan invasion).

[933] 56 AdG (1986) 29624 A, 30497 A; 57 AdG (1987) 30793A, 30934B, 31379A, 31428. See also Pukrop, "The Aouzou Strip." Libya and Chad resumed their diplomatic relations on 3 October 1988; 58 AdG (1988) 32605 A.

boundary with Libya had been conclusively determined by the 1955 Treaty of Friendship and Good Neighbourliness between France and Libya, and that pursuant to that treaty, the territory in question was Chadian. Libya argued that no delimitation had been carried out and that it had title to the disputed zone based on a coalescence of rights and titles: those of the indigenous population, the Senoussi order, and those of a succession of sovereign states (the Ottoman Empire, Italy, and Libya itself).[934]

On 31 August 1989, the two states concluded a framework agreement on the peaceful settlement of the territorial dispute.[935] The parties undertook to submit the dispute to the ICJ in the absence of a political settlement of their territorial dispute within a period of approximately one year. For the period up to the delivery of the final judgment, the agreement provided for measures concomitant with the legal settlement.[936] No reference was made to the post-adjudicative phase. A Mixed Commission was also established for the agreement's implementation, which was to be monitored by an *ad hoc* committee of the OAU.

The agreement did not specify the question for the Court to decide; the agreement referred to "the territorial dispute," the precise definition of which remained a matter for the parties' submissions. The essential conflict related to the existence of a boundary in the disputed area. In Libya's understanding, the dispute related to the attribution of territory, whereas Chad considered the location of the boundary the key point.[937] Both parties desired a common end from the Court—namely the delimitation of their respective territories—although they differed as to the means, either through a declaratory statement (pursuant to Chad) or through an act of attribution (pursuant to Libya). Their different perceptions of the nature of the dispute stemmed from their respective interpretation[938] of the Treaty of Friendship and Good Neighbourliness between France and Libya of 10 August 1955; it was not so much a controversy on the terms of reference than one on the

---

[934] Judgment of 3 February 1994, at 12–14, para. 17; and at 14–5, paras. 19–21.

[935] Framework agreement on the peaceful settlement of the territorial dispute, 31 August 1989, 1545 UNTS 101.

[936] Article 2: in the absence of a political settlement of their territorial dispute, the two Parties undertake:
(a) To submit the dispute to the International Court of Justice;
(b) To take measures concomitant with the legal settlement by withdrawing the forces of the two countries from the positions which they currently occupy on 25 August 1989 in the disputed region, under the supervision of a commission of African observers, and to refrain from establishing any new presence in any form in the said region.
(c) To proceed to the said withdrawal to distances to be agreed on;
(d) To observe the said concomitant measures until the International Court of Justice hands down a final judgment on the territorial dispute.

[937] Judgment of 3 February 1994, at 14–15, para. 19.

[938] Libya refrained from calling the 1955 treaty invalid while contesting that it had established any new boundaries, see ibid., at 19, para. 36, and at 22, para. 43. Chad claimed that the treaty had effected the delimitation in the area and subsidiarily relied on *effectivités*. Ibid., at 15, para. 21.

applicable law. An endorsement of Chad's position on the 1955 treaty would make Libya's claim for attribution of the territory redundant, as the Court would explain in the course of the judgment.[939] Given the consensus between the parties as to the ultimate objective of the litigation, it did not turn out to be problematic that the special agreement left the question submitted undefined.

At a summit in Rabat in August 1990, both countries' heads of state agreed to bring the dispute before the Court and highlighted the historic and cultural ties between both countries.[940] Libya notified the Court on 31 August of the 1989 agreement with reference to Article 40(1) of the ICJ Statute. An application by Chad against Libya founded on Article 2(a) of the 1989 agreement followed on 3 September, on 28 September supplemented by a statement that the two notifications related to one single case and that the 1989 agreement constituted a special agreement pursuant to Article 40(1) of the Statute of the Court, a finding in which the Libyan agent concurred.[941] Accordingly, the Court could rely on the agreement as basis for its jurisdiction.[942] The UN Secretary-General's trust fund to assist states in the settlement of disputes through the ICJ helped to defray some of the costs of the proceedings;[943] the overall climate between the parties during the litigation was rather positive.[944]

---

[939] The Court did not attach importance to this distinction, explaining that if it found that there was an established borderline, this would answer both parties' questions. Ibid., at 20, para. 38.

[940] Tensions still existed, as were visible in the Chadian foreign minister's refusal to sign the final communiqué. 60 AdG (1990) 34829 A.

[941] Judgment of 3 February 1994, at 6–9, paras. 1–8, Letter from the Secretary of the People's Committee of Foreign Liaison and International Co-operation of the Socialist People's Libyan Arab Jamahiriya to the Registrar of the International Court of Justice, 31 August 1990, The Minister for Foreign Relations of the Republic of Chad to the Registrar of the International Court of Justice, 1 September 1990, The Agent of the Government of Chad to the Registrar of the International Court of Justice, 28 September 1990, http://212.153.43.18/icjwww/icases/idt/ iDTpleadings/idt_iapplication_specialagreement.pdf.

[942] Judgment of 3 February 1994, at 12–13, paras. 18, 22.

[943] Chad's agent Abderahman Dadi expressed his country's gratitude for the support by the trust fund in his closing statement in the oral proceedings before the Court, 14 July 1993, CR 93/ 32, http://212.153.43.18/icjwww/icases/idt/iDT_cr/iDT_iCR9332_19930714.PDF. The Secretary-General's Reports on the trust fund do not disclose the recipients, although the description of the situation in which assistance was provided in 1991 fits to the case under consideration, see Report of the Secetary-General, Secretary-General's Trust Fund to Assist States in the Settlement of Disputes through the International Court of Justice, 7 October 1992, A/47/444, at 2; and idem, 10 October 2001, A/56/456, at 2.

[944] See the closing statements by both countries' agents: Abderahman Dadi (Chad), thanking the Libyan team for the cordiality during the proceedings, *supra* n. 943; Abdulati Ibrahim El-Obeidi (Libya), Public Sitting of 8 July 1993, C/93/29, http://212.153.43.18/icjwww/icases/idt/ iDT_cr/iDT_iCR9329_19990708.PDF, expressing his appreciation of the friendly spirit shown by the agent of Chad and his team. Michael E. Pukrop *supra* reports that tensions between the two countries were eased in late 1990 when a *coup d'état* in Chad brought into power a government favorable to Libya. For details on the *coup d'état*, see 60 AdG (1990) 35125 A. The rebel forces of the *Mouvement patriotique du salut* led by Idriss Déby took over the power; it had been supported by Libya. Déby was appointed new president of Chad on 4 February 1990; Libya celebrated this

In its judgment of 3 February 1994, the Court ruled by 16 votes to 1 in favor of Chad: it found that the treaty of 1955 established the boundary between Libya and Chad and defined the border line in accordance with Chad's sub-missions.[945] The immediate implication of the decision was that Libya was occupying Chadian territory and was under the obligation to withdraw from that area.[946] The two governments affirmed in letters to the Security Council from 9 and 23 March 1994 their readiness to abide with the judgment.[947] Nevertheless, there were fears that Libya might refuse to withdraw and that hostilities might break out again,[948] which eventually proved unfounded.

Negotiations between the parties rapidly brought about the conclusion of an agreement on the implementation of the ICJ judgment on 4 April 1994, which laid down the practical modalities: withdrawal of the Libyan adminis-tration and forces; removal of mines; crossing points for persons and prop-erty; study of the question of joint monitoring of the frontier; maintenance of good-neighborliness; demarcation of the boundary; and further cooperation. The withdrawal was to take place from 15 April until 30 May under the supervision of a mixed team composed by Libyan and Chadian officers. UN observers would monitor the withdrawal operations and had to establish when the withdrawal was effected.[949]

On 13 April, the UN Secretary-General informed the Security Council about the agreement and his intention to send a reconnaissance team to conduct a survey in order to prepare recommendations on a possible UN role in the dispute.[950] In his subsequent report to the Security Council of 27

development and stated that the change in government would give impulses for good neighborli-ness between the two countries. See in contrast the former government's statements on the territorial dispute of 60 AdG (1990) 34751 A, where the tensions were still visible.

[945] Judgment of 3 February 1994, at 40. Libya's judge *ad hoc* Sette-Camara dissented, while Chad's judge *ad hoc* Abi-Saab voted with the majority. The boundary line determined by the Court's judgment coincided with Chad's claims. See Sketch Map 4 (Boundary Line determined by the Court's Judgment) and Sketch Map 1 (Claims of the parties), ibid., at 16, 39. For details of the judgment see *Kohen*, 99 RGDIP (1995), 258–300.

[946] The judgment's operative part is limited to the findings on the boundary. Judgment of 3 February 1994, at 40, in accordance with the parties' submissions (ibid., at 12–14), in which the question of a withdrawal had not been included, the obligation to withdraw is a logical conse-quence.

[947] S/1994/296, S/1994/332. Libya's head of state Kadhafi made a declaration on 4 March that the territorial dispute was definitely settled. See 64 AdG (1994) 38650 A.

[948] *Naldi*, 44 ICLQ (1995), at 690.

[949] Agreement on the implementation of the ICJ judgment concerning the territorial dispute, 4 April 1994, 33 ILM 619 (1994); 6 Afr. JICL 516, 516 (English) and 519 (French). Article 10 of the agreement provided for its notification to the United Nations; the parties notified the Secretary-General accordingly, see Letters dated 6 (Libya) and 7 April 1994 (Chad), S/1994/402 and S/1994/424.

[950] Letter dated 13 April 1994 from the Secretary-General addressed to the President of the Security Council, S/1994/432. In this context, the Secretary-General stated that the reconnais-sance team would need to visit Libya on a UN aircraft. By resolution 910 of 14 April 1994, the Security Council exempted the UN aircraft to be employed for that purpose from the flight restrictions under Security Council Resolution 748 (1992).

April 1994, the Secretary-General proposed the immediate deployment of an observer unit, the UN Aouzou Strip Observer Group (UNASOG).[951] Moreover, he reported the reconnaissance team's concerns about the welfare of approximately 4,000 inhabitants in the Aouzou strip who had been dependent on support by Libya and stated that it was envisaged that a representative of the United Nations Development Program assisted in assessing the potential humanitarian dimension.[952] UNASOG was established by Security Council resolution 915 (1994) of 4 May 1994: the deployment of 9 UN observers and 6 support staff was authorized for a single period of up to 40 days.[953]

On 30 May 1994, the governments of Libya and Chad issued a joint declaration stating that by that date, the Libyan withdrawal from the Aouzou strip had been effected to the satisfaction of both parties and monitored by UNASOG.[954] In his report to the Security Council from 6 June 1994, the Secretary-General declared that the mandate of UNASOG could be considered successfully terminated; he drew a positive balance of the whole case:[955]

The Governments of Chad and the Libyan Arab Jamahiriya agreed to submit their territorial dispute to the International Court of Justice for judicial settlement. The Court rendered a Judgment which the parties accepted and they requested the assistance of the United Nations in implementing the decision. The Security Council acted promptly in providing assistance to the two Governments. The accomplishment of the mandate of UNASOG amply demonstrates the useful role, as envisaged by the Charter, which the United Nations can play in the peaceful settlement of disputes when the parties cooperate fully with the Organization. I should like to thank the Governments of Chad and the Libyan Arab Jamahiriya for the cooperation they extended to UNASOG and for the spirit of friendship they exhibited to each other during the operation.[956]

---

[951] Secretary-General's Report concerning the agreement on the implementation of the ICJ judgment concerning the territorial dispute between Chad and Libya, 27 April 1994, S/1994/512.
[952] Ibid., at 4.   [953] S/RES/915 (1994), A 2.
[954] Joint Declaration by the Great Socialist People's Libyan Arab Jamahiriya and the Republic of Chad on the withdrawal of the Libyan administration and forces from the Aouzou Strip, Annex I to the Report of the UN Secretary-General on the United Nations Aouzou Strip Observer Group, 6 June 1994, UN Doc. S/1994/672, 4.
[955] Ibid., 1–3. He reported that only a few families had stayed in the Aouzou village (most people having moved to Libya) and gave some recommendation on the future development of the area (para. 7).
[956] Ibid., paras. 8–9. Similarly, ICJ President Mohammed Bedjaoui lauded the parties in an address to the UN General Assembly on 13 October 1994: "I wish to pay a special tribute to the Libyan Government and to the Government of Chad which spared no effort to implement the Court's Judgment without delay, and in a spirit of friendly understanding." Idem, "The Place of the International Court of Justice in the general system for the maintenance of peace, as instituted by the Charter of the United Nations, " ICJ YB 1994–5, The Hague 1995, 207–15, at 211, also retrievable under http://212.153.43.18/icjwww/ipresscom/SPEECHES/SpeechPresid entGa1994e.htm.

The Security Council welcomed the Secretary-General's Report and terminated UNASOG's mandate with immediate effect by resolution 926.[957]

The case is exemplary in terms of the rapid and comprehensive implementation of the judgment. Several factors could have led to problems with compliance. Chad's total victory in the final decision could have caused some difficulties, for example, especially since the Court had failed to respond to some of Tripoli's arguments.[958] Moreover, the judgment obliged Libya to withdraw from a strategic area it already occupied that was inhabited by a population with which it had close ties. The history of armed conflict over the border was another potential breaking-point. Yet the dispute was settled efficiently and rapidly in accordance with the ICJ judgment, demonstrating the greater importance of positive factors in this case, including the desire of both parties for a judicial settlement, the conclusion of a special agreement for that purpose, and the financial support available during the proceedings. Both of the parties expressed their acceptance of the judgment, and received prompt assistance from the UN, who took into consideration the humanitarian dimension of implementation.

XXIII. *Maritime delimitation and territorial questions between Qatar and Bahrain*

In this case, the Court settled a centuries-old dispute between Qatar and Bahrain, described as one of the most explosive disputes in the Persian Gulf and which had brought the two countries to the verge of armed conflict in 1986.[959]

1. Areas at dispute between Qatar and Bahrain and settlement attempts

The dispute concerned the maritime delimitation between the two countries and sovereignty over five territories: Zubarah,[960] the Hawar Islands,[961] the

---

[957] S/RES/926 (1994) of 13 June 1994.   [958] *Kohen*, 99 RGDIP (1995), at 331–2.

[959] For more detailed history of case see Judgment of 16 March 2001, paras. 36–69.

[960] Zubarah is a townsite located on the north-west coast of the Qatar mainland. It has been abandoned since its destruction in the nineteenth century. Bahrain's interest derived from the fact that it was the ancestral home of the present rulers of Bahrain. The International Estimate Inc., Dossier: The Bahrain–Qatar Border Dispute: The World Court Decision, Part 1, The Estimate, Vol. 13 (2001), No. 6 (23 March 2001). http://www.theestimate.com/public/032301. html.

[961] The Hawar islands are a Bahrain-occupied island group located adjacent to the coast of Qatar. They were a key issue in the dispute between the two countries since sovereignty over them was directly linked to petroleum resources. While Bahrain claimed title to these islands on the basis of a British decision of 11 July 1939, Qatar founded its claim on proximity and a prior title. Judgment of 16 March 2001, paras. 99–109.

island of Janan/Hadd Janan,[962] Quit'at Jaradah,[963] and Fasht ad Dibal.[964] The dispute could be traced to economic interests—control over petroleum and gas resources, tourism[965]—as well as to tribal and dynastic rivalries.[966] For decades, the conflict seemed to elude resolution; whenever Qatar raised its claim to the Hawar Islands, Bahrain reiterated its claim to Zubarah.[967]

Since 1976, Saudi Arabia had engaged in attempts at mediation (sometimes referred to as good offices). Two sets of documents resulting from this mediation were to gain particular relevance in the proceedings before the ICJ. The first was a 1987 exchange of letters between the Saudi king and the emirs of Qatar and Bahrain, in which the two emirates accepted Saudi-backed proposals, including one that "all the disputed matters shall be referred to the International Court of Justice, at the Hague, for a final ruling binding upon both parties, who shall have to execute its terms" and another proposal that called for the formation of a Tripartite Commission for the purpose of approaching the Court. The second set of documents was the minutes of the meeting of the Co-operation Council of Arab States of the Gulf at Doha in December 1990. Qatar had at that point accepted a formula defining the question to be submitted to the Court that had been suggested by Bahrain in 1988. The parties agreed to continue to make use of the good offices of Saudi Arabia's King Fahd until May 1991, and that they might submit the matter to the ICJ at the end of that period.[968] No resolution of the conflict was reached within that time limit.[969]

---

[962] Janan and Hadd Janan are located off the south-western tip of the Hawar Islands proper. Ibid., para. 35. It was disputed whether Janan and Hadd Janan were a single island or two (at low tide, they formed a common territory) and whether they formed part of the Hawar Islands and thus shared in their fate. Ibid., paras. 149–56.

[963] Quit'at Jaradah is a tiny, uninhabited, and barren parcel situated between the main island of Bahrain and the Qatar peninsula. Ibid., para. 219. The parties disagreed on whether it was an island or a low-tide elevation. Ibid., paras. 191–4, 196.

[964] Fasht ad Dibal is a low-tide elevation with oil and gas reserves located off the north-west coast of Qatar, north-east of Bahrain. Ibid., paras. 35, 200. The sovereignty dispute brought the two countries to the verge of armed conflict in 1986. Qatar responded to Bahrain's building up of the reef around Fasht ad Dibal and its establishment of a coastguard post there by sending helicopters and arresting 29 persons working for Bahrain. Gunboats of the two countries exchanged fire. Saudi intervention prevented an escalation; the Qatari army withdrew shortly and the arrested persons released. The reef was dredged so that it was again below the water line, but the question of the control over the oil and gas resources remained open. The International Estimate Inc., Dossier: The Bahrain–Qatar Border Dispute: The World Court Decision, Part 2, The Estimate, Vol. 13 (2001), No. 7 (6 April 2001), www.theestimate.com/public/040601.html; *Rousseau*, 90 RGDIP (1986), at 963–4; *Saal*, 32 AFDI (1986), at 1055.

[965] Gulf Centre for Strategic Studies, "A New Dawn in Bahrain-Qatar Relations," in Bahrain Brief, Vol. 2 Issue 4 (2001), http://web.archive.org/web/20020111221833/http://www.bahrain brief.com/english/april-issue2001.htm, explaining that the Hawar Islands are attractive for tourism development.

[966] The International Estimate, Part 1, *supra* n. 960.

[967] The International Estimate, Part 2, *supra* n. 964.

[968] The parties delivered different translations of the Arabic text of the minutes. See Judgment of 1 July 1994, at 119, para. 19.

[969] See the summary in the Judgment of 1 July 1994, at 116–20, paras. 15–20.

2. The proceedings before the ICJ

On 8 July 1991, Qatar filed a unilateral application instituting proceedings before the ICJ.[970] It founded the Court's jurisdiction on the two sets of documents, which in its view were agreements by which the two states had made express commitments to refer the dispute to the Court.[971] Qatar thereby implied that those two instruments were special agreements conferring jurisdiction on the Court under Article 36(1) of the ICJ Statute. Bahrain objected to the Court's jurisdiction and argued that the 1990 minutes did not constitute a legally binding document and that, in any case, Qatar did not have the right unilaterally to seize the Court.[972] While there was no denying the fact that the parties had agreed that the dispute should be submitted to the ICJ, it was controversial whether they had entered into a legally binding agreement that would entitle either state to bring the matter before the Court unilaterally.[973]

In its judgment of 1 July 1994, the Court held that the documents in question were, in fact, international agreements in which the parties had undertaken to submit "the whole of the dispute" to the Court as circumscribed in the instrument referred to in the 1990 minutes as "Bahraini formula," and it decided "to afford the Parties the opportunity to submit to the Court the whole of the dispute."[974] It stated that this submission could be effected by a joint act by both parties or by separate acts, that the result should be that all points mentioned in the Bahraini formula be submitted, and that this process should be completed within five months.[975] This part of the ruling responded to Bahrain's concerns that the Qatar application comprised only some of the elements of the subject-matter intended to form part of the Bahraini formula—a point acknowledged by Qatar, which had invited Bahrain to submit a separate application or a counterclaim.[976]

Although the judgment was made under the heading "jurisdiction and admissibility," the Court had not yet affirmed its jurisdiction, instead ruling on the parties' undertaking to submit the dispute.[977] One can assume that it

---

[970] http://212.153.43.18/icjwww/idocket/iqb/iqborders/iqb_iapplication_910708.htm.
[971] Ibid., para. 40.   [972] Judgment of 1 July 1994, at 120, para. 20.
[973] *Evans*, 44 ICLQ (1995), at 691.
[974] Judgment of 1 July 1994, at 120–5, paras. 21–38, 126–7, para. 41(1)–(3). The voting pattern on all sections of the operative part was 15 votes to 1, with both judges *ad hoc* concurring; the dissenter was Judge Oda (Japan). For details, see *Klabbers*, 33 AdV (1995), at 361–76; *McHugo*, 29 NYIL (1997), at 178–80.
[975] 1994 Judgment of 1 July 1994, at 125, para. 38, at 127, para. 41(4).
[976] Ibid., at 124, para. 36.
[977] Lauterpacht in Lowe/Fitzmaurice, *Fifty years of the ICJ*, at 470–1. See *Klabbers*, 33 AdV (1995), at 363, fn. 6 ("It is difficult to see, however, how the Court in a next decision could possibly deny jurisdiction."). But see *Cosnard*, 41 AFDI (1995), at 321 (seeing an implicit acknowledgment of the validity of some of Bahrain's submissions in 1994 judgment).

hoped that the parties might subsequently agree on terms for a joint submission so that there would be no need to establish whether the sets of documents served as a basis for jurisdiction.[978] The judgment was interlocutory in nature[979] and unprecedented in the Court's history. The Court did not dispose of the parties' submissions, instead "afford[ing] them the opportunity to submit the whole of the case," the concrete terms of which sounded rather like a request than the granting of the possibility. It demanded action at an interim stage, an unusual feature for an ICJ judgment.[980]

On 30 November 1994, Qatar broadened the scope of its earlier application and submitted to the Court "the whole of the dispute" in "the absence of an agreement between the parties to act jointly." On the same day, the Court's registry received a document from Bahrain insisting that the matter could only brought before the Court by both parties jointly and that in the absence of such a joint submission, the Court had no jurisdiction. This was based on a different interpretation of a provision in the 1990 minutes stating that "the parties" (in Qatar's reading, *al-tarafan* in Arabic) might submit the dispute to the ICJ; Bahrain latched a more restrictive connotation on the term, which it understood as meaning "the two parties" and deduced therefrom that the parties could only jointly seize the Court.[981] Bahrain argued that the Court had lacked jurisdiction when seized by Qatar and that Qatar's separate act of 30 November could not create jurisdiction.[982]

In its judgment of 15 February 1995, the Court held by 10 votes to 5[983] that it had jurisdiction to entertain the dispute, that it was seized with the whole of the dispute, and that Qatar's application as formulated on 30 November 1994 was admissible.[984] It interpreted the relevant phrase in the Doha minutes and concluded that it provided for a right of unilateral seisin of the Court.[985] By its order of 28 April 1995, the Court started the phase of written proceedings, which lasted until 30 May 1999. Oral proceedings were held from 29 May to 29 June 2000.[986] Fears voiced in the aftermath of the 1985 judgment that Bahrain would refrain from participating in the proceedings[987] did not materialize.

---

[978] See *McHugo*, 29 NYIL (1997), at 173.   [979] *Klabbers*, 33 AdV (1995), at 363, 370.

[980] *Cosnard*, 41 AFDI (1995), at 321; Lauterpacht in Lowe/Fitzmaurice, *Fifty years of the ICJ*, at 472–3, and at 479–83 on the Court's authority to make such a type of judgment.

[981] Judgment of 15 February 1995, at 18, para. 34.   [982] Ibid., at 9–10, paras. 12–13.

[983] Ibid., at 26, para. 50. Bahrain's judge *ad hoc* Valticos was among the dissenting judges.

[984] Ibid. Critical, see *Evans*, 44 ICLQ (1995), at 695–8; *McHugo*, 29 NYIL (1997), at 180–96 (admitting personal interest in the case at 171, since he served as counsel for Bahrain).

[985] Judgment of 15 February 1995, at 18–23, paras. 35–42.

[986] See the summary of the procedural history from 1995 onwards in the judgment of 16 March 2001, paras. 13–30.

[987] See *Evans*, 44 ICLQ (1995), at 698 (stating that "it seems unlikely [...] that Bahrain will participate in the later phases of the case").

3. The judgment on the merits

On 16 March 2001, the Court delivered its judgment on the merits—a Solomonic decision which effectively divided the disputed territories between the two parties.[988] The Court determined that Qatar had sovereignty over Zubarah, Janan (including Hadd Janan), and the low-tide elevation of Fasht ad Dibal; Bahrain had control over the Hawar Islands and Qit'at Jaradah. A unanimous Court affirmed the right of innocent passage enjoyed by Qatari vessels in Bahrain's territorial sea.[989] Moreover, the Court, by 13 votes to 4, drew a single maritime boundary dividing the various maritime zones; this line was definitive and not merely recommendatory ("the single maritime boundary [...] shall be drawn as indicated in paragraph 250 of the judgment").[990]

The Court had cut the Gordian knot.[991] The judgment was praised by both sides; each one considered itself as a winner. A public holiday was proclaimed in both countries to celebrate the verdict and there was relief that this long-standing dispute had found a solution.[992] Each party sent a letter to the ICJ registrar expressing its gratitude to the Court.[993] UN Secretary-General, Kofi Annan, congratulated the parties to the solution and stated: "The acceptance of the judgment delivered by the Court on 16 March has set an excellent example for other states of how disputes of this

---

[988] The International Estimate, Part 1, *supra* n. 960. The question of sovereignty over the Hawar Islands was more controversial than the question of Zubarah, with regard to which the Bahraini claims had been unlikely to succeed. Ibid. For assessments of which side gained more by the judgments, see The International Estimate, Part 2 ("[M]ost analysts would say that Bahrain won more than Qatar did [...]." But see Arabia Online Ltd., "Bahrain and Qatar both proclaim victory in border dispute," http://web.archive.org/web/20010817140328/http://www.arabia.com/news/article/english/0,1690,41986,00.html (quoting statement of Qatari foreign minister that "they obtained the Hawar islands, but we won four important points").

[989] Judgment of 16 March 2001, para. 252. The votes on Zubarah and Fasht ad Dibal were unanimous; on Janan, 13 to 4; on the two territories awarded to Bahrain, 12 to 5. Qatar's judge *ad hoc* Torres Bernárdez dissented in the ruling on the Hawar Islands, the island of Qit'at Jaradah, and on the single maritime boundary; Bahrain's judge *ad hoc* Fortier on Janan Island. Judge *ad hoc* Valticos had resigned with effect from 15 February 1995. Ibid., para. 12.

[990] Ibid., para. 252.   [991] The International Estimate, Part 2, *supra* n. 964.

[992] Arabia Online Ltd., *supra* n. 988; Gulf Centre for Strategic Studies, *supra* n. 988. The International Estimate, Part 2, *supra* n. 964; 24 Middle East Executive Reports (2002), No. 1, 8, Qatar–Bahrain dispute ended by World Court ruling. See also "Hawar Islands resolution opens new opportunities," Lloyd's List Int'l, 22 June 2001, 2001 WL 19251957L ("Within hours of the announcement Bahrain had invited international oil companies to start prospecting for oil and gas in the shallow seas around the Hawar Islands. Qatar has accepted the decision gracefully and mutual hostility is evolving into a full-blown love-in between the two former foes.")

[993] Letter of the Agent of the State of Qatar to the Registrar, 27 March 2001, http://212.153.43.18/icjwww/idocket/iqb/iqbjudgments/ijudgment_20010316/iqb_ijudgment_20010327_LetterQatar.pdf; Letter of the Agent of the State of Bahrain before the ICJ, 19 March 2001, http://212.153.43.18/icjwww/idocket/iqb/iqbjudgments/ijudgment_20010316/iqb_ijudgment_20010319_LetterBahrain.pdf. (In particular, Bahrain lauded the diligence and parity of the Court.)

nature should be resolved."[994] Hopes were voiced that the solution of the dispute might usher in a new era of cooperation between the two countries after decades of tensions and strengthen ties in the entire region.[995] Up to now, these hopes seem to have materialized: ties between Qatar and Bahrain are blossoming.[996] A project to build a bridge connecting the two states (referred to as Friendship Bridge) is under consideration,[997] which would bring closer relations as well as economic benefits.[998] A memorandum of understanding on Qatari gas supplies to Bahrain was signed in January 2002,[999] following a protocol on cooperation in the oil and gas sector signed in September 2001.[1000]

This case had elements that could have jeopardized the prospects for compliance—the tensions the conflict had created earlier, which had brought it close to escalation; important domestic interests, including questions of national pride; and a controversial consensual basis for the Court's proceedings.[1001] On the other hand, the parties had had a substantial interest in settling the dispute and neither party had lost face in the judgment on the merits. The Court's judgment was accepted, and the case is a success for the ICJ as an effective means of dispute settlement: a dispute that had soured the relations between the countries for decades and that had had a negative impact on cooperation in the Gulf[1002] was settled to open the way for a new era of friendship.

[994] UN Doc. SG/SM/7751 retrievable under http://212.153.43.18/icjwww/idocket/iqb/iqb judgments/ijudgment_20010316/iqb_ijudgment_20010323_statement%20kofi%20annan.PDF.

[995] "Hawar island decision brings optimism for future," US–Qatar J Online, 29 March 2001, www.qatarbusinesscouncil.org/newsletter/archives/issue11.htm (reporting that judgment brought "a pervasive sense of optimism" for the future of the Gulf Cooperation Council relations). Saudi Arabia and other states in the region praised the settlement of the dispute; the Secretary-General of the Gulf Cooperation Council was quoted as saying that this "historic event will reinforce the GCC and be beneficial to the two peoples"; see Middle East Executive Reports, *supra* n. 992.

[996] See also "Qatar—The political perspective," APS Review Oil Market Trends, 27 August 2001, 2001 WL 7300277 ("Settlement of the long-standing territorial dispute between Qatar and the neighboring island state of Bahrain marked a new era of cooperation for both emirates.")

[997] A Danish consortium was appointed to carry out a feasibility study in late September. If the project goes ahead as scheduled, both countries might be physically linked in 2006. The project was first unveiled in late 1999 and gathered momentum with the acceptance of the ICJ judgment by both countries. See "Cementing the ties," MEED, 26 October 2001, 2001 WL 8125455.

[998] "Special Report Bahrain: All change," MEED, 28 September 2001, 2001 WAL 6827845.

[999] "Old rivals push ahead with gas cooperation," Energy Compass, 11 February 2002, 2002 WL 7249760; "Qatar, Bahrain sign gas-supply act," Platt's Oilgram News, 10 January 2002, 2002 WL 12450445 (quoting Bahrain's oil minister as thanking the emir of Qatar and his people "for the constructive and friendly cooperation they have shown, which will enhance brotherly relations between the two countries").

[1000] "Qatari gas helps bring ex-foes together," Energy Compass, 14 September 2001, 2001 WL 20241930. On further plans for cooperation see Lloyd's List Int'l, *supra* n. 992.

[1001] See "Qatar seeks favored judgment over Hawar islands," US–Qatar J Online, 8 November 2000, www.qatarbusinesscouncil.org/newsletter/archives/issue3.htm (discussing impact of dispute on Gulf Cooperation Council relations).

[1002] See Middle Eastern Executive Reports, Qatar–Bahrain Border Dispute ended by World Court ruling, *supra* n. 992.

XXIV. Gabčíkovo–Nagymaros

1. Background of the case

On 16 September 1977, Hungary and Czechoslovakia signed a treaty[1003] to construct a system of locks on the River Danube for the development of energy and navigation as well as protection against flooding. The project envisioned a "joint investment" for the construction of locks at Gabčíkovo (then on Czechoslovak territory, now in Slovakia) and Nagymaros (in Hungary) as well as a dam at Dunakiliti (Hungary) and other works.[1004] The treaty neither contained a termination clause, nor did it explicitly provide for a right of either party to suspend or abandon the work unilaterally.[1005]

The treaty entered into force on 30 June 1978; works for the project started in the same year. In spring 1989, the work on the Gabčíkovo sector had reached a very advanced stage, while little construction had been carried out at Nagymaros. Political shifts in Central Europe led to increased attention to the project and its potential environmental impact in particular.[1006] While there were critical voices in both countries,[1007] opposition to the project grew particularly strong in Hungary. In the course of 1989, the Hungarian government first decided to suspend, then to abandon, the works at Nagymaros, against protests by Czechoslovakia, who expressed its openness to discuss modifying the original plans and stated that it might unilaterally start a provisional, substitute, project if Hungary continued to be in breach of the treaty. Attempts by the Hungarian government to achieve a termination of the treaty by mutual consent were unsuccessful. Czechoslovakia developed a provisional solution referred to as Variant C, which entailed a unilateral diversion of the Danube and, at its final stage, the construction of an overflow dam at Čunovo in Czechoslovakia. Work on Variant C began in November 1991, against the wishes of the Hungarian government. Further discussions between the parties broke down and, on 19 May 1992, Hungary transmitted a *note verbale* to the Czechoslovakian government terminating

---

[1003] Treaty on the Construction and Operation of the Gabčíkovo–Nagymaros System of Locks, 1109 UNTS 211, 32 ILM 1249 (1993). On the same day, the parties concluded the Agreement concerning mutual assistance in the construction of the Gabčíkovo–Nagymaros System of Locks (1724 UNTS 85), which, among other things, fixed the schedule of work. A number of related agreements were subsequently made. See Judgment of 25 September 1997, at 28, para. 26.

[1004] For a description of the project as originally envisaged see Judgment of 25 September 1997, at 17–24, paras. 15–20.

[1005] There was no controversy on this point, see ibid., at 35, para. 39.

[1006] While some of the environmental effects were foreseeable when the treaty was concluded in 1977, the full dimension of the potential environmental impact had not been clear prior to the late 1980s. *Reichert-Facilides*, 47 ICLQ (1998), at 839.

[1007] See Judgment of 25 September 1997, at 34, para. 38, with a statement from the Czechoslovak president of 15 February 1991 calling the project a "totalitarian, gigomaniac monument which is against nature."

the 1977 treaty. On 23 October 1992, Czechoslovakia proceeded to dam the river.[1008]

2. The proceedings before the ICJ

Hungary made an attempt to seize the Court unilaterally on 23 October 1992, demonstrating its desire for ICJ involvement, although it was aware that the Court lacked jurisdiction.[1009] At a meeting between Hungary and Czechoslovakia mediated by the European Commission on 28 October, the parties agreed that the matter would be submitted to the ICJ and that a tripartite group of independent experts would give suggestions as to emergency measures.[1010] Slovakia became an independent state on 1 January 1993[1011] and signed with Hungary a special agreement to turn their dispute over to the ICJ on 7 April 1993.[1012] They jointly notified the ICJ registry of the agreement by a letter dated 2 July 1993.[1013]

The questions before the Court were defined in Article 2 with a noteworthy precision. Under paragraph 1, the Court was asked to rule on Hungary's right to suspend and subsequently abandon the works at Nagymaros and on the part of the Gabčíkovo project for which it had been responsible under the 1977 treaty; Czechoslovakia's entitlement to proceed to the "provisional solution"; and the legal effects of the Hungary's notification of termination of the 1977 treaty. Article 2(2) requested the Court to determine the legal consequences arising from its judgment on the questions asked in the first paragraph, including the rights and obligations for the parties—demonstrating the desire of the parties to minimize potential disagreement on the form of implementation required.

The agreement gave due consideration to circumstances during and after the litigation. The parties committed to establish and implement a temporary water management régime pending the final judgment while explicitly ruling out the right of either party to request provisional measures under Article 41 of the ICJ Statute. The agreement provided that if either party believed its

---

[1008] See ibid., at 24–34, paras. 21–38. On Variant C, see also at 46–51, paras. 60–6. For additional background, see *Nakamichi*, 9 Ford. ELJ (1998), at 337–46.

[1009] Judgment of 25 September 1997, at 27, para. 24. The unilateral application thus represented an invitation to Czechoslovakia to give its consent to proceedings before the Court. It fell under Article 38(5) of the Rules of Court, and since Czechoslovakia took no action, the case was not entered in the Court's general list. See *supra* n. 9 on Article 38(5).

[1010] Ibid., at 27, para. 24.

[1011] Ibid., at 27, para. 25. On the issue of state succession see ibid., at 69–73, paras. 117–24.

[1012] Special Agreement for submission to the International Court of Justice of the differences concerning the Gabčíkovo–Nagymaros Project, 1725 UNTS 225, reprinted in: the Judgment of 25 September 1997, at 11–13, para. 2.

[1013] Judgment of 25 September 1997, at 10–13, paras. 1–2. The agreement had entered into force on 28 June 1993 (ibid., at 10, para. 1). By a letter of 9 August 1993, Hungary informed the Registry that its initial application was now without object and had lapsed (ibid., at 27, para. 25).

rights endangered by the conduct of the other in the period before the temporary régime was established or implemented, "it may request immediate consultation and reference, if necessary, to experts, including the Commission of the European Communities, with a view to protecting those rights." The parties accepted this commitment "as fundamental to the conclusion and continuing validity of the Special Agreement."[1014] Not only did the agreement stipulate that the parties would establish an interim régime between themselves so as to preclude the need for the Court to indicate provisional measures, but it also expressly excluded any recourse to Article 41 of the ICJ Statute, even before the establishment of a temporary régime—an unusual construction which indicated that the parties did not consider the Court an appropriate forum to grant interim protection in this case. The emphasis of the provision's fundamental character could be understood as a safeguard against a later request for provisional measures with an argumentation that not the special agreement but the Statute determined the Court's powers of interim protection, and that the clause therefore had to be left out of account: the validity of the agreement and thus the very basis for the Court's jurisdiction was made dependent on that provision.

A provision concerning the post-adjudicative phase demonstrated a common desire for an expedient settlement. The parties agreed to "accept the Judgment of the Court as final and binding upon them and [. . .] execute it in good faith" as well as to enter into negotiations on the modalities for its execution immediately after the judgment was delivered. If no agreement could be reached within six months, either party had the right to refer this determination to the Court for an additional judgment.[1015]

The establishment of the temporary régime proved difficult. On 1 December 1993, experts designated by the European Commission recommended the adoption of various measures that were not acceptable to both parties. A temporary agreement was finally reached on 19 April 1995 and designed to terminate 14 days after the judgment of the Court.[1016]

[1014] Special agreement, *supra* n. 1012, Article 4:
(1) The parties agree that, pending the final judgment of the Court, they will establish and implement a temporary water management régime for the Danube.
(2) They further agree that, in the period before such a régime is established or implemented, if either Party believes its rights are endangered by the conduct of the other, it may request immediate consultation and reference, if necessary, to experts, including the Commission of the European Communities, with a view to protecting those rights; and that protection shall not be sought through a request to the Court under Article 41 of the Statute.
(3) This commitment is accepted by both Parties as fundamental to the conclusion and continuing validity of the Special Agreement.
[1015] Special agreement, Article 5.
[1016] Judgment of 25 September 1997, at 27–8, para. 25. Agreement concerning certain temporary technical measures and discharges in the Danube and Mosoni Branch of the Danube, www.gabcikovo.gov.sk/doc/ia1995en/dohoda.html.

In the proceedings before the Court, Hungary argued that the suspension and abandonment of the works on its part had been justified by the existence of a "state of ecological necessity." Slovakia maintained that Hungary's assessment of the environmental impact was overly pessimistic and that, in any case, ecological problems were manageable and could have been accommodated through a modification of the original plan. Hungary, in turn, maintained that Variant C was a material breach of the 1977 treaty as well as of other obligations under international law. Slovakia defended its actions. With regard to Variant C, it invoked the "principle of approximate application," by which the provisional solution represented its only possibility to fulfill the purposes of the 1977, and stated that it had acted in accordance with its duty to mitigate the damage from Hungary's unlawful action. In the alternative, it sustained that its action was a legitimate countermeasure.[1017]

3. The judgment of 25 September 1997

On 25 September 1997, the Court delivered its judgment,[1018] in which it ruled that Hungary had not been unilaterally entitled to suspend and abandon in 1989 the works on Nagymaros and on the part of the Gabčíkovo project within its responsibility;[1019] that Czechoslovakia had been justified in proceeding to the "provisional solution" in November 1991,[1020] but not to put it into operation from October 1992;[1021] and that Hungary's notification of 19 May 1992 did not have the legal effect of terminating the treaty and its related instruments.[1022] The Court observed that the preceding findings had declaratory character and were confined to the past conduct of the parties (from 1989 to 1992). On the basis of these findings, it proceeded to define the required future conduct of the parties as requested by the parties in Article 2(2) of the special agreement.[1023] After affirming that Slovakia had become a party to the 1977 treaty as successor to Czechoslovakia,[1024] it found that the parties had to negotiate in good faith in the light of the

---

[1017] Judgment of 25 September 1997, at 35–8, paras. 40–5; and at 51–2, paras. 67–71. See also *Fuyane/Madai*, 1 IJ Glob.Env. Issues (2001), at 333–4.

[1018] For details see *Bekker*, 92 AJIL (1998), at 273–8; *Fitzmaurice*, 9 EELR (2000), at 83–7; *Koe*, 20 Syd. LR (1998), at 612–29; *Lammers*, 11 Leid. JIL (1998), at 287–320. Of note is the fact that the proceedings occasioned the first site visit ever taken by the World Court. See *Meadows*, 11 Leid. JIL (1998), at 603–8; *Tomka/Wordsworth*, 92 AJIL (1998), at 133–40.

[1019] Judgment of 25 September 1997, at 39–46, paras. 46–59 and 52–69, paras. 72–115. The decision was reached by 14 votes to 1, with Judge Herczegh (Hungary) casting the lone negative vote.

[1020] The decision divided the Court to a greater extent, garnering 9 votes to 6.

[1021] This decision was taken by 10 votes to 5.

[1022] The decision was made by 11 votes to 4. For issues relating to the law of treaties see *Fitzmaurice*, 11 Leid. JIL (1998), at 321–44.

[1023] Judgment of 25 September 1997, at 75–6, paras. 130–1.

[1024] Ibid., at 69–73, paras. 117–24. This decision was taken by 12 votes to 3. For issues relating to state succession, see *Klabbers*, 11 Leid. JIL (1998), at 345–55.

prevailing situation and take all necessary measures to ensure the achievement of the objectives of the 1977 treaty, and that a joint operational régime in accordance with the treaty of 16 September 1977 had to be established, unless the parties agreed otherwise.[1025]

Hence, the Court affirmed the validity of the 1977 treaty, but acknowledged that the treaty was no longer to be executed as originally envisaged and that modifications were required in order to adapt it to the changed circumstances: "What might have been a correct application of the law in 1989 or 1992, if the case had been before the Court then, could be a miscarriage of justice if prescribed in 1997."[1026] It explained that it could not ignore the facts that Variant C had been launched, operating in another mode than the one originally envisaged, and that not only had Nagymaros not been constructed, but "with the effective discarding by both parties of peak power operation, there is no longer any point in building it."[1027] The Court went on to state that it was for the parties to decide how the 1977 treaty's various objectives (including electricity generation, improvement of navigation, flood control, regulation of ice discharge, and the protection of the natural environment) could best be realized under the changed circumstances; it pointed out that the parties themselves had regarded the explicit terms of the treaty as negotiable and not as a rigid system.[1028] It emphasized that the environmental impact was necessarily a key issue for negotiations (for which it suggested third-party assistance)[1029] and that current environmental standards were to be taken into account.[1030] It regarded the establishment of a joint régime as a basic element of the 1977 treaty and therefore stated that such a régime should be restored, which could be effected by the transformation of Variant C into a treaty-based joint régime.[1031]

Finally, the Court ruled that Hungary had to compensate Slovakia for the damage caused by the suspension and abandonment of the works, and that Slovakia had to compensate Hungary for the damage it had sustained because of the operation of the "provisional solution." It observed that compensation issue could be resolved in an overall settlement if both parties abandoned all financial claims and counterclaims.[1032] However, the settlement of accounts for the construction of the works was regarded as a separate issue to be decided pursuant to the 1977 treaty; Hungary was to

---

[1025] Judgment of 25 September 1997, at 76–80, paras. 132–47. Those decisions were taken by 13 votes to 2. Ibid., at 83, para. 155(2)B, C.

[1026] Ibid., at 76, para. 134.   [1027] Ibid.   [1028] Ibid., at 76–7, paras. 135–9.

[1029] Ibid., at 79, para. 143: "When, after the present judgment is given, bilateral negotiations are held, both parties can profit from the assistance and expertise of a third party. The readiness of the parties to accept such assistance would be evidence of the good faith with which they conduct bilateral negotiations in order to give effect to the Judgment of the Court."

[1030] Ibid., at 77–9, paras. 140–3.   [1031] Ibid., at 76–80, paras. 132–47.

[1032] Ibid., at 81, para. 153.

pay a proportionate share in the building and operating costs of Čunovo if it was to participate in its operation.[1033]

The decision was carefully reasoned and reflected a rather conservative approach tailored to the specific case. Some commentators expressed their disappointment, be it for the reason that the Court had not taken the occasion to give guidance to the recent developments in the law relating to the environment or watercourses or because environmental matters had not been given more weight.[1034] Others regarded the Court's approach as constructive to the settlement of the dispute.[1035] The Court had sent both countries back to the negotiating table; given the difficulty of earlier talks and the complexity of the factors to be accommodated, it is not surprising that those negotiations have not turned out to be easy.

4. The follow-up to the judgment

At first, it seemed as if negotiations between the parties (in accordance with the special agreement)[1036] could bring about a speedy solution. On 27 February 1998, experts of the two governments prepared a framework agreement that, as a compromise, provided for the continued operation of Čunovo and the construction of a dam in Hungary, either at Nagymaros or at Pilismarót.[1037] The Hungarian government withheld its signature pending further studies on environmental impact and the economic feasibility;[1038] the ruling administration faced substantial domestic opposition on the matter.[1039] After May elections brought a change in government, the new prime minister rejected the dam-construction idea, although he offered talks on the meaning of the ICJ judgment.[1040]

[1033] Ibid., at 80–1, paras. 148–54, 83–4, para. 155(2)D, E. The decision on compensation was taken by 12 votes to 3; the decision on the settlement of accounts was made by 13 votes to 2.

[1034] See *Nakamichi*, 9 Ford. ELJ (1998), at 363–4, and 371; *Stec/Eckstein*, 8 YIEnvL (1997), at 41–50; *Koe*, 20 Syd. LR (1998), at 620, 623–5, 628–9 (acknowledging at 629 that the decision had positive aspects as "another small step in the gradual evolution of environmental norms in the context of legal relations between states" and that the Court "drew significant conclusions in respect of the law of treaties, the law of state responsibility and state succession"). Other commentators regarded the decision as a significant contribution to the evolution of international environmental law and the law of international watercourses. See e.g. *Bourne*, 8 YIEnvL (1997), at 6–12; *Boyle*, 8 YIEnvL (1997), 13–20; *Canelas de Castro*, 8 YIEnvL (1997), at 21–31.

[1035] See *Bekker*, 92 AJIL (1998), at 277 ("This case is a good example of how the ICJ gives and takes with a view to achieving a result that is acceptable to both litigants and that, consequently, stands the best chance of being complied with.") See also *Klabbers*, 8 YIEnvL (1997), at 32–40.

[1036] Ibid., Article 5(2).

[1037] The dam would be built either at Nagymaros (as planned in the original treaty) or at Pilismarót. See 68 AdG 42616 A, 42634 A (1998); *Fuyane/Madai*, 1 IJ Glob.Env. Issues (2001), at 339; *Fitzmaurice*, 9 EELR (2000), at 87.

[1038] See *Lammers*, 11 Leid. JIL (1998), at 319.   [1039] 68 AdG (1998) 42616 A.

[1040] "Slovakia's thinking on Gabcíkovo," Euro-East, 29 September 1998, 1998 WL 9410331. See also *Fuyane/Madai*, 1 IJ Glob.Env. Issues (2001), at 339–40.

Pursuant to the special agreement, the lapse of six months without an agreement on the judgment's execution triggered the right of both parties to request an additional judgment from the Court.[1041] The Slovak government blamed Hungary for its lack of willingness to comply with the judgment,[1042] and declared that a new Hague ruling would help to implement the original one.[1043] On 3 September 1998, it filed with the Court a request for an additional judgment, asking it to declare that Hungary was responsible for the failure to reach an agreement on the modalities for the 1997 judgment's execution and that the parties had to take certain measures to ensure the judgment's implementation (which were specified further), in particular, that they had to conclude a framework agreement to enter into force by 1 January 1999 and a final agreement by 30 June 2000, failing which the 1977 treaty would have to be complied with in accordance with its spirit and terms.[1044] A turnover in Slovakia's government after September elections opened the way for a new round of negotiations.[1045] Bilateral talks became a priority in the following months[1046] and Slovakia, although not formally dropping its suit at the ICJ, did not press for a continuation of the proceedings.[1047]

Disagreement exists as to the proper interpretation of the judgment—in particular, on whether it requires the building of new facilities; Hungary insists that the Court discarded Nagymaros.[1048] In spite of these difficulties, the negotiations were described as constructive.[1049] Rumors that UN

[1041] "Slovakia's thinking on Gabcíkovo," Euro-East, 29 September 1998, 1998 WL 9410331. See also *Fuyane/Madai*, 1 IJ Glob.Env. Issues (2001), at 339–40, Article 5(3).

[1042] "Hungary not showing will to fulfil Hague verdict," Czech News Agency, 4 September 1998, 1998 WL 13250463 (quoting the Slovak prime minister, Vladimir Meciar).

[1043] "Binder makes conditional offer to Hungary over Danube dam," Czech News Agency, 21 September 1998, 1998 WL 13251072.

[1044] The demands of Slovakia were rather specific, see ICJ Press Communiqué 98/28 of 3 September 1998, http://212.153.43.18/icjwww/ipresscom/iPress1998/ipr9828.htm. It is questionable whether the jurisdiction of the Court under Article 5(3) of the special agreement extends to findings on state responsibility.

[1045] "Slovakia seeks out-of-court solution to Gabcíkovo," Czech News Agency, 27 November 1998, 1998 WL 21340163.

[1046] "Hungarians ready to discuss Gabcíkovo with Slovakia," Czech News Agency, 18 November 1998, 1998 WL 21339563; "Dam Talks—Hungarian–Slovak Proposal," Hungarian News Agency, 29 January 1999, 1999 WL 10423231 (referring to common document on implementation of judgment, which was to be sent to ICJ).

[1047] The Court encouraged the parties to continue their negotiations, see Fitzmaurice, 9 EELR (2000), at 81. A notice by either party would be sufficient for a resumption of the proceedings: after the respondent has taken some step in the proceedings, the applicant cannot effect a discontinuance of the proceedings against the respondent's will. See Article 89(2) of the 1978 Rules of Court. In any event, Hungary could avail itself of the right to launch proceedings under Article 5 of the special agreement.

[1048] See *Fitzmaurice*, 9 EELR (2000), at 82, 87; *Fuyane/Madai*, 1 IJ Glob.Env. Issues (2001), at 339; "Another round of talks on Gabcíkovo fails," Czech News Agency, 10 March 1999, 1999 WL 5472945; "Hungary Not Building Dam on Danube," Hungarian News Agency, 16 March 1999, 1999 WL 10423998.

[1049] "Slovak, Hungarian Governments Hold Talks on Dam Project," 14 May 1999, 1999 WL 18737558.

Secretary-General, Kofi Annan, might mediate were not confirmed; the Slovak foreign minister pointed out that third-party assistance was not considered necessary.[1050] Both countries appear to prefer a continuation of negotiations to third-party assistance, in particular, to resubmitting the dispute to the ICJ.[1051] Meanwhile, the parties have agreed to prolong the validity of the temporary régime under the 1995 agreement until the conclusion of a treaty implementing the ICJ decision.[1052]

A solution is difficult, given the emotional climate surrounding the project. In Hungary, the project is regarded as an outdated and environmentally harmful leftover of the communist era; Slovakians, in contrast, tend to view the project more favorably.[1053]

A compromise seems difficult to attain: the construction of the Nagymaros dam or another downstream dam will either take place or not.[1054] One solution might be to carry out some additional works to optimize the operation of Gabčíkovo, but not to construct an additional large dam.[1055] Either way, neither party will be a clear winner, and both appear to prefer to continue futile negotiations rather than bear the political responsibility for a compromise. The Slovak government appeared to expect an improvement of its relations with Hungary following a conservative defeat in Hungary's 2002 elections,[1056] although there was reason for doubts on whether the new socialist/liberal government would pursue a substantially different course with regard to Gabčíkovo.[1057] Expectations that the upcoming EU accession

---

[1050] "Slovak premier turns down UN chief's offer of 'third party' help in dam feud," World News Connection, 11 September 2000, 2000 WL 26945435.

[1051] In an interview published 15 January 2001, the Slovak government commissioner, Kocinger, stated that his country was not interested at that time in bringing the matter before the Court, since it regarded the judgment as unambiguous. See "Slovak Commissioner Discusses Gabcíkovo Dam Project," World News Connection, 15 January 2001, 2001 WL 10141232.

[1052] Joint Annual Report on the environment monitoring in 2000, July 2001, www.gabcikovo. gov.sk/doc/jr2000en/preface.html.

[1053] See *Fitzmaurice*, 9 EELR (2000), at 81; *Fuyane/Madai*, 1 IJ Glob.Env. Issues (2001), at 331.

[1054] See Hungary, Slovakia reluctant to escalate feud over Gabčíkovo, Czech News Agency, 15 December 2000, 2000 WL 29620054.

[1055] *Fitzmaurice*, 9 EELR (2000), at 87.

[1056] "Dzurinda wants quick agreement with Budapest," CTK Daily News, 22 April 2002, 2002 WL 5789709; "Hungarian–Slovak relations could acquire new quality," CTK Daily News, 22 April 2002, 2002 WL 5789674. On relations during the Orban administration, see "Orban's diplomacy and the risks of manoeuvering," CTK Daily News, 19 April 2002, 2002 WL 5789593.

[1057] Both before and after their electoral victory, the socialists rebutted conservative allegations that they would build a dam on the Danube. See "MSZP–Fidesz-Duell," Budapester Zeitung, 22 April 2002, www.budapester.hu/news/printart.php?artikel_id=2543; "Hungarian Socialist premier candidate denies rumours about Danube dam plan," BBC Monitoring, 15 April 2002, 2002 WL 19296773; "Hungarians not to build Danube dam—Socialist leader," BBC Monitoring, 22 April 2002, 2002 WL 19301254. See "Far-right extremism cannot jeopardize Slovak EU entry bid," BBC Monitoring, 27 April 2002, 2002 WL 19947480 (quoting Slovak minister of foreign affairs, Kukan, as saying that, despite the positive outcome of the elections, a resolution of the dispute was not to be expected).

might force the parties into a settlement[1058] have not been confirmed; negotiations continue without a breakthrough.[1059]

5. Evaluation

There is no denying that the settlement of the dispute and the implementation of the judgment still face substantial difficulties. The Court cannot be held responsible for the delay; it made an effort to deliver a judgment conducive to compliance, resolving the legal questions submitted (which, as they were, did not permit a ruling prescribing specific action easy to implement) and indicating possible parameters for a practical solution.[1060] The Court has effectively required a good-faith renegotiation of the 1977 treaty,[1061] which, though still in force, is to be adapted to present needs and environmental standards.[1062] On the other hand, the Court did not rule out the necessity for new constructions in Hungary beyond stating that the original building plan for Nagymaros was now irrelevant. While it did not order Hungary to build Nagymaros, neither did it frustrate the Slovak investments.

Whenever parties have to negotiate to accomplish treaty objectives under changed circumstances, there will inevitably be some uncertainty as to how this can best be achieved. In this case, this is particularly difficult as an additional problem lies in the economic damage that both sides have inflicted on each other and for which accounts must be settled as well. The Court could do no more than offer a recommendation in this context (the mutual cancellation of claims); neither a precise assessment of the damages nor the determination of the practical way how compensation should be provided belonged to its tasks.

[1058] "Hungary, Slovakia reluctant to escalate feud over Gabčíkovo," Czech News Agency, 15 December 2000, 2000 WL 29620054.

[1059] Gyorgyi Jakobi, Slovakia and Hungary renew talks over the Gabcikovo Dam, 13 February 2004, http://www.incentraleurope.com/ice/article/50606; Hungarian Ministry of Foreign Affairs, The Renewal of the Talks on the Gabčíkovo–Nagymaros Water Barrage System, 13 January 2004, http://www.mfa.gov.hu/Kulugyminiszterium/EN/Ministry/Departments/Spokesmans_Office/Statements/040113_Gabcikovo-Nagymaros.htm; Ungarn will über Donaukraftwerk verhandeln, 19 December 2003, http://www.budapester.hu/news.php?kurzid=4758.

[1060] The Court suggested recourse to third-party assistance and the establishment of a joint régime over the installations already in place. For positive assessment shortly after judgment, see *Bekker*, 92 AJIL (1998), at 277.

[1061] *Boyle*, 8 YIEnvL (1997), at 14. See the respective section of the operative part, p. 83, para. 155(2)B: "[The Court] finds that Hungary and Slovakia must negotiate in good faith in the light of the prevailing situation, and must take all necessary measures to ensure the achievement of the objectives of the Treaty of 16 September 1977, in accordance with such modalities as they may agree upon."

[1062] *Bourne*, 8 YIEnvL (1997), at 9–11. There is no basis for a claim that the treaty be carried out in its original form, as the Court had explicitly stated that while the treaty was still in force, it was *not* to be executed as originally envisaged. In so far as Slovakia's request for an additional judgment could be understood as suggesting that the original treaty was to be executed failing other agreement, it would be unfounded.

Under the circumstances, the delay in the final implementation of the judgment is hardly surprising. Neither government seems willing to settle the matter for fear of a domestic backlash. Each apparently prefers to stick with its own interpretation of the ICJ judgment rather than risk an unfavorable subsequent judgment from the Court. The parties have spurned third-party involvement, which indicates their desire to retain control over the whole process. Despite the delays, it would seem incorrect to speak of "non-compliance" under Article 94(1) of the Charter, since the parties are in negotiations. While they could pursue a solution more forcefully, it would be difficult to establish by conclusive evidence that the delays were due to bad faith of one party or the other.

As for the terms of reference of the case as defined in the special agreement, it was a positive factor that the whole set of claims and counterclaims was submitted, and not only questions relating to past conduct but also those of the legal consequences. The Court could thereby deal with the legal questions of the dispute in a comprehensive manner. Moreover, the provision in the special agreement on the post-adjudicative phase might have had a positive impact: since both parties know that either one could seize the Court again at any moment, they have an incentive to keep negotiating. On the other hand, this Article does not lay down a procedure for the negotiations. If there had been some sort of institutionalized procedure,[1063] there might have been more pressure on the parties to reach an agreement; on the other hand, of course, third-party assistance is not of great help if unwanted.

A continuation of the proceedings before the ICJ does not seem to be desired by the parties, and it is doubtful whether it could even settle the dispute. The remaining problems are of essentially political character; the legal questions were resolved by the judgment.[1064] The question for the modalities of the 1997 judgment would most likely be answered in a similar manner as in the Haya de la Torre case:[1065] that it is for the parties and not for the Court to make a choice among the different possibilities for implementation.

XXV. Kasikili/Sedudu

This case addressed the question of sovereignty over a small, waterlogged, and uninhabited island known as Kasikili in Namibia and as Sedudu in Botswana and the course of the boundary in the Chobe River, which surrounds the island.[1066] Both countries were interested in developing a tourist

---

[1063] E.g. third-party assistance or the establishment of an independent commission. For proposals for a new international commission for the Danube and on the limitations of the existing commission, see *Nakamichi*, 9 Ford. ELJ (1998), at 366–71.

[1064] See *Bekker*, 92 AJIL (1998), at 278; *Fitzmaurice*, 9 EELR (2000), at 87.

[1065] See *supra* II 3.

[1066] Judgment of 13 December 1999, paras. 11–12. South of the river is Botswana's Chobe National Park, a protected reserve rich in wildlife; north of the river is the Namibian Caprivi strip.

infrastructure in the area; these efforts could not proceed while sovereignty over the area was under dispute. Their disagreement had complicated efforts to prevent poaching in the area. Although Namibia and Botswana stressed their commitment to good relations with each other, the question was a burden for their relations.[1067]

The dispute emerged shortly after Namibia gained independence, in March 1990. The principal legal issue was the interpretation of an 1890 treaty between Great Britain and Germany delimiting spheres of influence in South West Africa.[1068] The line in controversy had been defined as descending the center of the main channel (*Thalweg des Hauptlaufes* in the German text) of the Chobe River to its junction with the Zambesi.[1069] As the Chobe River splits in two branches north and south of the disputed island, the question arose as to which of the two branches constituted the main channel. "Main channel" was not a common legal term[1070] and, considering the geographical knowledge available to the parties at the time of the conclusion, the location of that main channel had been unknown. Botswana claimed that the border line was the northern branch, Namibia, the southern—each resulting in a claim of sovereignty over the island.[1071]

The parties called upon the good offices of the president of Zimbabwe to mediate the dispute. The three heads of state met in Kasane, Botswana, in May 1992 and issued a communiqué according to which the determination of the boundary around the island was to be submitted to a Joint Team of Experts. In its final report issued on 20 August 1994, the team revealed that it was deadlocked and recommended recourse to methods of peaceful settlement of disputes under international law. When the three presidents met again to consider the report, the decision was taken to submit the matter to the International Court of Justice.[1072] On 15 February 1996, Botswana and Namibia concluded a special agreement for that purpose; it entered into force on 15 May 1996. On 29 May 1996, they jointly transmitted the special

---

[1067] See on both parties' explanations on the origin of the dispute, their interests, and general relations: Memorial of Namibia, http://212.153.43.18/icjwww/idocket/ibona/ibonapleadings/ibona_ipleading_19971128_Memorial_Namibia.htm at paras. 5–11, Memorial of Botswana, http://212.153.43.18/icjwww/idocket/ibona/ibonapleadings/ibona_memorial_Botswana_1997022   8/Ibona_ipleading_19970228_Memorial_Botswana_TOC.html at paras. 30–6, Statement of Albert Kawana on behalf of Namibia before the Court on 15 February 1999, CR 99/01, http://212.153.43.18/icjwww/idocket/ibona/ibonacr/ibona_icr9901.html, Statement of Molosiwa L. Selepeng on behalf of Botswana before the Court on 22 February 1999, CR 99/06,http://212.153.43.18/icjwww/idocket/ibona/ibonacr/bona_icr9906_19990222.html.

[1068] Treaty between Germany and Great Britain respecting Zanzibar, Heligoland, and the Spheres of Influence of the two Countries in Africa, 1 July 1890, 173 CTS 271 (1890).

[1069] Id. Article III(2).

[1070] See on this issue the Declaration of Judge Higgins, 39 ILM (2000), 355–56.

[1071] On the facts and the parties' submissions, see Kasikili/Sedudu Island, Judgment of 13 December 1999, at paras. 9–16. For the background of the dispute, see *Perry*, 8 IBRU Int'l Bound. & Sec. Bull. (2000), at 80–2.

[1072] Judgment of 13 December 1999, paras. 15–16.

agreement to the Registrar.[1073] The special agreement asked the Court "to determine, on the basis of the Anglo-German Treaty of 1 July 1890 and the rules and principles of international law, the boundary between Namibia and Botswana around Kasikili/Sedudu Island and the legal status of the island."[1074] The rules and principles of international law applicable to the dispute were defined in another provision as those set forth in Article 38(1) of the ICJ Statute.[1075] Another provision alluded generally to a post-adjudicative phase, stating that the judgment would be "final and binding" and implemented as soon as possible by the parties.[1076]

In its judgment of 13 December 1999, the Court found by 11 votes to 4 that the boundary between Botswana and Namibia followed the line of the deepest soundings in the northern channel of the Chobe River around Kasikili/Sedudu Island and that the island formed part of the territory of Botswana, and unanimously, that nationals and vessels flying the flag of Botswana and Namibia were entitled to "equal national treatment" in the two channels around the island.[1077]

The parties had agreed that the Court was to deliver its decision on the basis of the 1890 treaty, which they recognized as applicable and binding. It had been controversial, however, whether the special agreement conferred on the Court further tasks: Namibia had asked the Court to declare that it had sovereignty over Kasikili/Sedudu Island based on the Anglo-German treaty as well as prescription. Botswana's position had been that under the special agreement, the Court was only asked to determine the boundary under the 1890 treaty and prescription could therefore play no role.[1078] The special agreement had been somewhat imprecise in this respect, particularly as to whether the determination of the boundary and the legal status of the island constituted a single question or two separate questions, and the manner in which the reference to the applicable law was to be understood.[1079]

[1073] Ibid., para. 1. The special agreement is retrievable under http://212.153.43.18/icjwww/idocket/ibona/ibonaorders/ibona_iapplication_960529.htm.

[1074] Article I.   [1075] Article III.

[1076] Article IX ibid. The other provisions concern the proceedings and the entry into force of the agreement.

[1077] Judgment of 13 December 1999, para. 104. The dissenting votes came from Judges Weeramantry (Sri Lanka), Fleischhauer (Federal Republic of Germany), Parra-Aranguren (Venezuela), and Rezek (Brazil); Judges *ad hoc* had not been appointed. For details of the judgment, see *Apostolidis*, 45 AFDI (1999), at 434–51; *Evans*, 49 ICLQ (2000), at 964–78; and *Perry*, 8 IBRU Int'l Bound. & Sec. Bull. (2000), at 82–7.

[1078] See Judgment of 13 December 1999, paras. 90–2.

[1079] Ibid., Sep. Op. Oda, paras. 9–21, suggesting that the parties should have been asked to clarify their position on the subject of the dispute. He goes as far as to state that the provisions of the special agreement were contradictory: "How can the Court deal with such a contradiction in this case? It is my belief that the *compromis* prepared by both States was not drafted in a proper manner." (ibid., para. 19). Judge Kooijmans's view was that the issues of the boundary determination and the legal status of the island were so intrinsically linked that the answer to one of them would implicitly have answered the other one; on this basis, he argued that the Court should have declared Namibia's alternative claim based on prescription inadmissible, see Sep. Op. Kooijmans, paras. 5–20.

Against Botswana's view, the Court held that it was not only authorized to interpret the treaty in light of the rules and principles of international law, but that it was also asked to apply those rules and principles independently. Hence, after it had decided on the definition of the boundary under the treaty, it proceeded to consider the question of prescription.[1080] However, it held that Namibia had not fulfilled the conditions which it itself had cited as necessary for the acquisition of territory through prescription.[1081] On the basis of its findings on the boundary pursuant to the 1890 treaty and its rejection of Namibia's claims relating to prescription, the Court reached the result that Kasikili/Sedudu belonged to Botswana.[1082] Consequently, while the Court followed Namibia's broader interpretation of the special agreement, this had no negative consequences for Botswana since Namibia's substantive claim was rejected.

The issue of national treatment in both channels of the river had been emphasized by Botswana in its pleadings; neither party had included a claim explicitly relating to this matter in its final submissions. Yet, the Court conceived of this issue as part of the question of the legal status of Kasikili/Sedudu,[1083] a finding conducive to a final settlement of the dispute.[1084] Namibia, while disappointed, agreed to abide by the decision. The Namibian president issued the following statement: "As a law-abiding nation and consistent with our undertaking, I wish to ensure the international community that Namibia will abide by the verdict of the ICJ and respect it fully."[1085] The president of Botswana commended Namibia for the positive handling of the dispute and called the case's outcome a "victory" for both parties' commitment to the peaceful settlement of disputes.[1086] The dispute was regarded as resolved[1087] and hopes emerged that remaining controversies over other parts of the border could be settled.[1088]

[1080] Judgment of 13 December 1999, para. 93. See also *Evans*, 49 ICLQ (2000), at 965–7.

[1081] Ibid., paras. 90–9. The Court therefore did not feel compelled to explain the conditions for prescription. See also Kohen, 43 GYIL (2000), at 254–8.

[1082] Judgment of 13 December 1999, paras. 100–1.

[1083] Ibid., paras. 102–3 (including a quotation from Botswana from the hearings). It referred in this context to the Kasane Communiqué of 24 May 1992. For the submissions of the parties, see ibid., para. 9.

[1084] See the Declaration of Judge Koroma on this point: "This important finding by the Court should not be regarded as extra-legal but finds a solid basis in international law and the jurisprudence of the Court. [. . .] [W]hile respecting the terms of a special agreement empowering the Court to determine the riparian boundary between two states, the Court is entitled to lay down terms which not only determine the boundary as such but would contribute to the peace and stability between the two states. The judgment, in my view, serves this purpose as well."

[1085] See Maletsky, "Kasikili KO," The Namibian, 14 December 1999, 1999 WL 10594387 and www.namibian.com.na/Netstories/December99/ko.html.

[1086] Maletsky, "Praise for Namibia on Kasikili," Africa News Service, 16 December 1999, WL 25960463.

[1087] The Economist Intelligence Unit Ltd, Country Profile Namibia 2000/2001, 2 August 2000, 2000 WL 10568377.

[1088] The Economist Intelligence Unit Ltd, Country Report Namibia 2nd quarter 2000, 1 April 2000, 2000 WL 17329646.

Both parties were interested in a rapid settlement of the dispute and in the removal of this irritant of their relations, and they had agreed that the ICJ was the appropriate dispute settlement body. The fact that the special agreement had submitted to the Court the questions of the boundary and of the legal status of the island was a positive aspect from the point of view of ensuring the comprehensive settlement of the dispute. The reference to Article 38(1) of the ICJ Statute in addition to the 1890 treaty probably aimed at excluding the possibility of a ruling *ex aequo et bono*[1089] in case the treaty had been deemed irrelevant.[1090] Still, it might have been preferable to define more precisely whether the delimitation and the legal status of the island were one or two questions, the degree to which these issues were interrelated, and how the relationship between the 1890 treaty and the principles and rules of international law was to be understood. The lack of precision of the special agreement might have led to difficulties; however, as explained, the broader interpretation had no negative effects for the party advocating the narrower interpretation.

Despite all positive factors, one has to bear in mind that questions involving territorial sovereignty are always delicate. The amicable route by which this dispute ended up before the ICJ was not lost upon the judges; as one observed: "It has not been unknown for similar disputes to be the source of serious tension between two states or even to give rise to armed conflict."[1091] On the other hand, the decision had no fundamental consequences for the life of people in the region—the island was uninhabited, after all—and the Kasane communiqué and judgment ensured a continuation of existing social and economic activities and navigation.

XXVI. LaGrand

This case concerned a dispute between Germany and the United States concerning the treatment of the German nationals Karl and Walter LaGrand, who were convicted of murder and sentenced to death by an American Court in proceedings violating the Vienna Convention on Consular Relations (VCCR).[1092] While the case received particular attention

---

[1089] See Article 38(2) of the Statute: "This provision shall not prejudice the power of the Court to decide a case *et aequo et bono*, if the parties agree thereto."

[1090] See *Kohen*, 43 GYIL (2000), at 257.

[1091] Judgment of 13 December 1999, Declaration of Judge Koroma.

[1092] Vienna Convention on Consular Relations, 24 April 1963, 596 UNTS 261. The relevant provision in this case was Article 36, which reads:

(1) With a view to facilitating the exercise of consular functions relating to nationals of the sending state:

(a) consular officers shall be free to communicate with nationals of the sending State and to have access to them. Nationals of the sending State shall have the same freedom with respect to communication with and access to consular officers of the sending state;

because it involved capital punishment, the subject-matter of the ICJ proceedings was not the permissibility of the death penalty under international law, but rather the scope of obligations under the VCCR and the consequences of its breach. Paraguay had instituted a similar case against the US one year earlier in which the Court had indicated provisional measures; the case had been discontinued in November 1998 before the LaGrand proceedings were instituted.[1093]

1. The facts and the institution of proceedings before the Court

Walter and Karl LaGrand were born in Germany in 1962 and 1963, respectively; their mother brought them to the US in 1967, where they took up permanent residence. On 7 January 1982, they were arrested in connection with an attempted bank robbery in Marana, Arizona, during the course of which a bank manager had been killed and another bank employee seriously injured. An Arizona state Court convicted the brothers of first-degree murder among other charges in February 1984 and handed down death sentences in December 1984. Subsequent appeals and petitions for post-conviction relief failed. At no point during the trial or appellate phases before the Arizona state Courts had the LaGrands been informed of their right to receive consular assistance under Article 36 of the VCCR. The German consulate with jurisdiction over Arizona had likewise never been notified of their arrest; it was only in July 1992 that officials became aware of the case through contact from the LaGrands themselves, who had learned from sources other than US officials about rights created by the VCCR. The brothers raised this issue in *habeas corpus* proceedings before US federal courts, which rejected this complaint on the basis of the doctrine of procedural default. Under this doctrine, a state criminal defendant must have raised

---

(b) if he so requests, the competent authorities of the receiving state shall, without delay, inform the consular post of the sending state if, within its consular district, a national of that state is arrested or committed to prison or to custody pending trial or is detained in any other manner. Any communication addressed to the consular post by the person arrested, in prison, custody or detention shall also be forwarded by the said authorities without delay. The said authorities shall inform the person concerned without delay of his rights under this sub-paragraph;

(c) consular officers shall have the right to visit a national of the sending State who is in prison, custody or detention, to converse and correspond with him and to arrange for his legal representation. They shall also have the right to visit any national of the sending State who is in prison, custody or detention in their district in pursuance of a judgment. Nevertheless, consular officers shall refrain from taking action on behalf of a national who is in prison, custody or detention if he expressly opposes such action.

(2) The rights referred to in paragraph 1 of this article shall be exercised in conformity with the laws and regulations of the receiving state, subject to the proviso, however, that the said laws and regulations must enable full effect to be given to the purposes for which the rights accorded under this article are intended.

[1093] For details of that case (Vienna Convention on Consular Relations), see *infra* C IX.

a claim in a state Court before being eligible for *habeas* relief based on that claim in federal courts, absent a showing of cause and prejudice. The US authorities officially notified the LaGrands of their right to consular access only in December 1998; a few weeks later, the Arizona Supreme Court set execution dates for the inmates for 24 February (for Karl LaGrand) and 3 March 1999 (for Walter LaGrand). Various interventions of the German government to stay the executions proved unsuccessful, as did further petitions and appeals for clemency by the LaGrands. Karl LaGrand was executed as scheduled.[1094] The facts were largely undisputed, with the exception of the precise time when the Arizona authorities had become aware of the LaGrands' German citizenship.[1095]

On 2 March 1999 at 7.30 p.m. local time The Hague, some 27 hours before Walter LaGrand was to be executed, Germany instituted proceedings before the Court by unilateral application and filed a request for the indication of provisional measures to stay the execution pending a final decision in the case.[1096] On 3 March 1999, the Court indicated provisional measures and unanimously ordered the United States to take all measures at its disposal to ensure that Walter LaGrand was not executed pending the proceedings.[1097] The execution nevertheless took place as scheduled.[1098]

2. The parties' submissions

Although a basic objective of the proceedings—saving Walter LaGrand's life—became moot after his execution, Germany upheld its application and asked for a declaration that the US had breached its international legal obligations under Article 36(1) of the VCCR to Germany (in its own right and in its right of diplomatic protection of its nationals) by failing to inform the brothers of their rights under Article 36(1)(b) of the VCCR without delay and by depriving Germany of the possibility of rendering consular assistance. The German submissions also called for findings that the US had violated its duty under Article 36(2) to give full effect to the rights accorded by the provision in the application of its domestic law—particularly the doctrine of procedural default, which had barred the LaGrands from raising their claims under the VCCR—as well as the Court's order on provisional measures. Furthermore, Germany requested a guarantee of non-repetition from

---

[1094] For the summary of the facts, see LaGrand (Germany v. United States of America), Judgment of 27 June 2001, paras. 13–34; and *Murphy*, 93 AJIL (1999), at 644–5.

[1095] Judgment of 27 June 2001, paras. 15–16.

[1096] http://212.153.43.18/icjwww/idocket/igus/igusapplication/igus_iapplication_19990302.htm and http://212.153.43.18/icjwww/idocket/igus/igusapplication/igus_iapplication_iprovmeasures_19990302.html.

[1097] Order of 3 March 1999.

[1098] The details on the provisional measures and their follow-up will be described below at Section C X.

the US, an assurance that the US would ensure the effective exercise of the rights under Article 36 VCCR in future cases involving German nationals and, in particular in cases involving the death penalty, provide for effective review of, and remedies for, criminal convictions impaired by a violation of Article 36.

The US on their part asked the Court to adjudge and declare that there had been a breach of the US obligations to Germany under Article 36(1)(b) VCCR by the failure promptly to notify the LaGrands, that it had apologized for that breach and was taking substantial measures aimed at preventing any recurrence, and that all further claims were to be dismissed.[1099] It contested Germany's submissions relating to violations of Article 36(1)(a) and (c) arising out of the (uncontroversial) violation of Article 36(1)(b) with the argument that the underlying conduct was the same as for the violation of Article 36(1)(b)—the failure promptly to notify the LaGrand brothers—and that the Court should reject "Germany's attempt to transform a breach of one obligation into an additional breach of a wholly separate and distinct obligation."[1100] In so far as Germany relied upon a violation of rights of the LaGrand brothers, the US contested that the Vienna Convention established any rights for individuals.[1101] The US held that the VCCR did not require states to establish in their domestic legal systems a remedy for individuals to assert a lack of notification under Article 36(1)(b) and that "the relevant laws and regulations" under Article 36(2) were only those relating to the exercise of specific rights under Article 36(1), such as the timing of communications, visiting hours, and security in a detention facility.[1102] With regard to the provisional measures order, the US claimed that the order did not have binding force and that it had done what had been called for by the order, considering the constraints on its ability to act posed by the federal structure of the United States and the practical matter of the short time between the issuance of the order and the time set for the execution.[1103] Concerning guarantees of non-repetition, the United States pointed to its current efforts to ensure compliance with Article 36 and argued that the German claim had no basis in the VCCR.[1104]

Germany founded the Court's jurisdiction on Article I of the optional protocol to the VCCR on dispute settlement (as the US had done in US

[1099] Final submissions of the parties, Judgment 27 June 2001, para. 12. For the submissions at earlier stages, see ibid., paras. 10–11: first, in the application, Germany had raised further state responsibility claims, asking the Court to declare the imposition of criminal responsibility on Karl and Walter LaGrand was void and was to be recognized as such by the US legal authorities, that the US should provide reparation in form of compensation and satisfaction for Karl LaGrand's execution and was to restore the *status quo ante* for Walter LaGrand; in the memorial, those claims were dropped and only the claim for a guarantee of non-repetition was maintained.

[1100] Judgment of 27 June 2001, para. 69.   [1101] Ibid., para. 76.
[1102] Ibid., paras. 84–7.   [1103] Ibid., paras. 94–7.   [1104] Ibid., para. 119.

Diplomatic and Consular Staff in Tehran),[1105] which conferred jurisdiction on the Court for disputes concerning the interpretation and application of the Convention.[1106] While the US had not filed preliminary objections, it raised some arguments relating to jurisdiction and admissibility: it contested the Court's jurisdiction for the German claim based on diplomatic protection as well as for the request for guarantees of non-repetition, arguing that those issues were not questions of the interpretation or application of the Vienna Convention, but matters of customary law for which there was no jurisdictional basis,[1107] and that the diplomatic protection claim was inadmissible because of a failure to exhaust local remedies.[1108] The US argued that some of Germany's claims were inadmissible because in granting them the Court would take up the role of an ultimate court of appeal in national criminal proceedings,[1109] and that the manner in which Germany had launched the proceedings had been such as to render its claim of non-compliance with the provisional measures order inadmissible.[1110]

Yet, as stated above, the US readily conceded its violation of the Article 36(1)(b) towards Germany, denying neither jurisdiction nor admissibility for this substantive claim.[1111] Most significantly, it did not use its acknowledgment of a breach to deny the existence of a dispute, but to the contrary even requested a ruling of the Court in this respect.[1112] This demonstrated that the United States at least up to a certain extent regarded the Court as an appropriate forum to settle the dispute, despite its opposition to many of Germany's submissions. While the United States disagreed with Germany about the extent of rights under Article 36 and the legal consequences of a breach of the duty to notify, it recognized the fundamental importance of effective implementation of Article 36(1)(b), given its own interest in the

---

[1105] See *supra* XIV 3.

[1106] Optional Protocol to the Vienna Convention on Consular Relations concerning the compulsory settlement of disputes, 24 April 1963, 596 UNTS 487. The US ratified on 24 November 1969; Germany, on 7 September 1971, see ST/LEG/SER.E/19, 123. Article 1 of the Optional Protocol reads: "Disputes arising out of the interpretation or application of the Convention shall lie within the compulsory jurisdiction of the International Court of Justice and may accordingly be brought before the Court by an application made by any party to the dispute being a Party to the present Protocol."

[1107] Judgment of 27 June 2001, paras. 40, 46.   [1108] Ibid., para. 58.

[1109] Ibid., para. 50.   [1110] Ibid., para. 53.

[1111] Unlike for Germany's claims of a violation of an obligation under this provision towards the LaGrand brothers, raised in the exercise of diplomatic protection: ibid., para. 40.

[1112] See the US final submissions, ibid., para. 12: "The United States of America respectfully requests the Court to adjudge and declare that (1) There was a breach of the United States obligation to Germany under Article 36, paragraph 1 (b), of the Vienna Convention on Consular Relations, in that the competent authorities of the United States did not promptly give to Karl and Walter LaGrand the notification required by that Article [. . .]; and (2) All other claims and submissions of the Federal Republic of Germany are to be dismissed." See also ibid., para. 39: "[The United States] does not deny that this violation of Article 36, paragraph 1 (b), has given rise to a dispute between the two States and recognizes that the Court has jurisidiction under the Protocol to hear this dispute in so far as it concerns Germany's own rights."

protection of American citizens abroad. Moreover, it reported to have taken a variety of measures to improve compliance with that obligation.[1113]

3. The judgment of 27 June 2001

The Court's judgment of 27 June 2001 was largely in Germany's favor.[1114] The Court found that the optional protocol conferred jurisdiction over all questions raised by Germany and that Germany's submissions were admissible.[1115] It ruled by 14 votes to 1 that the US had breached its obligations to Germany and to the LaGrand brothers under Article 36(1) and (2) of the VCCR.[1116] By 13 votes to 2, it decided that the US had breached the obligation incumbent upon it under the Court's order indicating provisional measures.[1117] Unanimously, it found that the commitment undertaken by the US to ensure implementation of its obligations under Article 36(1)(b) of the Convention had to be regarded as meeting Germany's request for a general assurance of non-repetition.[1118] By 14 votes to 1, it decided that should German nationals nonetheless be sentenced to severe penalties without their rights under Article 36(1)(b) having been respected, the US by means

---

[1113] Such as the publication of a brochure on consular rights and a pocket card, materials distributed to the competent domestic authorities. Ibid., paras. 119, 121, 123–4.

[1114] For details, see *Aceves*, 96 AJIL (2002), at 210–18; *Hillgruber*, 57 JZ (2002), at 94–9; *Kirgis*, http://www.asil.org/insights/insigh75.htm; *Oellers-Frahm*, 28 EuGRZ (2001), at 265–72; *Tams*, http://www.ejil.org/journal/Vol13/No5/sr1.html.

[1115] Judgment of 27 June 2001, para. 128(1), (2). The decision on jurisdiction was taken by 14 votes to 1 (with Judge Parra-Aranguren (Venezuela) dissenting), the decisions on admissibility ranged from 12 votes to 3 to 14 votes to 1 (first German submission (violation of Article 36(1): 13 to 2, with Judges Oda and Parra-Aranguren dissenting, second German submission (Article 36(2)): 14 votes to 1 (with Judge Oda dissenting), third German submission (violation of the order indicating provisional measures): 12 votes to 3 (with Judges Oda, Parra-Aranguren, and Buergenthal dissenting), fourth German submission (guarantees of non-repetition): 14 votes to 1 (Judge Oda dissenting).)

[1116] The obligations under para. 1 by not informing the LaGrands without delay of their rights under Article 36(1)(b), the obligation under paragraph 2 by not permitting review and reconsideration of the LaGrands' convictions and sentences after the violation of paragraph 1 had occurred, ibid., paras. 73–4, 77, 128(3), (4). Judge Oda dissented. The Court found that Article 36(1) established an interrelated régime for the implementation of the system of consular protection and that in cases of a violation of Article 36(1)(b), the sending state would be unable to exercise its rights under Article 36(1)(a) and (c); it concluded that the US had also violated Article 36(1)(a) and (c) as a result of the violation of Article 36(1)(b) (para. 74). Concerning the question whether Article 36(1) conferred rights on individuals, the Court based its affirmative answer on the "clarity of these provisions, viewed in their context" (para. 77). As to Article 36(2), the Court clarified that it was not the procedural default rule as such that violated Article 36(2), but the problem arose where the application of the rule resulted in preventing the detained individual from challenging the conviction and sentence (para. 90).

[1117] Ibid., paras. 112–15, 128(5). Judges Oda and Parra-Aranguren dissented. The Court carried out an interpretation of Article 41 of its Statute and concluded that its orders indicating provisional measures were binding. It examined the US behavior and found that it had failed to comply with the order. For details, see *infra* C X 3.

[1118] Ibid., paras. 124, 128(6).

of its own choosing would have to allow the review and reconsideration of the conviction and sentence by taking account of the violation of the rights set forth in the VCCR.[1119]

The judgment contains important findings likely to influence the development of international law. The Court's statements on the scope of the obligations under Article 36 effectively reinforced the significance of the right to consular assistance and affirmed that this provision contained rights for individuals as well as for states.[1120] Also the findings on state responsibility with regard to guarantees of non-repetition were important, and most significantly for the role of the Court, there was for the first time in its history an explicit statement to the extent that provisional measures under Article 41 of the Statute are binding. At the same time, it is noticeable that the Court cautiously avoided discussions not necessary to settle the dispute, leaving open the question whether, as Germany had claimed, the right of the individual to be informed under Article 36(1)(b) VCCR had the character of a human right.[1121] The Court deferred to the discretion of the US in choosing the appropriate means to fulfill its international obligations and sidestepped the issue of the illegality of a domestic law. Moreover, it abstained from comments on the permissibility and evaluation of the death penalty: this was a prudent approach, as the death penalty was explicitly not subject-matter of the proceedings and any unnecessary comments on this issue would have politicized the judgment and endangered its acceptability.[1122]

4. Action required by the United States in order to comply with the judgment

The subject-matter of the judgment is rather delicate, as it concerns domestic criminal proceedings, thereby affecting the US domestic sphere, and although the legality of capital punishment was not at stake, the case's political dimension is characterized by the fact that the death penalty had

---

[1119] Ibid., paras. 125–7, 128(7). Judge Oda dissented. The Court recognized that the US could not guarantee that violations of the VCCR would not occur ever again; this had not been contested by Germany.

[1120] See in particular *Vierucci*, 94 RDI (2001), at 686–710.

[1121] Judgment of 27 June 2001, para. 78. An affirmative finding on this question had been made by the Inter-American Court of Human Rights in its Advisory Opinion OC-16/99 of 1 October 1999, www.corteidh.or.cr/Serie_A_ing/Serie_A_16_ing.doc, at paras. 122, 124, 136. For details, see *Aceves*, 94 AJIL (2000), at 555–63. As the ICJ left the question open, the judgment cannot be taken to contradict the IACHR's advisory opinion; it was not quoted in the judgment. See also *Oellers-Frahm*, 28 EuGRZ (2001), at 267–8. Negative on a human rights character of the respective obligations, see *Vierucci*, 94 RDI (2001), at 701–7, 710.

[1122] See already the Order indicating provisional measures, at para. 25: "Whereas the issues before the Court in this case do not concern the entitlement of the federal states within the United States to resort to the death penalty for the most heinous crimes." See *Tams*, http://www.ejil.org/journal/Vol13/No5/sr1.html at 4 (welcoming Court's avoidance of "unnecessary discussion of matters of principle which might have endangered the acceptability of the judgment").

been imposed, a penalty generating intense controversy at both the national and international levels.[1123]

The section of the judgment's operative part decisive for the question of compliance is the finding that the US must allow for review and consideration of the conviction and sentence in future cases of imposition of severe penalties against German citizens where Article 36 VCCR had been violated.[1124] The finding is explicitly directed to future conduct of the US, whereas the preceding decisions are declaratory and evaluate past US behavior. It concerns such cases where the ordinary proceedings against an accused are concluded with a conviction; it does not decide the question of how a violation of Article 36(2) is to be cured during those proceedings.[1125] In order to understand the scope of the US obligation to allow for "review and reconsideration," it is useful to consider the respective findings in context with the other pronouncements of the judgment—in particular, with the findings on Germany's second submission relating to a breach of Article 36(2) through the application of US domestic law.[1126] The Court did not hold the doctrine of procedural default illegal, but decided that its actual application in the LaGrand case (which had prevented the violations of Article 36 of the Convention from being taken into account) had constituted a violation of Article 36(2). It explicitly stated that it had "not found that a United States law, whether substantive or procedural in character, is inherently inconsistent with the obligations undertaken by the United States under the Vienna Convention" and held that the US retained the choice of means to ensure the review and reconsideration.[1127] It did not specify steps under domestic procedural law through which review and reconsideration was to be effected (such as, for example, through an annulment of the sentence),[1128] or amendments of the law possibly required or recommendable. From the

---

[1123] See *Tams* http://www.ejil.org/journal/Vol13/No5/sr1.html at fn 2 with references to newspapers pointing to (alleged) implications of the judgment for the death penalty; *Mennecke*, 44 GYIL (2001), at 467–8.

[1124] Critical on the respective formula of the judgment's operative part dissenting opinion Judge Oda, para. 37: "I am utterly at a loss as to what the Court intends to say in this subparagraph."

[1125] This remains a question of interpretation of Article 36 VCCR (in the context of which the Court's reasoning might become relevant). As most effective implementation, one might think of the supression of evidence gathered in violation of the VCCR: American courts might analogize this with the so-called "Miranda warnings" concerning basic procedural rights (rights not to incriminate onself, to legal representation, etc.; derives from Supreme Court decision in Miranda v. Arizona, 384 US 436 (1966)), although most have refused to do so thus far. See *Paulus*, 23 StV (2003), at 58; *Woodman*, 70 JKaBA (2001), at 41–50. On possibilities for restitution, see also *Weigend* in Prittwitz, Festschrift für Lüdersen, at 469–70.

[1126] Judgment of 27 June 2001, paras. 79–91.   [1127] Judgment of 27 June 2001, para. 125.

[1128] For possible ways, see *Aceves*, 96 AJIL (2002), at 217. The Inter-American Court of Human Rights went further and stated that the imposition of the death penalty after proceedings including a failure to comply with Article 36 VCCR constituted a violation of the right not to be arbitrarily deprived of one's life, see OC–16/99 *supra* n. 1121, para. 137. Critical on this approach *Vierucci*, 94 RDI (2001), at 707–9.

perspective of compliance, the observation that the legislature has not taken action is, hence, inconclusive; the practice in future cases involving "severe penalties" against German nationals in scenarios such as LaGrand will show whether the US complies with the judgment.

It remains to be seen whether, and by which means, the US will give effect to its obligation. Clemency procedures alone might not suffice as there will be doubts on whether they are an effective remedy,[1129] and the fact that the Arizona governor had taken note of the violations of the Vienna Convention in her decision to proceed with Walter LaGrand's execution[1130] had not prevented the Court from finding that there was a violation of Article 36(2) VCCR in the concrete case.

The Court states that an apology will not be sufficient "in cases where the individuals concerned have been subjected to prolonged detention or convicted and sentenced to severe penalties,"[1131] which appears to imply that in lighter cases this *might* be sufficient.[1132] The Court speaks of severe penalties, not of the death penalty; at the very least, this will also comprise cases of the life sentence.[1133] The Court's reference to German nationals is due to the *inter partes* effect of the judgment:[1134] if the US were to disregard the Court's findings with regard to nationals of other states, it would not violate its obligation to comply with the Court's judgment under Article 94(1) of the UN Charter. Yet, there would not be any reason why the proper interpretation of the Vienna Convention should be any different in relation to nationals of other state parties. As ICJ President Guillaume observed: "... [S]ubparagraph (7) does not address the position of nationals of other countries or that of individuals sentenced to penalties that are not of a severe nature. However, in order to avoid any ambiguity, it should be made clear that there can be no question of applying an *a contrario* interpretation to this

---

[1129] See *Aceves*, 96 AJIL (2002), at 217; *Mennecke*, 44 GYIL (2001), at 459: "Only a judicial 'review and reconsideration' meets the terms of Germany's claim and the essence of the Court's formula."

[1130] See *infra* n. 1763.

[1131] Judgment of 27 June 2001, para. 125. The judgment's operative part only takes up severe penalties, not cases of prolonged detention, see para. 128(7).

[1132] Tams argues (http://www.ejil.org/journal/Vol13/No5/sr1.html at 3D) that by referring to cases of "prolonged detention [...] or severe penalties," the Court wanted to establish stricter obligations than for "ordinary" breaches of Article 26: "It is only with regard to the [...] narrower category of cases involving prolonged detention and and severe penalties that the ICJ expressly obliges the United States to adopt positive measures to change the present legal situation."

[1133] See Simma, Remarks, Consular Rights and the Death Penalty after LaGrand, [2002] Proc. ASIL 310, at 311. Simma, co-agent and counsel for Germany in the case, explained that Germany "would take up only those cases where a minimum prior sentence of five years is invoked." He reports that current cases of German nationals supposedly convicted in proceedings under breach of the Vienna Convention are not death penalty cases, so the classification of "severe penalties" might become relevant in practice.

[1134] See Article 59 of the Statute.

paragraph."[1135] Without doubt, it would violate the spirit of the judgment and harm the Court's authority if the US were to disregard the Court's conclusions in relation to other countries' nationals, even if it was no separate violation of Article 94(1) apart from a violation of the Vienna Convention.

At this time, it is still too early to assess US compliance with the judgment; instructive will be the practice in future cases, particularly the response by American courts.[1136] One example illustrates: in a case similar to the LaGrands', Gerardo Valdez, a Mexican citizen, had been sentenced to death in Oklahoma in 1990. Mexican authorities only became aware of the case in April 2001. Valdez's defense lawyers raised the LaGrand judgment with apparently positive results: on 1 May 2002, the Court of Criminal Appeals of Oklahoma granted Valdez's application for post-conviction relief and remanded the case for re-sentencing since relevant evidence had not been discovered due to the inexperience and ineffectiveness of Breard's court-appointed counsel—evidence that would have been discovered earlier with the assistance of the Mexican consulate (which would evidently have taken place)—and that this error had resulted in a miscarriage of justice.[1137] The

---

[1135] Declaration of President Guillaume.

[1136] See Brown, Remarks, Consular Rights and the Death Penalty after LaGrand, [2002] Proc. ASIL. 312, at 313. Brown, the deputy agent for the United States in LaGrand, stated: "[...] I identified at least a dozen of issues that will keep our courts busy for the next decade or so [...] [T]he judiciary will [...] have an important role in deciding what the US response will be." For steps that the federal government might take, see Quigley, Remarks, Consular Rights and the Death Penalty after LaGrand, [2002] Proc. ASIL at 315.

[1137] Valdez v. State, 2002 OK CR 20 (Okla. Crim. App. 2002), 2002 WL 809243. For an overview of the case, and the various stages of proceedings, and the opinion, see American University/Washington College of Law, Focus on Capital Punishment: Current cases—Gerardo Valdez, http://web.archive.org/web/20021022225745/http://www.wcl.american.edu/humright/deathpenalty/valdez.html, The International Justice Project, Gerardo Valdez, http://www.internationaljusticeproject.org/nationalsGValdez.cfm: on 20 July 2001, Oklahoma's governor rejected the parole board's clemency recommendation. He stated that he had consulted with the US Departments of State and Justice and pursuant to the ICJ verdict in LaGrand had carried out a review and reconsideration of the conviction and sentence. On 17 August 2001, the governor granted a 30-day stay referring, *inter alia*, to "complicated questions of international law presented by this case." The state criminal appeals court ordered an indefinite stay on 10 September 2001 (2001 WL 1715885) and ultimately remanded the decision for resentencing. The technical reason for remand was a violation of domestic law (ineffective assistance of counsel), not the violation of the Vienna Convention *per se*. The Oklahoma Court of Criminal Appeals held that it could not regard the LaGrand judgment as overruling the US Supreme Court in *Breard* v. *Greene*: "For this Court to decide the ICJ's ruling overrules a binding decision of the [...] Supreme Court and affords a judicial remedy to an individual for the violation of the Convention would interfere with the nation's foreign affairs and run afoul of the U.S. Constitution." (para. 23). It was hardly to be expected and not required under international law that a US domestic Court would explicitly state that the ICJ had invalidated a ruling of its highest Court. Decisive was in any case that the Court decision layed the basis for a judicial review and reconsideration of Valdez's conviction, enabling the Mexican consulate to provide the evidence which it would have presented had it timely been notified; the effects were therefore the same as a remand directly based on the violation of the Vienna Convention. See for details of the Oklahoma Court decision *Hoss*, RGDIP (2003), 401–14. For an assessment of the potential impact of *LaGrand* on the *Valdez* case prior to that decision, see *Mennecke*, 44 GYIL (2001), at 461–6.

Mexican ministry of foreign affairs praised the "unprecedented decision."[1138] It might be an indication that American courts and the executive will take a different approach to the impact of violations of the Vienna Convention on Consular Relations than before the LaGrand judgment;[1139] perhaps the Supreme Court will eventually again be seized with the matter.[1140] Speculations that similar cases might be brought before the ICJ again[1141] were confirmed when Mexico instituted proceedings in the Avena case on 9 January 2003 after just recently having acceded to the optional protocol to the Vienna Convention:[1142] the judgment in that case will provide

[1138] See Mexican Ministry of Foreign Affairs, Press Release No. 079/02, "The death sentence for a Mexican in the United States is annulled," www.sre.gob.mx/e-bulletins/2002/may/B-79.htm; Mark Warren, "Consular notification and assistance—a guide for attorneys," July 2002, www3.sympatico.ca/aiwarren/attorneys.htm (refering to case as "first domestic death penalty case to take full cognizance of the LaGrand decision").

[1139] For a rather pessimistic assessment prior to the Valdez decision, see Quigley, Remarks, Consular Rights and the Death Penalty after LaGrand, [2002] Proc. ASIL at 315: "The LaGrand judgment has had little impact on the practice of US courts. In the nine months since the judgment was rendered, US courts have continued to deny a remedy in cases involving Article 36 claims. They have not altered their analysis. Some have acknowledged the fact that the ICJ issued the LaGrand judgment but not indicated its content nor replied to it."
The recent death-row case involving the Mexican national Javier Suárez Medina aggravates the prevailing sense of pessimism. Mexican President Vicente Fox had personally intervened to halt the execution, invoking the violation of the Vienna Convention in the case. Nevertheless, the governor of Texas decided to proceed with the execution in August 2002. State and federal authorities made no efforts to halt the execution, which led to strong protest from Mexico. See "Texas executes Mexican murderer," BBC News, http://news.bbc.co.uk/2/hi/world/americas/2192464.stm.
Other actors such as the EU and the UN Subcommission on Human Rights had also called for a halt to the execution, making explicit reference to the LaGrand judgment. See letters of 23 July 2002 from the EU Delegation to the UN to the governor of Texas and to the Texas Board of Pardons and Paroles, www.eurunion.org/legislat/DeathPenalty/SuarezMedinaVTexGovPerry.htm, www.eurunion.org/legislat/deathpenalty/SuarezMedinaVTexBdPards.htm; Mexican Presidency press release, "Human Rights Subcommission urges United States to stay execution of Mexican national," 8 August 2002, www.presidencia.gob.mx/?P=42&Orden=Leer&Tipo=&Art=3481.

[1140] If there had been no remand for resentencing in Valdez, it might already have been the test case for the Supreme Court. See Brown, Remarks, Consular Rights and the Death Penalty after LaGrand, [2002] Proc. ASIL 312, at 315: "In any event, Valdez is probably the case in which the United States will decide, for our judicial branch, how the United States should respond to LaGrand." *If* the US Supreme Court were to change the direction it took in *Breard* v. *Greene*, American Courts would doubtlessly follow.

[1141] See Fitzpatrick, Introduction, Consular Rights and the Death Penalty after LaGrand, [2002] Proc. ASIL 309, at 310: The remedy problem may recur in future ICJ adjudications. US courts are making little headway in devising remedies that would deter violations of Article 36, leaving the responsibility with the executive branch and possibly Congress to improve compliance by both federal and state law enforcement agencies.

[1142] http://212.153.43.18/icjwww/idocket/imus/imusorder/imus_iapplication_20030109.PDF. Mexicans rank first among foreign nationals awaiting capital punishment in the US; violations of the Vienna Convention may be of relevance in many cases: American University/Washington College of Law, "Focus on Death Penalty," http://web.archive.org/web/20021102183120/http://www.wcl.american.edu/humright/deathpenalty/vccr.html; Death Penalty Information Center, "Foreign nationals and the death penalty in the United States," http://www.deathpenaltyinfo.org/article.php?did=198&scid=31.

further guidance on the findings in the LaGrand case, as a core question raised by Mexico is precisely the content of the remedies in the event of a breach of the obligations under Article 36 VCCR.[1143]

XXVII. Arrest warrant of 11 April 2000

1. Background of the case

The case concerned the legality of an arrest warrant *in absentia* issued by the Belgian judge Damien Vandermeersch for Abdulaye Yerodia Ndombasi, at that time foreign minister of the Democratic Republic of the Congo. The arrest warrant, which was circulated internationally, accused Mr Ndombasi of crimes against humanity and grave breaches of the 1949 Geneva Conventions and their 1977 Additional Protocols I and II, charges punishable under a Belgian act concerning grave breaches of international humanitarian law.[1144] The warrant alleged that in 1998, at a time when he served as President Laurent Kabila's principal private secretary (*directeur du cabinet*), Mr Yerodia had incited racial hatred leading to a massacre of Tutsi residents of Kinshasa through broadcast speeches, in which he had referred to ethnic Tutsis as "vermin" worthy of "extermination." Mr Yerodia was not a Belgian citizen and not present on Belgian territory; there were no Belgian citizens among the victims. Private individuals living in Belgium had initiated the complaint in Belgian courts.[1145]

The DRC protested, stating that Belgium had acted contrary to international law by issuing and circulating the arrest warrant. It submitted a unilateral application to the ICJ on 17 October 2000.[1146] A clear jurisdictional basis existed as both parties had made declarations under Article 36(2) of the Statute without reservations,[1147] although the wording of the DRC's

---

[1143] See Mexico's memorial, Ch. 6, http://212.153.43.18/icjwww/idocket/imus/imuspleadings/imus_ipleadings_20030620_memorial_06.pdf; and the US Counter-Memorial, Chapter VIII, http://212.153.43.18/icjwww/idocket/imus/imuspleadings/imus_ipleadings_20031103_c-mem_08.pdf.

[1144] Act of 16 June 1993 concerning the punishment of grave breaches of the Geneva Conventions of 12 August 1949 and their Additional Protocols I and II of 18 June 1977 as modified by the Act of 10 February 1999 concerning the punishment of grave breaches of international humanitarian law, reprinted in 38 ILM (1999), 918–25. For details, see *De Smet/ Naert*, 33 RBDI (2002), at 471–511.

[1145] See the summary of facts in the Judgment of 14 February 2002, at 13–20; and *Gray*, http://www.ejil.org/journal/Vol13/No3/sr1.html.

[1146] http://212.153.43.18/icjwww/idocket/iCOBE/iCOBEapplication/iCOBE_iApplication_20001017.PDF.

[1147] Declaration of Belgium recognizing as compulsory the jurisdiction of the International Court of Justice of 3 April 1958, 302 UNTS 251 (excluding only such disputes with regard to which the parties had agreed to another dispute settlement method), Declaration of Zaire recognizing as compulsory the jurisdiction of the International Court of Justice of 7 February 1989, 1523 UNTS 299.

application laid out the issue of jurisdiction somewhat vaguely.[1148] In the course of the oral proceedings on provisional measures, however, the DRC explicitly invoked the declarations under the optional clause after Belgium had contended that the Court prima facie lacked jurisdiction since the applicant had failed to refer to any particular jurisdictional provision.[1149] Both parties essentially agreed on the facts of the case essential for the proceedings before the Court.[1150] Controversial, however, was the applicable law, in particular, the scope of immunity to be granted to a foreign minister. The DRC application challenged the warrant based both on the Belgian judge's lack of jurisdiction and on the failure to respect the immunity of a foreign minister; the memorial and the final submissions invoked only the issue of immunity.[1151] The DRC explained that the question as to whether the arrest warrant was an exercise of excessive jurisdiction was only a secondary consideration, and that an examination of this question, if undertaken by the Court, would not be carried out at the request of Congo but rather "by virtue of the defense strategy adopted by Belgium."[1152] Belgium observed that considering the DRC's definition of its claims, the principle of *non ultra petita* prevented the Court from addressing the issue of universal jurisdiction.[1153]

The DRC argued that during their terms of office, foreign ministers enjoyed absolute immunity from criminal process with regard to all acts, including those committed in a private capacity or prior to their terms of office. It contended that the mere existence and circulation of the arrest warrant constituted a violation of Belgium's obligation to grant absolute

---

[1148] It had stated that "Belgium has accepted the jurisdiction of the Court and, in so far as may be required, the present Application signifies acceptance of that jurisdiction by the Democratic Republic of the Congo." Application, *supra* n. 1146, at 15.

[1149] See the statements on behalf of the parties in the hearings on provisional measures: Statement on Ntumba Luaba Lumu, counsel and advocate, on behalf of the Democratic Republic of the Congo, Public Sitting of 22 November 2000, CR/2000/34, No. 2, http://212.153.43.18/icjwww/idocket/iCOBE/iCOBEcr/iCOBE_icr2000-34.html; Statement of Daniel Bethlehem, counsel and advocate, on behalf of Belgium, Public Sitting of 21 November 2000, CR/2000/33, paras. 17–35, http://212.153.43.18/icjwww/idocket/iCOBE/iCOBEcr/iCOBE_icr 2000-33.html. At his next statement of 23 November 2000, CR 2000/35, http://212.153.43.18/icjwww/idocket/iCOBE/iCOBEcr/iCOBE_icr2000-35.html following Congo's explicit invocation of Article 36(2), Mr Bethlehem argued that the Court abstain from indicating provisional measures for reasons of procedural fairness, since the basis for jurisdiction had not been defined earlier (ibid., at paras. 7–10). The Court rejected that argument see Order of 8 December 2000, paras. 63–4. Critical on this point, see *Wickremasinghe*, 50 ICLQ (2001), at 674.

[1150] See Judgment of 14 February 2002, para. 15. It is important to remember that the question whether the charges against Mr Yerodia were founded in substance was not subject of the proceedings before the Court. Mr Yerodia supposedly admits to have used the words reported, but states that he was referring to aggressors in general and not to any particular race: Race charge against Congo minister, BBC News, 5 July 2000, http://news.bbc.co.uk/hi/english/world/africa/newsid_821000/821096.stm.

[1151] Judgment of 14 February 2002, para. 45.   [1152] Ibid., para. 42.

[1153] Ibid., para. 41.

immunity to an incumbent foreign minister, regardless of its execution.[1154] Belgium countered that a foreign minister's immunity covered only official acts and not those committed in a private capacity, that the charges against Mr Yerodia related to events prior to his period of office, and that immunities afforded no protection against charges of war crimes and crimes against humanity.[1155] It argued that the warrant could not infringe upon Congo's sovereignty because it did not oblige the authorities of another state to arrest Mr Yerodia in the absence of further steps by Belgium completing or validating it; for its execution within Belgium, the warrant contained an exception waiving its execution in the event Mr Yerodia was present in Belgium on an official invitation.[1156] As for remedies, the DRC asked the Court to order Belgium to cancel and withdraw the warrant. Belgium maintained that it was under no such obligation since there was no way the warrant could infringe upon an incumbent foreign minister's immunity since Mr Yerodia had left office.[1157]

2. The judgment of 14 February 2002

In its judgment of 14 February 2002, the Court found by 15 votes to 1 that the DRC's claims were admissible, that it had jurisdiction, and that the case was not moot despite the fact that Mr Yerodia was no longer occupying an official government position at the time of the judgment. By 13 votes to 3, it decided that the issuance of the arrest warrant and its circulation violated the obligation to respect the immunity from criminal jurisdiction and the inviolability enjoyed by a foreign minister under international law. By 10 votes to 6, it ordered Belgium to cancel the warrant by means of its own choosing and inform accordingly the authorities to whom it had been circulated.[1158]

In the evaluation of the legality of the arrest warrant, the Court found that as a matter of logic, the question of Belgium's jurisdiction under international law would have had to be decided prior to the one relating to the violation of immunities, but following Congo's final submissions that had not formally contained a claim of violation of the principles of jurisdiction, it addressed the question of immunity first.[1159] Since the Court then concluded

---

[1154] Judgment of 14 February 2002, paras. 47, 63–4.   [1155] Ibid., paras. 49, 50, 56.
[1156] Ibid., paras. 65–6.   [1157] Ibid., paras. 72–4.
[1158] On the first point, Judge Oda (Japan) was the only dissenting judge, the second point was adopted against the votes of Judges Oda (Japan) and Al-Khasawneh (Jordan) and Belgium's Judge *ad hoc* Van den Wyngaert, the third point was adopted against the votes of Judges Oda (Japan), Higgins (United Kingdom), Kooijmans (Netherlands), Al-Khasawneh (Jordan), Buergenthal (United States), and Belgium's Judge *ad hoc* Van den Wyngaert, see ibid., para. 78. For details of the judgment, see *Cassese*, http://www.ejil.org/journal/curdevs/sr31.html; *Czaplinski*, 78 F-W (2003), 63–75; *Verhoeven*, 33 RBDI (2002), at 531–5; *Wouters*, 16 Leid. JIL (2003), at 253–67.
[1159] Judgment of 14 February 2002, para. 46.

that the immunity was violated, there was no need to address the scope of universal jurisdiction; several judges did, however, take up the matter in separate opinions.[1160]

The Court found that, under customary international law, incumbent foreign ministers enjoy full immunity from criminal proceedings to ensure the effective performance of their functions, regardless of the nature and dates of the acts committed, and it saw no exception to this rule for national Courts.[1161] It affirmed, however, that immunity did not mean impunity, that the issues of immunity and criminal responsibility had to be distinguished, and that there were certain circumstances in which immunity did not represent a bar to criminal proceedings against a foreign minister. The Court mentioned four such scenarios. Foreign ministers may be tried by their own states. Their states may choose to waive their immunity since immunity served the state and not the foreign minister in a personal capacity. A third possibility is that after a foreign minister leaves office, a Court of another state might launch proceedings for acts committed prior to the term of office or for private acts committed during the term of office. Another possibility lies in international criminal tribunals, which might possess jurisdiction to conduct criminal proceedings against both former and incumbent foreign ministers.[1162] The Court did not explicitly state whether this list of scenarios was intended to be exhaustive, although the careful drafting and qualification as exceptions seem to suggest that it was.[1163] On the other hand, it is imaginable that those were simply the scenarios on which there was a consensus within the Court that prosecution was possible, whereas in other cases there was disagreement.[1164] In any event, this paragraph in the judgment represented an *obiter dictum*; the operative part was based on the preceding statement that there was no exception to the immunity of incumbent foreign ministers for national Courts.

Applying the findings of the scope of immunity to the concrete arrest warrant, the Court found that the warrant affected the DRC's conduct of its foreign affairs and that its issuance and circulation violated Mr Yerodia's immunity under international law.[1165] With regard to the remedies, it

[1160] See ibid., Sep. Op. Guillaume, paras. 4–17; the Sep. Op. Rezek, paras. 4–10; Decl. Ranjeva, paras. 6–12; Joint Sep. Op. Higgins, Kooijmans, and Buergenthal, paras. 19–65; Sep. Op. Judge *ad hoc* Bula Bula, paras. 63–83; Diss. Op. Judge *ad hoc* van den Wyngaert, paras. 40–67. For a critical comment on the Court's omission to rule on this issue, see *Czaplinski*, 78 F-W (2003), at 68–72; for the contrary view that the Court's silence was preferable so as to leave room for the further developments of the law, see *Cot*, 35 RBDI (2002), 546–53.

[1161] Ibid., paras. 51–8.   [1162] Ibid., paras. 59–61.

[1163] See *Cassese*, http://www.ejil.org/journal/curdevs/sr31.html, Nr.7a.

[1164] In a press statement of 14 February 2002 reporting on the Court's decision (http://212.153.43.18/icjwww/ipresscom/SPEECHES/iSpeechPresident_Guillaume_cobe%20judgement_20020214.htm), ICJ President Guillaume pointed to the Court's emphasis that "Ministers for Foreign Affairs do not enjoy any immunity from criminal jurisdiction under international law in their own countries."

[1165] Judgment of 14 February 2002, at para. 71.

followed the DRC's submissions and ruled that Belgium as *restitutio in integrum* had to cancel the arrest warrant and inform the authorities to which it had been circulated accordingly, and that the finding on Belgium's responsibility constituted a satisfaction for Congo's moral injury.[1166]

3. The implications of the judgment

The Court had laid out Belgium's obligations in clear terms: it had to cancel the arrest warrant and inform the states to which it had been circulated accordingly. However, would Belgium be free to issue a new arrest warrant against Mr Yerodia? At the time of the judgment, he no longer occupied a ministerial office; the terms of the judgment do not manifestly bar a Belgian magistrate from issuing a new warrant. The case would fall under one of the scenarios of permissible criminal proceedings which the Court had explicitly acknowledged: the case of a former foreign minister charged with acts committed *prior* to his or her period of office. Yerodia had been principal private secretary (*directeur du cabinet*) of the late President Kabila at the time of the events for which he was charged, a position with a domestic focus that cannot be equated to that of a foreign minister or head of state as regards immunity. The Court had construed the broad scope of a foreign minister's immunity by reference to the functional needs of that office. It had rejected the Congolese request for an indication of provisional measures on the basis that for the effective fulfillment of the office of a minister for education—the office Mr Yerodia was occupying from November 2000 through April 2001—there was less need to travel abroad in comparison to that of a foreign minister.[1167] A *directeur du cabinet* has probably even less need to travel abroad. One also has to bear in mind that the Court asked for the cancellation of the warrant as *restitution* of the *status quo ante* and its illegality at the time of the issuance, not on the basis of its actual *substance*. Further elucidation by the Court may have been desirable. If the terms of the judgment do not appear to preclude a new arrest warrant, one may ask what the purpose of an obligation of withdrawal is if it is combined with the possibility to issue a new warrant.[1168]

But even if Yerodia had already been foreign minister at the time of the 1998 speech, it is doubtful whether the judgment would present a bar to a new warrant, as he is no longer in office. The Court explicitly stated that after they leave office, former foreign ministers no longer enjoy full immunities and may be subject to prosecution for private acts committed during their

---

[1166] Judgment of 14 February 2002, at paras. 75–6.

[1167] Order of 8 December 2000, at para. 72.

[1168] See for a critical comment *Sands*, 33 RBDI (2002), 537–45, reprimanding also the scarcity of reasoning. For further critical remarks on this issue, see *Shaw*, 33 RBDI (2002), at 558–9.

terms of office; one could argue that Mr Yerodia's acts had been committed in a private capacity.[1169]

Beyond the question of what the Court had decided with binding force, the judgment's broader reaching implications merit further consideration.[1170] Although the judgment is only binding between Belgium and the Democratic Republic of the Congo, the same considerations would apply for similar cases launched in Belgium (and other countries) against the foreign ministers of other countries. The judgment's reasoning could apply equally to other high-ranking officials whose official duties to a similar extent necessitate international travel, in particular, heads of state and government.[1171] As to the scope of the obligation to respect the principle of immunity, one might ask whether it merely prohibits a state from taking any steps towards effecting an arrest or whether it represents an absolute bar to any form of criminal proceedings, including investigations.[1172] There is also the question of the applicability of the Court's findings to civil proceedings; those proceedings could also encompass judicial compulsion which similarly might result in similar obstacles for foreign ministers in the fulfillment of their functions. The judgment will certainly also trigger manifold discussions both on immunity and on universal jurisdiction.[1173]

4. The follow-up to the judgment

Belgium accepted the Court's ruling, withdrew the warrant, and made the required notifications on the day after the delivery of the judgment.[1174] The Belgian foreign minister acknowledged that some aspects of the 1993 law

[1169] See Joint sep. op. Higgins, Kooijmans, and Buergenthal at para. 85 referring to a trend in literature and state practice that serious international crimes could not be regarded as official acts. Moreover, it is not clear whether the Court wanted to set up an exhaustive listing of permissible exceptions, and its explanations on exceptions to immunity were *obiter dicta*. Critical on the Court's definition of the immunity for a foreign minister *Kamto*, 33 RBDI (2002), at 518–30; *Salmon*, 33 RBDI (2002), at 512–17.

[1170] See also *Pell/Bekker*, www.whitecase.com/case_icj_ruling_jurisdiction_ministers_pell_bekker.pdf.

[1171] See paragraph 53 of the judgment in which the Court compares the position of a foreign minister to that of heads of state or of government in the context of the explanation of the scope of immunity of a foreign minister: "The Court further observes that a Minister for Foreign Affairs, responsible for the conduct of his or her State's relations with all other States, occupies a position such that, like the Head of State or the Head of Government, he or she is recognized under international law as representative of the state solely by virtue of his or her office."

[1172] For an understanding of immunity as not preventing investigations, see the dissent of Judge Al-Khasawneh, at para. 4 ("[T]he opening of criminal investigations against [a Foreign Minister] can hardly be said by any objective criteria to constitute interference with the conduct of diplomacy"); *Gray*, http://www.ejil.org/journal/Vol13/No3/sr1.html.

[1173] For initial reactions, see Cassese, http://www.ejil.org/journal/curdevs/sr31.html; *Gray*, "Case concerning the arrest warrant of 11 April 2000," http://www.ejil.org/journal/Vol13/No3/sr1.html; *Pell/Bekker*, www.whitecase.com/case_icj_ruling_jurisdiction_ministers_pell_bekker. pdf.

[1174] "Le mandat retiré: et après?," La Libre Belgique, 15 February 2002, www.lalibre.be/article_print.phtml?art_id= 52589.

might have to be corrected;[1175] other officials went further and stated that a discontinuance of cases against foreign leaders entitled to immunity was to be expected.[1176] While human rights organizations expressed their disappointment, Mr Yerodia was reported to have opened a bottle of champagne and celebrated the verdict as a "victory for the Congolese people."[1177] The judgment received heightened media coverage, in part because of its implications for similar cases prosecuted in Belgium, most notably, the proceedings against other world leaders, including Israeli Prime Minister Ariel Sharon, Cuban leader Fidel Castro, Iraqi President Saddam Hussein, Côte d'Ivoire President Laurent Gbagbo, and Palestinian leader Yasser Arafat.[1178]

The withdrawal of the arrest warrant did not affect the continuation of the criminal proceedings against Mr Yerodia *per se*, as it merely removed the basis for an arrest.[1179] On 16 April 2002, the Court of Appeal (*Cour d'Appel*) of Brussels ruled that Mr Yerodia could not be tried in Belgium. The decision was not based on violation of immunity and the ICJ ruling, but instead on Mr Yerodia's absence from Belgian territory. Relying on a provision of the Belgian Code of Criminal Investigation (*code d'instruction criminelle*), the Court held that it could exercise universal jurisdiction under the 1993 Act for crimes committed outside of Belgium only if the accused was physically present in Belgium.[1180] Yet the *Cour de Cassation*, the highest Belgian

---

[1175] "Despite setback, Belgium minister defends war crimes law," Agence France-Press, 2002 WL 2340990. Article 5 §3 of the law (*supra* n. 1144) stated: "The immunity attributed to the official capacity of a person does not prevent the application of the present Act." See also Judgment of 14 February 2002, Sep. Op. Koroma, at para. 7.

[1176] The legal advisor to the Belgian foreign ministry was quoted with statements predicting that existing cases against senior foreign officials would be dropped. The matter was left to Belgian lawmakers, who could amend or repeal the law to adapt it to the Court's ruling. Lobe, "Rights: World Court ruling dismays rights activists," Inter Press Service, 14 February 2002, 2002 WL 4912874; see also "Scharon entgeht voraussichtlich Strafverfahren," Süddeutsche Zeitung, 16/17 February 2002, at 8; *Wielaard*, "Belgium told to halt war trials," Associated Press online, 14 February 2002, 2002 WL 13776482. Along similar lines, the royal prosecutor of Brussels expressed his expectation that criminal cases could not be pursued against foreign rulers while conceding that a thorough analysis of the judgment was still required. La Libre Belgique, Le mandat retiré: et après?, 15 February 2002, http://www.lalibre.be/article_print.phtml?art_id = 52589.

[1177] "Former DR Congo Minister hails ICJ decision to retract award," Agence France-Presse, 15 February 2002, 2002 WL 2341307; "L'immunité des hommes d'Etat en exercise ne cède que devant les tribunaux internationaux," Le Monde, Sélection hebdomadaire, 23 February 2002, at 2.

[1178] Leonard, "Brussels: Controversial leaders avoid 'arrest' in Belgium," 1 March 2002, Europe (Dow Jones), at 38, 2002 WL 14822450; Gibb, "Prosecution of Sharon is jeopardized," (London) Times, 15 February 2002, at 16, 2002 WL 4181474; "Vifs débats sur une justice à "compétence universelle," Le Monde, Sélection Hebdomadaire, 23 February 2002, at 2.

[1179] See "Brussels court postpones decision on accusations against DRC ex-minister," Agence France-Presse, 12 March 2002, 2002 WL 2362519 (quoting spokesman of the Brussels Court of Appeal, who explained that withdrawal of arrest warrant did not terminate proceedings).

[1180] Plaintes irrecevables dans l'affaire Yerodia, La Libre Belgique, 16 April 2002, http://www.lalibre.be/article_print.phtml?art_id = 58331; Former DR Congo minister cannot be tried in Belgium, Agence France-Presse, 16 April 2002, 2002 WL 2387158. In the only conviction to date made on the basis of the 1993 law, four Rwandans charged with genocide for massacres in Rwanda had been arrested while living in Belgium. See Richburg, "Rwandan nuns jailed in genocide," Washington Post, 9 June 2001, page A01, www.washingtonpost.com/ac2/wp-dyn/A42755-2001Jun8.

Court, cancelled the decisions in that case as well as in another one directed against Israeli Prime Minister Sharon and remanded them to the Court of Appeal for further consideration.[1181] In 1993, Belgium made fundamental changes to its laws on universal jurisdiction. Most importantly in the present context, the principle that an official position did not *per se* prevent application of the law has been made subject to the "limitations laid down in international law."[1182] Mr Yerodia, who meanwhile has taken up a government position again,[1183] will be unlikely ever to face Belgian criminal justice.

Belgium complied with its obligation under Article 94(1) of the UN Charter and beyond this obligation, which only concerned the Yerodia case, acted in conformity with the Court's reasoning as well.

The Court has another opportunity to provide guidance on immunity and universal criminal jurisdiction in the pending certain criminal proceedings in France case, launched by the Republic of the Congo against France.[1184]

XXVIII. Conclusion: An overall positive record of compliance with judgments

The overall record of compliance with ICJ judgments should be viewed as a positive one. Only on a few occasions have states openly and willfully chosen to disregard the Court's judgments: in the Corfu Channel, Fisheries jurisdiction, Tehran hostages, and Nicaragua cases. Even in these cases, the effects of non-compliance were mitigated to a certain extent, given eventual[1185] or partial[1186]

[1181] The Yerodia decision was made on 20 November 2002, "Plainte renvoyée devant la chamber des mises en accusation, http://www.lalibre.be/article.phtml?id=10&subid=83&art_id=90593, the Sharon decision on 12 February 2003, Ariel Sharon pourra être poursuivi, http://www.lalibre.be/article.phtml?id=10&subid=83&art_id=103067. Moreover, there are legislative initiatives under way with the aim of clarifying that war crimes committed abroad are to be covered even where the accused is not present in Belgian territory: Compétence universelle, adoptée en Commission du Sénat, http://www.lalibre.be/article.phtml?id=10&subid =83&art_id =100117; Amnesty International, Universal Jurisdiction, http://www.web.amnesty.org/ai.nsf/recent/IOR530012003?OpenDocument, footnote 16. On the Court of Appeal decisions, see, e.g. *Borloo*, "Compétence pour la Belgique, mais immunité pour Sharon?," Le soir, 16 May 2002.

[1182] The amendments to the law have fundamentally changed the character of the laws in question; generally a link to Belgium will be required. For details of the changes and their background, see *Ratner*, 97 AJIL (2003), 888–97; *Wouters*, 16 Leid. JIL (2003), at 264–7; and yet from the perspective prior to the amendment of the law *Winants*, 16 Leid. JIL (2003), at 491–509, on the former law and the necessary adaptations due to the judgment.

[1183] La retour de Yerodia, La Libre Belgique, 22 April 2003, http://www.lalibre.be/article_print.phtml?art_id=113155.

[1184] For the Congolese application, see http://212.153.43.18/icjwww/idocket/icof/icoforder/icof_iapplication_20020209.pdf.

[1185] Albania eventually payed compensation to the UK, so that the Corfu Channel case was finally settled in 1996 following an agreement reached in 1992. See *supra* I 4.

[1186] Iran partially complied with the judgment in the Tehran hostages case when releasing the hostages (although as part of an overall settlement). See *supra* XIV 5. That there was only partial compliance is often not sufficiently stressed.

compliance by the losing party, or changes in the law,[1187] or political[1188] scene that diminished the relevance of the original decision. Moreover, the judgments proved to be of some use for the applicants, even if only to a limited extent. Here the Fisheries jurisdiction case represents somewhat of an anomaly in retrospect; had the extraordinarily rapid development of the law been foreseen at the time the proceedings were launched, it is doubtful whether the UK and the Federal Republic of Germany would have initiated the litigation.

Over and above being cases of mere non-compliance, the aforementioned cases represented instances of outright defiance, with the respective respondents deliberately and openly taking action contrary to the judgments, vehemently criticizing the Court[1189] and challenging the bindingness of its decisions. Besides these extremes of the spectrum, cases of "simple" non-compliance may occur where the parties do not oppose the decision and, in fact, claim to comply with it, but whether their verbal commitment is matched by appropriate action remains disputed. Generally, it will be far more difficult to establish sufficient evidence for non-compliance in such situations, and in the concrete cases where complaints to this extent have been made, they appear too unsubstantiated to conclusively establish non-compliance by the opponent. In the Gabčíkovo–Nagymaros case, for example, Slovakia's application to the Court relating to Hungary's alleged non-compliance blames Hungary for the failure to renegotiate a treaty; in this case as in general in cases relating to obligations to negotiate, it will be very difficult to establish a violation, which may partially explain Slovakia's reticence in pressing its claim.[1190] Similarly, in the Land, Island and Maritime Frontier Dispute, Honduras's complaint that El Salvador failed to acknowledge the Court's findings relating to the régime of the Gulf of Fonseca does not appear sufficiently substantiated.[1191]

Some claims are *framed* as claims for compliance with a judgment, but actually aim at enforcement of rights not covered by the respective decision. An example arose in the Honduran claims in connection with the Land, Island and Maritime Frontier Dispute relating to the demarcation of the land boundary and the delimitation of maritime spaces where the obligations invoked do not appear to result from the judgment itself, but rather the special agreement.[1192] Further examples are the Asylum and the Rights of

---

[1187] The Court's findings in the Fisheries Jurisdiction case were superseded shortly after the decisions by the development of the law and the applicants' own behavior, and Iceland could no longer be held to be bound by its terms. See *supra* XII 5.

[1188] The US and Nicaragua reached a settlement to their dispute after the change in government in Nicaragua, which opened the way for an era of improvement of their relations. Support for Contra activities had already been continuously reduced before, as Reagan's Nicaragua policy became increasingly untenable on the domestic level. See *supra* XVIII 7–9.

[1189] An exception in this regard is the Corfu Channel case, where the respondent simply refused to obey.

[1190] See *supra* XXIV 4.   [1191] See *supra* IXX 4.   [1192] See ibid.

Passage cases. Peru's allegation that in order to execute the judgment in the Asylum case, Colombia was obliged to surrender Haya de la Torre was incompatible with the fact that the Court had held already a week after the Asylum judgment in the judgment on Request for the Interpretation of the Judgment of 20 November 1950 that the former had not ruled on the existence on such an obligation.[1193] Portugal claimed non-compliance on the part of India with the judgment in Right of Passage over Indian Territory, but actually tried to challenge India's occupation of formerly Portuguese-occupied territories, an issue not touched upon by the judgment.[1194]

In some cases, fears of non-compliance proved unfounded in spite of substantial grounds for concern because of important interest involved or past military clashes. Thailand followed through with its obligations under the judgment in Temple of Preah Vihear, despite its initial reactions to the decision.[1195] In the Territorial Dispute (Libya/Chad) case, Libya withdrew its troops from the area in questions despite fears that it might refuse to do so.[1196] These cases point positively to the respect of parties for the Court's role in the settlement of disputes, as it demonstrates that states will comply even with judgments contrary to their national interests.

Some cases that might have been problematical in terms of compliance did not reach the stage of a decision on the merits. It is unclear, for example, whether South Africa would have obeyed an unfavorable judgment by the Court in the South West Africa cases—it had already resisted broad international pressure concerning its continued presence in the former mandate area—and whether the enforcement procedure under Article 94(2) of the Charter would have been applied if it had not.[1197] The prospects for compliance would also have been unclear in Nuclear Tests assuming that a judgment of the Court had ordered France to desist from testing of any kind; the French reaction to the orders in that case might raise doubts as to the prospects for a positive response. Beyond the issue of Article 94(1) of the Charter, it seems highly unlikely that the People's Republic of China would have changed its nuclear testing policy because of a judgment of the Court against France; it was no party to the proceedings, but its disregard for

---

[1193] See *supra* II 2–3. Surprisingly, though, Colombia's reaction to the Asylum judgment is occasionally lisited as a case of non-compliance, see Nantwi, *Enforcement of international judicial decisions*, at 119; and *Charney* in Damrosch, The ICJ at a crossroads, at 294, 311 (arguing that Colombia refused to comply and that this was "found to be justified" in the Haya de la Torre judgment)—yet the Court explicitly decided in Haya de la Torre that: (a) in the Asylum judgment it had not decided on Colombia's obligation of surrender; and (b) that Colombia had no such obligation.

[1194] See *supra* VI 4.   [1195] See *supra* IX.   [1196] See *supra* XXII.

[1197] Of course, this is highly speculative, and it is noticeable that South Africa, unlike respondents in other cases, participated in the proceedings. See *supra* Ch. 2 n. 96 on the prospects for applying Article 94(1); and Rosenne, *World Court*, at 168–175 on the overall context.

the Court's findings would nevertheless have been considered a blow to the Court's authority.[1198]

In some cases, discussion of non-compliance would be misplaced even when in a non-technical sense, the Court's judgment was not strictly followed or even challenged. For instance, a challenge to the Court's findings by private persons whose action cannot be attributed to a state is no issue of a violation of Article 94(1) of the Charter, even though it might cause inconveniences for the state entitled under a judgment. For the judgment creditor, coping with such challenges is an issue of enforcement of its domestic laws and not a problem situated on the inter-state level. Hence, the occasional "invasions" of the Minquiers and Ecrehos by private French citizens opposing British sovereignty over the islets cannot take away from the fact that France has complied with the judgment in the Minquiers and Ecrehos case.[1199] Similarly, infractions of the maritime boundary between the US and Canada in the Gulf of Maine by local fishermen do not reopen the delimitation adjudicated by the Court.[1200]

Neither can one speak of non-compliance in cases where the parties jointly modify their legal relations following a judgment and thereby change a régime adjudicated upon by the Court. States are always free to modify their rights through agreements, be they confirmed by adjudication or not, and the content of compliance is first of all determined by the parties themselves. Thus, there is no reason to reprimand the parties in the Jan Mayen case for the fact that the coordinates in their treaty on maritime delimitation slightly deviated from those established in the judgment, or to investigate whether the North Sea Continental Shelf delimitation was the solution most faithful to the Court's indications.[1201]

Delays in the implementation of ICJ judgments not attributable to the bad faith of either side are likewise not examples of non-compliance in a strict sense. Difficulties are likely to arise, for example, when the subject-matter of the judgment is not more precise than an obligation of both sides to negotiate, particularly if the very reason the parties had seized the Court had been their inability to find a negotiated solution. In the Asylum/Haya de la Torre case, three judgments could not bring about a clear-cut situation, but the parties had to find a solution by negotiations; as a consequence, it took years until the asylum of Haya de la Torre was terminated. In the Land, Island and Maritime Frontier Dispute, the failure to implement the special agreement and demarcate the boundary appears to be a problem of allocation of resources and priorities, apart from the practical issues to be clarified given the settled population in the disputed area, raising questions of nationality,

---

[1198] See *infra* C III 5.   [1199] See *supra* V.   [1200] See *supra* XV.
[1201] See *supra* X and XX.

vested rights, etc.[1202] It remains to be stated that the implementation of ICJ judgments all in all has worked smoothly.

C. COMPLIANCE WITH PROVISIONAL MEASURES

I. Anglo-Iranian Oil Company case

The Anglo-Iranian Oil Company case marked the first instance in which the ICJ indicated interim measures of protection, the first instance in which such a measure was disregarded, and the first instance in which the subject-matter of the legal dispute was brought before the Security Council.

1. Background of the case

In this case, the British government exercised diplomatic protection against Iran on behalf of a company incorporated in the UK. In 1901, a concession agreement granted the financier William Knox D'Arcy the exclusive right to extract and process petroleum in a defined area in Iran; following this agreement, the Anglo-Persian Oil Company (later renamed Anglo-Iranian Oil Company) was founded in 1909. The agreement and the company's activities generated repeated tensions between the two countries, with Iran complaining that its national interests were not sufficiently met in the context of the exploitation of its oil resources. The Iranian government terminated the 1901 concession agreement in 1932. The company reached a new, 60-year agreement with Iran in April 1933 containing a requirement for arbitration in case of a breach of the agreement. In 1949, the parties signed a supplementary agreement aimed at increasing the benefits for Iran. The increase proved insufficient for the Iranian parliament, which refused to ratify the agreement and instead proceeded in March and April 1951 to cancel the concession by nationalizing the country's oil industry. The nationalization laws were the culmination of a political campaign to curb foreign influence over Iranian resources and economic affairs, responding to nationalist sentiments. This led to the dispute in which the British government intervened; nevertheless, all attempts to convince Iran to submit the matter to arbitration failed. The dispute became so intense that some speculations about a possible British military action came up.[1203]

[1202] See *supra* XX 4. It is no question of Article 94(1) in the strict sense.
[1203] On the background of the dispute, see 21 AdG (1951) 2859 B, 2890 B, 2923 D, 2933 J, 2945 D, 2954 A, and 2963 D; Ghosh, *The Anglo-Iranian Oil Dispute*; and Ford, *The Anglo-Iranian oil dispute*, 1–76; Frankel, 6 Yb WA (1952), at 56–74, and Judgment of 22 July 1952, at 102.

On 26 May 1951, the UK instituted proceedings against Iran by unilateral application before the ICJ, based upon declarations by both parties accepting the compulsory jurisdiction of the PCIJ.[1204] The UK asked for a ruling that Iran was bound to submit the matter to arbitration or that the Nationalization Act was illegal under international law and violated Iran's obligations under the 1933 concessions agreement. Although the concessions agreement had been concluded between Iran and the company, the UK claimed that in view of its own participation in the prior negotiations, it was also to be regarded as a treaty between the two governments. It also alluded to most-favored-nations clauses in treaties between the UK and Persia from 1857 and 1903.[1205]

It was not clear whether the Court had jurisdiction in the present case. The Iranian declaration on jurisdiction recognized the Court's competence only for "disputes arising after the ratification of the present declaration with regard to situations or facts relating directly or indirectly to the application of treaties or conventions accepted by Persia and subsequent to the ratification of this declaration." It excluded three categories of disputes, among those disputes with regard to questions which, by international law, fell exclusively within Persia's domestic jurisdiction.[1206] This reservation was not significant as the Court is *per se* barred from deciding matters within the exclusive domestic sphere of states.[1207] The former phrase, however, restricted Iran's acceptance to disputes about application of treaties and apparently—although the UK held a contrary view—only of those treaties concluded *after* the ratification of the declaration. Consequently, there were doubts on the applicability of the declaration in the present case, as the treaties between the two countries invoked by the UK had been concluded prior to Iran's declaration, and the UK argumentation relating to the character of the concessions agreement as a treaty between the two governments was questionable.[1208]

[1204] The UK declaration of 28 February 1940 and the Iranian declaration of 2 October 1940, see Judgment of 22 July 1952, at 103. Article 36(5) of ICJ Statute transferred this jurisdiction to the ICJ.

[1205] ICJ Pleadings, Anglo-Iranian Oil Company, at 8–44.

[1206] The declaration is reprinted in the judgment on jurisdiction: see Judgment of 22 July 1952, at 103.

[1207] See Article 2(7) of the United Nations Charter.

[1208] The agreement which the UK sought to enforce—a contract between a private company and the Iranian government—hardly qualified as a "treaty." With regard to the treaties of 1857 and 1903, the question was whether the words in the Iranian declaration "and subsequent to the ratification of this declaration" related to "situation or facts" or to "treaties and conventions." In the judgment on jurisdiction, the Court adopted the latter interpretation and held that it lacked jurisdiction because the treaties the application of which was controversial were concluded prior to the declaration and thus not covered by its terms, Judgment of 22 July 1952, at 103–10.

Concerned that the company's installations might be damaged, the UK made a request for the indication of provisional measures on 22 June 1951.[1209] On the following day, the ICJ President called upon Iran not to take action that might aggravate the dispute.[1210] The Iranian foreign minister responded to the request on 29 June,[1211] stating that Iran opposed the proceedings before the Court and the indication of provisional measures in particular since the Court lacked jurisdiction and the UK legal standing, not being a party to the concessions agreement. The Iranian government asserted that the nationalization was an exercise of its sovereignty and a matter within the sphere of its exclusive domestic jurisdiction. It criticized the concessions agreement as unjust and coerced, and leveled charges of breaches of the agreement by the company itself and criminal activities by company officials. Moreover, it argued that there was no basis for indication of provisional measures in the absence of a risk of irreparable damage, as material and human means for the exploitation of oil were to be maintained, foreign experts and technicians would continued to be employed and paid, and the government was to set up a bank account with a quarter of its current oil income with a view to compensating possible losses for the company.[1212]

On 30 June, the Court held a hearing on the request for interim measures. The Iranian side did not participate[1213] although it took part in the further stages of the proceedings.[1214]

2. The interim measures taken by the Court

The Court issued interim measures of protection by order of 5 July 1951. It indicated that both parties should ensure that no action was taken that might aggravate or extend the dispute or prejudice the rights of the other party in respect of the execution of any future decision on the merits. Both parties were ordered to ensure that no measure of any kind was taken designed to hinder the industrial and commercial operations of the Anglo-Iranian Oil Company, as they were carried out prior to 1 May 1951; the company's operations in Iran were to continue under the direction of its previous

---

[1209] Ibid., at 45–63.

[1210] Telegram from the Deputy-Registrar to the minister of foreign affairs of Iran, 23 June 1951, ICJ Pleadings, Anglo-Iranian Oil Company, 707–8.

[1211] Communication from the Minister of Foreign Affairs of Iran to the ICJ President, ICJ Pleadings, Anglo-Iranian Oil Company, 672–98.

[1212] Ibid., at 672–81.

[1213] Order of 5 July, 1951, at 92. The Court took note of the Iranian communication of 29 June: ibid., at 91.

[1214] Iran filed "preliminary observations" to the Court's jurisdiction within the time limit fixed for the presentation of its counter-memorial. In the Court hearings in June 1952, Prime Minister Mossadegh personally represented Iran. See Judgment of 22 July 1952, at 96–7.

corporate management.[1215] The Court also called for the creation of a board of supervision to oversee compliance with the other obligations and audit of the company's revenue and expenses. This board would be composed of two members appointed by each government and a fifth person to be chosen by agreement between the parties, or in default of such agreement and upon the joint request of the parties by the Court's President. All revenue in excess of normal operating expenses would be paid into bank accounts selected by the board.[1216]

The measures were for the most part of a noticeable precision. The Court did not limit itself to reiterating general obligations, deciding instead that the company's activities were to continue and the manner in which this had to take place. It provided for the establishment of an auxiliary body and defined its tasks and composition without having been requested to do so by either party. The measures were directed at both sides, unlike the unilateral tack of the UK request, although substantively they required an initial response by Iran in order to allow continued operation of the Anglo-Iranian Oil Company. In contrast, the duties to refrain from aggravating the dispute or frustrating a decision on the merits were not defined as precisely as the UK had asked.[1217]

After summarizing the British submissions and referring to the Iranian communication, the Court kept its reasoning on the actual measures and their legal basis very brief. On the question of jurisdiction, the Court stated that the UK complaint alleged a violation of international law and that it could not accept "*a priori* that a claim based on such a complaint falls completely outside the scope of international jurisdiction." It concluded that these considerations sufficed "to empower the Court to entertain the request for interim measures of protection"[1218] without further examining the applicability of both countries' declarations under Article 36(2) of the ICJ Statute. Hence, while not regarding it necessary to satisfy itself that it had jurisdiction before granting interim protection, the Court indicated that it would refrain from doing so only in cases of a manifest lack of jurisdiction.

The dissenting opinion of Judges Winiarski and Badawi Pasha took exception to this approach, arguing that the standard for examining jurisdiction should have been different and that the Court should not have granted interim protection: "We find it difficult to accept the view that if *prima facie* the total lack of jurisdiction is not patent, that is, if there is a possibility,

---

[1215] As constituted prior to 1 May 1951, subject to such modifications as may be brought about by agreement with the board of supervision. Order of 5 July 1951, at 93.

[1216] Ibid., at 93–4. The voting pattern was not disclosed; at least two judges (Judges Winiarski and Padawi Pasha) dissented. For details, see *Fenwick*, 45 AJIL (1951), at 723–7.

[1217] For the measures requested by the UK, see Request, *supra* n. 1205, at 51–2 (a request which was upheld in the hearings, see Order of 5 July 1952, at 92).

[1218] Ibid., at 93.

however remote, that the Court may be competent, then it may indicate interim measures of protection."[1219] The test which they suggested instead was a provisional finding that jurisdiction was "reasonably probable."[1220] The dissenters saw the jurisdiction on the merits and the power to indicate provisional measures as interrelated: "If there is no jurisdiction as to the merits, there can be no jurisdiction to indicate interim measures of protection."[1221] The judgment on jurisdiction in contrast located the power to indicate provisional measures and the competence to deal with the merits in separate articles of the ICJ statute—Articles 41 and 36, respectively.[1222] In keeping with this understanding of the applicability of Article 41, the Court carried out an examination of scope and applicability of Iran's declaration to recognize the compulsory jurisdiction of the Court only in the judgment and not in the order, although it had been aware of Iran's opposition to its jurisdiction.

As to the circumstances that required the indication of provisional measures, the Court provided no explanation beyond the statement that "the existing state of affairs justifies the indication of provisional measures of protection."[1223] It did not elaborate upon the necessity of interim protection as such or of the specific measures indicated—in particular, it did not address why any possible rights of the Anglo-Iranian Oil Company were not safeguarded through Iran's own measures to that extent.[1224]

In its judgment of 22 July 1952,[1225] the Court found that it had no jurisdiction based on an interpretation of the Iranian declaration accepting the compulsory jurisdiction of the Court.[1226] It found that since the provisional measures had been indicated pending the final judgment, the order ceased to be operative on the day of the delivery of the judgment and that the provisional measures lapsed at the same time,[1227] which indicated its view that the fact it had no jurisdiction did not detract from the validity of the measures in the first place. The relevant period for examining the compliance

---

[1219] Dissenting Opinion of Judges Winiarski and Padawi Pasha, ibid., at 97.

[1220] Ibid., at 96.

[1221] Ibid., at 97.

[1222] Judgment of 22 July 1952, at 102–3: "While the Court derived its power to indicate these provisional measures from the special provisions contained in Article 41 of the Statute, it must now derive its jurisdiction to deal with the merits of the case from the general rules laid down in Article 36 of the Statute. These general rules, which are entirely different from the special provisions of Article 41, are based on the principle that the jurisdiction of the Court to deal with and decide a case on the merits depends on the will of the Parties."

[1223] Order of 5 July 1951, at 93.

[1224] As stated *supra*, n. 1212, Iran had affirmed that the laws in question provided for a continuation of oil exploitation and for the deposit of 25% of the oil income for possible losses of the company.

[1225] Judgment of 22 July 1952, at 93–171.

[1226] For details, see Verzijl, *Jurisprudence of the World Court II*, 118–32.

[1227] Judgment of 22 July 1952, at 114.

with the provisional measures was thus the time from 5 July 1951 to 22 July 1952.

3. Iran's rejection of the provisional measures

While the UK government immediately welcomed the measures and expressed its willingness to nominate the members of the board of supervision,[1228] Iran took no steps to implement the order. In a telegram to the UN Secretary-General of 9 July,[1229] the Iranian government withdrew its declaration accepting the compulsory jurisdiction of the Court and vehemently criticized the Court's order. Three days later, it informed the UK government that it considered the order invalid.[1230] Iran's critique touched on various aspects, including the Court's lack of jurisdiction, the interference in Iran's domestic affairs, the short time between the application and the hearings on provisional measures (one week), and the substance of the provisional measures. Iran called the measure on a board of supervision a "crowning injustice" as the measure exceeded the scope of the UK request and the operation of this board would give the UK a right to intervene in Iran's domestic affairs. Moreover, it criticized the provision relating to the deposit of the company's excess of revenue over expenses with a bank, which failed to take into account that even if the concessions agreement was still valid, the Iranian government would have been entitled to regular payments. In its difficult financial situation, Iran argued that it would be put under inappropriate pressure not to pursue its nationalization policy if it were denied access to any gains.[1231]

In its preliminary observations to the Court in which it explained in detail the jurisdictional defects in the case, Iran further explained its opposition to the order, by which it did not consider itself bound.[1232] It criticized the Court's failure to give any justification for its competence over the matter or for its rejection of Iranian objections to its jurisdiction. Quoting the dissenting opinion of Judges Winiarski and Badawi Pasha, Iran argued that the relevant standard should be a probability of jurisdiction. It objected to the Court's display of an *excès de pouvoir* in prescribing substantive

---

[1228] Note presented by his Britannic Majesty's Ambassador in Tehran to the Imperial Government of Iran on 7th July 1951, Appendix No. 1 Annex 1a to the UK Memorial, ICJ Pleadings, Anglo-Iranian Oil Company, 64, at 129.

[1229] Telegram of 9 July 1951 from the Iranian Minister for Foreign Affairs to the UN Secretary-General, Appendix No. 3 to Annex 1a of the UK Memorial, ICJ Pleadings, Anglo-Iranian Oil Company, 130–4.

[1230] Note presented by the Imperial Government of Iran to his Britannic Majesty's Ambassador in Tehran on 12th July 1951, Appendix No. 2 to Annex 1a of the UK Memorial, ICJ Pleadings, Anglo-Iranian Oil Company, 129, at 130.

[1231] Telegram of 9 July 1951, *supra* n. 1229.

[1232] Observations préliminaires: Refus du Gouvernement impérial de reconnaître la compétence de la Cour, ICJ Pleadings, Anglo-Iranian Oil Company, 281, at 282–6.

measures rather than giving indications: its view was that the Court had no power to make injunctions and to intervene in Iran's domestic matters.[1233]

Iran's resistance went beyond the rhetorical. Oil production was halted at the refinery in Abadan, which Iranian troops seized on 27 September 1951.[1234]

4. The proceedings in the UN Security Council

In reaction to Iran's announcement ordering the company's remaining staff to leave the country by 4 October 1951, the UK decided to take the matter to the UN Security Council.[1235] On 28 September 1951, it filed a complaint about the Iranian non-compliance with the Security Council and requested the matter be placed on the Council's agenda.[1236] On the following day, the UK submitted a draft resolution calling upon Iran "to act in all respects in conformity with the provisional measures indicated by the Court and in particular to permit the continued residence at Abadan of the staff affected by the recent expulsion orders or the equivalent of such staff."[1237] No sanctions were envisaged. A legal basis for Council action was not indicated; the preamble referred to the Council's concern "at the dangers in this situation and at the threat to peace and security that may thereby be involved." The British draft included a phrase reprimanding Iran's action (the order of expulsion of the company's remaining staff) as "clearly contrary to the provisional measures indicated by the Court."

The Security Council decided on 1 October 1951 to include the UK complaint in its agenda despite protest from the USSR and Yugoslavia, who considered the matter one within the domestic jurisdiction of Iran.[1238] As for the legal basis of Council action, the UK representative, Sir Gladwyn Jebb, referred to Articles 34 and 35 of the UN Charter, both in Chapter VI, as well as to Article 94(2).[1239] He argued that the enforcement procedure of Article 94(2) applied to provisional measures as well as to judgments and that such measures had binding force.[1240] Beyond the legal arguments, he pointed

---

[1233] Ibid.

[1234] Reisman, *Nullity and revision*, 723–4; Ford, *The Anglo-Iranian oil dispute*, at 95–124 and at 275–81 for details on the events between the indication of provisional measures and the proceedings before the Security Council; 21 AdG (1951) 3139 A.

[1235] For a summary of the proceedings in the Security Council, see Ford, *The Anglo-Iranian oil dispute*, at 124–53; Grieves, *Supranationalism and international adjudication*, 113–16; Reisman, *Nullity and revision*, 724–8.

[1236] Letter dated 28 September 1951 addressed to the President of the Security Council and the Secretary-General from the UK deputy permanent representative to the UN, UN Doc. S/2357. The Security Council had been notified of the Order, Note by the Secretary-General of 11 July 1951, S/2239.

[1237] UN Doc. S/2358.

[1238] S/PV.559, at 10. The negative Soviet vote did not prevent a decision, given that it related to a procedural matter, see Article 27(2) of the UN Charter.

[1239] S/PV.559, at 20.   [1240] Ibid., at 20.

out that there was at the very least a compelling moral obligation to comply with such measures because they were an expression of the opinion of the highest international tribunal on what was necessary to preserve the parties' rights pending the proceedings. Furthermore, he pointed out that Iran's failure to respect those measures was such as to give rise to a potential threat to peace and security.[1241]

The Iranian representative opposed the discussion of the issue and requested an adjournment of ten days so as to allow members of the Iranian government to travel from Tehran to New York to present the Iranian view.[1242] The Security Council suspended the discussion,[1243] thus frustrating the UK's main objective, i.e. the prevention of the expulsion of the Company's personnel.

The next meeting took place on 15 October 1951. The Iranian government was represented by Prime Minister Mossadegh and Mr Allahyar Saleh. The UK representative began the meeting with the observation that the Anglo-Iranian Oil Company (AIOC) personnel had been expelled in the meantime, which rendered the earlier draft resolution useless and left the provisional measures partially without object.[1244] He referred to a revised UK draft resolution with a more limited scope, the aim of which it was to bring the parties together for negotiations "in accordance with the principles of the provisional measures indicated by the International Court."[1245] Thus, the UK did not any longer seek enforcement of the provisional measures but negotiations in accordance with the "principles of the provisional measures." The Iranian delegation stressed in the first place the country's motives for the

---

[1241] Ibid., at 21. *Tanzi*, 6 EJIL (1995), at 64, argues that this additional line of reasoning weakened the argument on the binding force.

[1242] S/PV.559, at 26. Iran was not a member of the Council at the time, but had been invited to participate in the discussions pursuant to Article 32 of the Charter, ibid., at 10–11.

[1243] Ibid., at 30.

[1244] Statement of Sir Gladwyn Jebb on behalf of the UK, S/PV.560, at 1–2: "As realists, we must also admit that there is not much point in our now suggesting that the Government of Iran should be called upon 'to act in all respects in conformity with the provisional measures indicated by the Court' [...] One has only to read these provisional measures [...] to see that they have, unfortunately, and to some extent now been overtaken by events [...]."

[1245] UN Doc. S/2358/Rev.1 of 12 October 1951. The preamble of the draft resolution refers to the Court's order (see *inter alia* the fifth paragraph: "Whereas the United Kingdom Government accepted the indication of the provisional measures and the Government of Iran declined to accept such measures"), the operative part called for "1. the resumption of negotiations at the earliest practicable moment in order to make further efforts to resolve the differences between the parties in accordance with the principles of the provisional measures indicated by the International Court of Justice unless mutually agreeable arrangements are made consistent with the Purposes and Principles of the United Nations Charter, 2. The avoidance of any action which would have the effect of further aggravating the situation or prejudicing the rights, claims or positions of the parties concerned." Sir Gladwyn Jebb explained further the purpose of that draft resolution, at 2: "[W]e are seeking agreement between the parties, at least on a provisional scheme, enabling the flow of oil to be resumed without prejudice to the ultimate agreed solution of the dispute [...] It is of course also with the object of upholding the rule of law that we have retained some reference to the International Court in the preamble."

nationalization: the desire to assert sovereignty over its natural resources and to improve its precarious economic situation. Turning to the legal questions, it argued that the Council had no jurisdiction over the matter, as it was within Iran's sphere of domestic jurisdiction, and that there was no threat to peace and security. Finally, it expressed the view that the particular measures indicated were invalid and that such measures in general were non-binding.[1246]

The Council continued its deliberations in the following meetings. The delegations of India and Yugoslavia submitted a joint proposal deleting the reference to the provisional measures in Britain's second draft resolution in order to make it acceptable to both sides.[1247] On the basis of these suggestions, the UK submitted a revised draft that left references to the provisional measures in the preamble, but omitted such reference from the operative part of the resolution;[1248] this revised draft was received favorably by the representatives of the US, France, the Netherlands, and Brazil.[1249] Several speakers questioned the Council's competence to deal with the matter, however. The USSR representative opposed any kind of resolution as interference with Iran's domestic affairs and violation of Article 2(7) of the Charter.[1250] The representative of Ecuador argued that the Council was not competent since neither the conditions of Chapter VI of the Charter nor of Article 94(2) were fulfilled, and that the Council should wait for the ICJ's decision as to whether the matter fell in Iran's domestic jurisdiction.[1251]

[1246] Statement of Prime Minister Mossadegh on behalf of Iran, S/PV.560, at 3–6; Statement of Mr Saleh on behalf of Iran, at 6–28. The main arguments against the order's validity were the Court's lack of jurisdiction and the interference with Iran's domestic affairs; moreover, Mr Saleh pointed out that the situation did not warrant the indication of the measures and that the UK had made abusive use of the Court, see ibid., at 9–12. With regard to the binding force of provisional measures, see ibid., at 12: Mr Saleh referred to the applicability of Article 94 to "binding" and "final" decisions and argued that only the judgment and not provisional measures possessed these attributes and that the language of Article 41 of the Statute was merely exhortatory.

[1247] UN Doc. S/2379, printed in S/PV.561, 15–16. The Indian representative discussed the effects of the departure of the AIOC technicians on the provisional measures and explained that the third, fourth, and fifth measures relating to a continuation of the activities of the AIOC were no longer capable of implementation, with only the first and the second measures (aimed at preventing action possibly aggravating the dispute or prejudicing rights under a future judgment) retaining relevance. As the same purpose was also pursued in the text of the draft resolution, he considered the reference to the Court's order unnecessary: see ibid., at 16.

[1248] UK, second revised draft resolution, S/2358/Rev.2, 17 October 1951. The revised draft resolution pursued the same objective as the earlier one: a resumption of negotiations.

[1249] S/PV.563, 17 October 1951: the US delegate (at 8–9), the French delegate (at 10), the Dutch delegate (at 32–4, expressing regret, though, that the provisional measures had not been paid more regard (at 33)), and the Brazilian delegate (at 40–1, expressing his relief at 40 that under the terms of the revised draft resolution, a decision on the questions of the concept of domestic jurisdiction and the bindingness of provisional measures was not required).

[1250] Statement of the USSR delegate, S/PV.561, at 21–2.

[1251] Statement of the Ecuadorian delegate, S/PV.562, at 3–10. He nevertheless suggested that the Council could facilitate agreement between the parties "without taking any action that would imply that it regarded itself as competent" (ibid., at 9) and "advis[e] the parties concerned to

On 19 October 1951, the French representative suggested that the Security Council suspend debate until the Court delivered its judgment on jurisdiction.[1252] The British representative did not oppose that proposal, recognizing that consensus on any type of resolution was impossible for the moment.[1253] He warned however that the Council's decision not to take action might create a dangerous precedent: "The tendency will surely be to diminish the prestige of the Security Council, the International Court of Justice and the United Nations itself."[1254] The Security Council followed the French proposal and adjourned discussion of the matter.[1255] It remained seized of the matter, but held no further discussions after the Court found that it lacked jurisdiction.[1256]

Consequently, in the proceedings in the Security Council, relatively little attention was given to the interim measures indicated by the Court: the discussion centered mainly on the domestic jurisdiction clause (Article 2(7) of the Charter) and the question of whether there was a threat to international peace and security.[1257] The Security Council did not take a stand on the issue of whether Article 94(2) applies to interim measures.[1258] It is unclear, though, whether one can deduce from this fact a general reluctance of the Council to take a role in the execution of provisional measures of the Court, or whether this was primarily due to the fact that the measures prescribing specific action had already become irrelevant when the main discussions took place between 15 and 19 October 1951. The precedential value of these Council proceedings for the question of enforcement of provisional measures was also limited in view of the doubts on the jurisdiction of both the Court and the Council.[1259] Moreover, it was clear that the Soviet side was opposed to any decision implying any kind of obligation on the part of Iran.[1260] Since the Soviet veto would have prevented all kinds of enforce-

---

reopen negotiations" (ibid., at 10). With regard to Article 94(2), his view was that the provision related only to judgments and not to provisional measures, although he supported a request for an advisory opinion on this issue, at 8.

[1252] Statement of the French delegate, S/PV.565, at 2–3.   [1253] Ibid., at 4.

[1254] Ibid., at 7–8.

[1255] Ibid., at 12. The USSR dissented, regarding the question as outside the Security Council's competences, ibid., at 4–5. Like in the first decision on an adjournment, the USSR's negative vote did not prevent the decision from being taken, as it was a decision under Article 27(2) of the Charter.

[1256] Ghosh, *The Anglo-Iranian Oil Dispute*, at 166, Elkind, *Interim Protection*, at 108.

[1257] Ghosh, *The Anglo-Iranian Oil Dispute*, at 162–6; Reisman, *Nullity and revision*, at 726.

[1258] *Mani*, 10 Ind. JIL (1970), at 368 fn. 37.

[1259] See *Schachter*, 54 AJIL (1960), at 23–4 (cited with approval by *Tanzi*, 6 EJIL (1995), at 565) (Council discussion added little to discussion of applicability of Article 94(2) to interim measures because of question's relating to Court's jurisdiction). See also Reisman, *Nullity and revision*, at 720 (stating that, while case does not clarify meaning of Article 94, it does highlight problems related to enforcement).

[1260] See Reisman, *Nullity and revision*, at 727.

ment action, not much could be expected from the Council in terms of bringing about compliance with the ICJ measure.

While the Security Council proved ineffective in mediating the conflict,[1261] it was political changes in Iran that paved the way for a solution. An army coup in 1953 overthrew the government of Prime Minister Mossadegh, who had been a key figure in the nationalization policy. The new regime reached an agreement with an international oil consortium and a compensation plan for the Anglo-Iranian Oil Company.[1262]

5. Conclusion

The case was not a good starting-point for the Court to develop jurisprudence on provisional measures as the dispute had heated political ramifications and the nationalization program had rallied nationalist sentiment in Iran against undue influences from abroad. Iran vehemently opposed the Court's involvement, and the basis for the Court's jurisdiction was dubious at first sight and subsequently rejected by the Court. Detailed legal reasoning behind the Court's measures would have been particularly desirable under those circumstances; the virtual absence of any justification did little to make the measures acceptable for Iran. In applying a very low standard for jurisdiction in interim proceedings, the Court did not respond to Iran's objections, and the circumstances requiring the indications of the measures were not explained further—particularly the necessity of those measures despite Iran's argumentation that its own laws included securities for possible compensation claims of the company. The lack of a reasoning on the necessity of the measures seems particularly ill suited considering that the Court's order exceeded what had been requested by the UK in so far as it provided for the establishment of the board of supervision and for the deposit of the excess of revenue over expenses in a bank, a fact which met the most intense criticism by Iran. Particularly with regard to the deposit of the company's gains, Iran's argument did not seem totally unfounded that, even in case of a continued validity of the concessions agreement, it would have been entitled to a certain percentage of the gains. Why the Court nevertheless felt that the entire profits would have to be put on hold required a justification. The absence of reasoning left unclear whether the Court considered those problems at all. It would have been desirable if Iran had chosen to participate in the hearings on provisional measures. Yet its non-participation did not relieve the Court from its duty to remain impartial and stay within its powers under Article 41 of the Statute.

[1261] Ghosh, *The Anglo-Iranian Oil Dispute*, at 166–7; *Frankel*, 6 Yb WA (1952), at 70–1, 74.
[1262] 23 AdG (1953) 4129 A, 24 AdG (1954) 4668 C, 4746 E. On private litigation launched by the Anglo-Iranian Oil Company in courts of several countries, see *O'Connell*, 4 ICLQ (1955), at 267–93.

For the question of jurisdiction, the Court apparently assumed that its competence to indicate provisional measures derived directly from Article 41. Yet the unfortunate situation presented by the fact that the Court had first indicated the measures and then found that it lacked jurisdiction begged the question of whether the alternative approach suggested by Judges Winiarski and Badawi Pasha would not have been the better one.

II. Fisheries Jurisdiction

The Fisheries Jurisdiction cases[1263] were unfortunate because the respondent decided to defy the Court's authority and because the Court's findings were short-lived, being superseded by subsequent legal developments.

1. The proceedings on interim measures

On 14 July 1972, after the main proceedings in the Fisheries Jurisdiction cases had been introduced, Iceland adopted regulations extending its exclusive fishery zone (EFZ) to 50 nautical miles and prohibiting foreign fishing within that zone as of 1 September 1972.[1264] The UK requested the Court to indicate interim measures of protection under Article 41 of its Statute on 19 July; the Federal Republic of Germany followed suit two days later.[1265] The requests aimed at the preservation of the *status quo ante,* i.e. the possibility to fish in the area between 12 and 50 nautical miles.[1266] As in the main proceedings, the applicants based the Court's jurisdiction on exchanges of diplomatic notes with the government of Iceland in 1961.[1267]

Iceland did not appear at the hearings,[1268] but made its views known through telegrams to the Court's Registrar.[1269] It argued that the Court could not indicate interim measures because it lacked jurisdiction and because the application related to economic interests of private actors rather than to legal positions of states. Moreover, it referred to its earlier explan-

---

[1263] For a detailed summary of the facts and the main proceedings, see *supra* B XII.

[1264] The Regulations are printed in ICJ Pleadings, Fisheries Jurisdiction, Vol. I, 79–80, as Annex A to the UK Request for the Indication of Interim Measures of Protection.

[1265] Request for the Indication of Interim Measures of Protection submitted by the UK Government, 19 July 1972, ICJ Pleadings, Fisheries Jurisdiction, Vol. I, 71–87. Request for the Indication of Interim Measures of Protection submitted by the Government of the Federal Republic of Germany, 21 July 1972, ICJ Pleadings, Fisheries Jurisdiction, Vol. II, 23–37.

[1266] See ibid.; and *Oellers-Frahm,* 32 ZaöRV (1972), at 566.

[1267] The UK request did not specify the basis for jurisdiction, but its application referred to the 1961 exchange of notes. The Federal Republic of Germany maintained that the 1961 exchange represented a basis for jurisdiction while emphasizing that an affirmative finding on jurisdiction was not necessary at the interim measures stage. *Supra* n. 1265, at 24–6.

[1268] Iceland did not formally participate at any stage of the proceedings, see *supra* B XII.

[1269] Orders of 17 August 1972, at 14–15 paras. 5, 6, 9 (UK), and at 32 paras. 5, 6, 9 (FRG).

ation of the reasons for extending the EFZ, that is, in particular, its exceptional dependency on the fisheries resources.[1270]

On 17 August 1972, the ICJ, by 14 votes to 1, indicated interim measures of
protection in the two cases.[1271] The Court stated that a party's non-appearance
as such could not prevent it from indicating provisional measures,[1272] and
that there was no need at the interim stage to satisfy itself that it had
jurisdiction "although it ought not to act under Article 41 of the Statute if
the absence of jurisdiction on the merits is manifest."[1273] It then affirmed that
prima-facie jurisdiction existed on the basis of the note exchanges,[1274] but it
did not yet examine the question of whether this agreement was terminated.[1275] Moreover, it decided that the matter was urgent because the regulations in question were due to become operative from 1 September onwards
and that there was a danger of irreparable harm to the rights claimed by the
UK and the Federal Republic of Germany.[1276]

The order in the case between the UK and Iceland stipulated that both
parties should take no action that might aggravate or extend the dispute or
prejudice the final decision of the Court. It also stated that Iceland should
refrain from enforcing its new EFZ against UK-registered vessels fishing
beyond the 12-mile fishery zone and from taking administrative, judicial,
and other sanctions against crews and ships. The Court ordered the British
government to ensure that the annual catch for UK vessels from the "Sea
Area of Iceland"[1277] did not exceed 170,000 metric tons and to provide
Iceland and the Court with all relevant information concerning the regulation of fishing activities in the area.[1278]

Analogous measures were indicated in the case between Germany and
Iceland,[1279] except that the annual limit was set at 119,000 metric tons.[1280]

[1270] Telegrams of the Minister for Foreign Affairs of Iceland to the Registrar, ICJ Pleadings,
Fisheries Jurisdiction, Vol. II, 388–90 (two of 28 July, one of 31 July 1972), 397–8 (two of 11
August 1972).

[1271] Orders of 17 August 1972, 12, 30. Padilla Nervo (Mexico) dissented. Iceland had not
appointed a judge *ad hoc*. For details on the orders, see *Favoreu*, 18 AFDI (1972), at 291–322.

[1272] Orders of 17 August 1972, at 15, para. 11 (UK), and 32–3, para. 11 (FRG). See on this
aspect *Favoreu*, 18 AFDI (1972), at 319–20.

[1273] Orders of 17 August 1972, at 15 para. 15 (UK), and 33 para. 16 (FRG). Judge Padillo
Nervo cited with approval the higher standard suggested by Judges Winiarski and Badawi Pasha
in the Anglo-Iranian Oil Company case (*supra* I 2), and argued that jurisdiction in the matter was
dubious: ibid., Diss. Op. Padilla Nervo, at 21–2 (UK) and 38–9 (FRG).

[1274] Orders of 17 August 1972, at 16 para. 17 (UK), and at 34, para. 18 (FRG).

[1275] Ibid., at 16, para. 19 (UK), and at 34, para. 20 (FRG): the Court merely announced that
this question "will fall to be examined by the Court in due course."

[1276] Ibid., at 16, paras. 17 and 22 (UK), and 33–4, paras. 17 and 23 (FRG).

[1277] Defined by the International Council for the Exploration of the Sea as area Va, at 17,
para. 26(1)(e) (UK), and at 35, para. 27(1)(e) (FRG).

[1278] Order of 17 August 1972 (United Kingdom v. Iceland), at 12–18. For a comment on the
interim measures, see *Perrin*, 77 RGDIP (1973), at 16–34; *Perry*, 7 Vand. JTL (1973–1974), at
512–20; *Oellers-Frahm*, 32 ZaöRV (1972), at 565–70.

[1279] Order of 17 August 1972 (Federal Republic of Germany v. Iceland), at 30–6.

[1280] Ibid., at 34–5, para. 27, 1(e).

In establishing the maximum catches, the Court stressed that account had to be taken of the need for the conservation of fish stocks in the Icelandic area and the exceptional importance of coastal fisheries to the Icelandic economy.[1281] The respective limits were calculated on the basis of the average annual hauls by fishing vessels of the two countries in the preceding five years.[1282]

Unlike in the Anglo-Iranian Oil Company case, the Court did not call for the establishment of a supervisory body like a control commission. Neither was there an explicit provision for the case that the decision on the merits would be in favor of Iceland, i.e. whether and to what extent Iceland would be entitled to compensation if it suspended the enforcement of its new fishery limits.

In both cases, the Court indicated that at an appropriate time before 15 August 1973, it would review the matter at the request of either party, provided that it had not yet delivered the final judgment in the meantime.[1283] When that date approached, the Court had already confirmed its jurisdiction in the judgments of 2 February 1973,[1284] but the proceedings on the merits were not yet concluded.

The Court's affirmative finding of its jurisdiction made it more difficult for Iceland to make a principled argument against the indication of provisional measures as such, which explains why Iceland's protest against the continuation of the measures focused more on substance—primarily the irreparable harm the measures posed for the Icelandic economy—than on lack of jurisdiction (although it still did not acknowledge the jurisdiction).[1285]

Both the UK and the Federal Republic of Germany requested a continuation of the interim measures and complained of Iceland's non-compliance with the earlier orders.[1286]

[1281] Orders of 17 August 1972, at 16–17, paras. 23–4 (UK), and at 34, paras. 24–5 (FRG).

[1282] The UK had suggested a limit of 185,000 metric tons; Germany, 120,000 metric tons. Both claims had been based on the annual catch from 1960 to 1969; the Court held that statistics for the period from 1967 to 1971 were more reflective of the then current situation. Ibid., at 17, paras. 25–6 (UK), and 34–5, paras. 26–7 (FRG).

[1283] Ibid., at 18 (UK), and 35–6 (FRG).   [1284] *Supra* B XII 2.

[1285] See Telegram of the Minister for Foreign Affairs of Iceland to the Registrar, 2 July 1973, ICJ Pleadings, Fisheries Jurisdiction, Vol. II, 447–8. The minister recalled earlier communications by Iceland (in which the argument had been made that the Court had no jurisdiction), but the telegram's main point was that "highly mobile fishing fleets of the distant-water fishing nations should not be allowed to cause dangerous fluctuations in the catch rates and inflict a constant threat of the deterioration of the fishstocks and thus endanger the viability of a one-source economy. It is submitted that the Court by endeavoring to freeze the present dangerous situation is completely ignoring the scientific and economic facts of the case."

[1286] Letter of the UK Agent to the Registrar, 22 June 1973, ICJ Pleadings, Fisheries Jurisdiction, Vol. II, 439–41; and Letter of the Agent of the Federal Republic of Germany to the Registrar, 22 June 1973, ibid., 441–6. While the UK asked for a continuation of the measures without modifications (see ibid., at 440), the Federal Republic of Germany, at 446, also requested the Court to add more weight to its earlier call: ("[...] the Government of the

On 12 July 1973, the Court decided by 11 votes to 3 that the provisional measures should remain operative[1287] and pointed out that these measures did not exclude an interim agreement possibly to be concluded by the parties in order to lay down other catch-limitation figures and related restrictions.[1288] The continuation of the measures was ordered without a re-examination of the situation; the orders were made only by reference to communications by the parties filed in the registry without hearings.[1289] The Court refrained from any comment on whether the earlier orders had achieved their purpose.[1290]

2. The parties' reactions

The UK and the Federal Republic of Germany complied with the order: they did not exceed the catches indicated by the Court and regularly informed the Court and Iceland about the measures taken in connection with the control and regulation of the fish catches.[1291] Iceland, in contrast, protested with harsh words against the measures: "[T]he Government of Iceland protests against the Court's right of jurisdiction in the said cases and it will not consider this Order by the Court binding in any way. The Government will firmly carry out its decision to extend the fisheries jurisdiction to 50 nautical miles as of September 1st 1972 in conformity with the resolution adopted unanimously by the Parliament of Iceland."[1292] This hardline position was reaffirmed in subsequent statements.[1293]

Iceland followed through on its words and enforced the new regulations,[1294] which resulted in frequent incidents between fishing vessels and

Republic of Iceland should be called upon to comply with the measures indicated by the Court in its Order of 17 August 1972 and in particular to refrain in future from any action against the vessels of the Federal Republic of Germany engaged in fishing activities in the waters around Iceland outside the 12-mile-limit") and to admonish the parties again to ensure that "no action of any kind is taken which might aggravate or extend the dispute submitted to the Court."

[1287] Orders of 12 July 1973, at 302–4 (UK), and 313–15 (FRG). The decisions were taken by 11 votes to 3. The dissenting judges held that a reappraisal was necessary in view of the incidents occurring after the first order.

[1288] Ibid., at 303, para. 7 (UK), and at 314, para. 7 (FRG).

[1289] Ibid., at 303, paras. 1–3 (UK), and at 314, paras. 1–3 (FRG).

[1290] Hence, it did not take up the FRG's request that Iceland be called upon to comply with the earlier order (see *supra* n. 1286).

[1291] Letter of the UK agent to the Registrar, 19 December 1972, ICJ Pleadings, Fisheries Jurisdiction, Vol. II, 405–20, Letter of the agent for the government of the Federal Republic of Germany to the Registrar, 21 May 1973, ibid., 423–38.

[1292] Telegram of the Prime Minister of Iceland to the Registrar, 18 August 1972, ICJ Pleadings, Fisheries Jurisdiction, Vol. II, 399. The prime minister pointed to the lack of jurisdiction of the Court, criticized the order's quota system, and regarded the order as an unfortunate interference with the ongoing negotiations.

[1293] Telegram of the Icelandic Minister for Foreign Affairs to the President of the Court, 4 December 1972, ICJ Pleadings, Fisheries Jurisdiction, Vol. II, 404.

[1294] *Perrin*, 77 RGDIP (1973), at 33.

the Icelandic coastguard; eventually, the British Navy got involved and the "Second Cod War" took place.[1295] The Icelandic coastguard ordered UK and German vessels to leave the 50-mile zone and in several instances cut the trawl wires of the poaching trawlers to prevent them from harvesting their catches. From 19 May 1973 onwards, the British Navy provided escorts for UK vessels in the disputed waters.[1296] Although this enabled UK fishermen to continue fishing, one can nevertheless not speak of "compliance" with the order on Iceland's part,[1297] since the Icelandic authorities made all efforts to prevent the British from fishing in the area. On the other hand, one may ask whether the active involvement of the British Navy constituted a violation of the obligation not to aggravate the dispute on the part of the UK. However, the UK policy was defensive in nature, aimed at preventing damage to British vessels and thereby enabling British fishing; the UK did not try to compel Iceland to take certain action. In view of this purely defensive character of UK action and its goal of ensuring that the Court's measures had their intended effect, the UK action did not represent non-compliance with the Order.[1298]

Neither the UK nor the Federal Republic of Germany made an attempt to seize the Security Council under Article 94(2) of the UN Charter. However, the UK sent a letter to the President of the Security Council following an incident in May 1973. The letter complained about Iceland's policy of forceful action against British vessels and its lack of respect for the Court's provisional measures and justified the UK naval escort policy.[1299] Iceland on its part protested to the Security Council against the "serious acts of aggression committed by the United Kingdom," without yet asking for concrete

---

[1295] The FRG never sent warships to the disputed zone and thus the denomination "Cod War" is inapt for relations between the FRG and Iceland, see Jónsson, *Friends in conflict*, at 153. The first "Cod War" (a series of incidents between Icelandic coastal patrol boats, British trawling vessels and the Royal Navy) had taken place between 1958 and 1961 as a consequence of the establishment of a 12-mile EFZ by the Icelandic parliament on 30 June 1958, see *Briney*, 5 Ga. JILC (1975), at 249. For a summary of the facts, see 44 AdG (1974) 18424 A.

[1296] UK Memorial on the Merits, ICJ Pleadings, Fisheries Jurisdiction, Vol. I, 267–432, at 285–7, 375–8, 421–32. German Memorial on the Merits, ICJ Pleadings, Fisheries Jurisdiction, Vol. II, 141–284, at 260–3, and 279–84; Jónsson, *Friends in conflict*, at 133–52. Iceland never disputed that it took enforcement measures. It protested against the action of the British Navy (Jónsson, *Friends in conflict*, at 142–5), but never claimed that the UK itself had violated the Court's interim measures. 43 AdG (1973) 17866 F, 17888 C.

[1297] But see for the opposing view, *Favoreu*, 20 AFDI (1974), at 306 (arguing that since British trawlers continued fishing, "execution" took place, albeit because of the power of the applicants). However, one cannot speak of "execution" when Iceland continuously engaged in efforts to enforce its regulations in spite of the provisional measures.

[1298] But see Declaration of Judge Ignacio-Pinto to the Order of 12 July 1973 (UK), 304–5, who, at 305, speaks of "flagrant violations of the orders of 17 August 1972 from either side."

[1299] Letter dated 28 May 1973 from the representative of the United Kingdom of Great Britain and Northern Ireland to the President of the Security Council, S/10936. The UK did not ask for action by the Council, but considered it appropriate "to bring the situation to your attention and to that of the Members of the Security Council."

action by the Council and without reference to the provisional measures.[1300] No meeting of the Security Council was scheduled in response to those two letters.

Iceland also complained to the NATO Secretary-General, and the matter was discussed in the North Atlantic Council, but without an outcome. Iceland also threatened to break off diplomatic relations with the UK.[1301] In general, the international community was reluctant to exert pressure on Iceland; the Scandinavian foreign ministers even expressed their support for Iceland's position at a meeting of 2 September 1972.[1302]

On 13 November 1973, the UK and Iceland reached an interim agreement that regulated the British fishing in the 50-mile zone for the subsequent two years.[1303] In the hearings before the Court, the UK counsel reported that there were no further incidents after the adoption of this agreement,[1304] and declared that the UK had decided not to pursue its claim for compensation raised in the memorial.[1305] The interim agreement transformed the legal relations between the two countries; it superseded the interim measures with another provisional régime.[1306] The fact that Iceland then no longer

---

[1300] Letter dated 29 May 1973 from the representative of Iceland to the President of the Security Council, S/10937. See the penultimate paragraph: "Finally, the Government of Iceland reserves its right to bring, at a later stage, the armed aggression by British warships in Icelandic waters formally before the Security Council, with a view to appropriate action by the Council in the matter."

[1301] Jónsson, *Friends in conflict*, at 144–7, 43 AdG (1973) 17977 B 4, 18172 C.

[1302] 42 AdG (1972) 17308 E. There were some fears that the Soviet Union might intervene in favor of Iceland; yet, this was unlikely in view of the Soviet opposition to fishery zones exceeding 12 miles, *Rüster* in Blumenwitz/Randelzhofer, Festschrift für Berber at 457, 42 AdG (1972) 17286 C, 17298 E.

[1303] Exchange of notes constituting an interim agreement in the fisheries dispute between the government of the United Kingdom of Great Britain and Northern Ireland and the Government of the Republic of Ireland, ICJ Pleadings, Fisheries Jurisdiction, Vol. II, 459–61. See also 44 AdG (1974) 18424 A.

[1304] Argument of Samuel Silkin, 25 March 1974, ICJ Pleadings, Fisheries Jurisdiction, Vol. I, at 446. *Rousseau*, 79 RGDIP (1975), at 220–1, reports another incident in July 1974 involving a British ship. However, that incident concerned fishing within the 12-mile-zone (a question definitely settled by the 1961 exchange of notes) and was therefore neither a matter of the interim measures nor of the interim agreement; both concerned the areas 12–50 miles from the baselines.

[1305] Argument of Samuel Silkin, *supra* n. 1304, at 447. The claims had been made under the heading "compensation for interference with British shipping" in the UK memorial on the merits, ICJ Pleadings, Vol. I, 267–432, at 375–8: the UK argued that Iceland's action violated the freedom of the high seas, that no authority or justification for such acts could be found under international law, and that they entailed Iceland's responsibility. In this context, the Court's orders were not given particular emphasis, but rather mentioned in passing: "Many British fishing vessels have felt justified in disregarding [the orders by Icelandic coastguard vessels to haul in their nets and to leave the area] for which, in the submission of the Government of the United Kingdom, the Icelandic officers concerned could claim no authority under international law and which, in addition, were incompatible with the Order made by the Court on 17 August 1972." (Ibid., at 375).

[1306] See Judgment of 25 July 1974 (UK), Sep. Op. de Castro, at 76: "This agreement deprives of effect as between the Parties the Orders of the Court [...] indicating interim measures. It establishes a temporary régime valid for a period of two years."

took enforcement action against British vessels was due to the interim agreement with the UK and not to the measures.

West German vessels continued to be subject to Icelandic enforcement action, in reaction to which the Federal Republic lodged additional claims before the Court (as the UK had done earlier)[1307] asking for a declaration that the acts of the Icelandic coastguard were unlawful under international law and that Iceland was obliged to provide compensation. In its memorial on the merits, the Federal Republic of Germany based its complaint about the enforcement action on non-compliance with the orders on provisional measures, although it also mentioned other grounds for illegality.[1308] It stated:

Since the Court has by its Judgment of 2 February 1973 decided with binding force between the Parties that it has jurisdiction in this case, and since under Article 94 of the United Nations Charter each Member of the United Nations has to comply with the decisions of the International Court of Justice in which it is a party, the Government of Iceland cannot, in law, any longer deny its legal obligation to pay due regard to the Order of 17 August 1972.[1309]

This was a rather cautious approach, which could be understood as conceding that the authority of an order indicating provisional measures would depend on the Court's jurisdiction on the merits. In the oral pleadings, the German agent argued that the Icelandic enforcement action was illegal because Iceland had intentionally disregarded the Court's order of 17 August 1972 confirmed by the order of 12 July 1973, but the main focus of his argument was on the impermissibility of the enforcement action under general international law.[1310] This state responsibility claim failed: while the Court held that it had jurisdiction to deal with this issue, it stated that insufficient evidence had been presented for the existence and amount of the concrete damages.[1311]

The Court was rather reticent in its comments on the follow-through with its provisional measures in the judgments on the merits of 25 July 1974. The Court held that the measures indicated in the case of Germany ceased to have effect from the day of the judgment, since Article 41 of its Statute was a competence only *pendente lite*.[1312] It noted that it had not been questioned or

---

[1307] See *supra* n. 1305.

[1308] Memorial on the Merits of the Federal Republic of Germany, ICJ Pleadings, Fisheries Jurisdiction, Vol. II, at 260–5.

[1309] Ibid., at 264.

[1310] Statement of Günther Jaenicke, Agent for the Federal Republic of Germany, 28 March 1974, ICJ Pleadings, Fisheries Jurisdiction, Vol. II, 346–8: the disregard of the orders is raised as the fifth reason for the illegality of the enforcement action.

[1311] Judgment of 25 July 1974 (FRG), at 204–5, para. 76. This decision was taken by 10 to 4 votes, at 206. While the Court saw its jurisdiction on this question as established, Judge de Castro adopted a narrower interpretation of the compromissory clause, Sep. Op. de Castro, 225–6, at 226.

[1312] Judgment of 25 July 1974 (FRG), at 202–3, para. 70. Such a statement was not included in the judgment in the case of the UK against Iceland because the interim agreement had led to a different situation, Judgment of 25 July 1974 (UK), at 17–20, paras. 35–41.

disputed that the UK and the Federal Republic had complied with the catch-limitation measure in the Court's order while Iceland had begun to enforce its new regulations "notwithstanding the Court's order."[1313] The Court seemed unwilling to go beyond that statement to express deeper disapproval of Iceland's action.

3. Conclusion

The interim measures in the Fisheries Jurisdiction cases failed in achieving their intended purposes. Their failure was in large part due to Iceland's opposition to the Court's involvement and its non-participation in the proceedings. In spite of Iceland's objections against its jurisdiction, the Court adopted a low standard for jurisdiction at the interim-measures stage. Apparently, it held that it was free to indicate those measures unless there was an obvious lack of jurisdiction. Its view that in the latter case it "ought not to act under Article 41 of the Statute" could be understood as a comment on propriety rather than on the limits to its competences.[1314] The Court recalled the dispute settlement clauses in the agreements of 1961, but without examining Icelandic objections to their applicability.[1315] On the other hand, Iceland's arguments against jurisdiction were rather weak, and when the Court ordered the continuation of the measures, it had already judged affirmatively on its jurisdiction and thus left no room for further doubt.

The interim measures were criticized by some commentators for various reasons: they were perceived as expressing disapproval of Iceland and lopsided against a small and relatively poor island state in favor of the more powerful applicant states, accepting nearly all of their arguments. The decision also put Iceland in an inferior position in the ongoing negotiations and aimed at suspending a politically important domestic regulation.[1316] Those factors might have increased the burden that the provisional measures represented for Iceland. Yet one could not put the blame on the Court if they constituted an appropriate exercise of its powers and the process was balanced and impartial; the Court cannot be expected to rule in favor of the defendant only because it is less powerful than the applicant.

[1313] Judgments of 25 July 1974, at 17, para. 33 (UK; omitting comments on the acts of the British Navy), and at 188, para. 32 (FRG).

[1314] Orders of 17 August 1972, at 15, para. 15 (UK), and 33, para. 16 (FRG): "Whereas on a request for provisional measures the Court need not, before indicating them, finally satisfy itself that it has jurisdiction on the merits of the case, yet it ought not act under Article 41 of the Statute if the absence of jurisdiction on the merits is manifest."

[1315] Orders of 17 August 1972, at 16, paras. 16–19 (UK), and 33–4, paras. 17–20 (FRG), see in particular 16, para. 19 (UK), and 34, para. 20 (FRG): "Whereas the contention of the Government of Iceland [...] that the above-quoted clause in the Exchange of Notes [...] has been terminated [...] will fall to be examined by the Court in due course."

[1316] *Favoreu*, 18 AFDI (1972), at 308–9; he concludes, at 322, that the measures were biased in favor of the UK and the Federal Republic of Germany.

On their face, the measures did not humiliate Iceland; they were designed to preserve the rights of both sides and put restraints on the UK and Germany as well, since they had to respect quotas for their fishing activities. Yet one might ask whether Iceland's rights were sufficiently protected. The Court emphasized the exceptional dependence of Iceland's economy on coastal fisheries and the need for conservation of fish stocks. Did it pay due regard to these factors when it limited fishing rights for the UK and the Federal Republic on the basis of their average catches in the five preceding years, or did it only pay lip-service to Iceland's exceptional dependence on coastal fisheries and the conservation needs? What if the applicants' average catch had been excessive and not reconcilable with Iceland's needs and the necessity for the conservation of fish stocks? Assuming that overfishing had taken place, Iceland's share would effectively be reduced if it was to guarantee conservation of the fish stocks, without the UK and the Federal Republic having to share the burden.

The issue of overfishing had been raised in the hearings on the interim measures: in the oral proceedings, the German agent, Günther Jaenicke, expressed doubts on whether the Icelandic concerns were justified. He pointed to statistics of the International Council for the Exploration of the Sea showing that the catches from 1960 to 1969 were rather constant and concluded that "at least at present, the danger of overfishing has not yet materialized."[1317] Some further explanations would have been desirable—if the danger had not yet materialized "at least at present," this did not rule out that it might do in the near future. Was a reference to a statistics that depicted average catches sufficient to rule out the existence of dangers for the fish stocks? Moreover, there was no differentiation with regard to categories of fish stocks. A closer analysis might have revealed that different régimes had to be set up for certain types of fish;[1318] the appropriateness of a maximum limit for all catches that leaves the conservation interests for certain fish stocks out of account might be questionable.[1319]

The UK counsel Sir Peter Rawlinson pointed out that there was no doubt that the fish stocks in the Icelandic area should receive the necessary protection, possibly including catch limitations, and that Iceland should get preferential treatment. His point was, though, that conservation measures should not be imposed unilaterally by Iceland, but had to be adopted through a multilateral mechanism: the North East Atlantic Fisheries

---

[1317] Oral Argument, 2 August 1972, ICJ Pleadings, Fisheries Jurisdiction, Vol. II, at 56.

[1318] As *Rousseau*, 76 RGDIP (1972), reports, at 898, fn. 124, the institute of maritime biology in Reykjavik had suggested a 50 % reduction in cod catches, predicting that stocks might otherwise be exhausted in two or three years.

[1319] For example, the Icelandic–German agreement of 28 November 1975, *supra* n. 425, that lays down that out of a maximum annual catch of 60,000 metric tons for vessels registered in the FRG in the Icelandic area, just 5,000 tons of which could be cod: point 2.

(NEAF) Convention.[1320] The UK reported that the permanent commission established under that convention had already recommended various conservation measures for the area.[1321] Here again, some more explanation would have been desirable. Was it certain enough that the NEAF Commission would be enabled to adopt effective measures soon, and did that rule out the need for protection in the meantime? The UK counsel had stated before that there had not been a decline in the average total catches.[1322] Still, there might be doubt whether this necessarily precludes any danger of overfishing, particularly for certain types of fish.

The question of overfishing was not among the questions on which the Court had asked the agents for clarification before adopting its interim measures.[1323] Admittedly, Iceland could have proposed a standard and informed the Court in detail about its needs and the conservation measures it considered appropriate.[1324] Still, this did not relieve the Court from its responsibility to safeguard the rights of either party, and since it had defined conservation needs and the needs of the Icelandic people as decisive criteria, one would have wished that the order reflected that those factors were taken seriously; from the wording of the order, it is not visible whether a proper balancing of interests had taken place.[1325]

[1320] North-East Atlantic Fisheries Convention, 24 January 1959, 486 UNTS 157.

[1321] Statement of Sir Peter Rawlinson on behalf of the UK, 1 August 1972, ICJ Pleadings, Fisheries Jurisdiction, Vol. I, at 116, reporting that conservation measures under Article 7(1) of the convention had already been adopted (including measures on the size of mesh of fishing nets, but not, however, on the amount of catch) that applied among others to the Iceland area and that the commission had proposed to the contracting states under Article 7(2) that it be empowered to recommend measures including catch limitations, a proposal approved by most parties except for three (Iceland, Belgium, and Poland), the formal approval of which was expected "shortly." The UK view was that, accordingly, there would soon be a basis for catch limitations for the area under this multilateral framework.

[1322] Ibid., 113.

[1323] Telegram of the UK agent to the Registrar, 3 August 1972, ICJ Pleadings Vol. II, 391–2, Telegram of the agent for the Federal Republic of Germany to the Registrar, 4 August 1972, ICJ Pleadings Vol. II, 393–5.

[1324] Iceland drew the Court's attention to its dependency on the resources and the need for conservation: Letters of the Minister of Foreign Affairs of Iceland to the Registrar of 29 May 1972 and 27 June 1972, ICJ Pleadings, Vol. II, at 380–2. Annexed was, among others, a memorandum by the Icelandic Ministry of Foreign Affairs entitled Fisheries Jurisdiction in Iceland, which is reprinted in: ICJ Pleadings I, 27–66, containing a report on related facts. Nevertheless, the Court's work would have been facilitated had Iceland provided more detailed information, such as concrete proposals on the catch limits it regarded necessary for the different types of fish stocks and the share it demanded.

[1325] But see *Langavant/Pirotte*, 80 RGDIP (1976), at 67, arguing that the Court set up the quota after the demonstration that there was no overexploitation. However, while the topic was mentioned, there was no deeper analysis. This is not to take sides or to express an opinion as to the need for establishing different catch limits—the analysis of that problem goes beyond the scope of the present study. However, those questions were controversial and were matters of the protection of the rights of either party; it would have enhanced the legitimacy of the measures if they had visibly been the result of a thorough examination and a balancing of interests.

The Court might have refrained from establishing a control commission given the limited success of the related measures in the Anglo-Iranian Oil Company case or out of doubts on whether it would have been authorized to do so.[1326] Such a control commission had not been requested, and in any case, there would have been no point in creating an organ of that type. Iceland would hardly have cooperated in its establishment. Although there was sharp disagreement between the parties, there was no climate of mutual suspicions and distrust. The dispute concerned the *law* and the need to adopt conservation measures. A commission to verify both sides' *activities* would therefore not have contributed much to the solution: Iceland never concealed that it was willing to enforce its regulations, and there were no conflicts on the issue of whether enforcement action took place.[1327]

The provision in the first orders that the measures were indicated for a limited period of time and were then subject to review was a positive factor, because thereby an automatic mechanism was introduced to make sure that the measures were up to date and efficient. One might doubt, however, whether the way the Court proceeded in the second orders was in any way constructive. A re-examination was not carried out, even though one would have thought that such a re-examination was the very purpose of a limitation of the first provisional measures for a certain time period. The Court apparently closed its eyes to the facts that the measures so far had failed to achieved their purpose and that an aggravation of the dispute had taken place; it did not even react to claims by the Federal Republic of Germany relating to non-compliance with the first measures. What is noticeable is that Iceland—the country that chose to ignore the provisional measures and boycott the Court—was in general committed to the rule of law and democracy, and that it violated the provisional measures towards countries with whom it had close ties and much in common. At the same time, one has to bear in mind that the fisheries policy had broad domestic support, and that "vital interests" had been involved; there were no doubts on the exceptional dependence on Iceland's economy on coastal fisheries.[1328]

III. Nuclear tests

In these cases, Australia and New Zealand challenged the legality of French nuclear testing in the South Pacific.

1. Background: France's nuclear weapons program

This litigation centered on highly political questions. The French government had decided to build nuclear weapons in the 1950s; it detonated its first

---

[1326] *Favoreu*, 18 AFDI (1972), at 304, 306.   [1327] But see ibid.
[1328] See further the report on the judgments, *supra* B XII.

fission bomb on 13 February 1960 in the Algerian desert. A series of atmospheric and underground tests followed, triggering strong protests, particularly from African states, and a number of resolutions in the UN General Assembly.[1329] In 1963, France announced that it would not become a party to the Limited Nuclear Test Ban Treaty.[1330] It moved its test center to French Polynesia in the Pacific Ocean; the main firing site was the Mururoa Atoll, located approximately 6,000 kilometers from the Australian mainland, 4,600 kilometers from New Zealand, and 1,950 kilometers from the Cook Islands, a self-governing state linked in free association with New Zealand. In order to exclude aircraft and shipping from the test area, France created "prohibited zones" for aircraft and "dangerous zones" for aircraft and shipping.[1331] The first test explosion at the atoll took place on 2 July 1966.

The French government justified its nuclear program by pointing to the necessity to protect its safety and independence as long as the requirements for complete disarmament were not met. It felt unable to rely entirely on its allies since their strategic doctrines might change in the future. The possession of nuclear weapons would also give France a major political role in international affairs, raising it to the same level as the other permanent members of the UN Security Council who were nuclear powers, and ensuring greater influence in possible negotiations on nuclear disarmament. While an intense national debate ensued on the *force de frappe* (the independent nuclear strike force), the government forged ahead with the nuclear program, which it styled as a cornerstone of the foreign policy of the Fifth Republic.[1332]

Between 1966 and 1973, France conducted a total of 34 tests in the South Pacific region, all of them in the atmosphere.[1333] Measurable quantities of radioactive matter dissipated into the environment, as confirmed by the UN Scientific Committee on the Effects of Atomic Radiation.[1334] France argued

---

[1329] Resolution 1379 (XIV) of 20 November 1959 expressed grave concern over France's intention to conduct nuclear tests in the Sahara and requested it to refrain from nuclear tests, Resolution 1652 (XVI) of 24 November 1961 called for a cessation of nuclear tests in Africa.

[1330] Treaty banning nuclear weapon tests in the atmosphere, in outer space, and under water of 5 August 1963, 480 UNTS 43. See *Ris*, 4 Denv. JILP (1974), at 113–15, on its significance in this case.

[1331] See the summary of the facts in the judgments of 20 December 1974, at 258, paras. 17–18 (Australia), and at 461–2, paras. 17–18 (New Zealand). See further Goldblat, *French nuclear tests*, at 12–13, 33; Hoog/Schröder-Schüler, *Die französischen Nuklearversuche im Pazifik*, at 43–62; *Ris*, 4 Denv. JILP (1974), at 112–13.

[1332] *Cot*, 19 AFDI (1973), at 253. For details on the French official position, see *de Lacharrière*, 20 AFDI (1974), at 235–51; and French Ministry of Foreign Affairs, White Paper on the French nuclear tests, June 1973; on the domestic discussion, see Goldblat, *French nuclear tests*, at 13–16; and *Rousseau*, 78 RGDIP (1974), at 796–8. See also *Ris*, 4 Denv. JILP (1974), at 111–12.

[1333] See Goldblat, *French nuclear tests*, at 12–13 and Table: "French Nuclear Tests in the South Pacific 1966–73," Appendix to a Report of November 1973 by the New Zealand National Radiation Laboratory, ICJ Pleadings, Nuclear Tests, Vol. 2, 310.

[1334] See the summary of the facts in the Judgments of 20 December 1974, at 258, paras. 17–18 (Australia), and at 461–2, paras. 17–18 (New Zealand).

that while its tests caused radioactive fallout all over the world, including in Australia and New Zealand, the doses were negligible and produced no health risks. It also noted that precautions had been taken to minimize the potential impact of the tests.[1335] Civil society groups and governments from around the world[1336] joined South Pacific states in protests against continued nuclear tests in the region.[1337]

2. Australia's and New Zealand's applications and requests for the indication of provisional measures

From 18 to 20 April 1973, the Australian attorney-general met with the French justice and defense ministers in Paris, in which the French side insisted on the necessity of the nuclear tests and rejected the idea of jointly submitting the dispute about their legality to the ICJ.[1338] New Zealand's vice prime minister discussed the matter with French President Georges Pompidou later that month, but left Paris without a promise from France to cease further tests.[1339] On 9 May 1973, the Court's Registry received unilateral applications against France from Australia[1340] and New Zealand[1341] requesting a declaration that further atmospheric nuclear weapon tests in the South Pacific Ocean would violate the applicable rules of international law and an order barring France from conducting such tests. The applicants claimed that atmospheric nuclear tests in general were not permissible under international law, that the tests violated their territorial integrity since radioactive fallout could be registered in both Australia and New Zealand, and that France violated the freedom of the high seas—on the one hand, through setting obstacles for navigation and aircraft by its "prohibited and dangerous in the zones" around the test sites, on the other hand, through the pollution caused by the tests.[1342] As jurisdictional basis, the applicants cited an article of the 1928 General Act for the Peaceful Settlement of International

---

[1335] See White Paper, *supra* n. 1332.

[1336] Hoog/Schröder-Schüler, *Die französischen Nuklearversuche im Pazifik*, 5–13, 16–20, 33, 25–42, 51–62; *Rousseau*, 78 RGDIP (1974), at 800–10.

[1337] On 17 April 1973, the South Pacific Forum adopted a declaration calling for the immediate termination of the tests: 43 AdG (1973) 17870 E.

[1338] 43 AdG (1973) 17868 A 1.   [1339] 43 AdG (1973) 17868 A 2.

[1340] Application instituting proceedings by Australia, ICJ Pleadings, Nuclear Tests, Vol. 1, 3–39.

[1341] Application instituting proceedings by New Zealand, ICJ Pleadings, Nuclear Tests, Vol. 2, 3–45.

[1342] See orders of 22 June 1973, at 103, para. 22 (Australia), and 139–40, para. 23 (New Zealand). The parties' submissions were not wholly identical: the Australian application referred to the conduct of "atmospheric tests," whereas the New Zealand one spoke of nuclear tests giving rise to radioactive fallout in general. The Court's judgments treated the applications in the same way; critical on the Court's approach *Elkind*, 9 Vand. JTL (1976), at 57–9.

Disputes[1343] in connection with Articles 36(1) and 37 of the ICJ Statute and, alternatively, Article 36(2) of the ICJ Statute. Australia and New Zealand had issued declarations recognizing the compulsory jurisdiction of the Court, as had France;[1344] however, the French declaration in force had been made under a reservation relating to disputes concerning activities connected with national defense.[1345] In requests for the indication of interim measures of protection submitted on the same day as the applications instituting proceedings, Australia[1346] and New Zealand[1347] asked the Court to order that France desist from conducting any further nuclear tests giving rise to radioactive fallout pending the proceedings in the case.[1348]

France objected to the proceedings and did not formally take part in them at any stage,[1349] although it did present its views in a letter to the ICJ's Registrar on 16 May 1973. It argued that the Court was manifestly not competent and requested that the case be removed from the docket.[1350] It recalled that its declaration under the optional clause had been made with a reservation relating to "disputes concerning activities connected with

[1343] General Act for the Pacific Settlement of Disputes of 26 September 1928, 93 LNTS, 343–63. Article 17 reads: "All disputes with regard to which the parties are in conflict as to their respective rights shall, subject to any reservations which may be made under Article 39, be submitted for decision to the Permanent Court of International Justice, unless the parties agree, in the manner hereinafter provided, to have resort to an arbitral tribunal. It is understood that the disputes referred to above include in particular those mentioned in Article 36 of the Statute of the Permanent Court of International Justice." In 1931, Australia, France, and New Zealand acceded to the General Act, see 107 LNTS 531–2, 529, and 532–4. For details on the Act and its history, see *Heydte* in EPIL II, at 499–502.

[1344] Declaration recognizing as compulsory the jurisdiction of the International Court of Justice, 10 May 1966, 562 UNTS 71.

[1345] "On behalf of the Government of the French Republic, I declare that I recognize as compulsory ipso facto and without special agreement [. . .] the jurisdiction of the Court, in conformity with Article 36, paragraph 2, of the Statute, in all disputes which may arise concerning facts or situations subsequent to this declaration, with the exception of [. . .] (3) disputes arising out of a war or international hostilities, disputes arising out of a crisis affecting national security or out of any measure or action relating thereto, and disputes concerning activities connected with national defence."

[1346] Declaration recognizing as compulsory the jurisdiction of the International Court of Justice of 6 February 1954, 186 UNTS 78.

[1347] Declaration recognizing as compulsory the jurisdiction of the Permanent Court of International Justice of 8 April 1940, printed in ICJ YB 1972–3, at 72–3.

[1348] Request for the indication of interim measures of protection submitted by Australia, ICJ Pleadings, Nuclear Tests, Vol. 1, 43, at 57, Request for the indication of interim measures of protection submitted by New Zealand, ICJ Pleadings, Nuclear Tests, Vol. 2, 49, at 59.

[1349] Judgments of 20 December 1974, at 256, para. 13 (Australia) and at 460, para. 13 (New Zealand). For a defense of the French non-participation see *de Lacharrière*, 20 AFDI (1974), at 249–50 (regarding non-participation as the "clearest and most honorable choice" ("*choix le plus net et plus honorable*") and questioning the seriousness of the alternative). Critically, *Cot*, 19 AFDI (1973), at 271; for a report on the opposing views among French commentators, see *Thierry*, 20 AFDI (1974), at 288–9.

[1350] Letter from the French ambassador in the Netherlands to the Registrar, ICJ Pleadings, Nuclear Tests, Vol. 2, 347–57. This was reaffirmed in a letter from the French ambassador in the Netherlands to the Registrar of 21 May 1973, ibid., 363.

national defense" and that the French nuclear tests in the Pacific Ocean represented precisely such activities.[1351] In a detailed annex, it explained that the 1928 General Act could not provide a jurisdictional basis as it had lapsed with the demise of the League of Nations and in any case could not override the subsequent reservation with regard to national defense matters.[1352] The Court took note of these French submissions in its orders,[1353] although the applicants objected because the submissions were not made in the regular manner in the proceedings.[1354]

3. The orders of 22 July 1973

By its orders of 22 July 1973, the Court indicated by 8 votes to 6 that both sides should ensure that no action was taken that might aggravate the dispute or prejudice the rights of either party, and, in particular, the French government should avoid nuclear tests causing the deposit of radioactive fallout on the territory of Australia, New Zealand, the Cook Islands, Niue, and the Tokelau Islands.[1355] Although the disputes related to the same events and the argumentation of the applicants was similar, the proceedings were not joined; Australia and New Zealand did choose the same judge *ad hoc*, however.[1356]

The order does not contain an actual discussion of issues relating to jurisdiction. On the relevant standard, the Court pointed out that although a final determination of its jurisdiction on the merits was not required, "it ought not to indicate such measures unless the provisions invoked by the Applicant, appear, *prima facie*, to afford a basis on which the jurisdiction of the Court might be founded." Thus, it indicated as relevant criterion a possibility of jurisdiction.[1357] Here, the Court laid an emphasis that

---

[1351] Letter from the French ambassador in the Netherlands to the Registrar, ICJ Pleadings, Nuclear Tests, Vol. 2, at 348.

[1352] Ibid., at 349–57; see Order of 22 June 1973, at 102, para. 15 (Australia).

[1353] Orders of 22 June 1973, at 101–2, para. 15 (Australia), and 137–8, para. 16 (New Zealand).

[1354] See statement of Senator Lionel Murphy on behalf of Australia, Public Sitting of 21 May 1973, ICJ Pleadings, Nuclear tests, Vol. 1, 166, at 183, and the statement of A. M. Finlay on behalf of New Zealand, Public sitting of 24 May 1973, ICJ Pleadings, Nuclear tests, Vol. 2, 100, at 103.

[1355] Orders of 22 June 1973, at 106 (Australia), and at 142 (New Zealand). Dissenting opinions were filed by Judges Forster (Senegal), Nagendra Singh (India), Petrén (Sweden), and Ignacio-Pinto (Dahomey). For details, see Frankel, 7 NYU JILP (1974), at 163–76.

[1356] Both sides selected Sir Garfield Barwick, Chief Justice of Australia, to sit in the case. Judgments of 20 December 1974, at 255, para. 3 (Australia), and at 458 (para. 3).

[1357] See *Frankel*, 7 NYU JILP (1974), at 167; *Ris*, 4 Denv. JILP (1974), at 128; see also the declarations by Judge Nagendra Singh, Orders of 22 June 1973, at 108–10 (Australia), and 145–6 (New Zealand), and by Judge *ad hoc* Barwick, ibid., at 110 (Australia) and 146 (New Zealand). But see also Diss. Op. Petrén, ibid., at 126–7 (Australia), and at 161–2 (New Zealand) (considering Court's test as one of probability rather than mere possibility, a condition not considered to be met in the case).

somewhat differed from the earlier cases of interim protection in so far as the stipulated test did not refer to the *absence* of a manifest *lack* of jurisdiction, but instead to the *presence* of a *possible basis* for jurisdiction, thus representing a higher threshold for the applicant: a *positive* test.[1358] Yet, the actual application of the test did not show whether this had effectively led to a stricter standard. After summarizing the parties' arguments in this respect, the Court limited itself to the statement: "Whereas the material submitted to the Court leads it to the conclusion, at the present stage of the proceedings, that the provisions invoked by the applicant appear, *prima facie*, to afford a basis on which the jurisdiction of the Court might be founded; and whereas the Court will accordingly proceed to examine the Applicant's request for the indication of interim measures of protection."[1359] The reasoning does not reveal whether any thorough analysis of the bases for jurisdiction had taken place. One might wonder whether this brief statement was well advised in the wake of the Fisheries Jurisdiction cases, in which the Court had also faced non-appearance on part of the respondent and sharp protests against its jurisdiction. While the jurisdictional basis, although disputed, had been fairly clear in the Fisheries Jurisdiction cases (as confirmed in the judgments on jurisdiction), the Court's competence in the Nuclear Tests cases rested on shakier ground. All the more would some further explanation have been desirable.[1360] It was rather questionable whether the French declaration under Article 36(2) could have provided jurisdiction since the development of the French nuclear arms force reasonably falls within the rubric of activities "connected with national defense," thereby exempting the dispute from the Court's jurisdiction.[1361] This conclusion is all the more persuasive in that the filing of that reservation seems to have been motivated precisely by the desire to protect France's nuclear program from judicial scrutiny.[1362] The French arguments against the validity of the 1928 General Act could also not be easily dismissed.[1363]

[1358] See *Cot*, 19 AFDI (1973), at 262–3. For a critique of a prima facie standard, see Orders of 22 June 1973, Diss. Op. Forster, at 111 (Australia) and 148 (New Zealand); and *Lellouche*, 16 Harv. ILJ (1975), at 617–19 (suggesting that question of jurisdiction should have been ruled on first).

[1359] Orders of 22 June 1973, at 102, para. 17 (Australia), and at 138, para. 18 (New Zealand).

[1360] *Cot*, 19 AFDI (1973), at 259.

[1361] See para. 3 of the declaration, *supra* n. 1344.

[1362] The preceding French declaration under the optional clause of 10 July 1959, 337 UNTS 65, had contained a narrower exception; its exception number 3 partly corresponded to the one in the 1966 declaration but did not encompass "disputes concerning activities connected with national defense." It is hardly a coincidence that the reservation had been extended in 1966—precisely at the time when the nuclear test phase in French Polynesia was being launched. A nuclear armament research and development program might reasonably be presumed to fall under the category of "activities connected with national defense." See also the French Ministry of Foreign Affairs' White Paper, *supra* n. 1332, at 20; *Cot*, 19 AFDI (1973), at 260.

[1363] See *Lellouche*, 16 Harv. ILJ (1975), at 628–31; *Cot*, 19 AFDI (1973), at 260.

The Court indicated the measures on the basis that the relevant information did "not exclude the possibility that damage to Australia might be shown to be caused by the deposit on Australian territory of radioactive fallout resulting from such tests and to be irreparable."[1364] While this argumentation was criticized as protection against an "uncertain violation of an uncertain right,"[1365] it lies within the nature of interim proceedings before the Court that the existence of a right might still be unclear during the interim proceedings. Two strands of argumentation on this point should be distinguished. One claim held that the nuclear tests were prohibited regardless of whether they resulted in damage for the respective country's population; here, the facts were undisputed, unlike the existence of the legal principles to this extent. On the other hand, there was reference to a right not to suffer negative health effects; here, the French did not contest the legal principle as such, but argued that the minimal fallout posed no risk. The order's reference to "damage" leans towards the latter concept—in other words, that the right afforded protection was not the general right to be free of nuclear tests, but a right to be free from *damage* caused by nuclear fallout, a principle that was not disputed *per se*, but whose relevance under the given circumstances was not entirely clear.[1366] The Court should perhaps have elaborated further on why the danger of irreparable harm was important enough to outweigh the French interests and clarified the relevant threshold. The potential damage of a suspension of the tests for France was not even discussed. This is not to say that the decision taken by the Court was wrong—it is advisable to proceed with caution in a case where the health risks are not predictable—but provisional measures are more palatable for both sides if the reasoning demonstrates that both perspectives were duly considered.[1367] On the other hand, France's non-participation did not facilitate this balancing of interests and thus the French government might have had only itself to blame. Yet the fact that a state refrains from participating in the proceedings does not release the Court from its obligation to remain impartial and to consider all relevant evidence.[1368]

4. The situation after the orders

France's first reactions were not promising for compliance. In a statement on 23 June 1973, a speaker for the French ministry of foreign affairs repeated the

---

[1364] Orders of 22 June 1973, at 105, para. 29 (Australia), and 141, para. 30 (New Zealand).

[1365] *Lellouche*, 16 Harv. ILJ (1975), at 620. See also *Cot*, 19 AFDI (1973), at 265.

[1366] See on the potential damage *Ris*, 4 Denv. JILP (1974), at 115–17.

[1367] One of the points raised in Judge Forster's dissenting opinions is that the order fails to protect the rights of either of the applicants or France, Orders of 22 June 1973, at 114 (Australia), and 148 (New Zealand).

[1368] See Judgments of 25 July 1974, at 257, para. 15 (Australia), and at 461, para. 15 (New Zealand).

official line that France did not recognize the Court's jurisdiction in the case.[1369] On 28 June 1973, the French government published a statement on its nuclear tests policy, the White Paper on French Nuclear Tests, in which it presented itself as unimpressed by the international protests and by the proceedings launched by Australia and New Zealand.[1370] The defensive and at times rather emotional tone of the document can hardly be overlooked.[1371] In particular, the paper voiced the suspicion that ulterior motives might lie behind the opposition against the nuclear tests:

The question then is whether the demonstrations and proceedings organized against our nuclear tests have not been motivated by something other than a concern for the preservation of the environment, protected absolutely, and for the norms of international law, respected absolutely. Behind certain of these campaigns does there not lie a willingness to obstruct our defense policy and to oppose our will for independence? The French government will however not allow the fundamental objective of the country's security and independence to be called in question.[1372]

French defense minister, Robert Galley, announced France's intention to find appropriate sites for underground tests in French Polynesia, but cautioned that this might take several years; in the meantime, the government pledged to continue atmospheric testing as long as it remained necessary for national defense.[1373] The tone later grew more conciliatory, and a series of statements were made according to which the atmospheric tests were to be replaced by underground tests after 1974.[1374]

France did not comply with the provisional measures, conducting two further test series in the Pacific in the summers of 1973 and 1974.[1375] Since it had been required to abstain from testing, each test represented an individual violation of the order that could not be cured by subsequent compliance

---

[1369] 43 AdG (1973) 18343 B.

[1370] Ibid., and White Paper, *supra* n. 1332. For further explanations of the French government's legal opinion, see *de Lacharrière*, 20 AFDI (1974), at 235–51.

[1371] For example, White Paper, *supra* n. 1332, at 1, the preamble ends: "Against those who think they can restrict the freedom of a state by a series of campaigns which are based on uncertain or fallacious arguments, the French government will set not only the clear conscience it has of national interests but also facts which have not been refuted. For those who are not swayed by emotion and for those who do not want to be swayed by campaigns which challenge objectivity, this White Paper will provide useful information." See also conclusion, ibid., at 21: "The hostile campaigns against the French nuclear tests in the Pacific have no sound scientific basis. Legally they rest on the rule of law [. . .]."

[1372] Ibid., at 21. In an interview on 24 July 1973, the French foreign minister again affirmed the necessity of nuclear armament in ensuring the country's independence and security, see 43 AdG (1973) 18343 B 2. The arguments explained in the White Paper were also reiterated in a statement of French President Georges Pompidou on defense policy of 27 September 1973, 43 AdG (1973) 18344 B 3.

[1373] 43 AdG (1973) 18344 B 2.

[1374] See those reported in the Judgments of 20 December 1974, at 265–7, paras. 34–41 (Australia), and at 469–72, paras. 35–44 (New Zealand).

[1375] The tests were carried out from 21 July to 29 August 1973 and from 16 June to 15 September 1974. 43 AdG (1973) 18343 B 2, 44 AdG 18932 A (1974).

with the interim measures. Australia and New Zealand reported that nuclear fallout was registered in their respective territory and informed the Court accordingly.[1376] Both issued notes of protest to France for the disregard of the order and called upon France not to commit further violations.[1377] The wave of international protests against the 1973 test series was considerably stronger than in previous years.[1378] Peru went as far as to break off its diplomatic relations with France on 23 July 1973 when the tests resumed.[1379] The UN response was surprisingly muted. No attempt was made to enforce the order through the Security Council.[1380] During the general debate in the General Assembly in September and October 1973, a few delegates voiced criticism of the French tests,[1381] some making express reference to the ICJ orders.[1382] But even the statements of the representatives of Australia and New Zealand were rather reserved as far as non-compliance with the orders was concerned.[1383] The French representative, on the other hand, did not explicitly comment on the ICJ order in his speech at the general debate,

---

[1376] Judgments of 20 December 1974, at 258–9, para. 19 (Australia), and 462, para. 19 (New Zealand).

[1377] See the various notes from the Australian government to the French government and public statements printed in ICJ Pleadings, Nuclear tests, Vol. 1, 545, 547, 549, 551, 552. For New Zealand, see the note of 22 July 1973 from the New Zealand Embassy to the French Ministry of Foreign Affairs, Annex XIII to the New Zealand Memorial, ICJ Pleadings, Nuclear Tests, Vol. 2, at 245, explicitly complaining of the violation of a "binding order," and further letters, ibid., 299–301.

[1378] See Goldblat, *French nuclear tests*, at 18–19; Hoog/Schröder-Schüler, *Die französischen Nuklearversuche im Pazifik*, at 23, 25–42, 51–62; Rousseau, 78 RGDIP (1974), at 820–821.

[1379] 43 AdG (1973) 18343 B 2. On 7 August 1975, the two states announced a resumption of diplomatic relations, 45 AdG (1975) 19630 C.

[1380] Of course, any such attempt would not have been likely to succeed given France's veto right as a permanent member of the Security Council.

[1381] See the statement of Peru's representative on 24 September 1973, UN Doc. A/PV.2124, at 7 and 8, and the statement of the representative of Ecuador during the same meeting (at 13) as well as the statements of representatives of the following countries at subsequent meetings: A/PV.2129, 26 September 1973, Mongolia (at 4), New Zealand (at 6–8); A/PV.2131 of 27 September 1973, Uruguay (at 3), Fiji (at 7), Colombia (at 13); A/PV.2138 of 3 October 1973, Australia (at 7–8).

[1382] See the Colombian delegate, A/PV.2131, at 13, para. 144: "In the case at issue there was also a formal judgment handed down by the International Court of Justice at the request of Australia and New Zealand, and our deepest hope is to see the highest court of the United Nations fully respected by the Member States when it intervenes in matters of peace." and Fiji's delegate, ibid., at 8: "France has ignored the call of the international community for the halting of all atmospheric nuclear-weapon testing in the Pacific or elsewhere, and its call for all states that have not done so to adhere to the partial test-ban Treaty. It has chosen to disregard the terms of an interim injunction granted by the World Court." See also the Peruvian delegate, A/PV.2124, at 8: "Despite the pronouncements of the General Assembly, of the United Nations Conference on the Human Environment, of the International Court of Justice and of the coastal states of the South Pacific, atmospheric tests on the atoll of Mururoa continue."

[1383] New Zealand, A/PV.2129, did not even explicitly mention the order, but stated (at 7): "In every way possible—by protests to the Governments concerned, by action in the General Assembly, by application to the International Court of Justice—we have made every effort to bring about the cessation of nuclear testing. But the testing in the Pacific zone has still persisted." Australia stated, A/PV.2131, at 7: "We find it regrettable that the Governments of two nuclear

instead defending his country's policy in terms similar to those of the White Paper.[1384] The General Assembly adopted two resolutions on the urgent need for suspension of nuclear and thermonuclear tests[1385] in line with earlier resolutions on the matter,[1386] but this time with a more intense call for an end to the tests:

The General Assembly [...] (1) emphasizes its deep concern at the continuance of nuclear weapon tests, both in the atmosphere and underground, and at the lack of progress towards a comprehensive test ban agreement; [...] (3) insists that the nuclear-weapon states which have been carrying out nuclear weapon tests in the atmosphere discontinue such tests forthwith [...][1387]

At the time the resolutions were adopted, only China and France still carried out atmospheric nuclear tests, with France conducting far more than China.[1388] France was, therefore, one of the addressees of paragraph (3), if not the primary one. The resolutions made no reference to the ICJ orders, however, and the verbatim records of the session where the vote was taken do not indicate that that issue was addressed.[1389]

In addition to the non-compliance with the orders, the French government expressed its dissatisfaction by terminating its declaration recognizing the compulsory jurisdiction of the ICJ in January 1974 and denouncing the

Powers have continued to conduct nuclear-weapons testing programs in the atmosphere [...] despite the repeated expressions of disapproval by the United Nations and other international bodies and other international bodies and by individual countries, I take the opportunity to recall that on 22 June last the International Court of Justice gave an order for interim measures to restrain the Government of France from conducting atmospheric nuclear tests in the Pacific which would deposit radioactive fallout on Australia."

[1384] Statement by the French delegate, A/PV.2147, 10 October 1973, at 2. His view was that "certain slanderous campaigns have sought to cast slurs upon our very idea of national independence, shared by so many others [...] Illusions, wars, more illusions and war again: this has been our fate. Henceforth, we rely primarily on ourselves, on our own efforts. [...] We have been distressed, I would say hurt, to hear from our friends and from people for whom we have affection statements made here or there whose lack of reality in comparison with the facts or the actual situation in the world seems surprising to me. [...] [I]t is a matter of national independence for a nation which does not want to be the pawn of world strategy."

[1385] A/RES/3078 A and B (XXVIII) of 6 December 1973. Res. 3078 A was adopted by 89 votes to 5 with 33 abstentions, Resolution 3078 B by 65 votes to 7 with 57 abstentions. France voted against both resolutions, see UN Doc. A/PV.2192, at 3–4.

[1386] See those quoted in Resolution 3078 A, preamble, in particular the directly preceding one, Resolution 2934 of 29 November 1972.

[1387] Resolution 3078B, 1, 3. Resolution 3078A addressed the situation in more general terms: "The General Assembly [...] condemns once again with the utmost vigor all nuclear weapon tests; [...] urges once more the Governments of nuclear-weapon States to bring to a halt without delay all nuclear weapons tests either through a permanent agreement or through unilateral or agreed moratoria."

[1388] See the statistics on nuclear explosions in Goldblat, *French nuclear tests*, at 37–8.

[1389] See A/PV.2192. The resolutions are based on draft resolutions suggested by the First Committee, see the Report of the First Committee on Agenda Item 36, 30 November 1973, A/9364.

General Act.[1390] To the present day, France has not made a declaration to restore the Court's compulsory jurisdiction under the optional clause.

5. The judgments of 20 December 1974

In its judgments of 20 December 1974, the Court found by 9 votes to 6 that France's intervening public statements had created a binding commitment not to conduct further atmospheric nuclear tests and that, as a result, Australia's and New Zealand's claims were moot and that the Court was no longer called upon to deliver a decision thereon,[1391] declining to address the questions of jurisdiction and admissibility.[1392]

The Court stated that the order on provisional measures ceased to be operative upon the delivery of the judgment and that thereby the measures lapsed.[1393] As to compliance, the Court confined itself to noting the complaints of Australia and New Zealand that there had been "a clear breach by the French government of the Court's Order of 22 June 1973."[1394] The Court refrained from further comments in spite of the evidence for a violation of the order.[1395] As if to counter the possible reproach that it might have shied away from deciding the case, the Court stated:

[1390] Memorandum of the Secretary-General of the United Nations to the Permanent Representative of Australia to the United Nations, 12 June 1974, ICJ Pleadings, Nuclear Tests, Vol. 1, 553–4, at 553; 44 AdG (1974) 18456 A; Jean Charpentier, Pratique française du droit international—Justice internationale, 20 Annuaire Français de Droit International (1974), 1052–4, France held that the General Act had lapsed; however, it denounced the Act for those states claiming it had not. See also 907 UNTS 129. Critically on France's decision: *Cot*, 19 AFDI (1973), at 253, 271. On the controversy among different French international lawyers, the motivations for the denunciation and the prospects for a new declaration under Article 36(2), see *Thierry*, 20 AFDI (1974), at 289–91, 295–8.

[1391] Judgments of 20 December 1974, at 268–72, paras. 47–62 (Australia), and at 473–8, paras. 50–65 (New Zealand). The dissenting judges were Onyema (Nigeria), Dillard (USA), Jiménez de Aréchaga (Uruguay), Waldock (United Kingdom), de Castro (Spain), and the judge *ad hoc* for Australia and New Zealand, Barwick, ibid., at 274 (Australia) and 478 (New Zealand). For a detailed analysis of the judgment, see *Bollecker-Stern*, 20 AFDI (1974), at 299–333. Critical on the judgment, *MacDonald/Hough*, 22 GYIL (1977), at 337–57; *Lellouche*, 16 Harv. ILJ (1975), at 621–7; but see *Juste Ruiz*, 20 GYIL (1977), at 373–4 (arguing that decision was only feasible solution) and *Thierry*, 20 AFDI (1974), at 291–5.

[1392] Judgments of 20 December 1974, at 260, para. 24 (Australia), and at 463, para. 24 (New Zealand): it treated the existence of a dispute as a preliminary question. Critically *Lellouche*, 16 Harv. ILJ (1975), at 628–34. On the same day, the Court issued two orders in which it stated that the two applications of Fiji for permission to intervene of 16 and 18 May 1973 had lapsed since there were no longer proceedings before the Court, see Orders of 20 December 1974, at 530–31 (Australia), and 535–6 (New Zealand).

[1393] Judgments of 20 December 1974, at 272, para. 61 (Australia), and at 477–8, para. 64 (New Zealand).

[1394] Ibid., at 258–9, para. 19 (Australia), and at 462, para. 19 (New Zealand).

[1395] Critical on the Court's assumption that France had been willing to undertake an actual commitment at a moment while it was not complying with the order *Lellouche*, 16 Harv. ILJ (1975), at 624–5.

This is not to say that the Court may select from the cases submitted to it those it feels suitable for judgment while refusing to give judgment in others. [...] In refraining from further action in this case, the Court is [...] merely acting in accordance with the proper interpretation of its judicial function.[1396]

Yet some observers suggested that the Court had merely sought a way to avoid having to make a judgment on the merits in view of the political implications and because of concerns of non-compliance.[1397] Whether France would have obeyed a judgment comprehensively prohibiting nuclear tests is doubtful. Certainly, China would have been unlikely to conform to a judgment prohibiting nuclear tests. Even though it would as a non-party not have been technically bound by the judgment,[1398] Chinese tests in the face of a judgment against France would have certainly struck a blow to the Court's authority.[1399]

6. A sequel in court: the proceedings in 1995

In the judgment of 1974, the Court had left the door open for further proceedings in the event that France failed to heed its commitments. The Court had stated that the applicants could "request an examination of the situation in accordance with the provisions of the statute" if "the basis" of the judgment "were to be affected," regardless of France's denouncement of the General Act.[1400] This paragraph became relevant in 1995, when New Zealand filed a request for an examination of the situation alongside a request for provisional measures after France on 13 June had announced a final series of underground nuclear weapons tests in the South Pacific scheduled to start in September.[1401] The Court decided by 12 votes to 3 that the

---

[1396] Judgments of 20 December 1974, at 271, para. 57 (Australia), and 477, para. 60 (New Zealand). But see *Juste Ruiz*, 20 GYIL (1977), at 367–4 for an account of policy factors influencing the Court's decision.

[1397] See *Dugard*, 16 Va. JIL (1976), at 485–6. See on the Court's dilemma in arriving at a decision on the merits—in the absence of international consensus, it would have either had to run counter all nuclear disarmament efforts or adopt a judgment unlikely to be complied with and condemning an activity that had been considered perfectly lawful when the US and the USSR were still carrying out nuclear tests, *Lellouche*, 16 Harv. ILJ (1975), at 616–17, 632–4; and *Juste Ruiz*, 20 GYIL (1977), at 367–8.

[1398] See Article 59 of the Statute.

[1399] *Lellouche*, 16 Harv. ILJ (1975), at 616–17 (adding that, on the other hand, a decision upholding nuclear tests might have hurt efforts to limit testing). See on the Chinese attitude Goldblat, *French nuclear tests*, 29–30.

[1400] Judgments of 20 December 1974, at 272, para. 60 (Australia), at 477, para. 63 (New Zealand).

[1401] For New Zealand's request of 21 August 1995 and the applications of interventions by various other countries, see http://212.153.43.18/icjwww/icases/inzfr/inzfr_pleadings/inzfr_ipleadings_toc.html. New Zealand asked the Court to declare the proposed nuclear tests unlawful and issue provisional measures to stop them, Further request for the indications of provisional measures, http://212.153.43.18/icjwww/icases/inzfr/inzfr_pleadings/inzf_ipleadings_19950821_ RequestExam_NewZealand_RequestProvMe.pdf.

request did not fall under paragraph 63 of the 1974 judgment since that judgment had dealt exclusively with atmospheric tests and not with underground tests, and consequently there was no basis for an indication of provisional measures either.[1402] What is noteworthy is the change in the French attitude *vis-à-vis* the Court. This time, France participated in a meeting with the ICJ President, filed an *aide-mémoire* in accordance with what had been agreed upon during that meeting, and presented oral statements during the hearings before the Court on 11 and 12 September 1995. It again affirmed that the Court lacked jurisdiction, but this time without taking the route of non-appearance but rather showing cooperation.[1403] It is worth bearing in mind, however, that France was already very close to terminating its nuclear testing program at this point and that the test series had been announced as the last one.[1404]

7. Non-compliance with the order: relevant factors

The non-compliance in this case can be attributed to a variety of factors. France took a radical stand: it had strongly opposed the involvement of the Court beforehand and did not even show enough respect for the Court to appear at any stage of the proceedings—this at a time when other cases of non-appearance had undermined the Court's authority.[1405] It had been unwilling to compromise in earlier discussions with Australia and New

---

[1402] Order of 22 September 1995, at 305–6, paras. 62–65 and at 307, para. 68. Since the further request for provisional measures and the applications for intervention by other states were proceedings incidental to the request for an examination, they were also dismissed, ibid. at 306–307, paras. 67–68. Paragraph 63 of the 1974 Judgment (Judgment of 20 December 1974 (New Zealand v. France) at 477) stated that if the basis of the judgment was affected, the applicant could request an examination of the situation in accordance with the provisions of the Statute, regardless of the denunciation of the General Act by France on 2 January 1974.

[1403] See Order of 22 September 1995, at 292–301, paras. 13–43: France participated in a meeting with the President of the Court, filed an *aide-mémoire* in accordance with what had been agreed upon during that meeting, and presented oral statements during the hearings before the Court on 11 and 12 September 1995.

[1404] See Chronologie des initiatives françaises en matière de désarmement et de non-prolifér-ation nucláires, http://www.diplomatie.gouv.fr/actual/dossiers/nucleaire/chrono1.html: France conducted the last test on 27 January 1996. In the course of 1996, it signed and ratified the three protocols to the South Pacific Nuclear Free Zone Treaty (Treaty of Rarotonga, 1445 UNTS 177–186, for the text of the protocols, see http://www.state.gov/www/global/arms/treat-ies/spnfz.html) and has now assumed unequivocal treaty obligations not to conduct further nuclear tests in the area. It signed the Comprehensive Test Ban Treaty on 20 September 1996 and ratified it on 6 April 1998. The treaty has not yet entered into force; its text is retrievable under http://pws.ctbto.org/treaty/treaty_text.pdf, for updated information on the status of rati-fications, see http://pws.ctbto.org/. See further *Torrelli*, 41 AFDI (1995), at 755–77.

[1405] See *Juste Ruiz*, 20 GYIL (1977), at 371. All the contentious cases on the Court's docket in 1973 and 1974 took place without participation of the respondent, see *supra* II and B XII on the Fisheries Jurisdiction case; in the Case concerning trial of Pakistani prisoners of war which was discontinued on 15 December 1973, India had refused to participate in the proceedings: Trial of Pakistani prisoners of war (Pakistan v. India), Order of 15 December 1973, at 347–8.

Zealand, insisting on its "vital interests" as a sovereign nation.[1406] Apart
from the question how *many* further tests were to be conducted (where one
could have imagined some margin for negotiations), the question of *whether*
to carry out tests left little room for compromise: either the French government would cede the pressure and desist from further tests, or they would
not. The highly political character of the controversy hardly needs to be
stressed: with the invocation of "security" and "independence," France had
brought forward vital interests to which it gave utmost priority, and it had
insisted on its perspective in spite of international and domestic protests. The
legal predicaments were unclear; the law on nuclear disarmament and non-
proliferation was in a state of transition and there was no consensus in the
international community.[1407] There were arguments against the Court's
jurisdiction and the jurisdiction was, in fact, highly contested by France;
the Court did not address these concerns as diligently as it could have.[1408]

In spite of the non-compliance with the orders, the interim measures were
useful for the applicants. The proceedings gave Australia and New Zealand
publicity and sympathy for their cause,[1409] and ultimately atmospheric testing
in the area came to an end. In the statements on which the Court had relied in
order to establish a commitment on part of France to desist from further
atmospheric tests, the French government had brought forward technological
reasons for its decision and had never conceded that atmospheric tests were
not in accordance with the law.[1410] Yet it is to be assumed that the wave of
protest—steadily increasing from 1971 onwards and particularly strong for
the 1973 and 1974 test series after the interim measures had been indicated—
had a decisive impact on the decision to switch from atmospheric testing to
underground testing.[1411] Further atmospheric tests would have been far
cheaper and easier for France than the underground tests,[1412] so absent any
pressure to cease the tests it might just as well have continued as before.

[1406] See White Paper, *supra* n. 1332; and *Juste Ruiz*, 20 GYIL (1977), at 368.

[1407] *Lellouche*, 16 Harv. ILJ (1975), at 615–16; and *Juste Ruiz*, 20 GYIL (1977), at 368.

[1408] Critical on the Court's argumentation, *Juste Ruiz*, 20 GYIL (1977), at 370.

[1409] This might have been one of their primary goals, see *Juste Ruiz*, 20 GYIL (1977), at 374;
and *Frankel*, 7 NYU JILP (1974), at 176: "It seems apparent [...] that the Nuclear Tests Cases
were instituted not so much to secure compliance with the Court's decision as to gain publicity
and sympathy for a cause." See also *Ris*, 4 Denv. JILP (1974), at 132.

[1410] See Judgments of 20 December 1974, at 265–7, paras. 34–41 (Australia), and 469–72,
paras. 35–44.

[1411] *Lellouche*, 16 Harv. ILJ (1975), at 635–6. See also *Juste Ruiz*, 20 GYIL (1977), at 372–3
(observing France's inability to maintain its position of challenging the Court's authority and
resist domestic and international pressures). See already the assumption by Goldblat, *French
nuclear tests*, at 29, prior to the judgment: "France could refuse to accept the ruling, as it refused
to comply with the ICJ interim measures, but it would not be able to ignore entirely its moral
weight. The judgement might prompt a speedier termination of the French atmospheric testing
programme." Similarly, *Ris*, 4 Denv. JILP (1974), at 131, predicting that the "barrage of negative
reaction" was "bound to have some influence on French attitudes."

[1412] See *Lellouche*, 16 Harv. ILJ (1975), at 635.

Still, the case does not mark a happy chapter in the Court's history. It was another instance of non-appearance in the proceedings and defiance of an order of the Court. The orders and the judgment were not entirely free from contradictions when compared to each other and caused disappointment both by advocates of judicial restraint and by those favoring stronger involvement. Moreover, the withdrawal of France's acceptance of the Court's compulsory jurisdiction was a further blow to the Court's authority at a time of declining prestige.[1413]

IV. United States diplomatic and consular staff in Tehran

The facts of the case were explained before: the seizure of the US embassy in Tehran and the consulates in Tabriz and Shiraz, and the taking of hostages by militant Iranian groups. The immediate facts were undisputed and received worldwide attention through the media coverage,[1414] but the views of Iran and the US differed as to the broader context in which they were embedded, i.e. the history of Iran–US relations, and the respective facts. The proceedings took place in a climate of hostility, a refusal of Iran to perceive the dispute as a legal one, and its opposition to any involvement of the Court.[1415]

1. The proceedings on interim protection and the Court's order

On 29 November 1979, the day of its application introducing proceedings against Iran, the US also requested the indication of provisional measures. The US demands included a call for the release of the hostages; the restoration of US control over its diplomatic and consular properties; a guarantee of freedom of movement for all persons attached to the embassy and consulate should the US, subject to Iranian approval, decide to maintain its missions in Iran; assurances that no hostages would be subject to trial; and an abstention from action that might prejudice the Court's decision on the merits.[1416] The request partially overlapped with the application introducing proceedings, in which the US asked the Court to declare "that [...] Iran is under a particular obligation to secure the release of all US nationals

---

[1413] See *Lellouche*, 16 Harv. ILJ (1975), at 636–7. But see *Elkind*, 9 Vand. JTL (1976), at 97: "In this case, the dexterity of the Court can only be admired. Both sides were able to claim a moral victory." He questioned, though, whether the Court was still performing a judicial function (rather than acting on policy concerns) and predicted that it was unlikely that significant issues would be submitted to the ICJ in the future.

[1414] See Judgment of 24 May 1980 at 9, para.12.

[1415] For details, see B XIV 1.

[1416] Request for the indication of provisional measures of protection submitted by the Government of the United States of America, ICJ Pleadings, United States Diplomatic and Consular Staff in Tehran, 11–12.

currently being detained within the premises of the United States Embassy in Tehran and to assure that all such persons and all other United States nationals in Tehran are allowed to leave Iran safely."[1417] On 30 November 1979, the ICJ President, Sir Humphrey Waldock, reminded the parties of "the need to act in such a way as will enable any Order the Court may make on the request for provisional measures to have its appropriate effects."[1418]

Iran refused to participate in the proceedings and instead transmitted a telegram on 9 December 1979, one day before the hearings for the provisional measures, stating that the Court could not take cognizance of the case.[1419] It restated the arguments indirectly submitted to the Court in the main proceedings,[1420] pointing out that the issue involved only a marginal and secondary aspect of an overall problem, that the application could not be considered separated from its broader context, which was highly political and involved twenty-five years of violations of international law on the part of the United States, and that the repercussions of its revolution were not a matter of application of treaties, but one essentially within the national jurisdiction of Iran. Two objections specifically concerned the indication of provisional measures: first, that the granting of such measures would imply an interim judgment breaching the norms governing the Court's jurisdiction; and, second, that the measures proposed were unilateral, incompatible with the concept of the Court's interim protection, "since provisional measures are by definition intended to protect the interests of the parties."[1421] As in the main proceedings, Iran basically used legal reasoning only as far as procedure was concerned, not on substance. It complained about the "unilateral character" of the measures requested, but it did not advance any right of its own that might require protection, or, in particular, a right that might be prejudiced by the indication of provisional measures, as for instance a right to prosecute the hostages for espionage that would suffer irreparable damage if the Court acceded to the US request. This posture reflected Iran's unwillingness to perceive the dispute as a legal one. As Iran itself did not show any desire to receive protection by the Court and had not put forward any rights requiring protection, it would suffice for the measures to include the general measure requiring that both parties ensure that no action was being taken that might aggravate the tension between the two countries or render the existing dispute more difficult to resolve.

[1417] Ibid., 8. In the oral proceedings on interim protection, the US delegate pointed out that this duplication was a result of "an excess of caution on the part of the United States" and the release of hostages "should have appeared only in our pending request for the indication of provisional measures:" ICJ Pleadings, US Diplomatic and Consular Staff, at 32. See on the issue of an overlap *Gross*, 74 AJIL (1980), at 404–5.

[1418] Telegrams transmitted by the Registrar to the Parties, 30 November 1979, ICJ Pleadings, US Diplomatic and Consular Staff, 495–6.

[1419] Order of 15 December 1979, at 10–11, para. 8. [1420] Ibid.

[1421] Ibid., at 11, para. 8(4).

A few days before the oral proceedings on provisional measures, the Security Council had already issued a unanimous call for a release of the hostages in Resolution 457 (1979), and the Secretary-General was already actively involved in the matter. The Court did not regard this parallel action of other UN organs as an obstacle to its exercise of function.[1422] On 15 December 1979, it unanimously indicated interim measures along the lines of those requested by the US, namely calling upon Iran to restore control over the premises of the embassy, chancery, and consulates to the US and to release the hostages immediately,[1423] and informed the Security Council of its action.[1424] These measures, while similar to those requested by the US, were not identical; the call to refrain from action likely to aggravate the tensions was directed at both sides and was broader in scope than the US request that Iran should ensure "that no action is taken which might prejudice the rights of the United States in respect of carrying out of any decision which the Court may render on the merits, and, in particular neither take, nor permit, action that would threaten the lives, safety, or well-being of the hostages."[1425] The question of jurisdiction raised no difficulties, since there were treaty clauses providing for the Court's jurisdiction and there was no reason to doubt their applicability.[1426] The Court therefore could conclude that a basis for jurisdiction was "manifestly" established,[1427] and did not have to decide on the degree of certainty on jurisdiction required for the adoption of provisional measures.[1428]

The Court correctly rejected the Iranian argument that the matter was just a "marginal and secondary aspect of an overall problem." The seizure of foreign missions and detention of internationally protected persons could not be treated as marginal or secondary, particularly given that the Security Council had referred to the events as posing a "serious threat to international

---

[1422] In the order, this issue was not even discussed; the Court took note of the respective organ's action, at 15, para. 23. In the judgment, the Court held that its competence to decide the case had not been affected by the actions of the Secretary-General and the Security Council, Judgment of 24 May 1980, at 20–2, paras. 39–40.

[1423] Judgment of 24 May 1980, at 20–21, para. 47: Iran should restore US control over the embassy, chancery and consulates, and ensure the inviolability of the premises; Iran should ensure the immediate release of all American citizens held as hostages; Iran should afford the diplomatic privileges and immunities, including immunity from criminal prosecution, and freedom to leave the country to the US diplomatic and consular staff; both governments should refrain from action that might aggravate the tension between the two countries or render the existing dispute more difficult of solution and should ensure that no such action was taken. Iran had not appointed a judge *ad hoc*. For details on the provisional measures, see *Gross*, 74 AJIL (1980), at 395–410; *Coussirat-Coustère*, 25 AFDI (1979), at 297–313; *Paul*, 21 Harv. ILJ (1980), at 268–74.

[1424] S/13697. This notification was made in accordance with Article 41(2) of the ICJ Statute.

[1425] See the final submission on the request during the oral proceedings, Order of 15 December 1979, at 12–13, para. 12, in comparison with the measures indicated (ibid., at 21, para. 47), see *Gross*, 74 AJIL (1980), at 409.

[1426] See *supra* B XIV 4.   [1427] Order of 15 December 1979, at 13–14, paras. 14–20.

[1428] *Rafat*, 10 Denv. JIL (1981), at 438–40.

peace and security" and that Iran was free to bring its own complaints before the Court. As the Court stated: "No provision of the Statute or Rules contemplates that the Court should decline to take cognizance of one aspect of a dispute merely because that dispute has other aspects, however important."[1429] Concerning Iran's claim that the matter was one within its domestic jurisdiction, the Court found that the matter was governed by international law and hence fell into the sphere of international jurisdiction.[1430]

A problematic issue was the fact that the US asked not only for an act of omission but for a positive act: the release of the hostages. Did this not amount to a request for an interim judgment, as Iran had argued in its telegram? The Court had to consider the jurisprudence of its predecessor, the Permanent Court of International Justice, which declined to indicate measures in the Chorzów Factory case because the request was "designed to obtain an interim judgment in favor of a part of a claim."[1431] The ICJ held that the circumstances in the earlier case (relating to partial satisfaction for a monetary claim) were entirely distinguishable, and that in the present case, the purpose of the measures was not to obtain an interim judgment, but rather to preserve the substance of rights claimed pending litigation.[1432] After recalling the fundamental importance of the rights in question, the Court concluded that "continuance of the situation [...] exposes the human beings concerned to privation, hardship, anguish and even danger to life and health and thus to a serious possibility of irreparable harm."[1433]

2. Iran's reaction

Iran did not comply with the provisional measures order. Tehran refused to return control over the premises to the US, much less free the hostages. The Court noted that the Iranian foreign minister publicly rejected the order the day it was issued, and Ayatollah Khomeini reaffirmed on 23 February and 7 April 1980 that there would be no hostage release.[1434] In a letter to the Court dated 16 March 1980, the Iranian government restated its argumentation as presented in its December telegram,[1435] despite the Court's rejection of those arguments in granting the provisional measures.

[1429] Order of 15 December 1979, at 15, paras. 22–4.
[1430] Ibid., at 15–16, para. 25.
[1431] Factory at Chórzow (Indemnities), Order of 21 November 1927, PCIJ Series A, No. 12, 9–11, at 10.
[1432] Order of 15 December 1979, at 16, para. 28. The rights for which the US claimed protection were in the Court's view the rights of its nationals to life, liberty, protection and security, the diplomatic and consular privileges and immunities, and the right for inviolability and protection of the diplomatic and consular premises. Ibid., at 19, para. 37.
[1433] Ibid., at 19–20, paras. 38–43.
[1434] Judgment of 24 May 1980, at 35, para. 75.   [1435] Ibid., at 8–9, para. 10.

The United States complained to the Security Council in a letter of 22 December 1979.[1436] On the same day, the Secretary-General issued a report describing his futile attempts at lending good offices.[1437] The Security Council dealt with the matter from 29 to 31 December 1979, again without Iran's participation.[1438] Although the discussion centered on the non-compliance with the earlier Security Council resolution, the material breaches of diplomatic and consular law, and the tensions between the two countries, many speakers made a reference to the Court's order.[1439] The fact that the order was not given primary attention is perhaps not surprising given the dimension of the breaches of international law by Iran even if the Court's order was to be left out of account and its lack of respect for a unanimous resolution of the Security Council. Resolution 461 reaffirmed the call for a release of the hostages and explicitly mentioned the Court's order, deploring "the continued detention of the hostages contrary to its resolution 457 (1979) and the Order of the International Court of Justice of 15 December 1979." It is noteworthy that the original version of the draft resolution submitted by the US had adopted a harsher tone: "The Security Council [...] condemns the continued detention of the hostages contrary to its resolution 457 (1979) and the Order of the International Court of Justice of 15 December 1979."[1440] By deleting that paragraph, the US might have tried to placate the Soviets, who had expressed some sympathy with Iran although they had joined the call for a release of the hostages.[1441]

[1436] Letter dated 22 December 1979 from the US representative to the President of the Security Council, S/13705. It was a complaint of non-compliance with resolution 457 and with the Court's order. See the comment on the provisional measures therein: "On 15 December 1979, the International Court of Justice issued an Order calling for 'the immediate release, without any exception' by Iran of all Americans held in Iran and for their safe departure from Iran. [...] Iran has rejected the Order if the International Court of Justice. In fact, Iran has defied all of the decisions of the international community as well as the strong appeals for the release of the hostages by the Secretary-General, the President of the Security Council, and the President of the General Assembly, and by numerous Governments and world leaders of every political persuasion and religious belief."

[1437] Report of the Secretary-General concerning the implementation of Security Council resolution 457 (1979), 22 December 1979, S/13704.

[1438] See the verbatim records of the meetings: S/PV.2182–4. When the Security Council dealt with the matter first, it had appeared as if Iran was willing to participate, but eventually the Iranian representative to the UN received instructions not to do so.

[1439] See the following statements in the 2,182nd meeting of 29 December 1979: S/PV.2182, 6 (USA), 11 (UK), 13 (Norway), 17–18 (Portugal), 21 (France), 22 (Federal Republic of Germany), 28–30 (Singapore). See also the following statements in subsequent meetings: S/PV.2183 at 16 (Jamaica), 18 (Bolivia), and 26 (Canada); S/PV.2184, 1 (Gambia).

[1440] United States of America: Draft Resolution, S/13711, 30 December 1979.

[1441] See, for example, the statement of the representative in the USSR in the Security Council's meeting of 1 December 1979, S/PV.2175, at 7: "The Soviet Union has deep sympathy for the Iranian people in its struggle for its interests, its democratic rights, and its genuine independence. The Soviet Union has consistently adhered in its relations with Iran to principles of respect for sovereignty, independence, territorial integrity and non-interference in domestic affairs. We understand full well the wish of the Iranian people to restore justice, trodden

In the last paragraph of Resolution 461, the Council decided to reconvene on 7 January 1980 "in order to review the situation and, in the event of non-compliance with the present resolution, to adopt effective measures under Articles 39 and 41 of the Charter of the United Nations." The reference to Chapter VII of the Charter hinted that enforcement action might be taken with a view to ensuring compliance with an ICJ order, among other consider-ations. However, in spite of this paragraph, there was no consensus in the Council on whether the situation was such as to fall under Chapter VII.[1442] A draft resolution submitted by the US on 10 January 1980 explicitly indicated Articles 39 and 41 as its basis and aimed at imposing economic and diplomatic sanctions on Iran.[1443] The Soviet Union vetoed the proposal based on its contention that Chapter VII was not applicable because there was no threat to international peace and security and the measures proposed were incompatible with the goal of a peaceful settlement of the US–Iranian conflict.[1444] In any event, the draft resolution of 10 January could not have been called an enforcement mechanism for the order in the strictest sense since the order received only passing reference in the preamble[1445] and none whatsoever in the operative part of the resolution. The United States had most likely drafted its proposal in this form for the same reason it had cancelled a condemnation of the violation of the order in draft resolution S/13711 of 30 December: to decrease the chances for a Soviet veto. Rather than actually enforcing the order, the draft resolution would have provided an alternative mechanism for achieving the goals of the provisional measures.

The Council was unequivocal in asking for a release of the hostages; Iran made no attempts to justify their continued detention.[1446] The Security Council joined many other actors, including the European Community and the Organization of American States,[1447] in exerting moral pressure on the

underfoot by the previous régime. That wish should be taken into account." Yet, he concluded "that the violation of the Vienna Convention on Diplomatic Relations—whoever commits the violation—constitutes an act that is contrary to international law." (ibid., 7–8). See further on the Iran–USSR relations during the crisis 50 AdG (1980), 23203.

[1442] Several representatives were critical on the reference to Chapter VII: see S/PV.2184, at 2 (Bangladesh), 4–5 USSR, Kuwait, Zambia).

[1443] United States of America, Draft resolution, S/13735, 10 January 1980.

[1444] S/PV.2191 of 13 January 1980, at 4 (for the vote), and at 4–6 for the statement of the USSR representative on the reasons on which he would base his vote.

[1445] "Having taken into account the Order of the International Court of Justice of 15 December 1979 calling on the Government of the Islamic Republic of Iran to ensure the immediate release, without any exception, of all persons of United States nationality who are being held as hostages in Iran and also calling on the Government of the United States of America and the Government of the Islamic Republic of Iran to ensure that no action will be taken by them which will aggravate the tension between the two countries."

[1446] See the verbatim records of the Security Council meetings where the matter was being primarily discussed: S/PV.2175, 2177, 2178, 2182, 2183, 2184, 2191.

[1447] In the course of the discussions of the Security Council, reference was made to statements from many international actors, see the verbatim records quoted above, n. 1446.

revolutionary government, although it stopped short in terms of taking actual enforcement action. No firm conclusions can be drawn on whether the deliberations and the resolution are indicative of an unwillingness of the Council to deal with breaches of ICJ orders or whether they are merely due to Cold War political patterns.

The intervention of UN Secretary-General, Kurt Waldheim, could not secure the release of the hostages. He made a personal visit to Tehran after some hesitation from Iran and met with Iran's foreign minister as well as with other Iranian officials from 1 to 3 January 1980, but returned to New York without a resolution to the crisis, which the Iranian leaders continued to link to the extradition of the former Shah and the return of assets allegedly taken out by him illegally.[1448] The Secretary-General's efforts should be understood as a parallel effort to achieve a release of the hostages and not as an attempt to enforce the ICJ order proper: while mentioning the Council resolutions, he did not refer to the order.[1449]

It remained to be seen how the Court was to react to the non-compliance with the interim measures in the judgment. After recalling its emphasis in the order of the cardinal importance of the obligations under the two Vienna Conventions, the Court expressed its "deep regret that the situation which occasioned those observations has not been rectified since they were made."[1450] It went on to say that it considered it "to be its duty to draw the attention of the entire international community, of which Iran itself has been a member since time immemorial, to the irreparable harm that may be caused by events of the kind now before the Court."[1451] The non-compliance with an interim measure as such was not explicitly mentioned as the reason for concern; the focus was on the obligations under the Vienna Conventions that had been so blatantly disregarded. However, since the order had asked Iran to desist from the behavior whose continuation was found to be in violation with international law, the finding of a continued breach of international law was tantamount to a statement that Iran had not complied with the order. A formal sanctioning of the breach of the order was not undertaken, however.

3. The US reaction: non-compliance?

The US engaged in measures of self-help, adopting several unilateral economic and diplomatic sanctions both prior to and during the

[1448] Report of the Secretary-General in pursuance of Security Council Resolutions 457 (1979) and 461 (1979), 6 January 1980, S/13730, at para.13.
[1449] See Report of 6 January, S/13730, and Report of 22 December 1979, S/13704. Resolutions 457 (at para. 4) and 461 (at para. 4) had explicitly asked the Secretary-General to lend his good offices.
[1450] Judgment of 24 May 1980, at 42, paras. 91–2.   [1451] Ibid., at 43, para. 92.

proceedings.[1452] An attempt was also made to free the hostages by force: during the night of 24 April 1980, one month before the delivery of the judgment, US President Carter unsuccessfully launched a military operation on Iranian territory with this aim. After this failed rescue attempt, President Carter stated the motivation for the mission had not been hostility towards Iran or the Iranian people, but humanitarian reasons, the protection of US national interests, and the alleviation of international tensions. He maintained that there had been increasing risks for the safety of the hostages and that the US had exercised its inherent right of self-defense.[1453]

The rescue attempt raised the issue of whether the US action constituted non-compliance with the interim measures.[1454] One might wonder whether the unilateral use of force was compatible with the part of the order requiring both parties to refrain from taking steps that would aggravate the situation. The Court commented on the incident in its judgment. While expressing sympathy with the US worries about the hostages and its frustration at Iran's failure to give effect to the Council resolutions and the provisional measures, it declared that it could not "fail to express its concern in regard to the United States' incursion into Iran."[1455] It referred to the fact that the proceedings were in course when the rescue attempt happened and felt "bound to observe that an operation undertaken in those circumstances, from whatever motive, is of a kind calculated to undermine respect for the judicial process in international relations; and to recall that in [its Order on provisional measures] the Court had indicated that no action was to be taken by either party which might aggravate the tension between the two parties."[1456] However, it proceeded to say that "neither the question of legality of the operation [...] nor any possible question of responsibility flowing from it, is before the Court. It must also point out that this question can have no bearing on the evaluation of the conduct of the Iranian Government over six months earlier [...] which is the subject-matter of the United States' Application."[1457] Thus while implying that the rescue attempt was not compatible with the order, the Court did not go as far as to characterize it explicitly as a violation.[1458] Its critique was instead framed in terms of the

---

[1452] Ibid., at 16–17, paras. 30–1.   [1453] Ibid., at 17–18, para. 32.

[1454] Another question, outside the scope of this study, is whether the US behavior was illegal under general international law by violating the prohibitions on the use of force and on intervention. On the general question of the right to self-help under the given circumstances, see *Schachter* in Kreisberg, American Hostages in Iran, at 327–38 (on the use of force) and 354 (on other sanctions); Hakenberg, *Iran-Sanktionen der USA*, 221–44 (on use of force), 46–220 (on other sanctions).

[1455] Judgment of 24 May 1980, at 43, para. 93.   [1456] Ibid.

[1457] Ibid., at 43–4, para. 94.

[1458] This leads *Papachristou*, 21 Harv. ILJ (1980), at 755, to the conclusion that the Court "resolved these problems squarely in favor of the United States." However, he does not suggest any clear alternative, and there is no denying the Court's criticism.

impact on judicial procedure[1459] based on the litigant's duty to exercise the right to judicial relief in good faith, akin to the common law notion of contempt of court.[1460] But the American transgression seems slight in comparison to the blatant disrespect Iran showed for the order; the aggravation of the situation could be seen as arising from Iran's non-compliance, with the US action being an understandable response. Yet the US had freely chosen to involve the Court in the dispute, it was therefore inappropriate for it to employ coercion pending the outcome.[1461] Measures usually allowed under general international law can be incompatible with a decision to pursue a judicial settlement and therefore be impermissible.[1462] The oral pleadings were already concluded and the judgment on the merits was expected when the rescue attempt took place; the United States did not show why the situation would have suddenly deteriorated to such a degree that it could not wait for the judgment.[1463] In this context, it was also noteworthy that the US itself had requested a delay of the scheduling of the oral proceedings.[1464] The rescue mission, in fact, was not of a character favorable to enhancing respect for judicial proceedings whose authority was already being undermined by Iran's non-compliance and the inability of the Security Council to react adequately. The Court apparently assumed that the obligation not to do anything likely to aggravate the dispute was still valid in spite of Iran's disregard of the provisional measures, rejecting reciprocity as an implied condition for that obligation.[1465]

For all the attention given to the US military action, the Court's majority did not comment on the non-forcible sanctions adopted unilaterally by the US after the Court's order. This silence seems to suggest that the economic measures were to be evaluated differently.[1466] In fact, although a priori recourse to interim protection by the Court seems to be incompatible with the adoption of new countermeasures and the pursuance of unilateralism instead of reliance on the judicial protection of rights, a state cannot be regarded as barred from taking any permissible countermeasures to enforce its rights if the interim measures turn out to produce no effect at all and are openly defied by their addressee. A contrary understanding would effectively

---

[1459] See *Stein*, 76 AJIL (1982), at 500–1.   [1460] Ibid., at 504–12.

[1461] *Stein*, 76 AJIL (1982), at 511–12; *Schachter* in Kreisberg, American Hostages in Iran, 341. This point was also highlighted by Judge Tarazi in his dissenting opinion, Judgment of 24 May 1980, at 63. Also Judge Lachs stated in his separate opinion, ibid., at 48: "[T]he applicant, having instituted proceedings, is precluded from taking unilateral action, military or otherwise, as if no case is pending."

[1462] *Schachter* in Kreisberg, American Hostages in Iran, at 340–1.

[1463] See *Stein*, 76 AJIL (1982), at 523, who reports, at fn. 99, that there was no reference to a new threat to the hostages.

[1464] Judgment of 24 May 1980, at 22, para. 41; and *Stein*, 76 AJIL (1982), at 514–15.

[1465] *Stein*, 76 AJIL (1982), at 504; *Schachter* in Kreisberg, American Hostages in Iran, at 342–3.

[1466] *Schachter* in Kreisberg, American Hostages in Iran, at 342.

protect the party in breach of the order and penalize the state in whose favor it had been indicated. In this context, forcible and non-forcible countermeasures deserve a different treatment in view of the potential of use of force to disrupt efforts to settle the dispute by adjudication—in the order's terms, "to aggravate the tension between the two countries or render the existing dispute more difficult of solution."[1467] This point should not be stretched too far; in view of the limited possibilities of the Court to ensure effective protection faced with a defiant government, protective use of force in emergency situations cannot be excluded under all circumstances and cannot require the state that actually complies with the order to endanger its existence.[1468]

The Court refused to penalize the US for the rescue mission by withholding relief.[1469] This was appropriate: the comparative gravity of the acts by the two states was ultimately quite different.[1470] Also, Iran had not submitted a formal claim that the Court should desist from granting the relief on the basis of the rescue attempt, and it might be questionable whether the Court should impose such a sanction on its own initiative.[1471] Different appraisals are apparent in the various dissenting opinions. Judge Morozov had voted with the majority on Iran's obligation to release the hostages and to hand over US property, but against the finding of state responsibility.[1472] With regard to the rescue mission, he argued that the Court should have explicitly rejected the US justification of self-defense.[1473] On the state responsibility claims, he stated that the US had "forfeited the legal right as well as the moral right to expect the Court to uphold any claim for reparations" by the rescue mission (qualified by him as "military attack") and the economic sanctions,[1474] upon which the Court's majority had not commented.[1475] In a similar vein, Judge Tarazi held that Iran should not have been held responsible without a finding on the US responsibility for its actions. He criticized US legislative initiatives for the compensation of victims and the rescue operation, but pointed out that it was not his task "to characterize that operation or to make any legal value-judgment in its respect".[1476] Judge

---

[1467] *Stein*, 76 AJIL (1982), at 515–23. Yet a state would not be precluded from acting in self-defense to threats not existing at the time of the issuance of the order, ibid., 522 with examples.

[1468] Ibid., at 342.

[1469] Judgment of 24 May 1980, at 44, para. 93.

[1470] *Schachter* in Kreisberg, American Hostages in Iran, at 344.

[1471] Further on the potential for the Court sanctioning contempt of court on behalf of the applicant, see *Stein*, 76 AJIL (1982), at 523–31; and *infra* Chapter 4 B IV 2.

[1472] Judgment of 24 May 1980, at 44–5, para. 95.

[1473] Ibid, Diss. Op. Morozov, at 56–7, paras. 8–9. He also argued that the US was precluded from relying on the Treaty of Amity given its own behavior from November 1979 onwards, ibid., at 52, para. 3.

[1474] Ibid., Diss. Op. Morozov, at 53–7, para. 59.

[1475] Apart from reporting them: ibid., at 16–17, paras. 30–1.

[1476] Ibid., Diss. Op. Tarazi, at 63–5.

Tarazi made no explicit statement on a violation of the order, nor on the binding force of provisional measures.

4. Conclusion

The provisional measures were not complied with, despite the fact that the jurisdiction of the Court was manifestly established, the facts concerning the seizure of the embassy were undisputed, the applicable law was clearly defined in treaties, and the terms of the order were clear and precise, and, at least apart from the obligation to refrain from action likely to aggravate the dispute, left no room for interpretation.

A variety of negative factors can be identified. As was already explained with regard to the judgment, the ramifications of the case were such as to present serious obstacles for a successful compliance. The relations between the litigants could hardly have been worse, and the official comments from the Iranian side were full of hatred. Communication between the parties was hardly possible due to Ayatollah Khomeini's prohibition of any contact, the parties represented values which were highly different, they did not agree on how to frame the dispute and not even about the relevance of the law. While the law itself was rather precise, Iran rejected the appropriateness of a legal evaluation of the situation without the broader context, and Ayatollah Khomeini, in whom the main power in Iran was vested, seemed to reject the notion of international law as such. Even though there was a rather clear basis for the Court's jurisdiction, Iran vehemently opposed the Court's involvement and refused to participate at any stage of the proceedings. Under these circumstances, the prospects for compliance were slim, yet the order added more weight and legitimacy to the political efforts to bring about a release of the hostages.[1477]

On the part of the US, the rescue mission was to be understood as a desperate attempt to prevent further suffering of the hostages. The Carter administration was under substantial pressure to free the hostages as the American public witnessed on their TV screens the day-to-day misery of the hostages. Under the circumstances of the case, the requirement not to take any action likely to aggravate the dispute was a high burden in the face of the flagrant violation of the order and various basic international obligations on the part of Iran. Any valid assessment of the US action must take these factors into account. Yet, as was stated above, the US had chosen the route of adjudication, and the unilateral military action was problematic from the point of undermining respect for judicial proceedings; furthermore, the US did not substantiate further why the situation for the hostages had gotten critical to such an extent for it, in effect, to take the law into its own hands.

[1477] See *Paul*, 21 Harv. ILJ (1980), at 274; see also *supra* B XIV 6.

V. *Frontier dispute (Burkina Faso v. Mali)*

An armed conflict broke out between Burkina Faso and Mali on 25 December 1985 after the parties had submitted their frontier dispute to the ICJ.[1478] Malian troops occupied parts of the disputed territory after Burkinabe authorities had conducted a census there. The Organization of African Unity (OAU) became involved the next day and an extraordinary session of the Council of Ministers of the regional Non-Aggression and Defence Pact (ANAD)[1479] was convened, as a result of which the parties reached a cease-fire agreement while deferring the question of troop withdrawal.[1480]

Shortly thereafter, the two countries submitted separate requests for provisional measures to the ICJ—the first case where such requests came explicitly from both sides.[1481] Each request asked the Chamber to order the two parties to refrain from acts likely to prevent or impede the implementation of a future judgment. In addition, Burkina Faso requested the Chamber to indicate that both parties abstain from action likely to impede the gathering of evidence as well as acts of territorial administration beyond the dividing line proposed in 1975 by the Legal Sub-Commission of the OAU Mediation Commission. It also called for a withdrawal of Malian troops from the disputed territory,[1482] which Mali opposed on the basis that this would prejudice the decision on the merits and that the issue was already being dealt with by the ANAD apparatus. It submitted that the Chamber could only call on the parties not to prejudice the rights under a future judgment and to refrain from any action that might aggravate the dispute.[1483]

On 10 January 1986, a unanimous Chamber issued provisional measures in the case. In addition to the requirement that the parties take no action that might extend the dispute or frustrate compliance with the future judgment, it ordered both parties to refrain from any act that might impede the gathering

---

[1478] For details on the background of the case and the proceedings before the ICJ, see *supra* B XVII.

[1479] Non-aggression and defence assistance agreement (Accord de non-agression et d'assistance en matière de défense), a regional security pact concluded at Abidjan on 9 July 1977 between Burkina Faso, Ivory Coast, Mali, Mauritius, Niger, Senegal, and Togo, 1354 UNTS 211.

[1480] *Gautron*, 32 AFDI (1986), at 203 and 208–109; Naldi, 35 ICLQ (1986), at 972; *Rousseau*, 90 RGDIP (1986), 416–17; 55 AdG (1985) 29457 A.

[1481] The requests of Burkina Faso and Mali were received on 2 January and 6/7 January 1986, respectively. Order of 10 January 1986, at 4, paras. 2–3. In the letter of 6 January, Mali asked the Court to examine *proprio motu* pursuant to Article 75 of the Rules of Court whether the circumstances required the adoption of provisional measures. On the following day, it filed a formal request under Article 73 of the Rules. Ibid., at 5–6, paras. 5–6.

[1482] These were the claims raised in the oral hearing before the Court on 9 January 1986. In its written application, the withdrawal of troops was just requested beyond the line proposed by the Legal Sub-Commission. Ibid., at 5, para. 4, and at 7–8, para. 8.

[1483] Ibid., at 6–7, para. 6.

of evidence (the first measure of this type ever issued by the ICJ),[1484] to continue to respect the cease-fire instituted on 31 December 1985, to withdraw their troops to such positions as to be determined in an agreement to be concluded within twenty days from the order, failing which the Court would indicate the terms of the withdrawal itself, and to maintain the status quo of the administration of the disputed areas as before the armed incidents.[1485] The prima-facie jurisdiction presented no problem: the Chamber's jurisdiction was manifestly established by a special agreement and both parties desired an indication of provisional measures.[1486] Regarding the substance of the measures, besides the novel feature of the measure on the conservation of evidence, the manner how the Chamber approached the issue of a troop withdrawal deserves attention, in particular, how it took into account the settlement efforts by the regional dispute settlement ANAD. The Court saw the clear need for a troop withdrawal, but recognized that, for the moment, it had no sufficient knowledge for the purposes of determining the locations of the positions to which both parties should withdraw; it was aware that the terms for a withdrawal were shortly to be determined in the ANAD framework.[1487] Its decision to set a deadline for the determination of the modalities of the withdrawal by agreement, failing which it would itself prescribe these modalities, balanced between two extremes: one might have imagined that the Court would refrain from indicating measures in this respect, trusting in ANAD's capacity to contain the dispute;[1488] conversely, that it would indicate provisional measures without any recognition of the ANAD

[1484] On this issue, the Chamber referred to the possibility that evidence might be destroyed and to its power to indicate measures in order to prevent an aggravation of the dispute, especially when incidents occurred that were not only likely to aggravate the dispute but amounted to a use of force incompatible with the principle of peaceful settlement of disputes (ibid., at 9–10, paras. 17–21).

[1485] Ibid., at 11–12, para. 32. The formulation in the English text is "should"; however, the language of the authoritative French text is clearly mandatory : "les gouvernements [...] veillent à éviter," "[l]es deux gouvernements s'abstiennent de tout acte," "[l]es deux gouvernements continuent à respecter", "retirent leurs forces armées," "la situation antérieure [...] ne soit pas modifié." For details, see *Naldi*, 35 ICLQ (1986), at 973–4.

[1486] Order of 10 January 1986, at 8, para. 10.

[1487] Ibid., at 10–11, para. 27: "Whereas the measures which the Chamber contemplates indicating, for the purpose of eliminating the risk of any future action likely to aggravate or extend the dispute, must necessarily include the withdrawal of the troops of both parties to such positions as to avoid the recrudescence of regrettable incidents; whereas, however, the selection of these positions would require a knowledge of the geographical and strategic context of the conflict which the Chamber does not possess, and which in all probability it could not obtain without undertaking an expert survey; and whereas in these circumstances the Chamber, while remaining seised of the question, notes that the Heads of States, acting in the framework of ANAD, are shortly to define the detailed terms of the troop withdrawal which the Chamber considers it should indicate as a provisional measure."

[1488] See *Gautron*, 32 AFDI (1986), at 210. In the Aegean Sea Continental Shelf, the Court had refused to grant interim protection which it saw as superfluous in light of an an intervening binding resolution from the Security Council, Aegean Continental Shelf Case (Greece v. Turkey), Interim Protection, Order of 11 September 1976, at 13, paras. 41–2.

developments. While the first approach would not have been desirable considering the fact that both parties had explicitly requested action by the Chamber,[1489] the second approach would have ignored the potential of the regional peace framework, which had been successful in arranging the cease-fire. The ANAD members had expertise and knowledge of the local situation which the Chamber did not possess and which it would have had to acquire through time-consuming processes. The Chamber's order set a short time frame for achieving a withdrawal agreement, failing which the Court reserved power to prescribe the necessary steps. This intervention created an incentive to accelerate ANAD process and ensured that the expertise of this apparatus and of the parties was taken into account. It also promoted the adoption of a mutually acceptable solution and provided for a remedy in case diplomatic efforts were in vain. Had a second order been required, the Chamber would have been able to take the results of the ANAD efforts into account.

After the order, the relations between the parties continuously improved. The heads of state of the two countries publicly reconciled at an ANAD meeting that took place on 17–18 January 1986. On 18 January, the parties concluded an agreement providing for troop withdrawal under ANAD auspices.[1490] On 1 February, ANAD reported that the bilateral troop withdrawal had been completed without incident.[1491] The parties resumed diplomatic relations in June[1492] and in November, the defense ministers of both countries met in Burkina Faso to reaffirm their commitment to fraternal relations.[1493]

The Chamber stated that the order indicating provisional measures ceased to be operative upon the delivery of its judgment of 22 December 1986 and that it was "happy to record the adherence of both Parties to the international judicial process and to the peaceful settlement of disputes."[1494] Hence, the Frontier Dispute case marks an instance of successful compliance with provisional measures. While some negative factors can be identified— tensions that had led to the armed conflict, a need for positive action (a withdrawal) beyond the cease-fire—there were various factors conducive to compliance. There was no doubt that the Court's jurisdiction was established on the basis of a special agreement. Furthermore, both parties requested the indication of interim measures, although they differed as to their content.

[1489] Admittedly, the Malian delegation did not extend its request to the determination of a troop withdrawal; nevertheless, it asked for measures to eliminate the risk of an aggravation of the dispute.

[1490] *Rousseau*, 90 RGDIP (1986), at 417; *Naldi*, 35 ICLQ (1986), at 975 fn. 24 quoting "The Guardian" of 20 January 1986. 56 AdG (1986) 29532 A. According to *Gautron*, 32 AFDI (1986), at 213, the shortness of the deadline established by the Court in fact accelerated the political settlement. The Court was informed of the settlement by a communiqué of the co-agent of Mali. Judgment of 22 December 1986 at 559, para. 10.

[1491] 56 AdG (1986) 29592 A.   [1492] Allcock, *Border and territorial disputes*, 224.

[1493] 56 AdG (1986) 30527A.   [1494] Judgment of 22 December 1986, at 649, paras. 177–8.

Finally, there was a regional settlement mechanism already actively involved in the matter, and the Court took a prudent approach in balancing its judicial task with parallel diplomatic efforts to end the conflict.

The order indicating provisional measures had several novel features. It was made in response to requests filed by *both* parties by a *Chamber* of the court, not the whole court, and issued in proceedings introduced by the notification of a special agreement. It was also unusual in substantive terms in that it called for the preservation of evidence and conferred responsibility for the determination of the conditions for the withdrawal on the parties, with the Court retaining the decision if negotiations failed. Finally, it marked the first occasion in which provisional measures were followed and at its time one of the few cases of interim proceedings in which both sides had participated.

VI. *Military and paramilitary activities in and against Nicaragua* (*Nicaragua case*)

Together with its application instituting proceedings against the US, Nicaragua filed a request for the indication of interim measures on 9 April 1984.[1495] The US opposed the proceedings in general and the indication of interim measures in particular: it argued that the Court had no jurisdiction and that the indication of interim measures was inappropriate as it might interfere with the multilateral negotiations in the framework of the Contadora process.[1496] Oral proceedings on the provisional measures took place from 25 to 27 April 1984, in which the United States explained its position on the lack of jurisdiction as well as on inadmissibility.[1497]

Nicaragua asked the Court to indicate that the US should immediately cease military and paramilitary activities in Nicaragua and refrain from the use and threat of force in its relations with Nicaragua. It also asked that the US desist from providing any support to any nation, group, or individual conducting military and paramilitary activities in Nicaragua and that the US

[1495] The facts of the case concerning military and paramilitary activities in and against Nicaragua were described in detail at **B XVIII 1**.

[1496] Letter of the US Ambassador to the Netherlands to the Registrar, 13 April 1984, ICJ Pleadings, Military and Paramilitary Activities in and against Nicaragua, Vol. 5, 359–60; Letter of the Agent of the United States of America to the Registrar, ibid., 365–8.

[1497] The US challenged the Court's jurisdiction on the basis of an alleged invalidity of Nicaragua's declaration accepting the compulsory jurisdiction and of the Shultz letter excluding disputes with Central American States from the US declaration under Article 36(2) of the Statute. Its arguments against admissibility centered on the absence of necessary third parties, the danger of interferences with the Contadora process, the inappropriateness of judicial settlement mechanisms for the dispute, and the primary responsibility of the Security Council. See the statements on behalf of the US in the Oral arguments on the request for the indications of provisional measures, ICJ Pleadings, Military and Paramilitary Activities in and against Nicaragua, Vol. 1, at 81–116, 127–9. See for further details *supra* B XVIII 2.

not take any action likely to aggravate the dispute.[1498] The US, in turn, did not request protection for its own rights through provisional measures, but asked the Court to dismiss Nicaragua's claims and to remove the case from its list for a manifest lack of jurisdiction.[1499]

In its order of 10 May 1984, the Court rejected the US request and indicated several interim measures. It unanimously indicated a measure that the United States should immediately cease from action restricting, blocking, or endangering access to or from Nicaraguan ports, and, in particular, the laying of mines. The second measure, adopted by 14 votes to 1 with the US Judge Schwebel dissenting, stated that "the right to sovereignty and to political independence possessed by the Republic of Nicaragua, like any other State of the region or of the world, should be fully respected and should not in any way be jeopardized by any military or paramilitary activities which are prohibited by the principles of international law," in particular referring to the prohibition of the use of force and the principle of non-intervention. As third and fourth measures, the Court unanimously indicated that neither government should take any action that might aggravate or extend the dispute or prejudice the rights of the other party in respect of a future decision rendered in the case. Moreover, it decided to keep the matters covered by the order under review and to have proceedings on the questions of jurisdiction and admissibility.[1500]

1. Content of the measures

The measures indicated by the Court differed from those requested by Nicaragua. The first measure established an unconditional obligation for the US to refrain from acts against Nicaraguan ports. The third and fourth measures reiterated the general obligations of parties to pending litigation and were clearer in so far as they were directed at both sides without distinction.

The actual requirements of the second measure were somewhat murkier. The measure addressed the right of Nicaragua to have its sovereignty respected and not to suffer any military and paramilitary activities *prohibited by international law*. What this is actually meant—i.e. whether this barred the US from continuing its support for the Contras—could not be determined without further investigation of the facts (in particular, relating to the question whether Nicaragua was itself engaging in military activities in neighboring countries) and an interpretation of the relevant legal norms (notably, whether the US was entitled to self-defense). Therefore, it remains

---

[1498] Order of 10 May 1984, at 173, para. 8. [1499] Ibid., at 173, para. 9.
[1500] Ibid., at 186–7, para. 41. See for details: *Deatherage*, 26 Harv. ILR (1985), at 280–6; *Labouz*, 30 AFDI (1984), at 340–71; *Leigh*, 78 AJIL (1984), at 894–7; *Rucz*, 89 RGDIP (1985), at 83–111.

unclear what the measure contributed beyond a general appeal to respect the law; it appeared to state something obvious: the United States had never disputed that Nicaragua, as any other state in the world, could, in principle, claim that another state might not take unlawful military actions against it; the decisive question was whether the situation was such as to permit collective self-defense and whether and to what extent the US had the right to provide support to the Contras. One could read the measure somewhat differently, though, taking into account that Article 41 of the ICJ Statute serves to indicate such measures as deemed *necessary* in order to protect the rights of either party. Viewed in this context, the second measure could be understood as an interim signal in favor of Nicaragua,[1501] since it reflected the Court's understanding that this measure was, in fact, considered *necessary* under the given circumstances for protecting Nicaragua's rights.[1502] The emphasis on Nicaragua's right of sovereignty and political independence shows that the Court apparently saw a prima-facie risk to those rights.

Yet the measure remained somewhat ambiguous; it did not rule out a contrary interpretation pursuant to which it could be read as an order to cease only *unlawful* use of force, which did not cover US action taken in the exercise of the right of collective self-defense. Under this interpretation, the measure would represent a gesture to promote respect for international law rather than an actual remedy for the applicant.[1503] The second interim measure could be read in this light with its equation of the Nicaragua's individual right of sovereignty with the general right of sovereignty of "any other state in the region or of the world." It would thus be no more than a general statement, although only Nicaragua is specifically mentioned.[1504] The general character of the statement and its validity for, as well as against, Nicaragua is stressed by the separate opinion of Judges Mosler and Jennings in which they affirmed that the duties to refrain from use of force and intervention were "duties which apply to the Applicant State as well as to the Respondent State."[1505] Moreover, one has to bear in mind that the Court indicated this measure instead of the more specific one requested by

---

[1501] See also Reichler (one of the counsels for Nicaragua), 42 Harv. ILJ (2001), at 34: "The Court's condemnation of US support for the Contras was unmistakable." Similarly, Gill, *Litigation Strategy at the World Court*, at 145: "[The Order] was undoubtedly viewed politically as a censure of the confrontationist policies of the United States towards Nicaragua, in particular of the laying of mines by the CIA in Nicaraguan harbors."

[1502] See *Rucz*, 89 RGDIP (1985), at 106, arguing that by following Nicaragua's request, the Court considered that there was a risk of irreparable damage for the rights that were the subject of the litigation if the US intervention did not cease.

[1503] See *Labouz*, 30 AFDI (1984), at 369.

[1504] This a necessary consequence of the general applicability of the prohibition of the use of force and of intervention, already visible in para. 2; the fact that both the applicant and the respondent are bound by those principles is particularly stressed by Judges Mosler and Jennings in their Separate Opinion to the Order of 10 May 1984, at 189.

[1505] Ibid., at 189.

Nicaragua. Then, however, one might wonder why the Court did not direct its call for respect for the prohibition of use of force at both sides. The measure's lack of clarity might have been the bargain struck for a nearly unanimous decision,[1506] although it could not be seen as conducive to ensuring compliance. Effectively, the second measure permitted both states to stick with their opinions based on their respective versions of the facts: Nicaragua could claim that the US violated the measure through unlawful use of force; the US could counter that its behavior was not unlawful. The required behavior could not be determined easily, as controversial facts played a decisive role.

2. Reasoning of the order

The Court was again faced with a request for provisional measures in a case where its jurisdiction was extremely controversial. Reaffirming that, at the interim stage, no final determination of jurisdiction on the merits was required, it added that it neither had to finally satisfy itself that an objection to its jurisdiction was well founded and stated that it yet ought not indicate such measures "unless the provisions invoked by the Applicant appear, *prima facie*, to afford a basis on which the jurisdiction of the Court might be founded."[1507] It thus followed the line of endorsing a *positive* test of prima-facie jurisdiction rather than the negative one of a manifest lack of jurisdiction initially taken. It remained unclear, though, how the test was to function precisely, in particular, how the reference to objections to the Court's jurisdiction was to be understood. Would prima-facie applicability of such objections remove the *prima facie* showing of jurisdiction, or was full evidence required? The standard also remained unclear as to the degree of possibility or probability required. In the present case, it seems as if "a provision that prima facie appears to afford a basis on which the jurisdiction might be founded" was understood as "possibly might": a rather low threshold for the applicant.[1508] After reporting the submissions of the parties as to the validity of Nicaragua's declaration under the optional clause, the Court stated that Nicaragua had deposited a declaration recognizing the compulsory jurisdiction of the ICJ without need for ratification and no limitation of time. The Court stated without further explanation that the absence of an effective ratification of the Permanent Court's Statute did not preclude the operation of Article 36(5) of the Statute.[1509] As far as the effect of the Schultz letter is

---

[1506] Judge Schwebel's dissent was directed against the fact that the measure emphasized the rights of Nicaragua in a case where Nicaragua itself was charged with violating the sovereignty of its neighbors; he criticized the order's failure to enjoin alleged Nicaraguan violations of international law, Diss. Op. Schwebel, at 190–9.

[1507] Ibid., at 179, para. 24.

[1508] See Stern, *20 ans de jurisprudence*, 321: the Court gave Nicaragua the benefit of the doubt. Similarly, *Labouz*, 30 AFDI (1984), at 355–7.

[1509] Order of 10 May 1984, at 180, para. 25.

concerned, the Court apparently saw no need for a detailed examination at the interim stage.[1510] The way the Court proceeded with regard to both the Nicaraguan and the US declaration seems to suggest that where it was satisfied that prima facie, there was an instrument conferring jurisdiction, the burden of proof for the applicability of *exceptions* such as reservations would fall on the party contesting jurisdiction.[1511]

As Judge Schwebel observed in his dissent:

> The nub of the matter appears to be that, while in deciding whether it has jurisdiction on the merits, the Court gives the defendant the benefit of the doubt, in deciding whether it has jurisdiction to indicate provisional measures, the Court gives the applicant the benefit of the doubt. In the present case, the Court, in my view, has given the applicant the benefit of a great many doubts.[1512]

Ambiguous standards and cursory legal reasoning can, of course, be problematic for a decision's authority, particularly where the jurisdiction is vehemently disputed by the respondent,[1513] and such a lax standard could be a disincentive for states to submit declarations under the optional clause if they cannot be sure that a proper review of the scope of their declarations will be undertaken in interim proceedings.

Similarly, the standard for the "circumstances" that *required* the indication of provisional measures remains somewhat unclear. The Court's decision mentions US objections that Nicaragua's factual statements were false, that Nicaragua had engaged in aggression against neighboring countries who had turned to the US for assistance, and that interim measures could interfere with the Contadora process. Yet the order seemed to gloss over these concerns without comment.[1514] There were no further explanations, no sign of the Court's deliberative process. A thorough discussion of the submissions

---

[1510] The Court stated ibid., at 189, para. 26: "Whereas the Court will not now make any final determination of the [...] question whether, as a result of the declaration of 6 April 1984, the present Application is excluded from the scope of the acceptance by the United States of the compulsory jurisdiction of the Court; whereas however the Court finds that the two declarations do nevertheless appear to afford a basis on which the jurisdiction of the Court might be founded."

[1511] See *Rucz*, 89 RGDIP (1985), at 96–7, with the assumption that the Court would only take into account such reservations which would render it manifestly incompetent, e.g. those imposing a restriction *ratione temporis*.

[1512] Order of 10 May 1984, Diss. Op. Schwebel, at 207.

[1513] This critique remains valid although the Court explicitly confirmed its jurisdiction half a year later in a judgment, *supra* B XVIII 2, as the relevant moment for evaluating the legitimacy of provisional measures is the moment of their issuance; moreover, the suspicion might come up that the decision in the order might unduly influence the judgment on jurisdiction. Admittedly, in this case the Court at least refined the test and developed it further in comparison to earlier cases, for instance, by including the reference to objections.

[1514] Order of 10 May 1984, at 186, para. 39: the Court merely stated: "Whereas in the light of the several considerations set out above, the Court finds that the circumstances require it to indicate provisional measures, as provided by Article 41 of its Statute, in order to preserve the rights proclaimed."

would have been desirable to justify why provisional measures were required under the circumstances, in particular, the specific measures indicated.[1515] This was particularly true as the case involved the right to self-defense—the Court should have shown that it had paid sufficient regard to the security implications and had the necessary expertise.[1516]

Relating to the impact of the political implications, the parallelism between judicial and diplomatic settlement mechanisms, and the situation forming part of a larger context, the Court's decision seems in keeping with its prior decision in the Tehran hostages case, in which the US (as the applicant) had advanced that these issues did not preclude the Court from indicating provisional measures.[1517] It would have been desirable for the Court to demonstrate that it had taken the US concerns into account in devising its order. Even in relation to Nicaragua, the Court did not respond to all its submissions. It does not explain, for example, why it only partially acceded to its request.

Charges that the order's content demonstrated bias against the United States[1518] seem exaggerated. Judge Schwebel's dissent criticized the Court for taking a slanted approach when indicating the measure urging respect for Nicaragua's sovereignty and political independence without invoking the respective principles of international law against Nicaragua as well and failing to pay sufficient regard to the security of El Salvador, Costa Rica, and Honduras. However, the measure's reference to the respective right of "any other State of the region or of the world" could plausibly—if not convincingly—be understood as encompassing the right of those three states as well.[1519] Even assuming that the measure was an indication against the United States, it did not yet prejudge the Court's decision on the merits; moreover, the US itself had not requested the indication of provisional

---

[1515] See *Rucz*, 89 RGDIP (1985), at 104.

[1516] How can a state be expected to accept the Court's interpretation of its right of self-defense when it cannot even be sure on which basis the Court reached its conclusion as to the security requirements? Is it possible that the Court had enough information so as to recognize the impact of its decision for international peace and security despite the limited fact finding undertaken in interim proceedings? The Court should have demonstrated through its reasoning that such concerns were unfounded.

[1517] Still, there were significant differences with the Hostages case. The Nicaragua case presented a situation of ongoing armed conflict. Moreover, there was already a Security Council resolution in the Hostages case, whereas a US veto scuttled a similar resolution in the Nicaragua case. See Stern, *20 ans de jurisprudence*, at 321–3, for parallelism and divergences between the Nicaragua and the Tehran Hostages cases.

[1518] See *Franck*, 79 AJIL (1985), at 381; *Moore*, 81 AJIL (1987), 159.

[1519] But see *Leigh*, 78 AJIL (1984), at 896: "Although in a formal sense the decision of the Court to indicate provisional measures does not prejudge the merits of the case, it nevertheless suggests that there are significant questions regarding the validity, under international law, of US involvement in Nicaragua's internal conflict." Yet, as such significant questions necessarily arise in cases of support of military activities in another country and the general rule is the prohibition of force, with the burden of proof on the party trying to justify military action, it cannot be taken as a bias without further particulars.

measures. This did not automatically exclude the Court from indicating measures in this respect, as the Court is not restricted to the parties' requests in granting interim protection.[1520] Nevertheless, the lack of a request for provisional measures was significant: the US decision not to ask for an indication of provisional measures in its favor indicated its understanding that it saw no need for interim protection of its rights. The mere fact that the Court followed this logic cannot be taken as a sign of a bias against the US. Moreover, the US had the opportunity to make its own request for provisional measures at a later stage, although it declined doing so.[1521]

3. The follow-up to the order

The first measure (relating to mining operations) was apparently complied with. In its judgment on the merits, the Court noted that mining operations had been conducted prior to the order, constituting violations of international law, but that there had not been additional complaints of such activities after the order.[1522]

Compliance with the other measures was another matter. For the next few months following the order, Nicaragua complained several times that the US was still engaging in military activities and thus not respecting the remaining measures. On 25 June 1984, it addressed a communication to the Court requesting the indication of further measures, arguing that the US was violating the order of 10 May 1984.[1523] In this context, it requested "that, until such time as the United States ceases and desists from all activities that do not comply with the Order of 10 May 1984, the facilities of the Court shall not be available to the United States for the purpose of rendering a decision in its favor in any other pending or future case, and the United States shall not be permitted to invoke the Court's aid in any matter."[1524] The request

---

[1520] Article 75(2) Rules of Court: "When a request for provisional measures has been made, the Court may indicate measures that are in whole or in part other than those requested, or that ought to be taken or complied with by the parties which has itself made the request" (see also Article 75(1): "The Court may at any time decide to examine proprio motu whether the circumstances of the case require the indication of provisional measures which ought to be taken or complied with by any or all of the parties.")

[1521] For a different explanation see *Rucz*, 89 RGDIP (1985), at 109, arguing that the dispute before the Court concerned the US intervention in Nicaragua and not Nicaragua's intervention against its neighbors. This, however, seems to be too narrow an understanding of the subject-matter of the dispute. Since the US had explicitly invoked the right of collective self-defense, this right was equally a matter submitted to the Court, and the Court had to make sure that in protecting Nicaragua's rights, it did not unduly restrict the right of self-defense. It could entirely ignore the situation in the other countries.

[1522] Judgment of 27 June 1986, at 45–8, paras. 75–80, 143–4, para. 286.

[1523] Ibid., at 144, para. 287.

[1524] Excerpt from the Nicaraguan communication as quoted in the Letter of the ICJ President to the Agent of Nicaragua of 6 July 1984, ICJ Pleadings, Military and Paramilitary Activities in and against Nicaragua, Vol. 5, 382–3.

seemed to suggest that the Court should withhold its judgment in the Gulf of Maine case, the other case involving the US pending before the Court at the time.[1525] ICJ President Elias advised the Nicaraguans that they should await the outcome of the proceedings on jurisdiction and that the Court considered the withholding of its services in other cases as an impermissible measure. He restated the Court's view that "the Court naturally expects [the US] to comply with the Order of 10 May 1984 in strict accordance with its terms"—a statement which excluded an interpretation of provisional measures as merely hortatory.[1526] In its judgment on jurisdiction and admissibility, the Court stated that the interim measures were to remain operative until the delivery of its final judgment.[1527] Nicaragua made no subsequent request for further provisional measures.

Nicaragua also lodged complaints with the Security Council and argued that US aid to the Contras constituted "a flagrant violation of the duty of states to abide by the decisions of the International Court of Justice, in this case the Order of 10 May 1984."[1528] An urgent meeting of the Security Council was convened on 7 September 1984[1529] at the request of Nicaragua, who did not invoke Article 94(2) of the Charter in this context, instead referring to a "new escalation of aggression."[1530] The order was just one of the points mentioned in the course of Nicaragua's complaint against the US.[1531] The US representative at the Security Council meeting deflected the criticism by pointing to Nicaragua's oppressive political system and its increasingly close military ties to the Soviet Union.[1532] He did not mention the ICJ order; neither did the last speaker, the Soviet representative, who used the opportunity to decry US interventionism.[1533] No decision was ultimately taken at the meeting.

[1525] On the Gulf of Maine case, see *supra* B IXX.

[1526] *Supra* n. 1524. ICJ President Elias stated that a withholding of its services in other cases would unduly restrict the Court from exercising its normal functions and that there was no basis for such a request in the ICJ Statute or in the Rules.

[1527] Judgment of 26 November 1984, at 442, para. 112.

[1528] Letter dated 4 September 1984 from the representative of Nicaragua to the President of the Security Council, S/16730, transmitting a note from the Nicaraguan minister of foreign affairs to the US secretary of state complaining about widespread use of aircraft supplied by the US Central Intelligence Agency to mercenary groups, following the shooting-down of a military helicopter by the Sandinista Army. For further complaints, see the following letters from the representative of Nicaragua to the President of the Security Council: Letter dated 30 August 1984, S/16728, Letter dated 11 September 1984, S/16740, Letter dated 12 September 1984, S/16744, Letter dated 18 September 1984, S/16745.

[1529] S/PV.2557.

[1530] Letter dated 4 September 1984 from the representative of Nicaragua to the President of the Security Council, S/16371.

[1531] Statement of Mr Chamorro Mora on behalf of Nicaragua, S/PV.2557, at paras. 12–13.

[1532] Statement of Mr Sorzano on behalf of the United States, S/PV.2557, at paras. 58–73.

[1533] Statement of Mr Ovinnikov on behalf of the USSR, at paras. 79–84, 89.

Despite these complaints, the situation calmed substantially after the order. Nicaragua achieved its main strategic objective—the interruption of assistance to the Contras, although this might have been due to reasons other than the ICJ order. Official US military support for the Contras ceased on 30 September 1984 when the Reagan administration's appropriations request faltered in the House of Representatives after having been approved by the Senate. As a compromise solution, the Continuing Appropriations Act for 1985 in principle prohibited the use of funds for direct or indirect support of military or paramilitary operations in Nicaragua by any group, but provided $14 million in the event that the president could prove to the satisfaction of Congress that such aid was necessary after 28 February 1985. President Reagan tried to gain access to the funds in April 1985 with the pledge that it would only be used for humanitarian support, but the House balked at the idea. For the fiscal year 1986, Congress approved an appropriation of $27 million for humanitarian assistance under the condition that it not be administered by the CIA or the Department of Defense. It was only for fiscal year 1987 that Congress renewed aid for military and paramilitary activities of the Contras in addition to a continuation of humanitarian assistance.[1534]

A look at the judgment shows that the factual basis for several of the principal Nicaraguan claims related to times preceding the order or just overlapping with it for some time: the Court saw a direct involvement of US personnel in military and paramilitary activities as established for a period of time between 13 September 1983 and 4 April 1984, the production of the controversial CIA manual had happened in 1983, and military assistance for the Contras was delivered up to September 1984.[1535]

By an executive order of 1 May 1985, President Reagan imposed a general trade embargo against Nicaragua,[1536] an act not compatible with the duty to abstain from acts likely to aggravate the dispute. While the embargo hurt the Sandinista government, it was perhaps not quite as central an issue as the military assistance to the Contras.[1537] The termination of official US assistance substantially weakened the Contras; accordingly, while the order was not fully complied with, the overall situation after the indication of provisional measures improved for the Nicaraguan government.

[1534] See Judgment, at 55–8, paras. 95–9, "US Legislation relating to Nicaragua," 26 International Legal Materials (1987), 433–78. Humanitarian assistance was defined as "provision of food, clothing, medicine, and other humanitarian assistance, and it does not include the provision of weapons, weapon systems, ammunition, or other equipment, vehicles, or material which can be used to inflict serious bodily harm or death.", ibid. See for further details on Congress action to regulate Contra aid, *Hayes*, 88 Col. LR (1988), at 1566–8; Colella, 54 Br. LR (1988), at 131–69; Scheffer, 81 AJIL (1987), at 713–18.

[1535] Judgment of 27 June 1986, at 45–8, paras. 75–81, at 55–8, paras. 95–9, and 65, para. 117.

[1536] Judgment of 27 June 1986, at 70, para. 125. Other US acts that still took place after the order were overflights over Nicaraguan territory, ibid., at 51–3, paras. 87–91.

[1537] The halt to military assistance was most important: *Reichler*, 42 Harv. ILJ (2001), at 23.

The Court commented on the provisional measures in the judgment on the merits. Referring to the third and fourth measures,[1538] it stated:

When the Court finds that the situation requires that measures of this kind should be taken, it is incumbent on each party to take the Court's indications seriously into account, and not to direct its conduct solely by reference to what it believes to be its rights. Particularly is this so in a situation of armed conflict where no reparation can efface the results of conduct which the Court may rule to have been contrary to international law.[1539]

Thus, it stopped short of saying that provisional measures are binding, but emphasized that states are not free on how to react to them. The fact that the Court felt obliged to make a statement on this point at all seems to indicate that it was not satisfied with the order's implementation.

As was revealed in late 1986 after the delivery of the judgment, high-ranking officials of the Reagan administration had been involved in continued military-related assistance to the Contras at a time when this had been prohibited by Congress, partially financed through gains from secret weapons sales to Iran, and through the establishment of an organization channeling contributions of private persons and foreign governments (giving rise to the Iran Contra affair).[1540] There were also suspicions that funds allocated for humanitarian aid had been diverted to provide military assistance.[1541] The second and third measures had therefore been violated through covert action attributable to the US government.

Although US action with regard to Nicaragua did not wholly come to a halt, the provisional measures had proven useful for Nicaragua, bolstering its morale, decreasing its sense of isolation, and—probably to some degree— restraining US policy decisions during the litigation process.[1542] The danger stemming from the Contras significantly decreased following the official

---

[1538] The obligations not to take action likely to aggravate the dispute and not to prejudice the rights of the other party with regard to the implementation of the judgment, see *supra* 1.

[1539] Judgment of 27 June 1986, at 143–4, paras. 286–88.

[1540] See *Weinraub*, "Iran payment found diverted to Contras; Reagan Security Adviser and Aide are out," New York Times, 26 November 1986, retrievable under http://www.nytimes.com/learning/general/onthisday/991125onthisday_big.html; Final report of the independent counsel for Iran/contra matters, Lawrence E. Walsh, www.fas.org/irp/offdocs/walsh; *Hayes*, 88 Col. LR (1988), 1569–74; *Michaels*, 7 Bos. C. TWJ (1987), at 254–60. See also the panel of the American Society of International Law on "Congress and the executive: who calls the shots for national security?," Proceedings of the American Society of International Law, 81st annual meeting 1987, at 239–58.

[1541] *Michaels*, 7 Bos. C. TWJ (1987), at 254–5.

[1542] *Reichler*, 42 Harv. ILJ (2001), at 34; Gill, *Litigation Strategy at the World Court*, 145 ("It [...] provided ammunition for the Reagan Administration's Congressional opponents, who managed partially as a result to block the President's request for additional financial aid to the contra guerrillas at the time. It also contributed to the United States Government's decision to desist from the further laying of mines.") The refusal by the House of Representatives to appropriate Contra aid in 1984 had to be seen in context with the revelations of the covert mining activities: *Hayes*, 88 Col. LR (1988), at 1568.

334 Compliance with Decisions of the International Court of Justice

interruption of US aid, and bearing in mind that Nicaragua's foremost priority had been to put an end to US military support to the Contras,[1543] the official suspension of that support during the proceedings was a huge success for them.

4. Conclusion

A variety of factors made this case problematical. Besides the US opposition to an involvement of the Court and its eventual non-appearance, it is noteworthy that the Court dealt with a multilateral dispute in a bilateral setting; that it was a situation of ongoing armed conflict that involved claims of collective self-defense; and that the parties were ideologically in opposition and at the low mark of their bilateral relations (with Reagan, a strong opponent of communism, claiming that the Sandinistas were aligning with the Soviet Union). The facts were highly disputed; the Security Council had not been able to address the situation in more than very general terms. The order itself could be criticized for a lack of precision of the measures and for the brevity of its reasoning, particularly as concerned the standard for jurisdiction and for the "circumstances" requiring the adoption of provisional measures. This was unfortunate since the ramifications of this case made a convincing reasoning particularly desirable.

The partial success and the usefulness of the measures for the applicant should not be overlooked, despite the limits of the measures' efficiency. The temporary refusal by the US Congress to grant further Contra aid could be understood as a partial implementation of the order, although the weight of the provisional measures in the corresponding decision-making process was probably rather low. The continued support for military activities by covert action was attributable to the United States, but it was a problem of domestic as of international law and one involving criminal activities. The first measure, which was the most specific one (relating to the mining operations), was complied with.

VII. Application of the Convention on the Prevention and Punishment of the Crime of Genocide

The facts relating to the humanitarian tragedy in Bosnia and Herzegovina remain fresh in the memory of the international community. Power struggles broke out along ethnic lines in Yugoslavia after the collapse of communism in 1989. Slovenia and Croatia declared their independence on 25 June 1991, moves that were met with strong resistance by the mainly Serb federal authorities. Bosnia and Herzegovina declared its independence in October

---

[1543] *Reichler*, 42 Harv. ILJ (2001), at 23.

1991. After the recognition of Bosnia and Herzegovina (hereinafter Bosnia) by the European Union and the United States on 7 April 1992, the situation there escalated into war. Bosnian Serbs proclaimed a "Serbian Republic of Bosnia and Herzegovina," and "ethnic cleansing" campaigns to create ethnically homogenous areas and consolidate territorial claims occurred. The Muslim population was forced to flee and numerous persons were killed or placed in detention camps. There were many indications that the Bosnian Serbs were supported by the Federal Republic of Yugoslavia (Serbia and Montenegro) (hereinafter Yugoslavia).[1544]

1. Bosnia's application and the first proceedings on interim protection

On 20 March 1993, Bosnia instituted proceedings against Yugoslavia for violations of the 1948 Genocide Convention and other legal instruments relating to humanitarian law, human rights, the prohibition of the use of force, and of intervention. Moreover, Bosnia requested a declaration that it had the right to self-defense under Article 51 of the Charter, that all Security Council resolutions had to be construed in a manner as not to impair that right, and that all UN members had the right to come to its assistance. It also asked for reparation for damages caused by Yugoslavia's violations of international law.[1545]

On the same day, Bosnia filed a request for the indication of provisional measures.[1546] It claimed protection for a broad range of legal rights, including the right of its citizens to survive as a people and as a state and to self-determination, their basic human rights and the right to be free from acts of genocide. It asked the Court to order Yugoslavia to cease and desist from all acts of genocide, and from all direct or indirect military and paramilitary activities against Bosnia, as well as to abstain from the threat or use of force. It sought an order that Bosnia had the right "to seek and receive support from other states in order to defend itself and its people, including by means of immediately obtaining military weapons, equipment, and supplies" and the right "to request the immediate assistance of any state to come to its defense, including by means of immediately providing weapons, military equipment and supplies, and armed forces." The request also called for an order to the effect

---

[1544] See on the background Baer, *Der Zerfall Jugoslawiens*, at 30–44; *DeWeese*, 26 Denv. JILP (1998), at 628–32; *Wiebalck*, 28 CILJSA (1995), at 84–5. As for the name of the defendant, the name of the Federal Republic of Yugoslavia was changed into Serbia and Montenegro following a change of the constitutional structure, in 2003, see http://www.un.org/Overview/unmember. html. The Court has renamed pending cases and left the former denomination for completed cases. In the present context, as far as Court decisions in cases involving this country are cited, the citations are given in the form that was valid at the time the respective decision was delivered. As the present section deals with past events, it will use the name Yugoslavia.

[1545] See Order of 8 April 1993, at 4–7, para. 2, and http://212.153.43.18/icjwww/idocket/ibhy/ ibhyorders/ibhy_iapplication_19930320.htm.

[1546] Ibid., at 7, para. 3.

that any state had the right "to come to the immediate defense of Bosnia—at its request—including by means of immediately providing weapons, military equipment and supplies, and armed forces."[1547] Bosnia's strategy was therefore twofold: under the heading of a request for interim measures—measures directed at safeguarding either party's rights pending the proceedings—it did not only request measures directed at Yugoslavia but also desired a statement on its right to self-defense, its rights *vis-à-vis* the international community, and the right of the international community to come to its assistance. Its claim concerning its entitlement to receive arms can be understood as a request for a pronouncement that the arms embargo for Yugoslavia was not applicable to Bosnia.[1548] This arms embargo had been imposed by Security Council Resolution 713 (1991) and had been reaffirmed in subsequent resolutions, and it was also applied to Bosnia after its independence.[1549]

Bosnia founded the Court's jurisdiction on Article IX of the Genocide Convention. During the oral proceedings on provisional measures, it invoked as additional basis of jurisdiction a joint letter of 8 June 1992 by Montenegro's President Bulatovic and Serbia's President Slobodan Milosevic, acting on behalf of Yugoslavia, to Robert Badinter, Chairman of the EC Arbitration Commission on Yugoslavia, in which the two presidents expressed their opinion that remaining issues between the republics of the former Yugoslavia should be submitted to the ICJ if not resolved by agreement.[1550] In Bosnia's view, Yugoslavia had thereby made an offer to submit the dispute to the ICJ.[1551] Yet it was highly doubtful that the letter had intended an immediate commitment that would have entitled Bosnia to bring any dispute before the Court without further requirements.

Issues relating to jurisdiction *ratione personae* and *ratione materiae*[1552] raised problems. Under Article 35(1) of the ICJ Statute, the Court is open to all parties to its Statute, and under Article 93 of the UN Charter, all UN members are parties to the Statute. Whether Yugoslavia qualified as a party to the Statute under these provisions was doubtful. Bosnia, a UN member

---

[1547] See Order of 8 April 1993, at 4–7, para. 2, and http://212.153.43.18/icjwww/idocket/ibhy/ ibhyorders/ibhy_iapplication_19930320.htm.

[1548] See *Scott et al.*, 16 Mich. JIL (1994), at 2.

[1549] Ibid., at 7, 136. Security Council Resolution 727 (1992) had reaffirmed the embargo and decided that it was to apply "in accordance with paragraph 33 of the Secretary-General's report"; in the respective paragraph, it had been stated that the arms embargo was to apply to all areas that had been part of Yugoslavia, see Scott *et al.*, at 137, fn. 417. On 18 December 1992, the General Assembly adopted a resolution calling upon the Security Council to lift the arms embargo for Bosnia (GA Res. 47/121), but the Security Council did not follow this request, see *Gray*, 43 ICLQ (1994), at 706.

[1550] The letter was an answer to a letter by Badinter directing three questions on state succession to the presidents of Bosnia and Herzegovina, Croatia, Macedonia, Montenegro, Serbia, and Slovenia, and the presidency of the Federal Republic of Yugoslavia.

[1551] Statement of Francis Boyle on behalf of Bosnia and Herzegovina, Public Sitting of 1 April 1993, printed in: Boyle, *The Bosnian people charge genocide*, 102–3.

[1552] The first relates to the capability of the subject to be party before the Court (Article 35 of the Statute); the second to the issue of whether relating to the subject-matter there is a jurisdictional link.

since 22 May 1992,[1553] contested Serbia and Montenegro's claim to be a UN member in continuity with the former Yugoslavia,[1554] an original member of the United Nations:[1555] issues of state succession were also relevant with regard to the subject-matter jurisdiction. Yugoslavia had ratified the Genocide Convention in August 1950;[1556] on December 1992, Bosnia had filed a notice of succession to the convention with the UN Secretary-General with effect from 6 March 1992. Yugoslavia contested Bosnia's right to assert unilaterally its adherence to the convention.[1557]

Yugoslavia also opposed an indication of provisional measures because of the action taken by the Security Council under Chapter VII of the UN Charter, which, in its view, made interim protection by the Court "premature and inappropriate."[1558] On the other hand, Yugoslavia did not seem to be generally opposed to the involvement of the Court and to the exercise of its powers to grant interim protection: in its written observations, it had on its own requested the Court to indicate provisional measures, including the requests to order Bosnian authorities[1559] to respect a cease-fire; to observe humanitarian law and human rights of the Serbs living in Bosnia; to disband prisons and detention camps in which Serbs were being held; and to put an end to discrimination based on nationality or religion and the practice of "ethnic cleansing" against the Serb population of Bosnia.[1560]

On substance, the prohibition of genocide was undisputed;[1561] the parties disagreed, however, on the responsibility for any atrocities committed. Yugoslavia argued that the war in Bosnia was a civil war in which it was not involved, and that it was not responsible for any acts of genocide, while raising accusations against Bosnia in this context. Bosnia, on the other hand, claimed that Serbia and Montenegro were responsible for military and paramilitary activities by Serb forces and members of the former Yugoslav National Army and thus for acts of genocide while contesting any involvement in acts of genocide against the Serb population.[1562]

[1553] General Assembly Resolution A/RES/46/237.

[1554] Order of 8 April 1993, at 12, para. 15.

[1555] ST/LEG/SER.E/19, at 3–4. The treatment of the Federal Republic of Yugoslavia (Serbia and Montenegro) by the UN organs was ambiguous. Order I, at 12–14, paras. 15–18. For further details, see Gray, 43 ICLQ (1994), at 707–9.

[1556] ST/LEG/SER.E/19, 132.

[1557] Order of 8 April 1993, at 15–16, para. 24; see *Gray*, 43 ICLQ (1994), at 711.

[1558] Order of 8 April 1993, at 18–19, para. 33.

[1559] The Yugoslav request referred only to "the authorities controlled by A. Izetbegovic" in an effort not to recognize Izetbegovic as the legitimate president of Bosnia and Herzegovina. Ibid., at 9–10, para. 9.

[1560] Ibid.

[1561] Yet, the precise features of acts qualifying as genocide seemed somewhat unclear, see the enumeration of acts in Bosnia's request, ibid., at 8, para. 3, No. 1. See also on the practice of "ethnic cleansing," Judge *ad hoc* Lauterpacht's separate opinion to the Order of 13 September 1993, at 431–2, paras. 68–70.

[1562] Order of 8 April 1993, at 21, paras. 41–3.

2. The order of 8 April 1993

The Court treated the matter with particular urgency: the hearings were held on 1 and 2 April 1993, and an order indicating provisional measures was issued on 8 April 1993. After highlighting the importance of the matter given alleged violations of the Genocide Convention,[1563] a unanimous Court called on the Yugoslavian government to "take all measures within its power to prevent commission of the crime of genocide, in pursuance of its undertaking in the Genocide Convention." By 13 votes to 1, it ordered the Yugoslavian government to ensure that armed units it controlled or indirectly supported do not commit or incite acts of genocide against the Muslim population of Bosnia or any other groups.[1564] Unanimously, the Court issued a measure calling on both parties' governments not to take any action and ensure that no action was being taken "which may aggravate or extend the existing dispute over the prevention or punishment of the crime of genocide, or render it more difficult of solution."[1565]

The measures differed from those requested by the parties. The last measure had not been requested by either,[1566] although it is a common feature in interim protection granted by the Court. The first two measures related to the prevention of genocide only, so that Bosnia's other objective—namely, to get a declaration that it was entitled to arms deliveries—was not satisfied. In contrast to the Bosnian request, genocide was not further defined, although reference was made to the Genocide Convention. Even though the Court

---

[1563] Ibid., at 23, para. 49: "Whereas the crime of genocide 'shocks the conscience of mankind, results in great losses to humanity [. . .] and is contrary to moral law and to the spirit and aims of the United Nations,' in the words of General Assembly Resolution 96(1) of 11 December 1946 on 'the Crime of Genocide,' which the Court recalled in its Advisory Opinion on Reservations on the Convention on Genocide (ICJ Reports 1951, 23)."

[1564] The precise text of the first two measures reads: "The Government of the Federal Republic of Yugoslavia (Serbia and Montenegro) should immediately, in pursuance of its undertaking in the Convention on the Prevention and Punishment of the Crime of Genocide on 9 December 1948, take all measures within its power to prevent commission of the crime of genocide; The Government of the Federal Republic of Yugoslavia (Serbia and Montenegro) should in particular ensure that any military, paramilitary or irregular armed units which may be directed or supported by it, as well as any organizations and persons which may be subject to its control, direction or influence, do not commit acts of genocide, of conspiracy to commit genocide, of direct or public incitement to commit genocide, or of complicity in genocide, whether directed against the Muslim population of Bosnia and Herzegovina or against any other national, ethnical, racial or religious group." The Russian Judge Tarassov dissented on the second measure because it could be inferred that the Yugoslav government was, in fact, involved in genocidal acts, so that it came close to a prejudgment of the merits. Declaration of Judge Tarassov, ibid., 26–7.

[1565] Order of 8 April 1993, at 24, para. 52. For details, see Daniele, 76 RDI (1993), at 375–84; *Maison*, 5 EJIL (1994), at 382–9, 394–6; *Oellers-Frahm*, ZaöRV 53 (1993), at 641–54; *Wiebalck*, 28 CILJSA (1995), at 84–97.

[1566] Bosnia had maintained, however, that the Court should exercise its powers to grant interim protection "with a view to preventing the aggravation or extension of the dispute whenever it considers that the circumstances so require:" Order of 8 April 1993, at 23, para. 48.

followed Bosnia in so far as it directed the order to prevent genocide at Yugoslavia only, it left open whether there was any Yugoslav involvement; the Bosnian request, on the other hand, had spoken of "Yugoslavia (Serbia and Montenegro) together with its agents and surrogates in Bosnia and elsewhere."[1567]

The fact that only measures relating to genocide were indicated in addition to the measure relating to the aggravation of the dispute resulted from the fact that the Court saw a prima-facie basis for its jurisdiction only in Article IX of the Genocide Convention.[1568] The Court was not satisfied, however, that the 1992 letter[1569] on its face represented an immediate commitment binding on Yugoslavia, and even in the affirmative, whether it related to more than the three questions which it sought to answer.[1570] In keeping with its jurisprudence, the Court stated that it could not indicate provisional measures unless a prima-facie jurisdictional basis existed;[1571] in this context, it had to consider the question of jurisdiction *ratione personae* for the first time in addition to that of *ratione materiae*. Relying on Article 35(2) of the Statute, the Court held that Article IX provided a sufficient prima-facie basis for its jurisdiction even in the event that the respondents were later determined not to be a party to the ICJ Statute, and it therefore left the question of UN membership open.[1572] The concurrent involvement of the Security Council in the matter presented no difficulties for the Court. Confirming its earlier jurisprudence, it stated that the Court and the Council had separate but complementary functions and that it was not barred from taking action where the Council was seized.[1573]

The existence of an obligation of Yugoslavia to take all measures at its disposal to prevent genocide was something obvious; even outside the formal

---

[1567] See Order of 8 April 1993, 8, para. 3(1).

[1568] Concerning jurisdiction *ratione materiae*, i.e. the applicability of Article IX of the Genocide Convention as between the parties, the Court noted Yugoslavia's commitment to honor the international treaties concluded by the Socialist Federal Republic of Yugoslavia and Bosnia's status as having succeeded (rather than acceded) to the convention, as well as the subsequent lapse of the three-month period stipulated in Article XIII for accessions to become effective. The Court was thus satisfied that Article IX provided a prima-facie basis for jurisdiction. Ibid., at 14–16, paras. 20–6.

[1569] Ibid., at 19, para. 35; 20, para. 38.

[1570] Ibid., at 16–18, paras. 27–32. In the judgment on preliminary objections of 1996, the Court found that the letter, in fact, could not serve as a basis for jurisdiction, see *infra* n. 1624.

[1571] Ibid., at 11–12, para. 14. New elements were added to the usual formula. First, the Court referred to "the provisions invoked by the applicant or found in the Statute," indicating somewhat of an autonomy *vis-à-vis* the parties' submissions. Second, the Court explicitly stated that prima-facie jurisdiction also had to be established with regard to jurisdiction *ratione personae*. See *Daniele*, 76 RDI (1993), at 376-7.

[1572] Order of 8 April 1993, at 12–14, paras. 15–19. See *supra* Chapter 2 C II on Article 35(2) of the Statute on the conditions under which the Court is open to states not party to its Statute.

[1573] Ibid., at 18–19, para. 33. It also explained that the Yugoslav submissions on this point were primarily targeted at those aspects of Bosnia's request for which the Court had already found a lack of prima-facie jurisdiction.

framework of the Genocide Convention, the prohibition of genocide has a firm basis in customary law and its status as a norm of *jus cogens* is widely acknowledged. By reaffirming this obligation, the Court merely pointed to the need for the observance of a norm that was incumbent on Yugoslavia anyway, as upon any other state. If this is so, one may ask why the Court did not direct its call for the observance of the prohibition of genocide to both sides. This could be understood as one-sided, an implicit indication of Yugoslavia's guilt.[1574] The extent of evidence submitted by each side might have led the Court to different assessments as to the necessity of interim measures.[1575] This might have motivated the Court not to direct a measure at Bosnia to prevent genocide, although it explicitly stated in its reasoning that both states were under that obligation.[1576] Yet the reasoning remains short and somewhat ambiguous in this respect;[1577] in the second order, the Court would provide further explanations.[1578]

The Court did not provide for any role of the United Nations Protection Force (UNPROFOR) (*inter alia* deployed in the territory of Bosnia) for the supervision of the observance of the interim measures—unsurprising, given that UNPROFOR was a subsidiary organ of the Security Council, not the Court: it was therefore up to the Council to define its tasks.[1579]

3. Events subsequent to the order

Unfortunately, the order did not bring an end to the humanitarian catastrophe in Bosnia. Just a few days after the order, on 16 April 1993, the Bosnian UN representative addressed a letter to the Security Council concerning military attacks by Yugoslavia, in particular on Srebrenica. He qualified this assault as act of genocide which constituted a "direct violation"

[1574] See *Gray*, 43 ICLQ (1994), at 713–14.

[1575] In contrast with Bosnia's extensive submissions, Yugoslavia's written observations merely indicated its intention to submit evidence supporting its allegations of genocide being committed against Serbs: Order of 8 April 1993, at 21, paras. 40–1, 43.

[1576] Ibid., at 22, para. 45 "whereas in the view of the Court, in the circumstances brought to its attention and outlined above in which there is a grave risk of acts of genocide being committed, Yugoslavia and Bosnia-Herzegovina, whether or not any such acts in the past may be legally imputable to them, are under a clear obligation to do all in their power to prevent the commission on any such acts in the future."

[1577] The affirmation of both parties' obligation to prevent genocide is made with reference to the concrete circumstances; it would have been desirable if the Court then would have explained more clearly why only one party is addressed in the operative part.

[1578] See *infra* section 5.

[1579] UNPROFOR, in operation from February 1992 to March 1995, was originally established in Croatia to facilitate an overall settlement of the Yugoslav crisis; its mandate comprised the demilitarization and protection of the "United Nations Protected Areas" in Croatia and was subsequently extended to cover responsibilitites in to Bosnia and Herzegovina such as the assurance of humanitarian aid deliveries: see United Nations Department of Public Information, Former Yugoslavia: UNPROFOR, Background, September 1996, http://www.un.org/Depts/DPKO/Missions/unprof_b.htm.

of the second provisional measure and concluded: "Pursuant to Article 94, paragraph 2 of the Charter of the United Nations, request is hereby made that the Security Council take immediate measures under Chapter VII of the Charter to stop the assault and to enforce the Order of the International Court of Justice."[1580] Hence, recourse was taken to the Security Council under Article 94(2), although action was requested under Chapter VII. Another letter issued by the Bosnian representative on the same day indicated no legal basis for Council action.[1581]

The operative part of Resolution 819,[1582] unanimously adopted by the Security Council on the same day, deals comprehensively with the situation in Bosnia and in particular in Srebrenica without explicitly reinforcing the Court's order.[1583] The resolution's preamble noted the Court's order and its first measure directed at Yugoslavia to prevent genocide.[1584] The legal basis for Council action was not indicated; Article 94 of the Charter is not mentioned.[1585] The verbatim records of the meeting do not shed any light on this issue.[1586] Many factors explain the silence on Article 94 and speak for the

---

[1580] Letter dated 16 April from the permanent representative of Bosnia and Herzegovina to the UN addressed to the President of the Security Council, S/25616.

[1581] Letter dated 16 April from the permanent representative of Bosnia and Herzegovina to the UN addressed to the President of the Security Council, S/25609. The Bosnian representative referred to the "horrifying situation in Srebrenica" and demanded "with all moral and legal right, that the Security Council take all necessary measures, as a matter of utmost urgency, to guarantee the safety of the remaining inhabitants of Srebrenica," without indicating a legal basis for Council action.

[1582] S/RES/819 (1993), 16 April 1993.

[1583] It condemns acts of "ethnic cleansing" and the taking of territory by use of force; it orders Yugoslavia to stop supplying arms to Bosnian Serb units. It calls for a treatment of Srebrenica as a safe area, the unimpeded delivery of humanitarian assistance, and a guarantee of safety and free movement for UNPROFOR and other UN personnel, etc. S/RES/819 (1993), 16 April 1993. See further 63 AdG (1993) 37799A/4.

[1584] Ibid., preamble, second paragraph: "taking note that the International Court of Justice in its Order of 8 April 1993 in the case concerning application of the Convention on the Prevention and Punishment of the Crime of Genocide (Bosnia and Herzegovina v. Yugoslavia (Serbia and Montenegro)) unanimously indicated as a provisional measure that the Government of the Federal Republic of Yugoslavia (Serbia and Montenegro) should immediately, in pursuance of its undertaking in the Convention on the Prevention and Punishment of the Crime of Genocide of 9 December 1948, take all measures within its power to prevent the commission of the crime of genocide."

[1585] Chapter VII was only mentioned in the context of UNPROFOR, see the last paragraph of the preamble: "recalling the provisions of resolution 815 (1993) on the mandate of UNPROFOR and in that context acting under Chapter VII of the Charter of the United Nations." Resolution 815 had been adopted on 30 March 1993.

[1586] Provisional verbatim record of the 3199 meeting, 16 April, S/PV.3199, 1–3. No objections were made to the matter. The draft resolution (S/25617) had been a result of previous consultations of the Council, S/PV.3199, 2. Prior to the vote, the President of the Security Council referred to the two letters of the Bosnian representative of 16 April 1993 and to another letter of 5 April 1993, S/25529 where Bosnia complained of continued aggressions "by Serbian and Montenegrin aggressors and their proxies in Bosnia and Herzegovina" in the region of Srebrenica, despite the call of the Security Council's president of 3 April 1993 for strict compliance with all relevant Security Council resolutions. The resolution referred to the information provided by the Secretary-General on the rapid deterioration of the situation in Srebrenica and surroundings (preamble, 7th para.).

resolution's classification as a Chapter VII resolution: the resolution dealt with the situation in Srebrenica in a context much broader than non-compliance of an ICJ order, the order was just a small aspect in a situation which involved armed attacks against an area that had been designated a safe area, violations of international humanitarian law and various earlier Security Council resolutions, "ethnic cleansing," attacks against UNPROFOR, etc. Furthermore, one principal group addressed by the resolution—Bosnian Serb paramilitary units—had not been addressed by the Court's order, as the parties before the ICJ were Bosnia and Yugoslavia only. Resolution 819 was one in a series of Council resolutions dealing with the human tragedy in Bosnia; in the first paragraph of its preamble, it reaffirms resolution 713 (1991) of 25 September 1991[1587] and all subsequent relevant resolutions that had been adopted without connection to an ICJ decision. Also, since the draft for Resolution 819 had been prepared during the Council's prior consultations, the text might indeed already have been drafted before the Bosnian complaint of non-compliance had been received by the members of the Security Council. Considering all these factors, it is understandable that the focus of the resolution is not on non-compliance with an ICJ decision and that the order is just mentioned marginally. In the end, the resolution would not have looked different had there been no ICJ order.[1588] The precedential value of Resolution 819 for the interpretation in practice of Article 94(2) is therefore limited.[1589] The Court mentioned the resolution in its second order indicating interim measures of 13 September 1993 without further comment.[1590]

4. The second proceedings on interim protection

On 27 July 1993, Bosnia again turned to the Court with an additional request for provisional measures "because the respondent has violated each and

---

[1587] S/RES/713 (1991) imposed a general embargo on delivery of weapons and military equipment to Yugoslavia even before the independence of the several republics was recognized.

[1588] With the exception of the second paragraph, obviously, which reads: "Taking note that the International Court of Justice in its Order of 8 April 1993 in the case concerning application of the Convention on the Prevention and Punishment of the Crime of Genocide (Bosnia and Herzegovina v. Yugoslavia (Serbia and Montenegro)) unanimously indicated as a provisional measure that the Government of the Federal Republic of Yugoslavia (Serbia and Montenegro) should immediately, in pursuance of its undertaking in the Convention on the Prevention and Punishment of the Crime of Genocide of 9 December 1948, take all measures within its power to prevent the commission of the crime of genocide."

[1589] *Fleischhauer* in Schachter/Joyner, UN legal order, at 236 fn. 12, argues that Resolution 819 is "probably not a resolution under Article 94," since it does not relate to a judgment, but to an order indicating provisional measures. See also *Tanzi*, 6 EJIL (1995), at 565–8.

[1590] Order of 13 September 1993, at 348, para. 54. On the enforceability of provisional measures under Article 94, see ibid., Sep. Op. Ajibola, at 400–3. There is no record of Security Council discussions concerning the second order, see Rosenne, *Law and Practice III*, 1461 fn. 100.

every one of the three measures of protection on behalf of Bosnia that were indicated by this Court on 8 April 1993."[1591] For the first time, the Court conducted further proceedings on the basis of another request by the applicant despite the continued validity of an earlier order.[1592] Bosnia provided a chronology of violations of the Court's order in which the events at Srebrenica occupied a prominent place, besides many other incidents reported: this shows its attempt to have the breach of the earlier sanctioned through another order.[1593] This was not the only goal, as a variety of measures was requested beyond a mere reinforcement of the earlier ones—including, most importantly, "the desire to have the Court protect the very existence of the people and state of Bosnia."[1594] The Bosnian agent pointed out that if the additional measures were not granted, Bosnia would not be able to argue its case on the merits.[1595]

The Court was requested to indicate a number of additional measures to force Yugoslavia to stop providing support to insurgent groups in Bosnia and attempting to partition or in any other way dismember Bosnian territory. Bosnia asked for declarations that any annexation or incorporation of Bosnian territory was illegal, null and void *ab initio*; that it "must have the means to prevent the commission of genocide against its own people and to defend its state against partition and dismemberment by means of genocide"; and that all contracting parties of the Genocide convention were under the obligation to prevent genocide in Bosnia. With regard to the availability of military supplies, Bosnia sought a two-sided declaration that it was entitled to such aid and that such aid from parties to the Genocide Convention was lawful. The request also aimed at securing humanitarian relief through the Council's UNPROFOR mission in the Bosnian city of Tuzla.[1596]

Following the request, the President of the Court directed a message to both parties on 5 August 1993, calling upon them to act in a way as to enable any future order to have its appropriate effects and to comply with the first order:

I do now call upon the Parties so to act, and I stress that the provisional measures already indicated in the Order which the Court made after hearing the Parties, on 8 April 1993, still apply. Accordingly I call upon the Parties to take renewed note of the Court's Order and to take all and any measures that may be within their power to prevent any commission, continuance, or encouragement of the heinous international crime of genocide.[1597]

[1591] Boyle, *The Bosnian people charge genocide*, at 182.

[1592] As stated above (*supra* II 2) in the Fisheries Jurisdiction cases, further measures were indicated because of a lapse of the first measures. In the Nicaragua case, there was an informal request for provisional measures, and the Court did not see a sufficient basis for new proceedings on interim protection, *supra* VI 3.

[1593] Boyle, *The Bosnian people charge genocide*, at 185–219.   [1594] Ibid., at 183.

[1595] Ibid., at 230–2.   [1596] Ibid., at 231–2; Order of 13 September 1993, at 332–3, para. 6.

[1597] Order of 13 September 1993, at 333–4, para. 10.

Bosnia proposed several additional sources of jurisdiction beyond that arising from the Genocide Convention, including the 1919 Treaty of Saint-Germain-en-Laye between the Allied and Associated Powers and the "Kingdom of the Serbs, Croats and Slovenes" on the Protection of Minorities.[1598] Furthermore, Bosnia again pointed to the 1992 letter, without additional arguments why the Court should arrive at an evaluation different from the order of April, and it made a general reference to the principles of the international laws of war and international humanitarian law, without mentioning a specific jurisdictional clause; those arguments were unlikely to convince the Court, as it was not recognizable where one could see a prima-facie basis for jurisdiction.[1599]

Beyond that, Bosnia argued that the Court's jurisdiction was established in accordance with the doctrine of *forum prorogatum*, as Yugoslavia itself had requested provisional measures beyond the Genocide Convention in April 1993.[1600] At the same time, though, Yugoslavia had constantly asked the Court to reject Bosnia's request as "outside the jurisdiction of the Court," casting doubts on the applicability of the doctrine of *forum prorogatum*.[1601]

Through the second request, Bosnia sought to have the Court deal with the matter in a broader context than in the first order (through which it had received interim protection to a far smaller extent than desired) and, in particular, to clarify Bosnia's rights towards the international community (third states and UNPROFOR) and the right of third states not to apply the arms embargo to Bosnia. To achieve that goal, Bosnia pursued a twofold strategy: on the one hand, it referred the Court to additional bases of jurisdiction; on the other hand, it framed its claims—even those related to other legal principles such as Article 51 of the UN Charter—as claims of prevention of genocide; thus, it argued that the prohibition of genocide comprised the protection of the existence of a state.

[1598] Bosnia claimed that Yugoslavia had succeeded to the rights and obligations of the Kingdom of the Serbs, Croats, and Slovenes, which had agreed to PCIJ jurisdiction under certain provisions of the treaty; ibid., at 339–40, paras. 29–30.

[1599] Ibid., at 340–1, paras. 32–3.

[1600] It made a subsequent request for provisional measures in the context of the second proceedings on interim measures, but this time only relating to the Genocide Convention: "The Government of the so-called Republic of Bosnia and Herzegovina should immediately, in pursuance of its obligation under the Convention on the Prevention and Punishment of the Crime of Genocide of 9 December 1948, take all measures within its power to prevent the commission of genocide against the Serb ethnic group." Request dated 9 August 1993, ibid., at 334, para. 12, again submitted in the hearings, ibid., at 336, para. 19. Yugoslavia later formally raised counterclaims alleging genocide against the Bosnian Serb population, but it withdrew those counterclaims in 2001, see ICJ Press Release 2001/22, http://212.153.43.18/icjwww/ipress-com/ipress2001/ipresscom2001-22_bhy_20010913.htm.

[1601] Order of 13 September 1993, at 334, para. 11; at 335, para. 15; at 335–6, para. 19; and at 341, para. 34.

5. The order of 13 September 1993

As was to be expected, the Court did not see a basis for its prima-facie jurisdiction beyond the Genocide Convention.[1602] It refused to accept the 1919 treaty as such a basis given that on its face, it covered only protection of minorities within a state's own territory. It rejected the further bases of jurisdiction for the reasons indicated above.[1603]

The Court did not accept the broad range of rights claimed by Bosnia (such as its right of physical existence as a state) as appropriate for interim protection in the framework of the proceedings, but prima facie saw only the right to be free from genocidal acts as possible subject-matter of a judgment under Article IX of the Genocide Convention.[1604] It felt unable to accede to Bosnia's request in so far as it exceeded the framework of the bilateral relations of the parties to the proceedings and amounted to a clarification of Bosnia's rights towards the international community.[1605] What it found to remain from Bosnia's request was basically identical to the claims on whose basis the April order had been adopted.[1606]

The Court rejected Yugoslavia's request for the indication of provisional measures concerning genocide against the Serb ethnic group in Bosnia. In view of the available evidence and information, it recognized the existence of some risk to the persons whose protection Yugoslavia sought, but it stated that the relevant question was whether the circumstances were such as to *require* the indication of provisional measures. Referring to a paragraph of the April order in which it had stated that both states were under the obligation to prevent genocide, and to the fact that the third provisional measure of that order—the obligation not to take any action likely to aggravate the dispute—had been directed at both sides, the Court found that for the time being, there was no need for more specific measures being directed at Bosnia to reaffirm its undoubted obligations.[1607] This argumentation seemed to imply doubts on the Yugoslav observance of the Genocide Convention: with regard to Bosnia, the Court found it sufficient to restate its obligations in its reasoning, while in relation to Yugoslavia, it regarded it necessary to adopt a measure explicitly recalling this obligation.

In its evaluation on whether the indication of new measures was required, the Court then commented on the events subsequent to the April order. It did not close its eyes to the fact that neither its order nor the Security Council

[1602] Ibid., at 342, para. 36.
[1603] Ibid., at 341, para. 32 (for the 1992 Letter); at 341, para. 33 (for the general reference to the laws of war and international humanitarian law); and at 341-2, para. 34 (for the doctrine of *forum prorogatum*).
[1604] Ibid., at 343-4, paras. 38-9.   [1605] Ibid., at 344-5, paras. 40-1.
[1606] Ibid., at 346, para. 43.
[1607] Order of 13 September 1993, at 346-7, paras. 44-6. Criticism was voiced on that point by Vice-President Oda, ibid., Decl. Oda, at 351-2.

action had succeeded in preventing that "great suffering and loss of life has been sustained by the population of Bosnia-Herzegovina in circumstances which shock the conscience of mankind and flagrantly conflict with moral law and the spirits and aims of the United Nations."[1608] It stated that the risk of an aggravation or extension of the dispute had deepened and referred to Resolution 819; Resolution 859 (1993), in which *inter alia* the continuing membership of Bosnia in the United Nations was affirmed; and to the establishment of the International Crimes Tribunal for the Former Yugoslavia.[1609] The Court then explicitly commented on the compliance with the former order: "Whereas the Court, while taking into account, inter alia, the replies of the two Parties to a question put at them at the hearings as to what steps had been taken by them 'to ensure compliance with the Court's Order of 8 April 1993,' it is not satisfied that all that might have been done has been done to prevent commission of the crime of genocide in the territory of Bosnia-Herzegovina, and to ensure that no action is taken which may aggravate or extend the existing dispute or render it more difficult of solution."[1610]

This statement appeared to imply that the Court found that both parties had failed to comply with the order of April: Yugoslavia with regard to all three measures; Bosnia with regard to the duty not to aggravate or extend the dispute, which was the only measure of which it had been an addressee.[1611] The Court recalled its finding in the 1986 Nicaragua judgment that when the Court finds that the situation requires that measures of this kind should be taken, "it is incumbent on each party to take the Court's indication seriously into account."[1612] It concluded that what was required was not the indication of additional measures, but rather "immediate and effective implementation" of the measures already indicated.[1613] Accordingly, it reaffirmed by 13 votes to 2 the provisional measures indicated in paragraph 52 A(1) and (2) (relating to the prevention of Genocide), and by 14 to 1 votes the one in paragraph 52 B of the order.[1614]

[1608] Order of 13 September 1993, at 348, para. 52.   [1609] Ibid., at 348, paras. 53–7.

[1610] Ibid., at 348–9, para. 57.

[1611] See *DeWeese*, 26 Denv. JILP (1998), at 639: "The Court was clearly frustrated at the continued fighting taking place, despite numerous Security Council resolutions condemning the ethnic cleansing and other violations of international law [...]."

[1612] Order of 13 September 1993, at 349, para. 58: it is stressed that this was particularly so in the present situation "where no reparation could efface the results of conduct which the Court may rule to have been contrary to international law." See for the reference from the Nicaragua case *supra* VI 3 and n. 1539.

[1613] Order of 13 September 1993, at 349, para. 59.

[1614] Paragraph 52 A(1) and (2) were the measures calling for to the prevention of genocide, B the measure requesting the parties to abstain from measures aggravating the dispute. The Court urged that these measures "should be immediately and effectively implemented." Ibid., at 349–50, para. 61. Judge Tarassov dissented on the former part, repeating his concerns on the first order as well as criticizing the failure to address both sides, ibid., Diss. Op. Tarassov, at 449–52.

Several of the judges commented further on the issue of compliance with the first order in their separate opinions. Judge Shahabuddeen stated: "In my opinion, the evidence warrants a finding of non-implementation on part of Yugoslavia"[1615] and suggested that this fact should have been given weight when dealing with Yugoslavia's request for provisional measures:

Yugoslavia, not having implemented the provisional measures indicated by the Court, now seeks provisional measures of its own. I do not go as far as to suggest that the non-implementation necessarily or automatically debars Yugoslavia from making its request (as well it might in a corresponding case in some domestic jurisdictions); but it is, in my view, something which legitimates the conclusion that, in all the circumstances, it would not be correct for the Court, at this stage, to act on the material presented by Yugoslavia in support of the particular measures it requests.[1616]

Judge Weeramantry stated: "The Applicant has placed before the Court information from a diversity of independent sources in support of its contention that, after the date of the Court's Order of 8 April 1993, there has been a continuing series of acts which constitute a clear violation of the order."[1617] He referred to three types of materials: independent media reports, statements of neutral and independent observers, and statements by the respondent and the government of the Republic of Serbia, which provided extensive evidence for non-compliance with the order on the part of the respondent, even if one left the media reports out of consideration. On the other hand, he saw no sufficient proof by independent material for any non-compliance by Bosnia, although he also acknowledged the sufferings by Serbian people in Bosnia.[1618] Judge Ajibola referred to a lack of sufficient implementation of the measures on the part of both states, as shown by their insufficient answer to his question on the measures taken for that purpose. He expressed the view that a court might refuse to make a further order if it is not satisfied that an earlier order was complied with by both sides, and that it was on this basis that he concurred with the Court in the decision to reaffirm the earlier measures.[1619] Judge *ad hoc* Lauterpacht went as far as to conclude from the evidence at hand: "The Respondent stands behind the Bosnian Serbs and it must, therefore, be seen as an accomplice to, if not an actual participant in, this genocidal behaviour."[1620]

He dissented even though he had voted in favor of the first measure in the earlier order; even in his declaration to that order, however, he had voiced opposition to the fact that it had not been directed to both sides. The Yugoslav Judge *ad hoc* Kreca dissented on the entire operative part. For further details on the order, see *Daniele*, 98 RGDIP (1994), at 931–49; *Wiebalck*, 28 CILJSA (1995), at 97–103.

[1615] Order of 13 September 1993, Sep. Op. Shahabuddeen, at 365.   [1616] Ibid., at 368.
[1617] Order of 13 September 1993, Sep. Op. Weeramantry, at 371.   [1618] Ibid., at 371-3.
[1619] Order of 13 September 1993, Sep. Op. Ajibola, at 393-7, 406.
[1620] Order of 13 September 1993, Sep. Op. Lauterpacht, at 432, para. 69.

6. Assessment

Despite the second order, further atrocities took place; two years after its
designation as a UN protected zone, Srebrenica would become the synonym
for one of the darkest chapters in the war in Bosnia and in the history of
Europe since the Second World War: Bosnian Serb forces, after a long period
of siege, captured the city and killed thousands of unarmed Muslim men.[1621]
In 2001, the International Criminal Tribunal for the former Yugoslavia
(ICTY) found the former Bosnian Serb General Krstic guilty of genocide
for the Srebrenica massacre.[1622] For those events, as well as for various
others in Bosnia in the period 1 March 1992–31 December 1995, the former
president of Serbia, Slobodan Milosevic, is charged with genocide and other
crimes by the ICTY.[1623] Assuming he is found guilty, there will be hardly any
way to deny Yugoslavia's international responsibility for acts of genocide
and a violation of the ICJ orders. The World Court is, of course, not bound
by the findings of the ICTY and will undertake its own review of the facts;
yet, the evidential weight of an ICTY judgment against the former Serbian
leader would be enormous.

It will be up to the ICJ to reach an ultimate finding on whether the
provisional measures were complied with in its judgment on the merits: the
measures relating to the prevention of genocide coincide with the claims on
the merits as far as the time period subsequent to the order of 8 April 1993 is
concerned. The Court confirmed its jurisdiction under Article IX of the
Genocide Convention and the admissibility of Bosnia's application in its
judgment on preliminary objections of 11 July 1996; it dismissed the further
bases of jurisdiction invoked by the applicant and, hence, arrived at the
same result as already in the orders of 1993.[1624] The case is still pending
before the Court, and the applicant does not appear to push for a rapid
decision.[1625]

[1621] BBC News, Srebrenica timeline, 20 January 2003, http://news.bbc.co.uk/2/hi/europe/
675945.stm, BBC News, Bosnia remembers Srebrenica, 11 July 2000, http://news.bbc.co.uk/hi/
english/world/europe/newsid_828000/828390.stm; 65 AdG (1995) 40167A/5, 40205A/4. See also
DeWeese, 26 Denv. JILP (1998), at 625–7, 641, 650–3.
[1622] Judgment of Trial Chamber I of 2 August 2001, www.un.org/icty/krstic/TrialC1/judge
ment/index.htm, BBC News, General guilty of Bosnia genocide, 2 August 2001, http://news.
bbc.co.uk/hi/english/world/europe/newsid_1469000/1469896.stm. The matter is still pending
before the Appeals Chamber; for the current status, see the information on the ICTY website
at http://www.un.org/icty/cases/indictindex-e.htm.
[1623] Indictment of 22 November 2001, www.un.org/icty/indictment/english/mil-ii011122e.
htm. For an overview of all the charges against Milosevic, see http://news.bbc.co.uk/hi/english/
world/europe/newsid_1402000/1402790.stm, for the current status of the case, see http://www.
un.org/icty/cases/indictindex-e.htm.
[1624] Judgment of 11 July 1996, at 623–4, para. 47. For details, see *Maljean-Dubois*, 42 AFDI
(1996), at 357–86; *DeWeese*, 26 Denv. JILP (1998), at 642–7.
[1625] As the Bosnian constitutional organs also have Serb members, the lawsuit is not uncontroversial on the domestic level, in particular since there is an interest in an improvement of the

What is certain is that, despite the provisional measures, further atrocities happened in Bosnia, and, as is explained in several separate opinions and is the understanding of the majority, there is evidence suggesting that Yugoslavia could have done more to prevent acts of genocide on Bosnian territory and thus violated the provisional measures indicated by the Court; in fact, there seems to be ample evidence for non-compliance with the order on behalf of Yugoslavia.[1626]

The orders fulfilled a purpose for Bosnia as the measures to prevent genocide were directed at Yugoslavia only. Yet the measures remained rather general and central questions as to whether the acts happening in Bosnia qualified as genocide and whether Yugoslavia was involved were not yet answered by the first order,[1627] although the second order seemed to take a clearer stand in that direction. Further important objectives of its requests for provisional measures were not met, as the Court limited the measures to the bilateral relations of the parties (as a result of which Bosnia did not achieve a clarification of its rights towards the international community, namely, an interpretation of the arms embargo exempting Bosnia) and to the Genocide Convention. The usefulness of the measures for Bosnia was therefore limited to start with, as those measures indicated fell far short of Bosnia's request.[1628]

---

relations after the demise of the Milosevic régime in Belgrade. There are financing problems, as the Serb delegates have opposed inclusion of funds for the proceedings in the state budget. See Agence France-Press, 31 May 2002, Bosnian Parliament adopts budget enabling IMF, World Bank Loans, 2002 WL 2419781, BBC Monitoring, Bosnia to set up foundation to finance lawsuit against Yugoslavia, 26 May 2002, 2002 WL 21783315, BBC Monitoring, Bosnian Presidency Member outvoted on issue of Hague Lawsuit against Yugoslavia, 8 March 2002, 2002 WL 15938447, BBC Monitoring, Bosnia without budget until lawsuit against Yugoslavia dropped—deputy speaker, 6 February 2002, 2002 WL 12800569, BBC Monitoring, Bosnian Premier says genocide charges should not harm ties, 18 December 2001, 2001 WL 31754688, World News Connection, 6 December 2001, B-H: HINA speculates Sarajevo, Belgrade in secret negotiations on genocide suit, 2001 WL 31644260. On 23 April 2001, the respondent made a request for revision of the 1996 judgment, arguing that it had been admitted a member of the United Nations on 1 November 2000 and that this was a new fact showing that there had been no jurisdiction *ratione personae*: Application for Revision of the Judgment of 11 July 1996, http://212.153.43.18/icjwww/idocket/iybh/iybhapplication/iybh_iapplication_20010424.PDF; this delayed the proceedings further. The Court ruled in its Judgment of 3 February 2003 that the request for revision was not admissible. Accordingly, the affirmative finding on jurisdiction in the 1996 judgment stands. Even in the event that the Court might not arrive at a final decision on Yugoslavia's involvement in genocide in Bosnia and Herzegovina, that question will be examined by the International Tribunal for War Crimes committed in the Former Yugoslavia.

[1626] The case is generally referred to as a case of non-compliance, see *Ajibola* in Bulterman/Kuijer, Compliance with judgments, at 36; *Oda* in Lowe/Fitzmaurice, Fifty Years of the ICJ, at 548 ("No real effect has been observed with respect to the Court's Order.")

[1627] *Daniele*, 76 RDI (1993), at 384.

[1628] For some time, it looked as if Bosnia might take an alternate route to pursue its strategy of using the ICJ as a tool to influence international opinion *vis-à-vis* the arms embargo. On 15 November 1993, it announced its intention to institute proceedings against the United Kingdom for the imposition and maintenance of the arms embargo in violation of Article 51

Still, the Court's call for prevention of genocide was of political significance, and it would probably have been regarded as a sign of weakness if the Court had felt unable to adopt any kind of measure. In its interpretation of the jurisdictional clauses, the Court adopted a rather cautious approach in rejecting all but Article IX of the Genocide Convention; this way, it avoided the undesirable result of adopting measures on the basis of a jurisdictional clause that it would reject at a later stage. The point where its reasoning was perhaps the most debatable was the jurisdiction *ratione personae*; however, since in this context, the Court was in line with Yugoslavia's general policy concerning continuity of its obligations with the former Yugoslavia, this was not a point where significant resistance on its part was to be expected.[1629] All in all, the Court took the test of prima-facie jurisdiction seriously. While it is certainly desirable that all aspects of a complex situation are addressed and some commentators therefore expressed their regret that the Court had only referred to the Genocide Convention,[1630] the Court has to be cautious not to overstep its judicial powers, and its decisions were in line with the prima-facie test in the preceding orders on provisional measures and developed the criteria further.

No miracles could have been expected through interim protection by the Court. In this crisis, a variety of mechanisms of peaceful settlement had already been unsuccessfully employed by the international community and the Security Council. It would have been unfair to have expected too much from the Court: it was a situation where the law had reached its limits, as horrible and tragic as that was.[1631] The Court and the Council both pursued

---

of the UN Charter and for complicity in genocide: Statement of intention by the Republic of Bosnia and Herzegovina to institute legal proceedings against the United Kingdom before the International Court of Justice, printed in Boyle, *The Bosnian people charge genocide*, at 365–6. The UK was the only permanent member of the Security Council with a valid declaration under Article 36(2) of the Statute and was one of the opponents of an exemption for Bosnia and Herzegovina. However, no such proceedings were introduced: on 20 December the UK and the Bosnian government issued a statement that Bosnia did not intend to launch proceedings and that both countries were committed to work for a negotiated political settlement: Joint statement by the government of Bosnia-Herzegovina and the United Kingdom, printed ibid., at 368. Boyle ibid., at 371, contests the validity of the agreement between the two countries not to pursue the case.

[1629] At that time, Yugoslavia had an interest in being treated as a UN member; Bosnia and Herzegovina had put its UN membership in question. Order of 8 April 1993, at 12, para. 15.

[1630] *Wiebalck*, 28 CILJSA (1995), at 96–7, referring to the Nicaragua case as an instance in which broader measures were indicated; this argument fails to take into account, though, that in that case, the basis for the Court's prima-facie jurisdiction had been declarations under the optional clause, not a jurisdictional clause relating to the interpretation of a treaty.

[1631] See *Maison*, 5 EJIL (1994), at 399–400, expressing regret over the failure of positive international law to respond adequately to such situations and promoting support for individual criminal responsibility, *Oellers-Frahm*, ZaöRV 53 (1993), at 638–9, 651–2, on the limited effectiveness of the provisional measures. See also *DeWeese*, 26 Denv. JILP (1998), at 628: "The Bosnian war and the case it spawned before the ICJ serve as a reminder that violence in the form of genocide and warfare cannot be stopped in the courtroom. Perhaps the ICJ is not the place to settle disputes over issues as pressing as genocide."

the objective to prevent further atrocities, but peace was restored to the region only with the Dayton Peace Accords.[1632]

VIII. Land and maritime boundary between Cameroon and Nigeria

1. Background of the proceedings

In its application of 29 March 1994, Cameroon seized the Court with a dispute with Nigeria concerning sovereignty over the Bakassi peninsula.[1633] Cameroon claimed sovereignty over Bakassi and stated that Nigerian troops were engaging in acts of aggression since late 1993 and had occupied several localities in the peninsula. Economic interests in natural resources lay behind the dispute.[1634] Despite fraternal relations, to which the parties referred frequently during the proceedings, they had not achieved a diplomatic settlement.[1635] Cameroon asked the Court to confirm its sovereignty over Bakassi and to order Nigeria immediately and unconditionally to withdraw from the area and provide reparation. It also called on the Court to determine the maritime boundary between the two countries, which had only been partially delimited, "up to the limit of the maritime zones which international law places under their respective jurisdictions."[1636]

In an additional application of 6 June 1994,[1637] Cameroon submitted several questions concerning sovereignty over a part of territory in the area of the Lake Chad and asked the Court to "specify definitely" the frontier of the two states from Lake Chad to the Atlantic Ocean. As basis for jurisdiction, Cameroon referred to the two countries' declarations under Article 36(2) of the ICJ Statute: Nigeria's declaration of 3 September 1965 and Cameroon's declaration of 3 March 1994.[1638] Both declarations had been made without reservations.

[1632] 35 International Legal Materials (1996), 75–183.

[1633] http://212.153.43.18/icjwww/idocket/icn/icnorders/icn_iapplication_toc.htm.

[1634] Oil and gas resources were particularly important, as well as the fishing industry. Africa Analysis, 20 March 1998, Trouble ahead for oil-rich Bakassi, 1998 WL 8631556; Africa Review of World Information, Cameroon: Country profile, 14 August 2001, 2001 WL 26372205; *Garcia*, 42 AFDI (1996), at 409.

[1635] See, for example, the order of 15 March 1996 at 24, para. 47: "Whereas in the course of the present proceedings the representatives of the two parties have, on several occasions, referred to the fraternal relations which have always existed between their peoples." On the background of the dispute, see *Bekong*, 9 Afr. JICL (1997), at 288–92.

[1636] See *supra* n. 1633.

[1637] Application additional to the application instituting proceedings brought by the Republic of Cameroon, http://212.153.43.18/icjwww/idocket/icn/icnorders/icn_iapplication_940329_1.htm. Nigeria had no objections to treating the additional application as an amendment to the initial one in accordance with Cameroon's wish, and the Court confirmed that it saw no problems in this respect in an order of 16 June 1994, see Judgment of 15 March 1996, at 16, para. 12.

[1638] ICJ YB 1994–5, 84 (Cameroon's Declaration), 106 (Nigeria's Declaration of 14 August 1965).

Nigeria filed eight preliminary objections challenging the Court's jurisdiction and the admissibility of Cameroon's claims on 23 December 1995.[1639] Pointing to the fact that Cameroon had filed its application immediately after the deposit of its declaration recognizing the Court's jurisdiction under Article 36(2), Nigeria noted that it had had no knowledge of Cameroon's declaration when the proceedings were instituted and argued that there was a lack of "substantive reciprocity."[1640] It denied the existence of a legal dispute with regard to several claims; moreover, it maintained that the case implicated interests of third states and that other dispute settlement mechanisms had not been exhausted.[1641] Before the conclusion of the proceedings on these preliminary objections, the Court was seized with a request for the indication of provisional measures.

2. The incidents of February 1996 and the proceedings on interim protection

Although the precise details were murky, an armed skirmish between the two countries began on the peninsula on 3 February 1996.[1642] On 10 February 1996, Cameroon made a request for provisional measures and asked the Court to order a bilateral withdrawal to positions occupied before the "Nigerian armed attack of 3 February 1996" and a cease-fire along the entire boundary pending the judgment. It also called for an order for the conservation of evidence in the case.[1643] Interestingly, unlike requests in other cases, Cameroon's request related to measures directed at both parties, not only at the respondent, although the wording "Nigerian armed attack" implied a

---

[1639] Land and Maritime Boundary between Cameroon and Nigeria, Preliminary Objections, Judgment of 11 June 1998, at 284–9, para. 16, Preliminary objections of the Federal Republic of Nigeria, http://212.153.43.18/icjwww/idocket/icn/icnpleadings/icn_ipleadings_951201_preliman aryobjectionsnigeria.htm. See also *Bekker*, 92 AJIL (1998), at 751–4.

[1640] Preliminary objections of the Federal Republic of Nigeria, December 1995, *supra* n. 1639, Ch. 1.

[1641] Nigeria argued that Court could not be validly seized before exhausting these mechanisms (bilateral talks and the Lake Chad Basin Commission), Judgment of 15 March 1996, at 284–9, para. 16.

[1642] According to Cameroon, Nigerian forces had attacked Cameroonian troops along the entire cease-fire line of 1994, resulting in fatalities, and several localities had fallen in the hands of the Nigerian forces. Order of 15 March 1996, at 17–18, para. 18, Statement of Douala Moutoume, Agent for Nigeria, CR 96/2, 5 March 1996, at 23–8, see also the letter dated 22 February 1996 from the minister for foreign affairs of the Republic of Cameroon addressed to the President of the Security Council, S/1996/125 (transmitting also a letter from the Cameroonian minister for foreign affairs to his Nigerian counterpart). Nigeria attributed the fights to a surprise attack by Cameroon on Nigerian positions. It maintained that its own response had been limited in scope and proportionate to the need for self-defense, and that its military positions had not advanced in comparison to the situation prior to 3 February 1996. See the following statements before the Court on behalf of Nigeria: Chief M.A. Agbamuche (Agent), CR 96/3, 8 March 1996, 11–18, Sir Arthur Watts, Counsel and Advocate, CR 96/4, 8 March 1996, 80–90, Ian Brownlie, Counsel and advocate, ibid., 102. See also a Letter dated 26 February 1996 from the minister for foreign affairs of Nigeria addressed to the President of the Security Council, S/1996/140.

[1643] Order of 15 March 1996, at 18, para. 20.

finding against Nigeria. This language was unlikely to be accepted by the Court at the stage of interim proceedings, given the insufficient evidence for arriving at a clear attribution of responsibility.[1644]

Nigeria responded to Cameroon's request in a communication to the Court of 16 February 1996. Besides recalling its position in the main proceedings, it complained about municipal elections held in Bakassi by the Cameroonian authorities on 21 January 1996 and invited the Court to "note this protest and call the government of Cameroon to order." It requested that the government of Cameroon "should be warned to desist from further harassment of Nigerian citizens in the Bakassi Peninsula" pending a final judgment in the case.[1645] The issue of those elections was not given a central place in the interim proceedings. During the oral proceedings, Nigeria stated that this communication did not represent a counterclaim for the indication of provisional measures[1646]—probably with a view to avoid legitimating the jurisdiction and admissibility of the complaint.[1647] Still, this "invitation to the Court" could be understood as an acknowledgment that, despite the general objections against jurisdiction and admissibility, Nigeria did not regard the Court's involvement in the matter as inappropriate *per se*, unlike respondents in other cases who had taken a course of fundamental opposition against the Court.

On 17 February 1996, the foreign ministers of Nigeria and Cameroon agreed to a cease-fire upon mediation of the Togolese president.[1648] The President of the Security Council, Madeleine Albright, addressed the two parties on 29 February 1996 in two identical letters, in which she explained that the Council members had noted that the case was already pending before the Court and stated:

The resumption of fighting, therefore, also threatens respect for peaceful settlement mechanisms. Neither side should take any unilateral action, particularly the use of force, to complicate the dispute settlement process. The members of the Council urge you to redouble your efforts to reach a peaceful settlement through the International Court of Justice. The Council members of the Security Council also welcome bilateral and regional efforts undertaken to assist such a peaceful resolution of the dispute.

[1644] The Security Council did not see the situation clearly enough as to take sides. The same held true for the European Union, which directed a call at both sides to refrain from military intervention and to return to the positions which they had occupied before the dispute was referred to the ICJ. S/1996/125, 4 (Annex II).

[1645] Order of 15 March 1996, at 19, para. 23. There is no hint at any causal link between those elections and the February incidents, see *Sztucki*, 10 Leid. JIL (1997), at 342.

[1646] Order of 15 March 1996, at 20, para. 26.

[1647] Cameroon, in fact, made the argument that Nigeria's "request" implied a recognition at least of the prima-facie jurisdiction: Alain Pellet, Counsel and advocate, CR 1996/2, 5 March 1996, 53, Maurice Kamto, co-agent, CR 1996/4, 8 March 1996, 25.

[1648] Order of 15 March 1996, at 22, para. 37, S/1996/140, 2 (Annex I), S/1996/125, 2 (Annex I).

354 Compliance with Decisions of the International Court of Justice

Albright called on the parties to respect the cease-fire and to take the necessary steps to return their forces to the positions they occupied before the dispute had been referred to the Court. She also welcomed the Secretary-General's proposal to send a fact-finding mission and urged the parties to cooperate fully with this mission.[1649] The Security Council thus addressed the parties in an informal way, not by way of a resolution or a formal presidential statement. From their content, the Council's calls partially coincided with the request of Cameroon in so far as the parties were asked not to aggravate the dispute further, to abstain from military action, to withdraw to their earlier positions,[1650] and to cooperate with the fact-finding mission. However, the Security Council refrained from identifying one party or the other as the "aggressor," opting for a neutral formulation. The issue of conservation of evidence was not mentioned.

In the oral proceedings on interim protection, the parties disagreed on the Court's jurisdiction and the admissibility of Cameroon's claims, on the facts (in particular, about the cause of the armed clashes), and on the need for the indication of provisional measures.[1651] As in the main proceedings, Nigeria brought forward objections against jurisdiction (based on a lack of "substantive reciprocity") and against the admissibility (based on a duty to settle boundary disputes through bilateral machinery and on the absence of a dispute).[1652] These arguments did not appear to be particularly strong: both countries' declarations accepting the compulsory jurisdiction of the Court had been made without reservations. Nigeria had made its declaration under the sole condition of reciprocity; there did not seem to be an impediment for the establishment of a jurisdictional link from the moment when Cameroon deposited its declaration. Neither the Statute nor the Nigerian declaration made the actual knowledge of another country's declaration a condition for the acceptance of the Court's compulsory jurisdiction. Nigeria could have prevented being taken to the ICJ by surprise by making its declaration under a reservation relating to the deposit of the declaration of the respective applicant within a certain time frame, something Nigeria, in

[1649] S/1996/150. The letters are quoted in the order of 15 March 1996, at 23–4, paras. 45–6.

[1650] But note that, unlike Cameroon's request, the Security Council alluded to the positions occupied before the dispute was referred to the Court and not before the outbreak of violence in February 1996.

[1651] See for Nigeria's arguments against the indications of provisional measures the statements of Chief Agbamuche, Agent for Nigeria, CR 1996/3, 6 March 1996, 10–21, and of the following counsels and advocates for Nigeria: Ian Brownlie (absence for reasons for the indication of provisional measures), Sir Arthur Watts (mootness of the request, absence of a current conflict, lack of prima-facie jurisdiction), 30–47, James Crawford (lack of prima-facie admissibility, coincidental character of Cameroon's request), 47–59. See also *Sztucki*, 10 Leid. JIL (1997), at 343–4; *Bekong*, 9 Afr. JICL (1997), at 296–8. The proceedings took place on 5, 6, and 8 March 1996.

[1652] Order of 15 March 1996, at 20–1, paras. 29, 32.

fact, did[1653] shortly before the Court was to confirm its jurisdiction in the judgment on the preliminary objections in 1998.[1654] Nigeria's challenge to the prima-facie admissibility was not convincing either: the existence of a duty to settle boundary disputes by bilateral machinery was doubtful and, even if it existed, the outbreak of violence had proven this machinery inadequate. The existence of a dispute with regard to the Bakassi peninsula—the protection of the rights over which was the main object of the interim proceedings—could not be denied and was not even challenged by Nigeria.[1655]

3. The order of 15 March 1996

In its order of 15 March 1996, the Court partly took up what Cameroon had suggested and adopted further measures that had not been requested, referring to Article 75(2) of the Court's Rules and its power to "indicate provisional measures with a view to preventing the aggravation or extension of the dispute whenever it considers that circumstances so require" under Article 41 of the ICJ Statute.[1656]

On the issue of jurisdiction, the Court noted Nigeria's preliminary objections and recalled that the relevant criterion at the interim stage was whether the "provisions invoked by the Applicant appear, *prima facie*, to afford a basis on which the jurisdiction of the Court might be founded." It considered

---

[1653] See Nigeria's declaration of 30 April 1998, ICJ YB 1999–2000, at 129–30. The new declaration exempts nine categories of disputes from Nigeria's acceptance of the Court's compulsory jurisdiction, in particular: "(i) disputes in respect of which any party of the dispute has accepted the jurisdiction of the Court by a Declaration deposited less than twelve months prior to the filing of an Application bringing the dispute before the Court after the date of this amended Declaration," "(iv) disputes in respect of which the any other party to the dispute has accepted the jurisdiction of the Court in relation to or for the purposes of the dispute," "(viii) disputes concerning the allocation, delimitation or demarcation of territory [...]," and "(ix) disputes in relation to matters which arose prior to the date of Nigeria's independence, including any dispute the causes, origins or bases of which arose prior to that date." If the 1965 declaration had been made under these terms, the proceedings in the present case could not have taken place unless Nigeria would have given its specific consent. Of course, this new declaration could not interfere with the pending proceedings.

[1654] In its judgment of 11 June 1998, the Court ruled that it had jurisdiction and that Cameroon's application was admissible (at 325–6, para. 118). For the decision on the first preliminary objection (jurisdiction under the declarations under Article 36(2) of the ICJ Statute), see ibid., at 290–300, paras. 21–47, it was taken by 14 votes to 3 (Judges Weeramantry and Koroma, and Judge *ad hoc* Ajibola dissenting).

[1655] See Sir Arthur Watts, counsel and advocate for Nigeria, CR 1996/3, 36: "Of course, the underlying dispute as to the merits of the parties' positions regarding Bakassi still exists—but the present proceedings are not concerned with those merits, but only with the more limited issue arising from the localized incidents which have taken place, and as regards that limited issue, does it any longer 'genuinely exist'? No, it does not." However, the issue was not the existence of a dispute concerning the February 1996 events, but whether there was a need for interim protection with regard to the Bakassi peninsula in view of those events.

[1656] Order of 15 March 1996, at 24, para. 48.

that the declarations under Article 36(2) of the Statute made by the parties without reservation constituted such a basis.[1657]

On Nigeria's arguments concerning admissibility, the Court stated:

Whereas without ruling on the question whether, faced with a request for the indication of provisional measures, the Court must, before deciding whether or not to indicate such measures, ensure that the Application of which it is seized is admissible prima facie, it considers that, in this case, the consolidated Application of Cameroon does not appear prima facie to be inadmissible in the light of the preliminary objections raised by Cameroon.[1658]

This statement is somewhat confusing as to the applicable standard. As the Court gives no further reasoning, the test as stated *in abstracto* appears to be a positive one requiring an affirmative finding on admissibility (*"is* admissible"*) rather than a negative one limited to a finding of a lack of inadmissibility, yet the way this test was actually applied rather sounds like a negative one (*"does not* appear *inadmissible"*). Nigeria's argumentation was not strong on this point, which might explain the brevity of the reasoning in the order. The Court will hopefully shed light on the precise standard in its future jurisprudence.

Confronted with contradictory versions of the facts, the Court could not assign blame for the conflict to either party. It did note, however, that military incidents had occurred in the Bakassi peninsula resulting in fatalities and major material damage.[1659] The Court could thus conclude that the events had caused irreparable damage to the rights the parties might have over the peninsula and that there was a risk of further damage;[1660] moreover, it referred to the risk of an aggravation or extension of the dispute, a risk that equally entitled it to indicate provisional measures.[1661]

[1657] Order of 15 March 1996, at 21, paras. 28–31. See *Garcia*, 42 AFDI (1996), at 412–14; *Sall*, 9 Afr. JICL (1997), at 185–6.

[1658] Order of 15 March 1996, at 21, paras. 32–3; see *Sztucki*, 10 Leid. JIL (1997), at 346–7.

[1659] Order of 15 March 1996, at 22, para. 38.

[1660] It is noticeable that the Court acknowledged the risk of loss of life as a justification for the indication of provisional measures, rejecting an understanding pursuant to which such danger did not represent a risk of "irreparable damage" given the possibility to pay compensation. This strengthened the role of human rights by providing a mechanism for their protection in the context of a dispute not primarily involving human rights. See *Higgins*, 36 Col. JTL (1997), at 107: "[The Order] made clear that disputes about frontiers are not just about lines on the ground but are about the safety and protection of the peoples who live there. It was on that ground that both parties were called on to ensure that no action was taken by their armed forces which might prejudice the rights in respect of a future judgment of the Court."

[1661] Order of 15 March 1996, at 23, para. 42: "Whereas the events that have given rise to the request, and more especially the killing of persons, have caused irreparable damage to the rights that the Parties may have over the Peninsula; whereas persons in the disputed area and, as a consequence, the rights of the Parties within that area are exposed to serious risk of further irreparable damage; and whereas armed actions within the territory in dispute could jeopardize the existence of evidence relevant to the present case; and whereas, from the elements of information available to it, the Court takes the view that there is a risk that events likely to aggravate

The Court indicated a number of concrete measures directed at both parties.[1662] The Court ordered unanimously that both parties "should ensure that no action of any kind, and particularly no action by their armed forces, is taken which might prejudice the rights of the other in respect of whatever judgment the Court may render in the case, or which might aggravate or extend the dispute before it." With the sole dissent of the Nigerian Judge *ad hoc* Ajibola, the Court also adopted measures calling for an observance of the February 1996 cease-fire agreement, the conservation of evidence relevant to the case, and assistance in the Secretary-General's proposed fact-finding mission. An additional measure adopted by 12 votes to 5 required the parties to ensure that the presence of their armed forces did not extend beyond their positions prior to 3 February 1996.[1663] Several judges felt that this measure was too imprecise to be implemented successfully, as the location of the parties' armed forces prior to 3 February was controversial and therefore the measure, rather than preventing an aggravation of the dispute, had the potential for creating new conflict.[1664] The relevant line was left undefined, and it is noticeable that the order, unlike Cameroon's request and the letter of the Security Council President, does not even use the term "withdrawal." This leaves it open to both sides to stick with their perspectives regarding the occurrence of troop movements: Nigeria could maintain that it had not further advanced its troops, whereas Cameroon could argue at the same time that a withdrawal was requested as the troops had been in different positions earlier.[1665] Whether the benefit of adopting this measure in addition to the measure calling for the parties to respect the cease-fire outweighed its potential for additional conflict is debatable. As one of the dissenting judges noted:

A provisional measure should be framed in self-executing terms, in the sense that it should contain all legal elements required for its interpretation and application. In the case of a provisional measure limiting the movement of armed forces, an essential element is the prescription of a clear physical benchmark, in the nature of a stipulation

---

or extend the dispute may occur again, thus rendering any settlement of that dispute more difficult." See ibid., at 22–3, para. 41, for the Court's power to indicate interim measures to prevent an aggravation or extension of the dispute.

[1662] See on the object of the provisional measures, *Sall*, 9 Afr. JICL (1997), at 192–4.

[1663] Order of 15 March 1996, at 24–5, para. 49. The dissenting judges were Shahabuddeen, Weeramantry, Shi, Vereshchetin, and Judge *ad hoc* Ajibola.

[1664] Ibid., Decl. Shahabuddeen, 28: "[The Order] may provide a basis for a fresh dispute, in that, in the circumstances of this case, there could be argument between the Parties as to what position or positions each occupied prior to 3 February 1996." Joint Decl. Weeramantry, Shi and Vereshchetin, at 31: "The Court's Order [. . .] in effect leaves it up to each Party to determine what that position was and to act upon that determination. These positions may well be contradictory, thus leaving open the possibility of confusion upon the ground. The Order may thus be interpreted as containing an internal contradiction."

[1665] But see *Sall*, 9 Afr. JICL (1997), at 193.

of positions or lines in relation to which it could be easily determined whether the required limitation has been observed.[1666]

One might have thought that the lack of clarity was not quite as much a reason for concern as the facts were shortly to be assessed by a fact-finding mission to be dispatched by the UN Secretary-General. Yet at that point, this mission was nothing more than a proposal. It was not certain if and when it would deliver results which could serve as a basis for the withdrawal of troops.[1667]

The measure relating to troop withdrawal is also noteworthy for another reason: while the interim measures are identical with the indications by the Security Council with regard to the cease-fire, this is not true for the withdrawal. The Security Council called for a return to the positions occupied before the dispute was referred to the ICJ (i.e. prior to Cameroon's application of 29 March 1994). The Court, on the other hand, took as the decisive date 3 February 1996, the date of the outbreak of violence that had given rise to the interim proceedings before the Court.[1668] This was in accordance with Cameroon's request—i.e. it corresponded to what Cameroon regarded as necessary pursuant to Article 41—and the situation appeared to have been largely quiet until that date. In fact, little importance appeared to have been accorded to this difference, either by the Court or the parties. In a 1998 report to the General Assembly, for example, the ICJ President noted the concurrent political and judicial means of dispute settlement in this case without even mentioning the different dates: "[B]oth the Security Council [...] and the Court [...] called on the parties to respect a ceasefire and to take the necessary steps to return their forces to the positions which they had occupied before the outbreak of the fighting."[1669] In a similar vein, in welcoming news of the interim measures, Cameroon transposed the ICJ's cut-off date with the Security Council's: "[T]he return of the forces to the positions held prior to the submission of the case to the Court is the only way to ensure peace and security in the region until the Court hands down its final decision. It is in this spirit that we endorse the protective measure decreed by the Court in this regard."[1670]All in all, despite some slight

---

[1666] Order of Decl. Shahabuddeen.

[1667] Ultimately, it never took place; even if it had, the results of that mission would not have been binding (the order had not provided for such an effect) and there would have been room for further conflict. See in contrast the Frontier Dispute (Burkina Faso/Mali) case, in which the Court had ordered the parties to positions to be agreed upon between themselves within twenty days, failing which it would prescribe the details of the withdrawal itself: *supra* V.

[1668] Judge Oda stated that although he voted in favor of this provisional measure, the decisive date should have been 29 March 1994, but he does not explain this further: Order of 15 March 1996, Decl. Oda at 26, para.1.

[1669] Speech of President Schwebel, 27 October 1998, A/53/PV.44, 2–3.

[1670] S/1996/287, Letter dated 15 April 1996 from the Chargé d'Affaires a.i. of the Permanent Mission of Cameroon to the United Nations addressed to the President of the Security Council,

differences,[1671] the Council and the Court's calls pursued similar objectives. There is some indication for an " 'active' support for the Security Council,"[1672] as the order specifically reports the phrases employed in the Security Council President's letter on the cease-fire and the troop withdrawal and reports the call for support of the fact-finding mission made in the same letter.[1673] The measure demanding cooperation with the fact-finding mission took up an element of the Security Council letter that had not been requested by Cameroon.

4. The follow-up to the order

Although the situation calmed down after the indication of the provisional measures,[1674] it appears that the measures have not always been respected: both Cameroon and Nigeria complained about incidents whose occurrence they attributed to the other side. As Cameroon had introduced a formal claim relating to the non-compliance with the order[1675] and Nigeria had filed counterclaims that partially related to events subsequent to the indication of provisional measures,[1676] the Court had to deal with the compliance of the measures in its judgment on the merits.[1677] Neither country had contested the validity and binding force of the measures, and Nigeria did not object to

transmitting a Letter from the President of Cameroon to the President of the Security Council dated 12 April 1996. This is all the more surprising given that Cameroon itself had indicated 3 February 1996 as the decisive date in its request for provisional measures, *supra*. In the letter of 12 April, Cameroon also welcomed the fact-finding mission of the Secretary-General and assured its cooperation and all assistance necessary for that mandate.

[1671] Besides the differences relating to the withdrawal, the measures included issues not addressed by the President of the Security Council, such as the question to conserve evidence—a measure that made sense in ICJ proceedings rather than before the Council. Consequently it was not surprising that the Council remained silent on this issue.

[1672] *Sztucki*, 10 Leid. JIL (1997), at 348–9, 357, identifies this as the distinct novel feature of the order.

[1673] Order of 15 March 1996, at 23–4, paras. 45–6.

[1674] See Maurice Kamto, co-agent for Cameroon, CR 2002/1, 18 February 2002, at 35, para. 13: "[L']ampleur des mesures conservatoires décidées par votre Cour [...] étaient à la mesure de la gravité de la situation qui prévalait alors, et *qui du reste a connu quelques accalmies depuis lors*." (emphasis added).

[1675] Final submissions of Cameroon, CR 2002/25: the Court is *inter alia* asked to adjudge and declare "(g) Qu'en ne respectant pas l'ordonnance en indication de mesures conservatoires rendue par la Cour le 15 mars 1996, la République fédérale du Nigéria a manqué à ses obligations internationales. (h) Que la responsabilité de la République fédérale du Nigéria est engagée par les faits internationalement illicites exposés ci-dessus et précisés dans les écritures et les plaidoiries orales de la République du Cameroun."

[1676] See Nigerian Counter-memorial. May 1999, Part VI, 808–10, http://212.153.43.18/icjwww/idocket/icn/icnpleadings/icn_ipleadings_19990501_countermemorial_nigeria_chp25.pdf. Nigeria has not raised a formal claim of non-compliance, though; see Nigeria's final submissions, CR 2002/26, http://212.153.43.18/icjwww/idocket/icn/icncr/icn_icr200226_20020321.pdf, at 39.

[1677] In the Judgment on the preliminary objections of 11 June 1998, in which the Court ruled that it had jurisdiction and that the Cameroonian application was admissible, there are no comments on the provisional measures besides a reference in the procedural history of the case, at 280, para. 10. For further details on the judgment, see *Bekker*, 92 AJIL (1998), at 751–5.

the fact that Cameroon, relying on the Court's judgment in the LaGrand case, introduced a complaint of non-compliance with the order as a formal submission to which it also extended its state responsibility claims.[1678] Hence, shortly after the judgment in the LaGrand case, which for the first time sanctioned a breach of provisional measures through a declaration of non-compliance, that judgment was invoked as an authority for sanctioning a similar breach, and a more far reaching claim was made: a claim for state responsibility, a step not taken by Germany in LaGrand.[1679] In its judgment on the merits, however, the Court found that neither the facts relating to non-compliance with the order nor their imputability to either side had been sufficiently substantiated and proven.[1680]

The dispute as to whether the provisional measures were respected related partly to the facts and partly to the scope of obligations stemming from the order.

The call for a cease-fire in Bakassi did not prevent further hostilities; armed clashes took place in late April and May 1996.[1681] Both parties played the blame game: Cameroon immediately complained about Nigerian aggression to the UN Security Council,[1682] while it took Nigeria until 21 June 1996 to lodge its complaint—notably with Cameroon's foreign minister only, not the Security Council.[1683] Nigeria's behavior following the clashes might cast

---

[1678] See *supra* n. 1675. For the reference to the LaGrand judgment, see the statement of Christian Tomuschat, CR 2002/7, 58–9, paras. 3–4.

[1679] For a further discussion on the potential for sanctioning the violation of provisional measures in the judgment, see *infra* Chapter 4 B IV 2; on this aspect of the LaGrand judgment, see *infra* X 3.

[1680] Judgment of 10 October 2002, at paras. 320–4.

[1681] [no author], Bakassi cease-fire broken, 4 IBRU Boundary and Security Bulletin (Summer 1996) 33, Nigeria and Cameroon clash over peninsula on the border, New York Times Abstracts, 7 May 1996, Section A 3,1996 WL 7504885; Nigeria: Review 1997, Africa Review World of Information, 1 February 1997, 1997 WL 10204078 The parties agreed that clashes had taken place, but disagree on who was responsible: See Chief Akinjide, co-agent for Nigeria, CR 98/1, 2 March 1998, para. 70; Christian Tomuschat, CR 2002/7, 60, para. 6; Sir Arthur Watts, CR 2002/14, 8 March 2002, 36, para. 47. There were reports of further clashes: Nigeria refutes attack on Cameroon, The Week, 16 March 1998, 24, 1998 WL 12491706; Army Chief says Cameroonian Troops Fire at Nigerians, World News Connection, 24 January 2000, 2000 WL 12121330; Cameroon denies shooting at Nigerian lookouts, Hart's Africa Oil and Gas, 9 February 2000, 2000 WL 9169716; Nigeria urges France to broker territorial dispute with Cameroon, Xinhua News Agency, 8 January 2002, 2002 WL 7934349, Troops massing on Bakassi, 6 IBRU Boundary and Security Bulletin (Summer 1998), 24.

[1682] Letter dated 30 April 1996 from the Minister for Foreign Affairs of Cameroon addressed to the President of the Security Council, S/1996/330 (see in particular at 3: "This new aggression by Nigeria is a flagrant violation of the protective measures brought to the attention of our two Governments by the Order of 15 March 1996 of the International Court of Justice.")

[1683] Sir Arthur Watts, CR 2002/14, para. 47, Counter-memorial of Nigeria, May 1999, http://212.153.43.18/icjwww/idocket/icn/icnpleadings/icn_ipleadings_19990501_countermemorial_nigeria_chp25.pdf, 807, para. 25.17: the Nigerian minister of foreign affairs stated in this context: "If [the attacks which occurred in April 21, 22, and 23, to May 1 1996] were not in utter contravention of the provisional measures of the ICJ, and the calls by the international community for restraint, one wonders what else they were." The full letter was submitted as Annex 361 to the Nigerian Counter-memorial.

doubts on its version of the facts;[1684] yet, it argued that it had to undertake a thorough investigation of the facts and that no negative inferences could be drawn from the time period between the events and its protest.[1685] The Court, as stated, did not see a sufficient basis to attribute any responsibilities.

The Court's failure to define the line of partition between the two countries' armed forces (i.e. the positions before 3 February 1996) in the order makes it difficult to assess compliance with the measure relating to this point. Despite the potential usefulness of the fact-finding mission, no clarity was achieved on where the line was to be located; the mission never became operative as originally envisaged, but was reduced to a mere goodwill mission.[1686] Cameroon complained that the fact that the mandate of the mission was transformed was due to Nigeria's resistance against a broader mandate.[1687] Nigeria argued that the nature of the mission had been "a political matter to be determined in New York," that the goodwill mission had been the one to come into existence, and that it fully cooperated with it.[1688] The Secretary-General did not make statements criticizing any lack of cooperation on the part of Nigeria in this respect.[1689]

Concerning the obligation to conserve evidence, Cameroon complained about a lack of access to its archives in the part of Bakassi allegedly occupied by Nigeria and about the destruction of boundary pillars.[1690] Nigeria countered that the obligation relates to conservation and there was no evidence of destruction of archive materials; with regard to the boundary pillars, Nigeria questioned their relevance as evidence in some locations and the attributability of the destruction of pillars to Nigerian officials in others.[1691] These claims, again, were hardly substantiated.[1692]

[1684] This was Cameroon's point: Christian Tomuschat, CR 2002/16, 11 March 2002, at 64–5, para. 34.

[1685] Sir Arthur Watts, CR 2002/20, 15 March 2002, at 34, paras. 36–7.

[1686] In any case, Cameroon complained that fighting had taken place on "its" side of the line. Christian Tomuschat, CR 2002/7, 26 February 2002, at 64–6, paras. 15–16.

[1687] Christian Tomuschat, CR 2002/7, 26 February 2002, 63–4, para.13, CR 2002/16, 63–4, paras. 32–3.

[1688] Sir Arthur Watts, CR 2002/14, 8 March 2002, at 36–7, para. 49, CR 2002/20, 15 March 2002, 33, para. 35.

[1689] The Secretary-General had reported in a letter to the President of the Security Council of 29 May 1996 (S/1996/330) that the Cameroonian president had stressed that his country would obey the ICJ Order and welcomed the fact-finding mission and the Nigerian president "in deference of this order [...] accepted in principle the idea of such a mission." In a letter dated 9 October 1996 to the President of the Security Council (S/1996/891), the Secretary-General reported that a goodwill mission had been carried out, without indicating on whose initiative the mandate had been transformed: "After close consultation with the Governments of Cameroon and Nigeria, I obtained their agreement to sending a goodwill mission to the two countries [...]" (at 1). He stated: "The mission has reported that it obtained the fullest support and cooperation from all parties." (at 2).

[1690] Christian Tomuschat, CR 2002/7, 64, para. 14.

[1691] Sir Arthur Watts, CR 2002/14, 37, paras. 50–3.

[1692] With regard to the archives, as far as Cameroon's complaint related merely to lack of access to evidence, rather than the physical destruction of evidence, no violation of the

Cameroon raised some claims of non-compliance with the measure relating to preventing an aggravation of the dispute. Here, the controversy centered mainly on the scope of the obligations stemming from the measure. The facts were undisputed: Nigeria had created a commune of Bakassi in October 1996,[1693] issued a prohibition of overflights at low altitude applicable to the entire Bakassi peninsula in December 1996,[1694] and organized municipal elections in Bakassi in December 1998 and gubernatorial elections in January 1999.[1695] In 1996, the Nigerian president had announced that the troops stationed in Bakassi would be reinforced.[1696] While the third measure indicated by the Court related to location of troops, not to numbers,[1697] and would therefore appear unaffected by this act, it would not seem exaggerated to qualify it as a violation of the obligation not to aggravate the dispute, unless Nigeria could refer to legitimate concerns. With regard to its further activities on Bakassi, Nigeria argued that there had been nothing in the Court's order putting a halt to all civilian administration.[1698] One may doubt, however, whether the creation of new administrative structures and the assumption of jurisdiction to regulate air traffic over Bakassi in its entirety did not go beyond "arrangements for the health, the education and the social welfare of the Nigerian population of Bakassi,"[1699] or whether they effectively intended to create greater allegiance to Nigeria and thereby make its exercise of state functions a *fait accompli*. There seems to be some basis for the claim that those measures had the potential of aggravating the dispute and prejudicing the rights that Cameroon might have under the judgment, not necessarily by creating an irreversible situation, but as a source of future logistical problems in the course of the eliminating the Nigerian presence in the event of a finding in favor of Cameroon (which was the eventual result). With regard to the organization of local elections, it is interesting to recall Nigeria's complaint relating to elections organized by Cameroon in January 1996 in Bakassi: in its communication to the Court of 16 February 1996, Nigeria had stated that Cameroon's right to conduct elections in its territory "cannot and should not extend to areas in dispute between the Republic of

---

provisional measure could have arosen in this respect, as the Court had called for conservation of evidence, not for access to it.

[1693] Christian Tomuschat, CR 2002/7, 65–67, paras. 17–21.

[1694] Christian Tomuschat, CR 2002/7, 68, para. 25.

[1695] Christian Tomuschat, CR 2002/7, 67–8, paras. 22–4. Following the municipal elections, Cameroon immediately complained to the Nigerian embassy in Yaoundé and to the President of the Security Council about a violation of the ICJ order: S/1998/1159, 11 December 1998 (transmitting letters dated 10 December 1998).

[1696] Cameroon admitted, though, that it had no knowledge on whether an increase in troops had actually taken place. Christian Tomuschat, CR 2002/7, at 62–3, para. 12.

[1697] Sir Arthur Watts, CR 2002/14, at 36, para. 48.

[1698] Sir Arthur Watts, CR 2002/14, at 38, para. 54, see also *idem*, CR 2002/20, 15 March 2002, 34–5, paras. 38–40.

[1699] Sir Arthur Watts, CR 2002/14, at 38, para. 54.

Cameroon and the Federal Republic of Nigeria" and called the elections a "flagrant violation of this cardinal principle."[1700] Clearly, this argumentation does not square with subsequent Nigeria-sponsored elections in Bakassi. Yet the Court did not comment on this issue.

While Cameroon complained about non-compliance with the order to the Security Council,[1701] it did not formally request any enforcement action, and the Council did not take action. The UN Standing Advisory Committee on Security Questions in Central Africa[1702] addressed the dispute between Cameroon and Nigeria several times and directed its call specifically to Nigeria "to comply strictly with the interim measures of protection laid down by the Court"[1703]—a diplomatic measure with the aim of increasing the pressure for compliance.

5. Conclusion

Again, as in earlier cases, provisional measures were requested in a situation involving hostilities. In general, the parties had good relations and shared values, but their border disputes had already led to armed incidents. The Security Council had made a call on the parties, and while the Court's measures were not wholly identical to the Council indications, they went into the same direction.

[1700] See Order of 15 March 1996, at 19, para. 23.

[1701] See S/1996/330, 2 May 1996 (concerning renewed fighting in late April 1996, see *supra*), S/1996/1052, 17 December 1996 (transmitting a protest note of the Cameroonian minister of foreign affairs to the office of the high commissioner of Nigeria in Yaoundé of 12 December 1996, complaining of a Nigerian drinking-water supply project as "flagrant violation of the protective measures" S/1998/1159, 11 December 1998 criticizing the holding of municipal elections in Bakassi). See also S/1998/228, 13 March 1998 (in which there is no statement on non-compliance, although Cameroon asked Nigeria to respect the interim measures).

[1702] The United Nations Standing Advisory Committee on Security Questions in Central Africa was established by the UN Secretary-General on 28 May 1992 pursuant to General Assembly resolution 46/37 B of 6 December 1991. It is a mechanism for dialogue and confidence-building in the region; it is composed of eleven countries from the Central African region: Angola, Burundi, Cameroon, Central African Republic, Chad, Congo, Democratic Republic of the Congo, Equatorial Guinea, Gabon, Rwanda, and Sao Tome and Principe: United Nations, "United Nations Standing Advisory Committee on Security Questions in Central Africa," http://disarmament.un.org:8080/CAB/sacsqca.html. Admittedly, Cameroon is a member while Nigeria is not, which might raise concerns of partiality; yet, one has to bear in mind that Cameroon is only one of eleven countries forming part of the committee.

[1703] Report of the 13th ministerial meeting of the United Nations Standing Advisory Committee on Security Questions in Central Africa, A/54/889–S/2000/506, 30 May 2000, at 8 ("The Committee expressed deep concern at the information provided by the delegation of Cameroon on the persistent attempts at infiltration and repeated acts of provocation by Nigerian forces on the Bakassi peninsula and called on the two parties to refrain from any action that could heighten tensions while awaiting the decision of the International Court of Justice, which Cameroon had seized of the matter.") This statement also appeared in the subsequent reports, Report of the 14th meeting, A/55/505–S/2000/1005, 20 October 2000, at 5, Report of the 15th meeting, A/55/940–S/2001/483, 15 May 2001, at 4, Report of the 16th meeting, A/56/378–S/2001/890, 21 September 2001, at 4.

The respondent opposed the involvement of the Court in the matter—with regard to the interim proceedings as well to the merits of Cameroon's claims—and made a new declaration under Article 36(2) so as to prevent similar matters from being brought before the ICJ without its specific consent; yet, it participated at all stages of the proceedings and stressed its respect for the Court. It did not oppose the measures once they were indicated. Although it is not entirely certain whether its rhetorical commitment was always matched by the appropriate practical action, Cameroon could not substantiate and prove its non-compliance claims sufficiently. There was no defiance of the Court's authority; both states acknowledged the validity and bindingness of the order, claimed to have complied with the measures, and blamed the other side for incidents that occurred after the measures were indicated—in this context, their disagreement partially related to facts, partially to the interpretation of the obligations under the order.

While the measures were only partially implemented as cease-fire violations occurred (the responsibility for which seems unclear), it appears as if the measures had some calming effect.

It would have been preferable if the measures had been framed more precisely, given that the scope of the obligations later turned out to be a source of conflict; on the other hand, the Court apparently felt that it lacked the factual basis for more concrete orders, and it might have been interpreted as a sign of weakness if the Court had remained silent where an outbreak of violence had resulted in fatalities and it was yet uncertain if the cease-fire would hold.[1704]

IX. Vienna Convention on Consular Relations (Breard case)

This case involved a dispute between Paraguay and the United States concerning the failure of US authorities to comply with Article 36(1)(b) of the Vienna Convention on Consular Relations[1705] (VCCR) in the context of criminal proceedings against the Paraguayan national Angel Francisco Breard. The case was similar to the LaGrand case between Germany and the United States that would be submitted to the Court one year later.[1706]

[1704] *Koroma* in Boisson de Chazournes/Gowlland-Debbas, The International Legal System in Quest of Equity, at 600: on the provision that both parties withdraw behind their 3 February 1996 position: "such calls appear to have had a positive impact on the disputes themselves, putting an end to the clashes or preventing their resumption while the disputes were before the Court. On the other hand, failure to have called for such restraints, especially in situations of armed conflict where fatalities had already occurred and would recur if the conflict were allowed to continue, would have deprived the provision of positive substantive meaning, and could have led to an aggravation of the conflicts, with serious implications for international peace and security."

[1705] For the text of Article 36(1)(b), see *supra* n. 1092.

[1706] For details of LaGrand, see *supra* B XXVI and *infra* X.

1. Background

On 1 September 1992, Breard, a US resident, was arrested in Virginia on suspicion of attempted rape and murder. Although the authorities knew that Breard was a Paraguayan national, Breard was not informed of his rights to consular assistance under Article 36(1)(b) of the Vienna Convention on Consular Relations, nor was the Paraguayan consulate informed of Breard's detention. A Virginia Court convicted Breard on 24 June 1993 and sentenced him to death on 22 August 1993.[1707] Paraguayan officials first learned about the case in 1996. Breard filed a writ of *habeas corpus* in a US federal Court, alleging violations of the Vienna Convention; Paraguay initiated a civil suit on the same issue. Both actions failed before the Courts of first instance and the appellate Courts; petitions for a writ of *certiorari* were still pending in the US Supreme Court when Paraguay decided to bring the matter before the ICJ. On 3 April 1998, it seized the ICJ by unilateral application and made a request for the indication of provisional measures.[1708] The applicant founded the Court's jurisdiction on Article I of the optional protocol on compulsory dispute settlement to the Vienna Convention on Consular Relations,[1709] to which the United States and Paraguay are parties.[1710]

The applicant argued that the US had violated its international obligations towards Paraguay in its own right and in the exercise of diplomatic protection on behalf of its national, that Paraguay was entitled to *restitutio in integrum*, and that in any future criminal proceedings against Breard or any other Paraguayan nationals, the US was to respect its obligations under the Vienna Convention. It called for a declaration that Bread's conviction was null and void and orders for the US to restore the *status quo ante* and to provide a guarantee of non-repetition of the illegal acts.[1711]

In its request for provisional measures, Paraguay asked the Court to order

(a) that the Government of the United States take the measures necessary to ensure that Mr Breard not be executed pending the disposition of this case;
(b) that the Government of the United States report to the Court the actions it has taken in pursuance of subparagraph (a) immediately above and the results of those actions,

[1707] For the facts and the proceedings before American courts, see Application instituting proceedings submitted by the Government of Paraguay, ICJ Pleadings, Vienna Convention on Consular Relations, 3, at 4–6 (also retrievable under http://212.153.43.18/icjwww/idocket/ipaus/ipausorder / ipaus_iapplication_980403.html), and the Supreme Court decision of 13 April 1998, Breard v. Greene, 118 S. Ct. 1352 (*per curiam*). See also *Charney/Reisman*, 92 AJIL (1999), at 666–75.
[1708] Application, *supra* n. 1707; Request for Provisional Measures of Protection Submitted by the Government of Paraguay, *ibid.*, 13–14 (also retrievable under http://212.153.43.18/icjwww/ idocket/ipaus/ipausorder/ipaus_iapplication_980403_provisionalmeasures.html).
[1709] Application, *supra* n. 1707, 6–7. For the text of Article I, see *supra* n. 1106.
[1710] The US ratified the optional protocol on 24 November 1969, Paraguay acceded to it on 23 December 1969, ST/LEG/SER.E/19, 123.
[1711] Application, *supra* n. 1707, at 8.

(c) that the Government of the United States ensure that no action is taken that might prejudice the rights of the Republic of Paraguay with respect to any decision this Court may render on the merits of the case.[1712]

Little time was left, as, on 25 February 1998, a Virginia circuit Court had fixed the execution date for 14 April 1998, eleven days after the date of the request for interim measures. On the very day of the request, the acting President of the Court directed letters to both parties to draw their attention "to the need to act in such a way as to enable any Order the Court will make on the request for provisional measures to have its appropriate effects."[1713] Hearings before the ICJ took place on 7 April 1998, where the US acknowledged that Breard had not been informed of his rights to consular assistance; it claimed, however, that he had had all necessary legal assistance, that consular assistance would not have altered the outcome of the proceedings as his guilt had been well established, and that the restitution of the *status quo ante* was not an available remedy for violations of the Vienna Convention.[1714] Moreover, the US argued that the measures requested would prejudge the merits and represent an undue intervention in domestic judicial proceedings. With regard to the Court's jurisdiction, the US contested the existence of a dispute on the interpretation or application of the Vienna Convention (referring to its expression of regret for the failure to notify, its consultations with Paraguay, and its steps to ensure compliance with the VCCR).[1715]

Most of the US arguments related to the merits stage and were thus unlikely to succeed, as the success on the merits is generally no criterion for the indication of provisional measures. The US left the central issue unanswered: if Paraguay claimed that Mr Bread's conviction was null and void and that it was entitled to a re-trial, how could this be achieved despite the execution? The danger of an irreparable damage to the rights claimed by Paraguay was imminent and obvious; consequently there was a need for provisional measures.

2. The order of 9 April 1998

On 9 April 1998, the ICJ unanimously indicated that "the United States should take all measures at its disposal to ensure that Angel Francisco Breard

---

[1712] Request, *supra* n. 1708, at 14.   [1713] Order of 9 April 1998, at 252, para. 12.

[1714] The US brought these arguments (that actually related to the merits stage) as arguments for a lack of jurisdiction and for the inappropriateness of provisional measures: see statement of John Crook, counsel for the US, at the public sitting of 7 April 1998, ICJ Pleadings, at 42–7; see also Order of 9 April 1998, at 254, para. 20: "[W]hereas it pointed out that provisional measures should not be indicated where it appears that the Applicant's argument will not enable it to be successful on the merits."

[1715] This argument was not convincing as there was a controversy as to the appropriate redress. For details of the US argumentation, see *ibid.*, at 253–6, paras. 18–22, 28–9, 32. See also for details of the parties' submissions, *Shank/Quigley*, 9 Crim. LF (1999), at 104–11; *Rieter*, 16 NQHR (1998), at 480–2.

is not executed pending the final decision in these proceedings, and should inform the Court of all the measures which it has taken in the implementation of this Order."[1716]

The Court largely followed the request of Paraguay, but did not explicitly order the US to refrain from action that might prejudice the rights of Paraguay under a potential future decision of the Court; as the essential action prejudicing such those rights was the execution of Breard, there was no compelling reason to make that general indication besides the more specific one to take all measures to halt the execution. The formulation with regard to the stay of Breard's execution was also different: while Paraguay's request called upon the United States to "take the measures necessary to ensure that Mr Breard was not executed," the order urged the United States to take "all measures at its disposal" to prevent the punishment. It is somewhat surprising that the Court felt the need to change this formulation. Its intention might have been to indicate that the obligation was none of result.[1717] However, as Breard was in custody and his execution necessarily required action of some state official, it is hardly imaginable how it could take place without an act attributable to, and controlled by, the US; the distinction between obligations of conduct and of result would not have appeared to make a practical difference.[1718] Moreover, the wording differed from the request in so far as the Court addresses "the United States"

[1716] Order of 9 April 1998, at 258, para. 41. On the same day, the Registrar informed the Security Council of the order pursuant to Articles 41(2) of the Statute and Article 77 of the Rules: Letter dated 9 April 1998 from the Registrar of the International Court of Justice addressed to the Secretary-General, S/1998/315. For comments on the order, see Bekker/Highet, http://www.asil.org/insights/insigh17.htm; *Shank/Quigley*, 9 Crim. LF (1999), at 111; *Rieter*, 16 NQHR (1998), at 483–4. Although the decision was reached unanimously, two judges expressed a certain unease: President Schwebel explained that he voted in favor of the order for necessity to protect the rights claimed by Paraguay, yet he recalled that the US had apologized and taken steps to improve its practice under the Vienna Convention, and that the claim for the remedy advanced by Paraguay was unprecedented: Order of 9 April 1998, Decl. Schwebel at 259. Judge Oda stated that he would rather have dismissed the claim because he saw no prima-facie jurisdiction and no Paraguayan "rights." He explained his affirmative vote on the basis of "humanitarian reasons:" Order of 9 April 1998, Decl. Oda at 260–3. This argumentation might imply that the Court had acted *ultra vires*, which could be used as justification for non-compliance. A court is either empowered to make a decision or not; if the legal conditions are not fulfilled, it must not issue an order on a moral basis.

[1717] The Court would make a statement to this extent on the identical formulation in the LaGrand case: "As to the first measure, the Court notes that it did not create an obligation of result, but that the United States was asked to take all measures at its disposal to ensure that Walter LaGrand is not executed pending the final decision in these proceedings." LaGrand, Judgment of 27 June 2001, para. 111. See also *Forlati*, 94 RDI (2001), at 717–18 (pointing to the differences of the obligation to take "all necessary measures" and "all measures at its disposal" as denoting the difference between obligations of conduct and of result and interpreting the Court's formulation as reference to the former).

[1718] This distinction relates to the question of the party bearing the risk for a failure to achieve a certain result despite all attempts. *Aznar-Gómez*, 102 RGDIP (1998), at 936, nevertheless argues that the obligation in this case is an obligation of result. *Forlati*, 94 RDI (2001), at 718, expresses doubts on the appropriateness of a due diligence obligation in the LaGrand case. The

as a whole, not the US government in particular. As the responsibility to ensure compliance with its international obligations falls upon the state as a whole and there did not seem to be a particular reason why the call should be specifically directed at the government, this formulation seemed not only more logical but also more in line with Paraguay's objectives.

The Court held that it had prima-facie jurisdiction under Article I of the optional protocol to the VCCR, as there was a dispute concerning the application of the Vienna Convention, relating to the questions of whether the relief sought by Paraguay was a remedy available under that instrument and whether Paraguay was entitled to it under the concrete circumstances.[1719] The relief sought by Paraguay was dependent on a stay of Breard's execution; the Court was thus satisfied that there was a danger of irreparable harm to the rights claimed by Paraguay, and there was urgency in view of the execution date.[1720] The Court emphasized that it had not made any pronouncement on the legality of the death penalty as such and not taken up the role of a court of criminal appeal.[1721]

3. The US reaction

Despite the order, the execution would take place as scheduled.

On 13 April, US Secretary of State, Madeleine Albright wrote a cautiously worded letter asking the Virginia governor to stay the execution while avoiding the appearance of an "order." Albright considered the ICJ order as non-mandatory: "Using non-binding language, the Court said that the United States should 'take all measures at its disposal to ensure that Angel Francisco Breard is not executed pending the final decision in these proceedings.'"[1722] She acknowledged the seriousness of the crime, but expressed worries about "potential harm to Americans abroad" and requested "with great reluctance" that Mr Breard's execution be

---

Court might also have pursued the intention of giving more emphasis to the obligation; there is no indication in the reasoning that a substantive change to Paraguay's request had been intended.

[1719] Order of 9 April 1998, at 255–7, paras. 23–34. On the prima-facie jurisdiction in this case, see *Addo*, 10 EJIL (1999), at 716–18.

[1720] Order of 9 April 1998 at 257, paras. 35–7.

[1721] Ibid., at 257, para. 38: "Whereas the issues before the Court in this case do not concern the entitlement of the federal states within the United States to resort to the death penalty for the most heinous crimes; and whereas, further, the function of this Court is to resolve international legal disputes between States, inter alia when they arise out of the interpretation or international conventions, and not to act as a court of criminal appeal."

[1722] Letter from Madeleine K. Albright, US secretary of state, to James S. Gilmore III, governor of Virgina, 13 April 1998, Annex 22 of the Paraguayan Memorial, reprinted (to a large extent) in *Charney/Reisman*, 92 AJIL (1999), at 671–2.

postponed.[1723] The potential harm to the authority of the ICJ apparently played a subordinate role.[1724]

On the same day, the Department of Justice submitted a brief to the US Supreme Court signed by the legal advisor of the department of state in which that Court was asked not to intervene in the execution. The brief referred to "substantial disagreement among jurists" as to whether ICJ orders on provisional measures were binding and stated that "the better reasoned position is that such an order is not binding." Moreover, it pointed out that the specific order in question contained precatory rather than mandatory language, that the "measures at [the US] disposal" were those available under domestic law, and that the federal system in the specific case did not allow for additional measures on part of the federal government beyond persuasion.[1725] The ICJ order was thus merely considered one of a variety of factors to be taken into account.[1726]

On 14 April, the US Supreme Court denied the petition for *habeas corpus* and the petitions for *certiorari* in a 6:3 decision. It ruled that Breard's claim had become procedurally defaulted by his failure to raise the violation of the Vienna Convention in state court proceedings and rejected Paraguay's petition *inter alia* on the basis that the Vienna Convention did not establish a

---

[1723] "In light of the Court's request, the unique and difficult foreign policy issues, and other problems created by the Court's provisional measures, I therefore request that you exercise your powers as Governor and stay Mr Breard's execution. It is only with great reluctance that I make this request, especially given the aggravated character of the crime for which Mr Breard has been convicted and sentenced and our view of the merits of Paraguay's legal claims. As Secretary of State, however, I have a responsibility to bear in mind the safety of Americans overseas. [...] The immediate execution of Mr Breard in the face of the Court's April 9 action could be seen as a denial of the United States of the significance of international law and the Court's processes in international relations and thereby limit our ability to ensure that Americans are protected when living or travelling abroad."

[1724] Department of State, Daily press briefing, 13 April 1998, http://secretary.state.gov/www/briefings/9804/980413db.html.

[1725] Brief for the United States as Amicus Curiae, Breard v. Greene, U.S., 118 S. Ct. 1352 (1998), Annex 21 to the Paraguayan Memorial, reprinted in excerpts at *Charney/Reisman*, 92 AJIL (1999), at 672–3. Critical, *Shank/Quigley*, 9 Crim. LF (1999), at 112–17. A group of international law professors, on the other hand, submitted an *amicus curiae* brief that urged the Court to issue a stay and pointed to the potential consequences for the US. See Statement Amicus Curiae of International Law Professors George A. Bermann, David D. Caron, Abram Chayes, Lori Fisler Damrosch, Richard N. Gardner, Louis Henkin, Harold Hongju Koh, Andreas Lowenfeld, W. Michael Reisman, Oscar Schachter, Anne-Marie Slaughter, and Edith Brown Weiss, Republic of Paraguay v. Gilmore, 118 S. Ct. 1352 (1998) (No. 97–1390); see on this brief *Bradley/Goldsmith*, 92 AJIL (1998), at 676.

[1726] See Department of State spokesman James Rubin on 13 April, *supra* n. 1724: "[...] Obviously, the United States is a country of laws that is going to give due respect to the ICJ. That doesn't mean we have to agree with it. It just means that we will give respect to it and we will act accordingly and make our decisions based on our laws and our constitution, and the extent to which we want to see the principles of international law respected." See also *idem* on 15 April, http://secretary.state.gov/www/briefings/9804/980415db.html: "That Court's decision was not a binding decision, it was not written in a binding form," 2.

private right of action for a foreign nation to set aside a criminal conviction and sentence.[1727] The Supreme Court stated:

It is unfortunate that this matter comes before us while proceedings are pending before the ICJ that might have been brought to that court earlier. Nonetheless, this Court must decide questions presented to it on the basis of law [. . .] If the Governor wishes to wait for the decision of the ICJ, that is his prerogative. But nothing in our existing case law allows us to make that choice for him.[1728]

The Supreme Court did not even touch upon the issue of binding effect of provisional measures: its reasoning seems to suggest that the decision on whether to comply with the ICJ order was not a matter of law, but of politics. The dissenting judges did not explicitly refer to a requirement of compliance with ICJ provisional measures either, but saw a need for more time for the consideration of the case.[1729]

Applications for emergency relief to stay or enjoin the execution were rejected by a US district Court in Virginia, decisions affirmed in a federal appeals Court.[1730]

The Virginia governor refused to block the execution, which took place as scheduled on 14 April 1998.[1731] He issued a statement in which he reported the proceedings before the Supreme Court and mentioned that "the US Department of State has argued forcefully that the rulings of the International Court of Justice are not enforceable by the courts of the United States, that the International Court of Justice has not authority to intervene in the criminal justice system of the Commonwealth of Virginia [. . .]." He stated that he had given serious consideration to the concerns of the secretary of state, but that they were just one of the various aspects he had to take into account. He stressed that it was his first duty to ensure safety

---

[1727] *Supra* n. 1707; for critical comments on the decision, see *Paust*, 92 AJIL (1998), at 691–7; *Damrosch*, 92 AJIL (1998), at 697–704; *Shank/Quigley*, 9 Crim. LF (1999), at 125–7; *Rieter*, 16 NQHR (1998), at 488–91; *Sastre*, 103 RGDIP (1999), at 147–68.

[1728] The department of state, on the other hand, had shifted the responsibility to the Supreme Court: see James Rubin, *supra* n. 1724: "The question of whether this court's request for a stay of execution should be granted is something the Supreme Court is considering [. . .]" at 4, 6.

[1729] *Supra* n. 1707, also retrievable under www.yale.edu/lawweb/avalon/diana/breard/42498-1.html. Dissenting opinions of Justice Stevens and Justice Breyer, ibid. Justice Stevens argued that Virginia's schedule for the execution did not leave the Supreme Court the time normally available for deliberation: "There is no compelling reason for refusing to follow the procedures that we have adopted for the orderly disposition of noncapital cases. Indeed, the international aspects of this case provide an additional reason for adhering to our established Rules and procedures." A similar argument is made by Justice Breyer, who adds: "More time would likely mean additional briefing and argument, perhaps, for example, on the potential relevance of proceedings in an international forum." Similarly, Justice Ginsburg explains that she would have granted the application for a stay of execution in order to consider the instant petition.

[1730] Memorial Paraguay, 111, paras. 2.44–2.45.

[1731] Amnesty International Report AMR 51/27/98, May 1998, United States of America: the execution of Ángel Breard: apologies are not enough, http://web.amnesty.org/library/Index/engAMR510271998, Memorial Paraguay, 111, para. 2.47.

for the residents of Virginia, a responsibility which he could not cede to the ICJ:

I am concerned that to delay Mr Breard's execution so that the International Court of Justice may review this matter would have the practical effect of transferring responsibility from the courts of the Commonwealth and the United States to the International Court. Should the International Court of Justice resolve this matter in Paraguay's favor, it would be difficult, having delayed the execution so that the International Court could consider the case, to then carry out the jury's sentence despite the rulings [of] the International Court.[1732]

In other words, he saw benefits in creating an irreversible situation by executing Breard contrary to the order so that he could avoid the situation where he would have to take a decision on whether to comply with an ICJ judgment in the case. Referring to Mr Breard's unquestioned guilt and the denial of the petitions of Breard and Paraguay by the US Supreme Court, the governor concluded that he saw no reason to interfere with Breard's sentence.[1733] After the execution, the department of state stated that there had been no legal obligation to grant a stay and that it had made a good faith effort to implement the ICJ order by submitting a request to the Virginia governor, who had reached a sovereign discretionary decision.[1734]

The ICJ order had thus failed to achieve its purpose. All institutions and persons mentioned above were public authorities and officials whose behavior was attributable to the US under international law.[1735] Considering the action taken by the various actors involved, one can hardly say that the United States had taken all measures at its disposal to prevent Breard's execution. In fact, the governor had pursued the contrary objective: he had acted precisely in a manner so as to *deprive* the proceedings of their object. The department of state had taken a half-hearted and thereby insufficient approach: the secretary's letter to the Virginia governor had alluded to the "non-binding language" of the order, thus reducing its potential persuasive effect. Moreover, the department had backed the solicitor-general's brief to the Supreme Court, in which that Court had been asked not to intervene and the position had been taken that ICJ provisional measures were non-binding.[1736] Finally, the Supreme Court had failed to stay the execution.[1737]

[1732] Commonwealth of Virginia, Office of the Governor, Press Office, Statement by Governor Jim Gilmore concerning the execution of Angel Breard, 14 April 1998, Annex 24, the large part of which is reprinted in: *Charney/Reisman*, 92 AJIL (1999), at 674–5.

[1733] Ibid.   [1734] Department of State, *supra* n. 1726.

[1735] The organization of a state in a federal system is no excuse for the failure of a state to observe its international obligations, see Article 27 Vienna Convention on the Law of Treaties, 1155 UNTS 331; *supra* Ch. 2 C I; *Henkin*, 92 AJIL (1998), at 680; and *Rieter*, 16 NQHR (1998), at 491–3.

[1736] Critical *Richardson*, 12 Temple ICLJ (1998), at 128–9: "Here in full public view the Executive spoke with two voices, and thus any court or public official inclined to defer would necessarily be confused about the proper direction of their deference."

[1737] See *Henkin*, 92 AJIL (1998), at 680–1: "Secretary Albright heard the voice of the International Court and acted upon it. But the Solicitor General seemed to be under the

The US complied with the order as far as it had been requested to deliver information on the measures taken in the implementation of the first measure.[1738] As this measure was not the essential one, but it was rather meant to secure compliance with the other measure staying the execution,[1739] this did not make the non-compliance with the principal measure appear significantly better; still, it was a sign of respect for the Court and an indication of a certain willingness to respect the order and cooperate with the Court, and the US expressed its assessment that it had done all that could be expected by the order. While it was a case of non-compliance, the US pretended to have respected the provisional measures; they had not acted out of *defiance* for the Court.

4. The further proceedings

The essential objective of Paraguay's application—a re-trial of Mr Breard under observance of the provisions of the Vienna Convention—was frustrated through the execution. Paraguay at first nevertheless continued with the ICJ proceedings, adapting to the new situation by filing an amended application,[1740] in which it added claims relating to non-compliance with the order. It asked the Court

impression that the ICJ Order was not addressed to him (or that he was not bound by it). The Supreme Court was also under the impression that the ICJ Order was not addressed to it, that it was not bound by it, or that it had no responsibility (or no means) to honor it. The Department of Justice did not take other measures to obtain compliance by the state of Virginia with the treaty obligation of the United States to stay the execution. Governor Gilmore seemed to be under the impression that the International Court of Justice was not addressing him; perhaps he did not think he was required to honor Secretary Albright's request. In response to the Order, the Secretary of State wrote to the Governor of Virginia formally requesting that he exercise his powers as Governor to stay the execution. In doing so, the Secretary took a measure at the disposal 'of the United States.' But 'the United States' did not take 'all measures as its disposal.'" On the means that should have been employed, see *idem*, 681–3; *Addo*, 10 EJIL (1999), at 727–8; *Shank/Quigley*, 9 Crim. LF (1999), at 117–19; *Slaughter*, 92 AJIL (1998), at 708–12; *Vázquez*, 92 AJIL (1998), at 683–91.

[1738] The US agent sent two letters to the Court's Registrar for that purpose, highlighting that the order was transmitted to the governor of Virgina and to the US Supreme Court and referring to Secretary Albright's letter to Governor Gilmore, the Solicitor-General's Brief to the Supreme Court, the Supreme Court *per curiam* opinion, and the ultimate decision of Governor Gilmore not to halt the execution: Letter of the agent of the United States of America to the Registrar, 9 April 1998, ICJ Pleadings, 194, Telefax of the agent of the United States of America to the Registrar, 15 April 1998, ICJ Pleadings, 194–5. He concluded: "The United States has taken 'the Court's indications seriously into account,' case concerning military and paramilitary activities in and againts Nicaragua (Nicaragua v. United States of America), Merits, Judgment of 27 June 1986, para. 289. Through its actions, culminating in the Secretary of State's April 13 request to the Governor of Virginia to stay Mr Breard's execution on account of this Court's indication of provisional measures, the United States took all measures lawfully at its disposal to do what the Court requested." (Telefax of 15 April 1998, 195).

[1739] See *Aznar-Gómez*, 102 RGDIP (1998), at fn. 83.

[1740] Amended application instituting proceedings submitted by the government of Paraguay, 9 October 1998, ICJ pleadings, Vienna Convention on Consular Relations, 73–81.

(c) to adjudge and declare that the United States violated its international legal obligation to comply with the provisional measures [...] by failing to take all measures at its disposal to ensure that Angel Francisco Breard was not executed; and (d) to adjudge and declare that the United States violated its international legal obligation not to undertake any kind of action that might prejudice any eventual decision in the case or aggravate the dispute by failing to halt the execution [...].[1741]

Moreover, Paraguay made state responsibility claims for compensation and moral damages for the breach of those obligations.[1742] Hence, Paraguay went further than Germany would about a year later in the LaGrand case.[1743] If the present case had reached the merits stage, the Court would not only have had to decide on the binding force of provisional measures and on the commission of a breach of the order, but also on the conditions under which a violation of provisional measures can give rise to an entitlement for compensation and moral damages.[1744] However, the proceedings never reached that stage: in a letter to the Registrar of 2 November 1998, Paraguay expressed its wish to discontinue the proceedings and requested that the case be removed from the Court's docket, which was quickly welcomed by the US.[1745] Accordingly, the ICJ proceeded as requested and removed the case from its list.[1746]

5. Conclusion

This case has several aspects likely to have had a negative impact on compliance with the provisional measures.

[1741] Ibid., at 80–1, para. 45.

[1742] Ibid., "May it please the Court [...] (h) to adjudge and declare that, as a remedy for the United States' breach of the provisional measures Order and of its international legal obligation not to undertake any action which might prejudice any eventual decision in the case or aggravate the dispute, the Republic of Paraguay is entitled to payment by the United States, in an amount to be determined by the Court in a subsequent proceeding, of (1) compensation, and (2) moral damages as satisfaction." See also "(g) to adjudge and declare that in light of the United States' actions rendering it impossible for the Court to provide the remedy of restitutio in integrum, Paraguay, in its own right and in the exercise of diplomatic protection of its national, is entitled to payment by the United States, in an amount to be determined by the Court in a subsequent proceeding, of (1) compensation, and (2) moral damages as satisfaction."

[1743] Germany did not make a claim for compensation for the breach of provisional measures, but only requested a declaration that the United States had violated the order. See *supra* B XVI 2.

[1744] It is not surprising, therefore, that the order and the US reaction gave rise to a renewed debate on the binding force of provisional measures: see *Aznar-Gómez*, 102 RGDIP (1998), at 915–36; *Rieter*, 16 NQHR (1998), at 479–80; *Shank/Quigley*, 9 Crim. LF (1999), at 113–20. On the line of argument regarding the violation of the Order and state responsibility, see *Aznar-Gómez*, 102 RGDIP (1998), at 936–48.

[1745] Letter of the agent of Paraguay to the Registrar, 2 November 1998, ICJ Pleadings, 198, Letter of the agent of the United States of America to the Registrar, 3 November 1998, ICJ Pleadings, 199. In a statement of 3 November, the US acknowledged the violation of the Vienna Convention, conveyed its apologies to Paraguay, and announced efforts to ensure respect for consular rights: US Department of State, Press Statement by James P. Rubin, 4 November 1998, http://secretary.state.gov/www/briefings/statements/1998/ps981104.html.

[1746] Order of 10 November 1998, at 426–7.

Most notably, there had been doubts as to the binding force of the provisional measures, which appear to have had a significant role in the domestic debate. The stands taken by both the state department and the solicitor-general were regrettable[1747] as they stripped the secretary's request of much of its persuasive force.[1748]

There was also the problem of international law enforcement in a federal system, with the involvement of authorities on state level with less sensibility for the requirements of international law.[1749] A state governor, conscious of the potential reaction of local constituents and future re-election and usually only active in a cross-border context to a limited extent, has perhaps naturally less concern for foreign policy and the need for compliance with international law. Had a stay been ordered by the Supreme Court or another domestic Court, compliance would likely not have presented as great a problem. Yet it cannot be entirely discarded that the governor might have acted differently if he had been aware of the existence of an actual *obligation* under the Court's order, even without any compulsion by the federal government.[1750] His argument that "it would be difficult to carry out the jury's sentence despite a ruling of the International Court"[1751] appeared to acknowledge the binding force of an ICJ judgment and the resulting obligation to obey. Consequently, given its apparent awareness of the need to honor an ICJ *judgment*, he might have showed respect for the ICJ order as well if there had been no doubts about its bindingness. However, particularly the *substance* of the case was one as to lead to concerns about the governor's reaction. Although the order did not concern the legality of the death penalty as such, it related to a case where that penalty had been imposed, a politicized matter with different emotional connotations at the local and federal levels. Judging from his statement that he had "to meet his responsibility for the safety of the residents of Virginia", a responsibility which he could not "cede to the International Court," the governor might have been concerned that any deference to the ICJ could be interpreted as weakness and undue subjugation under an international jurisdiction. Yet his argument was totally unfounded given that a *stay* of the execution was requested, not a re-trial— let alone a release.[1752] Such a stay would by no means have put the public

---

[1747] See *Henkin*, 92 AJIL (1998), at 683: "It is regrettable that the Department of State saw fit to conclude, and to announce, that the Order of the ICJ used 'non-binding language.' That created the impression that the United States did not recognize a legal obligation to comply with the Order; it removed, or relaxed, pressure on all who were 'the United States.'"

[1748] If the federal government had taken a different perspective, the Supreme Court and the governor might have given more weight to the ICJ order as well. See *Addo*, 10 EJIL (1999), at 728–9; *Richardson*, 12 Temple ICLJ (1998), at 129–30.

[1749] See *Duxbury*, Cal. W. ILJ (2000), at 141–76, at 171, ascribing the lack of compliance to problems of implementing international law in a federal system.

[1750] See Addo, 10 EJIL (1999), at 729.   [1751] *Supra* n. 1732.

[1752] See *Kirgis*, 92 AJIL (1998), at 707.

safety in Virginia at hazard. Finally, another negative factor might have been concerns about the case leading to more litigation, as there were reports about numerous deficiencies in the implementation of the Vienna Convention on part of the US.[1753]

X. LaGrand

This case presents a fact pattern similar to that of the Breard case: two German nationals, Karl and Walter LaGrand, had received death sentences in a US state Court as a result of proceedings in which the Vienna Convention on Consular Relations had been violated.[1754]

1. The order of 3 March 1999

After the execution of Karl LaGrand, Germany instituted proceedings against the US before the ICJ and requested an indication of provisional measures to stay the execution of his brother Walter scheduled for 3 March 1999.[1755] The request was patterned after the terms of the Court's order in the Breard case[1756] and was received by the Court on 2 March at 7.30 p.m., The Hague time. The lateness of the application was allegedly due to the fact that German officials had learned only a week prior that Arizona authorities had been aware of the LaGrands' nationality as early as 1982.[1757] The German foreign minister requested that his American counterpart urge the Arizona governor to stay the second execution pending a ruling from the ICJ.[1758]

The Court reacted swiftly to the request. The Court's acting President urged the US government to act in such a way as to enable any order on provisional measures to have its appropriate effects.[1759] No formal hearings were held in the little time available; the Court only met with representatives of the parties on the morning of 3 March to determine the subsequent course of proceedings. The US raised concerns about the Court making an order

---

[1753] See *Addo*, 10 EJIL (1999), at 731.   [1754] For details, see *supra* B XXVI.
[1755] See *supra*, n. 1096.
[1756] Request, *supra* n. 1096: "The United States should take all measures at its disposal to ensure that Walter LaGrand is not executed pending the final decision in these proceedings, and should inform the Court of all the measures which it has taken in the implementation of that Order." Judgment of 27 June 2001, para. 30. As in the case concerning the Vienna Convention on consular relations, the Court's jurisdiction was based on Article I of the Optional Protocol to the VCCR, see ibid., at para. 1.
[1757] Judgment of 27 June 2001, at paras. 54, 56; Order of 3 March 1999, at 14, para. 20. Even assuming this was so, one fails to understand why the request and application could not have been made earlier than the night before the execution. Regardless of whether an earlier application would have made a difference, the extreme haste was unlikely to have a positive impact on the prospects for compliance.
[1758] Judgment of 27 June 2001, at para. 30.   [1759] *Ibid.*, para. 3.

proprio motu, whereas such action was requested by Germany.[1760] At 7.15 p.m., The Hague time, four hours before the execution was to take place in Arizona, the Court unanimously indicated the following measures:

(a) The United States of America should take all measures at its disposal to ensure that Walter LaGrand is not executed pending the final decision in these proceedings, and should inform the Court of all the measures which it has taken in implementation of this Order;

(b) The Government of the United States of America should transmit this Order to the Governor of the State of Arizona.[1761]

The order conformed to Germany's request and added another measure (b) with a view to facilitating compliance with the first measure: the duty to transmit this order to the state governor could be understood as a means to ensure that the governor was sufficiently informed within the little time left. It also could be understood as an attempt to involve the Arizona governor to a greater extent and to ensure her compliance with the order, given that another state governor had given insufficient consideration to the provisional measures order issued in the Breard case.[1762] There was the danger that a similar course of events might take place, given that Arizona's governor had issued a statement on 2 March 1999 pointing out that she had decided to have the execution go forward as scheduled "in the interest of justice and with the victims in mind,"[1763] despite a recommendation of the state clemency board that a 60-day reprieve be granted having regard to the German application before the ICJ.[1764]

The Court's reasoning with regard to prima-facie jurisdiction, irreparable damage, and urgency was similar to the order in the Breard case.[1765] It was the first time for the Court to indicate provisional measures *proprio motu*[1766] and without hearings,[1767] and the Court felt obliged to include additional comments on its unprecedented action.[1768] Although the order was adopted

---

[1760] *Aceves*, 93 AJIL (1999), at 925.

[1761] Order of 3 March 1999, at 16, para. 29. For details, see *Aceves*, 93 AJIL (1999), at 925–6.

[1762] See in this direction also Order, at 16, para. 28: "Whereas the international responsibility of a State is engaged by the action of the competent organs and authorities acting in that State, whatever they may be; [. . .] whereas, according to the information available to the Court, implementation of the measures indicated in the present Order falls within the jurisdiction of the Governor of Arizona; whereas the Government of the United States is consequently under the obligation to transmit the present Order to the said Governor; whereas the Governor of Arizona is under the obligation to act in conformity with the international undertakings of the United States."

[1763] Statement of Governor Jane Dee Hull on the case of Walter LaGrand, 2 March 1999, Annex 33 to the German memorial.

[1764] Judgment of 27 June 2001, para. 31.

[1765] Order of 3 March 1999, at 13–16, paras. 13–18, 22–7.

[1766] See Article 75 of the 1978 Rules of Court.

[1767] For details on this aspect of the case, see *Addo*, 10 EJIL (1999), at 719–20; *Mennecke/ Tams*, 42 GYIL (1999), at 199–203.

[1768] Order of 3 March 1999, at 14, paras. 19–21.

unanimously, the same judges that had expressed their unease with the Breard order—Judges Oda and Schwebel—did so with regard to the LaGrand order as well. The American Judge Schwebel explained in his separate opinion that he did not oppose the substance of the order and therefore had not voted against it, but that he had "profound reservations about the procedures followed both by the Applicant and the Court" as the US had not been afforded the opportunity to be heard.[1769]

Certainly, the Court's power to indicate provisional measures without a hearing is a competence that has to be made use of with caution, since the right of each side to present its view to the Court is a fundamental principle of the judicial process. None the less, Article 75(1) of the Rules of Court provide for the competence to issue an order *proprio motu* to be able to ensure interim protection in cases of utmost urgency where the holding of the normal procedure would frustrate the request—particularly in cases such as this one where, in view of the little time remaining, there was no other way of preserving the subject-matter of the proceedings. Moreover, one has to bear in mind that the US had presented its position in the parallel Breard case just one year earlier and it was to be assumed that a similar stance would be taken. While under normal circumstances this would not in itself have justified a refusal to hold a hearing, it made the recourse to the exceptional competence to grant interim protection without a hearing less worrisome, as the Court had been aware of the US primary concerns from the experience of the former case.

2. The follow-up to the order

In the few hours left before the execution was to take place, Germany tried to enforce the ICJ order and achieve a stay of execution before the US Supreme Court. The US solicitor-general filed a letter with the Supreme Court adopting a position against the binding force of ICJ provisional measures more extreme than in the Breard case, arguing that "an order of the

---

[1769] Ibid., Sep. Op. Schwebel, at 21–2. Despite his affirmative vote, Judge Oda appended a declaration (ibid., at 18–20) rather resembling a dissenting opinion. In his own words at a later time, its dissenting opinion to the Judgment of 27 June 2001, at para. 15: "It should [. . .] be clear from my declaration appended to the Court's Order of 3 March 1999 that I was, in substance, opposed to the Order." He stated that he "considered that the request for the indication of interim measures [. . .] should have been dismissed," arguing that the Court could not act as a court of criminal appeal, that the judicial procedure in the US courts would have been the same in the absence of a breach of the Vienna Convention, and that there was no danger of a right of Germany being irreparably prejudiced. Also, he pointed to the extremely late filing of Germany's request and expressed concern that the case might set a dangerous precedent. Yet, he explained his affirmative vote by "humanitarian reasons." As pointed out *supra* n. 1716, it might be preferable for a judge to cast a negative vote if he argues so strongly against an order. In fact, Judge Oda himself points out in his dissenting opinion to the judgment at para. 15 that he regretted his vote in favor of the order "since I did so against my judicial conscience."

International Court of Justice is not binding and does not furnish a basis for judicial relief."[1770] The Supreme Court denied Germany's motion and declined to exercise its original jurisdiction.[1771] Two of the concurring judges explicitly referred to the solicitor-general's position.[1772] Two justices dissented and stated that "in light of the fact that both the International Court of Justice and a sovereign nation have asked that we stay this case," a preliminary stay would be appropriate to allow time to consider "the jurisdictional and international legal issues involved."[1773] The federal government took no steps apart from transmitting the ICJ order to the governor of Arizona; unlike in the Breard case, the secretary of state made no attempt at persuading the governor.[1774] Walter LaGrand was executed in the evening of 3 March 1999. At a press briefing on the following day, a spokesman for the state department referred to a lack of opportunity to take action beyond transmitting the order to the governor and mentioned the fact that the order had been made without a hearing.[1775] On 8 March 1999, the US informed the Court of the measures taken in the implementation of the order: it reported that the order had been transmitted by the state department to the governor of Arizona and that "in view of the extremely late hour of the receipt of the Court's order, no further steps were feasible."[1776] The subsequent allegation of the US to have complied with the order can be followed only as regards the complementary measure of transmitting the order to the state authorities and informing the Court of the action taken. It is apparent, however, that the US did not comply with the principal measure "to take all measures at its

[1770] Letter of Seth P. Waxman, solicitor-general, to the Supreme Court, 3 March 1999, Annex 28 to the German Memorial. Without indicating details, he referred to the Amicus Curiae brief for the United States in the Breard case; yet, that brief had at least pointed to "substantial disagreement among jurists" about this question, see *supra* n. 1725.

[1771] Federal Republic of Germany v. United States *et al.*, 119 S. Ct. 1016 (1999). See also *Murphy*, 93 AJIL (1999), at 646–7.

[1772] Justice Souter with whom Justice Ginsburg joined, concurring: "[. . .] In exercising my discretion, I have taken into consideration the position of the Solicitor General on behalf of the United States." (*supra* n. 1771).

[1773] Justice Breyer with whom Justice Stevens joined, ibid. The Supreme Court also denied Walter LaGrand's motion that challenged the execution method (lethal gas) and vacated an injunction on the execution that had been issued by the US Court of Appeals for the Ninth Circuit Court with regard to the execution method. LaGrand v. Arizona, 119 S. Ct. 1137 (1999) (Justice Breyer, joined by Justice Stevens, dissenting, under reference to the dissenting opinion in Federal Republic of Germany v. United States, *supra* n. 1771.). Stewart v. LaGrand, 119 S. Ct. 1018 (1999).

[1774] Judgment of 27 June 2001, at para. 111. The US acknowledged that the transmission of the order to the governor of Arizona had been the only step taken by the federal government in its implementation, arguing that "the United States' ability to act" had been constrained by the extraordinarily short time period left for a response and the character of the United States as a federal state: US Counter-memorial, 27 March 2000, http://212.153.43.18/icjwww/idocket/igus/iguspleadings/iGUS_ipleading_CounterMemorial_US_20000327.htm at paras. 116–26.

[1775] Statement of James B. Foley, US Department of State Press Briefing, 4 March, reprinted in: *Murphy*, 93 AJIL (1999), at 647.

[1776] Judgment of 27 June 2001, at para. 111, see also US Counter-memorial, para. 127.

disposal" to prevent Walter LaGrand's execution.[1777] Neither state nor federal officials took a single substantive measure to prevent the execution; instead, through behavior of state officials attributable to the United States, the execution was carried out, precisely the contrary of what had been ordered by the Court.

3. The further proceedings: the judgment as a vehicle for sanctioning the breach of an ICJ order

Proceedings before the ICJ continued despite the second execution and ended with a judgment in favor of Germany.[1778] The judgment contained important novelties for provisional measures. Similar to Paraguay, Germany made the non-compliance with the order a formal part of the proceedings. It requested a declaration that the US "violated its international legal obligation to comply with the Order on Provisional Measures [...] and to refrain from any action which might interfere with the subject-matter of a dispute while judicial proceedings are pending."[1779] This German submission allowed the Court for the first time in its history to make a pronouncement about the binding character of provisional measures, and opened the way for litigants to use the final judgment as a mechanism for sanctioning the breach of an ICJ order—in this case, through a declaration of non-compliance, as the applicant had not raised state responsibility claims in this regard.[1780]

The US did not challenge the Court's jurisdiction to decide on the violation of the order,[1781] even though one might have expected the argument that this issue involved an interpretation of Article 41 of the ICJ Statute rather than an interpretation or application of the Vienna Convention.[1782] The Court found that it had jurisdiction, as the dispute over the non-compliance with the order arose directly out of the dispute between the parties as submitted to the Court (i.e. the one relating to the breaches of the Vienna Convention and their legal consequences). The Court recalled its finding in the Fisheries Jurisdiction case that in order to consider the dispute in all its aspects, it might also deal with submissions based on facts subsequent to the

---

[1777] See *Mennecke/Tams*, 42 GYIL (1999), at 203. But see Judge Oda in his dissenting opinion at para. 35: "I believe that that Order was complied with by the United States, which took all measures at its disposal in an attempt to respect the terms. At any rate, the stay of an execution, in this case of Walter LaGrand, could not be—and, in fact, was not—mandated by the Court in its Order indicating provisional measures." However, at para. 17 he points out that the provisional measures aimed at staying the execution. He does not explain further what kind of obligations the Order generated in his view nor why the United States would have taken all measures at its disposal even though the execution was carried out by public officials whose behavior is attributable to the United States.

[1778] *Supra* B XXVI 3.   [1779] Judgment of 27 June 2001, at paras. 11–12.
[1780] See Chapter 4 B IV 2.   [1781] See Judgment of 27 June 2001, at para. 43.
[1782] This was the view of Judge Gonzalo Parra-Aranguren, see his separate opinion, at para. 15.

filing of the application, but arising directly out of the question subject-matter of the application.[1783]

The US had argued that the German claim of non-compliance with the order was inadmissible because of the tardiness of Germany's application and request for provisional measures.[1784] The Court disposed of these claims by stating that irrespective of the circumstances of the filings, it had considered the granting of interim protection appropriate and Germany was consequently entitled to challenge non-compliance.[1785]

After having established its jurisdiction and rejected the US claims of inadmissibility,[1786] the Court moved on to the merits and the US arguments that it had, in fact, complied with the order, which it believed had not been mandatory under its concrete terms and in light of the function of ICJ interim measures, which had in the American view not been designed to create legal obligations.[1787] For the first time in its history, the Court ruled that orders adopted under Article 41 of its Statute had binding force.[1788] Then, it turned to the specific order and stated that it had not been a mere exhortation, but had been adopted pursuant to Article 41, and that it consequently had been binding and created legal obligations for the US.[1789]

Finally, the Court examined the conduct of the US.[1790] It concluded by 13 to 2 votes—the American Judge Buergenthal voting with the majority—that, based on the behavior of the federal and state governments and of the US Supreme Court,[1791] the US had breached the obligation incumbent upon it under the order.[1792] Noteworthy is that the Court deemed it appropriate to

---

[1783] See Judgment of 27 June 2001, at para. 45, quoting *Fisheries Jurisdiction* (Federal Republic of Germany v. Iceland), Judgment of 25 July 1974, at 203, para. 72. See (already prior to the judgment) *Mennecke/Tams*, 42 GYIL (1999), at 216. Critical on this point Diss. Op. Judge Oda, para. 21.

[1784] Moreover, the US had also based the inadmissibility on the argument that the Court could not act as an ultimate court of appeal in criminal proceedings with regard to Germany's other claims; as reported above, the Court rejected this arguments since the legal rules which it was asked to apply were purely rules of public international law, not domestic law: see *supra* B XXVI 3 and Judgment of 27 June 2001, at paras. 50–2.

[1785] Judgment of 27 June 2001, at paras. 57 and 128(2)(c); the decision was taken by 13 votes to 3, with Judges Oda, Parra-Aranguren, and Buergenthal dissenting.

[1786] The Court found that an assessment on whether the US had violated an order pursuant to Article 41 of the ICJ Statute did not convert it into a court of appeal: Judgment of 27 June 2001, paras. 50–2.

[1787] For a summary of these US arguments, see ibid., paras. 95–7.

[1788] Ibid., paras. 98–109. On this aspect of the judgment, see *Aceves*, 96 AJIL (2002), at 213–14, 217–18; *Hillgruber*, 57 JZ (2002), at 98; *Mennecke*, 44 GYIL (2001), at 445–9, and *supra* Chapter 1 B II.

[1789] Judgment of 27 June 2001, para. 110.   [1790] Ibid., paras. 111–16.

[1791] Ibid., paras. 111–15.

[1792] Ibid., para. 128(5). The dissenting judges were Oda and Gonzalo Parra-Aranguren (Venezuela). Judge Buergenthal had voted against the admissibility, though, see para. 128(2)(c). Judge Parra-Aranguren explained that his vote was due to his conviction that the Court lacked jurisdiction to decide on this issue since it related to the interpretation of the ICJ statute and not of the Vienna Convention, Dissenting Opinion Parra-Aranguren, para. 15. Judge Oda held that the US had complied with the order and that the question of whether this had happened should never have been raised, Diss. Op. Oda, at para. 35.

recall that the US obligation to "take all measures at its disposal to ensure that Walter LaGrand is not executed" had not been an obligation of result.[1793] Yet, as Walter LaGrand was in custody, it is hardly imaginable how he could be executed without action by state officials. In other cases, the distinction between obligations of result and of conduct makes sense so as to establish who is to bear the risk that all implementing action might fail; in this case, however, the adoption of "all measures at its disposal" on the part of the US (understood as comprising all branches of both federal and state governments) *would* have led to a stay of execution.[1794] The Court might have been influenced by a certain consideration for the problem of implementation of international law in a federation through the language used for the analysis of federal organs *vis-à-vis* state organs: the Court's comments on the failure of the state governor to halt the execution appear somewhat milder than those of the federal organs, although the governor's action was the most obvious and direct violation of the order.[1795] Yet, one should not read too much into the slight linguistic difference in the Court's reference to state (as opposed to federal) organs. The assessment of the governor's action was made in the context of analyzing the violation of the order on behalf of the different US actors and the conclusion that "the United States" had not discharged its obligations under the order came subsequently. The order itself had emphasized the Governor's obligation "to act in conformity with the international undertakings of the United States."[1796] The Court's reasoning should therefore not be understood as suggesting that only federal, but not the state, organs had been obliged to comply with the measures: the behavior of both groups of actors was attributable to "the United States." Interestingly enough, after two orders failing to achieve halts to an execution,

---

[1793] Ibid., para. 111.

[1794] Of course, this would be different if one assumed that only federal organs had been obliged by the order; however, as explained above (see *supra* Chapter 2 C I), public international law considers the entire state as a unit, and the order's language had already aimed at involving state authorites.

[1795] On this point, the Court stated (Judgment of 27 June 2001, at para. 113): "It is noteworthy that the Governor of Arizona, to whom the Court's Order had been transmitted, decided not to give effect to it, even though the Arizona Clemency Board had recommended a stay of execution for Walter LaGrand.". See, in comparison, ibid., para. 112: "The [State Department's] mere transmission of [the] Order to the Governor of Arizona without any comment, particularly without even so much as a plea for a temporary stay and an explanation that there is no general agreement on the position of the United States that orders of the provisional measures are non-binding, was certainly less than could have been done even in the short time available. The same is true of the United States Solicitor General's categorical statement in his brief letter to the United States Supreme Court [...]" and para. 113: "The Supreme Court rejected a separate application by Germany for a stay of execution [...]. Yet it would have been open to the Supreme Court, as one its members urged, to grant a preliminary stay [...]." Interestingly, it seems as if the Court was more sympathetic to problems of federal *vis-à-vis* state organs than to considerations of separation of powers.

[1796] Order of 3 March 1999, para. 28.

the Court turned away from the "all measures at its disposal" formula to endorse an "all necessary measures" formula in the Avena case.[1797]

4. Conclusion

As in the Breard case, non-compliance with the order had various aspects. Significant was the US position that provisional measures were not binding, as a result of an incorrect interpretation of Article 41 of the ICJ Statute and this question not being clarified by the ICJ, as well as questions relating to the implementation of international law in a federal system and the emotional climate surrounding issues of capital punishment.

While regardless of the legal status of provisional measures, there might be reason for concern about an insufficient awareness of the requirements of international law in subunits of a federal state,[1798] it is difficult to assess the outcome of this case under the hypothesis that there had already been clarity on the binding force of provisional measures. The state clemency board had demonstrated some sensitivity for the need to pay respect for international proceedings when it had recommended a reprieve; the pressure on the state executive towards halting the execution may have been greater had no doubts existed that her behavior violated the US obligations under international law. With the ICJ having settled the question of binding force of provisional measures, there is hope that the outcome in similar scenarios will be different in the future. By creating a mechanism for the sanctioning of provisional measures through a declaration in the final judgment, the LaGrand ruling is of tremendous general significance.[1799] Its impact on the pending Avena case remains to be seen.

[1797] Avena and other Mexican Nationals, Order of 5 February 2003, at para. 59I(a): "The United States of America shall take all measures necessary to ensure that Mr. César Roberto Fierro Reyna, Mr. Roberto Moreno Ramos and Mr. Osvaldo Torres Aguilera are not executed pending final judgment in these proceedings."

[1798] It is noteworthy that the execution of Walter LaGrand was not considered important enough an issue as to be included in the News Archive for March 99 of the governor's website: http://web.archive.org/web/20021228072235/http://www.governor.state.az.us/news/releases/march99/index.html, thus considered a matter less important than, for example, "Governor launches comprehensive transportation study," the news for 3 March 1999. The Arizona Department of Corrections's 1999 Annual Report on Executions, http://adcprisoninfo.az.gov/AR99/99httpExecutions.htm reports the case as follows: "The LaGrand executions received worldwide attention for another reason. Since they were German citizens, the German Consulate, German Chancellor and the World Court became involved in an international appeal to halt the executions, as the death penalty is not used in Germany." It is worrisome that a state authority depicts the situation in such a seriously flawed manner.

[1799] See *infra* Chapter 4 B IV 2 for a further discussion of this mechanism.

XI. Armed activities on the territory of the Congo (DRC v. Uganda)

1. Background of the case

By a unilateral application of 23 June 1999,[1800] the Democratic Republic of Congo (hereinafter DRC) instituted proceedings against Uganda for acts of armed aggression on DRC territory, based on both countries' declarations under Article 36(2) of the Statute.[1801] The DRC requested the Court to declare that through military and paramilitary actions, illegal exploitation of Congolese resources and oppression against Congolese nationals, Uganda had violated several norms of international law, including the prohibition of the use of force, and to order the immediate and unconditional withdrawal of all Ugandan armed forces and nationals from DRC territory, in addition to financial compensation.[1802] On the same day, the DRC initiated similar proceedings against Burundi and Rwanda, which were later discontinued.[1803] The case against Uganda is still pending; oral proceedings had been scheduled for November 2003, but were postponed at the DRC's request to allow for negotiations in an atmosphere of calm.[1804]

[1800] http://212.153.43.18/icjwww/idocket/ico/icoapplication/ico_iapplication_19990623.pdf.

[1801] Both Congo and Uganda made unconditional declarations accepting the compulsory jurisdiction of the ICJ. Democratic Republic of Congo, Declaration of 8 February 1989, ICJ YB 1998–9, 96–7, Uganda, declaration of 3 October 1963, ibid., 129.

[1802] See Application, *supra* n. 1800.

[1803] Armed Activities on the Territory of the Congo (Democratic Republic of Congo v. Burundi), Order of 30 January 2001; Armed Activities on the Territory of the Congo (Democratic Republic of Congo v. Rwanda), Order of 30 January 2001. The Democratic Republic of the Congo launched new proceedings against Rwanda for "massive, serious and flagrant violations of human rights and of international humanitarian law" on 28 May 2002 (http://212.153.43.18/cijwww/cdocket/ccrw_capplication_20020528_requete.PDF). Its application was joined by a request for the indication of provisional measures (http://212.153.43.18/cijwww/cdocket/ccrw_capplication_20020528_demand.PDF), which the Court rejected, Armed activities on the territory of the Congo (New Application: 2002), Order of 10 July 2002, given a lack of prima-facie jurisdiction. The case is still pending before the Court.

[1804] ICJ Press Release, 7 November 2003, http://212.153.43.18/icjwww/ipresscom/ipress2003/ipresscom2003-39_co_20031107.htm: in a letter of 5 November 2003, the DRC suggested a postponement until April 2004. This initiative is in line with the DRC's efforts to normalize its relations with its neighbors, including Uganda, see Progress report of the Secretary-General on the recommendations of the Security Council mission to Central Africa, 20 January 2004, S/2004/52, paras. 16 and 18; see also "Kagame hails improving relations with Kampana", 20 February 2004, http://www.irinnews.org/report.asp?ReportID=39608&SelectRegion=Great_Lakes&SelectCountry=RWANDA-UGANDA. A new schedule for the hearings has not yet been fixed. Once the case is ready for a decision and unless it is settled out of court, the Court will have to decide about a Ugandan counterclaim as well: in its counter-memorial filed on 20 April 2001, Uganda had made various counterclaims concerning: alleged acts of aggression by the DRC; the responsibility of the DRC for attacks on Ugandan diplomatic premises and personnel in Kinshasa and on Ugandan nationals; and alleged violations of the Lusaka Agreement on the part of the DRC. In an order of 29 November 2001, the Court had held the first two counterclaims admissible and the third inadmissible: Armed activities on the territory of the Congo, Order of 29 November 2001.

The motivations of the several actors relate to security concerns as well as to economic interests. A UN expert panel traced the main source of conflict to disputes over access, control, and the trade of five key mineral resources in the mineral-rich Congo region.[1805] In May 1997, Laurent Kabila overthrew the régime of Mobutu Sese Seko in Zaire, later rechristened as the Democratic Republic of the Congo. Kabila had received assistance from Rwanda and Uganda, who had an interest in stopping insurgents against their governments based on DRC territory. However, Kabila himself later took advantage of those insurgent groups, and his former allies turned against him. The conflict soon spilled over the borders of the DRC, embroiling several other states and rebel groups in the conflict: the DRC government received support from Zimbabwe, Angola, and Namibia while being opposed by Uganda, Burundi, and Rwanda. A cease-fire agreement concluded in Lusaka on 7 July 1999[1806] has still not been fully implemented. The DRC government maintains control over a smaller part of the Congolese territory than its adversaries. New hopes have arisen for the peace process since Kabila was assassinated and succeeded by his son Joseph.[1807]

2. Security Council Resolution 1304 and Congo's request for provisional measures

In early May 2000, serious fighting took place between Ugandan and Rwandan forces in Kisangani (Eastern Congo); an agreement on a troop withdrawal

---

[1805] Report of the Panel of Experts on the Illegal Exploitation of Natural Resources and Other Forms of Wealth of the Democratic Republic of the Congo, transmitted by the Secretary-General to the President of the Security Council on 12 April 2001, S/2001/357 (in particular 41–2, paras. 213–18). See also Addendum to the Report of the Panel of Experts on the Illegal Exploitation of Natural Resources and Other Forms of Wealth in the Democratic Republic of the Congo, November 2001, S/2001/1072 (in particular 20 para. 100: "There is a link between the continuation of the conflict and the exploitation of the natural resources, in the case of Uganda", and 26–7, paras. 143–51), Interim Report of the Panel of Experts on the Illegal Exploitation of the Natural Resources and other Forms of Wealth of the Democratic Republic of the Congo, May 2002, S/2002/565.

[1806] Agreement for a cease-fire in the Democratic Republic of the Congo with annexes, reprinted in: 11 African Journal for International and Comparative Law (1999), 529–41. It was signed by the representatives of Angola, the DRC, Namibia, Rwanda, Uganda, and Zimbabwe.

[1807] Report of the Security Council Mission to the Great Lakes Region, 15–16 May 2001, S/2001/521: "The Security Council mission found much that was encouraging in its visit to the Great Lakes region. For the first time since the outbreak of the conflict, the outlines of a solution appeared to be taking shape [. . .] Prominent among these positive indications was the attitude towards the peace process and towards MONUC of President Joseph Kabila, who is clearly committed to the implementation of the Lusaka Ceasefire Agreement and the restoration of peace and democracy to the Democratic Republic of the Congo." (ibid. at 15, para. 111). On the background, see Gray, *International Law and the Use of Force*, 52–4; Leader, "The Congo Crisis," 30 April 2001, http://web.archive.org/web/20020620020331/http://fundforpeace.org/resources/perspect/leader03.htm. For recent developments, see Report of the Security Council Mission to Central Africa, 7–16 June 2003, S/2003/653, Progress Report of the Secretary-General on the recommendations of the Security Council mission to Central Africa, 20 January 2004, S/2004/52.

and a demilitarization of the city was reached on 21 May.[1808] Renewed fighting broke out on 5 June. As a response, the Security Council adopted Resolution 1304 on 16 June.[1809] Acting under Chapter VII, the Council expressed its deep concern at the continuation of the hostilities in the DRC and its outrage at the renewed fighting between Ugandan and Rwandan forces in Kisangani and the failure of Uganda and Rwanda to cease hostilities and withdraw from the area. It deplored a lack of cooperation of the DRC government concerning the Inter-Congolese dialogue.[1810] The detailed resolution included a series of specific demands directed at all belligerents, including a cease-fire and troop withdrawal, demilitarization of Kisangani, the implementation of the Lusaka cease-fire agreement, Inter-Congolese dialogue, respect for human rights and humanitarian law, and cooperation with MONUC, the UN Mission in the Democratic Republic of the Congo, and the International Committee of the Red Cross.[1811]

[1808] Third report of the Secretary-General on the United Nations Organization Mission in the Democratic Republic of the Congo, 12 June 2001, S/2000/566, at 2–3.
[1809] S/RES/1304 (2000).   [1810] Ibid., preamble.
[1811] To see the degree of precision and comprehensiveness of the Resolution, it is worthwhile having a look at its whole operative part: "The Security Council [. . .] acting under Chapter VII of the Charter of the United Nations,
1. *Calls on* all parties to cease hostilities throughout the territory of the Democratic Republic of the Congo and to fulfil their obligations under the Ceasefire Agreement and the relevant provisions of the 8 April 2000 Kampala disengagement plan;
2. *Reiterates* its unreserved condemnation of the fighting between Ugandan and Rwandan forces in Kisangani in violation of the sovereignty and territorial integrity of the Democratic Republic of the Congo, and *demands* that these forces and those allied to them desist from further fighting;
3. *Demands* that Ugandan and Rwandan forces as well as forces of the Congolese armed opposition and other armed groups immediately and completely withdraw from Kisangani, and *calls on* all parties to the Ceasefire Agreement to respect the demilitarization of the city and its environs;
4. *Further demands*:
   (a) that Uganda and Rwanda, which have violated the sovereignty and territorial integrity of the Democratic Republic of the Congo, withdraw all their forces from the territory of the Democratic Republic of the Congo without further delay, in conformity with the timetable of the Ceasefire Agreement and the 8 April 2000 Kampala disengagement plan;
   (b) that each phase of withdrawal completed by Ugandan and Rwandan forces be reciprocated by the other parties in conformity with the same timetable;
   (c) that all other foreign military presence and activity, direct and indirect, in the territory of the Democratic Republic of the Congo be brought to an end in conformity with the provisions of the Ceasefire Agreement;
5. In this context *demands* that all parties abstain from any offensive action during the process of disengagement and of withdrawal of foreign forces;
6. *Requests* the Secretary-General to keep under review arrangements for deployment of the personnel of the United Nations Organization Mission in the Democratic Republic of the Congo (MONUC), as authorized and in conditions defined by resolution 1291 (2000), to monitor the cessation of hostilities, disengagement of forces and withdrawal of foreign forces as described in paragraphs 1 to 5 above and to assist in the planning of these tasks, and *requests also* the Secretary-General to recommend any adjustment that may become necessary in this regard;

Three days later, Congo submitted a request for the indication of provisional measures in connection with the events in Kisangani.[1812] This request was only made in the proceedings against Uganda and not those against Rwanda and Burundi, which were still pending at that time.[1813] The DRC

7. *Calls on* all parties, in complying with paragraphs 1 to 5 above, to cooperate with the efforts of MONUC to monitor the cessation of hostilities, disengagement of forces and withdrawal of foreign forces;

8. *Demands* that the parties to the Ceasefire Agreement cooperate with the deployment of MONUC to the areas of operations deemed necessary by the Special Representative of the Secretary-General, including by lifting restrictions on the freedom of movement of MONUC personnel and by ensuring their security;

9. *Calls on* all the Congolese Parties to engage fully in the National Dialogue process as provided for in the Ceasefire Agreement, and *calls in particular on* the Government of the Democratic Republic of the Congo to reaffirm its full commitment to the National Dialogue, to honour its obligations in this respect and to cooperate with the Facilitator designated with the assistance of the OAU and to allow for the full participation of political opposition and civil society groups in the dialogue;

10. *Demands* that all parties cease all forms of assistance and cooperation with the armed groups referred to in Annex A, Chapter 9.1 of the Ceasefire Agreement;

11. *Welcomes* efforts made by the parties to engage in a dialogue on the question of disarmament, demobilization, resettlement and reintegration of members of all armed groups referred to in Annex A, Chapter 9.1 of the Ceasefire Agreement, and *urges* the parties, in particular the Government of the Democratic Republic of the Congo and the Government of Rwanda, to continue these efforts in full cooperation;

12. *Demands* that all parties comply in particular with the provisions of Annex A, Chapter 12 of the Ceasefire Agreement relating to the normalization of the security situation along the borders of the Democratic Republic of the Congo with its neighbours;

13. *Condemns* all massacres and other atrocities carried out in the territory of the Democratic Republic of the Congo, and *urges* that an international investigation into all such events be carried out with a view to bringing to justice those responsible;

14. *Expresses* the view that the Governments of Uganda and Rwanda should make reparations for the loss of life and the property damage they have inflicted on the civilian population in Kisangani, and *requests* the Secretary-General to submit an assessment of the damage as a basis for such reparations;

15. *Calls on* all the parties to the conflict in the Democratic Republic of the Congo to protect human rights and respect international humanitarian law;

16. *Calls also on* all parties to ensure the safe and unhindered access of relief personnel to all those in need, and *recalls* that the parties must also provide guarantees for the safety, security and freedom of movement for United Nations and associated humanitarian relief personnel;

17. *Further calls on* all parties to cooperate with the International Committee of the Red Cross to enable it to carry out its mandate as well as the tasks entrusted to it under the Ceasefire Agreement;

18. *Reaffirms* the importance of holding, at the appropriate time, an international conference on peace, security, democracy and development in the Great Lakes region under the auspices of the United Nations and of the OAU, with the participation of all the Governments of the region and all others concerned;

19. *Expresses* its readiness to consider possible measures which could be imposed in accordance with its responsibility under the Charter of the United Nations in the case of failure by parties to comply fully with this resolution;

20. *Decides* to remain actively seized of the matter."

[1812] http://212.153.43.18/icjwww/idocket/ico/icoapplication/ico_iapplication_requestinterim-measures_20000619.pdf.

[1813] *Supra*, n. 1803. On the DRC's request for provisional measures in the new case instituted against Rwanda in 2002, see *supra* Chapter IV A IV 2.

pointed to the risk of immediate grave and irreparable prejudice for the country and its inhabitants and asked for the six measures: the withdrawal of the Ugandan army from Kisangani; a cease-fire on DRC territory; an assurance that Ugandan units would respect international humanitarian law; an end of oppressive policies against the population in the occupied zones; a discontinuation of illegal transfers of DRC mineral wealth; and respect for the sovereignty and territorial integrity of the DRC.[1814]

3. The relation between the request and the resolution

As the Security Council resolution obviously overlapped with the measures requested by the DRC, the question arises as to the additional benefits that the DRC expected from turning to the Court for interim protection. In the presence of Security Council resolutions on the same subject-matter, a state can have various reasons for seeking interim protection. It may desire re-inforcement of the resolution where its validity or relevance is disputed. Alternatively, it may try to prevent a Security Council resolution or claim the invalidity of a potential or actual resolution, as happened in the Lockerbie cases.[1815] In the present case, the situation was yet another, as the DRC request made reference to the resolution in order to strengthen its own

---

[1814] *Supra*:
"(1) the Government of the Republic of Uganda must order its army to withdraw immediately and completely from Kisangani;
(2) the Government of the Republic of Uganda must order its army to cease forthwith all fighting or military activity on the territory of the Democratic Republic of the Congo and to withdraw immediately and completely from that territory, and must forthwith desist from providing any direct or indirect support to any State, group, organization, movement or individual engaged or preparing to engage in military activities on the territory of the Democratic Republic of the Congo;
(3) the Government of the Republic of Uganda must take all measures in its power to ensure that units, forces or agents which are or could be under its authority, or which enjoy or could enjoy its support, together with organizations or persons which could be under its control, authority or influence, desist forthwith from committing or inciting the commission of war crimes or any other oppressive or unlawful act against all persons on the territory of the Democratic Republic of the Congo;
(4) the Government of the Republic of Uganda must forthwith discontinue any act having the aim or effect of disrupting, interfering with or hampering actions intended to give the population of the occupied zones the benefit of their fundamental human rights, and in particular their rights to health and education;
(5) the Government of the Republic of Uganda must cease forthwith all illegal exploitation of the natural resources of the Democratic Republic of the Congo and all illegal transfer of assets, equipment or persons to its territory;
(6) the Government of the Republic of Uganda must henceforth respect in full the right of the Democratic Republic of the Congo to sovereignty, political independence and territorial integrity, and the fundamental rights and freedoms of all persons on the territory of the Democratic Republic of the Congo."
[1815] Questions of Interpretation and Application of the 1971 Montreal Convention arising from the Aerial Incident at Lockerbie (Libyan Arab Jamahiriya v. United Kingdom), Provisional Measures, Order of 14 April 1992; Questions of Interpretation and Application of the

position, although Uganda had not opposed the resolution as such. During the oral proceedings on interim measures, a DRC counsel pointed out that

the Security Council adopted a resolution [...] in which it demanded that Uganda withdraw its troops not only from Kisangani but also from the whole of Congolese territory, without further delay. The withdrawal of the Ugandan troops is in essence what the Democratic Republic of Congo requests the Court to indicate, not as a political measure to maintain international peace and security but as a judicial measure.[1816]

Accordingly, its request encompassed a measure urging Uganda "to withdraw immediately and completely" from Congolese territory.[1817] This reliance on an *immediate* withdrawal from the *entire* territory appears to have been a main reason for the DRC request for interim protection. On the question as to why the DRC request was not moot despite Uganda's expressed readiness to withdraw from Kisangani in response to Resolution 1304, the DRC highlighted that the respective Ugandan declarations concerned only the Kisangani region.[1818] The DRC's reading of the resolution's provision concerning the troop withdrawal from the whole Congolese territory, however, omitted the context of the obligation to withdraw as part of the Lusaka agreement and the Kampala disengagement plan (and later the Harare agreement)[1819] and the respective timetable which provided for a reciprocal withdrawal of all parties at each phase.[1820] It was only for the

---

1971 Montreal Convention arising from the Aerial Incident at Lockerbie (Libyan Arab Jamahiriya v. United States of America), Provisional Measures, Order of 14 April 1992. There was a Security Council resolution under Chapter VI prior to the request for interim protection and one under Chapter VII that was adopted after the hearings, but before the order on provisional measures. See ibid., 11–14, paras. 29, 32, and 35–6 (Order UK), and 123–6, paras. 31, 34, and 38–9 (Order US).

[1816] Statement of Olivier Corten on behalf of the DRC, public sitting of 26 June 2000, http://212.153.43.18/icjwww/idocket/ico/ico_cr/ico_icr2000-20_translation.htm. Already in its request (in the context of reporting the events at Kisangani), the DRC referred to the condemnation of these events in Resolution 1304 and stated that the Council had urged Uganda to start withdrawing all its forces from Congolese territory without further delay Request, *supra*, 2 "Ces agissements ont fait l'objet d'une condemnation unanime, y compris par le Conseil de sécurité de l'ONU qui, agissant en vertu du chapitre VII de la Charte, a exigé, que l'Ouganda [...] qui (a) porté atteinte à la souveraineté et à l'intégrité territoriale de la République démocratique du Congo, commenc[e] à retirer toutes [ces] forces de son territoire sans plus tarder' ((S/RES/1304), du 16 juin 2000)."

[1817] See request, *supra* n. 1812, at section 2.

[1818] Order of 1 July 2000, para. 20, and Statement of Olivier Corten on behalf of the Democratic Republic of the Congo, 26 June 2000, http://212.153.43.18/icjwww/idocket/ico/ico_cr/ico_icr2000-20_translation.htm (who, however, also argues that earlier Ugandan commitments had remained unheeded, see also Statement of Michel Lion on behalf of the Democratic Republic of the Congo, 28 June 2000, http://212.153.43.18/icjwww/idocket/ico/ico_cr/ico_icr2000-24_translation.htm).

[1819] See Security Council Resolution 1355 (2001) of 15 June 2001, S/RES/1355 (2001).

[1820] See also, for example, the Report of the Security Council's Mission to the Great Lakes Region, S/2001/521, at 15: "The mission reaffirmed the respective obligations of the parties as

Kisangani area that the Council had urged an *immediate* withdrawal, while referring to the Lusaka agreement and related instruments for the rest of Congolese territory.[1821] This was apparently not acknowledged by the DRC, who argued during the oral proceedings that the measures requested aimed at a reinforcement of the resolution (the text of which it considered clear and unambiguous), that there was no incompatibility between the resolution and the request, that the timetable of the Lusaka agreement had long expired, and that the reference to that timetable consequently was to be understood as emphasizing the call for a withdrawal without delay.[1822] However, the resolution had been adopted in full consciousness of the expiry of the respective timetable and had nevertheless set the withdrawal in context with these instruments, which implied that there was a difference between the resolution's sections 3 (concerning an immediate and complete withdrawal from Kisangani) and 4 (concerning the withdrawal from the entire territory, where reference was made to the Lusaka agreement supplemented by the Kampala disengagement plan and later the Harare agreement).[1823] Section 4(b) explicitly stipulated that the withdrawal had to take place in phases reciprocated by the withdrawal of the other parties.[1824] Yet what the DRC aimed at was to interpret these two sections in the same manner, so that Uganda had to withdraw *immediately* from the *entire* Congolese territory without further conditions. Hence, under the heading of a request for measures "compatible" with the resolution, even representing its *reinforcement*, the DRC actually applied for a different measure, an immediate withdrawal, a claim that also formed part of its submissions in the main proceedings.[1825] Another motive might have been that the DRC desired to increase pressure on Uganda individually (which in the Security Council resolution was just

specified in the resolutions of the Security Council, including resolution 1304 (2000), particularly that all foreign forces must withdraw from the Democratic Republic of the Congo. This withdrawal must be conducted in a phased and orderly manner and proceed on a mutual and reciprocal basis according to pre-negotiated plans accepted by all the parties."

[1821] Compare sections 3 and 4 of the resolution's operative part, *supra* n. 1811.

[1822] Statement of Olivier Corten on behalf of the DRC, public sitting of 28 June 2000, http://212.153.43.18/icjwww/idocket/ico/ico_cr/ico_icr2000-24_translation.htm. For the timetable, see Annex B to the Lusaka Agreement, *supra* n. 1806 at 539–40.

[1823] See Security Council Resolution 1355 (2001) of 15 June 2001, S/RES/1355 (2001).

[1824] *Supra* n. 1811. See also, for example, the Report of the Security Council's Mission to the Great Lakes Region, S/2001/521, at 15: "The mission reaffirmed the respective obligations of the parties as specified in the resolutions of the Security Council, including resolution 1304 (2000), particularly that all foreign forces must withdraw from the Democratic Republic of the Congo. This withdrawal must be conducted in a phased and orderly manner and proceed on a mutual and reciprocal basis according to pre-negotiated plans accepted by all the parties."

[1825] In its application instituting proceedings, *supra* n. 1800, the DRC had similarly asked the Court to adjudge and declare that "Ugandan armed forces shall forthwith vacate the territory of the Democratic Republic of the Congo."

one of the addressees): the measures requested were directed at Uganda only, creating at least a presumption of illegal behavior on its part.[1826]

There are some factors which might raise doubts on whether Congo acted in good faith when making its request. In particular, its insistence that the timetable of the Lusaka agreement had expired might appear disingenuous if one considers the failures by the DRC itself to implement that agreement.[1827]

Uganda opposed the indication of provisional measures and held that the request was inadmissible because of the existence of Resolution 1304, or, at least, that it should not be granted because of judicial propriety; moreover, it argued that the Lusaka cease-fire agreement formed a comprehensive system of public order in the region and that the focus should be on its implementation, and that the Kabila regime bore the greatest responsibility for the delays. It also invoked issues of procedural fairness and security and claimed that the prerequisites of urgency and a risk of an irreparable damage were not fulfilled.[1828]

4. The Court and the Security Council resolution: possible routes

The Court could certainly not ignore the Security Council resolution, a decision binding on the parties under Chapter VII. A possible course of action for the Court could have been a refusal to indicate provisional measures in the presence of the resolution. Uganda asked the Court to proceed this way,[1829] based on the Court's previous case law: the orders rejecting requests for interim measures in the Lockerbie[1830] and Aegean Continental Shelf[1831] cases. However, the situations were distinguishable. Unlike the applicant in the Lockerbie cases, the DRC did not ask the Court to set aside a Security Council resolution, but rather to enforce a certain interpretation of a given resolution. On the other hand, the Aegean Continental Shelf

---

[1826] The Security Council Resolution stated at section 4 a that Uganda had violated the sovereignty and territorial integrity of the DRC, see *supra* n. 1811.

[1827] For example, in its Third Report on the United Nations Mission in the Democratic Republic of the Congo of 12 June 2000, the UN Secretary-General criticized the DRC government's lack of cooperation with MONUC and of commitment to the Inter-Congolese dialogue. He summarized: "The people of the Democratic Republic of the Congo desire peace. The Government, the rebel groups and the governments of the belligerent countries have to demonstrate that they also desire it. Their repeated undertakings to cooperate with MONUC are not always supported by action." S/2000/566, 8–9.

[1828] See the statements of Bart Katureebe, Ian Brownlie, and Paul Reichler on behalf of Uganda, Public Sitting of 28 June 2000, http://212.153.43.18/icjwww/idocket/ico/ico_cr/ico_icr2000-23.html. For a summary of both parties' submissions, see *Kritsiotis*, 50 ICLQ (2001), at 663–5; *Lovelace*, www.asil.org/insights/insigh48.htm, at 1–3; and the Order, paras. 18–31, 39 ILM at 1104–8.

[1829] See Order of 1 July 2000, para. 26.   [1830] *Supra* n. 1815.

[1831] Aegean Sea Continental Shelf (Greece v. Turkey), Interim Protection, Order of 11 September 1976. See for the details of the case *Oellers-Frahm*, "Aegean Sea Continental Shelf Case," in EPIL I, at 48–50 with further references.

case was also rather different: in that case, the Court had rejected Greece's request for the indication of provisional measures following a Security Council resolution adopted fifteen days after the request for provisional measures and while the oral proceedings on the interim measures were taking place,[1832] arguing that it was not to be presumed that either party would fail to heed the recommendations of the Security Council and that therefore, no action by the Court was required.[1833] In this context, the Court could rely on a statement from the Greek foreign minister expressing his trust that the resolution "would clear away the obstacles to a resumption of the dialogue [with Turkey] and lead to the solution of the problem."[1834] In contrast, in the present case, the DRC seemed far more skeptical of the potential effectiveness of Resolution 1304, given that it submitted its request *after* the resolution had been approved.[1835]

There were several precedents where the Court had decided that it was not barred from exercising its judicial function when the Security Council was concurrently seized with a matter.[1836] This made it unlikely that the Court would reject Congo's request for the mere reason that the matter was before the Security Council. On the other hand, it was not to be assumed that the Court would entirely set aside the resolution and ignore the expertise and primary responsibility of the Council concerning the maintenance of international peace and security. The situation had apparently somewhat improved since the resolution, as Uganda's commitment to withdraw from Kisangani[1837] demonstrated. There was no reason to cast doubts on the validity of the resolution, and none of the parties had contested that it was valid and binding. The question was whether and to what extent the Court would feel the need to deviate from the resolution, and whether it would make an explicit reference to the Security Council resolution in the operative part of the order.

5. The order of 1 July 2000

The Court indicated interim measures in the case, albeit not in strict accordance with the terms of the DRC request. The operative part of its order of 1 July 2000, reached by unanimous decision, reads:

[1832] Order of 1 July 2000, at 4, para. 2; 5–6, para. 9; and 12, para. 38.

[1833] Ibid., at 12–13, paras. 37–41. The respective resolution had been Security Council Resolution 395 (1976).

[1834] Ibid., at 12–13, para. 40; it also quotes the Turkish foreign minister with a positive comment on the resolution.

[1835] Anyhow, the Court's decision majority in the 1976 order had been criticized for perceiving its judicial functions too narrowly. See *Oellers-Frahm*, "Aegean Sea Continental Shelf Case," in EPIL I, at 48.

[1836] See, for example, the Tehran Hostages case, *supra* B XIV 4.

[1837] See *supra* n. 1818.

Both parties must, forthwith, prevent and refrain from any action, and in particular any armed action, which might prejudice the rights of the other Party in respect of whatever judgment the Court may render in the case, or which might aggravate or extend the dispute before the Court or make it more difficult to resolve;

Both parties must, forthwith, take all measures necessary to comply with all their obligations under international law, in particular those under the United Nations Charter and the Charter of the Organization of African Unity, and with United Nations Security Council resolution 1304 (2000) of 16 June 2000;

Both parties must, forthwith, take all measures necessary to ensure full respect within the zone of conflict for fundamental human rights and for the applicable provisions of humanitarian law.[1838]

Interestingly, the language in the order differs from all former orders in so far as it uses the word "must" instead of "should." This may have been a reaction to the follow-up of the Court's orders in the Breard and LaGrand cases, where the United States had *inter alia* contested the binding force of those orders on grounds of the language used; by an unambiguous wording, the Court might have intended to strengthen the order's authority.[1839]

The order reinforced obligations already incumbent on the parties, in particular, those under Security Council Resolution 1304. One may ask which parts of Resolution 1304 are thereby reinforced, as the scope of the resolution transcends the legal relations between the parties to the proceedings before the Court, encompassing other countries and non-state actors in addition. To answer this question, it is useful to look at the Court's definition of the rights subject of the dispute and necessitating protection: Congo's rights to sovereignty, territorial integrity, the integrity of its assets and natural resources, its rights to respect for the rules of international humani-

---

[1838] Order of 1 July 2000. Although Judge Oda voted in favor of the order, his declaration rather reads like a dissenting opinion, and one might think that it should have been termed as such: he expresses his belief that the Court was not in a position to grant provisional measures because the case was inadmissible. Here again, as already in the Breard and LaGrand cases, it seems contradictory for a judge to put the legitimacy of his own vote in question by taking part in a decision which the Court—in his view—is not empowered to take. Judge Oda's reasoning might be based on his rejection of a binding force of provisional measures. But even so, it implies an *ultra-vires* action on behalf of the Court and Judge Oda himself. A judge convinced that the Court lacks authority to adopt a certain measure should rather file a dissenting vote, even if the respective decision might be one that "few would ever disagree on."

[1839] Of course, the authoritative text was the French one, and the French formulation was identical to the earlier cases: "La Cour indique [...]: Les parties doivent [...]." Still, although the authoritative version was the French version, the English version stemmed from the Court as well (see the last paragraph of the order: "done in French and English, the French text being authoritative;" on the process of drafting the decision in the two languages, see Rosenne, *World Court*, at 134–5), and it will hardly have been a coincidence that another formulation was chosen. This is confirmed by the fact that in the next case where the Court indicated provisional measures with English as the authoritative language, the Avena case, an unambiguous language ("shall") was chosen: Avena and other Mexican Nationals (Mexico v. United States of America), Order of 5 February 2003, at para. 59.

tarian law, and for the instruments relating to the protection of human rights; on that basis, the Court concluded "that it is upon the rights thus claimed that the Court must focus its attention in its consideration of this request for the indication of provisional measures."[1840] Hence, the provisions of the resolution reinforced by the order as between the parties are in the first place those aimed at the protection of these particular rights, namely, the calls for a general troop withdrawal, a cease-fire in Kisangani and a withdrawal from that area, and respect for humanitarian law and human rights.

But what about, for instance, the DRC's obligations relating to the Inter-Congolese dialogue and both parties' obligations to cooperate with MONUC and the International Committee of the Red Cross? The fact that the order reaffirmed the obligations of both parties and addressed the existence of a serious risk of an aggravation or extension of the dispute advocates in favor of a broad interpretation of the order, to the extent that all those aspects of the resolution with a potential impact on the conflict between Congo and Uganda are covered. One could be inclined to criticize the order's wording for lack of clarity on how the obligations arising from the resolution were supposed to operate in the bilateral relations between the parties. Yet it is questionable whether it would have been appropriate and whether it would have made any difference if the order had singled out individual paragraphs from the resolution and adjusted them to the bilateral framework of the proceedings before the Court. The resolution acknowledged that the war in the Congo involved a variety of parties, and treated it not as a sum of several bilateral disputes but as a multilateral conflict with many interrelated aspects. In this complex situation, it was difficult to predict, for example, the precise repercussions of a failure to cooperate with MONUC or the ICRC. Similarly, a failure of the DRC to engage in the Inter-Congolese dialogue might have led to renewed fighting between government troops and rebels, which could affect Uganda's security interests and precipitate an aggravation of the dispute with Uganda as well. The Secretary-General had repeatedly stressed the significance of the Inter-Congolese dialogue for the settlement of the conflict as a whole.[1841] Therefore, it seemed rather appropriate not to isolate single factors of the resolution as irrelevant for the Ugandan–Congolese relations. A second question is whether a more precise formulation would have made a difference. It is important to bear in mind that the validity of Resolution 1304 was not actually disputed, nor was the content of the applicable international law. Bearing this in mind, it seems unlikely that it would have produced different results if the Court had picked phrases from the resolution and specifically tailored them to the

---

[1840] Order of 1 July 2000, para. 40.
[1841] For example, 3rd report, S/2000/566, 9 and 4th report of the Secretary-General, S/2000/888, 13.

bilateral relations between the DRC and Uganda.[1842] If the parties—at least verbally—do not oppose a resolution, there would not be much reason to assume that that they would pay more regard to an excerpt of the resolution than to the resolution in its entirety.

The order did not follow the DRC request, nor did it provide specific indications explicitly incorporating sections of the relevant resolution as the Court had done in the Genocide case.[1843] Unlike those requested, the measures indicated were directed at both parties. Through the reference to Resolution 1304, the order contained obligations more precise than the ones not to aggravate the dispute and to observe international law, since the resolution had prescribed a variety of concrete measures with a view to a comprehensive settlement of the dispute.[1844] Still, the calls for respect for the respective resolution and international law remained general in character: the measures indicated were, as Judge Oda observed, "measures on which few would ever disagree"[1845]—nobody, not even the parties, contested that they were bound to respect the resolution as well as international law. The implementation was yet likely to be difficult, as neither the parties' verbal acknowledgment of the bindingness of Resolution 1304 nor of their obligations relating to human rights, humanitarian law, and the sovereignty over natural resources had prevented violations of international law before (which raised the question of the will and/or capacity of both sides to prevent such violations in the future, independent of verbal commitments).[1846] With regard to one particular obligation under the resolution—the troop withdrawal from the entire DRC territory—the Court's blanket reinforcement of the resolution left the dispute about the substance of that obligation unsettled: this was a question that required a legal analysis, as the resolution had placed this obligation in the framework of the Lusaka agreement. The interpretation of this provision had been a sticking point in the hearings on interim protection, and the Court failed to give explanations, which limited the potential impact of the order. As this question of substantive law remained unanswered, both parties could stick with their position: Uganda pointing to its security interests and the overall framework of the Lusaka

---

[1842] But see *Kritsiotis*, 50 ICLQ (2001), at 669, in whose view "it would have doubtless enhanced the determinate nature and potential effectiveness of the measures articulated" if the Court had selected the particular provisions in mind and tailored them to the parties.

[1843] *Supra.*

[1844] In any event, the measures requested by the DRC had not been much more precise, see the text of the request, *supra* n. 1814. But see *Kritsiotis*, 50 ICLQ (2001), at 668, arguing that the interim measures "bear a marked contrast to the detailed measures sought by the DRC in its request."

[1845] Declaration of Judge Oda, 39 ILM 1113–1115, at 1113. See also *Kritsiotis*, 50 ICLQ (2001), at 667–8, expressing concern that the measures amounted to "nothing more than a series of basis but important generalities."

[1846] Admittedly, though, at the time of the issuance of the Order, it was too early to make a finding on the ultimate efficiency of Security Council Resolution 1304.

agreement; Congo to the lapse of the respective timetable and a resulting need for an immediate withdrawal.

6. The follow-up to the interim measures

This is a case where the question of the responsibility for the violations of the applicable rules of international law—to be decided in the judgment of the merits—and that of compliance with interim measures partially coincide.[1847] If the Court eventually holds Uganda responsible for violations of its obligations towards Congo for events subsequent to the indication of provisional measures, this will imply that Uganda violated the order of 1 July 2000. Therefore, the final judgment might include findings concerning compliance with the order, although they might not be explicitly mentioned as such.

At present, it seems safe to say that while the situation has improved and the resolution and order have generated a limited positive response neither has been fully implemented. A part of the objectives of both instruments was achieved: Uganda withdrew its troops from Kisangani, maintaining them at a distance of some 100 kilometers from its center.[1848] It had mainly been the events in Kisangani that had given the impetus for Security Council Resolution 1304 and the interim proceedings before the Court, so the implementation of the cease-fire there and Uganda's withdrawal from that area was a success. Already during the proceedings, there had been positive signs in this respect.[1849] While it is difficult to say how much of a role the ICJ order had played and whether Uganda would have respected the Security Council

---

[1847] See *infra* Chapter 4 B IV.

[1848] See the various Reports of the UN Secretary-General on the United Nations Organization Mission in the Democratic Republic of the Congo (MONUC): 8th Report 8 June 2001, S/2001/572, at 6; 7th Report, 17 April 2001, S/2001/373, 6; 6th Report 12 February S/2001/128, 4; 5th Report 6 December 2000, S/2000/1156, 6, 13; 4th Report 21 September 2000, S/2000/888, 5, 12. But see a letter from the DRC Government to the President of the Security Council of 26 February 2001 claiming that Ugandan forces had not been withdrawn from Kisangani contrary to Res. 1304 (2000): S/2001/174 at 3. However, most likely, thereby it was referring to a withdrawal from the region, not from the city itself. This is a broader understanding of No. 3 of Resolution 1304 than the one adopted by the UN Secretary-General, who, in the above-mentioned reports, stated that Uganda had limited its forces to a distance of some 100 km "in compliance with SC Resolution 1304(2000)": see, for example, S/2000/1156 p. 6. The rebel group Rassemblement Congolais pour la Démocratie (supposedly backed by Rwanda) has failed to comply with No. 3 of Resolution 1304; see Statement of the President of the Security Council of 24 July 2001, S/PRST/2001/19; Security Council Resolution 1355 of 15 June 2001, A 5; 10th report of the Secretary-General on MONUC, 15 February 2002, S/2002/169, 7–8, paras. 42–7. This rebel goup is an addressee of Resolution 1304, but not of the Court's Order. Peace and security for the inhabitants of Kisangani has still not been achieved; in May 2002 massacres took place, but there was no claim that Uganda had been involved, see Human Rights Watch Press Release, Congo: Kisangani residents again under fire, May 2002, www.hrw.org/press/2002/05/congo0524.htm; Statement of the President of the Security Council, 24 May 2002, S/PRST/2002/17.

[1849] Already during the hearings, Uganda had declared that it had withdrawn from Kisangani as required, Statement of Mr Paul Reichler, on behalf of Uganda, Public sitting of 28 June 2000, http://212.153.43.18/icjwww/idocket/ico/ico_cr/ico_icr2000–23.html. The Secretary-General's 3rd

resolution in any case, the order and the pending proceedings might have increased the pressure to effect the withdrawal. As regards the general cease-fire, initially, frequent violations were reported;[1850] then came a period of respect for the cease-fire from January 2001 until March 2002, when fighting resumed in some areas, but apparently not attributable to either party's action but to a rebel group.[1851] Hence, No. 1 of the resolution was respected to some extent, although not entirely.

It was just in 2003, following the conclusion of the Luanda agreement,[1852] that significant progress towards a troop withdrawal was reached.[1853] The question on whether this mere fact constitutes non-compliance hangs on the interpretation of the relevant provision of the resolution (section 4), a controversial issue not explicitly addressed by the Court. As explained above, the resolution set the obligation to withdraw in the framework of the Lusaka agreement and the Kampala plan. Therefore, the decisive question was

Report on MONUC of 12 June 2000 refers to reports indicating a northward retreat by Ugandan forces: S/2000/566, at 3. Congo had conceded in the hearings that Uganda's withdrawal had started, Statement of Mr Olivier Corten on behalf of the DRC, Public sitting of 26 June 2000, http://212.153.43.18/icjwww/idocket/ico/ico_cr/ico_icr2000–20_translation.htm, but stated that the completion was yet unconfirmed, Statement by Mr Michel Lion on behalf of the DRC, Public sitting of 28 June 2000, http://212.153.43.18/icjwww/idocket/ico/ico_cr/ico_icr2000–24_transla tion.htm: "[T]hey did not refer to the serious and important events that have taken place in Kisangani, apart from stating that they withdrew 120 km from Kisangani, *which is perhaps unconfirmed* [...]." (emphasis added).

[1850] See, for example, the assessment of the UN Secretary-General in his 4th report on MONUC, *supra* n. 1848: "I regret to inform the Security Council that there has been little progress, if any, in the implementation of the Lusaka Ceasefire Agreement. The cease-fire has been consistently violated in the intensified fighting between government and rebel and UPDF [= Ugandan People Defence Force] forces in northern Équateur province."

[1851] The violation of the cease-fire was attributed to RCD-Goma and to none of the parties before the Court. S/RES/1399 (2002) of 19 March 2002, 10th report of the Secretary-General on MONUC, 15 February 2002, S/2002/169, at 4, para. 22. See further Uganda to pull troops out, BBC News, 10 February 2003, http://news.bbc.co.uk/1/hi/world/africa/2744215.stm; Delayed Ugandan pull out begins, BBC News, 25 April 2003, http://news.co.uk/1/hi/world/africa/2971045.stm .

[1852] For the Luanda agreement (Agreement between the Governments of the Democratic Republic of the Congo and the Republic of Uganda on Withdrawal of Ugandan Troops from the Democratic Republic of the Congo, Cooperation and Normalisation of Relations between the Two Countries, 6 September 2002), see http://www.state.gov/t/ac/csbm/rd/2002/22627.htm.

[1853] See 8th report of the Secretary-General on MONUC of 8 June 2001, S/2001/572, 2. At 5–6 it is reported that the Ugandan withdrawal in the area of Batwasende is hampered by the rebel group RDC's refusal to permit them transit via the airport of Kisangani. In a statement of 7 May 2001 transmitted to the President of the Security Council, Uganda announced a withdrawal from ten locations, but maintained a presence in other zones and stated that it reserved the right unilaterally to withdraw from the Lusaka agreement: Statement dated 7 May 2001 by the First Deputy Prime Minister/Minister for Foreign Affairs on Uganda's troop withdrawal from the Democratic Republic of the Congo, Annex to a Letter dated 8 May 2001 from the chargé d'affaires a.i. of the Permanent Mission of Uganda to the United Nations addressed to the President of the Security Council, S/2001/461. Pursuant to the 10th report of the Secretary-General on MONUC of 15 February 2002, S/2002/169, a total of 6,655 Ugandan troops have been withdrawn, but Uganda insists on a presence of three of its battalions in the Eastern Congo, and there were some concerns that it might reinforce its presence there: paras. 23–4, 94.

whether Uganda could be said to have violated the provisions of the Lusaka agreement—which was difficult to answer.[1854] Since the resolution's provision for a total troop withdrawal is directed at the DRC as well, the DRC will in this context also have to account for the detrimental impact of its own behavior on the implementation of the Lusaka agreement and the Kampala plan. The UN Secretary-General's fourth report on MONUC stated that progress on the disengagement plan had been stalled since late July 2000, when the DRC government had withdrawn from the Joint Military Commission deliberations on this subject[1855] shortly after the indication of the provisional measures: the DRC itself had thus taken action likely to deteriorate prospects for Uganda's withdrawal. Uganda's security concerns also had to be addressed. While the Secretary-General continued to ask for the full implementation of the Lusaka agreement, he acknowledged that a withdrawal was not without risks: "The vacuum left by the withdrawal of foreign forces in some areas may permit the resurgence of conflicts which the presence of those forces might have helped to check."[1856] It was uncertain whether the DRC government would be able to exercise effective control over the whole territory[1857] while satisfying all of Uganda's security interests. As the Secretary-General acknowledged: "Borders can be considered truly secure only if all four governments are at peace with one another."[1858]

There are strong indications that in the eastern territory of the DRC controlled by Uganda, human rights violations have been taking place on a large scale, which were partially attributed to Ugandan officials in UN and NGO reports.[1859] A UN expert panel concluded that Uganda has illegally exploited Congo's natural resources on a large scale.[1860] The panel went as

---

[1854] Assigning blame for the lack of implementation of the Lusaka agreement would go beyond the scope of the present study; in the proceedings on the merits, the Court will have to deal with the question on whether Uganda's continued presence on DRC territory can be justified.

[1855] 4th Report of 21 September 2000, S/2000/888, at 12.

[1856] 7th Report of the Secretary-General on MONUC, 14, see also the addendum to the report of the panel of experts, *supra* n. 1805 at 20, para. 95: "Uganda [...] has some legitimate security threats, which prompted its military intervention in the Democratic Republic of the Congo."

[1857] See the Report of the Security Council Mission to the Great Lakes Region, S/2001/521, at 16.

[1858] Secretary General's 7th Report on MONUC, 16. As far as the remaining part of the Order is concerned—the call to the parties for compliance with all their obligations under international law—it would go beyond the scope of the present study to provide a full account of violations of international law in the relations between Uganda and the DRC; again, such questions will be raised in the proceedings on the merits.

[1859] See the reports by Human Rights Watch, "Uganda in Eastern Congo: Fuelling political and ethnical strife," March 2001, www.hrw.org/reports/2001/drc/drc0301-03.htm, "DR Congo: Scores killed in new ethnic fighting," 13 February 2002, www.hrw.org/press/2002/02/bunia0213. htm, "Attacks on civilians in Ugandan occupied areas in Northeastern Congo," 13 February 2002, www.hrw.org/backgrounder/africa/bunia0213bkg.htm. See also the UN Secretary-General's 7th Report, 12.

[1860] See *supra* n. 1805.

far as to state that Uganda's President Museveni has put himself in a position of an accomplice with regard to criminal activities by his relatives and Ugandan officials.[1861] The panel's findings were severely criticized by President Museveni,[1862] but as independent assessment by experts drawing from a variety of sources[1863] they cannot be easily dismissed, and all the more since subsequent reports of the panel (with a partially changed composition) confirm an involvement of Ugandan officials in the exploitation of DRC resources.[1864] The most recent reports suggest that some progress has been made and that at least some of the persons involved in the exploitation are being held responsible.[1865]

7. Conclusion

The precise extent of non-compliance with the provisional measures remains to be seen pending further examination in the proceedings on the merits, unless the case is discontinued before that point. The situation has somewhat improved and parts of the resolution (and thereby also of the order) have been implemented, although it is not quite clear whether the ICJ order had much of an impact in achieving this result. The order itself garnered no mention in UN documents such as the subsequent Security Council resolutions,[1866] statements of the President,[1867] and various reports.[1868] Still, the existence of the order and the pending proceedings might have constrained the parties' actions and therefore ameliorated the situation.

[1861] Panel's First Report, ibid., at 40–1.

[1862] Report of the Security Council Mission to the Great Lakes Region, 15–16 May 2001, S/2001/521, 14.

[1863] For an explanation of the methodological framework, see *supra* n. 1805 (first report), 4–5.

[1864] It should be noted that the subsequent reports omit a direct reference to President Museveni. Addendum to the Report, *supra* n. 1805 (see in particular 20, paras. 97–8: "While the effect of the Panel's report and the significant withdrawal of UPDF Troops have given the impression that the exploitation activities have been reduced, they are in fact continuing. [. . .] While the Government of Uganda does not participate directly in the exploitation activities, the culture in which its military personnel function tolerates and condones their activities.") and interim report, ibid. (confirming the earlier reports and speaking about the involvement of the foreign armies in general terms).

[1865] Final Report 2002, transmitted by a letter of the Secretary-General to the Security Council of Final Report 2003, transmitted by a letter of the Secretary-General to the Security Council of 23 October 2003, S/2003/1027, at para. 71: "The Panel's work has spurred Governments, NGOs and other organizations or associations to pursue their own investigations into the plundering of resources.(. . .) In Uganda, following his implication in exploitation in the Democratic Republic of the Congo by a government commission, thee head of the defence forces, General Kazini, was relieved of its post." See further on this case "Profile: Major General James Kazini, 9 June 2003, http://news.bbc.co.uk/1/hi/world/africa/2974496.stm. See also "Museveni's brother resigns amid corruption and looting charges," http://www.irinnews.org/report.asp?ReportID=38168& SelectRegion=Great_Lakes&SelectCountry=DRC-UGANDA.

[1866] S/RES/1332 (2000), S/RES/1341 (2000), S/RES/1355 (2001).

[1867] See, for example, S/PRST/2001/19 of 24 July 2001.

[1868] See the reports quoted *supra* 1805 and 1848.

Nevertheless, the content of the interim measures was not such as to assume that they would have a significant role or enjoy full compliance. The Court used general terms when it called on both parties to respect the Security Council resolution and international law; as both parties acknowledged the bindingness and relevance of the resolution as well as of international law as such, the order stated little beyond what the parties already agreed upon. The Court might have had good reasons for not adopting more concrete measures: not enough time had passed to assess whether the resolution had adequately addressed the conflict, and it would not have been appropriate to ignore the expertise of the Security Council.[1869] On the other hand, a refusal to indicate interim measures might have been interpreted as indifference in face of armed conflict and human suffering. In this situation, the Court might have regarded an appeal for the observance of the law as the best approach.

One should not expect miracles from such measures on which "few would ever disagree"[1870]—still, they might have some positive impact, if only for the reason that both countries had to present their case before the Court where there was the possibility of the adoption of further measures and of claims of state responsibility on the merits. As this case shows, measures that are broadly formulated are by their nature likely to attract some compliance and some non-compliance.[1871]

XII. Conclusion: A mixed record for provisional measures

A review of practice with regard to provisional measures leads to a balance altogether different from the experience in the case of judgments. Provisional measures were successfully implemented in only one case—Frontier Dispute; in the other ten cases, non-compliance was the rule, rather than the exception.[1872] At first sight, this scorecard may raise doubts as to the potential efficiency of the Court's ability to provide interim protection and even offer ammunition to deny the binding force of provisional measures.[1873] A closer inspection reveals a more differentiated picture, however. Over the last

---

[1869] But see *Kritsiotis*, 50 ICLQ (2001), at 669.

[1870] See the quotation of Judge Oda, *supra* n. 1845.

[1871] Critical *Kritsiotis*, 50 ICLQ (2001), at 669 fn. 50: "Formulations of provisional measures such as those indicated in the present Order could be advanced as a partial explanation on why the overall record of compliance with provisional measures has been described as 'not encouraging.'"

[1872] But see *Mennecke/Tams*, 42 GYIL (1999), at 208 fn. 69; and *Addo*, 10 EJIL (1999), at 721, who also quote Land and Maritime Boundary between Cameroon and Nigeria as a case of full compliance: an assessment that cannot be safely made given the developments in the case.

[1873] Indeed, the US cited the practice to support their argument that provisional measures are non-binding: US Counter-memorial, at para. 161: "The practice of States also shows that the Court's indications of provisional measures have not been understood to impose binding obligations. Indeed, for the most part, Parties have not carried the actions recommended by

decades, there has been some positive development and while implementation often left much to be desired, the measures in several cases fulfilled some useful purposes for the applicant.

The cases of non-compliance with orders indicating provisional measures fall into three main categories. At one extreme are the cases of defiance: those cases in which the state in question openly refuses to implement the decision and to accept it as binding, thereby directly attacking the authority of the Court. These include all the orders made up to 1984: Anglo-Iranian Oil Company, Fisheries Jurisdiction, Nuclear Tests, United States Diplomatic and Consular Staff in Tehran, and—to a certain extent—Military and Paramilitary Activities in and against Nicaragua.[1874] The second category comprises the cases where the provisional measures were accepted by both sides, but it is disputed whether the verbal commitment of both sides was, or is, being matched by sufficient action. In these cases, the dispute centers on facts, and some measures confirmed legal rules that were not the actual point of controversy. In principle, the Court's authority remains untouched, as the parties acknowledge the existence of the norm; yet, doubts are cast as to the Court's efficiency and its ability truly to provide interim *protection*. Falling under this category are the orders in Application of the Convention on the Prevention and Punishment of the Crime of Genocide, Land and Maritime Boundary between Cameroon and Nigeria, and Armed Activities on the Territory of the Congo.

The two cases on consular assistance (Breard (Vienna Convention on Consular Relations) and LaGrand) form a category unto themselves, with the respective orders being made in similar situations under almost identical terms. There, the implementation problem had two dimensions. On the one hand, there was uncertainty as to the binding force of ICJ provisional

---

the Court into full effect, leading one commentator to observe, albeit reluctantly, that: 'It is at least open to argument that States themselves have built up a body of practice, treating interim measures as nonbinding. In other words, it could be argued that there has been a de facto clarification of Article 41.'" (fn. omitted). Critical on this argumentation *Mennecke/Tams*, 42 GYIL (1999), at 208–9. See also *Addo*, 10 EJIL (1999), at 725: "It is possible to argue that Article 41 of the ICJ Statute has lost some or all of its binding character as a consequence of the continuing disregard with which most respondent states have treated the provisional orders directed at them. However, the state practice on the matter is an ineffectiveness of provisional measures in practice rather than of their non-binding nature." (fn. omitted).

[1874] The last case somewhat differs from the former in that there had been some positive response: the US House of Representatives halted official aid for Contra military activities some time. *Oda* in Lowe/Fitzmaurice, Fifty years of the ICJ, at 555, observes that the respondent did not seem to comply fully with the order, "although there was no open act of defiance on its part." Yet, the US reaction in so far as there was no compliance can be classified as defiance; the Reagan administration never accepted the measures in principle nor made an attempt of implementation; moreover, the non-compliance is to be seen in context with the US government's overall policy concerning the proceedings, particularly after the judgment on jurisdiction. Admittedly, though, the provisional measures were less of an object of attack than the judgments in the case.

measures, in general, and of the specific measures, in particular: before the Court, the alleged lack of bindingness was used as argument to justify non-implementation. On the other hand, there were heterogeneous domestic structures in the enforcement of international law, with the government having an interest in observing the respective ICJ order, but being unwilling or unable under the domestic constitutional order to compel compliance by a subunit with less concern for the demands of international law. This third category is unique in so far as after the LaGrand judgment, which confirmed the binding force of the Court's provisional measures in unequivocal terms, no state can any longer sustain in good faith a lack of binding force of provisional measures. Should similar cases occur in which a local governor refuses to implement an ICJ order despite being on notice of the bindingness of provisional measures, it would have to be classified as a case of defiance—with the respective negative impact on the Court's authority. It is a positive sign for the Court that cases of defiance have not occurred since the order in the Nicaragua case in 1984. While the initial observation that full compliance arose in only one case must consequently be modified, the record remains troublesome, as in most cases, the Court's measures did not prove efficient protection for the rights subject to adjudication.

Focusing solely on full compliance and on the deviation from the *ideal* follow-up may be viewing the matter too narrowly. A broader optic that takes even partial responses into account—regardless of violations—will reveal the extent to which the measures had some ameliorative effect and actually prevented the worst-case scenario. Even in cases of outright defiance, such as Military and Paramilitary Activities in and against Nicaragua,[1875] or in Land and Maritime Boundary between Cameroon and Nigeria,[1876] and Armed Activities on the Territory of the Congo,[1877] in which a fear of further escalation existed, the behavior of parties after the order can be seen as contributing to a calming of tensions.

Interim orders in most cases fulfilled some useful purpose for the litigant, irrespective of actual compliance.[1878] In Nuclear Tests, for example, the orders might have played a role in exerting diplomatic pressure on France and speeding up its eventual decision to terminate atmospheric nuclear tests

---

[1875] See *supra* VI 3, 4: a calming of the situation, a halt of official aid for Contra military activities, and no further mining activities.

[1876] See *supra* VII 4; in general, the situation calmed down, which the parties' representatives acknowledged.

[1877] See *supra* XI 6: the withdrawal from Kisangani undoubtedly took place; in general, tensions somewhat eased.

[1878] Yet this cannot be said in the following cases: Anglo-Iranian Oil Company, Vienna Convention on Consular Relations and LaGrand. In Fisheries Jurisdiction, one might see at least some positive development in that the UK and Iceland reached an interim agreement; there does not appear to be any indication for an influence of the Court's provisional measures on that achievement, though.

(*inter alia* by strengthening domestic opposition).[1879] Similar goals were realized through the Court's orders in United States Diplomatic and Consular Staff in Tehran and Military and Paramilitary Activities in and against Nicaragua.[1880] In the Genocide case, the order was framed in such a way as to foreshadow an indication of Yugoslavian involvement in genocide in Bosnia, and thus strengthened the position of the applicant.[1881] In Land and Maritime Boundary between the Cameroon and Nigeria, besides the positive effect of a calming of tensions, Cameroon gained more publicity for its cause and made the Court aware of the precarious nature of the dispute and the need for rapid settlement. Similar objectives were reached through the order in Armed activities on the territory of the Congo.[1882] Finally, several cases raise the question whether the applicant had in the first place made its request in the true expectation that it would be complied with, or whether it had ulterior motives which the order did or did not satisfy. In the Genocide case and in Armed activities on the territory of the Congo, the applicants sought to achieve a certain interpretation of a Security Council resolution: Congo in the latter case to the extent that Uganda had immediately and unconditionally to withdraw from Congolese territory; Bosnia in the former through an order that it should be considered exempt from the arms embargo imposed by the respective resolution. In fact, in this case the desire for a declaration of its rights towards the whole international community was likely to have been one of Bosnia's principal motives, particularly in view of its second request attempting to broaden the basis of the Court's jurisdiction.

In sum, too big anxiety over the fact that full compliance arose in one case appears misplaced. None the less, the record of compliance and efficiency of provisional measures is far from satisfactory and offers a stark contrast *vis-à-vis* the overall positive picture of compliance with judgments. Factors relevant for the difference in the records of those two types of decisions will be taken up in the following chapter, which considers the lessons learned from an analysis of practice.

[1879] *Supra* III 4, 5, 7.
[1880] In addition to the huge benefit for Nicaragua of a halt of official aid to military activities to the Contras from 1984 to 1986, *supra* VI 3, 4.
[1881] *Supra* VII 6.
[1882] *Supra* VIII 4, 5; XI 6, 7.

4

Lessons to be Learned from the Practice

A. GENERAL OBSERVATIONS

The analysis of practice has shown a generally satisfactory compliance record for judgments and a more problematical (yet somewhat successful) one for provisional measures. For both types of decisions, the Nicaragua case marked a paradigm shift as the last in a series of instances of open defiance and non-appearance. The authority of judgments or provisional measures was not subsequently challenged. The limited efficiency of the provisional measures following the Nicaragua decision owes to reasons other than an overt non-compliance: all parties pretended to have complied with the provisional measures.

I. Compliance and usefulness

Compliance and usefulness are related, but not identical, concepts: in most cases of judgments and in several cases of provisional measures, the applicants derived some benefit from the respective decisions despite rejection by the other side or deficiencies in the implementation.[1] On the other hand, non-compliance will not be the only factor rendering a decision futile for the applicant. A favorable judgment will be of little use if it falls below its expectations, or if the situation changes so as to render the decision meaningless.[2]

II. Defiance and non-appearance before the Court: The Nicaragua judgment as a turning point

A common thread running through all cases of *defiance*, i.e. deliberate and open refusal to honor the Court's decisions, is the refusal of the respondent to participate in some stage of the proceedings.[3] It is unsurprising that a state that boycotts the proceedings based upon a principled argument denying the Court's competence to decide the dispute will stick to its position and refuse

---

[1] See *supra* Chapter 3 B XXVIII and C XII.

[2] See, for example, the Rights of Passage over Indian territory case and the Fisheries Jurisdiction cases, *supra* Chapter 3 B VI 3 and XII 5–6.

[3] In some cases, the respondent participated only in limited portions of the litigation. Albania boycotted the Corfu Channel proceedings on the assessment of the amount of compensation, contesting the Court's jurisdiction in this regard. The Anglo-Iranian Oil Company case's interim proceedings took place without the respondent, who did participate in the proceedings on jurisdiction. The US still participated during the interim measures phase in Military and

to honor the decision once delivered.[4] In fact, a change of position could be seen as acknowledgment of the untenability of its earlier position, although such a change could take place if, for example, the state benefits from the decision or there is a shift at the domestic level, such as a new government. The correlation between non-appearance and defiance relates to the extent that the former will likely contribute to the latter.

Fortunately, cases of defiance and non-appearance—which are surely the most worrisome for the Court as they amount to a direct attack on its authority—have not recurred since the Nicaragua case. There is no sufficient evidence suggesting non-compliance with subsequent judgments; as for provisional measures, the addressees have either refuted the *factual* allegations relating to compliance or framed *legal* arguments supporting the conformity of the behavior with the respective order.

Yet the absence of cases of non-appearance and defiance in recent times should not lead to a false sense of security. It is true that the political cost for states boycotting ICJ proceedings has substantially increased since the 1970s, when a series of non-appearances not only encouraged similar behavior but also might have made lawful behavior appear a sign of weakness.[5] Today, the Court enjoys a prestige higher than ever, there are no longer any significant allegations that it is biased in favor of certain groups of states, and it is seized by countries from the entire world with different cultural and ideological backgrounds. Non-appearance in ICJ proceedings will win little sympathy for the state concerned. Yet while all these considerations make recurrence of this phenomenon less probable, the Court must be aware that the threat of non-appearance still exists and that its means of addressing such a situation are limited. Moreover, the absence of cases of non-appearance in no way guarantees that cases of defiance will not occur; especially for judgments, it is very well imaginable that following an unfavorable judgment, a state might challenge that decision despite its earlier commitment to the settlement process.[6]

III. Delays and difficulties in implementation: Problems to some degree inevitable

Problems implementing decisions of the ICJ are inevitable to some degree. They may arise as a result of the subject-matter of the respective decision—be

paramilitary activities in and against Nicaragua, but withdrew after the Court's subsequent judgment on jurisdiction. Three respondents in the cases under revision completely boycotted proceedings: Iceland (Fisheries Jurisdiction), Iran (United States Diplomatic and Consular Staff in Tehran), and France (Nuclear Tests).

[4] See *Collins*, 234 RdC (1992) at 220.

[5] See *Oxman* in Damrosch, The ICJ at a crossroads, at 333.

[6] Hopefully the Land and Maritime Boundary between Cameroon and Nigeria will not become an example, see *supra* Introduction n. 12—at present it seems as if the parties are making efforts to arrive at a settlement.

it a matter of a broad character of the underlying legal rule, the features of the specific decision, or practical circumstances. Difficulties are unsurprising where the Court's decision calls for negotiation when the parties turned to the Court in the first place precisely because of the difficulty of arriving at some negotiated solution.[7] The lack of precision of the measures (rather than of the applicable law) might represent a source of conflict, such as when the Court orders the withdrawal of troops to positions whose location it does not specify further.[8] Decisions requiring substantial logistical efforts, such as transfers of a settled population, are clearly of a different magnitude than decisions on maritime delimitation, for example.[9]

In cases presenting likely obstacles for implementation, it is desirable for the parties to address such problems beforehand and include specific provisions to this extent in the special agreement or regulate controversial questions separately.[10] This might take the form of substantive provisions as well as provisions on recourse to further dispute settlement processes. Positive measures by the United Nations or regional organizations might be helpful. Even the Court has facilitated implementation—for instance, by appointing experts to assist in the demarcation, as requested by the parties in a special agreement.[11]

Where implementation is hindered by a lack of sufficient financial resources, a special trust fund set up by the Secretary-General has already proven an effective tool in one judgment.[12]

IV. Source of jurisdiction: Relation of non-compliance and cases of compulsory jurisdiction

In general, the situation where both parties desire an involvement of the Court and have concluded an agreement to that extent is viewed as the ideal scenario for compliance,[13] whereas compulsory jurisdiction provokes greater

[7] See *supra* Chapter 3 B XXVIII; examples are the Asylum/Haya de la Torre case and the Gabčíkovo–Nagymaros cases, *supra* Chapter 3 B II and XXIV.

[8] See the Land and Maritime Boundary between Cameroon and Nigeria case, *supra* Chapter 3 C VIII 3, 5.

[9] Examples are the Land, Island and Maritime Frontier Dispute and the Land and Maritime Boundary between Cameroon and Nigeria case; in the latter, local resistance appears to be a core problem for implementation, see *supra* Introduction n. 12.

[10] For example, in the Minquiers and Ecrehos case, the controversial issue of fishing rights had been dealt with beforehand, see *supra* Chapter 3 B V.

[11] See the Frontier Dispute (Burkina Faso/Mali) case, *supra* Chapter 3 B XVII.

[12] The full name of the fund is the Secretary-General's Trust Fund to Help States in the Settlement of Disputes through the International Court of Justice. See further *supra* Chapter 3 n. 943.

[13] *Oda*, 49 ICLQ (2000), at 257: "The parties to the dispute bring the case before the Court on the understanding that they will naturally comply with the judgment, and it goes without saying that disputes subject to a special agreement between States can most properly be settled by the Court."

suspicion, occasionally even put generally into question. The vast majority of the cases currently on the Court's docket were instituted on the basis of compulsory jurisdiction (i.e. by an instrument conferring jurisdiction on the Court in advance irrespective of a particular dispute). Judge Oda has expressed worries about resulting dangers of non-compliance in an article entitled "The compulsory jurisdiction of the International Court of Justice—a myth?"[14] However, does the analysis of state practice confirm that non-compliance is mainly a problem of compulsory jurisdiction? And has the Court's compulsory jurisdiction really proven inefficient? Reality suggests a more nuanced picture. Compliance problems have arisen both in cases of joint submission and in cases of compulsory jurisdiction, and cases launched without the respondent's consent have frequently produced significant results.

1. The alleged smoothness of proceedings based on specific consent

There are, in fact, many indications to suggest that defiance is less likely where states have given their specific consent to proceedings before the Court. The parties recognize the existence of a dispute and its legal character and agree that the Court is the appropriate settlement mechanism. The ability of the parties to reach a mutual understanding demonstrates at least a minimum of respect and of working channels of communication, as well as some readiness to compromise. The process of a joint formulation of the terms of reference will most likely ensure that all aspects of the dispute are submitted on which the parties consider adjudication desirable. Another positive aspect that can be found in many special agreements is the inclusion of provisions for the post-adjudicative phase.

The potential for dispute is further minimized if the parties reach agreement on the terms of reference: the more clearly defined, the better. On the other hand, where the very existence of a special agreement is disputed by the respondent, the case will come closer to one instituted on the basis of compulsory jurisdiction as a test for the Court's authority.

Table 4.1 shows all cases with an agreement relating to the submission of the specific dispute to the ICJ, irrespective of whether the case was instituted by notification of a special agreement or by unilateral application.[15]

---

[14] *Oda*, 49 ICLQ (2000), at 265: "The parties to the dispute bring the case before the Court on the understanding that they will naturally comply with the judgment, and it goes without saying that disputes subject to a special agreement between States can most properly be settled by the Court."

[15] The terminology is somewhat unclear as to the term "special agreement." Is it every agreement in which the parties undertake to submit a particular dispute to the Court, or only such that define the terms of reference and are notified to the Court according to Article 40(1) of the Statute, forming in themselves the subject-matter of the proceedings (unlike in cases of unilateral application, where this will be determined by the parties' submissions)? Rosenne suggests that only the latter are "true special agreements": Rosenne, *Law and Practice II*, at 663–4: a special agreement in the sense of the Statute and the Rules of Court is an agreement conferring jurisdiction in a concrete case and which is formally notified to the Court and thereby

Table 4.1. Cases with an agreement on the submission of a specific dispute to the ICJ

Cases instituted by notification of a special agreement
- Minquiers and Ecrehos (France/United Kingdom) (1951–3)
- Sovereignty over Certain Frontier Land (Belgium/Netherlands) (1957–9)
- North Sea Continental Shelf (FRG/Denmark; FRG/Netherlands) (1967–9)
- Continental Shelf (Tunisia/Libya) (1978–82)
- Delimitation of the Maritime Boundary in the Gulf of Maine Area (Canada/USA) (1981–4)
- Continental Shelf (Libya/Malta) (1982–5)
- Frontier Dispute (Burkina Faso/Mali) (1983–6)
- Land, Island and Maritime Frontier Dispute (El Salvador/Honduras) (1986–92)
- Territorial Dispute (Libya/Chad) (1990–4)
- Gabčíkovo–Nagymaros (Hungary/Slovakia) (1994–present)
- Kasikili/Sedudu Island (Botswana/Namibia) (1996–9)
- Sovereignty over Pulau Litigan and Pulau Sipadan (Indonesia/Malaysia) (1998–2002)*
- Frontier Dispute (Benin/Niger)(2002–present)*
- Sovereignty over Pedra Branca/Pulau Batu Puteh, Middle Rocks and South Ledge (Malaysia/Singapore) (2003–present)*

Cases instituted by a unilateral application lodged after parties had agreed to submit dispute to the Court
- Asylum (Colombia/Peru) (1949–1950) and Haya de la Torre (Colombia v. Peru) (1950–1)
- Arbitral Award made by the King of Spain in 1906 (Honduras v. Nicaragua) (1958–60)

Cases in which a special agreement was concluded during the proceedings
- Corfu Channel (United Kingdom v. Albania) (1947–9)

Cases under Article 38(5) Rules of Court (consent given after the proceedings were instituted)
- Certain criminal proceedings in France (Democratic Republic of the Congo v. France)*

Cases in which the existence of an agreement on the submission of the concrete dispute was controversial
- Maritime Delimitation and Territorial Questions between Qatar and Bahrain (Qatar v. Bahrain) (1991–2001)

*Compliance cannot yet be assessed/no decision delivered yet

The further one moves down the list in Table 4.1, the weaker the actual basis of consent on the submission of the dispute to the ICJ. Proceedings launched by unilateral application in spite of a preceding agreement might reflect difficulties of the parties in jointly defining the terms of reference, which might open a source for conflict.[16] In the Corfu Channel case, the fact that the UK had already unilaterally instituted proceedings might have persuaded Albania to conclude a special agreement (and thus include its own complaints in the subject-matter of the proceedings) than risk having the Court deal with the case on the basis of the UK application alone. Yet its attitude towards the Court proceedings might not have been as positive as this normally is in the presence of a special agreement. Similarly, despite France's acceptance of the Court's jurisdiction pursuant to Article 38(5) Rules of Court in the Certain Criminal Proceedings case, a state's attitude towards the Court's involvement will usually be more positive where both parties had an equal role in shaping the terms of reference. Finally, the Qatar/Bahrain case came already somewhat close to a case of compulsory jurisdiction in that the respondent opposed the Court's involvement in the matter and denied the acceptance of a binding commitment to take the matter before the Court.[17]

Examining compliance with the decisions in these cases is basically a question of compliance with judgments, as only one case of provisional measures relates to a case with a special agreement, and in that case, the order was successfully implemented.[18]

A look at the cases in the list shows that problems with compliance are not limited to those of compulsory jurisdiction, so that the general assumption that proceedings based on a special agreement work smoothly must be put in perspective. Even though the most extreme cases of defiance are absent from this list, there is the Corfu Channel case, an instance of open refusal to

---

produces the effect of the introduction of the proceedings. The Court's practice does not seem quite consistent, as it lists the Asylum case—a case launched by unilateral application—under "cases submitted to the Court by means of special agreements," whereas it does not for the similar situation in the Arbitral Award made by the King of Spain case, where a framework agreement on the submission of the dispute had been made prior to the unilateral seizing of the Court.

[16] This might partially explain why the Court had to deliver three judgments in the Asylum/Haya de la Torre case, *supra* Chapter 3 B II.

[17] While in cases of notification of a special agreement, the special agreement will determine the subject-matter of the proceedings, this will be the application for cases launched by unilateral application rather than an underlying agreement providing for the dispute's submission to adjudication. As this application comes from one side only, the other party might disagree on the definition of the dispute and a potential for conflict arises. The Qatar/Bahrain case was remarkable in that the Court ruled on the existence of an undertaking to submit the dispute to the ICJ and demanded that the subject-matter be broadened as Qatar's application was too narrowly framed if considered under the terms of the documents providing for submission to the Court.

[18] See Frontier Dispute (Burkina Faso/Mali), *supra* Chapter 3 C V.

comply for several decades (admittedly, though, not an orthodox case of a special agreement).[19] Cases of joint submission are not immune to difficulties; indeed, several cases can be found with delays and difficulties in implementation.[20] In several cases involving special agreements, claims of non-compliance were made, although such claims were unjustified[21] or at the very least not sufficiently proven.[22] Agreements providing for submission of a dispute to the ICJ can in themselves become a source of conflict. The parties might disagree on their interpretation, particularly with regard to the tasks conferred on the Court and the scope of their consent to jurisdiction, which might in the worst scenario result in refusal to comply (as in the Corfu Channel case).[23] Such disputes might be attributable precisely to the earlier inability of the parties to arrive at a less ambiguous formulation of the terms of reference.

Consequently, the variety of factors favoring a successful settlement in cases of joint submission by no means guarantees a smooth implementation. The parties can significantly contribute to minimizing the potential for conflict: terms of reference should be drafted in a precise manner and, if possible, in the desired language of the proceedings.[24] Provisions on an interim régime ensure that the subject-matter of the proceedings is protected in a manner acceptable to both parties without the need to recur to the Court for interim protection. References to the post-adjudicative phase can clarify

[19] This case, often left out of consideration in analyses to support the hypothesis of a lack of efficiency of compulsory jurisdiction, was unusual: the Court was first instituted by unilateral application of the UK, Albania first gave its consent but then denied having done so, and then, a special agreement was concluded and the Court notified accordingly, so that the Court proceedings were brought on another track. Admittedly, it is not a typical case of a special agreement, and Albania might have felt pressured to reach an agreement given the possibility that the Court would confirm its jurisdiction and then the case would be heard under the terms of reference as determined by the applicant only. Still, the case is closer to the "typical cases of special agreements" than to cases launched under the Court's compulsory jurisdiction.

[20] See the Asylum case, the Land, Island and Maritime Frontier case and the Gabčíkovo–Nagymaros case, *supra* Chapter 3 B II, IXX and XXIV. The percentage of cases with difficulties in the group of cases submitted jointly is accordingly rather high.

[21] See Asylum case and the Land, Island and Maritime Frontier case (relating to the demarcation of the land boundary and the delimitation of maritime spaces); in both cases, claims were made under the heading "compliance with the ICJ judgment" although the respective states were trying to enforce rights not expressly restated by those judgments, see *supra* Chapter 3 B XXVIII.

[22] See the Land, Island and Maritime Frontier case (relating to the regime of waters in the Gulf of Fonseca) and the Gabčíkovo–Nagymaros case, *supra* Chapter 3 B XXVIII.

[23] Disputes might concern the tasks conferred on the Court, the nature and extent of the dispute, or the applicable law; examples are Corfu Channel, Continental Shelf (Tunisia/Libya), Continental Shelf (Libya/Malta), Land, Island and Maritime Frontier and Kasikili/Sedudu Island, see Chapter 3 B I, XIII, XVI, IXX, XXV. Only in the first case did this disagreement appear to have had a role in the subsequent non-compliance. In Asylum, misunderstandings on the scope of obligations came up precisely because there had not been any joint definition of the terms of reference; the differences were only sorted out after two subsequent decisions.

[24] In the Continental Shelf (Tunisia/Libya) case, disagreement arose on the meaning of the special agreement; the fact that different translations were delivered, with one party choosing French, the other English, certainly added to the controversy, *supra* Chapter 3 B XIII 1.

the actual obligation under Article 94(1) (for example, by providing for an implementation schedule), allow for recourse to assistance in the implementation or further dispute settlement mechanisms (including perhaps diplomatic mechanisms where it is questionable whether all relevant questions might be settled through a judicial examination).[25] Obviously, states are the masters of the drafting process and weaknesses in the text of the special agreement might simply reflect an inability to reach agreement[26] or the willingness to retain control over certain aspects of the settlement process rather than to adopt the text that would appear the most reasonable from an academic perspective. Yet it is desirable for states to recognize that an ambiguously worded special agreement might cause more harm than good by shifting the conflict to another level rather than ensuring a comprehensive final settlement. The Court, on the other hand, should exercise caution in conforming to the actual basis of consent in the special agreement.

2. The experience in cases of compulsory jurisdiction

The most infamous cases of defiance of the Court's authority happened in cases of compulsory jurisdiction, be it under the optional clause (Article 36(2) of the Statute) or on some general treaty clause providing for ICJ jurisdiction for disputes under the respective treaty.[27] The repeated occurrence of such cases led some observers to question whether compulsory jurisdiction fulfills any useful purpose at all and whether it might not be more conducive to the Court's position to reserve its jurisdiction for cases of joint submission only.[28]

---

[25] The circumstances of each case will determine the most appropriate type of post-adjudicative procedure. The parties might even decide for a combination of judicial and extrajudicial mechanisms. In a case where political considerations will determine the implementing action—particularly in cases where the parties are sent back to negotiations—non-judicial mechanisms (such as a conciliation commission) might be helpful. Where their motivation is rather to cover the eventuality that the Court fails to address all the relevant aspects, the parties might decide to include a provision entitling each of them seize the Court again to request a ruling on additional aspects, or to take recourse to arbitration.

[26] See, for example, the compromise formula in the agreement between Libya and Malta, Continental Shelf (Libya/Malta), *supra* Chapter 3 B XVI.

[27] While the respondent openly refused to comply in the Corfu Channel case, this refusal was still of a different nature from the other cases of defiance. Albania's rejection concerned the earlier demand for the full sum; it had made an offer to pay part of it (albeit one that could hardly be taken seriously), keeping a rather low profile and declining to engage in verbal attacks on the Court to an extent comparable to other recalcitrant states. The question on whether proceedings were introduced based on the optional clause or on a treaty clause does not appear to have played a role in cases of defiance. While Tehran Hostages and Fisheries Jurisdiction were based on treaty clauses, Anglo-Iranian Oil Company was based on the optional clause; the Nuclear Tests cases and the Nicaragua case were based both on treaty clauses and the optional clause. The difference between these two possible bases of jurisdiction appears to have a role rather for the question on whether states can be convinced to agree in advance to the Court's compulsory jurisdiction.

[28] *Scott/Carr*, 81 AJIL (1987), at 74–6.

Cases of compulsory jurisdiction, in fact, appear to present a far greater challenge for the Court's authority, as a state dragged into the Court against its will might feel less obliged to respect the proceedings. Power distribution might also have an impact on the prospects for compliance.[29] Yet, the call for an abolition of compulsory jurisdiction appears unjustified, given the successful settlement of many cases introduced on this basis[30] and the fact that no further cases of defiance have occurred since the Nicaragua judgment. In all cases currently pending before the Court, including those introduced on the basis of compulsory jurisdiction, the respondents are participating in the proceedings and have not cast doubts on their respect for the Court. Studies claiming a failure of compulsory jurisdiction before the Court appear to be founded on the premise that only those cases where the respondent filed preliminary objections are true test cases for the Court's compulsory jurisdiction.[31] Yet this is based on the purely speculative assumption that cases where the respondent did not contest the Court's jurisdiction would eventually have been taken to the Court jointly. The basis for such an assumption is highly doubtful: what reason would the United States have had, for example, to take the issue of the execution of the LaGrand brothers to the ICJ; or Belgium to do so regarding the criminal proceedings against Mr Yerodia? Rather, there might be grounds to count discontinued cases of compulsory jurisdiction as successes, as, for example, the Nauru case, where it can be safely assumed that the Court's confirmation of its jurisdiction[32] had a positive impact for Nauru with regard to the terms of its settlement with Australia.[33] The general respect for the Court shown by parties in cases of compulsory jurisdiction—with the few infamous exceptions of defiance—demonstrates the inappropriateness of calling the Court's compulsory jurisdiction a failure or, in the words of Judge Oda, a "myth."[34]

Yet cases launched without the respondent's specific consent come with an increased risk of non-compliance compared to those launched by joint consent; in addition, there will be the risk that the state concerned might withdraw its declaration under the optional clause in response to an undesired decision.[35]

---

[29] Ibid., at 70.

[30] A successful case of compulsory jurisdiction despite serious fears to the contrary can already be found in the earlier phase of the Court: the judgment in the Preah Vihear case, see *supra* Chapter B IX.

[31] See *Scott/Carr*, 81 AJIL (1987), at 61, 63–4; for a similar argument, see *Oda*, 49 ICLQ (2000) at 258–9.

[32] Certain Phosphate Lands in Nauru (Nauru v. Australia), Judgment of 26 June 1992, ICJ Rep. 1992, 240.

[33] The case was discontinued due to an agreement between the parties, see Certain Phosphate Lands in Nauru (Nauru v. Australia), Order of 13 September 1993, at 322.

[34] See *Oda*, 49 ICLQ (2000), at 251.

[35] Similar to the course of events in the Anglo-Iranian Oil Company case, the Nuclear Tests cases, and the Nicaragua case, Nigeria filed a modified declaration after the introduction of proceedings in Land and Maritime Boundary between Cameroon and Nigeria, see *supra* Chapter 3 C VIII 1.

While this should not lead to exaggerated fears, it is important for the Court to develop predictable and convincing standards to ensure that the jurisdictional basis is not overstretched so as not to create concerns of an excess of powers and cast doubt on the legitimacy of its decision-making process.[36] When making declarations under the optional clauses or subscribing to treaty clauses, states should have certainty about the scope of their being subject to the ICJ's jurisdiction. The Court should apply utmost care not to overstep its powers, including in the situation where it finds it has no jurisdiction (or no prima-facie jurisdiction, as the case may be). Substantive comments should be avoided in such situations, as there is no basis for a competence for the Court to pass upon the substance in the absence of jurisdiction; otherwise, it would allow itself to become the pawn of one of the litigants. The Court would create an incentive to bring claims bereft of any jurisdictional basis as a political maneuver, in the hope that the Court might issue some statement lending credence to the applicant's claims. While the Court takes visible efforts to examine its competence, its order rejecting the Congolese request for interim protection in the Armed Activities case between the Democratic Republic of the Congo and Rwanda gives rise to some worries that the Court might not understand the full implications of having recognized a lack of (prima-facie) jurisdiction. Its remarks by way of *obiter dicta* expressing its deep concern about the situation in the Eastern Congo read rather similarly to the formulation it would have used if granting the order[37] and therefore do not square with its rejection of prima-facie jurisdiction. In the words of Judge Buergenthal:

The Court's function is to pronounce itself on matters within its jurisdiction and not to voice personal sentiments or to make comments, general or specific, which, despite their admittedly "feel-good" qualities, have no legitimate place in this order.[38]

While the preceding considerations show that compulsory jurisdiction fulfills a useful function, as long as the Court keeps attention not to overstep its powers, it might not be constructive to force states to accept compulsory jurisdiction when they are unwilling to bear the consequence of being taken to the Court against their will. A broader acceptance of the Court's jurisdiction is only desirable if it reflects a genuine commitment that would be likely to be upheld even in critical situations.[39]

---

[36] On the standard for prima-facie jurisdiction, see further *infra* B II 1.

[37] Armed activities on the territory of the Congo (New application: 2002)(Democratic Republic of the Congo v. Rwanda), Order of 10 July 2002, at paras. 54–6 and 93; and the convincing criticism in Judge Buergenthal's separate opinion.

[38] Armed activities on the territory of the Congo (New application: 2002)(Democratic Republic of the Congo v. Rwanda), Order of 10 July 2002, Separate Opinion Buergenthal, at para. 4.

[39] For a proposal to strengthen the Court's compulsory jurisdiction through acceptances under very specific terms, see *Sofaer*, 44 Rec. NYCBA (1989), at 478–80.

V. Non-compliance and highly political situations

A common feature of cases of defiance of judgments as well as most cases of provisional measures was the highly political character of the underlying dispute, which often involved the use of force. In several cases, at least one of the parties determined the matter to be of vital interest and doubted the adequacy of the judicial process for dealing with the matter. In several cases, various international dispute settlement initiatives had already proven futile and it appeared that the law had reached its limits. Even the cases of Breard and LaGrand—perhaps not major issues for the overall foreign relations of the US—touched upon sensitive issues such as the distribution of powers in a federal system and capital punishment. The Court has correctly noted that the political implications of a dispute do not prevent it from adjudicating upon the legal questions involved, as to decide otherwise would effectively prevent it from taking a role in precisely those disputes where the restraining influence of the law is most needed.[40] While it thus *should* use its powers in such situations, it should be no particular surprise that the practical effectiveness will often remain limited—more a sign of the limits of the law than of the actual impotence of the Court. It would be unfair to use disputes such as the Genocide case as examples for an alleged inefficiency of the Court. In that case, the international community as a whole had proven incapable of halting atrocities in the Balkans, and the assumption that a mere call by the Court alone would restore peace would have been naïve. Nevertheless, Court decisions in such situations may possess some symbolic value, and the possibility that they might have at least some limited impact—even if only to speed up the decision to return to legality—justified their issuance. Rejecting a request for interim protection only because of its supposed inefficiency would be unacceptable—it would effectively transmit the message that states which are victims of the breaches of the most fundamental rules of international law would be left without protection.

On the other hand, cases that had highly political dimensions and involved concepts of national pride were successfully settled, even when the decision involved the need for a troop withdrawal.[41] It would therefore be inappropriate to write off any role for the Court in disputes with highly political dimensions.

VI. Subject-matter of the proceedings

The legal topic addressed in the proceedings will have an impact on the prospects for compliance. Matters such as maritime delimitation will usually

[40] See, for example, the Tehran Hostages case, the Nicaragua case, the Genocide case, *supra* Chapter 3 B XIV and XVIII and C IV, VI, and VII.
[41] See, for example, the Temple of Preah Vihear and the Territorial Dispute (Libya/Chad) cases, see *supra* Chapter 3 B IX and XII.

be less problematic than those relating to title to territory, although in all cases a variety of factors will come into play, including the economic significance of the dispute and extent of public interest. The fact that the applicable law is well settled will usually be a positive factor; yet it might not help where the very concept of law is put in question, as in the Tehran Hostages case. The Court is particularly ill equipped for situations where the law is very much in development as in the Fisheries Jurisdiction case, where its findings were short lived. The Court obviously cannot pick and choose the cases submitted on their adequacy for settlement, but it has to develop mechanisms on issues such as political questions, impact of Security Council resolutions, and the determinacy of the law.

VII. Factors with a doubtful or non-measurable impact on compliance

1. Relations between the parties and form of government

Good relations between the parties will naturally foster the prospects for compliance. The existence of shared values and an understanding of the role of the law and dispute settlement favor a positive outcome, but cannot ensure it.[42] Moreover, bad relations are not necessarily fatal to successful implementation, which may succeed even in a climate of hostility between the parties.[43]

With regard to system of government, the track-record for liberal democracies has not been generally better than for other régimes. The group of defiant states includes countries such as the United States, France, and Iceland, while Libya, for instance, has an exemplary compliance record.[44] When discussing whether democratic structures might have a positive influence, it can by no means be taken for granted that public opinion will pressure a government into compliance with ICJ decisions.[45] To the contrary, where a government's behavior enjoys broad public support, irrespective of its evaluation under international law, democracies might even be less willing to cooperate with the ICJ than are other regimes. Where a local governor, for example, might even count on increased popularity by asserting alleged security concerns of his state against what the population might perceive as "encroachment" by the ICJ, democratic structures might

---

[42] While the general relations between the parties were bad in the Corfu Channel case, the Tehran Hostages case, and the Nicaragua case, this cannot be said of the Fisheries Jurisdiction cases (the UK, the FRG, and Iceland were partners in NATO and the Council of Europe and shared many commonalities), the Nuclear Tests cases, and the Breard and LaGrand cases.

[43] See, e.g. Temple of Preah Vihear, Chapter 3 B IX.

[44] See Continental Shelf (Libya/Malta), Continental Shelf (Libya/Tunisia), and Territorial Dispute (Libya/Chad), *supra* Chapter 3 B XIII, XVI.

[45] The broad public support across party lines for the Icelandic government made it unlikely that it would eventually respect the ICJ's decision, see *supra* Chapter 3 B XII 5–6.

even in a certain sense *disfavor* compliance. On the other hand, dictators who control their country to an extent that they can easily guarantee an easy and reliable implementation without local resistance might often be reliant enforcers of ICJ decisions.

Support for the rule of law will encourage compliance in scenarios where the support of domestic courts in the enforcement of ICJ decisions can be secured. While a country with an effective observance of the rule of law might regard defiance of international courts justified, it will obey its national courts as they form the very basis of its constitutional order. For example, if in the currently pending Avena case, the US Supreme Court were to order state governors to halt an execution pending a case before the ICJ, it would be almost certain that the respective governor would heed this call.[46] As explained earlier and seen in various cases, however, this form of assistance by national courts in the enforcement of ICJ decisions is by no means guaranteed and will be closely connected with the rank of international law in the domestic legal order.[47] It will be seen whether and to what extent US domestic courts will heed the ICJ's call.

2. UN membership

There is no evidence substantiating a higher probability of non-compliance in cases where the parties were not UN members; no case involving parties to the Statute under Article 93(2) of the Charter yielded provisional measures or a judgment requiring implementation.[48] Instances of non-compliance in disputes involving parties admitted under Article 35(2) of the Statute cannot be attributed to the fact that one party was a non-member.[49]

3. Voting patterns and dissenting votes

Voting patterns of the Court's judges could have various effects. A unanimous decision might appear particularly persuasive given that the Court with

---

[46] In fact, this appears to be acknowledged by the Texas governor who contested the Court's authority to halt the execution (see http://www.internationaljusticeproject.org/briefs WorldNews.cfm). A spokesman was quoted saying that state and federal courts provided adequate safeguards in criminal proceedings and were the appropriate forums in which to hear "issues such as consular notification on a case-by-case basis," and that orders from those Courts were the only ones Texas would follow.

[47] See *supra* Chapter 2 E III 5.

[48] The cases in which one of the parties was participating as a non-UN member state party to the ICJ Statute were Nottebohm, and Certain Phosphate Lands in Nauru (Nauru v. Australia).

[49] See the Corfu Channel case: Albania never tried to invoke this issue, and it did not reconsider its position either after becoming a UN member (in 1955) until the final settlement was reached in 1992. Iceland's response to the Court's provisional measures did not accord a different treatment to the UK, a founding member, and Germany, which only became a member during the proceedings (on 18 September 1973).

its diverse composition stands fully behind a decision.[50] On the other hand, it was suggested that a unanimous decision could be considered a humiliation of the addressee;[51] a divided opinion would have conveyed more of an impression that its concerns were taken into account. Refusals to comply, in any event, happened both with regard to decisions taken unanimously as well as in cases where the Court was divided.[52]

The fact that judges append individual opinions might be taken by the recalcitrant state as legitimization of their refusal of the respective decision. In fact, the US pointed to Judge Schwebel's dissenting opinion when expressing its disdain for the decisions in the Nicaragua case.[53] Allowing dissents, declarations, and separate opinions bears an inherent risk which is, however, outweighed by the advantages of such statements—in other words, the certainty that different perspectives were considered. Nevertheless, dissenting judges should be aware of their responsibility towards the Court as an institution and frame their critique in an appropriate manner.

4. Decisions of a Chamber *vis-à-vis* decisions of the full Court

There is no case of defiance of a Chamber decision; however, the empirical basis for evaluating compliance with Chamber decisions remains limited, with only three judgments requiring implementation and one case of provisional measures.[54] The fact that both parties must agree to Chamber proceedings[55] and approve of the Chamber's composition in a joint submission instituting proceedings imply that the parties will have a higher degree of trust and thus be more receptive to the eventual decision. In the one case of difficulties in implementation and complaints of non-compliance (Land,

---

[50] This appears to be assumed by *Szabó*, 10 Leid. JIL (1997), at 486, drawing attention to the fact that practically all orders indicating provisional measures from Tehran Hostages onwards were made unanimously and arguing that this "accentuates their 'moral' authority."

[51] See in this sense on the Fisheries Jurisdiction cases *Favoreu*, 18 AFDI (1972), at 308.

[52] The Court's judgment criticized by Albania in Corfu Channel—the one on the assessment of damages—was made by 12 votes to 1. The voting pattern on the provisional measures in the Anglo-Iranian Oil Company case was not disclosed, but at least two judges dissented, see *supra* Chapter 3 X I 2. The Fisheries Jurisdiction cases were based on solid majorities: 14 to 1 for the first series of orders; 11 to 3 for the second series of orders; and 10 to 4 for the judgments on the merits. The Nuclear Tests orders were more controversial with an 8:6 decision. The Tehran Hostages order was made unanimously, the judgment ranged from unanimous sections to 12:3 decisions. In the Nicaragua case, votes on the order ranged from a unanimous decision to a 14:1 decision and on the judgment from a unanimous to an 11:4 decision. There would not appear to be any point in examining the voting patterns beyond defiance cases, as in the cases of difficulties in the implementation or those where it is controversial whether the formal respect is matched by appropriate action, neither party questioned the legitimacy of the decision-making process.

[53] See *supra* Chapter 3 nn. 700, 756.

[54] The Gulf of Maine, the Frontier Dispute (Burkina Faso/Mali), and the Land, Island and Maritime Frontier Dispute (El Salvador/Honduras) cases. Another Chamber case—ELSI—did not result in a judgment requiring implementation.

[55] See Article 26(3) of the Statute.

Island and Maritime Frontier Dispute), nothing indicated that the fact that the decision emanated from a Chamber rather than from the full Court played any particular role.

VIII. *The role of the UN main organs*

UN involvement in the enforcement of ICJ decisions has been very limited. The analysis of practice has shown that this is in the first place due to a scarcity of genuine requests by the states that are creditors of a decision. Since the implementation phase is primarily the realm of the parties, there is no need for UN intervention, be it through compulsive or positive measures, absent a request from the creditor.[56] Consequently, where the parties have made complaints that did not appear to be backed by a genuine desire of the Council dealing with the matter, the Council rightly displayed reserve.[57] Similarly, the Assembly's reluctance to reprimand France for nuclear testing from the specific perspective of the provisional measures orders was irreproachable given that such action was apparently not desired by the entitled states.[58]

The dearth of requests reflects, on one hand, the lack of a need, given that most cases of judgments were successfully implemented. In the critical cases, as well as in cases of provisional measures, it might also reflect the recognition that UN action was either unlikely to happen at all, or that the Council was already actively involved in the matter and it was not to be expected that a reference to the order would add much. Cases of defiance regularly involved a permanent member either on the applicant or the respondent side, reinforcing the institution's Cold War stasis. Moreover, Council members might, in general, prefer to deal with disputes more in political terms than in legal ones.[59] As far as provisional measures are concerned, this might change as a result of the clarification of their binding force in the LaGrand judgment.[60]

That Council action hardly occurred even after the Cold War (with the change in power constellations making enforcement action appear more feasible) can also be explained by the absence of cases of defiance. Council

---

[56] In the Arbitral Award by the King of Spain case, the parties even provided for mandatory recourse to OAS settlement procedures prior to recourse to the Council under Article 94(2), see *supra* Chapter 3 B VIII.

[57] See, for example, the complaints in the Land, Island and Maritime Frontier Dispute, and the Land and Maritime Boundary between Cameroon and Nigeria case—neither of which requested the Council to put the matter on its agenda, see *supra* Chapter 3 B IXX 4 and C VIII 4.

[58] See *supra* Chapter 3 C III 4.

[59] References to the ICJ orders in draft resolutions in the Anglo-Iranian Oil Company case were deleted and in the Tehran Hostages case very limited, see Chapter 3 C I 4 and IV 2.

[60] See *infra* III.

action will be far more plausible in cases where a state openly and deliberately refuses to honor an ICJ decision. Where a state, on the other hand, emphasizes its faithful observance of the Court's decision although the other side complains of non-compliance, the Council will rarely see the situation as so clear as to envisage sanctions and will prefer to tackle the dispute in a cooperational rather than confrontational manner. This leads to a further field where UN action has been helpful: positive measures to assist in a decision's implementation. Such action, again, would depend on approval by the parties; however, an initiative by the Secretary-General can encourage movement in this direction.

B. THE WEAKER RECORD FOR PROVISIONAL MEASURES: EXPLANATIONS AND POSSIBLE REMEDIES

The examination of the practice has revealed a surprisingly big difference between the negative record for provisional measures and the largely positive one for judgments. One explanation for the different track-record might lie in the very nature of provisional measures as *provisional*. From the final judgment, the parties expect a conclusive determination of their legal relations and a settlement of their dispute. Interim protection, on the other hand, aiming at protecting rights whose existence is uncertain, limits their freedom of action pending the proceedings without creating clarity.[61] Moreover, despite all safeguard clauses, there is some danger that provisional measures will be perceived as a certain pre-indication of the future judgment on the merits and might thus cause resentments.[62]

However, these are general aspects that cannot sufficiently explain the difference in the track-record between the two types of decisions, as the same consideration would apply for all bodies granting interim protection. In exploring further reasons, one can identify aspects relating to the nature of the cases (showing the impacts of the circumstances under which the concrete orders indicating provisional measures were issued) as well as some inherent problems of interim protection before the Court. Finally, the role of the uncertainty about the binding force of provisional measures prior to the LaGrand decision will be assessed, and the potential for the Court to promote compliance through complementary measures and sanctioning mechanisms will be explored.

---

[61] See *Favoreu*, 18 AFDI (1972), at 308; *Cocâtre-Zielgien*, 70 RGDIP (1966), at 7–8 (explaining that the granting of interim protection in the exercise of the Court's powers cannot be taken as an infringement on sovereignty).

[62] See for the Fisheries Jurisdiction case, *Favoreu*, 18 AFDI (1972), 308.

I. Circumstances under which the orders were issued/nature of the cases

1. Form of introduction of proceedings

The first observation is that provisional measures were almost exclusively requested in cases launched by unilateral application against the respondent's will.[63] This shows that in cases launched by special agreement, the parties regularly do not see a need for interim protection.[64] The positive aspects of special agreements[65] can provide some explanation for the general absence of provisional measures in such cases: the communication and cooperation between the parties will usually work well enough for them to find some interim solution between themselves without the necessity of recurring to the Court. Provisions on interim régimes can be found in several special agreements.[66] Moreover, there has even been a case where the parties adopted a provision with the aim of *excluding* any possible recourse to Article 41, attaching decisive weight to retaining control over the adoption of an interim régime.[67] It might be even more appropriate for provisional measures than for judgments to assume that special agreements will favor successful implementation. Parties turning to the Court might have a special interest in ensuring that their action does not cast doubts on their commitment to adjudication pending the proceedings or give rise to negative inferences in the judgment. The sympathy of the judges similarly cannot be underestimated.[68] Bearing in

---

[63] Including those requests on which the Court did not take a decision: see the Pakistani Prisoners of War case, where Pakistan asked for a postponement of its request and later discontinued the case. In the Border and Transborder armed actions (Nicaragua v. Honduras) case, Nicaragua withdrew its request for provisional measures only ten days after it had been made. In both cases, the respondent contested the Court's jurisdiction; in the second case, the Court upheld its jurisdiction in a judgment made after the request for provisional measures was withdrawn. The only exception where provisional measures were made in proceedings based on a special agreement was the Frontier Dispute (Burkina Faso v. Mali) case, which is also the only case where these measures were fully successful.

[64] The situation in the Frontier Dispute case, where armed incidents occurred after the joint submission of a dispute to the Court, was thus somewhat of an anomaly. See further *Merrills*, 44 ICLQ (1995), at 138–9, stating that "if States are willing to co-operate, interim measures may well be unnecessary. [...] [C]ases like the Frontier Dispute case are likely to be the exception rather than the rule, and interim measures will frequently have to be used in cases of incomplete depoliticisation, with correspondingly little prospect of their being observed."

[65] See *supra* A IV 1.

[66] In Territorial Dispute (Libya/Chad), the special agreement provided for the adoption of concomitant measures. In Gabčíkovo–Nagymaros, the parties undertook to establish an interim régime. In Minquiers and Ecrehos, controversial aspects (fishery rights) were regulated beforehand. See *supra* Chapter 3 B XXII, XXIV and V.

[67] This happened in the Gabčíkovo–Nagymaros case, *supra* Chapter 3 B XXIV 2, where the parties raised the undertaking of establishing of an interim régime by agreement to the status of an essential basis of their special agreement, apparently linking their consent to the Court's jurisdiction to the exclusion of Article 41. What would have happened if one of the parties had nevertheless made a request for interim protection is debatable.

[68] See, in general, on the risks for a party in non-compliance with provisional measures *Oxman* in Damrosch, The ICJ at a crossroads, at 332–3.

mind the other positive factors inherent in the joint submission of a dispute, it is no coincidence that the only case where provisional measures can confidently be said to have completely fulfilled their purpose came in a case jointly submitted to the Court.[69]

Consequently, two observations are to be made. First, provisional measures are almost exclusively requested in situations where the proceedings were launched by unilateral application and the Court's jurisdiction was contested. Second, where provisional measures are indicated in cases of joint submission, there is a greater likelihood of compliance.

2. Attitude of parties towards the proceedings

During the Court's first four decades, the only instances where provisional measures were indicated were cases of fundamental opposition by the respondent against Court proceedings. Those cases were marked by non-appearance, non-participation, and vehement criticism of the decisions up to the point of claiming their invalidity and an excess of powers, coupled with defiance of the final judgment, where a judgment requiring implementation was reached.[70] As stated above, defiance has, in general, been a problem linked to non-participation: once a state goes as far as to boycott proceedings before the Court, it is not surprising to see it refusing to comply with decisions produced by these proceedings. From the cases on the Court's docket up until 1984, those in which provisional measures were indicated were precisely those where the respondent was extremely averse to submitting the dispute to adjudication.

A remarkable shift has taken place since then. In the Frontier Dispute case, both parties made requests for provisional measures, showing their joint understanding that interim protection was required. Subsequent respondents have evinced substantially less hostility towards the concept of

---

[69] See the Frontier Dispute case, *supra* Chapter 3 C V.

[70] In all cases of provisional measures from Anglo-Iranian Oil Company to Military and Paramilitary Activities in and against Nicaragua, the respondents boycotted at least some stage of the proceedings. While in the Anglo-Iranian Oil Company case the respondent eventually participated after the interim proceedings, the respondents in the Fisheries Jurisdiction, Nuclear Tests, and US Diplomatic and Consular Staff cases did not appear before the Court at any time. The US still participated in the provisional measures and the jurisdiction and admissibility phase of the Nicaragua case, but after the unfavorable judgment on jurisdiction and admissibility chose to desist from further participation. Judgments on the merits requiring implementation were made in Fisheries Jurisdiction, United States Diplomatic and Consular Staff in Tehran, and Military and paramilitary activities in and against Nicaragua. In Nuclear Tests, the final judgment did not require any implementation as the Court held the applicants' claims to be moot. Whether a judgment on the merits would have had any chance of being complied with would have depended on its precise terms. A judgment ordering France to desist from further atmospheric tests would have had a good chance of being complied with, as France had decided not to carry out further tests of that type anyway. The prospects for compliance with a more far-reaching decision prohibiting *any* kind of testing would appear slim, though.

interim protection than in the first decades. Cases of provisional measures were no longer limited to cases where the respondent challenged the Court's jurisdiction—and even where it did, the respondent's first reaction to a request for interim protection was to point to violations of its own rights by the other side, in remarkable contrast to the wholesale opposition of any Court involvement as in earlier cases.[71]

3. Political leverage

As indicated above, all orders indicating provisional measures were made in situations with highly political ramifications, including matters involving the failed use of force, with futile settlement attempts by the international community, matters involving "vital interests," or matters where the law had reached its limits. Such situations pose obvious problems in terms of compliance. A comparable assessment does not hold for judgments, many of which were delivered in disputes of only minor national interest.[72]

4. Preponderance of ulterior motives of the applicant of provisional measures

The inefficiency of provisional measures also appears in a different light when considering that requests for interim measures might occasionally not have been made strictly in the expectation that the other party would comply. Rather, the applicant might have sought a judicial forum for its grievances and publicity for its cause[73]—motives that are directly linked with its desire for eventual enforcement of the order. Similarly, it might have had an ulterior motive, such as in the Genocide case, where the applicant actually desired an affirmation of its rights *vis-à-vis* the international community. This should offer one explanation for the limited success of interim protection, albeit not a reason for its denial.

5. Low expectation of meaningful Security Council involvement

In most cases, orders of provisional measures were issued in situations where little material assistance could be expected from the Security Council and the

---

[71] See the Genocide and the Land and Maritime Boundary between Cameroon and Nigeria cases, Chapter 3 C VII and VIII.

[72] While, for example, the underlying issues in the North Sea Continental Shelf cases and the Gulf of Maine case were certainly of interest to the parties, they did not represent crucial national interests. In some cases, one might even say that the significance was negligible, as the Ambatielos case, the Minquiers and Ecrehos case, or the Certain frontier land case, or only of fleeting relevance, such as the Rights of US nationals in Morocco case, see Chapter 3 B X, XV, IV, V, III.

[73] See *Collins*, 234 RdC (1992), at 219; *Merrills*, 44 ICLQ (1995), at 139–42.

possibility of enforcement action could thus not serve as a deterrent. This owes either to the involvement of a permanent member or a state within its sphere of interests or the ongoing engagement of the Council in the matter, in which case the order was likely superfluous.

II. Inherent problems of interim protection before the Court

1. No final determination of the Court's jurisdiction

Interim measures might (and frequently will) come at a stage where the Court has not yet conclusively determined the existence of jurisdiction: instead, they follow the conclusion that, prima facie, a possible jurisdictional basis exists.[74] Conceptually, the Court's competence to indicate provisional measures resides in its power to grant interim protection (i.e. in Article 41 rather than Article 36).[75] This entails the need for a state to comply with the decision without the possibility of invoking a lack of jurisdiction as a valid defense for non-compliance. Everything else—be it the demand for a definite finding on jurisdiction prior to granting interim protection or the argument that the ultimate validity of the decision hangs on the later decision on jurisdiction— would be incompatible with the necessity for efficient interim protection. Admittedly, considering that consent forms the cardinal principle of ICJ proceedings, the expectation of obedience at a stage where there is no certainty on the question of jurisdiction places a rather high burden on the addressee.[76] Moreover, concerns might arise that the Court might be unduly influenced by its finding on prima-facie jurisdiction to avoid the unpleasant result of finding that there is no jurisdiction after having granted interim protection. On the other side of the coin, the very fact that the jurisdiction is not yet established beyond doubt might contribute to reluctance on the part of the international community in responding to failures of compliance.[77]

It is therefore imperative for the Court to develop a consistent, predictable standard for prima-facie jurisdiction that pays sufficient regard both to the need to ensure efficient interim protection even in cases of contested jurisdic-

---

[74] This was the case for all provisional measures except for the second series of orders in the Fisheries Jurisdiction cases, which came after the judgments on jurisdictions, and in the Frontier Dispute case where the jurisdiction was not disputed, see Chapter 3 C II 2 and V.

[75] See Anglo-Iranian Oil Company case, Judgment on preliminary objections of 22 July 1952, at 102–3: "While the Court derived its power to indicate these provisional measures from the special provisions contained in Article 41 of the Statute, it must now derive the jurisdiction to deal with the merits of the case from the general rules laid down in Article 36 of the Statute."

[76] See *Tomuschat* 281 RdC (1999), at 416 identifying the uncertainty on jurisdiction as a specific problem of the Court's provisional measures. It might discourage states from agreeing to the Court's compulsory jurisdiction if they cannot be certain that existing reservations will be taken into account in the context of interim protection.

[77] See the course of events in the Anglo-Iranian Oil Company case, where the Security Council adjourned the meeting to await the decision on the Court's jurisdiction, Chapter 3 C I 4.

tion and to the general principle of consent to the ICJ proceedings. Significant progress has been achieved in defining this standard, and the Court's recent decisions rejecting requests for provisional measures because of an absence of prima-facie jurisdiction show the Court's awareness of the need to take this test seriously.[78] In the Anglo-Iranian Oil Company case, its first order indicating provisional measures with a very low threshold had had unpleasant ramifications: the respondent defied the decision, and the Court later found that it had no jurisdiction[79]—the only case to date where this has happened.[80] While the test for prima-facie jurisdiction as stipulated in the first cases was whether there was an apparent lack of jurisdiction, the permanent formula used from the Nuclear Tests cases[81] onwards is a positive test: the Court has to determine positively that there is a prima-facie basis for its jurisdiction.[82]

There remains some uncertainty, which is reflected, for instance, in the fact that the 1996 edition of the information booklet "The International Court of Justice," published by the Court and prepared by the Registry under the supervision of the ICJ President, reports the applicable standard as follows: "[T]he Court will normally indicate provisional measures unless it manifestly lacks jurisdiction"[83]—a statement that does not quite square with the current standard test of a positive finding on prima-facie jurisdiction.[84] The degree of

---

[78] This is visible in the rejection of the various requests by Yugoslavia in the legality of use of force cases (see only Legality of Use of Force (Yugoslavia v. Belgium), Order of 2 June 1999; and of the DRC's request in Armed activities on the Territory of the Congo (New application: 2002) (Democratic Republic of the Congo v. Rwanda), Order of 18 September 2002.

[79] See the Anglo-Iranian Oil Company case, Chapter 3 C I.

[80] As *Merrills*, 44 ICLQ (1995), at 94, observes, the fact that in the judgment on jurisdiction in the Nicaragua case, the Court was seriously divided after having reached a unanimous order in which prima-facie jurisdiction had been affirmed shows that it is not impossible that a situation like in the Anglo-Iranian Oil Company case might occur again.

[81] Nuclear Tests, ICJ Rep. 1973, at 101, paras. 13 and 137, para. 18: "Whereas on a request for provisional measures the Court need not, before indicating them, finally satisfy itself that it has jurisdiction on the merits of the case, and yet ought not to indicate such measures invoked by the applicant appear, *prima facie*, to appear to afford a basis on which the jurisdiction of the Court might be founded." The Fisheries Jurisdiction orders were still somewhat ambiguous. The abstract formulation of the test read like a negative test, its actual application, however, like a positive test, see *supra* Chapter 3 C II 1.

[82] See *supra* Chapter 3 C XI. See further on the development since 1980 Merrills, 44 ICLQ (1995), at 91–100.

[83] ICJ, "The International Court of Justice", 4th edn., The Hague 1996, at 61–2 (quoting the decisions Anglo-Iranian Oil Company, Fisheries Jurisdiction, Nuclear Tests, United States Diplomatic and Consular Staff in Tehran, Military and Paramilitary Activities in and against Nicaragua). See *Oxman* in Damrosch, The ICJ at a crossroads, at 341.

[84] See *Oxman* in Damrosch, The ICJ at a crossroads, at 341, tracing the origin of the current standard in Judge Lauterpacht's Separate Opinion in the Interhandel case, Order of 24 October 1957, at 118–19: "The Court may properly act under the terms of Article 41 provided that there is in existence an instrument such as a Declaration of Acceptance of the optional clause, emanating from the parties to the dispute, which *prima facie* confers jurisdiction upon the Court and which incorporates no reservations obviously excluding its jurisdiction." But see *Collins*, 234 RdC (1992), at 221, arguing that the test is still the one endorsed by the Court's majority in the Anglo-Iranian Oil Company case.

probability required, the role of reservations, and the role of prima-facie admissibility all still need further clarification. This is perhaps unsurprising given that there is still only a limited number of decisions; the refinement of the prima-facie test is perhaps better relegated to the future jurisprudence of the Court than, for instance, to a revision of the Rules. The Court should, in any event, take this matter seriously, especially given that there is no longer room for doubt on the binding force of provisional measures.[85] Its recent decisions demonstrate this awareness and make it unlikely that interim measures would be indicated under circumstances such as those present in the Anglo-Iranian Oil Company case.

2. Practical problems: Time pressure and lack of knowledge and expertise

Time pressures and—depending on the subject-matter—ignorance of the facts or lack of expertise (e.g. relating to security implications) are problems the ICJ shares with domestic courts. They demand appropriate mechanisms, such as criteria for the weighing of risks, for incidental evidence, or for the burden of proof. In the Frontier Dispute (Burkina Faso/Mali) case, the Court has shown its ability to tailor the measures in a creative manner by involving both the parties and regional settlement efforts. Its two-step approach, leaving the parties some leeway as to the details while reserving its right to make the detailed prescriptions itself, might be an adequate step in similar future cases.[86] As far as security implications are concerned, the Court will be most successful when taking into account the potential of regional settlement mechanisms and the Security Council, where appropriate. While the Court cannot be reproached for insisting that neither security implications nor the fact that the matter is before the Council bars it from dealing with a case, it should nevertheless avail itself of the Council's special expertise in security matters. Time pressures vary substantially from case to case, and must therefore be confronted on an individual basis.[87]

3. Brevity of the reasoning

Unlike for judgments, the ICJ Statute does not contain an explicit requirement of an indication of the reasons for provisional measures.[88] Nevertheless, in view of the inherent problems of interim measures just explained, and

---

[85] Its recent decisions appear to reflect this awareness, see *supra* n. 78.

[86] See *supra* Chapter 3 C V.

[87] LaGrand was obviously the most extreme situation, see *supra* Chapter 3 C X 1. In Passage through the Great Belt, for example, there were more than two months between the initial request and the order rejecting Finland's request, see ICJ Rep. 1991, 12, at 14, para. 7; see further *Merrills*, 44 ICLQ (1995), at 142.

[88] See on judgments Article 56(1) of the Statute: "The judgment shall state the reasons on which it is based."

as implementation will be a matter for the parties in the first place, the Court would be well advised to convince through a thorough and transparent reasoning as proof of its deliberative process.[89] Although the Court's orders on interim protection have grown considerably in size over time and its effort to provide a truly reasoned decision are visible, more should be done to convince litigants through the quality of the reasoning. The decision should always attempt to address the parties' arguments comprehensively and make doubtlessly clear on which considerations it was based. This has not been the case in all the former orders; for example, the mere statement that the Court considers that the circumstances "required" the indication of provisional measures is no substitute for a rationale.

Admittedly, there are two restraining factors: on the one hand, the danger of a prejudgment of the merits; on the other hand, the short span of time between the provisional measures and the difficulty of acquiring sufficient expertise. These factors, however, are inherent to interim protection— domestic courts face them as well and have developed mechanisms to cope with them.[90] Keeping the reasoning short or intentionally vague will not be a solution, for if the Court saw interim protection as necessary, it should also reveal the considerations on which that decision was based. Anything else will cast doubts on its decision-making process and raise suspicions of an insufficient consideration or even a bias. It could also make it far easier for states to make complaints to this extent. The increasing length of orders on interim protection shows the Court's awareness of this issue;[91] of course, not only the length, but in the first place, the thoroughness of its argument on the fundamental issues will be the relevant factor.

4. Impression of bias/balancing of interests

The Court's impartiality was questioned in several cases of provisional measures.[92] Although these complaints were regularly unfounded, the Court must work to avoid even the impression of bias. It was not always visible whether and how competing interests had been balanced and how much regard the ICJ really gave to the considerations of the adverse party. The reasoning should have taken up those concerns.

---

[89] See in particular the brevity of the Order in the Anglo-Iranian Oil Company case, consisting only of 6 pages, ICJ Reports 1951, 89–95.

[90] Moreover, the time period between the request and the order cannot always be said to be overly short, see, for example, the Passage through the Great Belt, *supra* n. 87.

[91] The most recent example of an indication of provisional measures—Avena and other Mexican Nationals (Mexico v. United States of America), Order of 5 February 2003, that consists of 15 pages and 59 paras.

[92] See, for example, the Fisheries Jurisdiction cases and the Nicaragua case, *supra* Chapter 3 C II and VI.

The Court should work to integrate the other side in the litigation and create an environment conducive to compliance. This task will, of course, be easier where requests for interim protection come from both sides, as in the Frontier Dispute case, or where at least both sides show a constructive attitude towards the proceedings on interim protection. Yet the Court should not blindly rely on the existence of a request of the one side and the absence of the request by the other side, although it may, of course, take this as an indication that one side sees a need for protection of its rights whereas the other does not.[93] Yet the Court's power to provide interim protection has a feature entirely different from judgments: it is not dependent on a request of either party.[94] This makes it worth while to consider whether the Court should become involved to a higher degree in ensuring the efficiency and acceptability of provisional measures to both sides, taking advantage of oral proceedings and meetings of the President with the parties' agents to determine the further course of the proceedings.

5. Uncertainty about the recovery of potential losses and injuries

A significant issue for the addressee of provisional measures might be restitution for possible loss suffered as a consequence of its compliance with an order protecting a right that is later found to be inexistent.[95] The existence of securities could significantly mitigate concerns on the part of the respondent, as potential loss might be the main reason for its resistance against an order. Even a mere halt to certain activities can certainly be harmful, and the Court's Statute does not contain any provision providing for recovery. Such losses might be a high burden to pay for a party's commitment to the judicial settlement; it might be more appropriate to attribute the risk to have to bear such damage to the party applying for the provisional measures. There might be a convincing basis for a general principle of law on liability for damage caused by provisional measures, as stipulated in many legal orders, according to which a party requesting an injunction is liable for damages suffered by the other party as a consequence of an injunction if the Court later decides that the enjoined acts were legal.[96] This argument was

---

[93] See, for example, the Nicaragua case, *supra* Chapter 3 C VI 2.

[94] See Article 75(1) and (2) Rules of Court. The Court has, in fact, made use of its competence to indicate measures others than those applied for, as there were usually some deviations between the request and the order. See further *Merrills*, 44 ICLQ (1995), at 144.

[95] See *Oxman* in Damrosch, The ICJ at a crossroads, at 333, listing the issue of interim loss as a disincentive for compliance with provisional measures: "if [a state] ultimately prevails before the Court on jurisdiction or the merits, the interim loss was unnecessary, may be irreparable, and does not at present appear to be compensable from the other party."

[96] See, for example, § 945 of the German *ZPO* (Code of Civil Procedure): "Erweist sich die Anordnung [...] einer einstweiligen Anordnung als von Anfang an ungerechtfertigt [...], so ist die Partei, welche die Anordnung erwirkt hat, verpflichtet, dem Gegner den Schaden zu ersetzen, der ihm aus der Vollziehung der angeordneten Maßregel [...] entsteht [...]." ("If the order [...]

advanced by Denmark, the respondent in the interim proceedings in the Passage through the Great Belt case: for the case of an indication of provisional measures, it asked the Court to impose on Finland an obligation to compensate Denmark for the losses caused by the provisional measures in the event the Court were to reject Finland's submissions on the merits. "For otherwise, Denmark will be left to bear an enormous financial burden even though, ultimately, the Court finds Denmark to be acting lawfully."[97] Finland refuted these submissions, *inter alia* questioning the technique of recourse to a general principle under Article 38(1)(c) of the Statute and arguing that such liability might discourage states from taking recourse to the Court and that a request for interim protection was perfectly lawful.[98] This still does not answer why it should be up to the respondent to sustain the damage. The Court ultimately did not decide this issue as it rejected Finland's request, seeing no risk of irreparable damage.[99] Further research on this question would be highly desirable. While the Court will most likely be reluctant to raise this issue *proprio motu*, future parties might bring the matter to the table again.

6. Degree of precision of the measures indicated

The text of the measures will have a definite bearing on compliance. It is easier to establish compliance when measures are unambiguous and concisely worded; broadly formulated measures will leave states a wide discretion as to the manner of implementation, making proof of actual non-compliance rather difficult to establish. In such cases, there will likely be a mixture of compliance and non-compliance (as in case of the obligation not to take action likely to aggravate the dispute),[100] thus compromising, but not negating, the actual efficiency of such measures. A lack of precision might be a factor generating a potential source of conflict as to the required action for compliance; a measure whose scope can be objectively assessed will certainly be preferable. Measures that are dependent on a further examination of the law or the facts will be unlikely to have a constructive effect, as the precise scope of obligations stemming from them will be debatable and the parties

of a preliminary injunction proves to have been unjustified from its inception [...] the party who secured the order is liable to compensate the opponent for the damage arising from the execution of the ordered measure.") While there will be a basis for state responsibility claims where a state has intentionally brought an unfounded claim, this will hardly ever be proved.

[97] Argument of Mr Magid on behalf of Denmark, 1 July 1991, ICJ Pleadings, Passage through the Great Belt, 169–74.

[98] Reply of Mr Treves on behalf of Finland, 4 July 1991, ICJ Pleadings, Passage through the Great Belt, 198–201.

[99] Passage through the Great Belt, Order of 29 July 1991, ICJ Reports 1991, 12–21.

[100] See *Addo*, 10 EJIL (1999), at 726.

might thus simply decide to stick to their earlier positions.[101] Similarly, measures urging respect for the law in general will most likely enjoy only limited effectiveness, particularly where the existence of these legal rules is undisputed.

III. Uncertainty about the binding force

The significance of the Court's dicta on the binding force of provisional measures in the LaGrand judgment and the resulting hopes for a better compliance record have already been discussed.[102] Whether earlier non-compliance can be attributed to the fact that this question had not been authoritatively settled remains in question. Interestingly enough, Breard and LaGrand were the only cases where an alleged lack of binding force consti-tuted a central and principled argument.[103]

If the law of interim protection had been unambiguously worded so as to leave no room for doubts on the binding force, it is still questionable as to whether the response would have been very different in the types of cases of provisional measures prior to Breard and LaGrand.[104] In the cases of defiance up to the measures in the Nicaragua case, the recalcitrant states had opposed any Court involvement, to the point of boycotting the proceedings, contesting the validity of the respective decision, and ignoring the judgment in those cases that resulted in a judgment on the merits.[105] In the second category of cases, both sides claimed to have complied with the provisional measures; the facts and/or the law were disputed. In both categories of cases, reasonable doubts may exist as to whether the general question of binding force had a significant influence on the respective government's decisions. The impact of uncertainty on this issue is not dispositive. First, the inter-national community as well as the domestic actors might have paid substan-tially greater attention if they had been aware that non-compliance was more than the disregard of a recommendation, amounting instead to a breach of a

---

[101] Examples were the provisional measure in the Nicaragua case urging for respect of Nicaragua's sovereignty, or the measure relating to troop locations in the Land and Maritime Boundary between Cameroon and Nigeria case, see *supra* Chapter 3 C VI 1 and VIII 3.

[102] See *supra* Chapter 1 B II.

[103] There was one case where this argument came up in passing—the Anglo-Iranian Oil Company case, where it appeared as an additional argument alongside Iran's main claim that the decision was invalid because the Court had acted *ultra vires*. See *supra* Chapter 3 C I 4. Invalidity of the decision was clearly Iran's central argument, and one might even doubt whether this was not even in contradiction with the claim that the measures lacked binding force.

[104] See also *Mennecke/Tams* in 42 GYIL (1999), at 208: "[N]on-compliance with provisional measures [...] was not in all incidents due to the respondent's view that these measures were not binding. Rather this non-compliance was due to a general rejection of the Court's jurisdiction in the particular case, partially accompanied by a refusal to comply with the final judgment itself."

[105] Either partially or even completely, see the Fisheries Jurisdiction cases, the Tehran Hostages case, the Nicaragua case, *supra* Chapter 3 B XII, XIV and XVIII.

Charter obligation and an attack on the ICJ's authority.[106] Second, the possible scrutiny of a judgment—be it through a declaration of non-compliance or even in the form of a state responsibility claim—might have caused governments to show more respect for the Court, in that they were subject to far more pressure to justify their behavior.

While the findings on binding force in LaGrand cannot be taken as a guarantee against future problems, they were doubtlessly of tremendous significance in the promotion of compliance. First of all, *silence* of the Court on this issue, let alone a finding of non-bindingness, would certainly not have enhanced the readiness of those measures' addressees to take them seriously.[107] The confirmation of bindingness, on the other hand, resulted in a revalorization. The stakes for justifying non-compliance are substantially higher now that the status as binding decisions is no longer in question. The concrete circumstances of the cases submitted to the Court in the future will be a decisive factor. If the Court were another time seized with a dispute like the Tehran Hostages case, in which a régime rejects the concept of international law in its entirety, the level of deference to the Court's measures for interim protection would most likely not differ much from Iran's. On the other hand, if the Court were to indicate measures, say, in a case against Belgium under terms similar to those requested by the Democratic Republic of the Congo in Arrest Warrant, there would be a very high likelihood that the respondent would comply, a likelihood that can be considered to have increased through the Court's clear statement on the binding force. The Avena case will show how far the US non-compliance in the Breard and LaGrand cases could be explained on the basis of these doubts. Neither an alleged lack of binding force nor the reference to the federal structures would be a valid excuse if the three Mexicans were executed despite the Court's order, but this would inevitably have to be qualified as non-compliance.

---

[106] For example, the General Assembly might have been less reluctant to label non-compliance with the Court's order in the Nuclear Tests cases as such, see *supra* Chapter 3 C III 4.

[107] As the Court was pressed into giving an opinion of the matter, every answer short of a confirmation of the binding force (be it that the Court would have found some formal justification for not giving its opinion) would have been prejudicial to those measures' authority. Governments would most likely have been more hesitant to accept the disadvantages of unfavorable orders and might, in fact, face domestic criticism if they did. If the Court had regarded provisional measures as non-binding, it would have *ex post* lent legitimacy to the practice of non-compliance. States still complying might have been perceived as weak, and it would appear far more advantageous for them to rely on the diplomatic process only to find some interim solution. *Oxman* in Damrosch, The ICJ at a crossroads, at 333, refers to various potential costs for states of compliance with provisional measures: the government might lose the benefit of action restrained; it might suffer losses which it might be unable to recover even after a favorable judgment; it may weaken its bargaining position in negotiations with its opponent, and in view of the general record of non-compliance, domestic constituencies; the opponent and others might perceive its compliance as weakness or a lack of commitment or conviction.

IV. Decisions by the Court for improved compliance with provisional measures: Complementary measures, further orders, and sanctioning mechanisms in the judgment

1. Complementary measures and further orders to bring about compliance

Apart from ensuring the acceptability and legitimacy of the decision on provisional measures proper, the Court has complementary mechanisms at its disposal that may contribute to improved compliance. The Court's Presidents have regularly made use of their power under Article 74(4) of the Rules of Court to call upon the parties to ensure that any order the Court may make has its appropriate effects. While no miracles can be expected from such calls, they might contribute to sharpening the respective governments' awareness of the significance of the matter involved and the need to be prepared for a possible order. The Court made use of its power to require the states to request information about the implementation measures under Article 78 of the Rules. In the Breard and LaGrand cases, the order explicitly incorporated such complementary measures, thus showing the addressees that they would have to account for their behavior to the Court.

An entitled state might again turn to the Court to adopt a second order in view of the failure of the first order. While attempts in a similar direction had already been made earlier, the Genocide case was the first (and so far only) one where the Court issued a second order urging compliance with the first one. Such an approach might add weight to the first order, demonstrate the Court's dissatisfaction with the sufficiency of actions taken up to that point by the recalcitrant state, and increase the degree of attention of UN organs and the international community.[108] The Court might consider it possible and appropriate to adopt another order with measures of a higher degree of precision to ensure better compliance.[109]

2. Sanctioning non-compliance in the judgment on the merits

In certain circumstances, the Court might at the request of either party go one step further and sanction the breach of provisional measures in the judgment on the merits via a declaration of non-compliance, findings on state responsibility, or the withholding of relief. While some sanctioning mechanisms can

---

[108] The Security Council will be informed of the order, Article 41(2) of the ICJ Statute.

[109] This does not appear problematical as provisional measures do not enjoy force of *res judicata*: they can be revoked or amended at any stage anyway if a change in the situation justifies such action, see Article 76(1) of the Rules of Court. The Court had already indicated that it might adopt further measures in the Frontier Dispute (Burkina Faso/Mali) case, where there was ultimately no such necessity as the parties reached agreement on the terms of withdrawal between themselves, see Chapter 3 C V. It apparently saw no possibility beyond a reinforcement of the earlier measures in the Genocide case, given the limited scope for its jurisdiction.

already be found in implicit form in earlier cases, the findings in the LaGrand judgment make this phenomenon appear in a new light.

Implicit findings on breaches of provisional measures can be found in earlier orders where there was an overlap between the order and the questions under consideration in the merits. In the Tehran Hostages case, for example, the findings that Iran was obliged to free the hostages implied that its refusal to follow the same call in the order was illegal.[110] An explicit declaration of non-compliance as in LaGrand will only come where states have raised claims to this extent. In any event, the Court usually commented on problematic behavior of the parties in *obiter dicta* where such an occasion arose.[111] The extent to which a breach of the obligation of compliance entails the responsibility of the state and gives rise to a duty to provide reparation or indemnification is a question of the general rules of state responsibility, which is beyond the scope of the present study. Unlike Paraguay, Germany had not raised a claim for reparation or indemnification with regard to the measures; yet the Court by way of *obiter dicta* mentioned some criteria that might have been relevant if it had done so.[112] The Court will likely have to address such issues in the future, as litigants might well go that route.[113] The following remarks are intended to stimulate such a debate.

---

[110] *Supra* Chapter 3 C IV 2 (yet the Court did not speak of non-compliance). Similarly, the findings on the breach of the prohibition of the use of force and of intervention in the Nicaragua judgment implied that the US had violated the second provisional measure, as far as the violations concerned time periods after the indication of provisional measures.

[111] As the Court delivered no judgments on the merits in the Anglo-Iranian Oil Company case, the Nuclear Tests cases, and the Breard case, there was no such occasion there. In the Fisheries Jurisdiction cases, the Court stated that while no complaints had been made relating to the UK's and the FRG's compliance with the catch-limitation measure, Iceland had enforced its regulations notwithstanding the order, Chapter 3 C II 2. In the Tehran Hostages case, the Court expressed its deep regret that the situation giving rise to the order had not been rectified, which implied a breach of the order. On the other hand, its critical comments on the US military action to bring about the release of the hostages through self-help were rather arguments of contempt of court than of actual non-compliance with the order, Chapter 3 C IV 2–3. In the Nicaragua case, the Court stopped short of an explicit statement of non-compliance when recalling that in presence of provisional measures, states were not free to direct their conduct solely by what they believed to be their rights, Chapter 3 C VI 3. In the Genocide case, the Court emphasized in the second order that it was not satisfied that all that might have done had been done to prevent genocide in Bosnia and Herzegovina and to prevent an aggravation of the situation; this was particularly applicable for Yugoslavia, the only addressee of two of the three measures (the ones specifically relating to genocide), Chapter 3 C VII 5.

[112] LaGrand, Judgment of 27 June 2001, at para. 116: "[T]he Court points out that the United States was under great time pressure in this case, due to the circumstances in which Germany had instituted the proceedings. The Court notes moreover that at the time when the United States authorities took their decision on the question of the binding character of orders indicating provisional measures had been extensively discussed in the literature, but had not been settled by its jurisprudence. The Court would have taken these factors into consideration had Germany's submission included a claim for indemnification." For Paraguay's claims, see *supra* Chapter 3 C IX 4.

[113] See e.g. Cameroon's state responsibility claims in respect of alleged Nigerian non-compliance with the Court's provisional measures in the Land and Maritime Boundary case. See *supra*

Jurisdiction for non-compliance claims   Interestingly, the Court used its competence over the main claim in the LaGrand judgment as a jurisdictional basis for a claim of non-compliance with provisional measures.[114] If the Court has jurisdiction over the main claim, there are good grounds to assume that this jurisdiction will extend to state responsibility claims, given the Court's expansive formula for determining its jurisdiction with regard to the respective claim in LaGrand: "Where the Court has jurisdiction to decide a case, it also has jurisdiction to deal with submissions requesting it to determine that an order indicating measures which seeks to preserve the rights of the Parties to this dispute has not been complied with."[115] The generality of this statement intimates that in subsequent cases, a jurisdictional base would exist for the general question of non-compliance with provisional measures once jurisdiction is established on the main claims, irrespective of whether the complaint of non-compliance came from the applicant or the respondent. Conversely, a state entitled under an interim protection order probably cannot assign a non-existence competence to the Court when jurisdiction on the merits is wanting; such jurisdiction can only arise if some other basis is provided.

Admissibility of non-compliance claims   The next question relates to the impact of the complaining state's previous behavior on the admissibility of the claim. In the LaGrand judgment, the US had argued that the circumstances of Germany's request (i.e. the last-minute filing of its request) were such as to render Germany's non-compliance claim inadmissible.[116] The Court disposed of these claims in rather brief form, stating that the indication of provisional measures had been appropriate and that Germany was consequently entitled to challenge the non-compliance, even though Germany might be criticized for the manner in which it had made its filings.[117] One of the dissenting judges, the American Judge Buergenthal, specifically addressed the circumstances of Germany's application and argued that although it had been appropriate for the Court to issue the order, Germany's justification for its late filing did not withstand scrutiny, that the late filing itself had had serious negative consequences for the US position before the Court, and that the circumstances would have required the Court to hold the submission of non-compliance inadmissible.[118] Judge Buergenthal further

Chapter 3 C VIII 4. Cameroon's claim failed as it was insufficiently substantiated and proved; the burden of proof will be on the party claiming non-compliance, see Judgment of 10 October 2002, at para. 321.

[114] See *supra* Chapter 3 C X 3.

[115] LaGrand, Judgment of 27 June 2001, at para. 45. The Court appeared to acknowledge that further-reaching claims would be covered by its jurisdiction when referring to factors it would have taken into consideration "had Germany's submission included a claim for indemnification." (para. 116).

[116] See *supra* Chapter 3 C X 3.   [117] LaGrand, Judgment of 27 June 2001, at para. 57.

[118] Dissenting Opinion Buergenthal, paras. 1–19. Buergenthal noted that Germany could have had knowledge about the relevant facts at least since 1993, paras. 11, 14.

maintained that Germany itself had breached an obligation of elementary fairness towards the US when requesting provisional measures in the same terms as in the Breard case, even though it had been aware of the official US position in that case concerning the non-binding character of ICJ provisional measures.[119]

Indeed, the German request could have anticipated arguments relating to an alleged lack of bindingness of provisional measures. Yet it seems excessive to say that bringing counter-arguments in this respect would constitute behavior *mandated* by an obligation of elementary fairness. Germany was merely exercising its procedural rights when asking for the indication of provisional measures.[120] It is not the applicant's task to investigate whether domestic actors might be likely to ignore their international obligations.[121] The US *itself* should have been aware of the controversy regarding its stance on the binding character of provisional measures. The non-compliance with the order in the Breard case had generated great controversy particularly among US international lawyers,[122] and Paraguay had made a formal claim of non-compliance with the order in similar proceedings that were later discontinued.[123]

As regards the tardiness of the application, Judge Buergenthal's starting-point appears to be correct in separating the question of the appropriateness of the *indication* of provisional measures at the issuance of the order from the right of a state to bring a claim of non-compliance when its own behavior had contributed to making compliance more difficult and amounted in retrospect to an unjustified delay. Germany acknowledged that delay on the part of a claimant state might render an application inadmissible, but it had argued that there was no specific time limit and that it had only gained knowledge of all the relevant facts seven days prior to the application.[124] Questions arise as to whether Germany itself acted negligently when gathering the relevant information. Moreover, it is debatable whether the knowledge of the precise date that the local authorities were aware of the nationality issue could be so decisive a factor as to justify a last-minute application to the Court and require a week-long period of reflection at a time when the execution date

---

[119] Ibid., paras. 20–4.   [120] See *Oellers-Frahm*, EuGRZ 2001, at 267.

[121] But see Dissenting Opinion Buergenthal, para. 22: "There was nothing in the order Germany requested on 2 March 1999 that would have provided the authorities of the United States with a legal basis justifying the Solicitor General to reverse his official position adopted less than a year earlier. In the absence of such a justification, it would have been unprecedented for him not to adhere to its earlier view." It was not Germany's task to consider that the Solicitor-General had reasons to deviate from an official position that had not been in conformity with the US's international obligations; see on the violation of the order the Breard case *supra*.

[122] See the various contributions to "Agora: Breard" in 92 AJIL (1998), at 666–712.

[123] See *supra* Chapter 3 C IX 4.   [124] LaGrand, Judgment of 27 June 2001, at para. 56.

was imminent.[125] The judgment did not explicitly tackle these issues, which might imply a general rule that the claimant might raise a breach of the provisional measures at the merits stage whenever the Court had considered it appropriate to indicate provisional measures. Such a leap in logic, however, would be an oversimplification. It is well imaginable that the applicant's conduct complicated compliance to such a degree as to reduce its right to indemnification or to estop a claim of non-compliance although circumstances had necessitated the provisional measures. Certainly, if the applicant had *intentionally* rendered compliance difficult for the other side for the sole purpose of creating a possible non-compliance claim, the Court would most likely reject such a claim as inadmissible on the basis of some doctrine akin to the "clean hands" doctrine or the principle of good faith.

The relation between non-compliance claims and the main claim   In terms of substance, one may ask how closely non-compliance claims are connected with the merits of the main claim. May a state assert non-compliance with a decision in an effort to protect a right whose existence the Court denied in its decision on the merits?[126] The answer to this question depends on the locus of the obligation of compliance with provisional measures. If the basis for the obligation lies in a provisional measures order's status as a Court decision, compliance is always required as a sign of respect for the Court's authority. Alternatively, if the basis is the order's nature as a mechanism protecting a right, non-compliance may become a moot point in the event that the alleged right is later found to be non-existent.

There are better reasons to advocate for the former view: the actual existence of the right that is to be protected is not a precondition of the obligation of compliance under Article 41 of the Statute and Article 94(1) of the Charter. Effective interim protection could not be guaranteed if the debtor could raise a defense of non-existence of the obligation. A decision on provisional measures is binding because it was adopted as a binding decision under Article 41 of the Statute; the other side can assert compliance or non-compliance even if it loses the main claim. Yet there would be no basis for a claim for reparation or indemnification against the recalcitrant state, as the state entitled under the order could only claim "imaginary" (and thus not awardable) damages.

Withholding of relief   In extreme cases, it is imaginable that the Court could refrain from issuing a decision on the merits when the applicant continuously thwarts the dispute-settlement process—despite having initiated it—by not adhering to provisional measures, for example. Judge Morozov suggested

---

[125] See critically *Mennecke*, 44 GYIL (2001), at 443–4, in particular, at 444: "The enduring passivity of the German government conjures up questions whether for most of the time, motives such as the reluctance to bring the main ally United States before the International Court of Justice had been prevalent."

[126] A distinction should be made between such orders protecting the *res* and other decisions where there is a less intrinsic link with the subject-matter, such as measures to prevent an aggravation of the dispute, where this problem would not come up.

such a scenario in his dissenting opinion in the Tehran Hostages case, akin to "contempt of court" in national legal systems—although in that case, the US behavior certainly did not rise to such a level.[127] The likelihood of such cases is low since states deciding to pursue litigation before the ICJ will usually generally accord due respect to the Court—at least superficially.

The Court, however, would have no apparent basis under the Charter or Statute of withholding relief in other pending cases involving the recalcitrant state; falling short of non-compliance as this would unduly affect other proceedings and involve legal positions of other states.[128]

---

[127] See *supra* Chapter 3 C IV 3.

[128] Such action had been suggested by Nicaragua following its complaint of non-compliance with the Court's order, but this was correctly denied by the Court's president, see *supra* Chapter 3 C VI 3.

Concluding Remarks

There is reason for cautious optimism. The Court's prestige is at an unprecedented high. Even though compliance has not always been easy, there has been a marked shift in the attitude of parties to proceedings. Since the 1986 Nicaragua judgment, litigants have assumed a more respectful posture—in stark contrast to the open defiance of the Court in the 1970s—and not questioned whether the respective decision was, for example, a case where the Court had exceeded its powers. Problems have instead centered on the sufficiency of certain modes of implementation—for instance, whether a party's verbal commitment constitutes appropriate action. In these cases, however, the authority of the Court's decisions and the obligation of compliance were not put in question (with the Breard and LaGrand cases as special situations in which the bindingness of the decisions had been controversial). The reaction to the Court's most recent order and judgments[1] will hopefully continue the largely successful compliance trend. The nature of future cases will, of course, have a decisive impact on the risks for compliance. Since the Court cannot pick and choose among the cases submitted, it must take care to avoid the danger of political manipulation when addressing sensitive topics. The more critical a case might be in terms of future compliance, the more important it becomes that the Court's reasoning be thorough and conform to its former jurisprudence.

The relatively positive compliance record for ICJ decisions merits greater recognition and is all the more remarkable in light of the increasing diversity in terms of litigants before the Court. While attention is easily drawn to areas of criticism (e.g. the US government's rejection of the Nicaragua judgment, the relative weakness of enforcement mechanisms), the many cases of trouble-free implementation of judgments—including in cases of compulsory jurisdiction—often escape notice. The record for provisional measures deserves a more nuanced description than the mere reference to the Frontier Dispute case as the only case of doubtlessly perfect implementation. Enhancing awareness of the successful compliance record requires gathering information on follow-up to ICJ decisions and disseminating this information to a broad audience. The variety of sources that had to be consulted for the purposes of the present study shows the difficulty of finding such information; the Court itself has reported on implementation in its Yearbooks, but

---

[1] These include the judgments in the Land and Maritime Boundary between Cameroon and Nigeria, and in Sovereignty over Pulau Litigan and Pulau Sipadan, and the provisional measures in Avena and other Mexican Nationals.

only on an infrequent and seemingly random basis.[2] Some recent orders on provisional measures have called on parties to keep the Court abreast of measures taken in their implementation.[3] In addition to serving as an incentive for compliance in those concrete cases, since the states concerned knew that they had to account for their implementing action, the information requirement had the useful side effect of creating a new information source. Beyond this, a useful mechanism for gathering information might be creating a central depository for follow-up data, such as the Carnegie library at the Peace Palace, and requesting parties to provide pertinent information on a voluntary basis.[4] This could then function as a springboard for further scholarship as well as for efforts by the Court's information department to enhance visibility of the successful role of the ICJ.

---

[2] See, for example, the information on the UK–Albanian memorandum of understanding in the ICJ YB 1995–6, at 257.

[3] See *supra* Chapter 4 B IV 1.

[4] To make the delivery of such information mandatory would go too far, as would the establishment of an actual monitoring unit, as the parties might want to retain control over the post-adjudicative settlement process. Yet if the parties knew that such a central depository existed and if the Court were to inform all parties on a courtesy basis that it would appreciate their contributions, explaining the function of the depository in facilitating legal research and improving the visibility of the Court's action, it is very likely that almost all states will cooperate and submit some information.

Zusammenfassung (German Summary)

Der Internationale Gerichthof, Hauptrechtsprechungsorgan der Vereinten Nationen, erfreut sich seit einigen Jahren zunehmender Beliebtheit. Vor ihm sind mehr Fälle denn je zur Entscheidung anhängig. Die Streitparteien stammen nicht wie in den ersten Jahrzehnten seiner Geschichte fast ausschließlich aus dem westeuropäisch-amerikanischen Kulturkreis, sondern aus allen vier Kontinenten, mit einer bemerkenswerten Präsenz afrikanischer Staaten. Die Vielfalt in der Zusammensetzung der Richterbank, der Streitparteien und der relevanten Sachgebiete—Gewaltanwendung, Kriegsrecht, Völkermord, Meeres- und Landgrenzen, Vertragsrecht, Staatenverantwortlichkeit, nur um einige Beispiele zu nennen—lässt die inoffiziell verwendete Bezeichnung als "World Court"—Weltgericht—durchaus als angemessen erscheinen.

Trotz dieser Entwicklung sollte nicht aus den Augen verloren werden, dass sich der IGH nicht vor allzu langer Zeit—in den 70er und teilweise auch noch in den 80er Jahren—in einer tief greifenden Krise befand, in welcher er von einigen Beobachtern bereits totgesagt worden war, zumindest bezüglich seiner obligatorischen Zuständigkeit. Eine Serie von Fällen, in denen die Klagegegner das Verfahren zumindest in einem Teil boykottierten, die Miss-achtung einstweiliger Anordnungen und Urteile und das Unvermögen der berechtigten Staaten, ihre Rechte aus IGH-Entscheidungen wirksam durchzusetzen, haben der Weltöffentlichkeit vor Augen geführt, dass die wirksame Umsetzung dieser Entscheidungen im wesentlichen Maße von ihrer Akzeptanz durch die Streitparteien abhängt und Vollstreckungsmechanismen zwar existieren, aber sehr viel schwächer ausgeprägt sind als solche innerstaatlicher Gerichte. Die Tatsache, dass eine Vielzahl der Fälle, die derzeit vor dem IGH anhängig sind, gegen den Willen der betreffenden Klagegegner eingeleitet worden ist, könnte Anlass zur Befürchtung einer erneuten Zunahme von Widerstand gegen IGH-Entscheidungen bieten.

Eine Analyse der Befolgungspraxis des Gerichts ist ein Erfolgs- und Risikomesser für die Stellung des IGH: je besser die Entscheidungen des Gerichtes befolgt werden, umso mehr ist damit zu rechnen, dass die Befolgung zur *self-fulfilling prophecy* wird und dass es für einen Staat zunehmend schwerer wird, eine Nichtbefolgung zu rechtfertigen. Andersherum gesehen wird es eine Serie von Fällen der Nichtbefolgung dem betreffenden Staat nicht nur einfacher machen, sich ebenso zu verhalten, sondern es mag sogar zu einem gewissen Druck in diese Richtung führen, um keine vermeintliche Schwäche zu zeigen. Eine Analyse der Praxis dient weiterhin dazu, Faktoren aufzuzeigen, die für die Umsetzung der Entscheidungen von Bedeutung waren, um Mittel zur Förderung einer erfolgreichen Befolgungspraxis aufzuzeigen. Zu diesem Zweck müssen notwendigerweise die Rahmenbedingungen der jeweiligen

Fälle einbezogen werden, wie beispielsweise die Beziehungen zwischen den betroffenen Staaten, die anwendbaren Rechtsvorschriften, das Wesen der Streitigkeit, die dahinter stehenden Interessen. Es wäre naiv anzunehmen, dass das Bestehen einer Verpflichtung zur Umsetzung der Entscheidung der einzige Faktor ist, der einen Staat zur Befolgung einer Entscheidung veranlasst.

"Entscheidungen" im Sinne dieser Studie sind Urteile und einstweilige Anordnungen. Die Verpflichtung zu ihrer Befolgung ergibt sich aus Artikel 94(1) der UN-Charta und Artikel 41 des Statuts des Gerichtshofs. Die lange umstrittene Frage der bindenden Wirkung einstweiliger Anordnungen ist vom IGH im LaGrand—Urteil 2001 im positiven Sinne beantwortet worden. Diese Entscheidung ist als Aufwertung einstweiliger Anordnungen zu sehen. Andererseits steht damit die wahre Bewährungsprobe dieser Entscheidungen, für deren begrenzten Erfolg bislang unter anderem die umstrittene Bindungswirkung angeführt werden konnte, erst jetzt an. Weiterhin mag die Entscheidung einen gewissen Anreiz für rein politisch motivierte Anträge mit dubioser rechtlicher Grundlage bieten, für die der Gerichtshof vorbereitet sein sollte.

Hinsichtlich der Vollstreckung seiner Entscheidungen hat der Gerichtshof selbst nur sehr beschränkte Zuständigkeiten, was die Trennung zwischen gerichtlicher und vollstreckender Phase auf der internationalen Ebene verdeutlicht. Die Hauptverantwortung zur Umsetzung der Entscheidungen obliegt den Parteien. Während der IGH für einstweilige Anordnungen noch ein bestimmtes Instrumentarium an Durchsetzungs- und Sanktionierungsmechanismen hat, ist seine Aufgabe mit dem Erlass des Urteils im Prinzip abgeschlossen. Im Fall der Nichtbefolgung eines Urteils sieht Artikel 94(2) der Charta ein Recht des berechtigten Staates vor, sich an den Sicherheitsrat zu wenden, der nach Ermessen Empfehlungen oder Maßnahmen zur Durchsetzung des Urteils beschließen kann. Der Ermessenspielraums ist notwendig, da es dem Sicherheitsrat möglich sein muss, Erwägungen, die gegen eine sofortige Umsetzung eines Urteils sprechen könnten, zu berücksichtigen, insbesondere die Auswirkungen einer Vollstreckung auf die internationale Sicherheit. Andererseits ergibt sich dadurch die Gefahr eine Blockade durch ständige Mitglieder des Sicherheitsrats, insbesondere unter der Berücksichtigung der Tatsache, dass beteiligte Staaten nicht zur Enthaltung verpflichtet sind, sofern die Angelegenheit nicht als "Streitigkeit" unter Kapitel VI behandelt wird. Somit wird der Rückgriff auf den Sicherheitsrat in der Regel dann wenig hilfreich sein, wenn Interessenssphären der ständigen Mitglieder betroffen sind. In der Praxis hat der Sicherheitsrat noch nie Vollstreckungsmaßnahmen aufgrund von Artikel 94(2) ergriffen. Die geringe Praxis des Sicherheitsrats als Vollstreckungsorgans spiegelt in erster Linie die Zurückhaltung der Parteien wider, sich zu diesem Zweck an den Sicherheitsrat zu wenden. Für diese Zurückhaltung mögen verschiedenartige

Gründe bestehen: der betreffende Staat mag die Kontrolle über die Umsetzungsverhandlungen nicht verlieren wollen, oder er mag die Erfolgschancen für eine solche Initiative für gering halten, sei es, weil die Grundlage seines Befolgungsersuchens in rechtlicher oder tatsächlicher Hinsicht zweifelhaft ist, weil sein Anliegen auf wenig Sympathie stoßen würde, weil ständige Mitglieder oder ihre Interessengebiete betroffen sind oder weil der Sicherheitsrat ohnehin schon mit der Sache befasst ist.

Angesichts der Tatsache, dass die Chancen für effektives Handeln des Sicherheitsrats nach Beendigung der im Kalten Krieg bestehenden Blockadesituation größer geworden sind, könnte dem Sanktionsmechanismus des Artikel 94(2) in der Zukunft durchaus höhere Bedeutung zukommen. Allerdings wird in der Regel anzunehmen sein, dass eine Vollstreckung nach Artikel 94(2) nur dann in Frage kommen wird, wenn der betreffende Staat sich ausdrücklich weigert, das Urteil zu befolgen; eine Situation, die seit dem Nicaragua-Fall nicht mehr eingetreten ist. Zumindest wird der Sicherheitsrat ein hohes Ausmaß an Wahrscheinlichkeit dafür verlangen, dass eine Verletzung eines Urteils vorliegt, und es unter dieser Schwelle für wünschenswerter halten, durch positive Maßnahmen den Umsetzungsprozess zu unterstützen (Vermittlung, Beobachtung, etc.), anstatt durch Verhängung von Sanktionen Partei zu ergreifen. Im Rahmen von positiven Maßnahmen ist auch eine konstruktive Rolle der Generalversammlung, des Sekretariats und des Wirtschafts- und Sozialrats vorstellbar.

Als weitere Durchsetzungsmechanismen kommen Maßnahmen internationaler Organisationen, unilaterale Maßnahmen des berechtigten Staates und Hilfe durch Drittstaaten in Betracht. Eine Durchsetzung von IGH-Entscheidungen durch Einschaltung innerstaatlicher Gerichte könnte ein besonders effizienter Mechanismus sein, da es für einen Rechtsstaat undenkbar ist, die Entscheidung seines eigenen Gerichts ausser acht zu lassen und damit die Grundlage seiner verfassungsmäßigen Ordnung in Frage zu stellen.

Eine Analyse der Befolgungspraxis ist auf diejenigen Entscheidungen zu beziehen, die Umsetzungsakte erfordern. Für einstweilige Anordnungen liegt dies nach dem Wortlaut von Artikel 41 des IGH-Statuts in der Natur der Sache ("Maßnahmen (. . .) die zur Sicherung der Rechte der Parteien getroffen werden müssen"); für Urteile ist das Bestehen eines Umsetzungserfordernisses im Einzelfall zu untersuchen. Ausgeschlossen werden konnten alle Urteile, in denen die Klage abgewiesen wurde, es sei denn, damit waren Feststellungen verbunden, die eine Handlungspflicht implizierten. Gegenstand der Untersuchung sind demnach 27 Fälle für Urteile und elf Fälle für einstweilige Anordnungen (wobei Fälle, die parallel verliefen, als ein Fall gezählt wurden).

Die Erfolgsbilanz für Urteile ist weitgehend positiv. Zwar gibt es einige besorgniserregende Ausnahmen, bei denen die Adressaten die Rechtgültigkeit eines Urteils bestritten haben. Zu erwähnen ist hier der Korfukanal-Fall, der Isländische Fischereistreit, der Teheraner Geiselnahmefall sowie der Nicaragua-Fall. Selbst diese Fälle erscheinen jedoch aus heutiger Perspektive weniger schwerwiegend als zum Zeitpunkt ihrer Verkündung: der Korfuka-nal-Fall ist nach mehreren Jahrzehnten doch noch beigelegt worden, im Teheraner Geiselnahmefall wurden die Geiseln schließlich freigelassen (wenn auch nur im Rahmen einer Gesamteinigung; weiterhin bleiben andere Elemente der Entscheidungsformel bis heute unerfüllt), im Nicaragua-Fall eröffnete ein Regimewechsel die Chance für eine Neubewertung der Beziehung der beiden Staaten, so dass dem Urteil keine Bedeutung mehr zukam. Das Urteil im Fischereistreit-Fall wiederum wurde innerhalb von kurzer Zeit von der Rechtsentwicklung überholt, und der Fall wäre mit großer Wahrscheinlichkeit nie vor den Gerichtshof gebracht worden, wenn diese Rechtsentwicklung und insbesondere ihre enorme Schnelligkeit vorauszusehen gewesen wäre. Es gibt zwar einige weitere Fälle, in denen sich einzelne Staaten über Nichtbefolgung eines Urteils beschwert haben, aber diese Vorwürfe waren entweder ungerechtfertigt, weil sie auf einer unzutreffenden Auslegung des Verpflichtungsgehalts der jeweiligen Entscheidung beruhten, oder zumindest nicht hinreichend substantiiert. Das Auftreten von Schwierigkeiten oder Verzögerungen in der Umsetzung kann je nach Rechts- und Sachlage nicht völlig ausgeschlossen werden, insbesondere wenn das Urteils zum Ergebnis hat, dass die Parteien den Streit durch Verhandlungen zu lösen haben, nachdem der Grund, dass diese die Angelegenheit vor den IGH gebracht hatten, gerade das Scheitern solcher Verhandlungen war. Auch unzureichende Resourcen können eine Rolle spielen.

Die Erfolgsbilanz für einstweilige Anordnungen fällt deutlich negativer aus. Nur in einem Fall—dem Grenzstreit zwischen Burkina Faso und Mali—ist von vollumfänglich erfolgreicher Umsetzung der einstweiligen Anordnung auszugehen. Die übrigen Fälle können in drei Gruppen gegliedert werden. Die erste Gruppe sind die Fälle, in denen die Adressaten die Rechtmäßigkeit der betreffenden Anordnungen bestritten und sich geweigert haben, sie zu befolgen. Dies betrifft alle Fälle einstweiliger Anordnungen von Anglo-Iranian Oil Co. bis zum Nicaragua-Fall (im letzteren Fall nur mit Einschränkungen, da eine Teilbefolgung gegeben ist). Die zweite Gruppe bilden die Fälle, bei denen sich die Parteien über die Rechtsgültigkeit der Entscheidung einig waren, aber umstritten ist, inwieweit sie ihrer Verpflichtung tatsächlich nachgekommen sind. Die dritte Gruppe schließlich bilden die beiden Fälle über die Verletzung der Wiener Konsularrechtskonvention, Breard und LaGrand, in welchen neben der Behauptung, alles Erforderliche getan zu haben, ein Hauptargument des nichtbefolgenden Staates die angebliche Unverbindlichkeit einstweiliger Anordnungen war. Ein dahinter-stehendes Problem dieser Fälle war die Durchsetzung internationaler Verpflichtungen in einem Bundesstaat. Obwohl in allen dieser Fälle Anzeichen für eine Nichtbefolgung vorliegen, ergibt sich ein differenzierteres Bild, wenn man weniger auf die Abweichung von der idealen Befolgung abstellt, sondern im Gegenteil darauf, inwieweit sich die Lage ohne die Anordnung hätte verschlimmern können und ob sie nicht zumindest eine gewisse Mäßigung zur Folge gehabt haben könnte. Weiterhin mag bereits die Anordnung als solche einen Nutzen für die Antragsteller erfüllt haben. Lediglich für die Isländischen Fischereistreitsfälle und die Breard und LaGrand-Fälle muss wohl auch bei einer solchen Betrachtung jeglicher praktische Wert abgesprochen werden.

In der Gesamtbilanz ist der Nicaragua-Fall als Zäsur sowohl für Urteile als auch für einstweilige Anordnungen zu erkennen: Konflikte über die Umsetzung der Entscheidungen betrafen nach dem Nicaragua-Urteil nicht mehr die Rechtgültigkeit der jeweiligen Entscheidung, sondern ihre tatsächliche Befolgung. Diese Tatsache ist von enormer Bedeutung: Streitigkeiten darüber, ob das tatsächliche Verhalten einer Partei mit einer Anordnung übereinstimmt, sind a priori kein besonderer Grund zur Beunruhigung, sondern ein üblicher Bestandteil von Rechtsstreitigkeiten—die Autorität der Entscheidung und die Pflicht zu ihrer Befolgung werden nicht in Frage gestellt (wohl aber gegebenenfalls die Effizienz des Gerichts als Streitbeilegungsorgan). Der Respekt, den sämtliche Parteien seit dem Nicaragua-Fall dem Gerichtshof erwiesen haben (zumindest verbal), ist ein für die Stellung des IGH ermutigendes Zeichen. Dadurch sollte sich der Gerichtshof jedoch nicht in falscher Sicherheit wiegen. Zwei der jüngsten Entscheidungen, deren Befolgung noch nicht abschließend bewertet werden kann, könnten in der Tat die Autorität des Gerichts erneut angreifen: der Grenzstreit zwischen Kamerun und Nigeria, in welchem Nigeria das Urteil in ersten Stellungnahmen verworfen hatte, inzwischen aber über die Umsetzung verhandelt, sowie die einstweilige Anordnung im Avena-Fall, einem Parallelfall zu Breard und LaGrand, in welchem die USA aufgefordert sind, von der Hinrichtung dreier mexikanischer Staatsbürger während der Dauer des Verfahrens abzusehen. Die erste Stellungnahme von Seiten des texanischen Gouverneurs gibt Grund zu der Befürchtung, dass er möglicherweise die Anordnung nicht respektieren wird, sofern nicht innerstaatliche Gerichte oder die Bundesorgane ein völkerrechtsgemäßes Verhalten erzwingen.

Insgesamt lassen sich aus der bisherigen Befolgungspraxis eine Reihe von Schlussfolgerungen ziehen. Eine Verwerfung einer Entscheidung durch eine Partei hat bislang nur in denjenigen Fällen stattgefunden, in denen der betreffende Staat zumindest einen Teil des Verfahrens boykottiert hat. Dies ist aber kein notwendiger Zusammenhang. Es ist einerseits nicht auszuschließen, dass Staaten, die an einem Verfahren teilgenommen haben, und sei es unter ständiger Betonung ihrer Rechtstreue, eine aus ihrer Sicht unzumutbare Entscheidung schließlich doch als unrechtmäßig zurückweisen, möglicherweise unter Verweis auf eine angebliche Kompetenzüberschreitung des Gerichtshofs. Andererseits kann nicht ausgeschlossen werden, dass sich das Phänomen einer Nichtteilnahme an Verhandlungen wiederholen könnte, auch wenn die Hemmschwelle dafür sicherlich inzwischen sehr viel höher ist als in den 70er Jahren, in der eine Serie von Fällen des Nichterscheinens es für einen Staat fast schon legitim erscheinen lassen konnte, denselben Weg einzuschlagen.

Ein gemeinsames Element der Fälle der Erfüllungsverweigerung ist ihr politischer Charakter; viele Fälle bezogen sich auf Situationen von Gewaltanwendung. Zutreffend hat der Gerichtshof festgestellt, dass ihn die politischen Dimensionen einer Streitigkeit nicht an einer Entscheidung in dem betreffenden Fall hindern können. Dennoch dürfen die politischen Dimensionen nicht ignoriert werden, sondern der Gerichtshof muss Methoden entwickeln, um seine Instrumentalisierung zu vermeiden.

Die allgemeine Annahme, dass Fälle, in denen sich die Parteien über die Anrufung des Gerichtshofs im speziellen Einzelfall geeinigt haben, das für den Gerichtshof ideale Szenarium sind, bei dem grundsätzlich keine Befolgungsschwierigkeiten zu erwarten sind, bedarf einer Relativierung. Zwar sind in der Regel in solchen Fällen Faktoren gegeben, die für eine Befolgung förderlich sind, und das Risiko eines Widerstands gegen eine Entscheidung dürfte bei Fällen, bei denen eine Streitigkeit gegen den Willen eines Staates vor den Gerichtshof gebracht wird, höher sein. Dennoch liegt mit dem Korfukanal-Fall ein Fall vor, in dem die Befolgung eines Urteils trotz Bestehen eines *special agreements* (eines Abkommens über die Zuständigkeit des Gerichtshofs im Einzelfall) lange Zeit verweigert worden ist. Die Auslegung von *special agreements*, insbesondere das Ausmaß der dadurch übertragenen Zuständigkeit, hat in vielen Fällen zu Konflikten geführt. Dieses Konfliktpotential kann durch eine genauere Formulierung der Vertragsklauseln verringert werden; die Unschärfe der Formulierung mag jedoch gerade von der Unfähigkeit der Parteien herrühren, die dem Gericht vorzulegende Frage präziser zu formulieren. Eine problemlose Umsetzung ist auch in Fällen der Einigung über die Vorlage des Streites an den Gerichtshof nicht garantiert. Andererseits sollten die Erfolge in Fällen von obligatorischer Zuständigkeit (sei es unter der Fakultativklausel oder aufgrund von allgemeinen Streitbeilegungsklauseln in Verträgen) nicht in Abrede gestellt werden, auch wenn die berüchtigtsten Fälle der Befolgungsverweigerung in solchen Konstellationen geschehen sind. Daher erscheint der Ruf nach einer Abschaffung der obligatorischen Zuständigkeit ungerechtfertigt. Andererseits dürfte es für die Stellung des Gerichtshofs wenig hilfreich sein, Staaten ihre Zustimmung zu dieser Art von Jurisdiktion aufzudrängen, sofern sie nicht bereit sind, die Konsequenzen dieser Entscheidung sind zu tragen. Weiterhin sollte der Gerichtshof peinlich genau darauf achten, sich in den Grenzen seiner Zuständigkeit zu halten und das fundamentale Prinzip der freiwilligen Unterwerfung der Staaten unter seine Gerichtsbarkeit ausreichend zu berücksichtigen. Dies gilt insbesondere für einstweilige

Anordnungen. Zwar hat die bisherige Rechtsprechung schon große Fortschritte in Hinblick auf eine Präzisierung des Kriteriums der *Prima-Fazie-*Zuständigkeit gemacht hat, im einzelnen bleiben aber noch viele Fragen offen. Da einstweilige Anordnungen fast ausschließlich zu einem Zeitpunkt erlassen worden sind, zu dem der Gerichtshof noch nicht abschließend über seine Zuständigkeit entschieden hatte, sind überzeugende Standards besonders wichtig, die die Entscheidung voraussehbar machen, um die Akzeptanz der Entscheidung zu sichern.

Die Unterschiede in der Erfolgsbilanz von Urteilen und einstweiligen Anordnungen können auf eine Reihe von Faktoren zurückgeführt werden. Einstweilige Anordnungen wurden bis auf eine Ausnahme, den Grenzstreit zwischen Burkina Faso und Mali, der in der Tat auch der einzige Fall einer vollumfänglich erfolgreichen einstweiligen Anordnung war, in Fällen erlassen, die gegen den Willen des Klagegegners eingeleitet worden waren und in welchen der Klagegegner die Zuständigkeit des Gerichtshofs bestritten hatte. Für die Fälle der offenen Erfüllungverweigerung kommt hinzu, dass die Klagegegner eine Fundamentalopposition gegen jegliche Tätigkeit des Gerichtshofs in der Sache bis zum Punkt einer Boykottierung des Verfahrens (zumindest zu einem Teil) betrieben hatten. In einigen weiteren Fällen hat der IGH lediglich Rechtsregeln bestätigt, die zwischen den Parteien unstreitig waren und deren Anerkennung auch vor der Anordnung keine Rechtsverstöße hatte ausschalten können. Damit durften keine Wunder durch die Maßnahmen des Gerichts erwartet werden, was eher auf die Grenzen des Rechts als auf eine Schwäche des Gerichtshofs hinweist. Ein weiteres Problem ist die Unbestimmtheit der Anordnungen, die dazu führen kann, dass stets einige Aspekte für und andere gegen eine Befolgung sprechen werden (wie etwa bei der Pflicht, keine Maßnahmen zu ergreifen, die zu einer Erweiterung des Streits führen könnten); dennoch mag selbst ein Ausspruch solch unbestimmter Anordnungen eine gewisse mäßigende Wirkung ausüben und daher einem Nichthandeln vorzuziehen sein. Des weiteren war bedeutsame Hilfe von Seiten des Sicherheitsrats in den bisherigen Fällen nicht zu erwarten, da entweder ein ständiges Mitglied unmittelbar beteiligt oder der Sicherheitsrat ohnehin schon mit der Angelegenheit beschäftigt war.

Die Überzeugungskraft der einstweiligen Anordnungen wird im wesentlichen davon abhängen, dass die Staaten darauf vertrauen können, dass eine sachgemäße Abwägung aller relevanten Faktoren erfolgt ist und die Entscheidung auf rechtlichen Kriterien beruht. Dies sollte aus einer sorgfältigen und umfassenden Begründung ersichtlich sein. Eine solche ist nicht in allen Fällen gegeben worden. Die knappe Begründung zumindest der ersten Anordnungen hat sicher nicht dazu beigetragen, die Legitimität der betreffenden Entscheidung aus Sicht der Adressaten zu stärken.

Eine genauere Untersuchung der Frage, inwieweit einstweilige Anordnungen so gestaltet werden können, dass für beide Seiten ein Anreiz zur Befolgung besteht, ist wünschenswert. Insbesondere erscheint unklar, ob und inwieweit der Antragsteller dem Antragsgegner für Schäden haftet, die aufgrund der Befolgung einer einstweiligen Anordnung entstanden sind, die ein Recht zu schützen bestimmt war, welches der Gerichtshof später für nicht existierend gehalten hat. Das Bestehen eines allgemeinen Entschädigungsanspruchs entsprechend § 945 ZPO könnte dazu beitragen, Bedenken des Antragstellers gegen eine Befolgung der betreffenden Anordnung abzumildern, und würde gleichzeitig eine gewisse Abschreckung gegen ausschließlich politisch motivierte und rechtlich unfundierte Anträge auf einstweiligen Rechtsschutz bieten.

Die Zweifel an der Verbindlichkeit der einstweiligen Anordnungen scheinen bislang, die Breard und LaGrand Fälle ausgenommen, eher eine geringere Rolle für die Befolgung gespielt zu haben, da in den Fällen der Fundamentalopposition gegenüber dem Gerichtshof auch bei einer klareren Formulierung des Artikels 41 des Statuts wohl keine andere Reaktion zu erwarten gewesen wäre; in den anschließenden Fällen wiederum hat kein Staat die Maßgeblichkeit der einstweiligen Anordnung in Frage gestellt, sondern alle Parteien haben vorgebracht, sie befolgt zu haben. Dennoch kann nicht ausgeschlossen werden, dass sich die internationale Gemeinschaft gegenüber der Außerachtlassung von zweifelsfrei als verbindlich erkannten Anordnungen weniger gleichgültig gezeigt hätte, dass der Rechtfertigungsdruck auf den betreffenden Staat höher gewesen wäre, und dass die Aussicht, möglicherweise für sein Verhalten im Verfahren Rechenschaft ablegen zu müssen, einen Einfluss auf den Adressaten gehabt hätte.

Der LaGrand-Fall enthält im übrigen Ausführungen des Gerichts zum einstweiligen Rechtsschutz, die als Rahmen für einen Sanktionsmechanismus für einstweilige Anordnungen im Urteil ausgelegt werden können. Ansätze für solche Mechanismen sind schon in Fällen früherer Anordnungen erkennbar, da der Gerichtshof in der Regel in den Urteilen Kommentare zu den einstweiligen Anordnungen abgegeben hat. Des Weiteren bestehen gewisse Mechanismen zur Förderung der Befolgung einstweiliger Anordnungen insoweit, als der Gerichtshof Information über die Maßnahmen zur Umsetzung verlangen sowie erforderlichenfalls eine weitere Anordnung zum wirksamen Schutz der betroffenen Rechte erlassen kann.

Abschließend bleibt festzustellen, dass die Befolgungspraxis des Gerichtshofs durchaus Anlass zu vorsichtigem Optimismus hinsichtlich der zukünftigen Entwicklung gibt. Dass auch heutzutage in einigen Fällen darüber gestritten wird, ob bestimmte Entscheidungen befolgt werden, steht dem nicht entgegen, denn der entscheidende Aspekt ist, dass nicht mehr über die Rechtmäßigkeit der Entscheidungen und eine mögliche Kompetenzüberschreitung gestritten wird, sondern darüber, wie eine Entscheidung auszulegen ist und ob die vorgebrachten Tatsachen zutreffend sind. Dies sind Streitigkeiten, die ein normaler Bestandteil von Streitbeilegungsprozessen

und die Geltung der Norm über die Befolgungspflicht nicht in Frage
_en. Dennoch sollte der Gerichtshof nicht vergessen, dass er von der
_xzeptanz der Staatengemeinschaft abhängig ist, und sich nicht nur um
_achlich angemessene Standards bemühen, sondern auch durch die Begrün-
dung seiner Entscheidungen überzeugen und geeignete Mechanismen gegen
eine politische Manipulation entwickeln. Weiterhin sollte die positive Befolgungspraxis im höheren Maße in das Bewusstsein der Öffentlichkeit gebracht
werden. Hierzu könnte die Einrichtung einer zentralen Stelle zur Sammlung
von Informationen (z. B. in der Carnegie Library am Sitz des Gerichtshofs)
beitragen, für die der Gerichtshof die Parteien um Übersendung von Informationen über die Umsetzung der Entscheidungen auf freiwilliger Basis
bitten könnte.

Bibliography

Unless indicated otherwise, treatises will be cited with the last name of the author, the title or its first words, and the target page. Articles will be cited by the last name of the author, an abbreviated form of the source, and the target page. Where a source has more than three authors, only the first will be cited along with the indication *et al.*

News articles, UN documents, treaties, documents submitted in the proceedings, etc. are cited with full references in the footnotes, with cross-references in subsequent footnotes where appropriate.

Aceves, William J., Case concerning the Vienna Convention on Consular Relations (Federal Republic of Germany v. United States). Provisional measures order, 93 American Journal of International Law (1999), 924–8.

—— The Right to Information on Consular Assistance in the Framework of the Guarantees of the Due Process of Law, 94 American Journal of International Law (2000), 555–63.

—— LaGrand (Germany v. United States), 96 American Journal of International Law (2002), 210–18.

Addo, Michael K., Interim Measures of Protection for Rights under the Vienna Convention on Consular Relations, 10 European Journal of International Law (1999), 713–32.

Ago, Roberto, "Binding" advisory opinions of the International Court of Justice, 85 American Journal of International Law (1991), 439–51.

—— Las opiniones consultivas "obligatorias" de la Corte Internacional de Justicia: problemas de ayer y de hoy, in Manuel Montaldo (ed.), El derecho internacional en un mundo de transformación, Montevideo (1994), Vol. 2, 1081–98.

Ajibola, Bola, Compliance with Judgments of the International Court of Justice, in Mielle Bulterman/Martin Kuijer, Compliance with Judgments of International Courts, The Hague/Boston/London (1996), 9–38.

Allcock, John B., Border and territorial disputes, 3rd edn., Essex (1992).

American Society of International Law, Panel of the American Society of International Law on "Congress and the executive: who calls the shots for national security?", Proceedings of the American Society of International Law, 81st annual meeting (1987), 239–58.

—— Panel of the American Society of International Law on "Consular Rights and the Death Penalty after LaGrand," Proceedings of the American Society of International Law, 96th annual meeting (2002), 309–19.

Anand, R. P., Execution of international judicial awards: experience since 1945, 26 University of Pittsburgh Law Review (1965), 671–703.

—— Iceland's Fisheries Dispute, 16 Indian Journal of International Law (1976), 43–53.

Anderson, David H., The Icelandic Fisheries Cases—Professor Jaenicke as Agent and Counsel before the International Court of Justice, in Volkmar Götz/Peter Selmer/

Ꞁr Wolfrum (eds.), Liber Amicorum Günther Jaenicke zum 85.Geburtstag, Ꞁ *et al.* (1998), 445–63.

‚olidis, Charalambos, L'affaire de l'île de Kasikili/Sedudu (Botswana/Namibie), arrêt de la CIJ du 13 décembre 1999, 45 Annuaire Français de Droit International (1999), 434–51.

Ꞁttard, David Joseph, The Exclusive Economic Zone in international law, Oxford (1987).

Auburn, M., The North Sea Continental Shelf Boundary Settlement, 16 Archiv des Völkerrechts (1974/5), 28–36.

Azar, Aida, L'exécution des décisions de la Cour Internationale de Justice, Brussels (2003).

Aznar-Gómez, Mariano, Á propos de l'affaire relative à la Convention de Vienne sur les relations consulaires (Paraguay c. Etats-Unis d'Amérique), 102 Revue Générale de Droit International Public (1998), 915–50.

Bacot, Guillaume, Réflexions sur les clauses qui rendent obligatoires les avis consultatifs de la CPJI et de la CIJ, 84 Revue Générale de Droit International Public (1980), 1027–67.

Baer, Stephanie, Der Zerfall Jugoslawiens im Lichte des Völkerrechts, Frankfurt (1995).

Bailey, Sydney D./Daws, Sam, The Procedure of the UN Security Council, Oxford (1998).

Bains, J. S., India's international disputes, A legal study, London (1962).

Ball, M. Margaret, The OAS in transition, Durham (1969).

Barcía Trelles, Camilo, El derecho de asilo diplomático y el caso Haya de la Torre, Glosas a una sentencia, 3 Revista española de derecho internacional (1950), 753–801.

Beat, James A./Wolf, Christopher, Application of El Salvador to Intervene in the Jurisdiction and Admissibility Phase of Nicaragua v. United States, 78 American Journal of International Law (1984), 929–36.

Bedjaoui, Mohammed, The Reception by National Courts of Decisions of International Tribunals, in Thomas Franck/Gregory H. Fox (eds.), International Law Decisions in National Courts, Irvington-on-Hudson (1996), 21–35.

Bekker, Peter H. F., Gabčíkovo–Nagymaros Project (Hungary v. Slovakia), 92 American Journal of International Law (1998), 273–8.

—— Land and Maritime Boundary between Cameroon and Nigeria (Cameroon v. Nigeria), Preliminary Objections, 92 American Journal of International Law (1998), 751–5.

—— /Highet, Keith, ASIL Insight, International Court of Justice orders United States to stay execution of Paraguayan national in Virginia, April 1998, http://www.asil.org/insights/insigh17.htm.

Bekong, Njinkeng Julius, International Dispute Settlement: Land and Maritime Boundary between Cameroon and Nigeria—Origin of the Dispute and Provisional Measures, 9 African Journal of International and Comparative Law (1997), 287–310.

Benadava, Santiago, Las opiniones consultivas "obligatorias" de la Corte Internacional de Justicia, in María Teresa Infante Caffi, Solución judicial de controversias, Santiago de Chile (1995), 85–94.

Berg, Axel, Nordic co-operation, in Rudolf Bernhardt (ed.), Encyclopedia of Public International Law, Volume III, Amsterdam/London/NewYork/Tokyo (1997), 634–8 (*cited: Berg in EPIL III*).

Bermejo, Romualdo, Les principes équitables et les délimitations des zones maritimes: analyse des affaires Tunisie/Jamahiriya arabe libyenne et du Golfe du Maine, 1 Hague Yearbook of International Law (1988), 59–110.

Bernhardt, Rudolf, "Corfu Channel Case," in *idem*, Volume I, Amsterdam/London/ New York/Tokyo (1992), 831–3 (*cited: Bernardt in EPIL I*).

Bernstein, David, Case concerning military and paramilitary activities in and against Nicaragua, 28 Harvard International Law Journal (1987), 146–55.

Beveridge, Fiona, Case concerning the Arbitral Award of 31 July 1989 (Guinea-Bissau v. Senegal): Provisional measures, Merits, 41 International and Comparative Law Quarterly (1992), 891–6.

Bilder, Richard B., The United States and the World Court in the post-"cold war" era, 40 Catholic University Law Review (1991), 251–63.

Birt, Michael, A fishy tale, 4 Jersey Law Review (2000), 290–9.

Bishop, W. W., Case concerning sovereignty over certain frontier land, 53 American Journal of International Law (1959), 937–43.

—— Minquiers and Ecrehos Case (France v. United Kingdom), 48 American Journal of International Law (1954), 316–26.

Blum, Yehuda Z., Eroding the United Nations Charter, Dordrecht/Boston/London (1993).

Böckstiegel, Karl-Heinz, Streitentscheidungszuständigkeiten in der Internationalen Zivilluftfahrtsorganisation, in Institut für Völkerrecht und ausländisches öffentliches Recht der Universität Köln (ed.), Festschrift für Hermann Jahrreiß zum 80. Geburtstag, 5–18.

Bollecker-Stern, Brigitte, L'affaire des esssais nucláires français devant la Cour internationale de Justice, 20 Annuaire Français de Droit International (1974), 299–333.

Bourne, Charles B., The Case Concerning the Gabčíkovo–Nagymaros Project: An Important Milestone in International Water Law, 8 Yearbook of International Environmental Law (1997), 6–12.

Boyle, A. E., The Gabčíkovo–Nagymaros Case: New Law in Old Bottles, 8 Yearbook of International Environmental Law (1997), 13–20.

Boyle, Francis, Determining U.S. responsibility for Contra operations under international law, 81 American Journal of International Law (1987), 86–93.

—— The Bosnian people charge genocide, Amherst (1996).

Bradley, Curtis A./Goldsmith, Jack L., The abiding relevance of federalism to U.S. foreign relations, 92 American Journal of International Law (1998), 675–9.

Brandt, Niels, Das interamerikanische Friedenssystem- Idee und Wirklichkeit, Hamburg (1971).

Brauer, Robert H., International Conflict Resolution: The ICJ Chambers and the Gulf of Maine Dispute, 23 Virginia Journal of International Law (1983), 463–86.

Briggs, Herbert W., Nicaragua v. United States: Jurisdiction and Admissibility, 79 American Journal of International Law (1985), 373–8.

—— The International Court of Justice lives up to its name, 81 American Journal of International Law (1987), 78–86.

̦er A., The Icelandic Fisheries Dispute: A decision is finally rendered, ̦ia Journal of International and Comparative Law (1975), 248–56.

̦dward Duncan, The Libya–Malta Continental Shelf Case (1985), in Bin ̦g/Edward Duncan Brown (eds.), Contemporary Problems of International ̦. Essays in Honour of Georg Schwarzenberger on his Eightieth Birthday, ̦ondon (1988), 3–18.

Brown, Norman, The United States and India, Pakistan, Bangladesh, Cambridge, MA (1972).

Canelas de Castro, Paulo, The Judgment in the Case Concerning the Gabčíkovo–Nagymaros Project: Positive Signs for the Evolution of International Water Law, 8 Yearbook of International Environmental Law (1997), 21–31.

Carrillo Salcedo, Juan Antonio, Caso del templo de Preah Vihear (Camboya c. Tailandia). Sentencia del 26 mayo de 1961, 15 Revista española de derecho internacional (1962), 189–206.

Cassese, Antonio, When may senior state officials be tried for international crimes? Some comments on the Congo v. Belgium Case, http://www.ejil.org/journal/curdevs/sr31.html.

Castillo Daudí, María Vicenta, Tribunal Internacional de Justicia: Asuntos de la competencia en materia de pesquerías (Reino Unido c. Islandia y República Federal de Alemania c. Islandia). Fondo. Sentencias de 25 de julio de 1974, 29 Revista Española de Derecho Internacional (1976), 437–45.

Chacko, C. J., The World Court's Judgment on Portugal's Request for access to Dadra and Nagar Aveli, 1 Indian Journal of International Law (1960), 293–9.

Charney, Jonathan, Disputes implicating the institutional credibility of the Court: problems of non-appearance, non-participation, and non-performance, in Lori Fisler Damrosch (ed.), The International Court of Justice at a Crossroads, New York (1987), 288–319.

——Maritime delimitation in the area between Greenland and Jan Mayen, 83 American Journal of International Law (1994), 105–9.

——Progress in international maritime boundary delimitation law, 88 American Journal of International Law (1994), 227–56.

——/Alexander, Lewis M., International Maritime Boundaries, 2 vols., Dordrecht (1993).

——/Reisman, W. Michael, Agora: Breard—The Facts, 92 American Journal of International Law (1999), 666–75.

Chaturvedi, S. C., The North Sea Continental Shelf Cases analysed, 13 Indian Journal of International Law (1973), 481–93.

Cheng, Bin, Rights of United States Nationals in the French Zone of Morocco, 2 International and Comparative Law Quarterly (1953), 354–67.

Chimni, B. S., The International Court and the Maintenance of International Peace and Security: The Nicaragua Decision and the United States Response, 35 International and Comparative Law Quarterly (1986), 960–70.

Chinkin, Christine/Sadurska, Romana, The anatomy of international dispute resolution, 7 Ohio State Journal on Dispute Resolution (1991), 39–81.

Christie, Donna R., From the Shores of Ras Kaboudia to the Shores of Tripoli: The Tunisia–Libya Continental Shelf Boundary Delimitation, 13 Georgia Journal of International and Comparative Law (1983), 1–30.

Churchill, R. R., The Fisheries Jurisdiction Cases: The Contribution of the International Court of Justice to the Debate on Coastal States' Fisheries Rights, 24 International and Comparative Law Quarterly (1975), 82–105.

—— EEC Fisheries Law, Dordrecht (1987).

Clain, Levi E., Gulf of Maine—A disappointing first in the delimitation of a single maritime boundary, 25 Virginia Journal of International Law (1985), 521–620.

Clericetti, Dario, L'affaire Ambatielos devant la commission arbitrale, Geneva/Paris (1962).

Cocâtre-Zilgien, André, Affaire relative à la souveraineté sur certaines parcelles frontalières, 5 Annuaire Français de Droit International (1959), 284–91.

—— Les mesures conservatoires décidées par le juge ou par l'arbitre international, 70 Revue Générale de Droit International Public (1966), 5–48.

Colella, Frank G., Institutional Competence: Congressional efforts to legislate United States foreign policy toward Nicaragua—The Boland Amendments, 54 Brooklyn Law Review (1988), 131–69.

Collier, John/Lowe, Vaughan, The settlement of disputes in international law, Oxford (1999).

Collins, Lawrence, Provisional and protective measures in international litigation, 234 Receuil des Cours (1992) 9–238.

Colson, David A., Sovereignty over Pulau Litigan and Pulau Sipadan, 97 American Journal of International Law (2003), 398–406.

Conforti, Benedetto, L'arrêt de la Cour internationale de Justice dans l'affaire de la délimitation du plateau continental entre la Libye et Malte, 90 Revue Générale de Droit International Public (1986), 313–43.

—— Le nazioni unite, 5th edn., Padua (1994).

Conte H., Alessio B., El derecho de asilo y el caso Haya de la Torre (1951).

Cosnard, Michel, L'affaire de la délimitation maritime et des questions territoriales entre Qatar et Bahreïn (Compétence et Admissibilité). Les arrêts de la CIJ du 1er juillet 1994 et du 15 février 1995, 41 Annuaire Français de Droit International (1995), 311–27.

Cot, Jean-Pierre, Affaire des essais nucléaires (Australie c/France et Nouvelle Zélande c/France), Demandes en indication des mesures conservatoires, Ordonnances du 22 juin 1973, 19 Annuaire Français de Droit International (1973), 252–71.

—— Cour internationale de Justice. Affaire du temple de Préah Vihéar. Fond. Arrêt du 15 juin 1962, 8 Annuaire Français de Droit International (1962), 217–47.

—— Éloge de l'indécision. La Cour et la compétence universelle, 35 Revue Belge de Droit International (2002), 546–53.

——/Pellet, Alain, La Charte des Nations Unies, 2nd edn., Paris (1991) (*cited as: commentator in: Cot/Pellet, Charte, Article*).

Cotterau, Gilles, Affaire relative à la sentence arbitrale du 31 juillet 1989 (Guinée-Bissau v. Sénégal). Demande en indication de mesures conservatoires. Ordonnance du 2 mars 1990, 36 Annuaire Français de Droit International (1990), 368–89.

—— Validité de la sentence arbitrale du 31 juillet 1989 (Guinée-Bissau, Sénégal): arrêt de la CIJ du 12 novembre 1991, 96 Revue Générale de Droit International Public (1992), 753–76.

Coussirat-Coustère, Vincent, Indication de mesures conservatoires dans l'affaire du personnel diplomatique et consulaire des Etats-Unis à Teheran (Etats-Unis d'Amérique contre Iran), Ordonnance du 15 décembre 1979, 25 Annuaire Français de Droit International (1979), 297–313.

Crawford, James, Military Activities against Nicaragua Case (Nicaragua v. US), in Rudolf Bernhardt (ed.), Encyclopedia of Public International Law, Volume III, Amsterdam/London/New York/Tokyo (1997), 371–18 (*cited as: Crawford in EPIL III*).

Czaplinski, Wladyslaw, Crimes against humanity v. immunity of State officials revisited—Some remarks on the Congo v. Belgium case, 78 Friedens-Warte (2003), 63–75.

d'Amato, Anthony, The United States should accept, by a new declaration, the General Compulsory Jurisdiction of the World Court, 80 American Journal of International Law (1986), 331–6.

—— Nicaragua and International Law: The "Academic" and the "Real," 79 American Journal of International Law (1985), 657–64.

—— Trashing Customary International Law, 81 American Journal of International Law (1987), 101–5.

—— /O'Connell, Mary Ellen, United States Experience at the International Court of Justice, in Lori Fisler Damrosch (ed.), The International Court of Justice at a Crossroads, Dobbs Ferry (1987), 403–22.

Damrosch, Lori Fisler (ed.), The International Court of Justice at a Crossroads, New York (1987).

—— The justiciability of Paraguay's claim of treaty violation, 92 American Journal of International Law (1998), 697–704.

Daniele, Luigi, La prima ordinanza sulle misure cautelari nell'affare tra Bosnia-Erzegovina e Iugoslavia (Serbia e Montenegro), 76 Rivista di Diritto Internazionale (1993), 373–84.

—— L'apport de la deuxième ordonnance de la Cour internationale de Justice sur les mesures conservatoires dans l'affaire Bosnie-Herzégovine contre Yougoslavie (Serbie et Monténégro), 98 Revue Générale de Droit International Public (1994), 931–49.

Deatherage, Scott Dean, Interim decision in the case concerning military and para-military activities in and against Nicaragua (Nicaragua v. United States), 26 Harvard International Law Journal (1985), 280–6.

De Smet, Leen/Naert, Frederik, Making or breaking international Law? An international law analysis of Belgium's act concerning the punishment of grave breaches of international humanitarian law, 33 Revue Belge de Droit International (2002), 471–511.

Decaux, Emmanuel, L'arrêt de la chambre de la Cour internationale de Justice dans l'affaire du différend frontalier (Burkina Faso/République du Mali), 33 Annuaire Français de Droit International (1986), 215–38.

—— L'arrêt de la Cour internationale de Justice sur la demande en révision et en interprétation de l'arrêt du 24 février 1982 en l'affaire du Plateau continental (Tunisie-Libye), arrêt du 10 décembre 1985, 32 Annuaire Français de Droit International (1985), 324–49.

DeWeese, Geoffrey S., The failure of the International Court of Justice to effectively enforce the Genocide Convention, 26 Denver Journal of International Law and Policy (1998), 625–54.

Dhokalia, P., International Court in Transition: Challenges to its effectiveness from South-West decision to Nicaragua judgment, in R. P. Dhokalia/B. C. Nirmal/ R. N. Misra, International Court in Transition. Essays in Memory of Professor Darma Pratap. Allahabad (1994), 108–74.

Diaité, Ibou, Le règlement du contentieux entre la Guinée-Bissau et le Sénégal relatif à la délimitation de leur frontière maritime, 41 Annuaire Français de Droit International (1995), 700–10.

Dipla, Haritini, L'arrêt de la Cour Internationale de Justice en l'affaire de la délimitation maritime dans la région située entre le Groenland et Jan Mayen. 98 Revue Générale de Droit International Public (1994), 899–930.

Dolivet, M. L., The United Nations, London (1946).

Dugard, John, The Nuclear Tests Cases and the South West Africa Cases: Some Realism about the International Judicial Decision, 16 Virginia Journal of International Law (1976), 463–504.

—— The South West Africa/Namibia Dispute, Berkeley/Los Angeles/London (1973).

Duxbury, Alison, Saving lives in the International Court of Justice: The Use of Provisional Measures to Protect Human Rights, 31 California Western International Law Journal (2000), 141–76.

Eyffinger, Arthur, The International Court of Justice 1949–1996, The Hague/ London/Boston (1996).

Elkind, Jerome B., Interim protection, Dordrecht (1981).

—— Footnote to the Nuclear Tests Cases: Abuse of right—a blind alley for environmentalists, 9 Vanderbilt Journal of Transnational Law (1976), 57–98.

—— Non-Appearance before the International Court of Justice, Dordrecht (1984).

Evans, Alona E., The Colombian–Peruvian Asylum Case: Termination of the Judicial Phase, 45 American Journal of International Law (1951), 755–62.

—— The Colombian–Peruvian Asylum Case: The Practice of Diplomatic Asylum, 46 The American Political Science Review (1952), 142–57.

Evans, Malcolm, Case concerning the Land, Island and Maritime Frontier Dispute (El Salvador/Honduras)—The Nicaraguan Intervention, 41 International and Comparative Law Quarterly (1992), 896–906.

—— Case concerning Kasikili/Sedudu Island, 49 International and Comparative Law Quarterly (2000), 964–78.

—— Case concerning Maritime Delimitation and Territorial Questions between Qatar and Bahrain (Qatar v. Bahrain), Jurisdiction and Admissibility, 44 International and Comparative Law Quarterly (1995), 691–8.

——Case concerning maritime delimitation in the area between Greenland and Jan Mayen (Denmark v. Norway), 43 International and Comparative Law Quarterly (1994), 697–704.

Fahmi, Aziza Morad, The Fisheries Jurisdiction Case (UK v. Iceland), 30 Revue égyptienne de droit international (1974), 141–56.

Falk, Richard, The World Court's Achievement, 81 American Journal of International Law (1987), 106–12.

Famchon, Yves, Le Maroc d'Algésiras à la souveraineté économique, Paris (1957).

Farer, Tom J., Drawing the right line, 81 American Journal of International Law (1987), 112–16.

Favoreu, Louis, Les affaires de la compétence en matière de pêcheries (Royaume-Uni c/Islande et Allemagne Fédérale c/Islande), Arrêts du 25 juin 1974 (fond), 20 Annuaire Français de Droit International (1974), 253–85.

——Les ordonnances des 17 et 18 aout 1972 dans l'affaire de la compétence en matière de pêcheries (Royaume-Uni c Islande et Allemagne fédérale c. Islande). Contribution au droit procédural de la Cour en matière de mesures conservatoires, exceptions préliminaires et compétence en cas de défaut. 18 Annuaire Français de Droit International (1972), 291–322.

Fayat, Henri, Historische Übersicht über die Zusammenarbeit der Beneluxländer, 25 Österreichische Zeitschrift für öffentliches Recht (1974), 247–54.

Feldman, Mark B., The Tunisia–Libya Continental Shelf Case: Geographic Justice or Judicial Compromise?, 77 American Journal of International Law (1983), 219–38.

Fenwick, Charles G., The Order of the International Court of Justice in the Anglo-Iranian Oil Compay Case, 45 American Journal of International Law (1951), 723–7.

Fernandes, Carlos, El asilo diplomático, México (1970).

Ferrer Sanchis, Pedro A., Tribunal internacional de Justicia: Asuntos de la competencia en materia de pesquerías (Reino Unido c. Islandia y República Federal de Alemania c. Islandia). Jurisdicción del Tribunal: Sentencias de 2 de febrero de 1973, 29 Revista Española de Derecho Internacional (1976), 431–5.

Fitzgerald, Gerald F., The Judgment of the International Court of Justice in the Appeal Relating to the Jurisdiction of the ICAO Council, 12 Canadian Yearbook of International Law (1974), 153–85.

Fitzmaurice, John, The ruling of the International Court of Justice in the Gabčíkovo–Nagymaros Case: A critical analysis, 9 European Environmental Law Review (2000), 80–7.

Fitzmaurice, Malgosia, The Gabčíkovo–Nagymaros Case: The Law of Treaties, 11 Leiden Journal of International Law (1998), 321–44.

Fleischhauer, Carl-August, Inducing Compliance, in Oscar Schachter/Christopher C. Joyner, United Nations Legal Order, Vol. I, Cambridge (1995), 231–43.

Ford, Alan W., The Anglo-Iranian Oil Dispute of 1951–1952, Berkeley/ Los Angeles (1954).

Forlati, Serena, Il contenuto degli obblighi imposti dalle misure cautelari indicate nel caso LaGrand, 94 Rivista di Diritto Internazionale (2001), 711–22.

Forsythe, David P., The politics of international law, Boulder (1990).

Foucheaux, Daniel J., International Court of Justice: Iceland's Regulations Establishing a Fishery Zone with a 50-Mile Limit are not opposable to the United Kingdom and the Federal Republic of Germany. 10 Texas International Law Journal (1975), 150–71.

Franck, Thomas M., Fact-finding in the ICJ, in Richard B. Lillich, Fact-finding before International Tribunals, Ardsley-on-Hudson (1992), 21–32.

—— Icy day at the ICJ, 79 American Journal of International Law (1985), 379–84.

—— Some observations on the ICJ's Procedural and Substantive Innovations, 81 American Journal of International Law (1987), 116–21.

—— /Fox, Gregory H. (eds.), International Law Decisions in National Courts, Irvington-on-Hudson (1996).

—— /Lehrman, Jerome M., Messianism and Chauvinism in America's Commitment to Peace Through Law, in Lori Fisler Damrosch (ed.), The International Court of Justice at a Crossroads, Dobbs Ferry (1987), 3–18.

Franckx, Erik, Belgium and the Netherlands settle their last frontier disputes on land as well as at sea, 31 Revue Belge de Droit International (1998), 338–93.

Frankel, J., The Anglo-Iranian Dispute, 6 The Year Book of World Affairs (1952), 56–74.

Frankel, Kathie D., International Law—International Court of Justice has preliminary jurisdiction to indicate interim measures of protection: The Nuclear Tests cases, 7 New York University Journal of International Law & Politics (1974), 163–76.

Friedmann, Wolfgang, The North Sea Continental Shelf Cases—A Critique, 64 American Journal of International Law (1970), 229–40.

Fritzemeyer, Wolfgang, Die Intervention vor dem Internationalen Gerichtshof, Baden-Baden (1984).

Fuyane, Bukhosi/Madai, Ferenc, The Hungary–Slovakia Danube River dispute: Implications for sustainable development and equitable utilization of natural resources in international law, 1 International Journal of Global Environmental Issues (2001), 329–44.

Garcia, Thierry, Les mesures conservatoires rendues par la Cour internationale de Justice, le 15 mars 1996, dans le différend frontalier entre le Cameroun et le Nigéria, 42 Annuaire Français de Droit International (1996), 409–27.

Gardiner, Leslie, The Eagle spreads his claws: A history of the Corfu Channel Dispute and of Albania's Relations with the West, 1945–1960, Edinburgh/London (1966).

Gautron, Jean-Claude, Création d'une chambre au sein de la Cour internationale de Justice, mesures conservatoires et médiation dans le différend frontalier entre le Burkina Faso et le Mali, 32 Annuaire Français de Droit International (1986), 192–214.

Ghosh, Sunil Kanti, The Anglo-Iranian Oil Dispute, Calcutta (1960).

Gill, Terry D., Litigation Strategy at the International Court, Dordrecht (1989).

Glennon, Michael J., Protecting the Court's Institutional Interests: Why not the *Marbury* approach?, 81 American Journal of International Law (1987), 121–9.

Goldblat, Jozef/Stockholm International Peace Research Institute, French Nuclear Tests in the Atmosphere: The Question of Legality, Stockholm (1974).

Gonidec, P.-F., L'affaire du droit d'asile, 55 Revue Générale de Droit International Public (1951), 547–92.

Goodrich, Leland M./Hambro, Edvard, Charter of the United Nations, Commentary and Documents, 2nd and rev. edn., London (1949).

Goodrich, Leland M./Hambro, Edvard/Simons, Anne Patricia, Charter of the United Nations, Commentary and Documents, 3rd and rev. edn., New York/London (1969).

Goy, Raymond, Le sort de l'or monétaire pillé par l'Allemagne pendant la second guerre mondiale, 41 Annuaire Français de Droit International (1995), 382–91.

Gray, Christine, Application of the Convention on the Prevention and Punishment of the Crime of Genocide (Bosnia and Herzegovina v. Yugoslavia (Serbia and Montenegro), Orders of Provisional Measures of 8 April 1993 and 13 September 1993, 43 International and Comparative Law Quarterly (1994), 704–14.

—— International Law and the Use of Force, Oxford (2000).

Gray, J. C. R., Much fine gold: The history of a fifty-year negotiation, Harvard Center for International Affairs Fellow Paper, Cambridge MA (1997).

Gray, Kevin R., Case concerning the arrest warrant of 11 April 2000 (Democratic Republic of the Congo v. Belgium), http://www.ejil.org/journal/Vol13/No3/sr1.html.

Greenberg, Jonathan, Algerian Intervention in the Iranian Hostage Crisis, 20 Stanford Journal of International Law (1984), 259–89.

Greig, D. W., Nicaragua and the United States: Confrontation over the jurisdiction of the International Court, 62 British Yearbook of International Law (1991), 118–281.

Griesel, Etienne, The Lateral Boundaries of the Continental Shelf and the Judgment of the International Court of Justice in the North Sea Continental Shelf Cases, 64 American Journal of International Law (1970), 562–93.

Grieves, Forest L., Supranationalism and International Adjudication, Urbana (1969).

Gross, Leo, The case concerning United States Diplomatic and Consular Staff in Tehran: Phase of Provisional Measures, 74 American Journal of International Law (1980), 395–410.

Guillaume, Gilbert, De l'exécution des décisions de la Cour Internationale de Justice, 5 Swiss Review of International and European Law (1997), 431–47.

—— Enforcement of decisions of the International Court of Justice, in Nandasiri Jasentuliyana (ed.), Perspectives on international law, London (1995), 275–88.

Gulf Centre for Strategic Studies, "A New Dawn in Bahrain–Qatar Relations," in Bahrain Brief, Vol. 2 Issue 4 (2001), http://web.archive.org/web/20020111221833/http://www.bahrainbrief.com/english/april-issue2001.htm.

Guyomar, Geneviève, Commentaire du règlement de la Cour internationale de Justice adopté le 14 Avril 1978, Interprétation et pratique, Paris (1983).

—— Affaire de la sentence arbitrale rendue par le Roi d'Espagne le 23 décembre 1906, 6 Annuaire Français de Droit International (1960), 362–71.

Hafner, Gerhard, Die Gefährdung der Freiheit der Hochseefischerei: das Urteil im isländischen Fischereistreit im Lichte der 3. Seerechtskonferenz der Vereinten Nationen, in Rudolf Bernhardt/Walter Rudolf (eds.), Die Schiffahrtsfreiheit im gegenwärtigen Völkerrecht 15 Berichte der Deutschen Gesellschaft für Völkerrecht, Karlsruhe (1975), 195–232.

Hailbronner, Kay, Aerial Incident of 27 July 1955 cases, in Rudolf Bernhardt (ed.), Encyclopedia of Public International Law, Vol. I, Amsterdam/London/New York/ Tokyo (1992), 51–4 (*cited as: Hailbronner in EPIL I*).

Hakenberg, Michael, Die Iran-Sanktionen der USA während der Teheraner Geiselaffäre aus völkerrechtlicher Sicht, Frankfurt (1988).

Hambro, Edvard, Urteil des Internationalen Gerichtshofs vom 17. November 1953 in der Sache der Minquiers- und Ecrehos-Inseln, 4 Archiv des Völkerrechts (1953), 490–97.

—— The Ambatielos Arbitral Award, in 6 Archiv des Völkerrechts (1957), 152–73.

Hargrove, John Lawrence, The Nicaragua judgment and the future of the law of force and self-defense, 81 American Journal of International Law (1987), 135–43.

Hartzenbusch, Catharine A., Land, Island and Maritime Frontier Dispute (El Salv./ Hond.), 34 Harvard International Law Journal (1993), 241–57.

—— Arbitral Award of 31 July 1989 (Guinea-Bissau v. Senegal), 86 American Journal of International Law (1992), 553–8.

Hayes, Andrew W., The Boland Amendments and Foreign Affairs Deference, 88 Columbia Law Review (1988), 1534–74.

Henkin, Louis, Provisional Measures, US Treaty Obligations, and the States, 92 American Journal of International Law (1998), 679–83.

Herman, Lawrence L., The Court Giveth and the Court Taketh Away: An Analysis of the Tunisia–Libya Continental Shelf Case, 33 International and Comparative Law Quarterly (1984), 825–68.

Heß, Peter, Bangladesh, Tragödie einer Staatsgründung, Frauenfeld (1972).

Heydte, Friedrich August Freiherr von der, General Act for the pacific settlement of international disputes (1928 and 1949), in Rudolf Bernhardt (ed.), Encyclopedia of Public International Law, Vol. II, Amsterdam/London/New York/Tokyo (1995), 499–502 (*cited as: Heydte in EPIL II*).

Higgins, Rosalyn, Interim Measures for the Protection of Human Rights, 36 Columbia Journal of Transnational Law (1997), 91–108.

—— The Advisory Opinion on Namibia: Which UN Resolutions are Binding under Article 25 of the Charter? 21 International and Comparative Law Law Quarterly (1972), 270–86.

Highet, Keith, Evidence, the Court, and the Nicaragua Case, 81 American Journal of International Law (1987), 1–56.

—— Litigation implications of the U.S. withdrawal from the Nicaragua case, 79 American Journal of International Law (1985), 992–1005.

Hillgruber, Christian, Anmerkung, Fall LaGrand, 57 Juristen-Zeitung (2002), 94–9.

Hodgson, Douglas C., The Tuniso–Libyan Continental Shelf Case, 16 Case Western Reserve International Law Journal (1984), 1–37.

Honegger, Claude, Friedliche Streitbeilegung durch Regionalorganisationen, Zürich (1983).

Honig, Frederick, Die Rechtsprechung des Internationalen Gerichtshofs 1951–1953, 15 Zeitschrift für ausländisches öffentliches Recht und Völkerrecht (1953–4), 681–730.

Hoog, Günter/Schröder-Schüler, Heidi, Die französischen Nuklearversuche im Pazifik, Hamburg (1973).

Hoss, Cristina, A l'Ouest, Rien de Nouveau? L'affaire Valdez devant la Cour d'Appel de l'Etat d'Oklahoma à la lumière du droit international, 107 Revue Générale de Droit International Public (2003), 401–14.

Hudson, Manley O., The effect of advisory opinions of the World Court, 42 American Journal of International Law (1948), 630–2.

—— The Thirtieth Year of the World Court, 46 American Journal of International Law (1952), 1–39.

—— The Thirty-First Year of the World Court, 47 American Journal of International Law (1953), 1–19.

—— The Thirty-Second Year of the World Court, 48 American Journal of International Law (1954), 1–22.

—— The Twenty-Fourth Year of the World Court, 40 American Journal of International Law (1946), 1–52.

—— The Permanent Court of International Justice 1920–1942, New York (1943).

Huntzinger, Jacques, L'affaire de l'appel concernant la compétence du conseil de l'O.A.C.I. devant la Cour internationale de Justice (Arrêt du 18 Août 1972), 78 Revue Générale de Droit International Public (1974), 975–1016.

Inter-American Institute of International Legal Studies, The Inter-American System. Its Development and Strengthening, Dobbs Ferry/New York (1966).

Jaenicke, Günther, Fisheries Jurisdiction Cases (UK v. Iceland; Federal Republic of Germany v. Iceland) in Rudolf Bernhardt (ed.), Encyclopedia of Public International Law, Vol. II, Amsterdam/London/New York/Tokyo (1995), 386–9 (*cited as: Jaenicke in EPIL II*).

—— North Sea Continental Shelf Case, in Rudolf Bernhardt (ed.), Encyclopedia of Public International Law, Vol. III, Amsterdam/London/New York/Tokyo (1997), 657–60 (*cited as: Jaenicke in EPIL III*).

Janis, Mark Weston, Somber reflections on the compulsory jurisdiction of the International Court, 81 American Journal of International Law (1987), 144–6.

Jenks, Clarence Wilfred, The prospects of international adjudication, London/ Dobbs/Ferry/New York (1964).

Jennings, Robert Y., Nullity and effectiveness in international law, in Cambridge Essays in International Law, Essays in honour of Lord McNair, London/ Dobbs Ferry (1965), 64–87.

—— The judicial enforcement of international obligations, 47 Zeitschrift für ausländisches öffentliches Recht und Völkerrecht (1987), 3–16.

Jessup, Philip C., The birth of nations, New York/London (1974).

Jiménez de Aréchaga, Eduardo, Derecho constitucional de las Naciones Unidas, Madrid (1958).

—— The amendments to the Rules of Procedure of the International Court of Justice, 67 American Journal of International Law (1973), 1–22.

Johnson, D. H. N., Judgments of May 26, 1961, and June 15, 1962. The Case concerning the Temple of Preah Vihear, 11 International and Comparative Law Quarterly (1962), 1183–204.

—— The Minquiers and Ecrehos Case, 3 International and Comparative Law Quarterly (1954), 189–216.

——— Case concerning e arbitral award made by the King of Spain on 23 December 1906, 10 International and Comparative Law Quarterly (1961), 328–37.

——— The Case of the Monetary Gold Removed from Rome in 1943, 4 International Comparative Law Quarly (1955), 93–115.

——— The Case concerning rights of Nationals of the United States in Morocco, 29 British Yearbook of International Law (1952), 401–23.

Johnston, Douglas M., The Theory and History of Ocean Boundary-Making, Kingston/Montreal (1988).

Jones, Lenore, Opinions of the Court of the European Union in National Courts, in Thomas M. Franck/Gregory H Fox, International Law Decisions in National Courts, Irvington-on-Hudson (1996), 221–45.

Jónsson, Hannes, Friends in Conflict, the Anglo-Icelandic Cod Wars and the Law of the Sea, London/Hamden (1982).

Jully, Laurent, Deux récentes décisions de la Cour internationale de Justice, 49 Friedens-Warte (1949), 119–33.

——— L'asile diplomatique devant la Cour internationale de Justice, 51 Friedens-Warte (1951), 20–58.

——— Le premier arrêt de la Cour internationale à Justice, 48 Friedens-Warte (1948), 144–57.

Juste Ruiz, José, Mootness in International Adjudication: The Nuclear Tests Cases, 20 German Yearbook of International Law (1977), 358–74.

Kamto, Maurice, Le contentieux de la frontière maritime entre la Guinée-Bissau et le Sénégal, 101 Revue Générale de Droit International Public (1997), 695–735.

——— L'intitulé d'une affaire portée devant la C. I. J., 34 Revue Belge de Droit international (2001), 5–22.

——— Une troublante "immunité totale" du ministre des affaires étrangères, 33 Revue Belge de Droit International (2002), 518–30.

Kapoor, Shyam K., Enforcement of Judgments and compliance with advisory opinions of the ICJ, in Raama P. Dhokalia (ed.), International Court in transition, Allahabad (1995), 301–16.

Kelly, G. M., The Temple Case in historical perspective, 39 British Yearbook of International Law (1963), 462–72.

Kelsen, Hans, The law of the United Nations, London (1951).

Keohane, Robert O./Moravcsik, Andrew/ Slaughter, Anne-Marie, Legalized Dispute Resolution: Interstate and Transnational, 54 International Organization (2000), 457–88.

Kerley, Ernest L., Ensuring compliance with judgments of the International Court of Justice, in Leo Gross (ed.), The future of the International Court of Justice, Vol. 1, Dobbs Ferry (1976), 276–86.

Kirgis, Frederic L., Zschernig v. Miller and the Breard Matter, 92 American Journal of International Law (1998), 704–8.

——— World Court rules against the United States in LaGrand case arising from a violation of the Vienna Convention on Consular Relations, ASIL Insights No. 75, July 2001, http://www.asil.org/insights/insigh75.htm.

Klabbers, Jan, Cat on a Hot Tin Roof: The World Court, ate Succession, and the Gabčíkovo–Nagymaros Case, 11 Leiden Journal of In national Law (1998), 345–55.

—— Qatar v. Bahrain: The concept of "treaty" in intern onal law, 33 Archiv des Völkerrechts (1995), 361–76.

—— The Substance of Form: The Case Concerning he Gabčíkovo–Nagymaros Project, Environmental Law, and the Law of Tr es, in 8 Yearbook of International Environmental Law (1997), 32–40.

Klein, Laurent, Klein, Brigitte, Chronologie des f s internationaux d'ordre juridique (année 1976) 22 Annuaire Français de Dro International (1976), 1018–44.

Koe, Adriana, Damming the Danube: The In national Court of Justice and the Gabčíkovo–Nagymaros Project, 20 Sydney aw Review (1998), 612–29.

Kohen, Marcelo G., Le règlement des différe ds territoriaux, 99 Revue Générale de Droit International Public (1995), 258–3 .

—— L'uti possidetis revisité: L'arrêt du 1 septembre 1992 dans l'affaire El Salvador/ Honduras, 97 Revue Générale de Dr t International Public (1993), 939–73.

—— Uti possidetis, prescription et p ique subséquente à un traité dans l'affaire de l'Ile de Kasikili/Sedudu devant Cour internationale de Justice, 43 German Yearbook of International Law 2000), 253–75.

Koroma, Abdul G., Provisional Measures of Protection in disputes between African States before the Internati al Court of Justice, in Laurence Boisson de Cha-zournes/Vera Gowlland-D bbas (eds.), The International Legal System in Quest of Equity, Liber Amico m Georges Abi-Saab, The Hague (2001), 591–602.

Krenz, Frank E., Interna onal enclaves and rights of passage. With special reference to the case concernin right of passage over Indian territory, Geneva/Paris (1961).

Kritsiotis, Dino, Arme activities on the territory of the Congo (Democratic Republic of the Congo v. ganda): Provisional measures. International and Comparative Law Quarterly 5 (2001), 662–70.

Kutzner, Gerhard, Die Organisation Amerikanischer Staaten, Hamburg (1970).

Kwiatkowska, Barbara, Equitable Maritime Boundary Delimitation, as Exemplified in the Work of the International Court of Justice During the Presidency of Sir Robert Yewdall Jennings and Beyond, 28 Ocean Development and International Law (1997), 91–145.

—— The 200 Mile Exclusive Economic Zone in the new Law of the Sea, Dordrecht/ Boston/London (1989).

Labouz, Marie-Françoise, Affaire des activités militaires et paramilitaires au Nicar-agua et contre celui-ci (Nicaragua c. Etats-Unis d'Amérique): Ordonnance de la Cour internationale de Justice du 10 mai 1984 en indications de mesures conserva-toires, 30 Annuaire Français de Droit International (1984), 340–71.

Lacharrière, Guy de, Commentaires sur la position juridique de la France à l'égard de la licéité de ses expériences nucléaires, 20 Annuaire Français de Droit International (1974) 235–51.

Lammers, Johan G., The Gabčíkovo–Nagymaros Case seen in Particular From the Perspective of the Law of International Watercourses and the Protection of the Environment, 11 Leiden Journal of International Law (1998), 287–320.

Langavant, Emmanuel/Pirotte, Olivier, L'affaire des pêcheries islandaises, 80 Revue Générale de Droit International Public (1976), 55–103.

Laubadère, André de, Le statut international du Maroc depuis 1955, 2 Annuaire Français de Droit International (1956), 122–49.

—— Le statut international du Maroc et l'arrêt de la Cour Internationale de Justice du 27 août 1952, Paris (1952).

Lauterpacht, Elihu, "Partial" judgments and the inherent jurisdiction of the International Court of Justice, in Vaughan Lowe/Malgosia Fitzmaurice (eds.), Fifty years of the International Court of Justice, Essays in honour of Sir Robert Jennings, Cambridge (1996), 465–86, at 470–1.

Lauterpacht, Sir Hersch, The Development of International Law by the International Court, London (1958).

Leader, Joyce E., The Congo Crisis, 30 April 2001, http://web.archive.org/web/20020620020331/http://fundforpeace.org/resources/perspect/leader03.htm.

Leanza, Umberto, La piattaforma continentale del mare Mediterraneo e la sua delimitazione, in Vincenzo Starace/Ugo Villani (eds.), Studi in ricordo di Antonio Filippo Panzera, Vol. I, Diritto internazionale, Bari (1995), 451–85.

——/Sico, Luigi (eds.), Mediterranean Continental Shelf, 2 vols., Dobbs Ferry (1988).

Legault, Leonard H./Hankey, Blair, From Sea to Sea-bed: The Single Maritime Boundary in the Gulf of Maine Case (Delimitation of the Maritime Boundary in the Gulf of Maine Area–Canada–United States), 79 American Journal of International Law (1985), 961–91.

Leifer, Michael, Cambodia. The Search for Security, London/New York (1967).

Leigh, Monroe, Case concerning Military and Paramilitary Activities in and against Nicaragua (Nicaragua v. United States of America), 78 American Journal of International Law (1984), 894–7.

—— Case concerning the Continental Shelf (Libyan Arab Jamahiriya/Malta)–International Court of Justice, June 3, 1985, 80 American Journal of International Law (1986), 645–8.

—— Case concerning the Frontier Dispute (Burkina Faso/Mali), 81 American Journal of International Law (1987), 411–13.

Lellouche, Pierre, The Nuclear Tests Cases: Judicial Silence v. Atomic Blast, 16 Harvard International Law Journal (1975), 614–37.

Lipstein, Kurt, The Ambatielos case. Last phase, 6 International and Comparative Law Quarterly (1957), 643–56.

Lovelace, Leopoldo, Armed activities on the territory of the Congo: The International Court of Justice Orders the Parties to Refrain from Armed Action and to Ensure Respect for Human Rights, ASIL Insight No. 48, July 2000, http://www.asil.org/insights/insigh48.htm.

Lucchini, Laurent/Vœlckel, Michel, Droit de la mer, Vol. 2, Paris (1996).

Luque Angel, Eduardo, El derecho de asilo, Bogotá (1959).

Macdonald, R. St. J./Hough, Barbara, The Nuclear Tests Case revisited, 22 German Yearbook of International Law (1977), 337–57.

Magid, Per, Presentation (The post-adjudicative phase) in Connie Peck/Roy S. Lee, Increasing the effectiveness of the International Court of Justice, The Hague/ Boston/London (1997), 325–47.

Magiera, Siegfried, Die Rechtsprechung des Internationalen Gerichtshofs in den Jahren 1972 und 1973, 17 Jahrbuch für internationales Recht (1974), 326–40.

Maison, Rafaëlle, Les ordonnances de la CIJ dans l'affaire relative à l'application de la Convention sur la prévention et la répression du crime de génocide, 5 European Journal of International Law (1994), 381–400.

Maljean-Dubois, Sandrine, L'affaire relative à l'application de le convention pour la prévention et la répression du crime de génocide (Bosnie-Herzégovine c. Yougoslavie): arrêt du 11 juillet 1996, exceptions préliminaires, 42 Annuaire Français de Droit International (1996), 357–86.

Malloy, Michael M., The Iran Crisis: Law under Pressure, Transnational Resolution, 1984 Symposium, Wisconsin International Law Society, Wisconsin International Law Journal (1984), 15–98.

Mani, V. S., Interim Measures of Protection: Article 41 of the ICJ Statute and Article 94 of the Charter, 10 Indian Journal of International Law (1970), 359–72.

Manin, Aleth, Appel concernant la compétence du Conseil de l'OACI, 19 Annuaire Français de Droit International (1973), 290–319.

Marston, G. (ed.), United Kingdom Materials on International Law 1992, 63 British Yearbook of International Law (1992), 615–841.

Martin, Pierre-Marie, Les affaires de la compétence en matière de pêcheries. Les arrêts du 2 février 1973, 78 Revue Générale de Droit International Public (1974), 435–58.

Mathy, Denise, L'autodetermination de petits territoires revendiqués par des Etats tiers, 10 Revue Belge de Droit International (1974), 167–205.

Mcdorman, Ted L., The Libya–Malta Case: Opposite States Confront the Court, 24 Canadian Yearbook of International Law (1986), 335–67.

McHugo, John, The judgments of the International Court of Justice in the jurisdiction and admissibility phase of Qatar v. Bahrain: An example of the continuing need for fact-scepticism, 28 Netherlands Yearbook of International Law (1997), 171–96.

Meadows, Frances, The First Site Visit by the International Court of Justice, 11 Leiden Journal of International Law (1998), 603–8.

Mennecke, Martin, Humanization of the Vienna Convention on Consular Rights— The LaGrand case before the International Court of Justice, 44 German Yearbook of International Law (2001), 430–68.

——/Tams, Christian, The right to consular assistance under international law, 42 German Yearbook of International Law (1999), 192–241.

Merrills, J. G., International Dispute Settlement, 3rd edn., Cambridge (1998).

—— Interim Measures of Protection in the recent jurisprudence of the International Court of Justice, 44 International and Comparative Law Quarterly (1995), 90–146.

Michaels, Peter S., Lawless intervention: United States Foreign Policy in El Salvador and Honduras, 7 Boston College Third World Law Journal (1987), 223–62.

Modelski, George, The Asian States' participation in SEATO, in *idem* (ed.), SEATO. Six Studies, Melbourne/Canberra/Sydney (1962).

Monconduit, François, Affaire du Plateau Continental de la Mer du Nord, République Fédérale d'Allemagne c. Danemark, République Fédérale d'Allemagne c. Pays Bas, arrêt du 20 février 1969, 15 Annuaire Français de Droit International (1969), 213–44.

Moore, Andrew F., Ad hoc chambers of the International Court and the question of intervention, 24 Case Western Reserve Journal of International Law (1992), 667–98.

Moore, John Norton, The Nicaragua case and the deterioration of World Order, 81 American Journal of International Law (1987), 151–9.

——The Secret War in Central America and the future of World Order, 80 American Journal of International Law (1986), 43–127.

Morandière, Chr. de la, Une injustice au milieu du XXe siècle: Les archipels normands des Minquiers et des Écrehous sont devenus possession britannique, 21 Etudes Normandes (1956), No. 4, 17–36.

Moreno Quintana, Lucio M., Derecho de asilo. Buenos Aires (1952).

Morr, Hubertus von, Secretary-General, in Rüdiger Wolfrum (ed.), United Nations, Law, policies and practice, Vol. 2, Dordrecht/Boston/London (1995), 1136–46.

Münch, Fritz, "Consular Jurisdiction", in Rudolf Bernhardt (ed.), Encyclopedia of Public International Law, Vol. I, Amsterdam/London/New York/Tokyo (1992), 763–5 (*cited as: Münch in EPIL I*).

Munya, P. Mweti, The International Court of Justice and peaceful settlement of African disputes: Problems, challenges and prospects, 7 Journal of International Law and Practice (1998), 159–224.

Murphy, Sean D., Contemporary practice of the United States: Execution of German nationals who were not notified of right to consular access, 93 American Journal of International Law (1999), 644–7.

Nakamichi, Mari, The International Court of Justice Decision regarding the Gabčíkovo–Nagymaros Project, 9 Fordham Environmental Law Journal (1998), 337–72.

Naldi, Gino J., The case concerning the Frontier Dispute (Burkina Faso/Republic of Mali): *Uti possidetis* in an African perspective, 36 International and Comparative Law Quarterly (1987), 893–903.

——Case concerning the territorial dispute (Libyan Arab Jamahiriya/Chad), 44 International and Comparative Law Quarterly (1995), 683–90.

——Case concerning the Frontier Dispute between Burkina Faso and Mali: Provisional Measures of Protection, 35 International and Comparative Law Quarterly (1986), 970–5.

Nantwi, E. K., The Enforcement of International Judicial Decisions and Arbitral Awards in Public International Law, Leyden (1966).

Nordquist, Myron /Lay, S. Houston/Simmonds, Kenneth R., New Directions in the Law of the Sea, Documents, Vol. 7. VII, London *et al.* (1980).

Obozuwa, A. U., The Icelandic Fisheries Case, Nigerian Annual of International Law (1976), 101–23.

O'Connell, D. P., A critique of the Iranian Oil Litigation, 4 International and Comparative Law Quarterly (1955), 267–93.

O'Connell, Mary Ellen, The prospects for enforcing monetary judgments of the International Court of Justice: A study of Nicaragua's judgment against the United States, 30 Virginia Journal of International Law (1990), 891–940.

Oda, Shigeru, Provisional measures: The practice of the International Court of Justice in Vaughan Lowe/Malgosia Fitzmaurice (eds.), Fifty years of the International Court of Justice, Essays in honour of Sir Robert Jennings, Cambridge (1996), 541–56.

—— The Compulsory Jurisdiction of the International Court of Justice: A Myth?, 49 International and Comparative Law Quarterly (2000), 251–77.

—— The International Court of Justice viewed from the bench, 244 Receuil des Cours (1993), 9–190.

Oellers-Frahm, Karin, Aegean Sea Continental Shelf Case, in Rudolf Bernhardt (ed.), Encyclopedia of Public International Law, Vol. I, Amsterdam/London/New York/ Tokyo (1992), at 48–50 (*cited as: Oellers-Frahm, "Aegean Sea Continental Shelf Case," in EPIL I*).

—— Anmerkungen zur einstweiligen Anordnung des Internationalen Gerichtshofs im Fall Bosnien-Herzegowina gegen Jugoslawien (Serbien und Montenegro) vom 8.April 1993, 53 Zeitschrift für ausländisches öffentliches Recht und Völkerrecht (1993), 638–56.

—— Continental Shelf Case (Libyan Arab Jamahiriya/Malta) in Rudolf Bernhardt (ed.), Encyclopedia of Public International Law, Vol. I, Amsterdam/London/New York/Tokyo (1992), 795–8 (*cited as: Oellers-Frahm, "Continental Shelf Case (Libyan Arab Jamahiriya/Malta)," in EPIL I*).

—— Continental Shelf Case (Tunisia/Libyan Arab Jamahiriya), in Rudolf Bernhardt (ed.), Encyclopedia of Public International Law, Vol. I, Amsterdam/London/New York/Tokyo (1992), 798–803 (*cited as: Oellers-Frahm, "Continental Shelf Case (Tunisia/Libyan Arab Jamahiriya)," in EPIL I*).

—— Die einstweiligen Anordnungen des IGH im Fisheries Jurisdiction Case, 32 Zeitschrift für ausländisches öffentliches Recht und Völkerrecht (1972), 565–70.

—— Die einstweilige Anordnung in der internationalen Gerichtsbarkeit, Heidelberg (1975).

—— Die Entscheidung des IGH im Fall LaGrand—Eine Stärkung der internationalen Gerichtsbarkeit und der Rolle des Individuums im Völkerrecht, 28 Europäische Grundrechte-Zeitschrift (2001), 265–72.

—— Die Entscheidung des IGH zur Abgrenzung des Festlandsockels zwischen Tunesien und Libyen: eine Abkehr von der bisherigen Rechtsprechung? 42 Zeitschrift für ausländisches öffentliches Recht und Völkerrecht (1982), 804–14.

—— Gulf of Maine Case, in Rudolf Bernhardt (ed.), Encyclopedia of Public International Law, Vol. II, Amsterdam/London/NewYork/Tokyo (1995), 647–51 (*cited: Oellers-Frahm in EPIL II*).

Oliver, Covey T., The Monetary Gold Decision in Perspective, 49 American Journal of International Law (1955), 216–21.

Orcasitas Llorente, Luis, Sentencia del Tribunal Internacional de Justicia de La Haya de 20 de junio de 1959, recaida en pleito surgido entre Bélgica y Holanda, sobre la soberania de ciertas parcelas fronterizas, 13 Revista Española de Derecho Internacional (1960), 519–29.

——Sentencia del Tribunal Internacional de Justicia de La Haya sobre soberanía de las islas "Minquiers" y "Ecréhous" en el Canal de la Mancha, 7 Revista española de derecho internacional (1954), 531–49.

Ordonez, Sarita/Reilly, David, Effect of the Jurisprudence of the International Court of Justice on National Courts, in Thomas M. Franck/Gregory H. Fox, International Law Decisions in National Courts, Irvington-on-Hudson (1996), 335–71.

Orihuela Calatayud, Esperanza, La sentencia dictada por el TIJ en el asunto relativo a la delimitación de la plataforma continental entre la Jamahiriya Arabe Libia y Malta, 40 Revista española de derecho internacional (1988), 105–20.

Ortiz García, Antonio, Sentencia del Tribunal Internacional de Justicia sobre el arbitraje del Rey de España, 14 Revista española de derecho internacional (1961), 197–203.

Oxman, Bernard H., Jurisdiction and the power to indicate provisional measures, in Lori Fisler Damrosch (ed.), The International Court of Justice at a Crossroads, Dobbs Ferry (1987), 323–54.

Papachristou, Alexander, International Adjudication—Embassy Seizure, 21 Harvard International Law Journal (1980), 748–56.

Paul, Joel Richard, International adjudication: Embassy seizure—United States v. Iran, 21 Harvard International Law Journal (1980), 268–74.

Paulus, Andreas L., Urteilsanmerkung zu BGH, Beschluß vom 7. November 2001, 5 StR 116/01, 23 Strafverteidiger (2003), 57–60.

Paust, Jordan J., Breard and Treaty-Based Rights under the Consular Convention, 92 American Journal of International Law (1998), 691–7.

Peck, Connie/Lee, Roy S., Increasing the effectiveness of the International Court of Justice, The Hague/Boston/London (1997).

Pell, Owen C./Bekker, Pieter H. F., World Court finds broad immunity from criminal jurisdiction for sitting foreign ministeres, but leaves open prosecution of former officials by domestic courts, http://www.whitecase.com/case_icj_ruling_jurisdiction_ministers_pell_bekker.pdf.

Perrin, Georges, Les mesures conservatoires dans les affaires relatives à la compétence en matière de pêcheries, 77 Revue Générale de Droit International Public (1973), 16–34.

Perry, Alan, Caprivi Strip: World Court awards island to Botswana, 8 IBRU International Boundary and Security Bulletin (2000), No. 2, 80–7.

Perry, Edward N., International Court of Justice—Procedure—Temporary Relief in the Form of Interim Measures Granted on Prima Facie Evidence of Jurisdiction and Jurisdiction of the Merits found on Basis of Prior Agreement on Compulsory ICJ Jurisdiction, 7 Vanderbilt Journal of Transnational Law (1973–4), 512–20.

Piñol i Rull, Joan, Los asuntos de las actividades militares y paramilitares en Nicaragua y en contra de este estado (Nicaragua contra Estados Unidos de America), 39 Revista Española de Derecho Internacional (1987), 99–119.

Planas-Suárez, Simón, El asilo diplomático. Estudio jurídico y político sobre este execrable uso latinoamericano destructor de la soberanía nacional y de la cordialidad internacional, Buenos Aires (1953).

Politakis, George P., The 1993 Jan Mayen Judgment: The End of Illusions?, 41 Netherlands International Law Review (1994), 1–29.

Pomerance, Michla, The Advisory Function of the International Court in the League and UN Eras, Baltimore/London (1973).

Pozo Serrano, María Pilar, La sentencia de la CIJ de 14 de junio de 1993, sobre la delimitación de la región situada entre Groenlandia y Jan Mayen, 49 Revista Española de Derecho Internacional (1997), 117–33.

Puig, Juan Carlos, Caso Ambatielos/Caso de las pesquerías, Buenos Aires (1968).

Pukrop, Michael E., The Aozou Strip, www.american.edu/ted/ice/aozou.htm.

Quéneudec, Jean-Pierre, L'affaire de la sentence arbitrale du 31 juillet 1989 devant la CIJ (Guinée-Bissau c. Sénégal), 37 Annuaire Français de Droit International (1991), 419–43.

Rafat, Amir, The Iran Hostage Crisis and the International Court of Justice: Aspects of the Case Concerning United States Diplomatic and Consular Staff in Tehran, 10 Denver Journal of International Law (1981), 425–62.

Ranjeva, Raymond, Introduction to "The post-adjudicative phase," in Connie Peck/ Roy S. Lee, Increasing the effectiveness of the International Court of Justice, The Hague/Boston/London (1997), at 324–5.

Ratner, Steven R., Belgium's War Crimes Statute: A Postmortem, 97 American Journal of International Law (2003), 888–97.

Reichert-Facilides, Daniel, Down the Danube: The Vienna Convention on the Law of Treaties and the Case concerning the Gabčíkovo–Nagymaros Project, 47 International and Comparative Law Quarterly (1997), 837–54.

Reichler, Paul, Holding America to its own best standards: Abe Chayes and Nicaragua in the World Court, 42 Harvard International Law Journal (2001), 15–46.

Reisman, W. Michael, Has the International Court of Justice exceeded its jurisdiction?, 80 American Journal of International Law (1986), 128–34.

—— Nullity and revision, New Haven/London (1971).

—— The enforcement of international judgments, 63 American Journal of International Law (1969), 1–27.

Reynaud, André, Les différends du plateau continental de la Mer du Nord devant la Cour international de Justice, Paris (1975).

Richardson III, Henry J., The execution of Angel Breard by the United States: Violating an Order of the International Court of Justice, 12 Temple International and Comparative Law Journal (1998), 121–31.

Richardson, Elliott, Jan Mayen in perspective, 82 American Journal of International Law (1988), 443–58.

Rieter, Eva, Interim Measures by the World Court to suspend the execution of an individual: The Breard Case, 16 Netherlands Quarterly of Human Rights (1998), 475–94.

Ris, William K., French Nuclear Testing: A crisis for international law, 4 Denver Journal of International Law and Policy (1974), 111–32.

Robinson, Davis R./Colson, David A./Rashkow, Bruce C., Some Aspects on Adjudicating Before the World Court: The Gulf of Maine Case, 79 American Journal of International Law (1985), 578–97.

—— The management and resolution of cross-border disputes as Canada/U.S. enter the 21st century: The convergence of law and diplomacy in United States–Canada relations: The Precedent of the Gulf of Maine case, 26 Canada–United States Law Journal (2000), 37–45.

Roche, Alexander George, The Minquiers and Ecrehos Case, Geneva (1959).

Rodvell, Warwick, Les Ecréhous Jersey, Stroud (1996).

Rogers, William D./Beat, James A./Wolf, Christopher, Application of El Salvador to Intervene in the Jurisdiction and Admissibility Phase of Nicaragua v. US, 78 American Journal of International Law (1984), 929–36.

Rogoff, Martin A., International Politics and the Rule of Law: The United States and the International Court of Justice, 7 Boston University International Law Journal (1989), 267–99.

Rosenne, Shabtai, The International Court of Justice, Leyden (1957).

——L'exécution et la mise en vigueur des décisions de la Cour internationale de Justice, 57 Revue Générale de Droit International Public (1953), 532–83.

——The Law and Practice of the International Court 1920–1996, 4 vols., The Hague/Boston/London (1997) (*cited as: Rosenne, Law and Practice I/II/III/IV*).

——The World Court—What it is and how it works, 5th edn., Dordrecht/Boston/London (1995).

Ross, Alf, Constitution of the United Nations, New York (1950).

Rothpfeffer, Thomas, Equity in the North Sea Continental Shelf Cases, 42 Nordisk Tidsskrift for International Ret (1972), 81–137.

Rottem, Gideon, Land, Island and Maritime Frontier Dispute (El Sal./Hond.: Nicar. intervening.) 1992 ICJ Rep. 351, 87 American Journal of International Law (1993), 618–26.

Rousseau, Charles, Achèvement de la délimitation de la frontière établie par la convention de Maastricht du 8 août 1843 dans la région de Baarle-Nassau, 79 Revue Générale de Droit International Public (1975), 166–8.

——Chronique des faits internationaux. Cambodge et Thaïlande: Attaque du temple de Préah-Vihéar par des forces thaïlandaises, 70 Revue Générale de Droit International Public (1966), 1009.

——Cambodge et Thailande—Rupture des relations diplomatiques, Chronique des faits internationaux, 63 Revue Générale de Droit International Public (1959), 99–100.

——Chronique des faits internationaux—France, 78 Revue Générale de Droit International Public (1974), 793–822.

——Chronique des faits internationaux—Inde et Pakistan, 76 Revue Générale de Droit International Public (1972), 538–64.

——Chronique des faits internationaux, 90 Revue Générale de Droit International Public (1986), 963–4.

——Chronique des faits internationaux. Cambodge et Thaïlande: Attaque du temple de Préah-Vihéar par des forces thaïlandaises. 3 et 19 avril 1966, 70 Revue Générale de Droit International Public (1966), 1009–10.

——Chronique des faits internationaux. Grande Bretagne et Islande, 79 Revue Générale de Droit International Public (1975), 220–1.

——Chronique des faits internationaux-Islande, 76 Revue Générale de Droit International Public (1972), 890–9.

——Burkina-Faso et Mali: affrontements armés entre les deux Etats à propos de leurs revendications territoriales (25–30 décembre 1985), Revue Générale de Droit International Public, Vol. 90 (1986), 416–7.

Rowles, James P., "Secret wars," self defense and the Charter—a reply to Professor Moore, 80 American Journal of International Law (1986), 568–84.

Rucz, Claude, L'indication de mesures conservatoires par la Cour internationale de Justice dans l'affaire des activités militaires et paramilitaires au Nicaragua et contre celui-ci, 89 Revue Générale de Droit International Public (1985), 83–111.

Rüster, Bernd, Überlegungen zum Isländischen Fischereistreit, in Dieter Blumenwitz/ Albrecht Randelzhofer (eds.), Festschrift für Friedrich Berber zum 75. Geburtstag, München (1973), 449–6.

Saal, Agnès, Chronologie des faits internationaux d'ordre juridique (année 1986), 32 Annuaire Français de Droit International (1986), 1050–64.

Sall, Alioune, Actualité des conflits frontaliers en Afrique: L'Ordonnance du 15 mars 1996 rendue par la Cour internationale de Justice dans le différend frontalier entre le Cameroun et le Nigéria, 9 African Journal of International and Comparative Law (1997), 183–94.

Salmon, Jean, Libres propos sur l'arrêt de la C. I. J. du 14 février 2002 dans l'affaire relative au Mandat d'arrêt du 11 avril 2000 (R. D. C. c. Belgique), 33 Revue Belge de Droit International (2002), 512–17.

Sandifer, Durward V., Evidence before international tribunals, rev. edn. Charlottesville (1975).

Sands, Philippe (ed.), Manual on International Courts and Tribunals, London et al. (1999).

——What is the ICJ for?, 33 Revue Belge de Droit International (2002), 537–45.

Sastre, Michel, La conception américaine de la garantie judiciaire de la supériorité des traités sur les lois (A propos de la décision Breard c. Greene de la Cour suprême des Etats-Unis du 14 avril 1998), 103 Revue Générale de Droit International Public (1999), 147–68.

Satow, Ernest, A guide to diplomatic practice, 4th edn., London/New York/Toronto (1957).

Scelle, Georges, Théorie et pratique de la fonction exécutive en droit international, 55 Receuil des Cours (1936), 87–202.

Schachter, Oscar, International Law in the Hostage Crisis: Implications for future cases, in Paul H. Kreisberg (ed.), American Hostages in Iran. The conduct of a crisis. New Haven/London (1985), 325–73.

——International Law in Theory and Practice, Dordrecht et al. (1991) (*cited as: Schachter, International law*).

——The enforcement of International Judicial and Arbitral Decisions, 54 American Journal of International Law (1960), 1–24.

Scheffer, David J., U.S. Law and the Iran-Contra Affair, 81 American Journal of International Law (1987), 696–723.

Schenck, Dedo von, Die vertragliche Abgrenzung des Festlandsockels unter der Nordsee zwischen der Bundesrepublik Deutschland, Dänemark und den Niederlanden nach dem Urteil des Internationalen Gerichtshofes vom 20.Februar 1969, 15 Jahrbuch für Internationales Recht (1971), 370–98.

chneider, Jan, The Gulf of Maine case: The nature of an equitable result, 79 American Journal of International Law (1985) 539–77.

Shwebel, Stephen, Commentary, in Mielle Bulterman/Martin Kuijer, Compliance with Judgments of International Courts, The Hague/Boston/London (1996), 39–42.

—— The Roles of the Security Council and the International Court of Justice in the application of international humanitarian law, 27 New York University Journal of International Law and Politics (1995), 731–59.

Scot, Craig/Qureshi, Abid/Kalajdzic, Jasminka/Michell, Paul/Copeland, Peter/Chang, Francis, A memorial for Bosnia: Framework of legal arguments concerning the lawfulness of the maintenance of the United Nations Security Council's Arms Embargo on Bosnia and Herzegovina, 16 Michigan Journal of International Law (1994), 1–140.

Scott, Gary L./MacGregor Bothwell, Heather/Pennell, Jennifer, Recent activity before the International Court of Justice: Trend or cycle? 3 ILSA Journal of International & Comparative Law (1996), 1–29.

Scott, Gary L./Carr, Craig L., The ICJ and compulsory jurisdiction: The case for closing the clause, 81 American Journal of International Law (1987), 57–76.

Shahabudeen, Mohamed, Precedent in the World Court, Cambridge (1996).

Shank, S Adele/Quigley, John, Obligations to foreign nationals accused of crime in the United States: A failure of enforcement, 9 Criminal Law Forum (1999), 99–149.

Shaw, Malcolm N., Case concerning the Land, Island and Maritime Frontier (El Salvador/Honduras: Nicaragua intervening), Judgment of 11 September 1992, 42 International and Comparative Law Quarterly (1993), 929–37.

—— The Yeroia Case: Remedies and Judicial Function, 33 Revue Belge de Droit International (2002), 554–9.

Shelley, Anthony ., Law of the Sea: Delimitation of the Gulf of Maine (Judgment of Oct. 12, 1984), 2 Harvard International Law Journal (1985), 646–54.

Shihata, Ibrahim F ., The power of the International Court to determine its own jurisdiction, The Hague (1965).

Silagi, Michael, United States Nationals in Morocco Case, in Rudolf Bernhardt (ed.), Encyclopedia of Public International Law, Vol. IV, Amsterdam/London/New York/Tokyo (2000), 129–30 (cited as: Silagi in EPIL IV).

Simma, Bruno, Self-contained regimes, 16 Netherlands Yearbook of International Law (1985), 111–36.

—— The Charter of the United Nations, A commentary, 1st edn., Oxford (1995) (cited as: commentator in Simma, Charter, first edition, Article xy at notes xy).

—— The Charter of the United Nations, A commentary, Oxford (2002) (cited as: commentator in Simma, Charter, Article xy at notes xy).

Slaughter, Anne-Marie, Court to court, 92 American Journal of International Law (1998), 708–12.

Smith, Robert W., Exclusive Economic Zone Claims, Dordrecht/Boston/Lancaster (1986).

Smith, Roger M., Cambodia's Foreign policy, Ithaca (1965).

Sofaer, Abraham D., Adjudication in the International Court of Justice: Progress through Realism, 44 Record of the Association of the Bar of the City of New York (1989), 462–92.

Sohn, Louis B., International organisation and integration, Dordrecht/Boston/
Lancaster (1986).

Sonenshine, Marshall, Law of the sea: Delimitation of the Tunisia–Libya continental
shelf (case note), 24 Harvard International Law Journal (1983), 225–36.

Soto, J. de, L'arrêt de la Cour internationale de Justice du 27 août 1952, 80 Journal du
Droit International (1953), 516–83.

Stec, Stephen/Eckstein, Gabriel E., Of Solemn Oaths and Obligations: The Environmental Impact of the ICJ's Decision in the Case Concerning the Gabčíkovo–
Nagymaros Project, 8 Yearbook of International Environmental Law (1997), 4–50.

Stein, Ted, Contempt, crisis, and the Court: The World Court and the Hostage
Rescue Attempt, 76 American Journal of International Law (1982), 499–53.

Stern, Brigitte, 20 ans de jurisprudence de la Cour internationale de Justice
1975–1995, The Hague/Boston/London (1998).

Stummel, Dieter, Jan Mayen, in Rudolf Bernhardt (ed.), Encyclopedia of Public
International Law, Vol. III, Amsterdam/London/New York/Tokyo (1997), 1–2
(*cited as: Stummel in EPIL III*).

Sweeney, Joseph M., Rights of U.S. nationals in Morocco, 4 International and
Comparative Law Quarterly (1955), 145–6.

Szabó, Eelco, Provisional measures in the World Court, 10 Leiden Journal of International Law (1997), 475–89.

Sztucki, Jerzy, Case Concerning Land and Maritime Boundary (Cameroon v.
Nigeria): Provisional Measures, Order of 15 March 1996, 10 Leiden Journal of
International Law (1997), 341–58.

—— Interim Measures in the Hague Court, Deventer (1983).

—— Intervention under Article 63 of the ICJ Statute in the Phase of Preliminary
Proceedings: The "Salvadoran incident," 79 American Journal of International
Law (1985), 1005–36.

Tams, Christian, Consular assistance and rights and remedies: Comments on the
ICJ's Judgment in the LaGrand Case, http://www.ejil.org/journal/Vol13/No5/
sr1.html.

—— Das LaGrand-Urteil-IGH-EuGRZ 2001, 287, Juristische Schulung (2002), 324–8.

Tanzi, Attila, Problems of enforcement of decisions of the International Court of
Justice and the law of the United Nations, 6 European Journal of International
Law (1995), 539–72.

Tavernier, Paul, L'abstension des États parties à un différend (Article 27 §3 in fine de
la Charte) Examen de la Pratique, 22 Annuaire français de Droit International
(1976), 283–9.

The International Estimate Inc., Dossier: The Bahrain–Qatar Border Dispute: The
World Court Decision, Part 1, The Estimate Vol. 13 (2001), No. 6 (23 March 2001).
http://www.theestimate.com/public/032301.html.

The International Estimate Inc., Dossier: The Bahrain–Qatar Border Dispute: The
World Court Decision, Part 2, The Estimate Vol. 13 (2001), No. 7 (6 April 2001),
http://www.theestimate.com/public/040601.html.

Thierry, Hubert, Les arrêts du 20 décembre et les relations de la France avec la Cour
internationale de Justice, 20 Annuaire Français de Droit International (1974),
286–98.

Thirlway, H. W. A., Non-appearance before the International Court of Justice, Cambridge *et al.* (1985).

Thomas, Lili, Law of the Sea: Delimitation of the Libya–Malta Continental Shelf, 27 Harvard International Law Journal (1986), 304–13.

Thornberry, Cedric, The Temple of Preah Vihear (Cambodia v. Thailand), 26 Modern Law Review (1963), 448–51.

Tomka, Peter/Wordsworth, Samuel S., The first site visit of the International Court of Justice in fulfillment of its judicial function, 92 American Journal of International Law (1998), 133–40.

Tomuschat, Christian, General Assembly, in Rüdiger Wolfrum (ed.), United Nations: Law, Policies and Practice, Vol. 1, München (1995), 548–57.

——International Law: Ensuring the survival of mankind on the eve of a new century, General Course on Public International Law, 281 Receuil des Cours (1999), 9–348.

Torrelli, Maurice, La reprise des essais nucléaires français, 41 Annuaire Français de Droit International (1995), 755–77.

Torres Bernárdez, Santiago, L'intervention dans la procédure de la CIJ, 256 Receuil des Cours (1995), 193–457.

Tredano, Abdelmoughit Benmessaoud, Intangibilité des frontières coloniales et espace étatique en Afrique, Paris (1989).

Trendl, Thomas J., Maritime Delimitation and the Gulf of Maine Case: A Guide for the Future of Merely "Slicing the Pie", 12 South Illinois University Law Journal (1988), 599–653.

Tuncel, Erhan, L'exécution des décisions de la Cour internationale de Justice selon la Charte des Nations Unies, Neuchâtel (1960).

Urrutia-Aparicio, Carlos, Diplomatic asylum in Latin America, Guatemala (1960).

Ursúa, Francisco A., El asilo diplomático, Comentarios sobre la sentencia de la Corte Internacional de Justicia, México, D. F., (1952).

Van Essen, J. L. F., Some reflections on the Judgments of the International Court of Justice in the Asylum and Haya de la Torre Cases, 1 International and Comparative Law Quarterly (1952), 533–9.

Vázquez, Carlos Manuel, Breard and the federal power to require compliance with ICJ Orders of Provisional Measures, 92 American Journal of International Law (1998), 683–91.

Verdross, Alfred/Simma, Bruno, Universelles Völkerrecht, 3rd edn., Berlin (1984).

Verhoeven, Joe, Quelques réflexions sur l'affaire relative au *Mandat d'arrêt du 11 avril 2000*, 33 Revue Belge de Droit International (2002), 531–5.

Verzijl, J. H. W., The International Court of Justice, 1960, I. Case concerning right of passage over Indian territory (Portugal v. India), Merits. 7 Nederlands Tijdschrift voor Internationaal Recht- Netherlands International Law Review (1960), 211–42.

——The jurisprudence of the World Court, A case by case commentary, Vol. 2 (The International Court of Justice), Leyden (1966) (*cited as: Verzijl, Jurisprudence of the World Court II*).

Vierucci, Luisa, La tutela di diritti individuali in base alla convenzione di Vienna sulle relazioni consolari in margine al caso LaGrand, 94 Rivista di Diritto Internazionale (2001), 686–710.

Visscher, Charles de, L'affaire du droit de passage sur territoire indien devant la Cour International de Justice, 64 Revue Générale de Droit International Public (1960), 693–710.

Vorsey, Louis De/Vorsey, Megan C. De, The World Court Decision in the Canada–United States Gulf of Maine Seaward Boundary Dispute: A perspective from Historical Geography, 18 Case Western Reserve Journal of International Law (1986), 415–42.

Vulcan, Constantin, L'exécution des décisions de la Cour internationale de Justice d'après la Charte des Nations Unies, 18 Revue Générale de Droit International Public (1947), 187–205.

Wald, Martin, Committee of United States Citizens Living in Nicaragua v. Reagan, 83 American Journal of International Law (1989), 380–4.

Waldock, Sir Humphrey, The International Court and the law of the sea, The Hague (1979).

Wallace-Bruce, Nii Lante, The settlement of international disputes, The Hague/Boston/London (1998).

Weckel, Philippe, Les suites des décisions de la Cour internationale de Justice, 42 Annuaire Français de Droit International (1996), 428–42.

Wegen, Gerhard, Discontinuance of international proceedings: The Hostages Case, 76 American Journal of International Law (1982), 717–36.

Weigend, Thomas, Der Fall LaGrand–Völkerrecht bricht Strafprozeßrecht, in Cornelius Prittwitz et al. (eds.), Festschrift für Klaus Lüdersen, Baden Baden (2002), 463–79.

Weil, Jeffrey G., Law of the Sea—Exclusive Economic Zone—Iceland Accorded Preferential Fishing Rights in Water Adjacent to Its Coast-Duty to Negotiate Imposed upon Disputing Parties to Define Iceland's Rights Against the United Kingdom and its Historic Rights, 16 Harvard International Law Journal (1975), 474–90.

Weiler, Joseph H. H., The Constitution of Europe, Cambridge (1999).

White, N. D., The United Nations and the maintenance of international peace and security, Manchester/New York (1990).

Whiteman, Marjorie, Digest of international law, Vol. 3, Washington (1964).

Whyte, Brendan R., Bordering on the ridiculous: A comparison of the Baarle and Cooch Behar Enclaves, 53 The Globe (Journal of the Australian Map Circle) (2002), 43–61.

—— "En Territoire Belge et a Quarante centimetres de la Frontière," a historical and documentary study of the Belgian and Durch enclaves of Baarle-Hertog and Baarle-Nassau, Research Paper Series, SAGES (School of Anthropology, Geography and Environmental Studies), University of Melbourne, unpublished manuscript (working title) (forthcoming) Melbourne.

Wickremasinghe, Chanaka, Case concerning the arrest warrant of 11 April 2000 (Democratic Republic of the Congo v. Belgium), 50 International and Comparative Law Quarterly (2001), 670–5.

Wiebalck, Alison, Genocide in Bosnia and Herzegovina? Exploring the parameters of interim protection at the World Court, 28 The Comparative and International Law Journal of South Africa (1995), 83–106.

Winants, Alain, The Yerodia Ruling of the International Court of Justice and the 1993/1999 Belgian Law on Universal Jurisdiction, 16 Leiden Journal of International Law (2003), 491–509.

Wolfrum, Rüdiger (ed.), United Nations, Law, policies and practice, 2 vols. Dordrecht/Boston/London (1995).

Woodman, Rebecca E., International Miranda? Article 36 of the Vienna Convention on Consular Relations, 70 Journal of the Kansas Bar Association (2001), 41–50.

Wouters, Jan, The Judgment of the International Court of Justice in the Arrest Warrant Case: Some Critical Remarks, 16 Leiden Journal of International Law (2003), 253–67.

Wright, Quincy, Espionage and the Doctrine of Non-Intervention in Internal Affairs, in Roland J. Stanger (ed.), Essays on Espionage and International Law, Columbus (1962).

Wühler, Norbert, "Ambatielos case", in Rudolf Bernhardt (ed.), Encyclopedia of Public International Law, Vol. I, Amsterdam/London/New York/Tokyo (1992), 123–5 (*cited as: Wühler, "Ambatielos" in EPIL I*).

—— "Arbitral Award of 1906 Case (Honduras v. Nicaragua)," in Rudolf Bernhardt (ed.), Encyclopedia of Public International Law, Vol. I, Amsterdam/London/New York/Tokyo (1992), 210–11 (*cited as: Wühler, "Arbitral Award" in EPIL I*).

—— Monetary Gold Case, in Rudolf Bernhardt (ed.), Encyclopedia of Public International Law, Vol. III, Amsterdam/Lausanne/New York/Oxford/Shannon/Singapore:Tokyo (1997), 445–7 (*cited as Wühler in EPIL III*).

Zárate, Luis Carlos, El asilo en el derecho internacional americano, con un apéndice de la Corte internacional de Justicia y de anexos de la Cancillería de Colombia. Bogotá, Iqueima (1957).

Zoller, Elisabeth, L'affaire du personnel diplomatique et consulaire des Etats-Unis à Téhéran, 84 Revue Générale de Droit International Public (1980), 973–1026.

Index

Printed in the USA/Agawam, MA
June 23, 2020

757026.042